the
of

Newport, in 1970, Gerald Koonce and Ken Opper, sports editor and editor of the *Daily Independent*, review a story arriving from their new UPI machine; carriers show off their products before delivering the *Jonesboro Evening Sun* in 1910; Alex Washburn emerges from his *Hope Star* building to look at an accident; Dorothy Stuck receives the Woman of Achievement Award from the Arkansas Press Women in 1969; *De Queen Daily Citizen* newspaper carriers pose in 1950, before heading out to deliver their routes; Claude P. Holt of Sevier County carries the mail by horseback to Lebanon, Arkansas, sometime before 1900; Roy Evans of Newport receives a Golden 50 Service Award in 1980, the first year the award was given, for his long service to the newspaper industry.

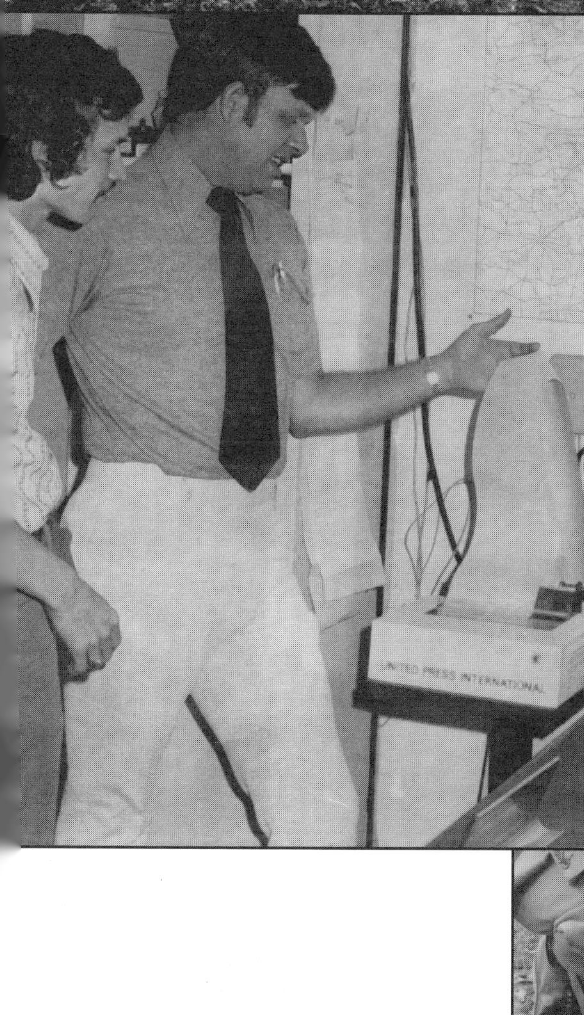

Community Diaries

Arkansas Newspapering 1819-2002

Michael B. Dougan

August House Publishers, Inc.
LITTLE ROCK

Published 2003 by August House Publishers, Inc., P.O. Box 3223, Little Rock, AR 72203,
www.augusthouse.com.

Printed in the United States of America
10 9 8 7 6 5 4 3 2 1

LIBRARY OF CONGRESS CATALOGING-IN-PUBLICATION DATA

Dougan, Michael B., 1944-
Community diaries : Arkansas newspapering, 1819-2002 / Michael B. Dougan
p. cm
ISBN 0-87483-722-7 (alk paper)
1. Newspaper publishing–Arkansas–History–20th century. 2. Newspaper publishing–Arkansas–History–19th century. 3. American newspapers–Arkansas–History–20th century. 4. American newspapers–Arkansas–History–19th century. 1. Title

PN4897.A8D68 2003
071'.67–dc21 2002043872

The paper used in this publication meets the minimum requirements of the American National Standard for Information Sciences—Permanence of Paper for Printed Library Materials, ANSI Z39.48-1984.

ON THE COVER: Attendees at the APA Convention posed in front of the State House on May 15, 1900.

"The job of the newspaper is to comfort the afflicted and afflict the comfortable."

Finley Peter Dunne, Chicago, 1902

Contents

Preface *by C. Dennis Schick* 4
Foreword *by Former U. S. Senator David H. Pryor* 5
Introduction 7
I. Origins of the Arkansas Press 11
II. The Antebellum Editor, or Tripods Under Fire 31
III. Editors in War and Reconstruction 63
IV. The Rural Press: Growing Up with the Country, 1875-1920 89
V. The City Press: Modernization Arrives, 1875-1920 133
VI. Publishing for Profit: The Press in the 1920s 187
VII. The Press Survives the Great Depression 215
VIII. Wars Foreign and Domestic 251
IX. O Brave New World 303
Presidents of the APA 360
Executives of the APA 362
APA Headquarters 363
Notes 364
Index 384

Preface

When the Arkansas Press Association Board of Directors began to consider projects to commemorate the 125th anniversary of APA's founding—October 15, 1873—their first decision was to create a history of the association and of newspapers in the state.

A book committee was formed, led by past president Tom Riley of North Little Rock, an author was interviewed and hired, and the difficult task of tracing the history of a statewide industry over 125 years began. As each chapter was completed, it was sent to readers for their input.

When I read the first drafts of early chapters, my first response was that they included too much history, that this was a newspaper book, not a history book. But as I read further, I realized that the histories of Arkansas and of its newspapers, even today, are closely intertwined. This brings to mind the many vital roles of newspapers in a free and open society:

· To disseminate news widely
· To interpret, to enlighten, to make people think
· To inform (from concerts and school menus, to meeting times, weather, and what's on sale)
· To entertain (comics, puzzles, sports, poetry, features, photos, recipes, etc.)

The newspaper is a fundamental institution in our communities, linking us to our families, our churches, our businesses, our schools, and our governments, as shown in the 1996 National Newspaper Week logo at the right, which APA designed.

Printed words have permanence. They can be cut and pasted and posted on refrigerators and saved in family Bibles. They can be mailed to relatives and glued in scrapbooks. The printed word is basic to education, learning, and progress.

It is significant that, in a poll of thought leaders at the end of the 20th century to determine the most important invention of all time, the choice was German Johannes Gutenberg's movable type and printing press in 1440. This single event opened wide the doors to spread wisdom and information throughout the world.

That is why there will always be newspapers; why newspaper readers have higher educations and higher incomes; why a higher percentage of newspaper readers go to the polls and vote. People who have "the newspaper habit" are thought leaders in their communities.

I want to thank all past and present people who love the newspaper business and help make it what it is today. I especially want to thank Batesville artist Craig Ogilvie whose cartoons appear throughout the book.

The newspaper is a diary of the community—a public diary—open for all the world to see. So read on, about the colorful histories of Arkansas and its newspapers.

— *C. Dennis Schick*

Foreword

When Michael Dougan gives us the colorful history of Arkansas "newspapering," he describes perhaps the most critical component of our state's political, economic, and social development. In readable, fascinating narrative, Dougan carefully traces Arkansas newspapers from 1819 to the present, along with the Association that has represented them for so long and so well. His book is truly a great recall of Arkansas history—at its best and even sometimes at its worst. He has rendered an immense contribution to the understanding and appreciation of the entrepreneurial, intriguing, and—many times—the courageous and cantankerous who owned and ran the "paper."

From a historian's insight, Dougan has reached into the deepest crevices of Arkansas's past. He has produced a treasure, a sobering and exciting account of the development and impact of the Arkansas press.

The early pioneers of Arkansas journalism faced obstacles and barriers that present-day owners might never dream of. Feuds, duels, fire, tornadoes, floods, and ultimately fierce competition added to the daily challenge of basic economic survival. For most of these newspapers, it became the "survival of the fittest." These publishers and editors took on the monumental duties of informing and educating the public, with hopeful anticipation of selling enough paid subscriptions and advertising to meet payrolls and heavy debt. Because so many of these individuals took positions not popular with their readership or the community, income for the enterprise was constantly threatened, often creating insurmountable odds.

The real measure of importance of Professor Dougan's work will be in the ultimate appreciation this and future generations will have for these individuals and families who made such great gifts to our state's fabric and meaning. Without these local newspapers, communities throughout Arkansas would have been denied not only access to news and commentary, but large segments of the population would have never experienced that central focal point that bound neighbors and communities together. The local papers told readers of current news, events on the horizon, and even who was visiting whom and where. They were the common denominator for rich and poor, rural and urban constituents. The country correspondent became one of the most important and best-read sections of the paper.

Professor Dougan performs yet another service in his look at the enormous changes in the equipment and machinery needed to publish a newspaper and the explosion of new technology that renders "hot lead," the flatbed press, and Linotype obsolete. Messrs. Woodruff, Heiskell, and Funk could have never envisioned these transformations and their impact.

Dougan observes the declining emphasis on local newspaper ownership and control with the reality of time and economics. His conclusions recount a remarkable transformation of merged ownerships of erstwhile "local" newspapers and give us reason for concern. What is happening to the local paper? Will attrition and changing laws of newspaper economics continue to be the major factors in family and corporate-ownership decisions? The late Speaker of the House "Tip" O'Neill proclaimed that "all politics is local." How much of the "local" flavor of the papers that serve Arkansas communities are we to protect and nurture?

For decades, the publicists and editors of Arkansas have belonged to what I've always believed to be one of our state's most exclusive fraternities: the Arkansas Press Association. Michael Dougan carefully treats this unique organization with great historical perspective and detailed attention. The APA has served as the gathering place for these men and women, their families and associates for generations. The Association has not only advocated those causes close to the hearts (and pocketbooks) of its members, it has always occupied the unique role of collective sounding board for those of the "fourth estate." When the APA takes a public position on issues like the Freedom of Information law or the protection of second-class mail permits, its voice is indeed a formidable force.

The opportunity to exchange ideas about "getting out the paper" and the most recent developments in machinery and technology have kept the organization vital, influential, and committed to a common purpose. For the politician who receives an invitation to address a winter or summer APA convention, it is an honor that mandates careful preparation. A public official has few opportunities to address and mingle with so many opinion-makers in one room.

The uniqueness of the "press meetings" mirrors the history of several generations of people and families who have so much in common. The members know each other. Their children have grown up with one another, and years and common challenges bind these families together. Dougan recounts the flood in Clinton in the early '80s—how fellow publishers and editors immediately rushed to the county seat town to help their colleagues Jay and Patsy Jackson "get the paper out." After all, the Jacksons would have been there for them in similar circumstances. The personal friendships and loyalties deepen over the years of association, as members share confidences and compare balance sheets.

One of the most critical functions of the Association is to give periodic solace and safe harbor by honoring the achievements or courageous positions taken by colleagues from sister Arkansas communities. The long shadows of the legends—Walter Lemke, Ernie Deane, Harry Ashmore, and the like—are still names embellished in hushed reverence at the "press meetings."

On a personal note, I look at many of these "newspaper people" throughout our history as some of our state's real heroes. Many times, they remained true to conviction in the face of economic loss. They were on the front line as advocates for better education, equality, justice, and local improvement when their safest position would have muted their feelings and compromised their duty. Week after week and year after year, those brave voices of reason and vision became embodied into the formation of our thoughts and beliefs. We are fortunate, as a people and as a state, to have had their willingness to lead and to provide the rest of us with the "paper."

—David H. Pryor

Introduction

"Journalism is too important, too crucial for our democracy, to be left unexamined."
—Marvin Kalb, *One Scandalous Story*, 2001

As the author selected to write a history for the Arkansas Press Association, I feel it incumbent upon me to lay before what in the 19th century was called the gentle reader an explanation or justification for my work. I am not a professor of journalism but have been a historian since the age of eight. Newspapers have played major roles in my life from my earliest days. A friend and I privately published a newspaper while we were in the third grade. One great-grandfather, Judge John R. Woodside of Thomasville, brought the first press into Oregon County, Missouri. His son, Captain J. Posey Woodside, served as editor of the *South Missouri Democrat* at Alton. My paternal grandfather, Archibald Patrick Dougan, was long the circulation manager for the Fargo (N.D.) *Courier-News*. During the 1930s, mother "gathered advertising," as she put it, for the weekly *Miner and Mechanic*.

As a child growing up in Neosho, Missouri, I was often in the family-owned *Times* building that sported a skylight and still proudly bore its name emblazoned in stone. From that building came a large framed picture of John Marshall which has been my constant companion. An editor of that newspaper was A.M. Sevier, a cousin to those Arkansas Seviers who grace the first chapters and to whom William Minor Quesenbury, the greatest of 19th century Arkansas editors, gave one of his paintings. Quesenbury, whose wife was a friend of my grandmother, retired to Neosho, where he died.

We were a newspaper-reading family. My father always bought newspapers everywhere we went. When visiting Salem, Missouri, his hometown, he always stopped by the newspaper office to meet old friends. At home two newspapers came daily, and another on Sunday. A friend brought over the *New York Times*, albeit a week late, on Sunday afternoon.

In graduate school at Emory University, where I studied under the legendary Civil War historian Bell I. Wiley, I wrote my master's thesis on the Little Rock press during the Civil War. An article drawn from that thesis appeared in the *Arkansas Historical Quarterly* in 1969, marking the beginning of my publishing career. During my early research days in the late 1960s, I spent much time in the library of the *Arkansas Gazette*, where I sat at the feet of Margaret Ross, who knew more about 19th century Arkansas than any living person, and whose "Chronicles of Arkansas" series from the *Arkansas Gazette* is consulted regularly even today. Her history of that famous newspaper appeared in 1969, and I am greatly indebted to her thoroughness. I also met John N. Heiskell, who was still active in the newspaper's management, Hugh Patterson, his son-in-law, and others. These were my first contacts with living Arkansas journalists.

After completing my doctoral dissertation on Confederate Arkansas, I joined the staff of Arkansas

State University in 1970 and found myself immediately involved in the Arkansas Historical Association. Through that body I came to know Ernie Deane, Wilson Powell, and other historically active journalists. Over the years, I have contributed both guest editorials and feature articles for Arkansas's newspapers.

In the course of preparing my adult one-volume state history, *Arkansas Odyssey: The Saga of Arkansas from Prehistoric Times to Present* (1994), I read rolls of the state's newspapers on microfilm. Even if there was no immediate project at hand, I still read whatever came my way. Once, when on a research grant at The Newberry Library in Chicago, I sat down with William E. Woodruff's personal bound volumes of the *Arkansas Gazette*, following it from 1819 to the 1870s. In the process I gained an increased understanding of the historical developments around the state. Another project, a life of William Minor Quesenbury, gave me a chance to research in depth the life of that eclectic genius.

In undertaking this project, I knew I wanted to write a book that would appeal to several audiences. The general reading public deserves to know about the history and roles that newspapers have played. Members of the profession, who in recent times have been shortsighted about the value and uses of history, need as well to see the heritage in perspective so that they may better live up to the high standards laid down earlier in the age of print. All the rest, as they say, is just history, but valuable nevertheless in its own light.

Through my researches I have come to respect and admire many now-forgotten editors and writers I never got to meet. These include such fine writers as Esther Bindursky, who toiled for years in the small east Arkansas town of Lepanto but whose mind was world-class; Mountain Home editor Tom Shiras, who lovingly recorded the doings and deeds of his adopted Ozarks even as he promoted the changes that would end its special way of life; Karr Shannon, the hill country boy editor who told how the woodpeckers destroyed the Izard County courthouse; Max Hampton, the bard of Booneville; Opie Read, a reporter who left Arkansas to become one of America's most popular novelists; and, most of all, Erwin Funk of the *Rogers Democrat*. Funk, whose commitment to the Arkansas Press Association started in the 1890s and ended in 1960, was in a host of ways the embodiment of the highest ideals and practices of journalism. Alas, I knew him only through his newspaper, his clipping files, his historical articles, and his diary.

In the course of my research I have been present spiritually as editors and publishers coped with natural and manmade disasters. I have seen them struggle with frozen presses, overheated politicians, competition of all sorts, and the day-to-day struggles to keep the newspaper coming out regularly in spite of floods, fires, and nonpaying subscribers. I have followed them in causes nearest to their hearts: the aged Confederate veterans Walter W. Raney of McCrory undertook to sponsor; the crusading Coughlin brothers of Crittenden County, who took on an entrenched county political machine; Christopher Columbus Danley, who tried to talk reason to Arkansans bent on rushing into a Civil War; and J.B. Parker of Conway, who opposed kissing, Sunday driving, and other sinful diversions. In this process I have read good newspapers and bad newspapers; I have seen newspapers come and go. And since so little of Arkansas's newspaper legacy survived to the age of microfilming, I have seen less and know less than I would like.

When traveler Alexis de Tocqueville observed that American history would be recorded through its newspapers, he was largely right. So much has been lost in Arkansas history because so many newspapers were not saved. In 1905, John Hugh Reynolds, on behalf of the newly organized Arkansas History

Commission, undertook a survey of existing files from the state's 200 editors. Few answered him; of those who did, the response from J.R. Stotts of Huntsville's *Madison County Democrat*—"old files were burned"—was all too typical. Much of the early collections of the Arkansas History Commission started with a donation from L.G. Gulley, who saved old newspapers from the state capitol from being carried to the dump. Another of Reynolds's discoveries was that overwhelmingly newspaper offices were not binding their issues. There were hundreds of newspapers for which today not one single issue exists that could have revealed much about the saga of Arkansas.

Unfortunately, the saving of newspapers for posterity has never been a high priority in Arkansas. At least 75 percent of all issues have been lost, and the figure may be even higher. Often I have written about newspapers on the strength of information that cannot be found today or from just one or two copies. In one dreadful instance years ago, I sat amidst 50 years of bound issues dumped on a floor in a shed and read issue after issue. Some years later these still unmicrofilmed volumes were consigned to the city dump. Of course this book is not intended to be a state history, but Arkansas history has informed every step taken by editors and publishers to make successes of their investments.

Special credit needs to be given to some of my predecessors. J.N. Smithee, the founding president of the Arkansas Press Association, was also that body's first historian. In the early Association a number of distinguished individuals held the constitutionally created office of Historian, and some took the work seriously. Then Frederick W. Allsopp, long of the *Arkansas Gazette*, wrote the *History of the Arkansas Press for a Hundred Years and More* in 1922. Allsopp had access to persons and copies of newspapers now no longer available, but his treatment was organized county by county with little attention being given to content or technological change. Clio Harper, the founder of the *Arkansas Publisher*, was devoted to press history. In addition, he used the *Publisher* to give an ongoing account of journalism during the late 1920s and early '30s. Just before his death there appeared the *History of the Arkansas Press Association* (1930).

In 1972 Professor Robert W. Meriwether updated the statistical information about newspapers and their owners from 1930 to 1972 in his useful volume that I carry with me everywhere I go. Histories of individual newspapers are rare. Margaret Ross's definitive account of the *Arkansas Gazette* extends only to 1867. The rest of newspaper history is scattered in articles in historical quarterlies or in past issues of the newspapers themselves. It is worthy of notice that a number of old-time editors and publishers recorded local newspaper history. In addition to Funk, O. Klute Braswell of Berryville, Harry Lee Williams of Jonesboro, and W.H. Plank of Bentonville, to mention a few, compiled much valuable information. By contrast, almost nothing has been written about the changes in Arkansas newspapers since the end of World War II. The saga of modernization since 1950 cries out for comprehensive treatment.

Meanwhile, historians have relied on the comprehensive history laid down by Frank Luther Mott in his classic volume, *American Journalism: A History, 1690–1960*. This was a book I had studied back in graduate school and to which I returned in the preparation of this history. As I saw it, I needed to build on the work done by my predecessors while adding stories about the contents and methods—the social, economic, and political realities—that underlay the roles newspapers played in Arkansas society.

Oral history was invaluable for the last chapters. I was fortunate enough to have interviewed Ray Kimball of De Queen, at 90, the oldest active publisher prior to his death in 1999. Other oral history interviewees have included: Sam H. Hodges,

Wilson Powell, J.E. Dunlap, Tom Dearmore, Roy Breeden, Dorothy Stuck, John Troutt, the late Margaret Woolfolk, Maurice and C. Edward Tudor, Charlotte and Melvin Schexnayder, Jay W. Jackson, Betty and Cone Magie, Bill Penix, Robert McCord, Jim Morriss, Hugh Patterson, Anita Floyd-Marshall, Van and Ginnie Tyson, Frank Martin, Pete Coughlin, Jon Kennedy, George Fisher, Rusty Fraser, Robert Fisher, Gene Herrington, Louie Graves, the late Betty Woods, Ted and Margaret Larimer, David Pryor and the last two managers of APA, Louise Bowker and C. Dennis Schick. Informally, I have talked to everybody I have met at APA conventions, stopped by local newspaper offices even when it was not convenient, and fired off e-mails in all directions.

I owe a great debt of gratitude to the inter-library department of the Dean B. Ellis Library at Arkansas State University, Bob Besom and the Shiloh Museum of Ozark History, the special collections departments at the University of Arkansas, the University of Arkansas at Little Rock, and the University of Memphis as well as the Butler Center for Arkansas Studies at Central Arkansas Libraries, Southwest Arkansas Regional Archives, and the Arkansas History Commission.

This manuscript benefited immensely from the work of its readers. The late Margaret Ross corrected errors of fact and challenged some of my conclusions; John Horn, Frank Granger, Bobby Ruff, John Thomas, and Gene Ballard saved me from making some mistakes on printing matters; and Roy Reed, Van Tyson, Jay W. Jackson, and Frank Robins criticized various chapters. Finally, a considerable debt of gratitude goes to C. Dennis Schick, who, while undertaking to move the Association into a new building in a new century, had to deal with the requests and needs of an author located halfway across the state who kept raising up old, long-forgotten issues. His editing skills and eye for layout were invaluable. The APA staff also has been supportive, and the favors I owe Nancy Gilchrist, Tres Williams, Terri Cobb, and Jan Schick are considerable.

The road has been much longer than anyone anticipated. I did not reckon on a driver running a stop sign, a softball line drive that shattered my jaw, or an indoor flood that demolished a large part of our home. However, the main cause of my delay was a desire to get the story as right as possible. For that, I make no apology.

Technological change has been at work in Arkansas since William E. Woodruff launched the *Arkansas Gazette* on a simple Ramage wooden press in 1819. There is little doubt that in the years ahead the newspaper "as we know it today" will undergo immense changes. Yet two things will remain constant. People want news, and they have a strong need to express themselves about the meaning and application of that news. Newspapers, in whatever form they may take, will remain the core medium.

Erwin Funk began his career as a boy editor in 1896, ending in 1960. During his life he served as president of both APA and NEA (now NNA). He was the consummate professional, taking advantage of every improvement in technology for his Rogers newspaper. His picture was on the very first issue of the *Arkansas Publisher* in 1927 (see page 192), and no one ever reflected better the high ideals and practical business sense that are needed to make a success of a newspaper. Welcome, dear reader, to the world of Mr. Funk.

—Michael B. Dougan
May 2003

Chapter I

Origins of the Arkansas Press, Together with an account of its earliest years and a collection of notable firsts

"I've always said that journalists are born just as musicians and artists are born."
J.N. Heiskill, 1972. Quoted in Robert Shaw, "Editor Reviews 79 Years as Journalist," *Arkansas Publisher*, November 1972, 3.

"That printing presses shall be free to every person; and no law shall ever be made to restrain the rights thereof. The free communication of thoughts and opinions is one of the invaluable rights of man; and every citizen may freely speak, write and print on any subject—being responsible for the abuse of that liberty."
Article II, Section 7, Constitution of the State of Arkansas, 1836.

"The present size and complexion of our paper does not exactly suit us; but this we intend to remedy as soon as our patronage will justify our procuring new materials, and enlarging its size."
Wm. E. Woodruff, *Arkansas Gazette*, November 20, 1819.

"Our territory is rapidly emerging from the sable gloom which so long shrouded and concealed its merits from the citizens of the States; and is beginning to assume a character which must ultimately equal that of any other section of the Union. The wilderness, which a short time since was the asylum of the buffalo, and the retreat of the marauding savage, at present presents a rich repast to the philosophic mind."
A Citizen, *Arkansas Gazette*, November 25, 1820.

"We have not received a regular mail from any quarter for about two months, nor any papers for about a month."
Arkansas Gazette, February 12, 1823.

Introduction

The idea of written communication in Arkansas is older than the first newspapers. In the prehistoric period, there appeared the petroglyph. These rock drawings imparted special messages, believed to be of a religious nature, to those Indians able to decipher them. Thousands of such messages were painted on Arkansas's rocks, of which today perhaps a few hundred survive. A second form of communication consisted of trail signs. Future editor William Quesenbury sketched one he encountered when on the trail to Texas with a group of Cherokees in 1845. Finally, there were smoke signals. "This is going to mean the end of newspapers," Benjamin Franklin is alleged to have said after first learning of this form of communication.[1]

Newssheets and newsbooks were just coming into existence when the Pilgrims landed at Plymouth Rock. Despite determined attempts at suppression in Europe, recognizable progenitors of modern newspapers were very much in circulation by 1690, the date of the first newspaper in English America. Seventeenth-century colonies had managed without newspapers. Despite the determined opposition of Virginia's longtime royal governor Sir William Berkeley ("But, I thank God, we have not free schools nor printing..."),[2] the 18th century saw an enormous growth in presses and newspapers. Governments found that they could operate better with a printing press, and printers found that issuing newspapers was a needed adjunct to job printing. William H. Lyon, Jr., in *The Pioneer Editor in Missouri* (1964), argued that four agents were necessary in order to found a newspaper: governments needed to publish laws; politicians desired to influence the public; a literate citizenry wished to be informed; and the printer and/or editor wanted to secure an income and even possibly do some good. Lyon's assessment, that at least two of these agencies were necessary catalysts, was as valid for the English colonial period as it was well throughout the 19th century.[3]

Arkansas's earliest history, however, was not a part of the English experience. Unknown during Arkansas's colonial period were the historic trial of John Peter Zenger in New York that began the process of breaking down the English common law of libel, or even the first internationally famous American printer, Benjamin Franklin, who retired from active printing to pursue a course of altruism. Although the European discovery of Arkansas began with the De Soto *entrada* of 1541–42, it was the French settlement at the Post of Arkansas in 1686, a small trading post not even consistently occupied until after 1700, that began more than a century of first French, then Spanish, rule. Despite the arrival of farmers as part of the John Law colonization scheme in the 1720s, the total population of the Post had reached only 107 by 1791.

Newspapers were not a part of the French-Spanish culture in the Mississippi River valley. New Orleans did not get its first newspaper until 1794. Although the area had been under Spanish control since 1764, the small octavo four-page *Moniteur de la Louisiane* was published in French. According to contemporary reports, the press run was 80 copies and most of those went to Europeans and other foreigners.[4] The merchants of the Post doubtless saw copies; because their trade depended on international developments, they needed the information newspapers imparted. Samuel Treat, the American factor who took charge of the Post's Indian trade after the Louisiana Purchase in 1803, complained of the absence of newspapers and requested repeatedly that newspapers be sent to him. The majority of the French, however, lived for dancing and gambling. Years later, according to traveler Washington Irving, they thought that the Americans "trouble themselves with cares beyond their horizon and import sorrow thru the newspapers from every point of the compass."[5]

After the Louisiana Purchase, the number of newspapers increased rapidly. Missouri took a strong interest in what until 1819 was its southernmost county. St. Louis, from the start, was focused on the west and southwest. This Missouri connection with Arkansas has continued in transportation, banking, sports, and other forms up to the present day. By contrast, New Orleans was largely wrapped up in itself and the river. Save for its importance in providing market access for antebellum cotton, teaching planters' sons the elegant delights of theatres, whorehouses, gambling halls, and the *code duello*, New Orleans had little direct impact on Arkansas.

Missouri's press history began in 1808 when Joseph Charless set up shop with a Ramage press in St. Louis. A refugee from Ireland, Charless had worked in Philadelphia before moving first to Lexington, Kentucky, and then on to St. Louis. Charless received not only an advance of $225 from Governor Meriwether Lewis but also a contract to publish the territory's laws. His newspaper's original title, the *Missouri Gazette and Louisiana Advertiser*, reflected the fact that the Territory of Orleans did not become the State of Louisiana until 1812. Everything north of the Territory of Orleans was still called Louisiana despite the fact that the area around St. Louis was called Missouri. Arkansas was a district in this territory after 1806.

Reflective of the large French population, Charless was forced to publish bilingually. Despite having strong opinions hostile to slavery and facing weekly problems with getting both adequate supplies of paper and reasonably new news, Charless enjoyed a monopoly for seven years.[6] His newspaper, later renamed the *Missouri Republican*, was for more than half a century one of the most widely read and quoted newspapers in the nation, being especially noted for its coverage of Arkansas.

While the nation was embroiled in following the controversy over admitting Missouri to the Union as a slave state, one aspect of Missouri's application for statehood attracted the interest of printers: In order to make Missouri of acceptable size for statehood, Arkansas had to be cut loose.

Creating the Arkansas Gazette

When Congress approved the creation of the Territory of Arkansas on March 3, 1819, there was no press within its bounds. Two years earlier, a failed St. Louis printer, Joshua Novell, had moved to Arkansas, and on his heels came another displaced editor, Sergeant Hall. Although the first newspapermen in Arkansas, neither played any subsequent role in its history.[7]

Closely following Arkansas affairs was William Edward Woodruff, then serving as the foreman of the *Clarion* and *Tennessee State Gazette* in Nashville. Born on Long Island, New York, on December 24, 1795, young Woodruff had grown up playing with John and James Harper, the future founders of a famous publishing firm, and B.L.E. Bonneville, later a famous Western military officer. After completing his formal apprenticeship at the *Suffolk Gazette* and the *Long-Island Star* under Alden Spooner, Woodruff became a journeyman printer on his 21st birthday.

Spooner's place in American history is secure, because in the 1830s another of his apprentices, who apparently never finished his term, was American poet Walt Whitman. Whitman later testified as to the value of his training in words Woodruff would no doubt have endorsed: "there you got your culture direct: not through borrowed sources—no, a century of college training could not confer such results on anyone."[8]

Forthwith, upon receiving freedom, Woodruff headed west. After a short and unhappy stay in Louisville, he and a friend, another printer named Henry Van Pelt (in 1841 the founder of the *Memphis Weekly Appeal*), shipped their trunks by keelboat (steamboats had not yet arrived in western waters) while they walked the distance from Louisville to Nashville. Unfortunately, these young men had arrived just as the Panic of 1818 was making its way west. Although Woodruff rose to the rank of foreman at the *Clarion*, he kept his eyes open for better opportunities. Arkansas was that opportunity.[9]

News of the territory's creation coincided with

the report that John M'Arthur of Ste. Genevieve planned to start a newspaper to be called the *Arkansas Herald*. McArthur (to use the more common spelling of his name)[10] bore a checkered reputation. Although his wife was the sister of future Senator Lewis F. Linn, McArthur had been accused of counterfeiting by Auguste DeMun. McArthur had challenged DeMun to a duel, but DeMun demurred on the grounds that McArthur was no gentleman. The printer, proving the point, retaliated by killing DeMun on the steps of the courthouse at Cape Girardeau; he was never prosecuted. McArthur not only announced his plans for a newspaper but even came to the Post and rented a house. Then he disappeared. Perhaps the thought of other DeMuns in Lawrence County prompted him to give up the project.

Just how Woodruff learned that McArthur had abandoned the field is not known, but by September the young printer had acquired a second-hand Ramage press (on credit) and other supplies. This simple wooden press, long standard, had been built by Adam Ramage, a Scottish-born printer who settled in Philadelphia in the 1790s. Woodruff's type, Binney & Ronaldson's Series No. 1, was the earliest type to be manufactured in the United States. Classified then as Small Pica Roman and Italic, it was renamed 11-point Oxford in 1908.

Woodruff left Nashville by keelboat in September 1819. In addition to the press and type, he carried such needed supplies as scissors, glue pot, inkwells, four bundles of paper, and a supply of printers' ink. Not expecting to find news in Arkansas, he also carried a stack of old newspapers with him and doubtless attempted to pick up others along the way.

Woodruff's route took him from Nashville down the Cumberland to the Ohio and thence to Cairo where that river joined the Mississippi. From there he descended the Father of Waters until coming to rest at Montgomery's Point. At this town, notorious for gambling and crime, Woodruff transferred his equipment to a pirogue carved out of a single cottonwood tree. His raftsmen, at first fearful that they were transporting some infernal machine, finally poled the boat up the White River and through the White River cut-off that connected to the Arkansas River. On October 31, Woodruff arrived at the Post.[11]

Already over a century old, the Post had failed conspicuously to flourish. During the French and Spanish period as well as during the first few years of American control, it had housed a military garrison in addition to a few farmers and the merchants who traded with the nearby Quapaw for furs and hides. Plagued by malaria and every other illness known to the West, the town at the time of Woodruff's arrival contained only some 30-odd houses but a collection of larger-than-life egos.

The French settlers had been largely displaced from any role in the new government. Only the merchants and a few farmers were literate, so Woodruff never needed to print his newspaper bilingually as in New Orleans and St. Louis. By the time Woodruff arrived, power rested with Robert Crittenden, the territorial secretary, who had arrived in late July. The first governor, War of 1812 hero James Miller, did not show up until five months later. By advancing Arkansas to a second-class territory soon after his arrival, Crittenden required voters to select an assembly and to elect a delegate to represent the territory in Congress. Those election campaigns were underway when Woodruff arrived. First Woodruff rented a two-room log cabin. If his memory 50 years later was correct[12], it was not in the French style but consisted of round logs and sported a waddle-and-daub (stick-and-mud) chimney. Then he began assembling his materials.

Three things were significant about that November 20, 1819, issue of the first newspaper in Arkansas. First, Woodruff had to make a choice as to how to spell his new home. His selection of

"Arkansas" rather than "Arkansaw" doubtless contributed mightily to the formal adoption of this spelling. Second, in styling his newspaper the "Gazette," he invoked a term that for over a century often had been used to denote an official publication.[13] Woodruff expected, as the territory's only printer, to be its official printer. It was his determination, which he proved to be unable to sustain, to avoid politics and personalities and offer only the news. Finally, in time, it would be long claimed that the *Gazette* was the oldest newspaper west of the Mississippi. (Technically, however, Missouri provided other competitors for this title.) Woodruff's legacy was lost when the *Arkansas Democrat* acquired the *Gazette* in 1991.

Woodruff's first shop, the two-room cabin he had rented, contained within one room the publisher's bed and office. Composing was done at an "editor's table," but whether Woodruff actually sat upon a tripod, a higher sort of milking stool which became synonymous with editing, is unknown. The smaller room housed the press. Woodruff did no cooking at his bachelor's quarters, taking his meals with a French lady.[14]

The first issue of the *Arkansas Gazette*, published on November 20, 1819, was curious in that it contained no prospectus. It had long been common to seek support by producing a broadside to announce plans for a newspaper. If perchance the newspaper came to reality, the first issue was certain to reprint the prospectus, usually running it for several months. Perhaps because the Post was so small and the rest of Arkansas's population so scattered and mail services so inadequate, Woodruff never felt the need even to issue one. Interestingly, Woodruff promised local subscribers home delivery.[15]

Woodruff's four-page newspaper had to be printed page by page. Standard practice for most of the century was to begin by setting the first and last pages, leaving for last an ever-narrowing space on the inside pages. Long-running advertisements, professional cards, and filler material constituted the first and fourth pages. Since newspapers relied heavily for distribution on the mails, and mailmen commonly subjected them to rough handling, almost all antebellum newspapers except those dailies sold directly by newsboys used this system.

The last thing Woodruff set was the newly arrived election returns. Each page measured 18 1/2 inches long by 11 1/4 inches wide, and four 14 1/2 pica columns constituted each page. Woodruff's skill as a printer was shown by having a two-column advertisement. This required Woodruff to break the brass column rule that held the type in place. Without that support, the type often showed a dangerous tendency to roll. Woodruff apparently filled the gaps by using a cutoff rule turned vertically.

Nineteenth-century newspapers commonly listed the editor and publisher, often combining the titles if one man or woman held both positions. In this case, under the *Arkansas Gazette* nameplate on the front page ran the tag "By Wm. E. Woodruff." With no way yet to attract outside advertisers, Woodruff collected his advertisements locally. All this work Woodruff did himself, serving as editor, publisher, foreman, compositor, pressman, devil, ball boy, and mail clerk. He may have even delivered the newspapers himself.[16]

Woodruff sent his newspaper off in all directions, although the subscription rate was three dollars a year if paid in advance and four dollars if on credit. At various times Woodruff claimed that he started with no subscribers, with fewer than 40 subscribers, and with 100. *Gazette* historian Margaret Ross speculated that all three versions could be in some way correct: he had no initial subscribers when he began setting type; there were 40 signed up on the first subscription list; and his first press run was 100 copies.[17]

Woodruff's first issue included two original contributions. One was a letter signed "A Citizen of the Territory" who protested the federal government's plans to move Cherokees into Arkansas; the other was an essay describing the Post. The latter piece's anonymous contributor, lawyer Samuel Calhoun Roane, soon began helping Woodruff get out his newspaper. Whether he was paid for his efforts is a matter of conjecture. Another feature was "Selected Poetry." Nineteenth-century newspapers invariably announced a commitment to Culture, and poetry columns long remained a popular item.

In Woodruff's time, assembling a newspaper meant three things. First, news would be gleaned from other newspapers. Every businessman and politician anxious to court the press saved old issues to drop off at the newspaper office. Editors graciously acknowledged these gifts of newspapers, thereby supplying the givers with some politically valuable name recognition. These supplemented the regular source of news, the exchanges. Newspapers kept an exchange list, sending off free copies and receiving the same by return mail. Within 10 years, Woodruff's list ran to nearly 100 newspapers. Woodruff would select what he thought his readers wanted or needed to read and print it in his newspaper. Ethics required giving credit to the newspaper of origin. Nineteenth-century journalists referred to this as the "scissors and pot paste" method. It was also common in the case of local obituaries to request republication in the deceased's hometown newspaper.

Nineteenth-century newspapers were strikingly different from their 20th-century counterparts. Conspicuously absent were headlines. Many important stories were simply paragraphs of varying length running one right after another. Headlines required breaking the columns, which printers were loath to do, and they required larger type sizes, which smaller shops often lacked. Well into the 20th century, shops still used old wooden block "boxcar" letters for creating headlines. Finally, it should be noted that newspapers were paid to publish laws and other documents. A presidential or gubernatorial address or the proceedings of a legislative session might start on page one, spill over into additional pages, or be continued in subsequent weeks. One of the most important of these early "legals" was the delinquent tax list.

The second source of news came from the editor himself. The idea that Woodruff went, like a modern reporter, to find stories and then wrote them in an impersonal manner was foreign to the operations of early 19th-century newspapers. Actually, local news that Woodruff might have covered was of little publishing value if the community already knew it. Fires and common affrays that might have made their way into print a century later were considered common knowledge. Early newspapers were very erratic in reporting marriages. Deaths and births were almost never mentioned. However, early Arkansas politicians were a violent bunch prone to duels, and since the loss of life of a territorial legislator or judge assumed regional importance, these events warranted coverage. Generally, the first column on the second page was presumed to contain the work of the editor. Little distinction existed between a news story and an editorial opinion. Subsequent columns, unless otherwise credited, contained mixtures of both news and editorial comment. In such stories, the separation of narrative from comment could be effected by the use of italics or capitals. The editor was personally responsible for what appeared unsigned or uncredited.[18]

The third source of news came in the form of contributions. Some of these were informational, like that of the aforementioned Samuel Calhoun Roane. Although Roane's piece had appeared without attribution, 19th-century editors generally granted credit to nonpolitical pieces. Woodruff did not accept for publication everything he received. On one occasion, he replied in print to "the herrikin morilist," noting that "it will require one better acquainted with dead languages than we are, to decipher some of the unknown characters in which it is written, or even to understand the subject which it treats on. It was unnecessary for the writer to have inform us, that he is no 'skoller.'"[19] On another occasion he refused to publish a letter "written in scriptural style" attacking slavery. "We can see no good that can result from a discussion" since it had been ordained that Arkansas would be a slave state.[20]

Election time brought forth a slew of contributions, often marked by such violent language that anonymity was considered necessary. And that first election, which Woodruff had arrived too late to cover, set in motion forces that shaped Arkansas from 1819 up to the Civil War. Since the history of the press became inexorably entwined with politics, some background is necessary.[21]

During the five months it took Governor James Miller to get to the Post, territorial secretary Robert Crittenden wheeled and dealed. This 22-year-old scion of a prominent Kentucky political family soon gathered around him a circle of other unmarried, ambitious young men whose careers he had the power to advance or retard. No middle ground was possible with Crittenden. Albert Pike, a future Arkansas editor whose career Crittenden advanced, called him "a thoroughly well-bred Kentucky gentleman"; Judge Thomas P. Eskridge, who knew him from the Post days on, denounced him as "the agitator of faction, the instigator of crime, the promoter of duels, the corrupter of youth, the open and shameless gambler, [and] the inmate of the vilest and most debasing associations of profligacy."[22]

Crittenden sought to promote an eastern, aristocratic faction, displacing both old settlers and keeping western Arkansans powerless. Early on, Crittenden was reportedly unhappy with Woodruff for allowing the secretary's opponents even to have access to the newspaper. Temperamentally, the high-toned aristocrat and the rising laborer were an unlikely combination. Well before their final break, the seeds of discord were being sown.

In the aftermath of that first election, which contained a closely contested race for territorial delegate and the election of the first legislature, Woodruff published a number of letters signed under pseudonyms. However, when "Tantamount" replied to "Silence" and neglected to provide Woodruff with his real name, Woodruff refused to publish the letter. His policy of refusing to publish letters unless he knew the author's name became standing policy at the *Gazette*.[23] Other early newspapers were not so careful, however, and editors often found themselves in trouble in consequence.

Despite a rocky start, the *Arkansas Gazette* was still being published when, on December 26, 1819, Governor Miller finally arrived, flying a flag with "Arkansaw" in large letters. By March 1820, Woodruff took in a partner, Robert Briggs, a Massachusetts-born printer. Briggs might have been responsible for the *Gazette*'s first weather reports. Styled "Meteorological Journal," it consisted of a monthly summary giving the daily temperature at three different times, the wind direction, and comments on each day's weather. Such features would become an irregular part of the Arkansas press for the remainder of the century.[24]

Woodruff and Briggs (as the firm was then styled) also printed the election announcement of Joseph Stillwell, an old settler, who had the *Gazette* set it in French as well as English. Since Woodruff lacked the fonts for French, improvisation was the order of the day. The acute and grave marks made it necessary to set each letter below the line. On another occasion when a cedilla was required in a French proper name, Woodruff simply inserted a "5."

Other improvements consisted of reporting the "prices current" from New Orleans and the first use of woodcuts. These were square generic pictures used for advertising. Woodruff had a horse for use in estrays, a three-story building for hotels (although no such building existed anywhere in Arkansas), and a steamboat for the *Comet*, the first such boat in Arkansas waters. In time, Arkansas editors would have a whole arsenal of such graphics.[25]

Finally, on February 22, 1820, Woodruff printed Arkansas's first "extra," President Madison's address to Congress delivered on December 7 but not received by Woodruff until two days before he put out his extra. Extras remained an occasional feature, diminishing in times of peace but reappearing during World War II and after the World Trade Center attacks in 2001.

More than personal piques were at stake in early Arkansas. A plan to move the Cherokees into western Arkansas threatened the very future of the territory and prompted a violent protest. The *Gazette* printed a variety of communications on this subject, again angering Robert Crittenden, who now began to find ways to withhold public printing from the *Gazette* while looking around for a competing printer.

Meanwhile, the first year rolled around, and Woodruff found himself with a bloated subscription list of nonpaying readers. Threats to sue delinquents, to publish names of nonpayers, to discontinue delinquent subscribers, and even to demand cash in advance all failed Woodruff.[26] They would fail every other publisher in Arkansas for the next 150 years.

Woodruff should have gotten the appointment from the Secretary of State in Washington for the printing of federal laws. The territorial delegate, James Woodson Bates, who was in Crittenden's pocket, apparently did nothing to disabuse the Secretary that Woodruff and not McArthur was the established printer. For a year and a half, this lucrative source of money was denied him.

Meanwhile, it was decided to move the territorial capital to a more central and healthier location. A little rock just below the big rock up the Arkansas River seemed the perfect site. In October 1820, the legislature authorized the removal of the government to Little Rock. However, locating the capital touched off a real estate war between rival sets of land speculators and their political allies over who owned what part of Little Rock.

When the first legislature met there in October 1821, they were greeted by their personal copies of the first Arkansas book. As authorized by the legislature, William E. Woodruff had published the *Laws of the Territory of Arkansas comprising The Organic Laws of the Territory of Missouri and Arkansas with their Amendments and Supplements Annexed* (to give the short title). Extra copies were sold for one dollar.

While in Little Rock, Woodruff attempted to collect moneys due him from the territorial secretary, but Crittenden threw every obstacle in his way. Although this controversy may have been rooted in personal differences between the two, it set a theme long common in Arkansas: that because Arkansas was poor, printers (and other trades as well) should be willing to accept less.

Woodruff had figured his bill in exact detail, charging one dollar per thousand ems of text and index, two dollars per ems for side notes, and one and a quarter cents average for the small type needed for signatures and titles. In addition, Woodruff had to bear the costs of binding and stitching. An extra journeyman had cost him $150. His total bill came to $336.89 1/2, payable in the territory's scrip (then being discounted 25 percent by local merchants). By the standards of American printing, the bill format was unexceptional, and the prices were in line with those of St. Louis, Woodruff's nearest point of reference. But Crittenden refused to pay more than $250, and Woodruff spent the next two years before he finally received the rest and that without any interest being paid on the balance.[27]

Meanwhile, the *Arkansas Gazette* had suspended publication, for Woodruff had to move his shop to the new capital. Snow and ice had come early in the winter of 1821–22, freezing the Arkansas River. Woodruff apparently used ox carts to move his press to the capital, where on December 29, 1822, he resumed the newspaper. Upon leaving the Post, he sold six town lots and several Spanish land grants. Whatever profits Woodruff had made he plowed into land purchases, and while for the next 30 years his claim to fame in Arkansas came from his newspapers, outside business activities constituted his primary source of income.

Little Rock, while strategically located for a capital, posed severe problems for its early inhabitants. Transportation depended on the floatability of the Arkansas River, and about half the time it was not. In consequence, Woodruff found himself faced with shortages of paper and of news, while getting his newspaper to subscribers elsewhere in the state was equally problematic.

The paper problem hit immediately, and Woodruff resorted to half-sheets to continue publication before suspending for two weeks. That newspapers would be wedded to the new technology became apparent when the first steamboat on the Arkansas, the *Eagle*, apparently brought Woodruff a supply of paper in March. Woodruff's next shipment of paper proved to be of a smaller size, forcing the publisher to narrow his margins. Historian Margaret Ross noted that during a period of 104 weeks running from December 29, 1821, to December 16, 1823, Woodruff missed two issues, printed 16 on half-sheets, 30 on smaller stock, 11 on stationary or book stock, and six on bright blue paper. In short, 65 out of the 104 issues presented unusual challenges.[28] Such conditions continued to plague newspapers well into the 20th century.

The mail, Woodruff's source for outside information, was just as bad. When, in 1823, the *National Intelligencer* in Washington concluded that communication with Arkansas was slower than with anywhere else in the world, Woodruff agreed. Indeed,

Woodruff complained that the failure of mail from and to Arkansas was largely due to the postmasters, "many of whom seem to be ignorant of the existence of such a country as the Territory of Arkansas" so that Arkansas's mail ended up at Arkansas, Illinois, or Little Rock, Alabama.[29] Fortunately, the mailman serving the Crawford County Court House (soon to be Van Buren) delivered subscribers their newspapers on his way.

Out on the edge of the frontier the *Gazette* reached the Quesenbury family. One of the earliest recollections of William (Cush) Quesenbury, later a famous editor, was growing up with the newspaper. "Do you know, dear old GAZETTE," Quesenbury recalled in 1871, "that yours was the first face I ever saw of the newspaper family? I almost heard your first words—you were a wonderful baby and talked as soon as you were born."[30] By 1823, Woodruff had 300 subscribers in all parts of the state, some of whom paid their bills. Otherwise, Little Rock merchants' advertisements replaced those from the Post, as that town dwindled into insignificance. At times Woodruff restored the weather column and, according to one calculation, published 65 original poems between 1819 and 1843.[31]

Since Woodruff was still the only printer in the territory, he continued to enjoy his monopoly status. Although he had adequate job facilities, as evidenced by his printing of the legislative acts and proceedings, he had remarkably little job printing business, issuing, as far as is known, only two years' minutes (1824 and 1825) for the Little Rock Association of Regular

This painting, which first appeared in print in 1910 and subsequently much reprinted, has several errors. Woodruff testified that only one pirogue (a large canoe made from one tree) carried the press. The two raftsmen poled, not paddled the boat; and since poling was skilled work, a novice like Woodruff would never have been allowed to help. The painting also failed to show that the two men were terrified of the supposed infernal engine they were transporting. (Courtesy UALR Archives and Special Collections)

First home of the Arkansas Gazette. *This drawing was made in 1877 under William E. Woodruff's personal direction. (Courtesy, Margaret Ross,* Arkansas Gazette: The Early Years, 1819-1866)

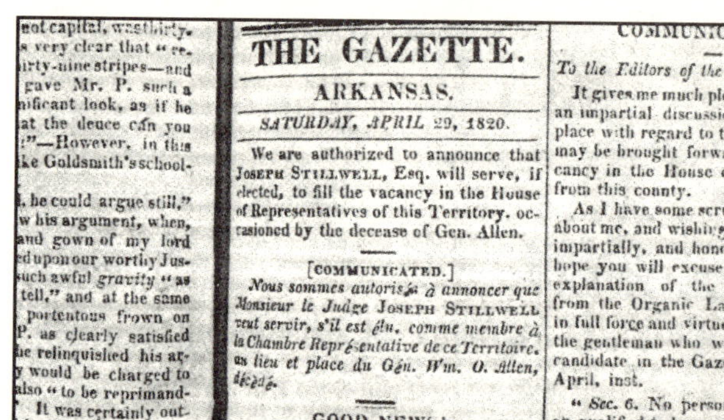

not capital, wasthirty-
s very clear that " re-
irty-nine stripes—and
gave Mr. P. such a
nificant look, as if he
at the deuce can you
!"—However, in this
ke Goldsmith's school-

, he could argue still,"
w his argument, when,
and gown of my lord
d upon our worthy Jus-
uch awful *gravity* " as
tell," and at the same
portentous frown on
P. as clearly satisfied
he relinquished his ar-
y would be charged to
also " to be reprimand-
It was certainly out-

THE GAZETTE.

ARKANSAS.

SATURDAY, APRIL 29, 1820.

We are authorized to announce that JOSEPH STILLWELL, Esq. will serve, if elected, to fill the vacancy in the House of Representatives of this Territory, occasioned by the decease of Gen. Allen.

[COMMUNICATED.]

Nous sommes autorisés à annoncer que Monsieur le Judge JOSEPH STILLWELL *veut servir, s'il est élu, comme membre à la Chambre Représentative de ce Territoire, au lieu et place du Gén. Wm. O. Allen, décédé.*

GOOD NEWS!

COMMUNICA

To the Editors of the A

It gives me much plea
an impartial discussion
place with regard to th
may be brought forwar
cancy in the House of
from this county.
As I have some scru
about me, and wishing t
impartially, and honor
hope you will excuse
explanation of the f
from the Organic Law
in full force and virtue
the gentleman who wa
candidate in the Gaze
April, inst.
" *Sec. 6.* No person
or qualified to be a re

The Arkansas Gazette *attempted to print a French announcement without the proper fonts. The French is a translation of the English above it.* (Arkansas Gazette, *April 29, 1820)*

Printer John Horn demonstrates the Ramage press to a group of students at Historic Arkansas Museum in Little Rock. (Courtesy Historic Arkansas Museum)

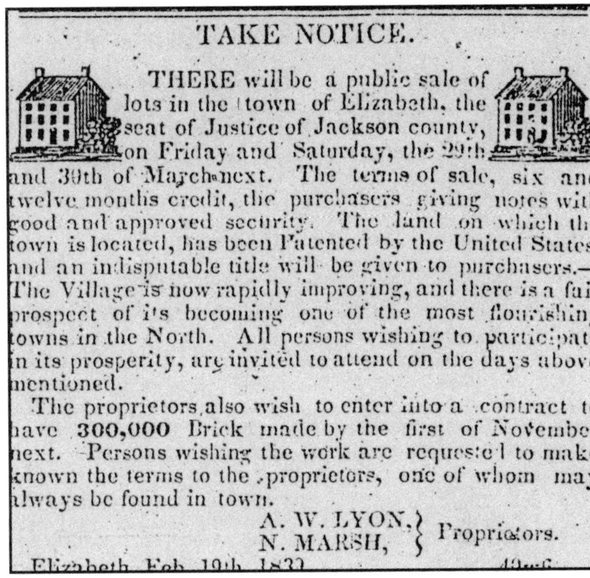

TAKE NOTICE.

THERE will be a public sale of lots in the town of Elizabeth, the seat of Justice of Jackson county, on Friday and Saturday, the 29th and 30th of March next. The terms of sale, six and twelve months credit, the purchasers giving notes with good and approved security. The land on which the town is located, has been Patented by the United States and an indisputable title will be given to purchasers.—The Village is now rapidly improving, and there is a fair prospect of it's becoming one of the most flourishing towns in the North. All persons wishing to participate in its prosperity, are invited to attend on the days above mentioned.

The proprietors also wish to enter into a contract to have 300,000 Brick made by the first of November next. Persons wishing the work are requested to make known the terms to the proprietors, one of whom may always be found in town.

A. W. LYON, }
N. MARSH, } Proprietors.

Elizabeth, Feb. 19th, 183[illegible]

An early classified ad. No three-story buildings existed at Elizabeth. Located on a ridge some ten miles back from the White River east of the future Newport, it failed to thrive. (The Batesville News, *February 21, 1839*)

An apprentice printer sits before the type cases. The sheet of paper in front gives the locations for the pieces of type. (Courtesy Historic Arkansas Museum)

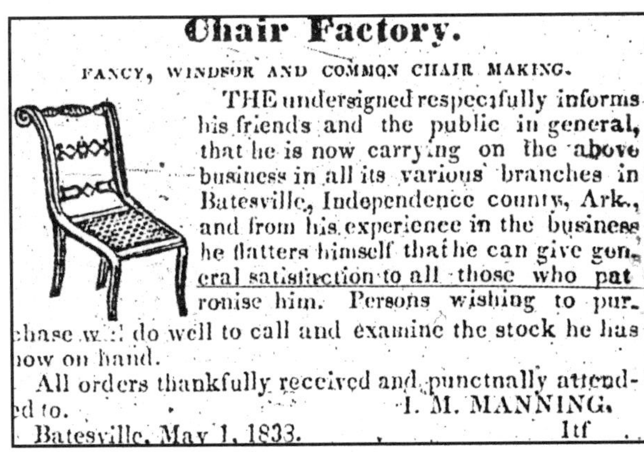

Chair Factory.

FANCY, WINDSOR AND COMMON CHAIR MAKING.

THE undersigned respectfully informs his friends and the public in general, that he is now carrying on the above business in all its various branches in Batesville, Independence county, Ark., and from his experience in the business he flatters himself that he can give general satisfaction to all those who patronise him. Persons wishing to purchase will do well to call and examine the stock he has now on hand.

All orders thankfully received and punctually attended to. I. M. MANNING.

Batesville, May 1, 1833. 1tf

Newspapers stocked common advertising cuts to illustrate specific products or services. Such cuts were generic, i.e., in the absence of evidence, it is doubtful that I.M. Manning's chair factory at Batesville actually made its chairs like the one pictured here. (The Batesville News, *August 9, 1838*)

Baptists and a collection of militia laws in 1826.[32]

What eventually caused Woodruff competition was the political fireworks that involved the territorial delegate, James Woodson Bates. Apparently, Crittenden switched his support to Henry W. Conway. Bates had planned to marry and had expressed doubts about running for a third term. However, his fiancée died, and Bates changed his mind. News of his decision did not reach Arkansas in a timely way, and Bates found himself out of the race. The *Gazette* was full of correspondence concerning the race, but Woodruff took no sides.

Meanwhile, Woodruff moved from a log cabin into a two-story brick building on the southwest corner of Cherry (Second) and Cumberland with a frame addition on its east side. Here he reestablished bachelor's quarters, and there the newspaper remained for the next three years. In 1939, the existing structures at this site became the Arkansas Territorial Restoration, which was expanded and renamed the Historic Arkansas Museum in 2001. Time and fires had wrought many changes, and there is strong evidence that the currently restored brick building is not the one that housed the *Gazette*.[33]

Woodruff prospered so much during this period that in 1827 he built an office building on the northeast corner of Scott and Markham streets. Flush to the street with two stories and an attic, it was a prestige address for a powerful institution. Directly opposite stood the new brick mansion of Chester Ashley.

Into Woodruff's employ came two individuals much associated with early Arkansas history. Hiram Abiff Whittington arrived on Christmas Eve 1826 from New York by way of New Orleans. A former employee of Alden Spooner, Woodruff's old master, Whittington served as foreman until 1832. Then, for health reasons, he established himself in Hot Springs, where he became one of the resort's founding fathers. About the same time, Charles Pierre Bertrand, the stepson of Little Rock's first doctor, Matthew Cunningham, entered the office as an apprentice. Woodruff had taken his meals with the Cunninghams on first arriving in Little Rock, which may have contributed to Bertrand's desire to learn printing.

At the same time, Woodruff expanded his land business. Creating the Arkansas Military Land Agency, he offered to take care of the territorial taxes for out-of-state owners. In time, he undertook all varieties of management for his clients as well as increasing his own speculations.

Although the political temperature had cooled after Conway's election, it again soared to fever heights, precipitating tales of revenge and sordid name-calling after Governor Miller submitted his resignation at the end of 1824. Miller had been out of state for 18 months straight at the time; so often had he been absent from his post that Secretary Crittenden's power was in reality superior to his. The new appointee, Major General George Izard (pronounced with the accent on the second syllable), did not intend to play second fiddle to the territorial secretary. At a minimum, the strict disciplinarian Izard expected to find a competently running government in Little Rock with all its affairs in order. Instead, he found Crittenden gone to Kentucky, thus depriving the territory of any executive, and the papers a mess, especially with regard to the territory's finances. Izard found comfort among Crittenden's opponents, notably Chester Ashley, a Massachusetts-born and Litchfield-trained lawyer who was Woodruff's closest friend. As Izard tried to make order, he found that many of Crittenden's friends had a lot of explaining to do. As sides took shape for the upcoming affray, Woodruff openly threatened to expose those "high in authority" who had abused their offices. He did not mean Delegate Henry W. Conway, who had illegally borrowed Quapaw moneys, for he did not know this at the time. But he did mean Crittenden.

Although Crittenden was reappointed secretary, he decided that Henry W. Conway had deserted him. Accordingly, when the next election rolled around in 1827, a close Crittendenite, Robert Oden, emerged as an opponent. Woodruff had been increasingly at odds with Crittenden, but now he was joined by Conway, Conway's cousin Ambrose Hundley Sevier, and Chester Ashley. For starters, Woodruff refused to print Oden's circular, claiming that it contained falsehoods for which he, Woodruff the printer, might be liable. Some of the libels, indeed, concerned Woodruff. Violence threatened as Oden's friends gathered outside the *Gazette* office, ready to horsewhip the editor, but when the newspaper's printers stood behind their man, no violence resulted. Oden was forced to send to Memphis to have his announcement printed. On the way back, his man carrying the circulars got lost. Eating sassafras leaves, blackberries, and crawfish (raw), the man "scarcely had the wherewithal to cover his nakedness" when he arrived in town.[34]

Hiram Whittington, Woodruff's printer, caught the atmosphere of the time in a letter to his brother in late July:

> Night before last, I saw four pistols presented to as many hearts, within six inches of each other, and had it not been for the interference of bystanders there would have been four or five persons killed. That there will be bloodshed before the election is over, there is not much doubt. Mr. Crittenden, Secretary of the Territory, has threatened to cut Mr. Woodruff's throat for publishing a communication concerning his official conduct, and, what is much worse, has threatened to cut off the nose of every printer in the place and pull down the printing office. Should he attempt either, he would be used up very soon. You have no idea what a set of villains inhabit this place. Mr. Woodruff and one of the young men in the office are sick with the fever; brought on, I believe, by fear.[35]

Instead of violence, Crittenden sued Woodruff for libel in the amount of $25,000, a huge figure at this time. The editor was in rather a tight spot in that his charges rested on the testimony of two men who were now dead. One of these, Isaac Watkins, had been murdered by a man he had accused of stealing hogs. An early settler of Little Rock, Watkins was tied to Woodruff in another way. On November 27, 1827, Woodruff had ended his bachelor days by marrying Watkins's niece, 17-year-old Jane Eliza Mills. The young couple started housekeeping in the Gazette Building. Living atop or in back of a newspaper business was a practice that continued into the 20th century.

The second of Woodruff's witnesses was Henry W. Conway. Despite, or perhaps because of, Crittenden's support for Oden, Conway easily turned back that challenge. What was not so easily deflected was the bullet on October 29, 1827, from Crittenden's dueling pistol that ended Conway's life. Fragments of the delegate's shattered toothbrush led to infection and death a week later. Ambrose H. Sevier succeeded his cousin as territorial delegate.

Fifty years later, Woodruff recalled: "In 1827 it was not very good. I found it difficult to avoid personal collision. I cannot say that I was afraid of my life but always went armed in those days."[36] And things got worse in 1828. On January 17 of that year, John T. Garrett, one of Crittenden's "satellites" (to use Woodruff's word) spent much of the day drinking and cursing Chester Ashley. Ashley, a married man, relied on that excuse to avoid duels, and Woodruff consistently denounced the duelling as barbaric. Garrett made one visit to the *Gazette* office with whip and pistol in hand but found too many persons present. After some more boozing, he returned to find only Woodruff and Ashley.

Exactly what followed was unclear at the inquest,

but as Garrett fired at Ashley, Woodruff deflected his aim, and a second pistol shot struck Garrett in the abdomen, resulting in his eventual death. Ashley fired his pistol but struck Woodruff instead. The mystery of the fatal shot was never satisfactorily resolved, but earlier in the day Garrett had flourished two pistols, of which only one was found across the street where he died. Although lawyer Ashley was more the object of Garrett's rage than editor Woodruff, there can be no disputing that Woodruff became the first Arkansas editor to survive an assassination attempt. The botched murder quelled the libel suit, as Woodruff and Crittenden worked out a temporary settlement of their difficulties.[37]

Meanwhile, on December 30, 1828, Woodruff celebrated the start of the *Gazette*'s 10th year. A new nameplate in Old English made it *The Arkansas Gazette*, and the size was now 13 inches wide and 21 inches long. Each page still contained five columns, but these were increased from 13 1/2 to 14 picas.

Along with an enlarged newspaper, Arkansas got a new governor. Izard had died in November 1828, and after the election of Andrew Jackson to the presidency the Senate had refused to confirm outgoing president John Quincy Adams's choice. Instead, on March 9, John Pope of Kentucky, ironically, the brother-in-law of Adams, was named governor. Pope, who had a monumental ego mismatched to miniscule skills, compared Arkansas to a plantation and himself to an overseer. Arkansans were not thrilled to be compared with slaves, and from the start Pope had an insurrection on his hands.

One victim of Jackson's "new broom sweeps clean" movement was Secretary Crittenden. His family members in Kentucky were violent Jackson opponents, and as soon as Congress adjourned, Jackson appointed an old friend, his former military secretary, William Savin Fulton, to the office. Crittenden, now out of a job and financially overextended, nevertheless engineered the creation of the second newspaper in Arkansas.[38]

The First Newspaper War: The Arkansas Gazette Fights the Arkansas Advocate

Charles Pierre Bertrand had not even reached his 21st birthday, qualifying for the end of his apprenticeship under Woodruff, when he issued a prospectus for a new newspaper to be styled the *Arkansas Advocate*. From the start, its policy was disingenuous. While "disavowing any connection to parties" and promising to "be open to all parties, and devoted to none," the prospectus committed the newspaper to Andrew Jackson. One small point of distinctiveness was that Bertrand offered to publish religious communications; Woodruff believed religion and newspapers did not mix.[39]

Bertrand became the first in a long series of Arkansas publishers who went to Cincinnati to obtain their presses. His first issue came out on March 31, 1830, and the reason for the pro-Jackson stance now became apparent: Bertrand wanted the federal and territorial public printing to be taken away from Woodruff, who was known personally (but not editorially) to have preferred the much despised John Quincy Adams over General Jackson. Behind the scenes, Crittenden and his still-loyal followers were providing Bertrand with editorials and those familiar anonymous letters. Arkansas was now old enough to have a memory, and one of the first things the *Advocate* dredged up was the Garrett murder case. Bertrand's stepfather, Dr. Matthew Cunningham, had presided over the inquest and now threatened to reveal all. Whatever the "all" might have been never came out.[40]

What did emerge was a three-sided struggle. On the one side, Crittenden still had influence in the legislature, and because he had a large house he could not afford, he wanted the territory to take it off his hands for use as a capitol building. Another faction centered on Sevier, Woodruff, and Ashley, who enticed territory secretary William S. Fulton to join them. Finally, Governor Pope plunged into the fray and soon found himself attacked by Charles Fenton Mercer Noland. Young "Fent" came from a prominent Virginia family but had been booted out of West Point and sent west for rehabilitation. One of Noland's newspaper letters accused the governor of "retailing liquor," and a nephew, William Fontaine Pope, decided to avenge the governor's honor. On February 5, 1831, Noland and Pope met in Texas. Pope was mortally wounded and died four months later.

This killing of the popular Pope by the popular Noland came as the result of newspaper accusations, and thus made newspapers contributors to the dueling. Public opinion was strongly against the practice, but the rhetoric of dueling continued, and other duels took place. All classes in Arkansas glorified personal violence to some extent, and rewarded brave politicians and brave editors. Inasmuch as Noland went on to edit the *Batesville Eagle*, he became the first editor in Arkansas who was a duelist.[41]

The full impact of having a rival printer became apparent when the territorial legislature assembled in October 1831. After opting to bid out the printing, the legislature examined Woodruff's bid, and when Bertrand offered to match it, the *Advocate* became the territory's printer. Justifiably, Woodruff felt he had been robbed and blamed his defeat on Crittenden's bribery of the legislators with "canvass hams."[42]

Woodruff's opposition to Crittenden intensified when the legislature agreed to accept the former secretary's offer to trade his home for the 10 sections of land that the federal government had granted Arkansas to fund building a capitol. The *Gazette*'s opposition helped fortify Governor Pope in vetoing the bill. Some legislators retaliated against Woodruff by canceling their subscriptions, and one, Dr. Nimrod Menefee, who used the floor of the house to denounce Woodruff in what the editor called "abusive and scurrilous" language, found himself exposed in the newspaper. Menefee's speech, Woodruff claimed, was "better suited to the meridian of a brothel, than the grave deliberations of a Legislative body." Later, while Woodruff was at work copying the House Journal at the clerk's table, Menefee attacked him with cane and knife. Woodruff grappled for his pistol, but in his haste fired it into the floor. Menefee managed to hit the editor over the head once before other members stopped the fight.

"The path is plain," Woodruff later proclaimed, "and though beset with difficulties and dangers, it shall be steadily and fearlessly pursued."[43] Although pusillanimous editors and timid publishers might inhabit Arkansas in time, Woodruff's credo of newspaper ethics never lacked for adherents in the 19th century. Besides being the first editor to survive an assassination attempt, he was also the first editor physically assaulted by an irate reader.

In order to keep readers informed of the laws after their legal printing passed to the *Advocate*, Woodruff continued their publication, not "By Authority," as before, but "Pro Bono Publico"—for the public good. This bore unexpected dividends when Bertrand ran out of paper and was forced to suspend publication, leaving the *Gazette* an open field.

Another noteworthy plum came Woodruff's way in 1831 when for four months he was Little Rock's acting postmaster. The association between the post office and the newspaper was well established in the 18th century when, in 1758, Benjamin Franklin of the *Pennsylvania Gazette* and William Hunter of the *Virginia Gazette* had been made joint deputy postmasters general for the colonies. Since so much of a newspaper's circulation and newsgathering depended on the mails, the connection was quite logical. Well into the 20th century, publishers received the patronage award of a postmastership as a reward for party services. As for Woodruff, he would hold that job again later in the 1830s.[44]

Woodruff used his office space for a variety of purposes. His lending library in 1826 offered 150 novels and plays at 12 1/2 cents per volume.[45] An indefatigable promoter, Woodruff lauded editorially at various times cotton, wheat, and even sugar cane. At the office, he not only sold seeds and plants but also acted as agent for the *Encyclopaedia Americana*. Woodruff began a tradition of local service by becoming a member of Little Rock's Town Council.

One of his constant complaints was about the town's crime rate and poor jail facilities. After criminals broke jail in 1835, a disgusted Woodruff suggested the public not "trouble our courts or juries with them."[46] Unfortunately, Woodruff's cure was at least as bad as the sickness, for the lynchings that followed added to Arkansas's already barbaric reputation.

Another of Woodruff's services was on the town's board of health. When Little Rock was invaded by smallpox in 1831, Woodruff became the first editor in Arkansas to advocate vaccination.[47] The following year, when cholera accompanied the massive migrations of Indians through Arkansas, Woodruff was active in the community's response. He also agitated in vain for doing something about Little Rock's deplorable sanitary conditions. One proposal was for a canal to carry away the filth. Woodruff thought that fixing the streets was the place to start.[48]

On a social level, Woodruff hosted noted American author Washington Irving on that worthy's return from the prairies. After leaving Little Rock, Irving stopped off at the Post and penned an essay on the quaint and simple ways of the remaining French. In the process, he popularized the term "the almighty dollar," an expression that passed into common speech before the century's end.

Despite the competition offered by the *Advocate*, Woodruff was prospering. The enormous growth of advertisements had led him to increase his supply of graphic materials. Eagle wings headed the column containing laws. Woodruff acquired a generic stagecoach, which, like his earlier hotel, reflected not at all the realities of Arkansas roads. Aside from cuts (graphics) for shoes, seeds, and other standard items, perhaps his most correct generic graphic was for runaway or captured slaves. Woodruff had both male and female versions of this heading.

Because politics had become far more central to his newspaper than he had originally planned and as advertising reduced the space for news, Woodruff first shrunk his type size to what would be five and a half points by modern standards. This added about 25 percent more content, but at some cost to the readers' eyes.

Then, on March 13, 1833, the *Gazette* came out much improved just in time for another vicious political campaign fought on two levels. First, lawyer William Cummins, a Crittenden supporter, attempted to instigate impeachment proceedings against Sevier's father-in-law, Judge Benjamin Johnson. Second, in the race for territorial delegate, Crittenden himself ran against Sevier only to lose by a two-to-one margin.[49]

Perhaps Crittenden's own declining personal popularity contributed to the makeup of the new legislature, for in 1833 Woodruff regained the title "Printer to the Territory." The *Advocate* counterattacked in letters written by a new arrival in Little Rock, Albert Pike.[50]

Pike, a Massachusetts native who had come west seeking adventure and fame, had ended up in western Arkansas teaching school when he encountered Crittenden, who encouraged the young man to seek his fame and fortune in the capital. Pike was an established poet as well as the author of *Prose Sketches and Poems, Written in the Western Country* (1834). Unfortunately, he left his school at Flatrock Creek for the capital only to be stopped by the law, as a friend accompanying him had some stolen otter skins in his possession.

Arriving in Little Rock just as the political picture was changing yet again, Pike found the rosy vision Crittenden had laid before him to be slightly exaggerated. Housed in a small shed at the back of the *Advocate* office, Pike was expected to do all the work, editorial as well as mechanical, in order to put out the newspaper. Extra income he found as assistant secretary to the territorial council, and it taught him the legislative process. The public printing controversy was still raging in the press, and Pike began by attacking Woodruff from the *Advocate*'s point of view—in poetry. A poetic treatment offered a change from the usual overheated rhetoric, but Pike's poetic lash stung. Woodruff replied by dredging up the otter-skins case.

Pike gained other experiences by joining the Little Rock Debating Society and by promoting a local theater group. He also began studying for the bar, under no one in particular it seems; he merely borrowed some of Crittenden's books. Finally, he fell in love and married Mary Ann Hamilton, a rich heiress.[51]

While Pike was getting his feet on the ground, Governor Pope and Secretary Fulton, who had been allied with the Woodruff-Sevier-Ashley faction, had a falling out over two issues. First, Sevier foresaw that in the wake of the Missouri Compromise, Arkansas would have to be admitted to the Union together with a Northern territory, and so unless Arkansas acted immediately, ready for statehood or not (and Arkansas was in no wise ready), territorial status would endure for possibly 25 years. Neither Pope nor Fulton was enamored with this proposition. Second, Fulton and Pope quarreled over the fate of the 10-section grant. Pope decided that Woodruff had not done enough to defend him and so imported a new editor, John Steele, who had recently set up the *Helena Herald*. Steele first tried to form a partnership with Woodruff under which Steele would be the editor; failing that, he offered to buy Woodruff out. When that failed, he started Little Rock's third newspaper, the *Political Intelligencer*, on July 10, 1834.

In his prospectus, Steele promised a newspaper printed on an imperial sheet but at twice the cost of the competition, five dollars a year. Larger and larger newspapers were then the rage. Already the *New-York Courier and Enquirer* had gone to eight columns on a page measuring 45 by 28 inches and a year later the size went to 54 by 48. Since Western newspapers were following the trend, Woodruff ordered a new iron press from Cincinnati. Meanwhile, the Bank of Maryland had failed, and Woodruff realized that hard times were on their way at a time when delinquent subscribers owed him nearly $10,000.[52]

Woodruff probably should have spared himself the extra expenses, for Steele proved to be a flash in the pan, his newspaper lasting only some five or six issues before expiring. Woodruff's delinquent subscribers never paid up, although Woodruff hired a collector and sent him into South Arkansas armed with a long list.[53]

Visiting English geologist G.W. Featherstonhaugh, who loathed the idea of free press, calling it a "cheap poison," offered an outsider's view of this fractious world. Little Rock had "no less than three *cheap* newspapers; which are not read but devoured by everybody; for what pleasure can be equal to that which—through the blessings of universal suffrage—those free and enlightened citizens called the 'common people' are made partakers of once a day, or at least three times a week…" Yet, while newspapers were all the rage, Featherstonhaugh reported: "I have never seen a Bible in the hands of any individual, even on Sunday." Nevertheless, the dyspeptic scientist had a high opinion of Woodruff, "one of the most indefatigably industrious men in the territory," and the editor showed him the very spot where Garrett had fallen.[54]

Meanwhile, Steele was otherwise occupied. Governor Pope had secretly given him the job of digesting and printing the laws of the territory. Woodruff congratulated Steele so well on his "good fat job" that this term took on a life of its own in Arkansas. Another, therefore, of Woodruff's firsts was the creation of the first political aphorism. Pope was Woodruff's intended victim, and having been taught by so many high-toned Southern gentlemen how to get nasty, the now-skilled gutter-fighter piled on the abuse. Pope, he charged, had given this job to Steele only because the editor swore he believed in "the infallibility of the Pope." And by keeping the arrangements secret, Pope intended to "finger" the appropriation for his private benefit.[55]

Woodruff's attack forced Steele to restart his newspaper. Calling Woodruff "a little narrow hearted YANKEE," Steele snapped at the bait. Woodruff had plenty of ammunition stored up to fire at Pope, but of Steele he knew little. On arriving in Little Rock with wife and family, Steele had been personally popular, but when his wife died, Woodruff was able to report rumors about Steele's Missouri past.[56] It is at least worthy of note that Steele accused Woodruff of being worth $50,000 but Woodruff would admit to only half of that amount.[57]

It was the first issue of the *Gazette*'s 16th year that saw the fruit of Woodruff's improvements. A new nameplate fit the new size, 21 inches in length by 15 inches in width, thus allowing six columns to the page. On December 18, 1834, five days before the beginning of the *Gazette*'s new year, Robert Crittenden died in Vicksburg after being stricken in the middle of arguing a case. Years of physical abuse had aged him beyond his 37 years. News reached Arkansas in January. One of Crittenden's friends contributed the obituary for the *Gazette*, but Woodruff did not drape the newspaper in mourning. No columns edged in black (an effect achieved by reversing the columns' rules so that the thick bottom replaced the usual narrow top) and no black borders marked the passing of one of the few important men who had arrived earlier than William E. Woodruff.

In the aftermath of Crittenden's death, Bertrand sold the *Advocate* to Albert Pike, who had just started his law practice. Pike would own the *Advocate* for only two years, but he financed or wrote for newspapers much of the rest of this life. "I am now, Sir," he wrote a New England friend, "Attorney and Counsellor at Law—Editor—Benedict—and a great man in Israel. I imagine I am settled here for my life time. After all there is something to being looked up to—even in Arkansas."

As editor, Pike rallied the now leaderless Crittenden faction, justifying his claim to being a great man in Israel, even if he never sought office. But Pike had other interests that were reflected in the newspaper. He covered the national literary scene intelligently; promoted the use of the tomato, which, though not a new plant in Arkansas, still had to overcome some prejudices; and, in an ongoing war with Woodruff, he defended law and order against lynching. One aspect of his New England background was his support for a public school system, putting him 50 years in advance of Arkansas popular opinion. In his earliest Western writings, Pike had written stories in the region's dialect. By 1836, he confessed to a friend, the language had "ceased to be odd or quaint," and he used it himself.

Pike's more literary approach to editing was best reflected in a column called "The Editor's Table" that dealt in all manner of topics. On one occasion he imagined Little Rock connected to the world by railroads and being able to travel 50 miles an hour. His conservatism was reflected in his popularization of the ideas of Whig legal theorist Chancellor James Kent. At the same time, Pike was a legal reformer, advocating building a penitentiary and opposing, if not capital punishment, then at least open displays of it. Like Woodruff before him, he had converted to the slaveholders' views concerning the "peculiar institution." By 1840, he used his wife's money to build a house occupying more than an entire city block. It was not in the suburbs—that distinction went to William E. Woodruff—but only a few others could rival it.[58]

Meanwhile, Steele sold his press to Andrew Jackson Hunt, a newcomer from Zanesville, Ohio, who renamed it *The Times*. One of Hunt's discoveries—another Arkansas first—was that he had been sold a padded subscription list. Steele, meanwhile, had gone into business with Lemuel R. Lincoln. Steele & Lincoln opened their doors on February 10, 1835, as Arkansas's first bindery. Their business, of course, was binding Steele's digest of the territory's laws, the "good fat job." If Steele expected further rewards from Pope, he must have been badly disappointed. With great glee, Woodruff published the news that Pope would not get a second term as governor from President Jackson; instead, that honor would go to William S. Fulton. As for Steele, as soon as the digest was bound, he sold his interest and said he was headed to New Orleans to buy goods. However, he never returned to Little Rock.

In the aftermath of Steele's departure, it was suggested that as a lawyer he had been the "front man" for an outlaw organization rumored to flourish along the Mississippi. The publication of an exposé in 1835, *A History of the Detection, Conviction, Life and Designs of John A. Murel* [sic], *the Great Western Land Pirate*, led many to cast nervous glances.

Law-and-order forces, editorially supported by Woodruff, were eager to try their hands at being "regulators," as the earlier period called vigilante justice. In Steele's case, he had not only acted as attorney for some known criminals but also had been in the business of finding lost slaves for owners—for a price. Just prior to his departure the suspicions appeared in print. If the charges were true, and there were reports that Steele was seen with outlaws in the Mississippi River valley, then Steele must be considered the first rogue editor in Arkansas.

Steele's departure coincided with an anti-gambling crusade tied to the Murrell outlaw stories. Gamblers had wide sway in early Arkansas, for this had been the principal recreational activity of many, especially in the Crittenden faction. When Woodruff reported approvingly how Vicksburg had dealt with its gamblers, Pike expressed his reservations and even let one gambler publish a letter in the *Advocate*. Name-calling followed, and a letter in the *Gazette* charged that Pike had been seen at a faro bank. While not denying the charge, "Who will throw the first stone?" rejoined Pike.[59]

The End of the Territorial Period

Under Governor William S. Fulton, the principal question agitating Arkansas was whether to advance to statehood. Woodruff led the way in supporting the proposition and was joined by Pike at the *Advocate*. The *Times* under A.J. Hunt opposed the move, but after Hunt's death in the fall of 1835, the new editor, John H. Reed, switched sides. Interestingly, just as Bertrand had trained at the *Gazette* before going on to the *Advocate*, so Jefferson Smith, another *Gazette* graduate, owned a half-interest and did the publishing part of the *Times*.[60] In time, the number of reporters, editors, authors, and printers who started their careers at the *Gazette* would loom large in Arkansas history.

The *Times* was able to get the territorial printing in 1835 over Woodruff and Pike, and it claimed to have 800 subscribers. The other two newspapers were reluctant to discuss numbers. Not until the 1930s did solid subscription figures exist for Arkansas newspapers. Meanwhile, with all the state's press now in favor of statehood, things moved rapidly.

In January 1836, a constitutional convention

assembled in Little Rock. Albert Pike got the "good fat job" of printing the proceedings, but Woodruff beat Pike to the punch by publishing an extra containing the convention's proposed constitution. Woodruff's version contained some errors that a later issue of the newspaper corrected.

Meanwhile, C.F.M. Noland had been chosen by the convention to take the official copy of the constitution to Washington for Congress's consideration. One of the losers in the voting had been "U.S. Mail." Given the uncertain winter weather, Noland chose to go by steamboat to New Orleans and hence by water to Washington. Meanwhile, the mail carried Woodruff's extra where it arrived eight days before Noland. Delegate Sevier turned the *Gazette*'s copy over to the House, which, by acting on it, sped the process of statehood. On June 15, 1836, President Jackson signed the authorizing legislation, thus insuring that Arkansas would be able to participate in the next presidential election that fall.[61]

In anticipation of these changes, Woodruff decided to retire as editor. On May 10, Woodruff sold an interest in the *Gazette* to Thomas Jefferson Pew. Woodruff's retirement and the entry of Arkansas into the Union marked the end of the first phase of Arkansas's newspaper history. The press in Arkansas—the *Gazette*, *Times*, and *Advocate*—was almost all located in the capital. The only other town boasting newspapers was Helena. There, Colonel Henry L. Biscoe, a prominent speculator, Crittendenite, and later the father-in-law of politician and Confederate General Thomas Carmichael Hindman, is reported to have established the *Arkansas State Democrat* in 1832. Later its name was changed to the *Southern Sentinel*, but it was gone by 1841.[62] John W. Steele's *Herald* of 1834 was of short duration.

Party lines were in the process of forming when Woodruff took his temporary retirement from the tripod. The Ashley-Woodruff-Sevier faction was enlarged by Sevier's marriage into another Kentucky political family, the Johnsons, for the vice-presidential candidate on the Democratic ticket with Martin Van Buren in 1836 was Colonel Richard H. Johnson, he of "Humpty-Dumpty, Colonel Johnson killed Tecumseh," fame. Meanwhile, Henry Conway's brothers, James S. and Elias N., followed their brother to Arkansas. Assorted other relations included members of the Rector family. In all, early Arkansas moved into statehood with Democratic politics being very much of a "family" affair; indeed, "family" and "Dynasty" were interchangeable terms for the ruling elite.

Crittenden's faction did not pass away but became instead the basis of the Whig party. Some were well-to-do planters, others town merchants and persons drawn from the professions. Arkansas, like the rest of the nation, sported a two-party system almost up to the Civil War.

Conclusion

The 25 years between statehood and the coming of the Civil War witnessed a renewed intensity to politics, and at the center of the maelstrom stood the Arkansas editor on his tripod. In 1828, English historian Thomas Babington Macaulay introduced the term "Fourth Estate." In so doing, he effectively described the power early Arkansas editors possessed to shape the policies and support or diminish the power of the men who ruled Arkansas.

Chapter II

The Antebellum Editor,
or,
Tripods under Fire

"His successor was a Mr. Wyatt, who was a weak brother of the quill."
Read Fletcher, 1876.

"After elections political leaders do not feel a very pressing necessity for the services of editors and a duel in which one or more meets his death, or by reason of which one or more has to leave the country, sometimes relieves a successful politician from the obligation of paying for political services with a lucrative office, or an unsuccessful one, from furnishing 'ways and means' of keeping above water until another canvass."
Arkansas State Gazette, July 14, 1860.

"Man's a vapor,
Full of woes;
Starts a paper,
Up he goes."
Anon.

"If we had not established banks when we did, our state would now in all probability be in a condition such as would rank her among the first of this glorious Confederacy. But a false step has burdened her with a debt which she cannot discharge for a quarter of a century. Her destiny must remain darkened for many years to come, not withstanding she has all the elements of greatness scattered in wild profusion around her."
Helena *Southern Shield*, August 3, 1860.

"Once arouse sectional feeling on this subject [railroads] and nothing will be accomplished. Each geographic division of the state and indeed every neighborhood, will be found advocating its immediate interests, and there is an end to the concentration of our means."
Washington Telegraph, March 24, 1852.

"Arkansas has caught the grand note of progress that is sounding around here; she has received the flow of spirit that actuates the great works, and she has fallen into the ranks of those who are pressing onward and upward."
Washington Telegraph, March 30, 1859.

Introduction

The Arkansas press from 1836 to 1861 operated in a strongly partisan atmosphere. Editors lived up to Alexis de Tocqueville's definition of newspapers as the "the chief democratic instrument of freedom." And with each editor acting as if the survival of the republic depended on acceptance of his positions, collegiality lay in the distant future. The newspapers at the capital led the way, devoting every spare space to political aggrandizement. While some of the content was ideological, personalities, the linchpin of territorial politics, appeared alternately as abuse or praise. No rising politician could afford to be without press support, and that goal was best achieved through covert ownership. The independence of the press was a lofty goal rarely practiced and for the most part not profitable.

Instead, the dominant trend was reported as early as 1817, when St. Louis editor Joseph Charless, piqued at his competition, reprinted an article from an eastern newspaper that showed how to get together a group of backers to purchase a press, and only then to find a compliant editor. This editor need not be a printer; he might be a young man trying to get a start, or a lawyer or doctor without clients. However, those who put up the money would determine editorial policy. This model competed with the older way, that of the printer-editor working for himself, and best exemplified by the young William E. Woodruff.

During the antebellum years, newspapers sprang up all over the state. Nevertheless, it is worthy of comparison that Missouri in 1860 had 15 dailies and 130 weeklies. Arkansas had no dailies and perhaps as many as 40 weeklies.[63] The telegraph, the key to producing a daily, had not yet arrived in Arkansas and would not until the very eve of the Civil War. Because of the great distances involved and the lack of major towns, Arkansas was the last state in the Union to be without the wonder-working wire. At the time of the Civil War, Little Rock's population had not even reached 4,000; most other towns numbered their residents in the lower hundreds. The lack of newspapers made journalists few and far between, thus helping explain why no formal professional organization emerged.

Whigs and Democrats

The destruction of the Second Bank of the United States by President Jackson proved to be the catalyst for restructuring America into a two-party system. In Arkansas, these ideological aspects rose to the surface in 1836, when William E. Woodruff sold part-interest of the *Arkansas Gazette* to Thomas Jefferson Pew. Pew's principal purpose was to undertake a stronger defense of the Democratic Party than Woodruff was likely to make. Determined to make the transition as difficult as possible, the *Times* called Woodruff first "the retired editor" and then "the pensioned editor," while Pew became "the hireling editor." Pew had had a stormy career in Kentucky and Louisiana before coming to Arkansas. George D. Prentice of the *Louisville Journal*, one of the most famous editors in America, had quarreled with Pew, exposing his past, and Arkansas's Whig editors reprinted Prentice's strictures. According to Prentice, Pew, who had been chosen as public printer in Louisiana, had sneaked out of the state. To keep from paying his debts, he claimed to be a minor. Pew's career in Arkansas was brief, for he left the *Gazette* in 1838. Alcoholism had effectively ended his career, and some years later he begged money from his hated rival, George D. Prentice. Although there were other candidates for this dubious distinction, strong evidence nominates Pew as the first Arkansas editor disabled by drink.[64]

In the age of Jackson, Democrats supported state rights, small government, and claimed to defer to the voice of the people. Whigs endorsed sound banking, internal improvements, a high tariff, education, and moral reform. In Arkansas, a Whig writer, Allen M. Scott, who had worked in the *Times* office, wrote a highly colored account of the period's politics largely critical of Ashley and Sevier, using a Biblical style of narration and with easily recognizable pseudonyms for all the participants.[65] This format proved so popular that William M. Quesenbury revived it in the 1850s. Anonymous letters continued apace, and those from Albert Pike, writing as "Casca," were directed at Chester Ashley and at least initially blocked Ashley's political ambitions.[66]

In the fall of 1836, William E. Woodruff celebrated statehood by buying a new nameplate. On October 11, 1836, his creation became the *Arkansas State Gazette*, a title that endured until after the Civil War. Meanwhile, in the first elections under statehood, the Democrats won easily. James Sevier Conway was elected governor, and the legislature sent Ambrose H. Sevier and William S. Fulton off to Washington as senators. Arkansas's sole congressman was the victorious Democrat, Archibald Yell.

Yell, the first truly charismatic candidate in Arkansas, eschewed newspapers and they chewed on him. Despite, or perhaps because of that, Yell was widely popular with the people. Whig David Walker, who opposed Yell in one race, recalled that at a beef shoot Yell won only to give the prize to a widow. At a revival he joined the choir and outsang them all. He also outpolled Walker.[67]

Following Pew's departure, Woodruff sold his entire interest in the *Arkansas State Gazette* to Edward Cole, a New York-trained former *Gazette* press foreman. Woodruff had grown increasingly disenchanted with politics. Elected state treasurer, he had been unable to collect all the money due the state from the federal government because of the banking collapse in the east. Instead of praising Woodruff for getting what he could, legislators censured him. Woodruff's income increasingly came from his growing land agency and now included the ferry at Little Rock, for which in 1838 he acquired a steamboat.[68]

At the *Gazette*, Woodruff now had some 66 agents collecting subscriptions, had raised his advertising rates (in conjunction with Pike at the *Advocate*), and claimed over 1,800 subscribers. Ominously, he was owed more than $30,000 in uncollected subscriptions. Cole bought the newspaper at the height of the "Flush Times," that remarkable boom period in the old southwest when land and slave prices went beyond reason and wildcat banks dumped paper money into an already overheated economy. Arkansas would not see the like again until the 1980s. In addition to promising to pay $5,000 for the newspaper, Cole moved its offices from Woodruff's home to a newly erected building on Markham and Main streets. This, too, he paid for in promissory notes.[69]

Cole was determined to run a clean newspaper. He refused to print stories about a crime committed at Fayetteville. "Crime begets crime," Cole declared, and published articles on agriculture instead. Cole tried humor on the topic of overheated editors, claiming that his "slight frame" had been wearing away "from unnecessarily making a portable armory of our pockets."[70] Meanwhile, another of the principal players had departed the scene. Albert Pike, on his way to being one of the most learned lawyers in the West, sold the *Times and Advocate* to Eli Colby, a newcomer who, like Cole, preferred to avoid bitter personalities. To Whig leaders led by lawyer William Cummins, Colby's restraint was proof that he was unsound. Albert Pike offered to buy back a half interest, but Colby denounced the plan as "officious and domineering." Forthwith a new newspaper, the *Arkansas Star*, cast a brief light on Little Rock.[71]

Editor David Lambert had served under famed editor Mordecai Manuel Noah of the *New York Evening Star*, hence his selection of a name for his newspaper. The first issue of the *Star* brought forth a critique from Cole. Newspapers, he believed, should be published by trained professionals, not lawyers who thought that editing consisted in writing personal attacks. Colby agreed with these sentiments and *Star* editor David Lambert responded by assaulting both editors on the streets of Little Rock. After the *Star* office was destroyed by a tornado on June 6, 1840, its press broken, its type pied, and its Whig flag supporting Harrison and Tyler blown away, Lambert left town, supposedly to get new supplies. Instead, he stopped in Lexington, Kentucky, never to return, thus leaving his sponsors some four or five thousand dollars the poorer. His was the first press office destroyed by a tornado; it was not the last. The sponsors had no choice but to revive the newspaper.

Meanwhile, the *Times and Advocate* was folding as Whigs left it to support the *Star*. As for Cole, he left town in October 1840, for the expected prosperity had not continued even as his debts multiplied. Woodruff, who regained his newspaper as well as Cole's other debts, wasted no time in finding another purchaser, and George H. Burnett, the *Gazette*'s business manager, assumed control. Cole found work surveying on the isthmus of Panama and later returned to his home in New York, where in 1855 he committed suicide, jumping into the East River.[72] His was the first suicide by an Arkansas editor.

George Burnett, who succeeded Cole, expressed the same determination to keep the newspaper clean of insulting language. The 1840s were relatively quiet, but the Depression that had hit the east insured that President Martin Van Buren would not be elected to a second term despite getting Arkansas's vote. Burnett, who got the state printing, had little luck collecting the *Gazette*'s past bills. Although he tried putting the newspaper on the cash system, then a new idea making its way west, he was willing to accept corn, wood, and other commodities in lieu of cash. Both the *Times and Advocate* and the *Star* joined in the movement. In addition to wanting cash in advance from subscribers, the newspapers also demanded advertisers pay in advance as well. It was all to no avail.[73]

The first legislature had founded two banks, the State Bank for the merchant community and the Real Estate Bank for the planters. Both were examples of how not to do business, and by 1844 Arkansas found its local circulating mediums to be worthless. Hints of these problems had surfaced as early as 1837. Speaker of the House John Wilson, who also served as president of the Real Estate Bank, quarreled with Randolph County Representative J.J. Anthony, a strong critic of the bank. There was on the floor a bill to issue bounty certificates for killing wolves. Anthony proposed as an amendment to the bill that the President of the Real Estate Bank sign the certificates. His attempt to defend his amendment enraged Speaker Wilson, who drew his knife, left his seat, and attacked Anthony. Despite taking a serious wound from Anthony, Wilson drove his knife "to the hilt" into Anthony's stomach and chest. On the house floor's new red carpet, Anthony expired; and the bounty bill was tabled.[74] After the killing, the atmosphere in Little Rock was extremely tense, but because the *Gazette* and the *Times and Advocate* both supported the banks, their coverage was greatly restrained. However, the *Gazette* did print a strong letter from "A Citizen" wherein Anthony was called "a representative of the ragged north." The author had written "rugged north," and the newspaper in its next issue apologized for an error which today would be called a "typo."[75]

In the 19th century, the word "typo" was short for typographer or printer. Such errors in newspapers could be embarrassing, as in 1855 when the Fayetteville *South-West Independent* apologized to the Camden *Southern Stamp* which it had called the *Southern Scamp*.[76] One reason for these errors was the aging of the type. The dulling of the edges made it harder for printers (who worked with their fingers) to feel the differences between the letters. When one sees in older prints a confusion between the "e" and the "c," old type is the best explanation. Printers actually preferred old type, errors and all, because it did not cut the fingers as did the new type.

The uncertainties in the nation's financial markets that had led to Woodruff's embarrassment cashing the state's federal deposit hit with a vengeance in 1840, and despite attempts by the press to downplay the extent of the disaster, the Flush Times came to an abrupt end. Suddenly, the *Gazette* bewailed, "Distress, ruin, and embarrassment pervade every village, neighborhood, and family. With but few exceptions, executions hang over every man's head, threatening to send him forth a beggar."[77] "These are ticklish times," a subscriber from Athens wrote the editor, advising him to cross out one R. Nichols who had fled to Texas "and never paid for anything."[78] At Napoleon, the editor of the *Messenger* disappeared, leaving his press and supplies behind. In Little Rock, first the *Star* suspended and then the press of the *Times and Advocate* was saved from an execution only at the last moment. To end it all, Burnett had contracted tuberculosis. He was only 27 when he died in December 1841. Once again, Woodruff had his newspaper back.[79]

A young lawyer, just barely older than the *Gazette* itself, became the new editor under Woodruff's ownership. Cyrus W. Weller, like his immediate predecessors, tried to stand on a platform of avoiding personalities. In Weller's extended discussion of his editorial philosophy, he came out boldly for temperance, which he defined as abstinence from alcohol as well as from violent language. When Jared C. Martin resolved not to continue the age-old lubrication process known as treating the voters in an upcoming election, his actions were duly lauded: "The practice of treating for votes is an awful spot on our glorious republican escutcheon."[80] In addition, Weller believed a newspaper owed its readers the truth, not distortions, denunciations, and spurious defenses.

The banking scandal hit hard at the reigning Democratic politicians. Sevier had a very tarnished record where the banks were concerned. At first, though, the legislature took its frustrations out on Woodruff, who had expected to get the public printing in 1842. Colby, his newspaper teetering on bankruptcy, offered a 33 percent lower bid, and won, even though he had no paper in stock and no line of credit. Woodruff's second complaint lay in wanting reversed the previous judgment that he was a defaulter in collecting the state's money back in 1837. After failing to get the printing or the redemption of his honor, Woodruff said he would sell the *Gazette* to the Whigs since the Democrats were not going to do him justice. He proved as good as his word, and on January 4, 1843, Woodruff announced that Benjamin J. Borden had acquired the newspaper.[81]

A North Carolina native and graduate of the University of North Carolina and the Georgetown law school, Borden had been in Arkansas less than four years when he took over the *Gazette*. At first, nothing betrayed the shift in political alliances, but Borden's professed desire to expose wrongdoing in high places meant attacking Senator Sevier and Governor Yell, neither of whom now had presses at their disposal. In Yell's case, vetoing the appointment of a state geologist would hardly excite the voters, and even publicizing his much earlier observation (lifted from a private letter), that "every man left his honesty and every woman her chastity, on the other side of the Mississippi, on moving to Arkansas," had little impact. On the other hand, Sevier's profiteering from bank funds had left him open to serious charges. Local Democrats banded together and raised the funds to start a new newspaper, the *Arkansas Banner*, for the party faithful. To edit it, they called on a young doctor, Solon Borland.[82]

A Virginia native and graduate of the Medical

College of Philadelphia, Borland mixed the practice of medicine with editing and politics. He had edited a newspaper in Memphis and arrived in Arkansas ready to take up the cudgels. The central purpose of the *Banner* was to insure that the Dynasty remained in control of the Democratic party. Dissident Democrat Richard C. Byrd had tried to get a newspaper called the *Independent Democrat* going in the summer of 1832, but its editor had disappeared. Borden, however did not disappear, and it had been 10 years since such biting language reigned in the Arkansas press. Borden suggested Borland's newspaper be called the "Family Quilt," and then the editors began comparing each other to various animals. After Borden suggested that Borland was lamb-like in reality although pugnacious in rhetoric, "which only proved how natural it is for one to prate loudest of that virtue to which he has the least claims," the doctor-editor attacked the lawyer-editor on the streets of Little Rock and, in Woodruff's account, "the doctor used Ben. Pretty roughly—having beaten his face into a jelly, and bro't the claret with every blow." An attempt to settle the matter failed, and the two editors met in Indian Territory. Borden was again the loser, firing his gun accidentally into the ground. Borland then shot him, just missing the heart. Borden recovered, however, and the war of words continued.[83]

Borland, who soon started a law practice in addition to his other activities, became the first Arkansas editor to become involved in a sex scandal. Madame d'Estimauville de Beau Mouchel, the founder of a fashionable girls' school in Little Rock before she relocated to Dallas County, was not only jilted by Borland but had to flee the state in a "condition" even as Borland was making an advantageous marriage. The scandal probably enhanced Borland's reputation with the all-male voters. Borland's other distinction was that he authored the first Arkansas medical book, a study of an often-fatal illness contracted by drinking the milk of cows who had eaten a poisonous weed. *An Essay on "The Milk Sickness" of the Human Subjects, or "The Trembles" of Animals; Embracing Its History, Cause, and Treatment* (1845) ran to 45 pages and is one of the rarest Arkansas imprints.[84]

Newspaper changes followed politics. After Eli Colby became the second Arkansas editor to die of tuberculosis, Weller became the editor of the *Times and Advocate*, giving that newspaper a Democratic orientation before its demise. Since Borland's duty was to the Dynasty, Chester Ashley needed support for his political ambitions, and Woodruff obliged, creating on May 21, 1846 a newspaper first christened the *Arkansas Democrat*, but soon renamed the *Arkansas State Democrat*.

The year 1846 was critical in Arkansas for a variety of reasons. The Mexican War began in the spring, and every aspiring politician hastened to get involved. Albert Pike, who had long commanded a local militia company, the Little Rock Guards, was not enthusiastic about leaving his law practice, but socially and professionally it would have been suicide not to have accepted his election as a captain. Borland took the war's opportunity to retire as editor of the *Banner*, for he, too, was elected a captain. Topping them all was Congressman Archibald Yell, who hurried home from Washington to enlist as a simple private—one immediately elected colonel of the regiment.

Since Yell was Ashley's biggest enemy, Woodruff at the *Democrat* hit hard on how Arkansas was now unrepresented in Washington by Yell's decision to become a soldier. After Woodruff generated so much pressure that Yell relinquished the office, Thomas W. Newton, a Whig, won the right to represent Arkansas for the 25 days remaining in Yell's term. This was the only victory in a statewide race the Whigs ever scored.

Wars have always been good for circulation, and the Mexican War was no exception. The two sources for news were private correspondents and copying from other newspapers. During the war, the Arkansas press employed both. Young volunteer William M. Quesenbury, already a skilled and nationally published writer, contributed for the *Gazette* a much reprinted account of the Battle of Buena Vista. The Battle of Palo Alto figured in another way. The *Banner* and the *Gazette* (but not Woodruff's *Democrat*) each appropriated a story from the *New Orleans Delta* without attribution. When the New Orleans newspaper found out, it took them to task: "We do not know if Little Rock, Ark., is a mean town—we should be sorry to insinuate that it is—but this we do know, it has got two mighty mean editors in it—him of the '*State Gazette*,' and his contemporary of the '*Banner*.' They are so mean that we wonder their shadows are not ashamed to keep them company." Borland, who had supplied the story to the *Banner*, dismissed the ethics charge as "a small concern, indeed." But in newspaper circles it really was not.[85]

Readers were also treated to maps. Borden had advanced beyond foundry cuts in 1843 when he printed seven plates from the book *Rambles in Yucatan*, which he received from a relative of the author. The first originally produced graphic, a simple map made to illustrate William Byrd Powell's planned dam on Fourche Bayou, appeared on May 31, 1843. Woodruff at the *Democrat* held rights to the first original publication of a map, that of Cerro Gordo, that accompanied a letter from former Arkansan Stephen S. Tucker. All of these maps were done in wood or type metal producing what was essentially a negative image—the background was black and the letters white.[86]

From reading the newspapers, readers learned that there was (a) a war with Mexico, and (b) a war between the Arkansas regiment and General John Wool, and (c) a war within the Arkansas Regiment. The Arkansas regiment headed southwest through Texas where it became part of General Wool's army. Wool despised what he considered the undisciplined rabble of the "Mounted Devils," and the regiment returned the disdain. Then the regiment's leaders fell out with each other. With the higher ranks full of men who wanted to displace Yell, the colonel was a sitting target. Chief among the archers was Borland, who, as his arrows hit their target, reported it all back to his Arkansas readers. However, Yell's postwar chances were somewhat seriously reduced when at the Battle of Buena Vista he fell, pierced by Mexican lances, at the head of those of his troops who had not run away.

As for Borland, he and a portion of the regiment sent out on scout had been captured at Hacienda Encarnacion after they camped for the night without posting guards and woke up the next morning surrounded by Santa Anna's entire army. Borland was locked away in a Mexico City prison when a new round of regimental infighting broke out. Captain Albert Pike, who had not witnessed Yell's death, having been on the other side of the battlefield, criticized Yell and the rest of regiment in one of his letters. Yell's successor, Colonel John Selden Roane, took offense by leaving the accomplishments of Pike's detachment out of his official report and describing Pike's letters as "the poisoned shafts of defamation from this polluted source."[87]

Two encounters followed. Lambert J. Reardon, editor of the *Banner*, took a hickory stick to John E. Knight, the junior editor of the *Democrat*, after Knight editorially defended himself for being born in Massachusetts. Neither man was hurt and Knight initially had no idea why he had been assaulted. The second encounter was between Pike and Roane, who met across the state line outside Fort Smith, firing twice at each other before the seconds and the surgeon forced the duel's end.[88]

Meanwhile, Chester Ashley won the Senate seat vacated by the death of William S. Fulton. Arkansas's

senior senator, Ambrose H. Sevier, resigned his seat in order to work on the peace negotiations with Mexico. He expected to have his Senate seat restored to him after the work was done, but Solon Borland, back from having escaped from prison in Mexico City and something of a national hero for his role in the capture of the city, took the appointment and promised to keep it. Borland's credentials were presented by Ashley, who later in the day took to his bed and died of a fever.[89]

Despite the election of Zachary Taylor to the presidency in 1848, the Whig party in Arkansas failed to make a dent in a land dominated by hardscrabble farmers. Whig editor Benjamin J. Borden explained part of the problem: "Sometimes the north has presented an unbroken front; and then again, the south; but never both at once."[90] Borden's response to the problem was to unload his unprofitable newspaper and turn to teaching. Chased by his creditors, Borden moved to Tulip and later Washington; after the war, he taught at Arkansas Industrial University. Thus he became the first of a long line of editors who became teachers, paralleling—but in the opposite direction—Albert Pike, who had turned from teaching to editing.

George B. Hayden borrowed the money to buy the *Gazette* in early 1848, keeping it loyal to the moribund Whig party. Thus, he was a mere observer when Ambrose H. Sevier's career imploded. Ashley's death left a vacancy in the Senate, thus offering a chance for compromise: Borland could take one seat, Sevier the other. But it was not to be. Woodruff at the *Democrat* attacked Sevier's increasing ineffectiveness. Borland scored greatly in the estimation of westerners by getting a new federal court established at Van Buren, a move Sevier opposed since it ended the judicial monopoly enjoyed by his father-in-law, federal judge Benjamin Johnson. Tempers ran high. Ashley's unexpired term went to William King Sebastian, known as the "milk and cider" man because he somehow managed to escape becoming entangled in controversies. Sevier, already gravely ill, had concentrated his energies on getting a full-term seat but again Borland was successful. Sevier retired to his father-in-law's plantation and died. Woodruff, who had largely masterminded his overthrow, "grieved because our ancient friend was no more" and he reversed the column rules on all four pages of the *Democrat*, which he had not done for Crittenden's death. Finally, Woodruff determined to break one more element of the Dynasty's control by engineering the election of Christopher Columbus Danley as state auditor.[91]

Danley, a tragic figure in Arkansas journalism, came from a Missouri family that had failed to prosper in Arkansas. His early education was limited, and among his youthful jobs was carrying the mail to Van Buren and working as a bartender at the Anthony House. He had served in the army of the Republic of Texas, taking part in the ill-fated Mier Expedition. Volunteering for the Mexican War, he came home a crippled hero. In an election that had all the earmarks of "Give a Veteran a Chance," Danley defeated Elias Nelson Conway, who had held the office of state auditor for 14 years.

Meanwhile, the state's governor, Thomas Drew,

resigned, and John S. Roane, who as a duelist was technically ineligible, became the third Mexican War hero to be elevated to office. The brief canvass resulted in a heated exchange in the press. L.A. Whiteley of the *Banner*, believing he had been maligned, challenged *Gazette* editor George B. Hayden to a duel. Perhaps because the charges involved veiled references to former Private Whiteley's looting practices during the Mexican War, Hayden declined to fight. A frustrated Whiteley then published a "card" pronouncing Hayden to be "a paltroon [*sic*], a liar, and a scoundrel, and beneath the notice of any honorable man." Hayden, after presenting evidence of Whiteley's peccadilloes, including the charge that he had stolen Captain Pike's brandy, retorted that duels were out of fashion and that he could not "afford to 'render satisfaction' to such an 'honorable man.'" The problem for Hayden was that he could not render satisfaction to his creditors. Woodruff had sold out at the right time, and none of his successors had been able to reverse the *Gazette*'s decline.[92]

Instead of dying, however, the *Gazette* was resurrected by its former owner, William E. Woodruff, who in February 1850 merged it with the *Democrat* to form the *Arkansas State Gazette and Democrat*. The front page contained the volume and issue numbers for both newspapers. A short time later, he bought an ornate nameplate that featured drawings of local scenes. This would be the first in a series of extravagant nameplates that occasionally the Arkansas press would sport.

At the "G & D," as it was commonly called, John Elliot Knight, who had worked for Woodruff at the *Democrat*, became the *de facto* editor, or, as he styled it, "an attaché of the Press." Knight also provided the lyrics for the first piece of sheet music written by an Arkansan, Benjamin F. Scull's 1857 song "I am Near Thee," dedicated to Mary Woodruff. This Massachusetts native was no friend to the rising tide

of Southern sectionalism triggered by the Mexican War and expressed his unionist sentiments in strong editorials not entirely to Woodruff's liking.[93]

In August, during the height of the Compromise of 1850 crisis, Knight and Woodruff parted company. Senator Borland's position was remarkably unclear, and indeed he spent much of the time in Arkansas explaining how he might have been voting had he been in Washington. Arkansas's congressman, Robert Ward Johnson, presented for Arkansas readers the Calhoun line that the South should either attain all its objectives for the protection and expansion of slavery or leave the Union. Ironically, Woodruff's new editor, Leon Trousdale, was if anything more extreme than Johnson. The firestorm that followed caught most editors and voters unprepared—ideological arguments, if not as rare as hen's teeth, normally were fodder for personalities rather than ends in themselves.[94]

One letter writer took Johnson to task for some of his more extreme sentiments. After vainly trying to get the *Banner* to publish it, the author got it in the *Gazette and Democrat*. Johnson was enraged, especially since he had heard of the letter second hand. Johnson was one of those who had not paid for his subscription during the last three years, and Woodruff had unceremoniously cut him off. It took deep pockets to adopt the cash system, but Woodruff had them by 1850.[95]

Cash got Auditor Danley in trouble when he found serious mistakes in the printing bills submitted by Lambert A. Whiteley of the *Banner*. The amounts were rather large, and the disagreement spread into the newspapers. Whiteley attacked Danley personally, making fun of the auditor's arm and leg injuries. A duel seemed out of the question; instead, Whiteley and senior editor Lambert Reardon encountered Danley and one of his brothers, Pulaski County sheriff Benjamin Franklin Danley, on Markham Street down from the capitol. The Danleys had passed them by when C.C. saw the *Banner* editors drawing pistols. C.C. used his one good hand to strike at Whiteley who nevertheless got off a shot at the sheriff. The Danleys chased Whiteley down an alley.

Solon Borland, a witness to the fight from the bar at the Anthony House, saw Reardon following the Danleys with pistol drawn. Borland knocked Reardon down only to have Gordon M. Peay, another bystander, intervene. As Reardon arose, a third Danley brother, William, hearing of the fray and that at least one of his brothers had been killed, came up and knocked Reardon unconscious. Meanwhile, back in the alley C.C. was unable, due to his lame leg, to catch up with Whiteley, but brother B.F. tried to hit him with his cane. B.F., another wounded veteran, had the use of only one hand, and Whiteley took away the cane and started beating the sheriff.

When C.C. caught up to the fight, Whiteley turned his attention on the auditor. B.F. fired a shot that grazed Whiteley, who headed back up the alley. Outside the Anthony House, he encountered brother William, whom he knocked down. While so occupied, C.C. came up the alley and felled Whiteley, ending the fight. Then followed a newspaper fight over what had really happened and who had started it, pitting the *Banner* on one side, while the Danley family provided the *Gazette* with their side.[96]

After Leon Trousdale moved on to Memphis, where he edited the *Appeal* and later the *Commercial*, Alden Mills Woodruff, the oldest of William Woodruff's sons, took over as junior editor, thus becoming the first son to join a father. After the Civil War, Alden would for a time even own an interest in the *Gazette*.[97]

Meanwhile Senator Borland, the head of the anti-Dynasty faction of the Democratic party, resigned his seat in order to become the minister to Central America. Violence followed Borland everywhere he went, for in Washington he had smashed in the nose of the elderly superintendent of the census; in Nicaragua he touched off a riot and had to be rescued by the U.S. Navy. Borland's resignation meant that the Dynasty regained control in Washington. Elias N. Conway, the ousted auditor, was elected governor in 1852, and Robert Ward Johnson moved from the House to the Senate. A younger brother, Richard Mentor Johnson, joined the *Banner*, which, with Whiteley and Reardon now gone, became the *True Democrat*, thereby claiming to be the only Democratic organ. The new title so offended Woodruff that he published a warning to correspondents about the 'bastard and piratical Newspaper established in this city, under the inappropriate title of '*The True Democrat*'…"[98]

The 1852 gubernatorial race was important in Arkansas newspaper history. The Whigs failed to field a candidate, and its last newspaper, the *Arkansas Whig* in Little Rock, soon expired. Shortly afterwards, the *Whig*'s former publisher, J.F. Butler, died at the hands of his brother-in-law, merchant tailor E. Marcus, outside the former Real Estate Bank. Marcus died as well in the shoot-out.[99] In the gubernatorial race Conway was opposed by an independent

Democrat, General Bryan Smithson, who fought on a platform of state internal improvements. Conway came out for good dirt roads and won.

Evidence of growing sophistication in the press included the use of original woodcuts. Several uncredited political cartoons appeared in the *Gazette and Democrat*. Edward Payson Washbourne, the young artist later responsible for "The Arkansas Traveler," has been suggested as one possible source.[100] A more likely candidate is William M. Quesenbury, already an accomplished artist in his own right and a former Whig.

On March 18, 1853, William E. Woodruff retired for the final time from the newspaper business. Already considered venerable at age 58, having outlived almost all of the figures in early territorial history, the old Nestor still had another 32 years to live.[101] For years he made it a practice to go down to the *Gazette* office to watch its progress and pick up his mail.

The sale was made to Captain Danley, who would own the newspaper until his death. Danley's first disaster came on February 21, 1854, when the newspaper office and all the equipment was lost in a fire. There was no insurance either there or at the *True Democrat* office nearby. The front and back pages of the *Gazette* and a long advertisement were saved and printed at the *Arkansas Whig* office. Then Danley borrowed the money to rebuild.[102]

The *Gazette* moved into a new office at the corner of Second and Scott, and it was there that a young Little Rock child first saw Danley in his office. The front room consisted of a table piled high with exchanges, some chairs, a bookcase, and a sawdust-filled box into which the editor spat. Part of Danley's spitting consisted of paper, for Danley told the young Dickison Brugman that, "Sometimes I am in doubt as to word or phrase I want to use in writing an editorial, and I chew the paper and in a few moments what I want comes to me."[103] Other editors succumbed to this practice as well, for little missing edges appear among the correspondence of Ray Kimball of the *De Queen Bee* and *Daily Citizen*.

Danley soon found himself out of the auditor's job and into political limbo. A crypto-Whig, in that his interests came to be similar to those of the merchant community, Danley orchestrated in 1854 a campaign to get Arkansas a new constitution. Many technical problems existed in the 1836 document, and supporters of a constitution claimed they wanted to expand the role of the voters. In addition, Amendment One, passed after the banking collapse, had banned banking altogether. Danley and the merchant community supported authorizing private banking as had been done in the rest of the nation. The Family, led by the *True Democrat*, called the old document "perfect and faultless" and assured voters that Arkansas had no need for such evil things as banks. Despite the support of the most of the state's press, voters in August rejected calling a convention.[104]

Danley had a weakness for Solon Borland, and after the ex-senator returned to Arkansas politically unemployed, Danley was induced against his better judgment to follow Borland into Know-Nothingism, a new movement sweeping the nation. This xenophobic fear of foreigners generally and Catholics in particular combined the talents of Albert Pike, the former Whig, and Borland, the former Democrat. Because Arkansas had only 1,468 foreign-born in the state and only seven Catholic churches, it was hard to excite the voters. At the national convention in 1856, Albert Pike bolted the party, claiming that Millard Fillmore, the presidential nominee, was unsound on slavery. Danley had little initial sympathy with the movement, but, mesmerized by Borland, he allowed the *Gazette and Democrat* to become the party's state organ.[105]

The struggle again descended to a personal level. After the *True Democrat* suggested that Borland had passed off his mistress, Madame d'Estimauville, as a suitable teacher, to the utter corruption of society, Borland replied that these matters were "indecent" for a newspaper to discuss and then brought up the matter of former Vice-President Richard Mentor Johnson's liaison with one of his slave women.[106] Danley's problems were different. After John E. Reardon took over as postmaster in Little Rock, Danley claimed the postmaster was keeping the *Gazette and Democrat* from reaching subscribers.[107]

After the Know-Nothings suffered a major defeat at the polls, Borland dropped out of politics in Arkansas, resurfacing in Memphis where he edited the *Enquirer*. Just before he left Arkansas, Borland wrote of his seven-year-old daughter, Fanny, who already talked in rhyme and metered verse. Six of her infant lines appeared in the newspaper on January 5, 1856; it was the start of a long poetic career that ended with her death in 1879 in the Memphis yellow fever epidemic.[108] Until letters to Santa Claus began to appear in the press at the turn of the century, she was surely the youngest writer to appear in Arkansas newspapers.

As for Danley, he took in a partner, William F. Holtzman, a practical printer, in 1856 and three years later dropped the *and Democrat* from his newspaper's nameplate, styling it simply the *Arkansas State Gazette*.[109] Danley's health was so bad that he enlisted others to do much of the work. One was "Fent" Noland, who, though suffering from the consumption that killed him in 1858, edited the newspaper at times and contributed articles of a very high level on early Arkansas history.

No one made a more accurate assessment of the risks of editing a newspaper than Noland during one of these stints:

> An editor's life is a hard one at best. He may toil and trouble to get some item of interest for his readers—he may spend sleepless nights in trying to make a readable paper, in short, he may do all that a decent man ought to do, and leave nothing undone, and the chances will be, that he gives more offense and less satisfaction to a certain class of beings, that if he left his paper to edit itself. It is no use to perpetrate a witty thing, or tell a good story, so far as some people are concerned, you but cast your pearls before swine. The only way for an editor to get along, and preserve his own self-respect, is to please himself, and let the rest of mankind take care of themselves.[110]

After Noland's death, William M. Quesenbury continued the local history series, writing about some of the exotic characters who had inhabited the frontier instead of the early politicians that Noland had treated. In addition, Quesenbury delighted readers with long letters written in his inimitable style. It is tempting to call him the first regular columnist in Arkansas journalism.

With Elias N. Conway reelected governor in 1856 and Robert Ward Johnson in the Senate, the Family seemed in complete control. At the *True Democrat* the junior editor was James W. Woodward, nicknamed "Dummy," for he was a deaf-mute. A great chess player and noted early teacher of the aurally and visually challenged, Woodward had been active in journalism for some 16 years when he joined the *True Democrat*. In his salutatory editorial, he said he had not considered his writings worth saving, and the *State Rights Eagle* at Camden took the hint: "We imagine there is a great unanimity upon that point."[111] Probably no other industry in Arkansas over time has presented disabled persons with more opportunities than the press.

The closing antebellum years were filled with agitations, alarms, and anxieties. A great expansion in cotton production in the state moved Arkansas closer to the Southern mainstream and away from the state's western moorings. As new lands opened and plantations sprung up, rumors of slave insurrections abounded. Alleged abolitionist plots were daily gossip. In the press, the *True Democrat* and the *Gazette* united in pushing for the expulsion of free Negroes from the state, and in 1859 this legislation passed.

The politician who benefited most from these developments was outside the Family. Thomas Carmichael Hindman came to Arkansas from Mississippi. A planter's son educated in New Jersey, Hindman had studied politics in Mississippi and sought to apply what he had learned in Arkansas. Marrying Henry L. Biscoe's daughter and establishing his own newspaper, the *State Rights Democrat* in Helena, was just the beginning. The Hindmans' honeymoon was spent in Little Rock so that the new husband could observe the legislature. Elected to Congress in 1858, Hindman embodied Southern extremism. By contrast, Robert Ward Johnson, Arkansas's first acknowledged follower of John C. Calhoun, appeared almost moderate.

What Hindman sought was a seat in the Senate, for that was where the real power lay. Accordingly, he established a newspaper in Little Rock, the *Old Line Democrat*, importing from Illinois Thomas C. Peek as editor. Hindman's name appeared in the first issue 38 times. Peek had been a pro-Stephen A. Douglas editor in Illinois, and during the course of his long Arkansas career proved adept at changing masters.

The warfare that raged in the state on the eve of the Civil War had much to with personalities and vaulting ambition and little to do with the crisis into which the nation was slipping. Hindman excelled at denouncing the Family, but overreached himself. When it was shown that some favorable reports on Hindman's successes on the stump had come from Hindman's own pen, great embarrassment followed. "Puffing" was expected, but that was what friends were for; one did not write one's own puffs unless selling patent medicine.[112]

Hindman did orchestrate the gubernatorial candidacy in the summer of 1860 of independent Democrat Henry M. Rector. Actually a minor member of the Family, Rector was hailed by Peek as "a poor honest farmer of Saline county, who toils at the plow handles to provide bread, meat and raiment for his wife and children."[113] Those who knew Rector laughed at this description of the lawyer-speculator, but the great increase in the state's population worked in Rector's favor. His gubernatorial opponent was Richard M. Johnson, the former *True Democrat* editor, who was by one account "slow, dry, and prosey in a painful degree" on the platform, a sharp contrast to those strongly virulent editorials for which he was noted.[114]

While Johnson was running for governor, the Family brought down from Fayetteville Elias Cornelius Boudinot to fill in as editor. An eastern-educated lawyer, Boudinot was an important leader of the Treaty faction in the Cherokee Nation. With anti-Treaty chief John Ross in power, Boudinot and other pro-Treaty leaders felt safer out of the Territory. Accordingly, he had founded the *Arkansian* in Fayetteville and loyally supported the Family in its struggles with Hindman.

Peek greeted Boudinot's arrival by suggesting that as an Indian he was no citizen. Peek's repeated comments about the "colored editor" failed to lead to a duel, but Boudinot did respond that such comments "have been the weapons with which other ignorant skulking poltroons have essayed to strike me down, and are well worthy of a man, who was purchased in Illinois, shipped to Arkansas, and bid by his owner to heap slander and abuse upon strangers and gentlemen."[115]

The highlight of the election, and an event long remembered in Arkansas political circles, was a set of cartoons together with commentary done by William M. Quesenbury. Boudinot had left Quesenbury temporarily in charge of the *Arkansian*, and Cush responded by making woodcuts of the candidates.

While not the first cartoons, these were the most memorable. One cut showed Richard M. Johnson and a whiskey barrel, a reference to the way in which Johnson's nomination had been won. But more to the point was Cush's observation that across the state there existed a "mournful and heavy list of delinquent subscribers of the True Democrat. They are expected to pay him or vote for him."[116] Alas, poor editor Johnson got neither.

The revolt against the Family proved successful, as Rector defeated Johnson by a slight margin. Nationally, Arkansans were not ready for the breakup of the Democratic party. Despite assurances from the *True Democrat* and the *Old Line Democrat* that John C. Breckinridge was the Democratic nominee and not Stephen A. Douglas, Douglas had strong localized segments of support in Arkansas, notably from the *Van Buren Press*. The Constitutional Union party enlisted the old Whig element, and Danley, who shared their nationalist sentiments, made the *Gazette* the leading voice for moderation and compromise.

Although Breckinridge carried Arkansas, it was a very close race, and statewide a strong conservative trend repudiating both the Family and Hindman was well underway. Just how this would play out when news came that Abraham Lincoln, the Republican candidate not even on the ballot in Arkansas, had been elected president, remained to be seen.

Early Newspapers Around the State

The early history of Arkansas newspapers tended to be Little Rock-centered because politics emanated from the capital and newspapers were largely political. As luck would have it, more files of those newspapers survived than almost anywhere else. Nevertheless, many important newspapers were to be found elsewhere in the state. Some followed the lead of William E. Woodruff and announced their independence and determination to avoid personalities. But none could avoid politics. Of those newspapers that survived for any length of time, only one, William M. Quesenbury's *South-West Independent*, failed to be partisan. Aspiring state politicians needed most a newspaper at the capital; but the typical non-capital newspaper was less focused on individuals and took on a political orientation only around election time. Most of all, every newspaper promoted its local community and region.

Helena continued to be an important newspaper town. In 1836, William T. Youman started the *Constitutional Journal*. Youman seems to have had a rather distorted sense of reality, for he is reported to have declared Helena to be a London in size and a Paris in beauty. The newspaper survived for perhaps two years.[117] The next newspaper was the *Arkansas State Democrat and Helena Commercial Advertiser* that started in 1839. A five-column affair, it listed William E. Butts as editor in 1840, but later in the year Thomas B. Hanly was in charge. Hanly, another man for whom the spelling of his name has occasioned great difficulties, was a Helena lawyer and later a prominent secessionist who served throughout the Civil War as Arkansas's fourth district Confederate congressman. The longwinded title apparently gave way to the *Southern Sentinel*, which did not long remain on guard duty, and of which no copies have survived.[118] There are a few issues of the *Helena Spy* from 1839, but the newspaper most associated with the town was the *Southern Shield*, founded by Q.K. Underwood. Whig in orientation, it championed Helena in its losing struggle to be the railroad terminus of Arkansas. That honor went to Memphis, and editor Q.K. Underwood spent much of his time denouncing the results. "Arkansas is to be made wholly tributary to our neighbors of the Chickasaw Bluffs," he wrote on one occasion, and "the press of Memphis has actually written itself into the belief that this State belongs, a fat province, to the town of Memphis."[119] Underwood's Democratic opponent,

W.W. Lewis of the *True Issue*, had a daughter who worked in the office as a compositor. J.W. Slayton, writing in 1875, believed she was the first woman so employed in Arkansas.[120] No earlier example has been uncovered.

Another short-lived Helena newspaper was the *Democratic Star*, whose editor, James M. Cleveland, died of yellow fever in the great epidemic of 1855 in which three-fourths of the town's residents fled.[121] Other short-lived newspapers were Hindman's *State Rights Democrat*, the *Independent Southron*, and the *Note-Book*. No other early Arkansas town boasted as many newspapers, but almost all of them vanished without leaving a trace.

Napoleon, another of Helena's rivals, was the town claimed for its own by the Mississippi River after the Civil War and immortalized by Mark Twain in his *Life on the Mississippi* (1883). Two early newspapers there were the *Journal* in 1839 that lasted only one year, and the *Messenger*, which seems to have been its continuation.[122] The *Weekly Planter* was being published there in 1859, and the issue of December 22 told of how some abolitionists had been frustrated in their efforts to ring the town bell to commemorate the execution of John Brown.[123] Conditions in Napoleon were best summarized by a message Thomas C. Hindman sent to local Democrats: "Say to Alf Eddington and others I can send them in ten days an editor who will fight."[124]

Batesville was another regional center. This White River town sported the *News* in 1838, followed by the *Eagle*. "Fent" Noland edited the *Eagle* for several years, but Noland's fame rested on his Pete Whetstone stories that appeared in a national publication, *The Spirit of the Times*. In these stories, Noland used a semi-fictional hunter to describe and satirize conditions in the old Southwest. After his early excesses, Noland became a champion of temperance, writing "Bust Head is Taking the Country." A number of newspapers came and went in Batesville. No copies survive of the *Commercial Standard*, but a small run exists of the *North Arkansas*. A continuation of the *Batesville News*, it used Nathaniel Hawthorne's story "The Two Widows" as filler in 1843 and printed a two-column woodcut of a horse. Next year came a three-column cut of a Durham short-horn cow. Cartoons appeared as well in this Whig newspaper, apparently the first ever published in an Arkansas newspaper.[125]

In 1856 came the *Independent Balance*, ably edited by M. Shelby Kennard. A strong newspaper until stopped by the Civil War, it campaigned against hogs running loose in the streets and the firing of pistols at night, and for better roads. "If ever a place needed a revival, Batesville does," Kennard observed in 1858.[126] Kennard, who like all editors, had trouble with the mail, denounced the "miserable, rickety, filthy, slab sided nuisances called mail coaches." One of his important observations, worthy of noting, provided a contemporary view of Arkansas's already legendary failure to modernize: "There is a strange and unaccountable disposition in our population which prevents their being united in sentiment upon any subject. In some cases sectarianism; in other political partizanship; in still others personal piques and jealousies distract and divide the people so that the accomplishment of any public enterprise in which the cooperation of a number of citizens is necessary is next to impossible."[127] Oft thought but ne'er so well expressed, these comments were echoed over and over again by frustrated editors trying to promote an unwanted progress. As for Kennard, after the war he went on to become a noted educator.

Kennard found his motto, "Independent in All Things! Neutral in Nothing!" tested in 1858 when he causally mentioned that Judge W.C. Bevens had adjourned court for the dedication of the Batesville Institute and added "as yet but little civil and hardly any of the chancery business has been disposed of." The day after the newspaper came out, Judge Bevens

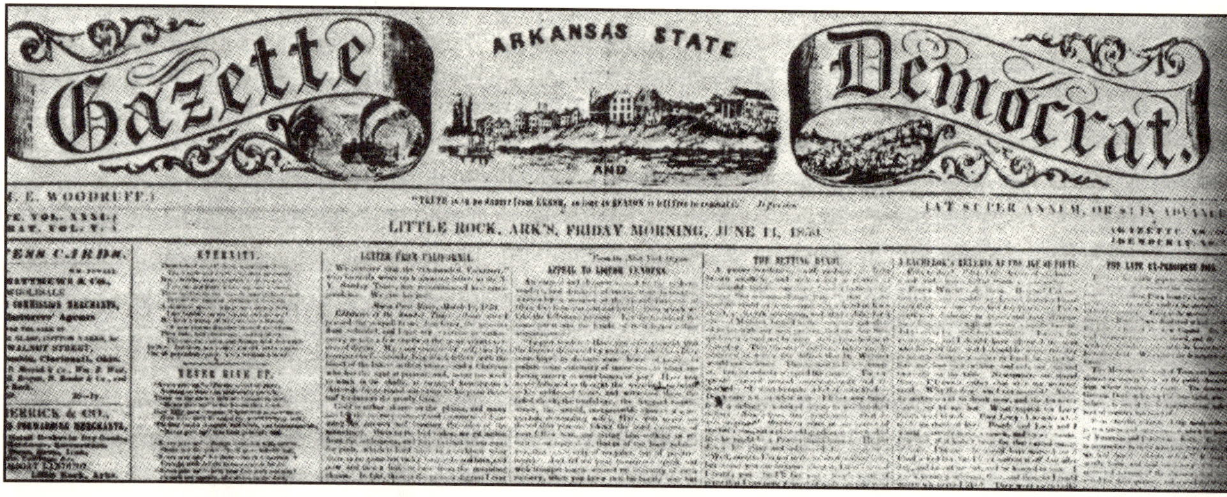

Gazette

ARKANSAS STATE

AND

Democrat.

LITTLE ROCK, ARK'S, FRIDAY MORNING, JUNE 11,

The first banner to contain scenes of Arkansas. (Arkansas State Gazette and Democrat, *June 11, 1854*)

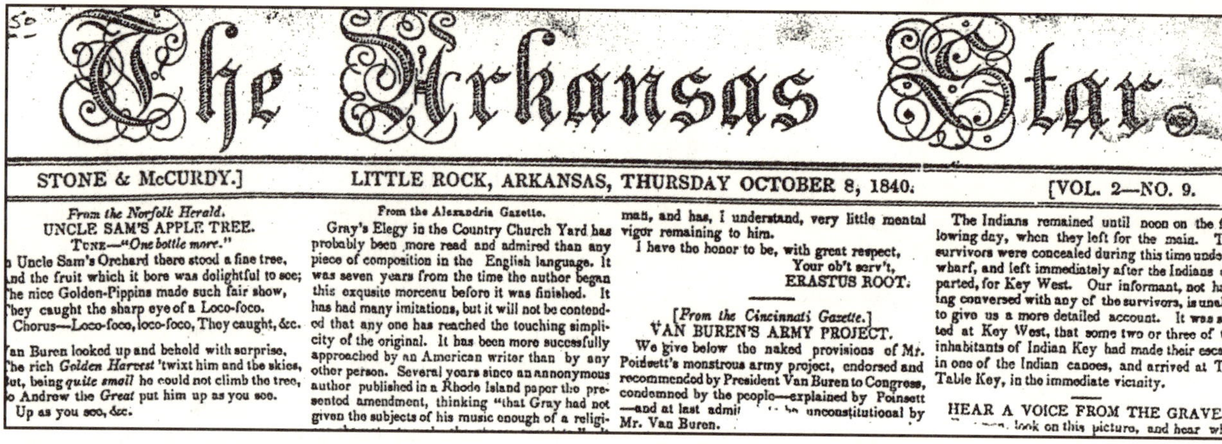

The Arkansas Star.

STONE & McCURDY.] LITTLE ROCK, ARKANSAS, THURSDAY OCTOBER 8, 1840. [VOL. 2—NO. 9.

From the Norfolk Herald.
UNCLE SAM'S APPLE TREE.
TUNE—*"One bottle more."*

Uncle Sam's Orchard there stood a fine tree,
nd the fruit which it bore was delightful to see;
he nice Golden-Pippins made such fair show,
hey caught the sharp eye of a Loco-foco.
Chorus—Loco-foco, loco-foco, They caught, &c.

an Buren looked up and beheld with surprise,
he rich *Golden Harvest* 'twixt him and the skies,
ut, being *quite small* he could not climb the tree,
o Andrew the *Great* put him up as you see.
Up as you see, &c.

From the Alexandria Gazette.

Gray's Elegy in the Country Church Yard has probably been more read and admired than any piece of composition in the English language. It was seven years from the time the author began this exquisite morceau before it was finished. It has had many imitations, but it will not be contended that any one has reached the touching simplicity of the original. It has been more successfully approached by an American writer than by any other person. Several years since an anonymous author published in a Rhode Island paper the presented amendment, thinking "that Gray had not given the subjects of his music enough of a religi-

man, and has, I understand, very little mental vigor remaining to him.

I have the honor to be, with great respect,
Your ob't serv't,
ERASTUS ROOT.

[*From the Cincinnati Gazette.*]
VAN BUREN'S ARMY PROJECT.

We give below the naked provisions of Mr. Poinsett's monstrous army project, endorsed and recommended by President Van Buren to Congress, condemned by the people—explained by Poinsett—and at last admi[...] unconstitutional by Mr. Van Buren.

The Indians remained until noon on the fol lowing day, when they left for the main. Th survivors were concealed during this time under wharf, and left immediately after the Indians de parted, for Key West. Our informant, not hav ing conversed with any of the survivors, is unabl to give us a more detailed account. It was sta ted at Key West, that some two or three of th inhabitants of Indian Key had made their escap in one of the Indian canoes, and arrived at Te Table Key, in the immediate vicinity.

HEAR A VOICE FROM THE GRAVE.

The Arkansas Star *of 1840 boasted an elaborate banner. Editors of the 19th century generally referred to the newspaper's name on the front page by the name "masthead", incorrectly. The term "banner" or "nameplate" is correct. On the second page a smaller box and cut would give the names of the editor and publisher, if separate, as well as other information about the newspaper: address, telephone number, hours open, etc. In many instances this masthead imight sport a differently worded or simplified title for the newspaper.*

STEAM-BOAT TECUMSEH At Auction.

WILL be sold, without reserve, t the highest bidder, at the landin at the city of Little Rock, on Mon-day, the 2d day of July next, th staunch and fast-running steam-boat TECUMSEH She has just undergone a thorough repair, and may b considered in first-rate order for one or two years' busi-ness, without further repair or expense.

Terms—CASH.

GLASGOW, HARRISON, & CO.

Little Rock, May 14, 1838. 22-7w

Times & Advocate six insertions.

REGULAR PACKETS FROM LIT-TLE ROCK TO MEMPHIS.

THE steamers ITASCA, Capt *A. Boyd*, and FOX, Capt. S *Buckner*, will make regular trip from this port to Memphis, dur-ing the season, and from their light draught, they will be able to get up at all times. They draw less water when light, than any boats ever in the trade

These cuts could be especially misleading. The first steamboat in Arkansas waters, the Comet, *got stuck and barely made it up to the Post. By the 1830s, steamboats were an important source of advertising revenue.*

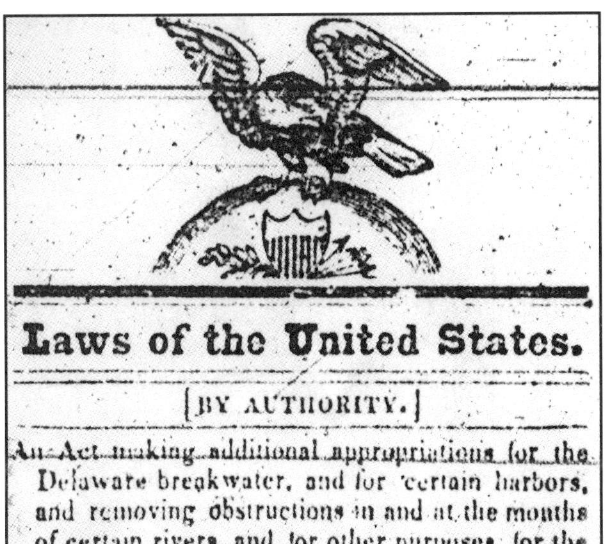

Laws of the United States.

[BY AUTHORITY.]

An Act making additional appropriations for the Delaware breakwater, and for certain harbors, and removing obstructions in and at the mouths of certain rivers, and for other purposes, for the

Some kind of eagle and shield adorned all official publications of laws and other documents.

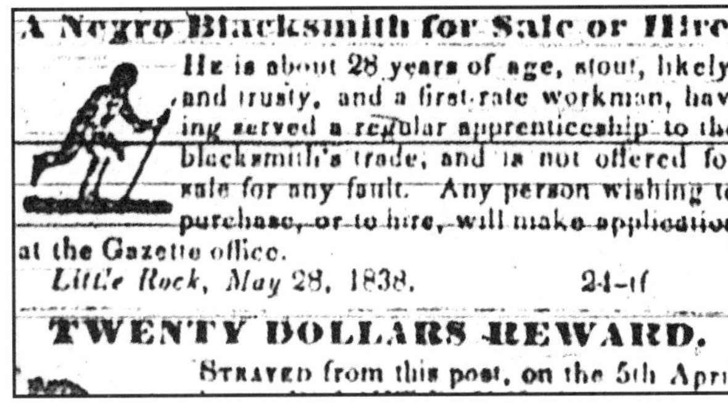

A Negro Blacksmith for Sale or Hire.

HE is about 28 years of age, stout, likely, and trusty, and a first-rate workman, hav-ing served a regular apprenticeship to the blacksmith's trade, and is not offered for sale for any fault. Any person wishing to purchase, or to hire, will make application at the Gazette office.

Little Rock, May 28, 1838. 24-tf

TWENTY DOLLARS REWARD.

STRAYED from this post, on the 5th April

Notice the cut for a blacksmith is hardly related at all to the subject matter of the advertisement. (Arkansas State Gazette, *June 20, 1838)*

The prosperity of Marshall and the Mountain Wave *are evident in this early 20th century photograph. (Author's collection)*

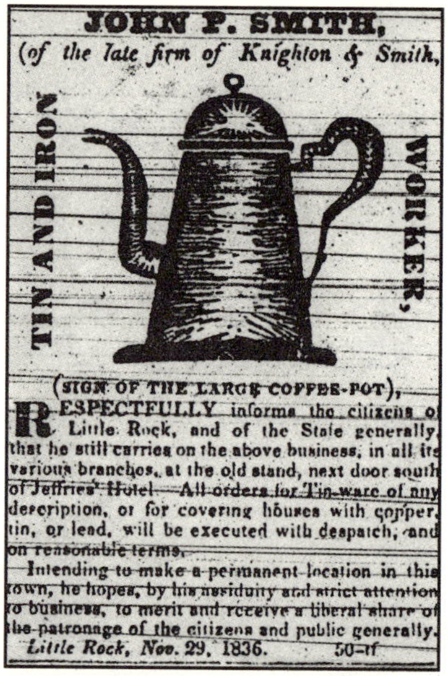

JOHN P. SMITH,
(*of the late firm of Knighton & Smith,*

TIN AND IRON WORKER,

(SIGN OF THE LARGE COFFEE-POT),

RESPECTFULLY informs the citizens of Little Rock, and of the State generally, that he still carries on the above business, in all its various branches, at the old stand, next door south of Jeffries' Hotel. All orders for Tin-ware of any description, or for covering houses with copper, tin, or lead, will be executed with despatch, and on reasonable terms.

Intending to make a permanent location in this town, he hopes, by his assiduity and strict attention to business, to merit and receive a liberal share of the patronage of the citizens and public generally.

Little Rock, Nov. 29, 1836. 50-tf

*One of the few cuts directly tied to a firm is the large coffeepot, which served not only for the newspaper advertisement but also to mark the store's location in Little Rock. (*Arkansas Gazette, *December 13, 1836)*

John R. Eakin. This longtime editor of the Washington Telegraph, *justice on the state supreme court, and agricultural promoter, was a strong believer in saving and recording the state's history. Eakin was editor for the* Washington Telegraph *throughout the Civil War. (Courtesy J.N. Heiskell Collection, UALR Archives and Special Collections)*

Charles Fenton Mercer Noland. *A Virginian from the planting class, Noland, a strong Whig editor at Batesville, killed a nephew of territorial governor John Pope in a duel but became nationally famous for his Pete Whetstone stories of the Arkansas frontier. (Courtesy Arkansas History Commission)*

Josiah Woodward Washbourne. The son of missionary minister to the Cherokees Cephas Washburn, Josiah, who changed the spelling of his last name, was a childhood chum of William Quesenbury and married one of the daughters of Major Ridge, an important Cherokee leader. (Courtesy J.N. Heiskell Collection, UALR Archives and Special Collections)

accosted the unarmed editor, swearing and raving. All this Kennard described in a subsequent issue of his newspaper, together with an analysis of the 83 cases on the docket. "Facts are stubborn things and they are dangerous too. The Honorable Gentleman charges that my statement is a lie. I fling the calumnious charge back in his teeth and I will prove from the record that what I stated is true." Kennard suggested the Judge's outburst was dictated by "too copious draughts of Dean's Whiskey," and the editor acquired a weapon, promising never to be bullied again. No fight took place, but in short order the Democrats established a competing newspaper in town, the *White River Arkansian*, which rallied to the Judge's defense during its brief life.[128]

Van Buren boasted the first newspaper in the west. Fittingly, it came about as the result of criminal activity. The head of one early criminal ring was Samuel G. Trowbridge, the mayor of Little Rock, who had an engraver make duplicate plates of Little Rock's scrip [paper money]. Francis M. Van Horne, a Philadelphia-trained printer, who in 1839 had come to Arkansas, where he found work first at the *Gazette* and then at the *Times and Advocate*, stole some type and ran off two batches of this counterfeit money. Van Horne used part of his share to buy a press, presumably that of the defunct *Arkansas Star*, and in partnership with Thomas Sterne, they moved it to Van Buren, establishing the *Arkansas Intelligencer* in 1842.

The *Intelligencer* claimed at the time of its founding to be farther west than any other newspaper in the United States. The law eventually caught up with Van Horne, who received a sentence of six years and six months. In the absence of other information, he was the first printer in Arkansas to be convicted of a felony. Sterne did not long stay with the newspaper, and John F. Wheeler, who came to Arkansas after being driven out of Georgia for printing the *Cherokee Phoenix* using Sequoyah's recently invented Cherokee

alphabet, stayed for a few months before moving on to Fort Smith, where he became the father of Fort Smith journalism. The *Intelligencer* then passed into, out of, and back into the hands of "the ever restless, uproarious, notorious Geo. W. Clarke."[129] Clarke fattened from time to time on government jobs, thus accounting for his irregular tenure. After the Civil War, he edited a bilingual newspaper in Mexico City. If the purity of Thomas B. Hanly's name suffered from having an "e" added, Clarke had the reverse problem.[130]

In 1846, local Whigs, who were strong in Van Buren, established a competing newspaper, the *Western Frontier Whig*, with John S. Logan as editor and former *Intelligencer* partner Thomas Sterne as publisher. During the election, Logan and Clarke dueled with words. Clarke christened his opponent "Big Mush," and Logan replied with "Toady Clarke." After the election, they met in a duel in Indian Territory using rifles instead of pistols but without fatalities. Logan then moved to Texas, the first Arkansas editor to head in that direction, and the *Whig* suspended. After Clarke left for one of his good fat jobs, C.D. Pryor and Josiah H. Washbourne took over at the *Intelligencer*.

Josiah H. Washbourne (to use his spelling) was a

son of missionary minister Rev. Cephas Washburn.[131] The elder Washburn had followed the Cherokees to Arkansas, and young Josiah grew up at Dwight Mission. A forceful Democratic writer and close childhood friend of Whig William M. Quesenbury, Washbourne married a daughter of Major Ridge, the prominent pro-Treaty Cherokee leader who had been murdered by the anti-Treaty faction. Washbourne, too, profited from good fat jobs and rarely was associated for long with any one newspaper. As early as 1843, the newspaper gave subscribers directions on how to deliver corn, wood, or vegetables to pay for subscriptions.[132] It also led the way in popularizing Thanksgiving in Arkansas, observing in 1847 that Arkansas was the only state without a designated date.[133] In response to a petition from Crawford County residents, December 9 was proclaimed as Thanksgiving for 1847. That year, celebrations were held in Fayetteville, Van Buren, and Huntsville.[134] The final owner of the *Intelligencer* was George W.'s brother, Anselm Clarke. After his death from tuberculosis in 1859, the newspaper closed.

Despite the changes in ownership, the newspaper was a relentless booster for the Southwest and served the nation as a principal source of news on Indian affairs. Since the anti-Treaty faction was busy murdering the pro-Treaty men and the violence spilled over into Arkansas, there was much to report. Thirty-four such murders took place just between 1845 and 1846.

Just before the start of the Civil War, J.S. Dunham, from Middleton, Connecticut, started the *Van Buren Press*. A graceful writer, Dunham was a force for moderation in the months before the Civil War. After the war, he reestablished the newspaper and remained at the helm until his death in 1912.

Fort Smith's newspaper history started with John F. Wheeler's *Herald* in 1847. The press from his former Cherokee newspaper, the *Phoenix*, was relocated to the Territory, and there Wheeler set scripture and tracts in the Cherokee alphabet. Years later, he recalled, "Although 30 years have elapsed since we saw a Cherokee case, we could take a composing stick and set the type, and can now read the language with as much ease as anyone can read Greek or Hebrew."[135]

In antebellum Arkansas, Fort Smith housed the military garrison while Van Buren had the federal court (courtesy of Senator Borland). Patronage and trade battles were intense, especially in the wake of the removal not only of the Cherokee but also of all the other Southern tribes and a mixture of Midwestern ones as well. At war constantly with its rival, Van Buren, Fort Smith presented a complicated newspaper history. Wheeler sold the *Herald* but later bought it back, merging it with another newspaper he had also started, the *Fort Smith Times*. After the *Intelligencer* went defunct, A.G. Mayers moved the plant to Fort Smith and started the *Thirty-Fifth Parallel*. Mayers served for a time as Fort Smith's postmaster and was deeply involved in Democratic politics.

Other antebellum newspapers included a Know-Nothing sheet, the *True American* (1855), as well as the *Southron* (1860), the *Picayune* (1860), and the *Tri-Weekly Bulletin* (1861). The short-lived *Daily Argus* of 1860 was the work of Charles Gordon Newman and George P.M. Turner. The newspaper did not endure, but the young men went on to distinguished careers: Major Newman joined the *Pine Bluff Commercial* after the Civil War, became its owner and edited it until 1902; Turner founded the *Memphis Scimitar*.

The principal problem both Van Buren and Fort Smith editors faced was the unreliability of the Arkansas River. Seven months during the winter of 1844–45 went by with no boats being able to ascend the river. In the absence of outside news, the newspapers generated their own. An extraordinarily large amount of locally produced poetry appeared, much of it by William M. Quesenbury and Josiah W. Washbourne. Once, when the *Fort Smith Herald* was duped into printing the graveyard poem, "Song of the Old Sexton" (at one time famous for its closing line, "I gather them in.") as if it were an original composition, Quesenbury exposed the fraud. His extended parody ended with:

"I gather them in," from living and dead,
I copy, I pilfer, wher'er I tread:
I've published much better, surely I ween,
Than what you complain of, the last you've seen:
You, printer, you reader, you ninnies, in rhyme,
But here by excuse for this time;
"I gather them in, I gather them in."

The *Herald* editor was not pleased and "permitted his temper to 'fly off the handle,'" attacking both author and newspaper. The *Intelligencer* sternly lectured his Fort Smith counterpart: "You must expect, occasionally, in your editorial career, such articles as 'Q in a Corner'; and you must either be prepared for them, or abandon the tripod."[136] It was good advice, for editing was not for the overly sensitive.

During its heyday in the 1840s, the *Intelligencer* printed a number of extended essays that made their way eastward to *The Spirit of the Times*, the nationally famous sporting magazine. Earlier, Arkansas had received national recognition from the works of Noland and Pike, and they were joined by William M. Quesenbury. His first essay reported his visit to the Upper Creek nation that included descriptions of a council meeting, a Stamp Dance, and an Indian ball game. In his second essay he followed up by describing the Lower Creeks, highlighting a dance and other diversions.

Fayetteville and other towns north of the Arkansas River were less fortunate. A newspaper entitled the *Fayetteville Witness* appeared in 1840 but was short-lived. William E. Smith's *Western Pioneer* in 1852 died quickly,[137] but Smith stayed on, later helping William Quesenbury at the *South-West Independent*. Just before the war, the *Arkansian* achieved statewide importance. Its rival was the *Fayetteville Democrat*, founded in 1860 and revived in 1869.

Washington was the early news center in the southwest. Today a state park, it was once an important stopping-off place on the road to Texas as well as being near the Red River Valley plantation lands. In 1836, the prospectus for the *Hempstead & Red River Inquirer* appeared in the *Gazette*, but in June its author, J. Garvin, died in Fulton, a town that ranked next to Helena as the state's most unhealthy site.[138] Then, in 1840 W.H. Etter started the *Washington Telegraph* even though it would be 20 years before a real telegraph started clacking in the state.

A native of Philadelphia, this "Dutchman" came to Arkansas in 1839, bringing the material for the office from his native state. At first he was assisted by his brother-in-law, John (or Joshua) Ruth, but he left to found the *Ouachita Herald* at Camden. Etter, who stood nearly six feet in height and weighed over 200 pounds, was primarily an editor rather than a printer.[139] Although he sold the newspaper in the 1850s, his family reclaimed it at various times, ending it in 1947, by which time Washington had become a ghost town.

A strong Whig, Etter and his successor editor, John R. Eakin, later a state supreme court justice, made the *Telegraph* a strong proponent of internal improvements. No editor was ever as eloquent on the subject of roads. "There is not such thing as a regular mail," Etter complained in 1844, noting that his New Orleans news now came from New York. [140] Conditions in 1848 were worse. Instead of regular post coaches, mail on this, the principal route to southwest, "arrives here semi-occasionally, sometimes on horseback, and sometimes in a rattle-trap sort of nondescript vehicle, which has been dubbed a stage. They were worn out and rotten, years ago, and are breaking down every trip."[141] Little wonder that the first thing to be tossed off were newspapers. After pronouncing the route a public nuisance, he added, "we would prefer that the mail should be carried on a wheel-barrow, and it shoved by a man with a wooden leg. It might, probably, not come through as quick, but it could be depended on with more certainty."[142]

In the absence of news to cut and paste, Etter fell back on fiction. Unlike some major metropolitan newspapers, Arkansas newspapers only printed stories and novels during times of drought. Instead of Charles Dickens or Harriet Beecher Stowe, Etter had "The Farmer's Daughter" in 1843, written by "A Lady of Maryland." It inflicted on its readers such telling lines as:

> "I cannot, indeed I cannot leave my mother, Henry! Oh, do not urge to do that which my heart and conscience alike condemn."
>
> "Then, Lucy, we must part to-night. I will not urge you to make any sacrifice which your own feelings do not prompt."

The story was, perhaps, for the times, not without some redeeming merit for Arkansas readers. That "the failure of the Bank of Maryland reduced the family from affluence to a state of comparative poverty,"[143] described a condition soon to prevail when the Real Estate Bank and the State Bank collapsed. Etter observed, and all antebellum editors would have agreed, "It is difficult for an editor to furnish his readers with any thing entertaining for some weeks after an election."[144]

Few newspapers did more to support funding for railroads. In 1852, Etter took editorial note of "a prejudice existing against Arkansas" on the part of emigrants: "The only thing needed to make Arkansas equal to any of her sister States, is an increased facility of communication with the commercial marts which afford her a market for her products."[145] Over the years, Etter and Eakin provided a running commentary on the state's failures: "Not a mile of turnpike, Plankroad, Railroad or Canal in the State—not a dollar that we ever heard of has been appropriated by the State towards the improvement of our common roads and streams—nothing has been done towards clearing out the obstructions from our navigable streams—not even a school-house has been built,—and yet the State is in debt upwards of three millions of dollars."[146] Only as the period ended did the newspaper strike a more optimistic note: Arkansas "has awakened from her Rip Van Winkle sleep—she has caught the grand note of progress that is sounding around her; she has received the glow of spirit that actuate the great works, and she has fallen into the ranks of those who are pressing onward and upward."[147]

It is not surprising that the Democrats resented the *Telegraph*, and Orville Jennings, later a prominent lawyer and politician, and Maine native J.S. Moore, whom printer's devil Sam Williams described as "a shrewd, smart, wide-awake chap, a thoroughly trained newspaper man," but who was also "bilious, dyspeptic, and altogether broken down in health," created the *Hempstead Democrat* in competition. After Moore's death, Jennings disposed of the newspaper to James M. Kilgore and John D. Kimbell. As no copies of the newspaper are extant, we have to rely on Williams's memory that Kilgore signed his editiorials with an asterisk (*) while Kimbell used a dagger (†). These two warred with Etter's editor, A.T. Hawley, a fine writer who, Williams recalled, "had an unfortunate habit of crooking his elbow and looking into the glass rather too frequently." Hawley fought his drinking habit, and after being converted in a Methodist revival, swore off drink for a time. So strong was the addiction that he used opium and other narcotics in his fight, but all to no avail. "Sam, this is worse than hell itself!" he exclaimed, "I can stand this torture no longer." Two bottles of whiskey later he was as "drunk as a lord" and soon migrated to California.[148]

The *Democrat* kept changing hands. Kimbell left for Little Rock where he worked at the *True Democrat* and other newspapers before settling in Hot Springs; Kilgore, a firm believer in spiritualism, went to Cincinnati to converse and shake hands with a dead relative. Joseph H. Black, another young lawyer, had the newspaper briefly before he, too, went into the *True Democrat*'s employ. The last owner was Kit Owsley (or Ousley), of whom Williams wrote: he "was inflated with the idea that he know more about running a newspaper than anyone else on the planet, but who in reality knew nothing at all about the business—a very common idiocy among certain young men even to this day." As Williams went on to note, "They labor under the foolish impression that two or three columns of platitudes on the editorial page constitutes the chief labor of the editor, and imagine that those two or three columns of 'fine writing' is going to astonish the world." Curiously, despite Williams's evident disdain for the man, he remained a figure in Arkansas journalism, being the co-founder of the *Hot Springs Sentinel* in 1877.[149]

The newspaper record in other parts of the state was spottier. At Camden, a Whig newspaper entitled the *Camden Herald*, metamorphosed into the *Ouachita Herald*. One antebellum editor was Adam Clark, later a founder of the Arkadelphia *Southern Standard*. The *Beacon*, the *Southern Stamp*, and the *State Rights Eagle* were other Camden newspapers. The *Eagle* was much quoted, and its editor, Anson W. Hobson, bore the nickname "Legs" on account of his height.

Pine Bluff also saw newspapers come and go. In 1847 William E. Smith, who made several tries for success, was brought in by James Yell, the governor's nephew. Smith "made no attempts at fine writing,"

but *The Jeffersonian* was "a very readable paper."[150] Smith then moved to Huntsville where he had the *Mountaineer* and hence to Fayetteville where he started the *Western Pioneer*. In 1850 the *Pine Bluff American* appeared. Read Fletcher, a strong Democrat, acquired the newspaper in 1855, where during the Know-Nothing canvass it competed against E.H. Vance at the *Pine Bluff Republican*. Upon the ruins of the *American* came the *Pine Bluff Democrat*, then the *Jefferson Enterprise*, and finally the *Independent*. Lawyer L.B. Luckie, who had started the *Republican* in 1850 and later edited the *Enterprise*, was exceedingly unlucky. Although "suave and gentle as the most gentle of women" when sober, his law partner, Read Fletcher, recalled, Luckie was killed in a fight while under the influence of alcohol. Another Pine Bluff figure was Major William F. Douglass, who in 1858 made the *Independent* "a live newspaper." Douglass, besides being "a graceful and ready writer," "was a gentleman of elegant leisure and good property, and to destroy the ennui of plantation life made the above investment."[151] Surely Douglass was the first for whom a newspaper was a hobby. Finally, J.N. Smithee, the first president of the Arkansas Press Association, worked in the office of the *Republican*.

El Dorado was another town served early on. In 1846 William H. Hines published the *Union*. Apparently after a long suspension, the newspaper resumed under the title the *Democratic Union*.[152] Just before the Civil War, J.B. Burton founded the *El Dorado Bulletin*.[153] Arkadelphia's press history started with the *Arkansas Sentinel* in 1850; then came a sheet called the *Arkansaw Traveler*, whose editor, S.M. Scott, in 1857 joined the trek to Cincinnati in quest of a new press.[154] Uncounted newspapers have borne the title "Arkansas Traveler," but J.N. Smithee nominated this one as the first.[155] The *Ouachita Conference Journal* of Rev. J.E. Cobb was one of, if not the first, religious newspapers in the state. At Monticello in Drew County there flourished *The Sage of Monticello*, which not surprisingly, claimed devotion to the ideals of Thomas Jefferson.

Des Arc, which tried to capture the state capital from Little Rock as well as boasting of a nonexistent gold mine, sported two newspapers. John C. Morrill founded the *Des Arc Citizen* in 1854, converting it to a semi-weekly just before the Civil War. A strong Democrat, Morrill got opposition in 1860 from the *Constitutional Union* of Weston H. Rhea, which, although created to be a party newspaper, was superior to the general run of that lot. The *Citizen* was revived after the Civil War. J.J. Baugh later moved it from Des Arc to Searcy, where it became the *White County Citizen*.

Newspapers came and went at Searcy, Jacksonport, Powhatan, Pocahontas, Bentonville, Warren, and other towns. Too often the state press greeted a newspaper's appearance with enthusiasm, quoting it a few times. If after a few months such notices no longer appeared, the newspaper probably was dead. Newspaper salutatories exceeded obituaries, making it hard to determine when many newspapers "suspended," the trade's euphemism for died.

A few otherwise lost newspapers left behind some small gems that other newspapers picked up and used. Hence, the *Messenger*, a newspaper from the now defunct town of Wittsburg in Cross County near the current site of Village Creek State Park, offered up the following which the *South-West Independent* thought worthy of copying:

> "Good morning stranger. Where are you moving to?"
>
> "To Ar-r-kansaw."
>
> "Where did you come from?"
>
> "From the State of North Caroliner."
>
> "Will there be much emigration from that State this year?"
>
> "A mighty sight I reckin—mighty hard times there this year. A heap of people is on the pint of starvin."
>
> "Why so—what's the matter?"
>
> "The 'simmon crap has failed, and I'm gwine to look for a better country."
>
> We mizzled.[156]

One reason the *Independent* printed the story was that too often the principal theme in the press was problems with Arkansas. "The very name," the *Powhatan Advertiser* complained, "conjures up to the benighted, misinformed stranger, the bloody bowie knife, assassins, cut throats, and highway robbers."[157]

The appearance of newspapers in remote parts added to the list of exchanges and increased the flow of Arkansas news reported in the state press in Little Rock. The late 1840s proved to be hard times to get newspapers going, due first to the Mexican War and then the California Gold Rush. The greatest period of expansion came in the 1850s, and with it the first call for a newspaper association. "We propose to our contemporaries, throughout the State, a Convention of *Editors* and *Publishers*," proclaimed the Arkadelphia *Arkansaw Traveler*, in the fall of 1854. The proposed meeting, to be held at the same time the legislature assembled, was promptly endorsed by the *Gazette and Democrat*. The purpose, the *Traveler* asserted, was for editors to become "personally as well as editorially acquainted," to promote harmony, and to establish uniform rates for advertising and job work.[158] Danley endorsed the idea, adding that, "The respectability of any profession depends entirely on those who are engaged in it. If they organize for their own protection, and stand up for their interests, as a class, they can and will make themselves respectable and respected."[159]

Nothing seems to have come of this meeting, but the same year saw the founding of *Arkansas Magazine*, the first state-related serial publication. It came out monthly but, although given strong editorial endorsement, soon failed. In a land where proud illiterates flourished, literary endeavors took time to find a local audience.[160]

There might have some connection between Danley's emerging professionalism and an article he cut from the *Richmond* (Virginia) *Republican* in 1853 entitled "Printers." "Printers, it is said, universally die at an early age," the article began, and continued with its litany of woe. Their hours were bad, their working conditions unhealthy, and they were poor: "they rarely ever receive a fair compensation for their services," and "their purse-strings are ever untied at the bidding of charity and their hard-earned 'dimes' are freely distributed for the relief of their fellow men." "Thus," the article concluded, "it is that they live poor and die poor; and if a suitable reward does not await them after death, sad indeed must be the beginning, the existence and end of the poor 'typos.'"[161]

Three years after Danley reprinted this article, Little Rock's printers met and organized a typographical union, with constitution, by-laws, and officers. In 1858 this group still existed, but what they might have accomplished or how long they endured is not known.[162] At this stage, when the lines between the offices of printer, editor and publisher were but poorly established, the conflict between labor and capital, which figured prominently in the mid-20th century, lay in the distant future.

William M. Quesenbury and the South-West Independent

One Arkansas newspaper stood preeminent, not on account of the length of its run, which was less than four years, but rather because through the surviving issues almost every essential element of antebellum newspapers save the political was encapsulated. And it was done in a style genuinely unique in the annals of the press. This newspaper was the *South-West Independent*, and its creator was William M. Quesenbury, who earlier made his appearance in this narrative.

Born in Arkansas Territory on August 21, 1822, Cush, as he early was nicknamed, came from a frontier family that figured in the founding of Tennessee. His mother, Susan Bean, was a sister to the Beans who owned the saltworks on the Illinois River in Indian Territory. Educated at the first school held in Fort Smith, Cush later attended St. Joseph's College, a Catholic school in Bardstown, Kentucky, along with other Arkansans, including Robert Ward and Richard Mentor Johnson. In his twenties he started lounging around the newspaper offices at Van Buren, where he learned some practical skills. During his trips across the mountains or into the Territory, he sometimes reported back to the *Intelligencer*. But even in Cush's earliest pieces there was nothing juvenile in his writing. His treatment of the graduation ceremonies at the Fayetteville Female Seminary became a small gem. Professor J.N. Maffitt gave the address. For years, Arkansas editors had respectfully printed his sermons and lectures, which were marked by both great verbal excess and a singular lack of substance. Cush took oblique aim, using the theatrical war going on in New York between two great actors as his starting point:

> The speaker was evidently suffering from debility, and though the address was not delivered in his usual manner, a circumstance observed by many, it was on this account the more pleasing to those who are affected chiefly by the matter of a discourse. Mr. Maffitt was on this day, to Maffitt himself, as is Macready to Forrest—by the one we see all the beauties of the author held up to view; the other continually keeps our attention to the *physique* of the actor; Macready acts Shakespeare, Forrest acts Forrest, Excuse me Mr. Maffitt.[163]

Cush's style was based on an exhaustive knowledge of the English and American classics. If he had a model, it surely was Laurence Sterne of *Tristram Shandy* fame. Conspicuously absent was the fractured, overheated political rhetoric espoused by most local writers.

That he could write with exactness and polished detail was displayed in his letter to the *Gazette* on the Battle of Buena Vista in the Mexican War. Cush, it should be noted, was honored by being mentioned in the dispatches, thus linking him, Borland, and Danley among the state's first war hero-editors. And this multi-talented genius had another side, too. He had begun drawing at an early age and studied at least informally with the great Western artist John Mix Stanley, who spent several months at Van Buren during 1843. Many of Cush's friends, both white and Indian, were captured on canvas by this ill-fated artist. (A number of Stanley's paintings were lost in a fire at the Smithsonian Institute in 1865.)

After returning from the Mexican War, Cush wrote a long poem about the battle of Buena Vista that reflected negatively on Albert Pike. Then he caught the Gold Rush fever. Traveling overland, sketchbooks in hand, he reached California. Prospecting for gold did not pan out, but he wrote for the California edition of the *New Orleans True Delta* and then took part in the founding of the *Sacramento Daily Union*. Its editor, John F. Morse, had been a charter member of Rev. Henry Ward Beecher's Plymouth Church in Brooklyn. A trained physician, Morse was a tireless promoter of public health and scientific agriculture. By late 1851, Cush was back in Arkansas, just as woodcuts were beginning to appear in the press. In addition, his drawing of the Fayetteville Female Seminary attained publication, making it the first published picture by an Arkansas editor.

Politics provided Cush with the job of Receiver of Public Moneys at Fayetteville and doubtless with the aid of family members, Cush decided to try his hand at owning a newspaper. Crossing the Boston Mountains, he took a steamer to Cincinnati where he ordered a Hoe cylinder press. His first press started for Arkansas on the steamboat *General Scott*:

> *Alas! Alas the fatal lot*
> *That haunts the name of General Scott—*
> *(The name this splendid craft has got;)*
> *For snags and floods, and fire all hot,*
> *Conspired with bad-luck in a plot*
> *Against the steamer as she shot*
> *Like a wild-goose through the waters,*
> *And quick as sinks a leaden chunk,*
> *Down, down, the mighty vessel sunk*
> *Among the fishes and the otters.*
>
> *A beautiful caper!*
> *Away went the paper,*
> *The hope of bread for the baby;*
> *Romance loving maid,*

A ca-fish had played
With these very letters, here—may be.[164]

Cush must have had insurance (perhaps another first), for another press ascended the river on the *Summit*, and on August 25, 1853, the first issue of what some had speculated would be called "Quesenbury's own" came off the press as the *South-West Independent*. Offered at two dollars a year, the newspaper promised to be "a journal for the encouragement of education, agriculture, internal improvements, fine arts, sciences, religion, political reformation, and the interest of everybody." "We shall write what we please," Cush averred, adding, "we shall write for the times—keeping as nearly as our judgment will permit, to the right point—which point, for a newspaper, we consider just in the advance or lead in all the great improvements and questions of the day."

In his first issue, Cush promised to "avoid all personalities, considering it cowardly and contemptible."[165] Unlike others who made that promise but soon broke it, Cush held to it successfully. During the 1856 campaign, when Know-Nothing leader Solon Borland came to Fayetteville, Cush gave him an extended notice, for, as he told readers, he and Borland had been together in the war: "Now some fool may think these remarks intended for a political purpose—to thrust Major Borland before the public. But fools think that way. We have nothing to do with the Major's political affairs."[166]

He had less luck with his other motto, "Pay the Printer." With his new Hoe press, apparently the first cylinder press in Arkansas, Cush could promise "fancy type, inks of all colors, and every article necessary for cards, hand bills, circulars, pamphlets, books, and every description of printing." The problem was that as long as Arkansas remained isolated and rural, these items were not in much demand and could do little to support an office.

The surviving issues of Cush's newspaper would suggest that he had taken Horace Greeley's advice on how to operate a successful weekly, except that Greeley's advice did not appear until 1860.[167] According to Greeley, a good newspaper should be "a perfect mirror of everything done in your county that its citizens ought to know." That included reporting who grew a mammoth beet; the erection of new churches, stores, mills, and houses; and the promotion of county fairs and home industry.

In Cush's case, he undertook to promote the relatively new national holiday of Thanksgiving. Fixing a national date for this celebration was delayed until the 1930s, when it became another of the New Deal reforms of the Roosevelt administration; earlier celebrations depended on governors' proclamations. When in 1854 Governor Elias N. Conway failed to act, Cush issued his own proclamation, setting two dates, December 25 and January 1 for the celebration.[168] It was a kind of covert action against the Democrats, and Danley rejoiced in reprinting it.

Agricultural improvements were also near to Cush's heart. Most other Southern states were ahead of Arkansas in holding county and state fairs when Cush unleashed his campaign in late 1853. First, he recalled a failed attempt in Crawford County in 1843, then a recent Sebastian County meeting that rejoiced in cow peas: "When planted it would spring forth like India-rubber on the ground, growing faster, higher and stronger than Jack's bean, and bearing rail roads and steam boats on its tendrils, cows on its leaves, and on opening the pods they could be found full of young calves."[169]

Despite, or perhaps because of, Danley's support in Little Rock, the cause of a state fair never got off the antebellum ground. However, in 1856 Washington County held its first fair, and Cush was there to report on it and to illustrate his story by a woodcut of "a large urchin on a big bay mare, followed by a healthy, fat young colt." Oratory was the order of the day. Major William D. Reagan "pictured Arkansaw as it ought to be with hogs on the hills—a hog for every acorn, colts in the pasture—a colt for every blade of grass,—and so on till Prosperity was presented complete in all." Then Judge David Walker took over, and "colt-show stock rose to 10,000 per cent premium. Agriculture took its stand at the top of human affections—all in the house—every man raised his hand—lawyer, doctor, merchant, mechanic, tinker, and exclaimed, 'Thank God I am a farmer.'"[170] The long association between agriculture and the state's press would form an important theme for more than a century and a half.

Cush found indirect ways for presenting controversial material. In one early issue, he invented a letter writer who asked why, at a recent convention in Fort Smith on railroad promotion, no one lower than the rank of colonel attended, and who also wanted to know who ranked highest among these officers. Although America was supposedly a democratic society without feudal trappings, every aspiring politician sought titles and, once attained, kept them. The once-famous anecdote of editor John Phoenix saying, "Good-bye, Colonel," as his ship pulled away from port and having 24 men on shore acknowledge the greeting, had its own parallel in Arkansas. "Everybody was a colonel," state historian Fay Hempstead later wrote, "unless he happened to be a 'Judge' or a 'Major.'"[171] Cush purported to explain to newcomer Robert Green, or "green Bob," that "we have none of the lower grade in Arkansas—the privates are all Colonels." And, as to who ranked highest, at least six of the men were over six feet tall.[172]

Once Cush got hold of a theme, he ran with it. A later issue reported after a visit to Fort Smith that he had met the colonels, and "there was very little of the military about them." One had accompanied Cush around town in his shirt sleeves, while "another sat, tailor fashion, on his table among his law papers and squirted tobacco juice over the floor in such a style as would have run an English tourist crazy."[173]

Like many county seat newspapers, the *South-West Independent* was located on the town square. The office, stocked with exchanges, Cush called a "cool quiet, virtuous place," and invited readers to drop by.[174] Apparently they did in such great numbers that they borrowed his books and did not return them and drove the editor to seek refuge in the nearby home of Jonas Tebbetts, a prominent lawyer and Democratic politician. Cush listed himself as editor rather than publisher, although the title "printer" appeared on his job work. J.C.M. Hicks, the compositor, figured occasionally in Cush's stories, and former printer William E. Smith lent his hand when Cush was out of town. Cush advertised for an apprentice aged from 14 to 16 and "from the country."

No antebellum editor left a better description of how local news in the absence of reporters was generated:

> Our ears are open, and we are awaiting the minute Capt. Chew shall haul out of his mail bags some startling or thrilling news of something extremely great, or extremely little, being done somewhere.
>
> This scarcity of news in the market puts the poor editor to as much trouble to fill out his paper, as the scarcity of bread troubles him to fill his basket. What are we do to then, to make our newspaper interesting? Somebody must do something, or else we shall not be able to make cut the records. Now, ye who always grumble at the paper, and we are very happy to state our subscribers don't, just to and perform some wonderful feat, discover some marvelous thing, or bring out some interesting news or tale, and we will have Hicks after it as quick as a flash.
>
> Our mental telegraph is in good order, and the lighting ready to bear any message which might be transmitted along its wires. But we do not want imaginary news. We want some real heart stirring news.—No great event can possibly transpire without our learning and noting it. Hurrah somebody and do something.[175]

On another occasion Cush resorted to poetry, explaining his daily routine in stanzas based on Manrico's off-stage serenade in Giuseppe Verdi's *Il Trovatore*:

> *Gaily the editor,*
> *Smoked his cigar,*
> *While he was scissoring*
> *News near and far—*
>
> *Looking for murders dire,*
> *Items or puffs,*
> *Devil say—devil say,*
> *"Ain't that enough!"*[176]

What set Cush apart from other editors was the way in which he turned ordinary events into extraordinary examples of humor. One good example came in the familiar case of acknowledgments. In one case, he listed 17 persons who had contributed things "eatable, wearable, rare or valuable." One gave him canned peaches, and Cush used the occasion to plug the still very rare process. Cherokee chief John Ross sent him prints of Red Jacket and Frelinghuysen, and his father-in-law supplied "a large *cornfed(!)* hog." Then Cush thanked J.J. Green, for supplying "*max j ellek vell ma ioof*," the secret pass word of the Know-Nothings.[177]

A familiar refrain in the country press was the weather. Cush was no exception, except in the way he treated it. In the spring of 1855, he wrote:

> The drouth, the dreadful drouth of the past season—who, who, what, what, have not felt its dire effects! The man who sells cabbage, sells little heads. Hens lay bluebird eggs, and all the hogs are pigs. Horses have dwindled down to colts, and all the cattle to calves. The loads of wood hauled to town are mere crows nests, and scarce any person can afford more fire than a single lucifer-match a day. Farmers are going about trying to sell pop-corn for large Tuscarora. Whiskey venders deal out pond-water for rot-gut. Doctors never get a more complicated case than the belly-ache; and attorneys think themselves the lawful children of Fortune if an eastern house sends them $6^1/_4$ cent claims for collection.[178]

Another of his observations was picked up by the *Washington Telegraph*:

QUESENBURY, of the *South-West Independent*, says, that hairy child which was born in Mississippi, spoke three words—"*seven years famine*"—and died, ought to have died, for had it lived, from the start it made, it would have become the most intolerable liar that ever infested the earth.[179]

Similarly, Cush was inspired by another type of weather. On January 28, 1854, he apologized for his newspaper's bad appearance. The week before, the cold had become so intense that "printing ink, writing ink, press joints—every thing that had a particle of oil or water about it became flinty hard. Types clogged, and the press became unmanageable." This prompted these lines:

THE English language—the language by which Milton and Shakespeare were immortalized, betrays its shabby poverty in any attempt at describing the late cold weather.

A faint conception of the intensity of the cold might be gained by a careful analysis of an expression of one of our farmers which came to our ears a day or so since; "I've been married nigh on to forty years, but I slept closer to Betsy last Friday night than I ever did before in my life."[180]

Fayetteville's remoteness was exacerbated by the drought, and Cush was reduced to printing a half-sheet for six months. Newspapers shared with each other, and in this case after running through some sheets from Van Buren and five bundles from Little Rock, he was rescued by the *Cherokee Advocate*,

thereby, enabling us to keep a record of the doings of the country; to tell who's dead, who's married; to pint [*sic*] the young to virtue; to encourage the timid and wavering; to give recipes for curing hams, and botts in horse, and oh! to make manifest the sighs of tender hearts, throbbing, sobbing, bobbing with emotions of love, in delicious jinglings at the ends of lines;—to acquaint of the state of the markets; to rake down the vicious; in fine, to sustain the honor of Fayetteville,—of the Northwest,—of all Arkansas,—of the whole World by continuing publication of the South-West Independent, straight along, regardless of distance, sandbars, and non-paying subscribers.[181]

Cush decided to turn to St. Louis for his supplies, even though this involved a long overland route. While visiting that city, he renewed an earlier acquaintance with the famous daguerrean John Fitzgibbon. Cush's account of having his picture taken was quoted at length by photographic historian Richard Rudisill, who assumed that Cush was just an ordinary country editor.[182] Since Cush had returned from California with J. Wesley Jones, who claimed to have 10,000 daguerreotypes of the Wild West and for whom Cush had worked as a sketch artist, Cush was really one of the most informed men in America on this subject.

Another of Cush's encounters consisted of a story related to Edward Washbourne. The young painter had set up in Fayetteville doing portraits when a countryman from War Eagle Creek came into the studio. The resultant dialogue focused on two issues. The young man's father had heard of pictures being taken on smoked glass and had created "smoke enough to cure all the bacon in Carroll County" without producing a picture. The daguerreotypist in Van Buren had charged only three dollars for a picture, and Washbourne wanted $50. "Why, daddy only giv two dollars for the paint to paint our big wagin, and it was the clur red and that war anough left to paint more nor the whole shoot of your picters. I reckon you needn't come over to War Eagle, stranger,—don't reckon you could git any picters to paint over thar."[183] This story received national circulation through *The Spirit of the Times*.

As time permitted, Cush continued to make woodcuts to illustrate some of his stories. One, known only by hearsay, was of a locomotive. According to a letter from the Choctaw Nation, "one warrior was so taken with it, that he determined to have him one, and requested me to write the 'print man send me one horse, tail stick high, smoke heap: me ride heap big man one horse tail smoke, squaw love smoke horse tail stick up."[184] In sharp contrast to Woodruff, well known for his diatribes against Indians, Cush was their defender, and many of his closest personal friends were among the Cherokees: "It has often been a matter of doubt whether we were not a Cherokee, for we were born among that people, and have grown up familiar with their customs, manners, and men and history."[185]

One of the hallmarks most remembered about Cush's editing was his poetry. At the end of 1853, he composed a long poem in the form of a carrier's address, and he used verse to describe the weddings of his friends. John Hunt's marriage to Sarah Jane Adair of the Cherokee Nation prompted these lines:

John's as brave as any man
That you'll meet anywhere,
But his friends will see he can
Quite calmly take Adair.

Or:

The night was dark and fearful,
The thunder made a racket,
When James Van Hoose was married
By the Rev. Mr. Hacket.

The longest poem, dedicated to Cush's former colonel, John S. Roane, urged all his bachelor friends to marry. The list included Captain Danley, who remained "a bachelor fusty, musty, crusty," and Elias Rector, the original of Albert Pike's poem, "The Fine Arkansas Gentleman," who did marry. The *Intelligencer* took offense, claiming that as a Van Buren resident, Roane belonged to it. Washbourne was apparently in charge of the *Intelligencer* (all copies for those years being lost), and only a fragment of the ensuing poetic warfare exists. At one point Cush complained, "The last Van Buren Intelligencer came down on us like a storm of shillelahs, tomahawks, wildcats, and fire. We survived, but a ruined being—a mere wreck of 'old Cush'—bruised, scalped, scorched, scratched, and we believe bit in three places." Cush ended his story with a line that soon became a proverb in Arkansas: "Be not affronted at a jest: if a man throws salt at thee, it will not hurt thee unless thou has sore places."[186]

Cush's most persistent campaign was for internal improvements. He journeyed off the mountain to attend a statewide railroad convention held in Little Rock. Louisville's George D. Prentice was the featured speaker, but tempers erupted when Prentice supported Memphis as an eastern terminus. The engineer of the proposed Little Rock and Helena railroad challenged the editor to a duel, but through the intervention of Albert Pike and "Fent" Noland, the visitor left Little Rock in one piece. Back on the mountain, Cush took aim at all the interested parties, who were too interested in playing to the crowd. Editor Danley at the *Gazette* stood back from the fray and admitted that Cush was right. Thereafter, Cush contented himself with advocating a canal to connect Van Buren and Fayetteville:

> Nature, oxen, wagons horses and mules will accomplish it, without a single direct effort to the purpose. The work has already begun. On the highest parts of the Boston Mountains some very fine excavations have been made, and in some of the valleys the work has been nearly completed. The only means necessary for the canal are those that have already been so successfully used—rain,

> and travel along the road. [Already] we have seen sixty yards of pretty good canal made by one hard rain where the road was favorable for washings...[187]

Not until the end of the 20th century was Fayetteville effectively connected by an adequate road through the Boston Mountains.

Another of Cush's innovations was a book review. New York newspapers had just started doing reviews when Cush ventured into the new format. A friend had sent him a copy of *Life and History of Samuel Phillips*, and Cush reviewed this Texas imprint known now only through his review. Phillips had lived in Arkansas and although he had reconstituted himself in Texas, old-timers like Cush, who had known the man in Van Buren, were not deceived.[188]

Despite its great popularity, the *South-West Independent* suspended. Its success, like that of so many early newspapers, depended on the editor's health, and Cush fell ill. At first, he tried to sell the newspaper to Stand Watie, the prominent Cherokee leader. According to Cush, he had 1,000 subscribers and the best-equipped office west of St. Louis. The job work brought in $1,000 a year and advertising $1,500. With the subscribers paying two dollars a year, his income should have been $4,500 while expenses ran to $1,500.[189] Watie did not bite, and the press was later sold to John F. Wheeler, who moved it to Fort Smith where he used it to print the *Times*

until it was lost in a fire. Cush apparently recovered his health late in the decade and continued to be a force in Arkansas journalism, serving as a correspondent for the *Gazette* and filling in at the *Arkansian*.

Conclusion

The antebellum press of Arkansas followed much of the rest of Arkansas in still being at the frontier stage at the start of the Civil War. In Little Rock, the *Arkansas Gazette* and the *True Democrat* claimed circulation statewide but still remained weeklies. Local newspapers were appearing in ever increasing numbers, but out of the hundreds that had at one time existed, only a few had lasted more than two or three years. All were about to be overwhelmed by events that changed Arkansas and the nation.

Chapter III

Editors in War and Reconstruction

"There is no medium ground—Southern slavery is either right or it is wrong."
Des Arc Citizen, May 18, 1859.

"We love the Union, but we love our rights better."
Chicot Press, March 1860.

"Arkansas, being without banks, feels the pressure of the times more severely than any other State in the Confederacy."
Little Rock *Daily State Journal*, November 12, 1861.

"Henceforth guns, sabres, bayonets, and all the paraphernalia of war should engage the energies of our people, and not letter writing and street argumentation."
William M. Quesenbury, *Arkansas State Gazette*, May 4, 1861.

"We find it impossible to make room for one half the communications sent to us. Long essays, however gracefully written, are unfitted for the times. Mister John D. Keith sends us a very pretty composition entitled 'Comfort to my mother,' which we would make room for if we could."
Little Rock *True Democrat*, March 20, 1862.

"This sheet has nothing to do with local or State matters."
Fayetteville *War Bulletin*, February 15, 1862.

"And what is Arkansas doing to keep pace with the spirit of improvement that is now rife in the country? Nothing—absolutely nothing."
Arkadelphia *Southern Standard*, March 6, 1869.

"[Editors] are a discontented, driveling, shabby mangy set. Nobody believes one word they say. They can't go on like their neighbors, making a livelihood in a decent, quiet way."
William Quesenbury letter, *Arkansas Daily Gazette*, December 1, 1866.

Introduction

Even after the firing on Fort Sumter, the coming of the Civil War was actually a gradual process. In the remote counties of Arkansas, the war was well underway before news of its arrival reached obscure mountain ridges. By contrast, Arkansas's editors were the most informed and among those most affected. Of particular note is that only one newspaper, the *Washington Telegraph*, managed to continue publishing throughout the war. When Union forces occupied Arkansas, they seized newspaper plants and started up new newspapers, laying the foundations for a Republican press during Reconstruction.

Reconstruction brought new challenges as old editors returned to reopen their newspapers, and the highly charged political atmosphere led to the founding of new publications. For the first time, Arkansas began to be linked to the rest of the nation by telegraph and railroads, and in time every county boasted not one but often dozens of newspapers. Out of this came the successful creation of the first professional body of journalists, the Arkansas Press Association.

The Press and Secession Crisis

No sooner did news reach Arkansas that Abraham Lincoln had been elected president than the newly installed governor, Henry M. Rector, proclaimed that the election by the North of a Republican automatically dissolved the Union, making Arkansas an independent state. This novel argument got little support, and if Rector expected it, he would have to "pay the printer." Instead, Congressman Thomas C. Hindman made his peace with the Family, abandoning Rector and shutting down the *Old Line Democrat* at the end of the year. Rector was thus left voiceless and practically without support in an increasingly hostile legislature.[190]

The new alliance of Hindman and the Family picked up another adherent in Albert Pike, a former Unionist during the Compromise of 1850 crisis. South Carolina seceded at the end of 1860, although Lincoln's term would not begin until March 4 of the next year. With the "Arkansas Comedian" Harry MacCarthy popularizing the song "The Bonnie Blue Flag," the other cotton belt states followed suit early in 1861.

Leading the opposition to secession was editor C.C. Danley at the *Arkansas State Gazette*. Danley argued that if the cotton states forced a war, it would be fought in the border states, of which Arkansas was one. In a view shared later by many historians, Danley felt that power and patronage were the real issues, not any direct threats to the South by Lincoln. By contrast, both the *True Democrat* and the last issues of the *Old Line Democrat* trumpeted "Dixie." Peek demanded that Arkansas follow South Carolina's lead: "Our destiny is irrevocably linked with that of the other cotton growing States; and we should not falter for one moment to seek that destiny, or pause to deliberate the consequences which may follow."[191]

In the last issue of his newspaper for 1860, Danley wrote: "An editor occupies a responsible position; and is under solemn obligation to proclaim the truth. Many who disagree with me upon almost all public questions, read it because they pay me the compliment to think that I write the honest convictions of my heart, and do not fear to defend the right because it may be unpopular, nor denounce the wrong though it may be popular."[192] And Danley was depressed. At the start of the new year he wrote a long and pessimistic editorial on the nation's condition. Feeling like a "skeleton at a feast," Danley believed the nation was set on a destructive course that only providence could avert.[193]

Meanwhile, the legislature had finally authorized a popular vote on the summoning of a convention to consider secession, but only at the end of the session when many of the members had left. Then, in February, alarmed by reports that Union reinforcements were headed for Little Rock and believing they had been summoned by the governor to save the state, secessionists descended on the capital ready for battle and forced the evacuation of the federal arsenal and its small caretaker force. If Governor Rector expected this display of state-sanctioned aggression to unite the people behind secession, he was wrong. Although in south Arkansas pro-secession mobs suppressed Unionist sentiments, in the north and west it was different. Perhaps at no other time were so many broadsides issued, the majority denouncing secession. At the polls a few weeks later, anti-secessionists won a majority of seats at the convention.

Galvanized by these events, a Union party had in fact formed, and when the convention met, they elected former Whig David Walker as chairman. Newly sworn-in president Abraham Lincoln uttered encouraging words, and the convention adjourned with Arkansas still in the Union. In all this, Danley's *Gazette* was the state's center for moderation. The *True Democrat* preached for "the Secession of the State from its unholy union with Black Republicans, Tariffites, Infidels, Abolitionists and Enemies," briefly establishing a daily edition to promote the cause.[194] For over one uneasy month, a tense quiet followed. When the Lincoln administration proposed naming Fort Smith merchant S.L. Griffith as Indian superintendent and former editor William M. Quesenbury as Creek agent, however, violent personal attacks on both men followed. Griffith met Fort Smith editor John F. Wheeler on the streets and shook his hand, "but it was to bid him *farewell forever*. Never in my life had my feelings [been] so hurt."[195]

The firing on Fort Sumter on April 12, 1861, had a profound but complex effect. The news arrived from Southern sources that colored the events in ways justifying the Confederacy. The Unionist leadership, unwilling to fight against the South, capitulated, but many of the rank and file did not. Danley was among those who gave up the cause, but he and the former Unionist leadership by no means contemplated a total surrender. When the *True Democrat* criticized the defeat of its chosen slate of officers in one of the regiments being formed, Danley rendered Quesenbury's famous proverb as: "Do not get mad if salt be thrown at you, for, if you have no sores, it will not hurt."[196]

On May 6, the secession convention was again called into session by chairman Walker. Danley and some other conservatives wanted the passage of a declaration of independence, but that was not to be. After the defeat of a move to require a vote of the people on the issue, secession passed with only five negative votes. Four of the delegates yielded to David Walker's plea to let Arkansas be unanimous, but one, Isaac Murphy of Huntsville, resolutely maintained his negative vote.

If the conservatives could not stop secession, they could use their control over the convention to redefine Arkansas. Cooperating with the Family, they discussed deposing Governor Rector. However, that worthy was saved by a compromise suggested by Hindman, by which a military board would assume control of the state's war power. One member of the three-man board was C.C. Danley. Another move was to write a new constitution for Arkansas that, among other things, opened the door for legalizing banks. Buried in the details was that two years were cut from Governor Rector's term of office. Those who perhaps thought that the coming of war would unite all the people and spell an end to politics were to be sadly disappointed.

The heightened political climate in Arkansas in 1860 and 1861 was reflected in other ways. Finally, the telegraph arrived in Arkansas, first in Fayetteville via Springfield and then on to Fort Smith. Appropriately, it was editors who exchanged the first telegraphic greetings. William Quesenbury, temporarily at the *Arkansian*, sent the "virgin" message to Fort Smith's John F. Wheeler. When in January Little Rock became connected to Memphis, *Enquirer* editor Solon Borland and his former disciple Danley exchanged the opening salutations.

For years, the nation's newspapers had experimented with publishing something more than a weekly and short of a daily. In Little Rock during the hot canvass in the summer of 1860, the *True Democrat* tried a tri-weekly, and to meet the competition, the *Old Line Democrat* resorted to a semi-weekly. Both failed to outlast the campaign. Then, in the fall just before it suspended, the *Old Liner* started Little Rock's first daily. It found little support, either for Rector, or with the reading public. The telegraph finally reached Little Rock in January 1861, but Danley, who toyed with the idea of a daily, was out of state at the time. On returning, Danley issued a prospectus, but no newspaper followed. The *True Democrat* got a march on the *Gazette* in March but found the public apathetic. Editor Richard H. Johnson later complained of the "feeble encouragement" and "considerable loss" that had attended this effort.[197] Thus, when the war began, all the newspapers in Arkansas were still weeklies.

With the Light Guns

Meanwhile, under the direction of the secession convention, Arkansas organized two armies, one in the northwest outside of Bentonville at the present site of Wal-Mart's headquarters, the other at Pitman's Ferry, where the Current River crossed into Arkansas.[198] Volunteers were plentiful at first, and the most enterprising chose to find a regiment that had enrolled for service in the Confederate Army, heading off for Virginia, "the seat of war."

The first impact on the press was that many new newspapers shut down, their editors, journeymen, and apprentices having enlisted. One was secession convention delegate and editor Anson W. "Legs" Hobson, who rose to the rank of major. J.N. Smithee was another, serving in the artillery under Captain William E. Woodruff, Jr. Former editor Albert Pike was off negotiating treaties with the tribes in Indian Territory, where his secretary was former editor William M. Quesenbury. On the other hand, J.S. Dunham of the *Van Buren Press* went north, returning only after the war's end. By the summer of 1862, Richard H. Johnson concluded that the number of newspapers had declined from 30 or 40 to only 10.[199] "I have been badly bit in newspapers this year—having paid in advance for no less than four, all of which have 'died off,'"[200] one planter complained.

For as long as the newspapers lasted, the principal topic was the war. At first, they speculated over how long the war would last. The notion that secession was constitutional and legal and therefore that the North would do nothing died away rapidly. Both Danley and Johnson expressed versions of the widely popular "Cotton is King" argument: without the South to tax, the North could not prosecute the war, and the need for cotton by England and France would result in foreign intervention. Johnson added another theme, that Southerners were a special fighting people, descendants of a conquering race.

The heady optimism was reinforced by the Confederate victory in July at Bull Run (First Manassas) in Virginia. Then in August, the northwest contingent of the Arkansas Army marched into Missouri where it joined with General Ben McCulloch's Confederate troops and the Missouri State Guard under the command of General Sterling Price. This allied army was attacked outside Springfield by the Federals under the command of General Nathaniel Lyon. At the Battle of Wilson's Creek (Oak Hills) on August 10, 1861, Lyon was killed and his army routed. Instead of following up the victory, McCulloch returned to Indian Territory, and the Arkansas Army marched back home where it voted to disband.

While the Federals regrouped at Rolla, the state's editors wanted to know why Arkansas had dropped out of the war. No one knew more than Editor Danley. As a member of the state's military board, Danley favored turning Arkansas's early recruits over to the Confederate government. Unfortunately, President Jefferson Davis showed little interest in the

Trans-Mississippi, and Rector made an alliance with the third member of the board, thereby outvoting Danley. An agreement to transfer the troops from state to Confederate service was scuttled when Rector and his militia officers campaigned against it. Thus, Arkansas's early war preparations went for naught.

Joining Danley in condemning the governor was Editor Johnson. The new alliance created quite a stir. When Rector finally created a newspaper for his defense in the fall of 1861, its editor, Thomas C. Peek, who was now married to a niece of Rector's, wrote: "that most wonderful combination, the *True Democrat* and the *Gazette* have got to billowing and cooing with each other like two suckling doves."[201]

Rector also took aim at the newspapers in his address to the fall session of the legislature. It was one of the nastiest things ever said by a public official about the press:

> More treason lurks in Arkansas, under the garb of patriotism, than most men conceive of. Libelous traduction of its authorities, gloatingly sought for, and swallowed by snarling cormorants of newspaper filth, well attest this fact. The press—the freedom of the press—once the synonym of liberty,—now, the covert and insidious vehicle for undeveloped treason—the hypocritical defender of public justice—its calling, lowered to the dignity of mercenary avarice—a blessing to the people when guided by enlightened patriotism—a dire curse, when marked by malice and ignorance.[202]

All this made little impression on the editors. "The press," Danley commented a month later, "regarded this about as much as it did the idle hissing of the wind, and pursued the even tenor of its way."[203] One of Rector's associates, his brother-in-law Edmund Burgevin, challenged Danley to a duel, listing Governor Rector as his second. Danley declined the challenge. "It was a bullying attempt to attack the liberty of the press, by overawing the editor, and thus preventing a free expression of opinion through the columns of the *Gazette*," Danley announced.[204] The crippled editor continued the attack, noting that Burgevin, a "vagabond," did not even know the rules of the *code duello*, which Danley explained in some detail.

The barrage of criticism prompted Rector to find both the newsprint and the money to start up his own newspaper. Thomas C. Peek assumed the tripod at the *Daily State Journal*, which during its short life tried to justify the governor and return the fire. In the spring, the *Gazette* and *True Democrat* had another issue to work with. The Union army under General Samuel Curtis invaded Arkansas and defeated a larger Confederate force under Earl Van Dorn at the Battle of Pea Ridge (Elk Horn Tavern) on March 6, 1862. One side issue to this battle was the role played by Brigadier General Albert Pike, who had agreed to take his Indian regiments out of the territory. Charges that they scalped Union dead and that Pike as their commander was responsible made him a war criminal in the minds of many Northerners.[205] Pike's other problem came from his alleged incompetence at the battle. Battle historians William L. Shea and Earl J. Hess concluded that Pike was "hopelessly inept," but others have tried to shift the blame for the defeat from Van Dorn to Pike, and, in a perverse fit of anti-intellectualism, claim that he was off writing poetry during the battle.[206]

Following the defeat, Van Dorn took the remainder of the army across the Mississippi River to Tennessee, where they arrived too late to participate in the Battle of Shiloh. Arkansas was left undefended, as Union victor General Samuel Curtis moved onward to Batesville. Rector denounced the Confederate government's abandonment in a proclamation in which he threatened to "build a new ark and launch it upon new waters." This threat to secede from secession met with total opposition. The

Washington Telegraph refused to carry the message, while the *Gazette* and *True Democrat* continued the attack on Rector. When the governor moved the archives and state offices to Hot Springs, an event caught in a drawing by former *True Democrat* editor J.W. Woodward, Johnson asked readers if "some patriotic gentlemen would relieve the anxiety of the public by informing it of the locality of the State government."[207] On returning to town, Rector accused Johnson of treason and then challenged him to a duel, with Burgevin serving as the governor's second. Nothing came of this challenge, either, but in *Danley and Johnson, ex parte* (1862), the state supreme court ruled that the new state constitution required a gubernatorial election that fall.

Rector vainly fulminated against the court and the editors. Peek's second newspaper had long been closed but a new Little Rock newspaper, the *Arkansas Patriot*, with the ubiquitous James D. Butler as publisher but no editor listed, supported Rector, as did the Camden *Ouachita Herald* and the Pine Bluff *War Bulletin*. All the rest of the state's press, together with a combination of former Unionists and secessionists, endorsed Harris Flanagin, a former Whig then serving as a Confederate colonel in the Army of Tennessee. James S.H. Rainey of Camden ran as well, his platform being, "whether, at public elections, should the votes of faction predominate by internal suggestions, or the bias of Jurisprudence?" The candidate, it was reported, "promptly and unqualifiedly endorsed this clause."[208] The most damage the *Ouachita Herald* could inflict was to claim that Flanagin was really an Irishman.[209]

With public disgust at Rector at a high, and weariness beginning to set in the wake of Confederate disasters east of the Mississippi River, Flanagin was an easy winner. Unfortunately, and for entirely different reasons, this strict Presbyterian ex-Whig proved to be as ineffective as the unlamented Rector in helping support the war.

Meanwhile, Arkansas's editors were fighting another struggle merely to survive. Prior to the war's start, Cincinnati was the source for newsprint. In May 1861, Danley ran out of paper and was forced to suspend. In the past, such suspensions often were greeted by smug satisfaction on the part of surviving newspapers. Not so this time. "The course of the *Gazette* during the war has been unselfish and patriotic in the highest degree," Johnson wrote.[210] And when Danley refreshed his paper supply and restarted in June, Johnson added, "The *Gazette* is a co-worker with us in a great cause, and we are glad to see the *Gazette* once more and welcome it to our office."[211] Danley's new supply lasted until February 21, 1863, when he was forced again to suspend. Augusta, Georgia, and Huntsville, Alabama, had become his paper sources. The wartime-inflated price of eight dollars per ream was two dollars more than good writing paper had cost before the war, and the transportation alone amounted to more than pre-war paper bought from Cincinnati or other Northern cities.[212]

The *True Democrat* had its problems as well. "By issuing a half sheet," Johnson wrote in April 1862, "we will have enough paper for 12 months."[213] Resupplied in December, the *True Democrat* ran continuously until July 1863. Reuben S. Yerkes, the publisher, had found paper in Georgia but because of the siege of Vicksburg could not get it across the Mississippi River. The last issue, dated July 8, 1863, appeared on wrapping paper.[214]

Part of the paper problem was due to the great increase in readers. In this, the *True Democrat* started with a distinct disadvantage in that it carried that long list of delinquent subscribers. In July 1861, Johnson reported an "unprecedented" circulation of 5,000. Of these, some 300 were from Texas, and the newspaper was said by a Texas colonel to have the largest circulation of any newspaper in that state.[215] As in colonial times, the number of readers greatly exceeded the number of subscribers, and Johnson estimated his readership at some 20,000.[216] This rising demand and the absence of any dominating political theme led Johnson to prune his subscription lists. In September 1861, he dropped 1,000 subscribers, complaining that they owed him $4,000 in unpaid subscriptions and another $16,000 for job work and advertising.[217] Meanwhile, more subscriptions poured in. The *True Democrat* had 10,000 subscribers when it suspended.[218]

By that time, the appearance of Arkansas's newspapers had changed. Often reduced to half-sheets of even smaller sized paper, newspapers abandoned the elaborate nameplates of the past. Also gone were poetry, elaborate advertisements, long obituaries, and finally any obituaries at all.

Faced with rising demand and higher costs, both newspapers raised their prices, and at the same time. In 1860 the *Gazette* charged four dollars a year, three dollars for six months, but only two dollars if paid "strictly in advance." Danley, too, had his delinquents, for in March 1862 he went to $2.50 for all customers. Rates rose to three dollars in October 1862 and five dollars in December. Readers responded by trying to unload worthless currency on the editors. Johnson specified that he would receive only Confederate money, war bonds, treasury certificates, and Texas state notes.[219] Would-be subscribers ignored these instructions and flooded both offices with what Johnson described as "half a bushel of trash." When a thief broke into the office and stole some of this "money," Johnson wrote: "We were often puzzled to know what to do with these shins [plasters], and wonder how we could get rid of them. The scamp has saved us the trouble, and we would like to know who it was to see what he will do with them. We pity him."[220] One cause for this problem was the law. Publishers either had to accept subscriptions received by mail carrying this worthless paper or write a letter and pay the postage to return it.

The patriotic tone of the Little Rock newspapers contrasted with a growing reaction against the war. General Curtis had cut through the northeastern part of the state in the spring of 1862, thoroughly burning and looting the region's farms and liberating the slaves on the plantations. The Union army reached Helena, where it remained until the fall of 1863, a potent reminder that Arkansas was now cut off from conquered Memphis and invested Vicksburg. If Rector took a certain amount of heat on one front, others blamed Arkansas's powerful Confederate senator, Robert Ward Johnson. At the fall session of the legislature in 1862, the first under Flanagin, it took Johnson 12 ballots to gain reelection, and the public printing was taken from the *True Democrat* and given to William Etter and John R. Eakin of the *Washington Telegraph*.

The principal reason for this discontent lay in the actions of Major General Thomas Carmichael Hindman. Appointed to command in Arkansas in the spring by General P.G.T. Beauregard, who had no authority west of the Mississippi River, Hindman tried his best to cope with Union General Samuel Curtis's invading army. By declaring martial law (which only President Davis legally could do) and adopting all sorts of illegal controls, Hindman warranted an entire chapter entitled "The Rogue Tyrant and the

Premodern State" in a recent study of Confederate civil liberties.[221] Hindman, by granting guerillas Confederate commissions, sanctioned a very uncivil warfare and imparted these lessons to General W. T. Sherman, who used them later in Georgia. Supported by both Little Rock newspapers, Hindman did as much as was humanly possible to put pre-industrial Arkansas on a war footing. However, in intercepting supplies and money intended for General Albert Pike in Indian Territory and giving direct orders to Pike's subordinates, Hindman found himself up against an opponent who bested him a war of words. Although Pike was twice arrested for treason and left the army, his broadside, *Albert Pike's Letter Addressed to Major General Holmes*, ranks as one of the nation's most outstanding examples of personal vituperation and well as an eloquent defense of civil liberties against military tyranny.[222] However, among the state's newspapers, only the misnamed *Arkansas Patriot* took up cudgels against Hindman. Etter and Eakins, safely removed from the threatening strife at Washington, spoke guardedly of "Stability not Tyranny."[223] As for Pike, he retreated first to a log cabin on Greasy Cove in Montgomery County, where he continued his work revising Masonic rituals. *Morals and Dogma of the Ancient and Accepted Scottish Rite of Freemasonry* (1881), to give the short title, certainly ranks as one of the great albeit arcane accomplishments of 19th century scholarship. On June 8, 1864, he was appointed an associate justice on the state supreme court, making him the first editor to ascend to the highest level of the judiciary.[224]

Hindman's last military action in Arkansas was an attempt to reclaim northwest Arkansas. At the Battle of Prairie Grove on December 7, 1862, he frittered away his early advantage and, after failing to dislodge the Union army, was forced to retreat down the Boston Mountains as his army dissolved. Hindman departed from Arkansas, not to return until Reconstruction. Hindman at least was energetic, but his successor, Theophilus Hunter Holmes, was not called "Old Granny" without good reason. Holmes did not long remain in command of the Trans-Mississippi, and after Richmond sent General Edmund Kirby Smith in early 1863, his duties were limited to Arkansas. Changes in command did not save Arkansas Post, which fell to a combined Federal naval and military force in January, and Holmes badly mismanaged his forces on a useless attack on Helena the same day that Vicksburg surrendered.

Meanwhile, the press struggled to print accurate war information for its hungry readers. At first, it appeared that the telegraph would provide a ready source of information. However, within a very short period of time, Arkansas editors turned away in disgust. John Eakin in Washington wrote: "The telegraphic lines keep working away to Little Rock from Memphis and bring us every week something which now and then turns out true, and often don't [*sic*]. We do not choose to bore our readers with all the contradictory mass of stuff as it reaches us—very often not worth knowing if true."[225]

An especially egregious example came in the spring of 1862, when headlines for a "Great and Glorious Victory" stated that McClellan's Union army outside of Richmond had losses of 65,000 killed and 47,000 wounded, figures greatly exceeding his total force, and that after Generals Lee and Johnston were killed President Davis took command. "They tried to make their escape," the report continued, "but were cut off by the Merrimack."[226] Newspapers generally stuck the telegraphic material in a separate column and rarely discussed it editorially. Curiously, there was talk of a printer's union in the fall of 1861 that would send a delegate to the Confederate National Union meeting in the spring. One planned item was to have been the organization of a Southern Telegraphic Associated Press, which proposed making available accurate news telegraphically at reasonable rates.[227]

As much as possible, newspapers continued to

rely on the old scissors-and-pot-paste method, albeit with a twist. Many formerly used sources were now enemy newspapers, and they were received very irregularly. However, on one occasion, the *True Democrat* was forced to copy an address delivered by President Jefferson Davis from a newspaper in Union-occupied Memphis.

The collapse of the mail system left editors in a bind. In February 1863 the *Gazette* lamented, "Since our last we have not received a paper from the South, nor have we heard of any thing coming from that direction."[228] Johnson responded to this problem by offering free subscriptions for those bringing in newspapers from east of the Mississippi.[229] In place of being about 10 days to two weeks behind, the newspapers fell to being a month out of touch.

The correspondent was another tactic newspapers employed. At the war's start, the only person so employed, William Quesenbury, became a major in the Confederate service under Pike in Indian Territory. No one took his place, although professional correspondents, soon to be called reporters, followed the Northern armies into Arkansas. Instead, the state's press had the usual letters from friends. The Battle of Wilson's Creek resulted in a torrent of accounts, but then the flow diminished. At the *True Democrat*, Johnson made arrangements for friends in each Arkansas regiment to supply regular reports, but the collapse of the Confederacy's mail service and military orders against divulging troop movements brought this system down.

Early on, however, one soldier in the Arkansas contingent in Virginia offered a useful commentary on "Stonewall" Jackson: "It is reported that he [General Loring] asked old Stonewall Jackson 'where the devil he was going,' when that officer cooly remarked that 'if he believed his own overcoat was acquainted with his plans, he would pull it off and burn it.'"[230] Such interesting stories stopped by the summer of 1862, however, when Johnson noted that the military had asked newspapers not to print soldier letters.[231]

Military reports were another source, but these came well after the events involved. They were suspect on another store, too. America's generals were politicians. Sterling Price, whom Danley strongly suspected of incompetence, had his own military newspaper, the *Army Argus*. Danley claimed that "the sole object of the publication seems to be the laudation of Gen. Price."[232] Danley became even more suspicious once the telegraph fell under military control. Reviewing the reports on the Battle of Corinth, he noted how each general's bravery and good sense was lauded, but, "notwithstanding the self-laudatory notices of the Generals, the fact cannot be concealed from the world that they suffered a defeat."[233]

In all, the state's press could do little to influence public opinion when accurate information was so hard to obtain. "I like the *Gazette* and *[True] Democrat*, too," wrote Mississippi County planter Mrs. M.B. Eskridge, "for they speak to the common sense and virtue of the reader, and they animate us in our retired homes to industry, management, and economy."[234] Such persons did not take kindly to Peek's *Daily State Journal*. One reader wanted it stopped because "I am tired of it"; another objected that the editor was "always snapping and snarling at the government at Richmond."[235]

As the defeats deepened and easy optimism disappeared, the people came to distrust the press, the government, and the military. To address these problems, John F. Wheeler suggested the creation of a historical society to collect and preserve the war's records. Organized on June 20, 1863, in the *Gazette* office, it chose Danley as its president. Among the vice-presidents were William M. Quesenbury, John R. Eakin, William E. Woodruff, John E. Knight, and John W. Woodward. U.M. Rose journeyed to Richmond and collected material on Arkansas's contribution to the war, but Federal control of the Mississippi River prevented him from bringing these archives home successfully.[236]

For the Little Rock press, many problems were solved on September 10, 1863, when the Union army occupied Little Rock and thus terminated the old regime. Danley took the news in bed. A year earlier, on October 29, 1862, he had started off to Richmond on government business. Two miles out of town the buggy wrecked, throwing Danley into the rocks on the side of the road. His arm was so badly broken as to require amputation, and he had a broken right thigh bone and a fractured patella. Two of Little Rock's leading physicians, Drs. Philo O. Hooper and Craven Peyton operated on the injured editor. Danley's life was saved, but he was left a permanent invalid. As for the doctors, their bills, amounting to almost $1,000, were still unpaid at the time of Danley's death nearly three years later.[237]

Fort Smith had fallen on September 1, while Batesville, Fayetteville, Pine Bluff, Camden, Helena, and other newspaper towns were either under Union control or had been largely destroyed. Although the *Memphis Appeal* had escaped capture and fled, relocating several times before the war's end, no Arkansas newspaper followed its example.[238] Left alone to survive the war and almost half of the 20th century was the *Washington Telegraph.*

In contrast to the strong editorial views of Danley and Johnson, *Telegraph* editor John R. Eakin followed a minimalist course. "Nothing could be more destructive to all hopes of success than opposition and dislike on the part of citizens to the military commander of the district," he observed, and even apologized for having printed a letter from Rufus K. Garland, the brother of Arkansas Confederate Senator Augustus H. Garland, who in the fall of 1863 unseated the incumbent Confederate congressman, Grandison D. Royston.[239] While the cynical view would hold that Eakin's reticence was due to the military supplying him with paper, the reality was that Eakin was a man of character. When given forged letters intended to discredit former Confederate Colonel E.W. Gantt, who had deserted to the Union, Eakin refused to publish them.

Eakin's principal problem was state government. State governor Harris Flanagin had retired to his home in Arkadelphia after the fall of Little Rock, apparently feeling that without a capital he was no longer governor. Eakin and others finally lit a fire under him to set up a government-in-exile. Washington became the new capital, and a rump legislature and supreme court (that included Albert Pike) took shape. Eakin hoped for Flanagin to procure him some paper, but General Kirby Smith became his angel. Meanwhile, *Telegraph* owner William Etter undertook the mission of buying cotton cards for the state. Etter died in Brownsville, Texas, and the much-needed cards never reached Arkansas. The rump Confederate government survived a Union invasion in the spring of 1864 that included Battles of Poison Springs, Marks' Mills, and Jenkins' Ferry.

By early 1865, the end was near. The continued existence of slavery was called into question, but Eakin argued that "we owe it to God to sustain it."[240] Flight to Texas had become an epidemic for those who could afford it. The army had not been paid in two years, and shortages existed everywhere. When news of Robert E. Lee's surrender at Appomattox reached the west, the Trans-Mississippi department dissolved. Flanagin took the state archives back to Little Rock, and later in the summer Federal troops came down to set up posts in Washington and other towns. Rebellion had failed.

Reuniting Arkansas

Union sentiment in Arkansas had never vanished despite initial impressions to the contrary. In the fall of 1861, a peace-society movement flourished across the mountain counties, its supporters claiming that they had no desire to go to war on either side. The vigorous suppression of this movement by the Confederates set the stage for a very uncivil war in the northern counties. Family feuds came into play and lingered for more than 30 years after the Civil War's official end.

President Lincoln's belief that the plain people of the South were not secessionists led to the creation of Arkansas Union regiments in Springfield and the appointment of former Springfield (Missouri) Congressman John S. Phelps, the legislative father of the licked postage stamp, as the state's first Union governor. Phelps wisely showed a reluctance to move to sickly Helena, choosing instead to set up his government at the Planter's Hotel in St. Louis. After the occupation of Little Rock, the move to establish a locally based government began in earnest.

Union Brigadier General John W. Davidson reportedly invited Danley to continue the *Gazette* as a Union newspaper, but Danley refused. Apparently, his partner, printer William F. Holtzman, was more amenable and took the loyalty oath that allowed him to remain and continue to work. After Danley proved uncooperative, Davidson turned the newspaper over to Unionist J.W. Demby. Only one issue of the *National Union* was issued, apparently because the newspaper was too conservative to suit the Radical Davidson. A second Union newspaper came from Dr. Cincinnatus V. Meador. In the 1860 election, Meador had edited a short-lived Douglas organ, the *National Democrat*, and he revived that title, renting the *True Democrat* plant. Up the Arkansas River at Fort Smith, there appeared the longer-lived *Fort Smith New Era*. Sporting a United States flag under the nameplate, the first issue listed "E Pluribus Unum" as the editor. "Traitors, and sympathizers with such, will be exposed unflinchingly, and their dark deeds of infamy put in proper light," Unum proclaimed.[241] A few issues later, Valentine Dell, a former schoolteacher of the town, revealed himself. A man of character in a town that prospered off the demoralized Indians to the west, Dell made his newspaper a strong Republican force for almost two decades.

Well before the Civil War was over, there appeared a distinction in Arkansas between Radicals and Conservatives.

Conservatives favored the reconstruction of the Union as it had been, possibly even with slavery intact. They were willing to forgive converted ex-Confederates and opposed loyalty oaths, disfranchisement, and confiscation. Ironically, the once-hated Lincoln was now seen as their leader. Radical Republicans grew nationally out of the abolitionist movement and thus were represented in Arkansas by those who either had suffered under the former Confederate regime or had come South during the war, carrying their emancipationist ideas with them. The military was divided: General Frederick Steele was considered too conservative by the Radicals.

Radicals and conservatives alike supported recreating Arkansas but divided on who and how to do it. At this early stage, two important Radical leaders were William F. Fishback (a future governor and APA honorary member) and Edward W. Gantt, both of whom had tarnished pasts. Fishback, an opponent of secession, had ended up voting for it at the secession convention. Later, he fled north and accompanied the Union army back to Arkansas, returning to Fort Smith. Gantt, elected to Congress before the war, had pledged his last drop of blood to the cause of secession but had been unwilling to shed the first. A Confederate colonel who took part in the disastrous battles of New Madrid and Island No. 10, he had gone over to the Union when the Confederacy failed to promote him.

On January 23, 1864, the first issue of the *Unconditional Union* appeared in Little Rock from Fishback and T.D.W. Yonley. The newspaper published the new constitution that a Unionist

Edward Bancroft. This Republican editor and railroad promoter during Reconstruction was the great-grandfather of another newspaper person, APA president (1981) Charlotte Tillar Schexnayder. (Courtesy Charlotte Schexnayder)

Adam Clark. Clark, the co-founder of the Southern Standard *in Arkadelphia along with Josiah Gaulding, made the* Standard *a strong weekly, much quoted around the state. (Courtesy Clark County Historical Association Archives, Ouachita Baptist University)*

William E. Woodruff, Jr., 1870. Called Major because of his Civil War title, "Buck" Woodruff guided the Gazette *during Reconstruction but later was accused of robbing the state during his term as state treasurer. He also authored a volume of Civil War memoirs. This unfinished painting by William Frye catches the man more closely to his days at the* Gazette *than later photographs. (Courtesy Historic Arkansas Museum)*

The three-color stationery of the post-war Arkansas Gazette *reflected its strong position in state affairs. (Courtesy Historic Arkansas Museum)*

Jacob Frolich, Jr. The German-born editor and Confederate veteran was accused of Ku Klux Klan activities and fled Arkansas during Reconstruction. He later held a number of offices in state government, the Arkansas Press Association, and at the Arkansas Gazette. *(Courtesy Arkansas History Commission)*

John McClure came to Arkansas during Reconstruction. A sometime editor and owner of the Republican party's state organ, chief justice on the state supreme court, and violent partisan, McClure was a fixture in the state's life until his death in 1915. This and subsequent cartoons appeared in the Arkansas Gazette *and then were reprinted in book form. No credit was given to the artist. (Courtesy Arkansas History Commission)*

convention had drafted. This document proposed the abolition of slavery and selected Isaac Murphy of Huntsville as the provisional governor subject to a March election. Lurking beneath the surface was the Federal Confiscation Act, which in the spring of 1864 was used to take the property of those who would or could not take a loyalty oath. Federal officials promptly seized both the *Gazette* and *True Democrat* offices. The inventories taken at the time are a useful clue to the operations of these capital-city newspapers. The *Gazette* had a new drum cylinder press, presumably the Hoe press purchased in 1860; a Lawyer jobber; a Superior Royal Hoe Washington press, a standing paper press; a Ruggles paper cutter; three marble composing stones; and the usual varieties of type. The *True Democrat* had four steam presses and six other presses. At the *Gazette*, Holtzman's one-third interest was safe, and at the *True Democrat* Yerkes had taken the oath, protecting his half interest. Danley, who had suffered enough for the now Lost Cause, relented at the last minute, saving his only source of income; Johnson, being the brother of a Confederate senator, did not.[242]

One man who took the oath was William E. Woodruff. This aged pioneer had had a busy time of it. In early 1862, he was on hand to dedicate the opening of the railroad linking the future North Little Rock to De Valls Bluff. During the war, he continued his management business for his old clients. Reportedly, he was in the trenches for a few weeks preceding the fall of Little Rock. After taking the oath to save his property, Woodruff explained his actions as being dictated by necessity in a letter he then took to the military authorities for permission to have it sent south. The military censors claimed Woodruff had lied in his oath and expelled the ancient editor from his home, wife, and four unmarried daughters. The *Washington Telegraph* tried to generate propaganda from the event, claiming that the Union made war on the elderly.

Woodruff was not the only person having trouble figuring out what was politically correct. Arkansas's fledgling Unionists were divided by ideology and personal ambition. As before, newspapers were at the center of things. After Danley took the oath of allegiance on April 1, 1864, he forthwith expelled the *Unconditional Union*. Calvin C. Bliss, the Secretary of State and its new owner, bought out Yerkes's half interest in the *True Democrat* and leased Johnson's other half from the Treasury Department, expelling Meador and the *National Democrat*. The doctor's response was to rent the *Gazette*'s office. Meador attacked Fishback so strongly that he was denied the privilege of covering the House of Representatives proceedings. Although Meador could not stop the somewhat irregular election of Fishback and Elisha Baxter as the new United States senators, in Washington Fishback's credentials were shredded by senators opposed to Lincoln's Reconstruction plans.[243]

The principal event in occupied Little Rock—and one that would resonate thereafter—was the trial of David O. Dodd, a former student of St. John's College, who had spied upon Union troop dispositions and been caught. His execution on January 8, 1864 turned him into the boy martyr, the Nathan Hale of Arkansas, for Fannie Borland and subsequent generations of Southern orators and poets.[244]

On April 17, 1865, a massive booming of cannons told Little Rock residents that the end of the Civil War was at hand. As matters stood, Arkansas's legal existence in the Union was recognized by the president but not by Congress. However, Congress considered the non-state competent to ratify the proposed 13th Amendment on April 20, 1865.

Without waiting for the formal surrender of the Trans-Mississippi, Christopher Columbus Danley resumed the tripod, beginning a new era in Arkansas journalism, as the *Arkansas State Gazette* was reborn, phoenix-like, from the ashes of the defeated Confederacy.

Calm Before the Storm

The tone Danley wanted for the new era appeared in the first issue of the revived *Arkansas State Gazette* on May 10, 1865. Preaching reconciliation, Danley promised "to bring about a feeling of confidence, faith and security among the people."[245] Elaborating on this theme as Confederate veterans began to return to the state, he said, "Let us have no more of bowie-knives and revolvers, and Sharp's rifles and other warlike tools. We should be a peaceful community, and our minds should be set upon steam engines and patent corn planters, printing machines and blacksmith's forges."[246] The high goals Danley set for himself and his newspaper his successors failed to keep.

Danley now felt that he could do no less than issue both a daily and a weekly. The daily came out Monday through Friday, the weekly on Saturday (later Tuesday). In July the daily bore a new nameplate reflective of its local audience, the *Little Rock Daily Gazette*. Both the daily and the weekly were the traditional four pages. The daily contained four columns, the weekly six. Danley tried to distinguish between the two newspapers so that the weekly claimed to be volume 44 (an incorrect calculation), and the daily started out as volume one. The daily cost 30 cents a week; the weekly four dollars a year. Single copies were 10 cents.

Charles Haight's news depot undertook the sale of individual newspapers, so Danley was at last able to free his office from the rabble of hangers-on who had once made it difficult to get work done. Thereafter, across the state, newsstands spread. A few operated as outdoor stands, more as either small hole-in-the-wall concerns or in conjunction with stationary stores, but all regularly carried newspapers that soon would arrive from all over the nation once Arkansas was linked into the emerging rail network.

That Danley and William F. Holtzman managed to get out their newspapers on a regular basis was one of the miracles of Arkansas journalism. Danley had never recovered from his wartime accident and was near death during the early summer of 1865. Holtzman was in the final stages of tuberculosis. Other than printers, there were no other employees. Danley subscribed to a telegraphic service, but all state and local news had to come from their own efforts.[247]

As refugees returned and tried to reestablish their lives, problems surfaced. For ex-Confederates who had served as officers in the army or state government, only a presidential pardon would suffice to restore their citizenship. After a less than successful Fourth of July celebration, Governor Murphy, who had been forwarding pardon applications to President Johnson, discontinued his efforts, disgusted at the "ingratitude and rebellious spirit" still in evidence. Arkansas's other pardon broker was Fayetteville's Jonas Tebbetts, who had a thriving business in Washington, and who secured William E. Woodruff's pardon.[248] However, unreconciled rebels could easily be found.

Meanwhile, a new economic order was emerging. The federally funded Freedman's Bureau was created to oversee the interests of the former slaves. In addition to establishing schools, its agents tried to guarantee rights for the freedmen in their contracts with white landlords. Determined not to work under slavery-like conditions, blacks did not want their women to have to do field work, and they would not live in the old slave quarters. Gradually, over the next 10 years, the sharecropping system arose. Seen by some as a new kind of freedom and by others as another form of slavery, it was in reality both. Prior to 1900 an ever-increasing number of blacks and whites who started cropping on shares managed to save enough to acquire their own farms; after 1900 landlords shut off advancement, and increasing numbers of both races fell into tenancy. Sharecropping endured as part of the state's agricultural way of life into the 1960s.

On October 3, 1865, Christopher Columbus Danley died at his rooms in the *Gazette* building. The Pulaski County Circuit Court was adjourned for his funeral, and the IOOF (The Independent Order of Odd Fellows) members wore badges for 30 days in remembrance of their former grand master. Since Danley had already deeded his interest in the newspaper to Holtzman, continuity was not interrupted. Holtzman, too, was determined to keep the newspaper out of politics, and in the fall elections made only one recommendation to the voters. On January 1, 1866, Little Rock regained self-government with a slate of old settlers led by Dr. J.J. McAlmont as mayor taking office. Holtzman's health continued to be a problem, and on June 29 he sold the newspaper to William E. Woodruff, Jr. A little over a month later, on August 12, Holtzman succumbed to his disease. One era had ended and another was just beginning. *Gazette* historian Margaret Ross summarized the situation this way:

> Only a few people were still living in Arkansas who had read the first issue of the Gazette, but there were many who had been subscribers before William E. Woodruff's retirement. Those who knew the Woodruff family well must have felt that the Gazette's future was secure when they saw the daily of July 2 and the weekly of July 7, 1866, with the statement of proprietorship, "By W.E. Woodruff, Jr.," under the nameplate.[249]

At first, Woodruff seemed likely to follow Danley's preaching: "Let's trade with the Yankees our asserted love of *politics*, for *energy*; our asserted love of *ease* and *leisure*, for *industry* and *perseverance*." But at the same time, this former Confederate artilleryman called for boycotting any celebration of the Fourth of July "while the rod is still uplifted."[250] Tensions between the Unionists and ex-Confederates escalated under Woodruff.

As long as cotton prices stayed high, rapid economic progress obscured other problems. With freed men and women earning wages, opportunities abounded for business. Some 20 steamboats braved the Ouachita River to supply Camden with goods, and four newspapers—three weeklies and a triweekly—opened. Only two predated the war. Fayetteville was equally blessed. The *Democrat* and the *Arkansian* had antebellum names if not the same owners, but the *Mountain Echo* and the *Observer* were completely new.

In Helena, Q.K. Underwood revived the *Southern Shield* but sold it to his son, Charles. The *Des Arc Citizen* was revived, as was John F. Wheeler's *Herald* at Fort Smith, and J.S. Dunham's *Press* at Van Buren. John R. Eakin retired from the *Washington Telegraph*, and the founder's son assumed control. New to the state in 1866 were the *De Witt Elector*, the *Jonesboro Register*, the *Magnolia Vindicator*, the *Ashley County Times*, the *Monticello Guardian*, the *Des Arc Crescent*, and best of all the *Pine Bluff Orthopolitan*. Almost all were as short-lived as the Reverend N.P. Moore's *Arkansas Baptist*. In less than four months the newspaper failed, its editor having fled to Texas, leaving the creditors with the shop. One of the few newspapers started at this time to have a long life was the *Southern Standard* at Arkadelphia, founded as a partnership between J.W. Gaulding and Adam Clark. Both had antebellum experience that many novices lacked at this time, and the highly revered Gaulding was "filled with noble and ennobling impulses, broad, conservative and charitable in all his view ..."[251]

Meanwhile, Arkansas enjoyed the postwar period's false prosperity. Ice barges arrived from the north, and synagogues arose in Helena and Pine Bluff. So great had the German population grown that there appeared in Little Rock the *Staats Zeitung*, Arkansas's first foreign language newspaper.[252] It might be assumed that such a newspaper limited its coverage to its special constituency, but this was not the case in 1870 when the arrival of the Brignoli opera troupe touched off a small war. After the *Morning Republican* claimed that Pasquilino Brignoli was "the best tenor in the world," the rival *Gazette* ignored these groundbreaking first opera performances until it discovered that Brignoli's soprano (and wife), Isabella McCulloch, was the daughter of a South Carolina plantation owner. Suddenly the *Gazette* discovered a passion for opera. Meanwhile, the *Staats Zeitung* editor reportedly said that Brignoli was "much sung out," claiming that "we have much better opera in the *faderland*." The *Gazette*, which now praised McCulloch and Brignoli to the skies, admitted Brignoli had a few gray hairs but nevertheless was "a regular old music box yet." The *Staats Zeitung* claimed it had been mistranslated—perhaps another first in Arkansas history—while the *Republican* contented itself with praising the contralto, Antonia Henne.[253]

The *Arkansas Gazette*, as it was henceforth called as Woodruff reverted to the original title, underwent a transformation. In the place of the old, worn-out equipment from Danley's last years, there were two new Hoe presses and three job presses, all powered by steam. The job office in 1869 printed Arkansas's first novel, R.H. Crozier's *The Bloody Junto*, for which no copies are recorded in the state today. In 1870, Woodruff recalled: "When we started in business our weekly subscriptions list did not number a dozen names of paid up subscribers, our daily was a thumb-paper in size and virtually printed for free distribution. Our last weekly issue was above 5000 copies sent to paid up subscribers, and the daily edition of today is equal, I believe, to the combined lists of all the other dailies in the city."[254]

Woodruff might have mentioned that the newspaper had joined the Associated Press for its telegraphic column. In 1873, the newspaper erected its own three-story building, housing not only the newspaper but also doctors, lawyers, and the offices of the Memphis and Little Rock Railroad. The office had the first central steam heat in Little Rock. The newspaper also installed a McFatrich addressing machine.

The *Gazette* had some labor troubles starting in 1867 when J.N. Smithee joined the staff. The ubiquitous James D. Butler, representing the typographers' union, tried unsuccessfully to get him removed.[255] Another crisis erupted in 1874, apparently over working conditions rather than rates. Woodruff replaced some seven or eight printers, winning this skirmish. "The old lady is all right again," he concluded.[256] And while the editor solemnly intoned that woman's suffrage was "ruthlessly essaying to destroy the most sacred images in the holiest of life's earthy temples," in the press room, "A feminine, with all the witchery of curl and costume, small hand and taper waist, has come in among them and demonstrated by her work her willingness and intention of assisting in the 'art preservative of all arts.' To bring it down to Saxon, a woman typer-sticker—a phenomenon in Little Rock—was at work in the GAZETTE office yesterday."[257] Soon the newspaper was advertising for women to work in its bindery.[258]

Yet there was continuity with the past. Old-time readers welcomed the occasional long letters from William M. Quesenbury in exile in Texas and Josiah W. Washbourne, living in retirement at Norristown. Historical articles appeared from time to time, as well.

But all this seeming prosperity was about to melt in the white-hot heat generated by the Reconstruction crisis. While much of it was rhetorical and political, well over 500 persons in Arkansas lost their lives due to politics between 1867 and 1874. On the Republican side, Congressman James Hinds fell victim to the Klan, while a Union League member assassinated Thomas C. Hindman. Historian E. Merton Coulter ranked Arkansas among the three most violent Southern states during these years.[259]

A War of Words

What made Reconstruction violent was the interaction between local conditions and federally imposed rules. In 1866, ex-Confederates had regained control of the legislature, giving the state printing to the *Arkansas Gazette*. These ex-Confederates were determined to bestow as few civil rights on the freedmen as possible, and they vented their hostility on Governor Murphy and other old Unionists. Conversely, Radical Republicans in Washington had concluded that merely abolishing slavery had been inadequate; the freedmen had to be made American citizens and given rights that the whites in the South could not take away. From Washington came the 14th Amendment that reversed the Dred Scott decision by granting citizenship to the freedmen. Radicals then offered the Southern states full restoration to the Union if the states would accept this proposed amendment. After only Tennessee agreed, Congress passed the 15th Amendment to keep the states from denying the right to vote because of color.

In the spring of 1867, Arkansas was put under military rule, and while Murphy was left in office, the legislature was sent home. A Republican party took form, and in the fall voters approved calling a new convention to write a constitution that Congress would accept. Dubbed the "Menagerie" by the *Gazette*, which led the Democratic opposition, the convention assembled in Little Rock in January and produced the state's fourth constitution. In some ways a forward-looking document, it pledged state support for internal improvements; protected blacks, women, and poor; and provided for public education. But, politically, it gave radicals control over the election machinery, created gerrymandered election districts, and disfranchised ex-Confederates. In Little Rock, John G. Price and John McClure (to use the more common spelling of M'Clure) started up the *Daily Republican* to serve as the party's official newspaper.

Ex-Confederates were determined to resist but had no workable plan. From Memphis, where Albert Pike was editing the *Daily Appeal*, came advice to avoid any participation that put a white man on the same level as a black. Those of this persuasion preferred the term "conservative," and found a voice in the *Arkansas Conservative*, put out by former Senator Robert Ward Johnson and Benjamin F. Danley, with the ubiquitous James D. Butler as publisher. On the other hand, many Democrats agreed with William E. Woodruff's call in the *Gazette* for total war:

> In the present political struggle we believe that the end we seek will justify the use of ANY means. We will not "play honest" with utter scoundrelism, but will use any and every weapon with which providence has gifted us to fight it.

These were not just editorial flourishes. To the conservative David Walker, long one of the state's leading jurists, Woodruff confided: "I think we are justified in conducting the canvass on war principles, 'to destroy the enemy' being first."[260]

Divided against themselves, the ex-Confederates were unable to stop the ratification of the constitution or the election of a new set of state officials.[261] During the summer, former Union army commander Powell Clayton, who had married a planter's daughter and settled outside of Pine Bluff, took over from Isaac Murphy as governor. Clayton had arrived for the ceremony sporting white gloves. After Murphy told him that "only dudes wear gloves in summertime," the abashed Clayton removed them. They stayed removed for the next three years.

The newly empowered Republicans were a mixed lot. Some were native Unionists, either mountain "boomers" or a few Southern planters and businessmen. Freedmen, although 90 percent illiterate, could now vote, and briefly were represented in the press by the newspaper *The Arkansas Freeman*, of which two issues have survived. Numerically the smallest group, Northern immigrants (carpetbaggers to the ex-Confederates) brokered their way to power. Clayton was Pennsylvania-born, but came to Arkansas from Kansas. Many were merchants looking for economic opportunities, but others were teachers and missionaries. From the start, the Republicans were divided against themselves, thus making the political history of the age a twisting kaleidoscope of personalities and issues.

Republican control was a godsend to some elements in the press. In order to establish their regime, Republicans saw to it that the press, both on the state and county levels, was well paid. The state printing went to the *Republican*, where John "Poker Jack" McClure wore three hats, chief justice of the Arkansas Supreme Court, editor of the party's newspaper, and state printer. Across the state, Republican newspapers sprang up to claim county printing privileges. An 1870 listing divided newspapers into five categories: Democratic, Republican, Radical Republican, Independent "or without any fixed policy," and Liberal Republican. At that time there were 47 newspapers. Leading the list was the *Helena Weekly Clarion*, "on both sides!" The two independent publications were the *Educational Journal* and the *Agricultural and Mechanical Journal*, neither of which ought properly to be classified as a newspaper.

The designation "Republican" meant supporting Governor Clayton, and there were 10 of these newspapers. Radical Republicans, those professing the strongest commitment to civil rights, consisted of nine, with Valentine Dell's *New Era* being the movement's oldest and strongest newspaper. Liberal Republicans, who rebelled against the endemic corruption that marred the presidency of U.S. Grant and called for universal amnesty, found support from four newspapers. Tabbs Gross's *Freeman* fell into this camp, as did the venerable *Southern Shield* in Helena. Keeping all this straight was not easy. The *Mountain Echo* in Fayetteville was owned by Republican legislator Samuel Bard. While Bard was in Little Rock, he left the newspaper in charge of Arthur F. Morgan, who, while supporting orthodox Republicanism in one place, criticized Carpetbaggers, notably John G. Price, in another. Bard unsuccessfully sued his quondam editor.[262] Interestingly, liberal Republican Edward Bancroft of the *White River Journal* at De Valls Bluff, a railroad promoter and distant relative of historian and politician Edward Bancroft, was the great-grandfather of future APA president and prominent Democratic legislator Charlotte Tillar Schexnayder.[263]

Twenty newspapers supported the Democrats, headed by the *Arkansas Gazette* and including the *Washington Telegraph*, the *Fayetteville Democrat*, the *Van Buren Press*, *The Des Arc Citizen*, the *Monticellonian* and the *Southern Standard* of Arkadelphia. Some of these newspapers endured for years, and some are alive, in altered form, at the time of this writing.[264]

Unfortunately, Reconstruction proved to be a hard time for Democratic newspapers. In Camden, Anson W. Hobson of the prewar *State Rights Eagle* established the *Constitutional Eagle* as a tri-weekly after the war. On August 2 or 3, 1866, the newspaper complained about soldiers from the garrison who came into town, got drunk, and made "obscene exhibitions" of themselves. Major George S. Peirce took offense at these remarks, and with the help of some 30 soldiers, attacked the office, destroying the press and dumping the type into the Ouachita River. In Little Rock, Arkansas's ranking officer, Major General E.O.C. Ord, discountenanced this action, and the major was court-martialed. Unfortunately, Hobson received no damages for his losses, which ran to about $2,000.

Republican officeholders used their powers to

make war on the Democratic press. The most egregious case came in Arkadelphia at the newly founded *Southern Standard* of J.W. Gaulding and Adam Clark. Clark County was a battleground between the parties, where several Republican newspapers came and went. The *Standard* criticized just about everything in Reconstruction, being especially opposed to freedmen serving on juries. However, when it attacked the circuit judge for dismissing a grand jury called to investigate election fraud, Judge E.H. Searle called out the militia and threw the senior editor, Gaulding, in jail and fined the junior, Clark, five dollars. The case attracted national attention, and from New York M.M. "Brick" Pomeroy, whose newspaper, *Pomeroy's Democrat*, had national readership, sent Gaulding money to help pay his fine. Gaulding replied that the citizens of Arkadelphia had already done that, but that he had given the money to the needy, in this case his own twins.

A third incident came from another troubled county, White. Here, a private detective Governor Clayton had sent to investigate Klan activity turned up dead down a well. One rather suspect witness told Republicans that the Klan had done the deed and named former Confederate Colonel Dandridge McRae as the region's commander and *White County Record* editor Jacob Frolich, Jr., as the Head Cyclops of the county's den. Rather than face charges, Frolich decamped to Canada, where he worked as a printer until he returned 14 months later and was cleared in court.[265]

Jacob Frolich, Jr., was an important figure in Arkansas journalism, and the first of note to be German. Born in Bavaria, his family had immigrated to America. Young Frolich was a trained printer who in later years delighted telling how he had "warmed rollers before the stove on wintry press days, in an open-floored and non-ceiled country printing office."[266] After serving in the Confederate army, he saved his money and bought a press outfit only to have it lost, together with his prized Confederate uniform, in a White River shipwreck. Frolich went back to work to buy a new press, and years later saw a black man in Vicksburg wearing his much-tattered Confederate coat, which the man told of fishing out of the White River.

Although Frolich was acquitted when finally put on trial, White County matters continued to vex the state. State Prosecuting Attorney E.W. Gantt's investigation into the Klan turned up the confession from Jesse N. Cypert, a well-known politician and former member of the 1868 constitutional convention, that he was a member of the Knights of the White Camellia. The local Republican newspaper in Searcy, the *Tribune*, printed what Cypert claimed was a distortion of his testimony, and in Little Rock the *Arkansas Gazette* accused the Republicans of judicial improprieties. Circuit Judge John Whytock responded by throwing editor William E. Woodruff, Jr., in jail.

Republicans soon realized the strategy had backfired. Woodruff was allowed to serve his five-day sentence largely with his family, taking his meals with them and attending to business as well. A reporter for the *Republican* wrote that he had been unable to find the prisoner in order to interview him, but Woodruff said he was only gone about three hours a day. Jailers charged visitors 50 cents to see the sometime-imprisoned editor, and his friends filled his cell with ale, brandy, flowers, a writing table, and newspapers. The county supplied him with a new water bucket, and he was able to bring his own bed from home. Not surprisingly, he was released early in order to avoid a planned grand parade with brass bands down Main Street.[267]

Although Woodruff managed to make himself and his newspaper into a useful martyr and doubtless enjoyed the sport, behind the scenes he was greatly alarmed. Apparently any serious investigation into the Klan in Pulaski County would have led to his door. Accordingly, the ownership of Woodruff and W.D. Blocher gave way to "The Gazette Publishing Company," thus opening the door for speculation about who really controlled the newspaper.

Certainly it was not clear who was writing the editorials. Thomas C. Peek, the former Hindman and Rector editor, came on board as did another pre-war figure, John M. Harrell, who later wrote two books of Arkansas history.[268] However, it was not from editorial comments but from a clipping that the next crisis arose.

Elias Cornelius Boudinot, formerly of the *Arkansian* and *True Democrat*, had served as the secretary of the secession convention and then during the war as the Cherokee representative at Richmond. Upon returning to the Territory, he opened a tobacco factory, believing that this endeavor was protected from federal taxation under treaty. From the larger legal standpoint, he doubtless was right, but Missouri tobacco interests and greedy Republican political appointees in the Treasury Department viewed it differently and seized Boudinot's factory. Boudinot exploded in a letter to the *Van Buren Press*, calling revenue official John McDonald, among other things, a "stupid ass" and a "self-convicted liar." McDonald's attorney filed suit, not against the "wild Indian" or the "obscure country paper," but against the *Gazette*, which was guilty of nothing more than using scissors and paste. McDonald wanted $30,000, and such a judgment would have put the newspaper out of business.[269]

The *Gazette*'s owners spared no expense in the defense, hiring Augustus H. Garland, a future governor; Uriah M. Rose, founder of the Rose Law Firm; and Elbert H. English, a former Arkansas Supreme Court reporter of decisions and future chief justice. By printing every scrap of evidence as well as the speeches of the lawyers, the newspaper managed to get maximum play out of the situation. English, for

example, argued, amusingly, at length that calling someone a "stupid ass" was not actionable. Woodruff testified he would have printed a response from McDonald but had never received one. Smithee, who seems to have managed the newspaper on a day-to-day basis, estimated the daily's circulation at from 400 to 500. Then the case rested for six months.

In October the jury, which, given the Republican laws, consisted only of voters who were overwhelmingly Republican because of disfranchisement, found the *Gazette* guilty but fined the newspaper one dollar. What lay behind the scenes in this settlement will never be known.[270]

The Press Associates

In the face of what can only be described as a climate far more hostile than that during territorial and early statehood days, the idea of a press association was reborn. The first revival of interest in the idea came in the fall of 1866. The *Pine Bluff Vindicator* seems to have launched the idea, but despite *Gazette* endorsement, nothing apparently happened.[271] Then, in the spring of 1868, two regional meetings were held in northeast Arkansas, where seven newspapers were represented in an effort to stabilize advertising rates. However, no further developments were reported.[272]

On October 16, 1869, representatives from nine newspapers met at the *Gazette* offices for a preliminary organizational meeting. W.D. Blocher called the meeting to order. Sam W. Mallory of the *Pine Bluff Republican* was elected temporary president and James Torrans of the *Washington Post* became secretary. On Monday, a fuller meeting took place. First styled the Publishers' Association of Arkansas, it had as its objects "the mutual protection of publishers, and to promote, encourage and forward the publishing business." Permanent officers were President John G. Price from the Little Rock *Republican*, James Torrans, vice-president, and William E. Woodruff, Jr., secretary.

Two of the three were Republicans, and it should be noted that the organization, renamed "The Press Association," admitted to membership Tabbs Gross of the *Arkansas Freeman*, thus making it the first integrated professional body in Arkansas. Since this was a publishers' association merely, its goals were limited to trying to set minimum prices for advertising. One of James Torrans's motions enacted by the meeting was that "no 'puffs' or editorial notices, except those notices calling attention to new advertisements, will be inserted in journals of the association unless paid for at usual rates."[273]

The officers of this association had interesting histories. John G. Price, the president, held a unique role in Arkansas. When Democrats discovered that Price was a former minstrel performer, they labeled his faction the Minstrels. Powell Clayton, of course, orchestrated and conducted the movement; Price was simply a performer/publisher. James Torrans, another newcomer and printer, had established the Radical *Post* in Washington in 1868 and later had an interest in another newspaper in Camden. His Republican loyalty was rewarded by appointment as United States Marshall for the Eastern District. Despite being a Republican, he apparently was well-liked and his early death was lamented even in Democratic circles. Samuel W. Mallory was best known for commanding a portion of the state militia Governor Clayton used to fight the Klan and for being pronounced dead from yellow fever when he was very much alive.

The failure of this organization to thrive was probably due largely to the era's politics. About the same time, an informal meeting styled the "Conservative Press Convention" discussed how to defeat the Republicans, who obviously were not represented there.[274] A secondary reason for failure was that a publishers' association was too narrow a base upon which to rest. Arkansas had about 45 newspapers, but only 11 were represented at the meeting.

The four years that followed the creation of this first body were as politically confused as at any time in Arkansas's history. Dissident Republican Joseph Brooks led a revolt against Governor Clayton. Brooks's faction was nicknamed the "Brindletails" in homage to Brooks's bull-like oratorical prowess; the Claytonites being called the Minstrels. The Democrat/Conservatives remained badly divided. They had gained additional seats in the legislature but needed the restoration of their voting rights to reclaim the state. Brooks offered them these rights and thus gained some support. The Minstrels, still managed by Clayton, who after 1871 was a United States senator, countered by running old-settler Elisha Baxter for governor and duplicated many of Brooks's promises. The gubernatorial election on November 2, 1872, was marked by the usual frauds. Since the Minstrels were in charge of the election machinery, they counted in Baxter as governor. However, when Minstrel congressional candidates tried to take their seats in Washington, their credentials were challenged and one was unseated. Brooks, meanwhile, and with considerable justification, went around claiming he had been robbed. However, Governor Baxter began drifting toward the Democrats. Although not clearly seen, the handwriting on the wall read that the end of Republican Reconstruction was at hand when on October 15, 1873, representatives from 17 of Arkansas's newspapers formed the Arkansas Press Association.

The timing was due to the holding of the state fair, which brought many editors into town. The idea for this celebration of agriculture dated to before the Civil War when William M. Quesenbury and C.C. Danley had been its principal proponents. Reflective of the planning that went into the meeting, the *Gazette* named those from "the press gang" who were in town and told them a meeting would be held "sometime to-morrow."[275] The next day's newspaper set the first meeting for 11 o'clock at the Chamber of Commerce rooms. Of the eight men who showed up that morning, not one was one of the visiting editors whose presence the newspaper had noted the day before, and two of the eight who did show failed to become members. B.F. Kearney from the *Lewisburg Empire* was so obscure as to be totally unknown to history, vanishing like the now extinct Conway County town where he had chosen to locate. William R. Burke, on the other hand, represented a still-living newspaper, the *Helena Weekly World*, that had been founded in 1871 by the Phillips County Democratic Committee.

As with the earlier attempt, bi-partisanship was in evidence, and James Torrans, now representing the *Daily Republican*, not only provided continuity with the old organization but also chaired this meeting. The presence of H.A. Pierce, a "correspondent," reflected the wider net this meeting cast. After scheduling another meeting for the next day, the session adjourned.

New arrivals on the second day included Jacob Frolich, Jr., from the *White County Record*, and Adam Clark from the Arkadelphia *Southern Standard*. During the day, the most important work was in drafting what today would be styled the mission statement. Instead a mere claim to economic self-interest, this body sought to "elevate its tone, purify its expressions, enlarge its usefulness, advance it in wisdom and justice, extend its influence in the work of true civilization, and to cultivate friendly relations and a spirit of fraternal regard among its members." Moreover membership was open to publishers, editors, and "correspondents." The *Arkansas Freeman* being extinct, no blacks were represented in the organization. J.N. Smithee became the first president, with James Torrans, vice-president; Jacob Frolich, Jr., secretary; and W.R. Burke, treasurer.

The membership was a mix of the old and new. Captain (so-called from his steamboat days) R.S. Yerkes, long the printing half of the *True Democrat*, dated back to before the war, but Charles Gordon Newman of the *Pine Bluff Commercial* and Dan O'Sullivan of the *Little Rock Chronicle* belonged to the new age. A banquet held at the Metropolitan Hotel that evening was a masterpiece of diplomacy. Of the eight toasts, about half were made by notable Republicans, including Logan Roots, a former federal marshall and congressman, who through his banking ventures was on his way to becoming the richest man in Arkansas; A.W. Bishop, the president of that Republican creation, the state university in Fayetteville; and Ozra A. Hadley, the former governor who had filled out Clayton's term. On the Democratic side, a toast to "Our Guests" came from Jacob Frolich, Jr., of Klan fame. One of the attendees was Miss Georgine Woodruff, the daughter of the *Gazette*'s founder, who was honored by the Association at its Fiftieth Jubilee meeting in 1923.[276]

More important than this first meeting was the second one a year later. That was largely due to the work of APA president, J.N. Smithee. Since there had been many previous meetings and much talk in the

past without sustaining power, Smithee's leadership was decisive in the infant Association's critical second year, 1874.

On March 16, 1874, Governor Baxter refused to authorize additional bonds to fund a Republican-controlled railroad. Three days later the party hatched a plan to get rid of the governor and install Joseph Brooks. Judge John Whytock, who earlier had sent Woodruff to jail, pulled out a long dormant case without informing Baxter's attorneys and held that Brooks was the real governor. Armed with a court order, Brooks and his armed followers invaded the State House on April 15 and threw Baxter out. Baxter retreated down the street to the Anthony House, and the Brooks-Baxter War was underway.

More than 200 persons lost their lives, and many more were wounded in military engagements around the state. Even innocent civilians suffered, like those caught between the lines when firing broke out in Little Rock between the two sides. One was a newspaperman. Irish-born charter APA member Dan O'Sullivan, who was connected with several Little Rock newspapers and was noted for his ability "to quote Latin on every occasion," was hit in the leg, probably by a stray bullet.[277]

Eventually, President Grant supported Baxter, and in June voters had another chance to consider the state's future. By an overwhelming margin, they decided to call a new convention and end Republican Reconstruction.

It was with the rubble as yet uncleared away and the State House a stinking wreck that "The Knights of the Pen and Scissors" held their second meeting on June 8, 1874. There were 17 members from 1873 and six more joined. In addition to having ready a body of by-laws, the meeting reelected Smithee as president, with James Torrans as vice-president and Jacob Frolich, Jr. as secretary. Then 13 of the delegates took advantage of an offer from the Cairo and Fulton Railroad (successively the St. Louis & Iron Mountain, the Missouri Pacific, and currently the Union Pacific) and departed to St. Louis on an editorial excursion, the first of many that the association would sponsor. Not only were Republican and Democratic editors on the trip, but D.H. Pope of the *St. John's College Record* went along. "No representative of the fair sex graced the party," the *Gazette* later reported, and the "excurts" toured the sights of St. Louis before returning home the next week.[278] Two of the 13 were destined to make marks in Arkansas journalism. Jacob Frolich, Jr. was a three-term Secretary of State and later business manager at the *Gazette*. H.C. "Cad" Allard was active at Fort Smith and later Hot Springs. Most importantly, the Association had survived, for in the midst of the rubble of the war and the new campaign for a constitutional convention, it would have been easy to put off the meeting, breaking the continuity.

Instead, members would look ahead to 1875, when they would find Arkansas much altered. Augustus H. Garland was now governor under the new "Thou Shall Not" constitution. With voters denied the right even to vote adequate taxes for schools, the public school system the Republicans had created disappeared, along with almost every other progressive program. Democrats repudiated the state debt, causing Arkansas again to become a state without credit. As Democrats regained control in state government, counties, and towns, Republican presses disappeared. After the *Arkansas Gazette* got the state printing, the *Daily Republican* sunk to a weekly before vanishing. On the county level, most Republican newspapers, except in pockets of strength, disappeared when the county printing was taken away.

All these changes the Arkansas Press Association weathered, but at the cost of becoming more homogenous. At any rate, from this time on the history of newspapers would have a focus, and the growth and development of the Association would be at the forefront of the modern way of organizing people by their trades, ideas, and commitments. Ten years later at the 1883 meeting, Association secretary W.A. Webber described the APA as "one of the brightest, living and progressive institutions of the

---

Editorial Excursions

From the time of the first meeting of the Arkansas Press Association until early in the 20th century, association meetings were the preludes to excursions. Editor Opie Read both explained and defended the practice in the third issue of his comic newspaper:

> An editorial excursion is one of the main features of the freedom of the press. A great many people do not understand why railroads will carry editors free and charge the members of a conference half rates. This has caused much complaint among delegates to religious assemblages, claiming that the business of promoting the spiritual welfare of man should receive as much courtesy at the hands of railroad corporations as the temporal work of publishing a newspaper. It should be remembered that the men do not grant free excursions to editors through a feeling of love. The editor is expected to give a long account of his trip, with complimentary description of the road. A newspaper man can do this with perfect consistency. He can dovetail a railroad puff into almost any kind of article and still preserve his dignity as a writer. It is different with a minister. He cannot with propriety weave a railroad puff into one of his sermons, neither could he, during prayer, ask the Lord to bless the Q.Q.&Z. road. How would it sound for him to say, "And at last, when the final trump sounds, may we all, including the Q.Q.&Z. railroad, be gathered unto our fathers?" The fathers, you see, would have no use for the road. No one would like to hear a minister say: "There was great excitement in Jerusalem. The fame of John the Baptist had gone abroad throughout the land. The people crowded around the depot of the Q.Q.&Z. railroad, waiting for an elegant dining car to take them out to Jordan." This would not be true, for there were no railroads in those days.
>
> The Arkansaw editors are preparing to make another extensive tour of the north. They always return with a dusty recollection of the trip. The trains on northern railways run so rapidly that passengers do not have time to get off the cars between stations, talk to the farmers awhile and then catch up with the train. The excursionists are hurried into a town, rushed onto another train and hurried to another town. An excursionist is not very presentable after his cheap duster has lost its original glaze and stiffness. A limp duster makes a man look as though he has been riding free and is ashamed of himself.*

* *Arkansaw Traveler*, June 18, 1882.

---

land. It has done much to build up journalism in the Southwest. It has done much to elevate the character of newspapers in the state—and to bring together and to harmonize the minds and feelings of those who are the makers of newspapers."[279] In short, the APA was one of the positive goods to come out of Reconstruction.

Conclusion

The long and sustained war of words and deeds known as Reconstruction created problems for the press. While most editors were strongly partisan, they were also determined to advance their communities and regions. But such progress was compromised by the violence. The Arkansas Press Association, by bringing members together for their common good, helped relieve the tensions.

Meanwhile, Arkansas had grown to the point where a parting of ways was in order. Daily newspapers took root in Little Rock, while country towns continued to be served by weeklies. But weeklies were losing their monopolies. The enormous expansion of railroads increasingly led to better mail service, and newspapers like Horace Greeley's *New York Tribune* circulated all over America. In Arkansas, the *Gazette* pioneered in tailoring its weekly to its state constituents, and its competitors would follow. As towns like Fort Smith and Pine Bluff continued to grow, they, too, provided fertile ground for venturing into the entirely different world of the daily newspaper. After 1875 these two journalistic streams flowed over different courses on their way into the great ocean of print.

Chapter IV

The Rural Press: Growing Up with the Country, 1875-1920

"Few avocations in life are as little understood and few men's services are as little appreciated by the general public as those of the man who presides over and shapes the destiny of the country press."
S.A. McNish, *Proceedings of the 27th Annual Session...1899*, 41.

"A number of our country housewives said they liked the big 8-column paper best as it is more adapted to use on pantry shelves, under carpets or even for papering rooms."
Erwin Funk, 1960.

"And please note that the word *weekly* is not spelled with an *a*."
Alfred Hawn, *Madison Record, Proceedings of the 60th Annual Session...1932*, 18.

"That old spinning wheel is sweeter music to our ears than the most scientific touch on organ or piano as it takes us back to brighter and happier days, ere sin had entered into our soul, and men and women were what they seemed and always paid their subscriptions to newspapers in advance."
Arkadelphia *Southern Standard*, October 27, 1877.

"I know as well as any one that printers' wood should be hauled up during warm weather."
Opie Read, *Len Gansett* (1888), 325-6.

"The boys will please remember that a printing office is no place to be dancing around, and that it is ill manners to be fingering with things lying around the office and reading copy over the compositor's shoulder. When you come to visit us, be as still as a mouse and your visit will be appreciated by both the editor and the printer and the printer's devil."
J.C.B. Lindsey, *Arkansas Wheel*, 1886.

Introduction

About the turn of the century, an Arkansas country editor was called before the throne of St. Peter and put on trial. Witness after witness came forth to give testimony. "What happened to the story you were going to write about the 40-pound radish that looked like a man?" demanded one man. "Why did you never warn me about what was really in those patent medicines for female complaints?" asked a woman who had become a drug addict. "Why was our wedding listed under the obituaries?" intoned a morose couple. "My best poem, and you ruined it by reversing two lines and misspelling five words," the town's poet proclaimed. Worst of all, five lynched black men said nothing, but by their silent demeanor told of an editor who had played with racial fire for political purposes.

The editor listened to this litany of woe and at last was given a chance to respond. "I'll tell you why we did not run the radish story," he said, "One hour after you brought it in there was a train wreck that claimed ten lives and filled every space we had. By the next week your radish looked more like a decomposed mummy than a man." "Yes, I had some inkling of what was in those 'patent' formulas," he responded to the drug-addicted woman, "but I was under contract to the ready-print company not to tell; that was the price I had to pay just to put out a paper." "Now, as for the couple whose wedding appeared as obituary. That turned out to be true, and everybody at the time knew it would be. But you really need to take that up with the tramp printer that came in the week before and claimed he really needed work. He appeared sober enough and did good work for awhile. After he claimed to be the brother of Alfred, Lord Tennyson and made a mess of your poem," he said pointing to the spinster, "is when I had to let him go. Except that he had already gone and had taken my whiskey with him." "As for causing that lynching, I always stood for law and order. If you black men hadn't tried to vote, if you had just left things up to us, who were your best friends, none of that trouble would have happened."

After staring at the witnesses for a few moments more while reckoning in his head, the editor turned before the mighty throne and made this eloquent plea: "Your honor, it is well established that the common law of England and America is, or least ought to be, the common law of God. This being so, I demand that the testimony of each of these witnesses be excluded and the charges dismissed." "What is your reason for this motion?" demanded the heavenly judge. "It is, your honor," said the editor with a look of quiet vindication in his eyes, "that not one of these witnesses ever paid for their newspaper subscriptions, and it is well established in heavenly law that no delinquent subscribers shall enter the Kingdom of Heaven." The case was dismissed.[280]

In short, the world of the late 19th-century editor was beset by difficulties, both internal and external. During the great age of personal journalism, the country press flourished—and floundered—all across the state.

Getting Started

Tennessean Opie Read heard from a friend, Harry C. Warner, about an opening in Carlisle, a newly formed town fronting the Memphis and Little Rock Railroad on Grand Prairie. "The chance of a lifetime," his friend said, as well as an opportunity "to print a paper on the level." A candidate for sheriff was providing backing, and Warner had ordered a complete outfit—a small hand press and type—from St. Louis. "So hop a train as soon as you can and come," he wrote, "Opportunity has not only knocked at the door but has busted through at the window."

Read jumped at the chance. First he spent a night in Pitzer Birdsong's saloon where he "earned" enough money to get him as far as Memphis. Stranded in the city park, and unable to get work without a union card, he witnessed three squirrels in a fight which he turned into a sketch. The *Appeal* editor rejected the piece on the grounds both that it was natural history and that it was unfitted for a family newspaper; the *Avalanche* took it, giving Read three dollars. So armed, he headed off to the nearest saloon where he failed to increase his capital enough to buy a full ticket to the new town. Read did get to Carlisle through the good graces of the conductor, and he and Warner lodged in the rear of a saloon, "a lively place but almost sure to quiet down after three o'clock, morning." Read was not impressed with Carlisle: "I looked about for the town, but as there were no street lights I couldn't find it, but I failed not to smell its outhouses."

The next morning, Read was introduced to the

newspaper office, which turned out to be an unused boxcar on a siding. In three days just as they had some 300 copies of the *Prairie Flower* ready to distribute a train stopped by, coupled up the boxcar, and carried publisher, editor, and press away to De Valls Bluff. "No doubt the best circulation the *Prairie Flower* will ever have," the rival newspaper commented.

The *Prairie Flower*'s candidate for sheriff failed to win and forthwith demanded payment on the note. "'Tomorrow,'" said Warner. When that day came, "in came a deputy sheriff, put a chain about our press and padlocked it. The weather had turned cool. The first frost had killed the *Prairie Flower*."

"I am going to get out of this ungrateful town for one thing," Warner stated. "We always took its part, lied and said it was bigger than Lonoke when everybody knew that Lonoke was bigger by least a hundred and fifty inhabitants." Before leaving, Warner stopped at the post office, where he found a letter from a friend describing a new town called Conway whose ex-carpetbagger founder, Colonel Asa Robinson, wanted a home newspaper. "The journalistic chance of a life-time," said Warner, who was ready to go. Read was less sure, preferring to stop in Little Rock and acquire a union card even though he hoped to get work as a reporter. Warner's response bespoke the values of the age: "That's all well enough but I want to tell you that's nothing like a man being his own boss. No man ever made any real headway to get on as a reporter."

Warner established in Conway a newspaper entitled the *Arkansas Traveler* and lured Read up from Little Rock to edit it. "I went," Read remembered, "and the town as he had said, was built on both sides of the railroad." Its main attraction was Bud Waller's saloon.[281]

In addition to the *Traveler*, there was another newspaper in the town, *The Spyglass*, put out by Conway's future merchant prince, Jo Frauenthal, who

recalled, "It fed upon the foibles of the 329 people who ventured here from civilization. Its wood-cuts tried to faithfully reproduce each of them. Some resented these cuts as caricatures, and hunted for the unknown editors. Upon the appearance of the paper, the refreshment stands on the four corners of the only block were filled, and the atmosphere was electric."[282] *The Spyglass* was printed at the *Traveler* plant, and one interesting feature of both newspapers was that the heads of horseshoe nails were pressed into service for the letters I and l.[283]

Read soon moved back to Little Rock, and Warner did not stay. In 1878, he founded *The Plebian* in Morrilton, the hometown of his new wife, and continued his penchant for odd names. After buying the *Springdale News* in 1882, he renamed it the *Springdale Yellow Jacket*. In keeping with the title, Warner published a column under the heading, "If You Don't Want to Get Stung, Keep Out of My Way."[284] The newspaper must not have been a stinger, and new owners changed the title to the *Journal*. Then it became the *Arkansas Locomotive*. In 1887, John P. Stafford (APA president, 1929) reverted to the title *Springdale News*. As for Warner, his next try was *The Incident*, reportedly the first newspaper in that emerging town across the river from the capital that at various times went by the names of Huntersville, De Cotillon, and Argenta before settling on North Little Rock.[285]

The careers of Warner and Reed reflected the partnership model. Usually, one man did the writing, the other the printing, but these arrangements were as different as the parties involved. The biggest obstacle to the successful operation of a partnership was that, in the overwhelming majority of markets, the income was too small to support even two single people.

The successful newspaper office rather than a college was the usual training school, even into the 20th century. In 1918, Austin C. Wilkerson of the *Batesville Record* bought the *Newport Independent*. Among those who trained in the latter office were James L. Bland, who with Wilkerson's assistance bought the Walnut Ridge *Times-Dispatch* in 1921; Oscar E. Jones, who after working at the newspaper while in college, bought the *Batesville Record*; and Roy Evans, owner of the *Tuckerman Record*.[286] In the rush to get started, two prominent Arkansas editors, John P. Stafford and Erwin Funk, began editing while still in their teens.

Funk realized that a high school education was inadequate to the new age, and he set out to rectify the situation. College journalism still lay in the future, so Funk signed up in the Murat Halstead Correspondence School of Cincinnati. Although in time, correspondence schools often got the reputation of diploma mills, this was not Funk's experience: "I never had regret for the dollars it cost me for I would send in my stories from the *Democrat*—and boy, how they did get blue penciled sometimes."[287]

The late 19th century witnessed a dizzying succession of town and newspaper creation. Underlying this boom period was a pattern. The main key to growth after the Civil War was the coming of a railroad. Carlisle was on the Memphis and Little Rock, that line, the future and now-abandoned Rock Island, having been completed during Reconstruction. Conway was on the Little Rock and Fort Smith, a road that became the "Whitewater" of American politics in the mid-1880s when Republican presidential hopeful James G. Blaine earned the nickname "The Continental Liar from the State of Maine" because of his involvement with its bonds.

Meanwhile, the Cairo and Fulton entered the state from the northeast, making its way through Little Rock and on to Texas, spurring the creation of towns from Walnut Ridge to Texarkana along the way. Paralleling it to the east some years later came the Cotton Belt. Along this line arose Corning, Brinkley, Stuttgart, and Fordyce.

Then the St. Louis and San Francisco ("Frisco"), which never made it west of Oklahoma, bought the line running from Springfield, Missouri, through Memphis, and also constructed a branch line into northwest Arkansas, resulting in the creation of Springdale and Rogers and connecting Fayetteville to Fort Smith.

The "Splitlog," subsequently the Kansas City Southern, skirted the state's western border. Decatur, Gravette, Gentry, and Sulphur Springs were among its towns in the northwest; Mena, De Queen, and Ashdown in the southwest. Early in the new century the St. Louis and Iron Mountain, which had acquired the Cairo and Fulton, ran a line up the White River through Batesville to Missouri. Finally the ill-fated Missouri and North Arkansas (Might Never Arrive) traversed the state from Neosho, Missouri, to Helena. Along this line Marshall, Berryville, Leslie, Alpena, Green Forest, Harrison, Heber Springs, and Searcy flourished.

Short-lines ran everywhere except in Newton County. Alongside the Jonesboro, Lake City and Eastern Railroad, Monette sprouted. By 1910, the state's railroad system was essentially complete.

Towns often appeared overnight. In the case of lumber towns, they sometimes decamped overnight.

News as well as supplies followed the rails. All of western Arkansas fell under the sway of Kansas City, for it was easier to get news from this source than it was out of Little Rock. On the other side of the state, St. Louis achieved primacy, and it replaced to a large extent Cincinnati as a source for presses and paper as well as news. For over half a century, both the *Kansas City Star* and the competing St. Louis metropolitan newspapers had many Arkansas readers.

Warner and Read's setting up in a boxcar was highly symbolic. James Graham and his stepson, Frank A. Mason, came to Rogers from Melbourne in 1881 to found the *Rogers New Era*. At that time, people were still living in tents and sheds along the tracks. Mason went to St. Louis, now far more accessible than in Quesenbury's day, and came back with a large job press. To his wife, who was still waiting to see if he made a go of it, Mason wrote, "I cannot say what the prospects are, but think they are tolerably fair." Already in place was competition, the *Rogers Champion*, but it was a Republican organ. Mason and Graham found an old man named Williams to help them, and the three "by the very hardest kind of work succeeded in getting out 500 or 600 copies of the paper yesterday."

An early issue showed that the newspaper was a six-column affair, and that the printers had neatly solved the problem of breaking the rule by taking all the two-column advertisements and setting them in one double column. Flanking this double column were single columns consisting mostly of professional notices. The *New Era* outlasted its first opponent. Erwin Funk recalled that both men were "outspoken, both in public debate and editorially, but neither had a reputation as troublemakers." Nevertheless, they found it necessary to carry pistols. After nine years they sold out, and the new owners, perhaps observing that Rogers had never had an old era and therefore

did not need a new era, changed the name to the *Democrat*.[288]

Another railroad story came from the opposite side of the state. When the Memphis and Little Rock crossed Crowley's Ridge, a new town arose at the site where ex-Confederate Nathan Bedford Forrest had his work camp. Its first newspaper, the *Free Press* of Thomas W. Ham that moved over from nearby Madison, was Republican in politics but opposed Governor Powell Clayton. After Reconstruction came the *Times*, the *Democrat*, and the *Herald*. The *Times* absorbed the *Democrat*, and then in 1915 the two survivors merged. This was one of the simplest newspaper histories Arkansas presented.

As the railroad achieved dominance in trade older towns died. Jacksonport, which over time boasted 14 newspapers because of its strategic location at the confluence of the White and Black Rivers, gave way to Newport. A vicious county seat war erupted, with Newport being the eventual victor. John H. Page, who later practiced his trade in Dermott, Warren, Perryville, and Little Rock, had Jacksonport's last newspaper, the *Democrat*, in 1887. An old army press, some second-hand type, a piece of tombstone for an ink slab, and strips off a billiard table for reglet made up his shop. The newspaper folded in two years.[289]

When the Cairo and Fulton Railroad missed Washington, a new town called Hope sprang up a few miles away. Its first newspaper, *The Star of Hope*, was perhaps named from the famous poem, but at any rate achieved national attention as having taken the same name as the New York prison newspaper at Sing Sing. The Hope editor replied to the publicity:

> I know nothing about the Sing Sing paper. I never was in that prison or any other, and I do not sing or yodel. I am endeavoring to publish a good newspaper in a growing town, and the government of our country and state is founded on faith, hope and charity. I have faith in the hope that I shall never need charity as long as the Star of Hope continues to guide and direct me in my efforts to enlighten the people and to help them make Arkansas the best state in the Union. If darkness has been over and around us, it is passing away, and the Star of Hope will show the way to brighter and better days.[290]

The *Star* outshone all its competition, 13 newspapers in nine years, some of which included the *Times*, the *News*, the *Telegraph*, the *Mercury*, the *Record*, the *Pine Torch*, the *Eagle*, the *Dispatch*, the *Radical*, the *Chronicle*, the *Arkansas Evening Herald* and the *Gazette*. At the last was Colonel W.W. Folsom (APA president, 1888), a strong prohibitionist. He and C.C. Colburn at the *Ozark Democrat* (APA president, 1884) published serially the entire New Testament; Folsom thought the project so useful that he was repeating the process at the time of his death.

Some towns relocated. There had been a Boonesville prior to the coming of the Choctaw, Oklahoma and Memphis Railroad. This line, built by a black contractor using black labor, extended the Memphis and Little Rock west and eventually became a part of the Rock Island system. At new Booneville, the company gave free lots to businesses who would relocate along the railroad, and a newspaper, the *Booneville Democrat*, arose with the new town. Occupying a 25 x 25 room were one small job press, a hand-operated newspaper press requiring one man to roll the ink and the other to run the press, three type cases (one single and two double), and two tables, one for business, one for folding.

Editor/publisher Harvey Theopolis Hampton was a Logan County farm boy born less than two miles from town. He had sought his fame as an editor, and had worked prior to 1897 in Paris, Greenwood, and Altus. A lawyer, he "practiced law for a living and ran a newspaper for the good he could do." He once held the office of county assessor, but was beaten for a second term when his opponents ran another man named Hampton. A sometime mayor of Booneville and codifier of its city digest, he was State Purchasing Agent in 1907. Hampton exemplified the independent editor. His motto, emblazoned on the *Democrat*'s banner, was "Having an Opinion; We Dare Express It." That meant, one local said, "he'll say what he da— pleases if it busts a suspender."[291]

Many newspapers had close ties to railroads, but none exceeded those of the *Mena Star*. Kansas City Southern Railroad president Arthur Stilwell convinced A.W. St. John, formerly of the *Carthage* (Missouri) *Press*, to set up shop in the as yet unnamed central division site the company had laid out as a town. When town lots for Mena went on sale on August 19, 1896, the newspaper was already in operation. Despite competition (eight newspapers known to early press historian Frederick W. Allsopp), St. John started a daily in 1898. The weekly edition, one of the strongest in the state, was adjudged one of the 19 best weeklies in the nation just prior to World War I.[292]

Another success story came at Springdale. John P. Stafford, a local boy from nearby Shiloh, started as a printer's devil at age 12 in the *Springdale Enterprise* office before moving to the *Fayetteville Democrat*. Only 18 when he purchased the *Locomotive*, he was, as he recalled later, "the entire force" for his renamed *News*, preparing the copy, setting the type, and printing and mailing the newspaper, all in a room measuring 14 feet square. His first circulation figure was 182. One Benton County newspaper took note of the event, observing, "The Springdale Locomotive has made its regular monthly change again," to which Stafford replied, "Yes, but she is here now to STAY, and don't you forget it."[293]

The newspaper he had purchased was a six-column, four-page affair of which two pages were patent insides. In 1888, Stafford replaced his old army press with a new Washington hand press and began moving into a succession of better buildings. By 1895, he had purchased a new Prouty press, giving him the capacity to print 1,500 copies in just two hours and 15 minutes. After three more moves, he built his own building on Emma Avenue in 1903. It boasted a skylight, a common feature to successful newspapers. This permitted, Guy Stafford recalled, "a flood of light that brought relief to eyes worn with searching dark places in other buildings."[294] Circulation, meanwhile, reached 1,200 in 1900 and 1,600 two years later. To keep up, he bought a Fairbanks-Morse gasoline engine to run the equipment in 1902 and converted to electricity in 1915.[295]

"Newspaper men of Arkansas have long looked upon The Springdale News as model weekly paper," wrote Walter J. Lemke in 1937. Lemke cited Stafford's on-going struggle for mechanical improvement, his careful organization of his country correspondents, and strong editorial views. "The Springdale News stood for all that was uplifting in community life," Lemke concluded. Stafford had moderated somewhat by the time of his death in 1933, but Lemke believed that was because Springdale had at last "become a safe and pleasant city in which to live."[296]

Stafford's strategies for success were varied. Producing special issues for free distribution were important advertising tools; Stafford printed over 4,000 copies on June 14, 1898, to publicize Springdale's Chautauqua. Every new industry received recognition. An 1896 stave mill led him to observe: "The News was never so happy in its life. We feel like giving a regular Fourth of July war whoop. Come to Springdale to live!" He shared every improvement he made mechanically to his newspaper with his readers. "No newspaper in Arkansas progressed so much through the work of the country correspondents as did The News and no publisher was more conscious of their worth to the paper or the interest created among the readers as was Dad," his son Guy recalled.[297]

Another key element common across the state was family involvement. In September 1889, Stafford's four-week-old infant son Guy made his first visit to the shop, where he grabbed an ink-smeared towel. "The odor of that towel," he recalled years later, "is with me today and to one raised in the print shop there is no perfume sweeter." At age five, he was placed on a stool in front of a type case, from which two hours later came six lines from the composing stick. "Needless to say the composition appeared without correction but with explanatory note." Guy's next jobs were sweeping out and lighting fires. Guy moved on to more complex jobs as younger brother Fay (John L.) followed. The introduction of gasoline and electric engines created numerous opportunities that turned both into practical engineers. During World War I, Guy scored 99.9 on a government test measuring mastery of gasoline engines.

One of Guy's early jobs was working the foot-powered job press. This resulted in him becoming a left-footed punter in high school football. Fay was selected to learn the new Junior Linotype, which required "many hours of brawn and brain" to force "the machine to live up to advance notices. Numerous were the times when all were tempted to take a sledge hammer and reduce the mechanical puzzle to a mass of wreckage." Father John was a strict taskmaster but still found time to play on a semi-pro baseball team. He and all three of his sons played in the town band.[298]

Having a family employed in the business allowed the elder Stafford to undertake a political career. During the two terms he served in the legislature, the sons had charge of the newspaper, but labored on strict instructions not to use their power in a partisan way. As Guy recalled, "There were times when his sons plead to be allowed to use the paper to besmirch political foes in return for unfair tactics. Tears were shed when he refused our wishes and time has proven the broadness of his teaching and the honor of his attitude."[299] John refused to run for a third term, stating, "I'd rather run my newspaper and discuss the other fellow in his job than be the one cussed." However, he did become the town's postmaster. In retrospect, Guy believed that his father's subsequent heart problems began with the strain of coping with two jobs.[300] The one common element missing there, the female, appeared after Guy went off to become the city editor of the *Los Angeles Times* and Fay became a banker. Although Edward Raymond (Marty) took over the newspaper, his wife, Glaphyra, better known as Bucket, was editor for seven years (1938-1945) during his illness.[301]

Entrepreneurship could take many forms. Clarksville had newspapers of short duration even before the Civil War. After the war, the appearance of a Republican newspaper, the *Clarksville Forum*, prompted the founding of the *Clarksville Democrat*. After both newspapers soon failed, there came the *Clarksville Enterprise*. In three years it was gone, and the *Vanguard* followed. After it failed, the shop was sold to Harry C. Warner at the *Arkansas Traveler* in Conway, whose former *Prairie Flower* press had remained in Carlisle.

In 1876 came the *Clarksville Herald*, which briefly became the *Laborer's Herald*. O.C. Ludwig, who at age 21 had been the editor of the *Atkins News* and who worked for a number of newspapers before embarking on a political career, established the *Arkansan*. It became the *Brothers of Freedom*, presumably an organ for the radical farmers' group in the late 1880s. The *Register* failed to register with readers, and *Western Journal* traveled into oblivion when it was merged with the *Clarksville Herald*. The new owners hoped to attain stability by selling stock to almost every businessman in town. This failed to work, however, and ownership and titles continued changing. A merger made it the *Herald-Democrat* in 1918, but the reason for selecting Clarksville from among the 100 some parallel cases is that it became home to one of the last upstart newspapers in Arkansas.

Thomas Paul Giacomini, a veteran correspondent who had always wanted his own newspaper, founded the *Picnic Post* in 1933. Giacomini tried as titles the *Clarksville Enterprise*, *Giac-Crax*, *Newsy News*, *Give It A Chance*, and *New Era*, all within a few months. In 1934 it became the *Johnson County Weekly Graphic*, a title that, sans the "weekly," has endured.[302]

The failure rate in the 19th century ran at over 90 percent. Yellville got a *Gazette* in 1873, but the next year its owners gave up on the town and moved to La Crosse in Izard County, establishing the *Post*. A year or so later they were at Melbourne with the *Clipper*.[303] One of the shortest careers was for the *Centre Point Courier*, which after two issues was sold and the plant removed to Texarkana to publish the *Democrat*. Camden's Jim Holmes, the poet laureate of the APA in 1877, observed that there were only two alive from the nearly half-dozen newspapers that he did not kill by being foreman. Such experiences no doubt prompted Holmes and John R. Ward, when they started the *Camden Beacon* in 1873, to declare that the *Beacon* "will float until the last spar is splintered."[304]

Hot Springs was one of the worst towns for achieving stability. In 1877, J.N. Smithee recorded that on the ruins of the *Courier* of 1869 came five newspapers in succession in eight years; another printing plant there put out three in six years.[305]

A Washington or "army" press was standard, but Harry Warner was not the only printer short of type. The *Chicot Press* office had been ransacked during the Civil War by visiting Union soldiers, who threw half the type into Lake Chicot and smeared the rest with ink before dumping it. Nevertheless, James McMurray and Major P.W. Gatewood managed to fish up and clean enough type to reopen the concern.[306]

A different tack was taken by John R. Huffman, founder of the *Sulphur Springs Speaker*, who made his own press, which he used for nearly 30 years.[307] As late as 1932, S.A. McCulloch, a former editor of the *Calico Rock Progress*, founded the *Ozark Times* using a press of his own construction.

Antebellum Arkansas had boasted J.W. Woodward, the deaf-mute; post-Reconstruction Arkansas had J.M. Cunningham of Star City. "The *Vidette*," Smithee noted, "is doubtless the first newspaper edited by a man with no arms. Mr. Cunningham, the editor, besides being a good lawyer and making a good newspaper, never had any arms. He uses his teeth in writing."[308]

Behind many newspapers at some point was a bank. The post-Reconstruction period saw a great growth in small-town banking. Every important element in a town or county's political configuration was represented by some combination of banks and newspapers. In addition, every mushroom town wanted a newspaper to boost its supposed glories. Thus it was that at Pettigrew, a village on the Frisco's St. Paul Branch, banker Charles Crawford corresponded with William A. Keithley, owner of a small weekly in Casey, Illinois. By 1918, Pettigrew was past its peak, and Keithley, after nearly 40 unprofitable years in the trade, was more interested in land speculation than running yet another newspaper. Nevertheless, he came, and on August 16 the first issue of the *Pettigrew Journal* was ready. Keithley had his second-class mailing permit, but he never registered his newspaper in the Ayer's and Son's directory nor did he join the APA. His wife died less than a year later, and the newspaper suspended. As for banker Crawford, he eventually had to foreclose on the small farm Keithley had left behind. A single issue of the newspaper survived.[309]

More complex was the situation at Calico Rock. In 1903, the first newspaper, the *Calico Rocket*, lived up to its name and took off in a few months. On August 18, 1904, the Bank of Calico Rock took possession literally, moving the Washington hand press to a backroom. During the next two years, the newspaper (now styled the *Progress*) had four different editors. One was S.A. McCullough, who came up from the *Cushman Elevator* after the Jones brothers decamped, and who later created a rival newspaper, the *Ozark Times*, using the press of his own construction. In 1912, Neill Brooks bought the *Progress*, keeping it, except for two interruptions, until 1955.[310]

At least one newspaper, the *Melbourne Times*, was first published out of a back room in a courthouse. Founder Henry A. Trevathan, the brother of George at the *Batesville Guard*, started off with a "handkerchief-size sheet." A subsequent owner was printer R.J. "Rufe" Estes, who in 1932 had the honor of being elected Izark County sheriff, although he had been dead for three days.[311]

Each early editor sought to seize the political and geographic high ground. "Bentonville First, and the World Afterwards," proclaimed the *Bentonville Sun* of H.L. Cross (APA president, 1903).[312] Cross's boast of "Our Fine Italian Climate" was "widely quoted," Erwin Funk recalled, "especially when we were having a spell of ice and snow in Benton County."[313] "The Future City of the Southwest" trumpeted Mansfield's "Sycamore Dan" Hogan, a fiery editor of the *Alliance Patriot* and APA poet in 1910 who took up the cause of the Farmers' Alliance before moving on to Socialism.[314] The *Arkansas Banner* of Searcy, the successor to the *Arkansas Populist*, went with "Equal Civil Rights: Equal Obligations."[315] Another Searcy newspaper, *The Southern Economist*, was foursquare and portentous with "Free Silver or Bust."[316]

One of the most curious newspapers was put out by George O. Agee. His *Fin de Siecle Sickle*, shorted to *The Sickle* after 1900, carried this warning: "This number for Grown Men Only!" Agee published Jeff Davis material as well as Arkansas historian and lawyer John Hallum's famous speech about adultery.[317] C.E. Cruce adopted "Covers the Petit Jean Country Like the Sunshine" for his 1896 *Morrilton Democrat*; it remained there until Gene Wirges went to a Biblical quotation ("Ye shall know the truth, and the truth shall make you free"—John 8:32) in 1979.[318] Jesse Matthews, whose newspaper office was located in a blackjack thicket outside of Salem, had "To Help Them That Help Me" for the *Fulton County Informer*. Apparently, readers helped, for that newspaper lasted about 10 years.[319] "In God and the Republican Party we trust, Everybody else CASH," was what John W. Casteel ran in the short-lived *Newton Herald* at Jasper in 1898.[320] A slightly different position was taken in Monticello, where "Devoted to the Interests of the Drew County and The Editor" survived the 1920 merger of the *Advance* and the *Monticellonian*.[321] The best example of this type of motto was at the little five-column, short-lived *Cane Hill News*: "Verily He That Tooteth Not His Own Horn; The Same Shall Not Be Tooted."[322]

The Life of a Printer

Well I remember my first newspaper work. It is a picture, I venture that but few of you can truly visualize. I was, at the ripe age of 14, "roller boy" on a Washington hand-press. It was not a very easy nor a very nice job, but a very essential part of the newspaper business in those days. Between press days I set type, the most awful bottled Brevier I have ever handled, and I well remember among the copy "Brown's Iron Tonic," popular at the time, but I suspect, now as little known as the Washington hand-presses.

After a time I graduated as roller boy and took the other side of the press, and those were proud days. A mere stripling in size, it was a joy to snap back that big lever to make the impression, and on gala occasions, when some big husky farmer would come around and watch how easily we did it, we would invite him to try for himself. He always tried, but we never saw one big enough to make ago of it. He didn't have the knack. As we would say now-a-days, in golf parlance, he didn't have the "follow through."*

*V.W. St. John, Mena Star, *Proceedings of the 59th Annual Session*....1927, 19-20. (See illustration on page 110.)

Some newspapers made historical statements. Valentine Dell's *New Era*, founded during the Civil War, in 1875 called itself the "Oldest Republican Paper in the Defunct Confederacy." Added in 1880 was "and only Republican Paper in the State."[323] As politics gave way to economics, mottoes changed. "A Family Newspaper Devoted to News of the Day, Literature, Manufacture, Politics, and Agriculture," proclaimed the *Boone County Record* of 1872.[324] The *Cleveland County Herald* was "Devoted to the Literature, Politics and the Interests of Cleveland County Generally."[325] W.A. Webber (APA president, 1885) used the motto "Challenge Those who Berate Progressive Arkansas of Today" in his *Saline County Digest* in 1877.[326] The *Newton County Times* used "Nesting in the Bosom of the Ozarks—Where You Can't Go Wrong."[327] The newspaper did go wrong, with one editor leaving the state to follow the barbering trade, and it was eventually sold to competitor J. Milam. For William R. Burke of the *Helena Daily World*, it was "Nerve and Vim are Sure to Come Out Ahead."[328] Mottoes often lacked vim and nerve in the 20th century. "Sketches About People You Know" was all that the *Dover Times* promised.[329]

The most common themes, expressed in various ways, celebrated both editorial independence and democracy. "A Non-Partisan Newspaper, Devoted to the Best Interests of the People," proclaimed the Fayetteville *Arkansas Times* of 1882.[330] The long-lived *Fayetteville Republic* of D.C. Ambrose promised "A Paper for All the People."[331] Editorial independence was also the theme for yet another Fayetteville newspaper, *The Arkansas Blade*, which vowed to "Hew to the Line, Let the Chips Fall Where They May."[332] On the other side of the state, the *Osceola Times* of Leon Roussan took to poetry: "Pledged to no party's arbitrary sway, we follow Truth where'er she leads the way."[333]

Mottoes were cheap; nameplates cost more money since they had to be made in St. Louis or some other factory town. *The Blade* of first Black Rock and then Walnut Ridge had one of the most elaborate dresses. After a sword bearing the inscription "In hoc signo vinces" that crossed the letters of the newspaper's name came pictures of fruits, a sheaf of wheat, a corn stalk, and a forest scene.[334] The various newspapers named "Sun" could hardly avoid using Old Sol.

When one of the best rural editors, De Witt's Bob Crockett, who practiced law downstairs and put out his newspaper upstairs, got a new banner, he celebrated the event in style: "Behold the beautiful new head of our paper, supplied by the St. Louis Type Foundry. We ordered a new head for the editor at the same time, but they regretfully acknowledged their inability to fill the order, heartlessly suggesting that if we would let Mrs. Gleaner catch us kissing another woman we might get a 'head put on us.' We've tried that and found it too painful for repetition."[335]

Several factors underlay the country editor's world. The growth of the telegraph and railroad shrunk the time it took news to arrive. Newspapers also got into the hands of readers more rapidly. Post-reconstruction Arkansas witnessed an enormous explosion in the number of post offices. Rural Free Delivery did not arrive until 1896, but with post offices every few miles, rural patrons got their mail far easier than before the Civil War. Better local mail service was essential for the development of country correspondents.

Ever-improving metropolitan newspapers reached out with weekly editions. The Sunday edition of the *St. Louis Republican* was "a marvel of modern newspaper enterprise," the Marshall *Mountain Wave* reported.[336] It possessed a world-wide news service; its magazine section included colored pictures as well as half-tones, fashion information, a piece of sheet music, cartoons, and high-class literature, all for only $2 a year by mail. Both the *Arkansas Gazette* and

Arkansas Democrat produced weekly versions for country distribution, but in content and construction were decades behind the *Republican.*

After the Civil War, the going rate for weekly newspapers was $1 a year. That rule applied "no matter how good or how poor, how big or how little. In every other line of business," Erwin Funk complained in 1916, "you pay according to value received. Not so in the newspaper."[337]

What prompted Funk's discussion was the great rise in prices that came with World War I. "Not a single paper can make expenses and show a profit at the $1 rate," he noted. According, the *Springdale News* of John P. Stafford, the *Rogers Democrat*, and other newspapers raised their rates to $1.50 a year.*

By the early 20th century, Arkansas appeared poised to shed itself of its earlier violent and backward reputation. Across much of the state, flourishing towns saw the building of two-story brick and stone businesses, often around a square in county seats, or fronting the new railroad tracks. Fine Victorian homes went up, and more and more farmers benefited from marketing fruit, stock, or grain, as well as the proverbial cotton. Canning and woodworking factories, mines, and other forms of industry were seen everywhere. Early in the 20th century, first gasoline and then electric engines changed town life radically, and such amenities as municipal water and sewerage became common.

Some editors flirted with issuing dailies. The Spanish-American War spurred many, for this was the first war Arkansans could follow almost instantaneously. In growing towns, editors like Springdale's John P. Stafford tried twice-a-week editions. These were big steps to take, and many waited to see if indeed the new century lived up to its rhetorical promises.

* The *Informer and Newton County Times* of Jasper still charged a dollar a year in 1956.

Among the Tripods

Politics remained the major reason for getting into the newspaper business. Republicans were no longer a major factor after 1874. By April 1875, only the Fort Smith *New Era*, the *Pine Bluff Republican*, and the *Batesville Register* remained of the once more than 20 party newspapers outside of Little Rock.[338] Immigration from the Midwest, starting in the 1880s and continuing for several decades, brought new Republicans to Arkansas.

The 1900 APA annual meeting, considering the topic worthy of note, got W.D. Mathews, a sometime editor of the *State Republican* in Little Rock, to undertake discussing the subject. Republican editors, he opined, were like freaks in side-shows. Men of "calibre and ability have jumped into the breech only to come out breechesless." Unable to make a dent against the Democrats, "many an editor has thrown up the sponge and turned his arsenal into a graveyard, where he quietly buried his fond dreams of evangelizing and converting the uncivilized Democracy." Such editors found themselves "dumped into the washing machine of the swampites and hillbillies and put through the squeezing rollers of the Democratic wringer, coming out smelling like an illicit distillery."[339] While the partisan Republican newspapers failed, many editors and publishers kept a private faith alive.

In general, the rural press pronounced itself independent but Democratic. For a majority of the newspapers that lasted longer than one election, this meant they would run every candidate's advertisements and for an additional financial consideration allow campaign literature to pass as news copy. Principled editors liked to think of themselves as kingmakers, or at least community guardians, but most were financially unable to sustain independence. In his early days, James L. Bland at the Walnut Ridge *Times Dispatch* was known locally as "Friday" because "he was the boss man's Friday, doing his bidding at all times," supporting a county machine led by S.E. "Bunk" Spike, Z.M. "Bear" McCarroll and others.[340]

During the late 19th century, pressing causes soon shook rural Arkansas. The various farmer groups of the 1880s, the Agricultural Wheel and the Brothers of Freedom, were suspicious of county-seat publishers whom they suspected (rightly) of being part of the political establishment. Both groups played on popular prejudices against squirrelly-headed editors but also founded their own organs, which often were edited by veteran squirrelly-heads. Following the defeat of this agrarian uprising came the Populist movement in the 1890s. It, too, was well represented, albeit briefly, in the press. Then there came out of the ranks of the Democrats the charismatic figure of Jeff Davis.

A regular Democrat during the crises of the 1880s and 1890s, Davis discovered that Populist rhetoric still stirred voters, that seemingly outrageous political ploys played well in rural regions, and that attacking newspapers appealed to the illiterate. Starting as state attorney general in 1898 and becoming governor in 1900, Davis used the new Rector Anti-Trust law to drive all the fire insurance companies out of Arkansas. Rural editors either cheered or condemned him; neutrality was not a serious option when during his three-term reign every month produced a new issue to debate. Davis's most famous campaign was against the building, already underway, of a new state capitol. Longtime Democratic organs often felt compelled to support him, at least at election time, simply because he was the Democratic nominee.

The short-lived Wheel and Populist newspapers were followed in the 20th century by Socialist sheets. The state party was founded in 1903, and in addition to the nationalization of industry, the Socialist platform endorsed equal rights for women; non-sectarian education; initiative, referendum, and recall; reduced working hours; unemployment compensation; national insurance; and old age pensions. The party sported organs in Jonesboro, Clarendon, Green Forest, Pine Bluff, Hot Springs, Judsonia, Piggott, Van Buren, and other towns. Dan Hogan edited the first newspaper, the Huntington *Southern Worker*, but A.M. Merrill of the *People's Friend* at Rogers endured longer than most, lasting until 1915. Merrill located his small job press on the second floor of a planing mill and set his tabloid entirely by hand. "A lone crusader against all the evils of the day—as he saw them," recalled Erwin Funk, Merrill served as secretary to the school board and publicized the heretofore unreported finances of the district.[341]

When Merrill suspended the *Friend*, Funk wrote a touching obituary. The newspaper's primary value was for Merrill's opinions: "While we know that Bro. Merrill often wandered off into devious and wondrous by-paths, his support of the schools, the park movement, the public library, and other local matters of importance, aided greatly and have been appreciated by all."[342]

The good relations that Funk shared with Merrill were the exception. If a town had two or more newspapers, the public expected to sit back and enjoy warfare waged to the hilt. "Far too prone to fight incessantly," V.W. St. John at Mena, recalled, "two newspapers in a single community meant diversion for the public, because of the lurid display of language each editor used to point the hopeless imbecility of the other."[343]

Although the coverage and opinions of the Little Rock press provided the main source of information for rural editors, it was common for the more literate legislators to send letters back to the home newspapers. At times, the *Southern Standard* at Arkadelphia kept its readers abreast of state doings in this way and did not hesitate to take the state press to task. The *Arkansas Gazette*, the newspaper wrote during the summer of 1877, "has become such a chronic sneerer that its nose stands up like the tower of Babel and its upper lip curled like a pig's tail in a gouber patch."[344]

Adam Clark and J.W. Gaulding were not afraid to criticize the nation's deflationary policy that was wreaking havoc on the South's agriculture, and they quoted approvingly the *Harrison Times*: "There is no reason why a farmer's home should not be as inviting, his furniture as tasteful and his children as intelligent as those of a lawyer, doctor, banker, or parson."[345]

The country Democratic presses flayed away on the race issue. Tensions between the races ran strong during Reconstruction and thereafter. In 1867, the *De Witt Elector* urged the establishment of a Sunday school because white boys were "jumping, running, and throwing brick bats at little 'niggers,'" actions that reflected no credit on the children or their parents.[346]

Typical of racial attitudes over much of the state was the *Southern Standard*. Bitterly opposed to Republican Reconstruction, it denounced having blacks on juries as "the worst curse of all the curses that Radical rule has inflicted upon the country."[347] Thus it was a real confession when the editors admitted that "the negro jury acquitted themselves with much credit, showing a disposition to do justice even against one of their own color."[348]

A similar change could be found on the subject of lynching. After a Negro was lynched for allegedly raping a white woman, the editors observed, "Served him right, he ought to have been tied to a stake and burnt."[349] But after an 1877 lynching in Hamburg, they editorialized against the practice.[350]

When the state passed civil-rights legislation that banned discrimination in public facilitiies, Democratic newspapers opposed it: "Only negroes who wish to create trouble or extort money will ever attempt to avail themselves of the provisions of this bill. Peaceable and well disposed negroes will never attempt to force themselves where they know they are not wanted."[351]

The political and newspaper history of Arkansas after Reconstruction saw the elevation of white supremacy to the very top of the Southern pyramid. Both in their editorials and in the way they handled stories involving race, newspapers reinforced these notions weekly.

The tortuous end of Reconstruction was marked by screaming headlines and national attention, but it merited this rebuke from the *Standard*: "The amount of gas, buncombe and bombast that has been expended at Little Rock within ten days past would have been sufficient to have seated and unseated half a dozen Governors if practical results ever followed such things."[352] Thus, in the midst of the worst of the Brooks-Baxter crisis, the newspaper fittingly turned its attention to the smells emanating from local slaughter houses.[353]

Flying high in the breeze of every local newspaper was the banner of town and county promotion. Getting a railroad came first at Washington: "Our very hair stands on end to think of the horrors of our situation—the land of the widow, the orphan and the poor man sold to the bloated speculator for a mere song to pay taxes…every day sinking our people lower and lower, and deeper in the depths of poverty, bankruptcy and ruin—and all for the want of a railroad."[354] There was great celebration when the railroad arrived in Arkadelphia, but few foresaw what changes it would make to the local economy.

Arkadelphia learned quickly, when the freight charges on the newly arrived town fire engine were four times the Chicago or St. Louis rates.[355] Arkadelphia had an additional woe. The Republican legislator decamped with $75,000 in bonds for the Ouachita Valley Railroad that was never built. A compliant Democratic legislature abolished Clark County in hopes that the debt would disappear, but the federal circuit court overturned this move.[356]

Clark County entered the new age bankrupt.

Prior to the coming of the railroad, most inland towns were largely self-subsisting. The railroad, by linking these towns to the national economy, brought in outside goods at lower prices, driving local factories and artisans out of business. Editors quickly perceived this, and were forced to balance the mixed impact of the new economics and some questions of ethics. Railroads gave editors free passes in exchange for advertising, and while some were only too happy to make full use of the passes, others found legitimate ethical objections. Many editors, while recognizing the need for railroads, began publicizing self-sufficiency at home and on the farm.

The pass system gave editors much freedom to travel around the country. Then, in 1906, Congress banned interstate passes. "It put a crimp in our travel," Erwin Funk recalled. For Funk and others from northwest Arkansas getting to Little Rock after 1906 posed problems. Since the Missouri Pacific rerouted its line into Oklahoma to avoid paying toll for using the Frisco bridge over the Arkansas River at Van Buren, a trip from Rogers to Little Rock became interstate travel.[357]

Nevertheless, high freight rates and the complete success railroad lobbyists enjoyed in the legislature provoked many editors. Railroad service could be a problem as well. A.I. Barnett, who in addition to publishing the *Leslie News* also ran a lumber mill on the Missouri & North Arkansas, wrote a long signed editorial on his difficulties.[358]

Editors were good at book farming and gave space to every new agricultural idea that came along. In northwest Arkansas it was tobacco, which flourished for a decade before being destroyed by Eastern monopolists. Colonel Peter Donan of the *Bentonville Advance* waxed eloquent: "Tobacco...to render every parlor and church pew just as nasty as his elevated Christian tastes require. No balmier breezes sign over Araby the blest or the Gardens of Gal in her bloom, than the sweetness-surfeited zephrys that linger in loving dalliance amid our rose beds and pig styes, japonica thickets, honey suckle arbors and frog-ponds."[359]

Colonel Bob Crockett added a stock column to his *Gleaner*, on one occasion illustrating every brand in use in Arkansas County.[360] The development of the peach and apple orchards in northwest and southwest Arkansas owed much to newspapers. The federal government supplied many reports and documents that lazy editors often delighted in using for filler, while state geologist John L. Branner produced a complete survey. Branner disappointed Bear (Montgomery County) residents by saying Arkansas lacked enough silver to warrant development. Some 1,500 prospectors hung Branner in effigy, and the state legislature stopped his funding, but J.L. Wadley (APA president, 1902) sold the *Bear Mountain News* forthwith, and soon only a ghost town remained.

Arkansas editors also tried to save local industries. "Arkansas Apples Best" ran the truthful headline in the *Rogers Democrat*. Funk went on to take growers to task for their failure to organize and market their products effectively, thus allowing apples from the Pacific northwest, "of inferior flavor and quality but fine appearance," to win out.[361]

The growth of county fairs after the Civil War gave editors a change to produce special editions devoted to the event. Often copies containing the names of winners were distributed generously in hopes that rural attendees might become subscribers. Small-town editors in the early 20th century produced richly illustrated progress editions. These required considerable financial backing in order for the publisher to be able to afford the large number of engravings. But if the business community thought it worthwhile, their support, both for pictures and the flattering biographies of individual bankers and merchants, guaranteed a large sale.

Since the work was frequently beyond the

capacities of small shops, there arose firms that specialized in this work. Their principal method was to sign up people who wanted to see their names "puffed" in the newspaper. "The write-up is so complimentary, is presented by such an oily-tongued solicitor, and appeals to so many of the weaknesses of the individual who is approached, that it is hard for him to turn down the canvasser," Frederick Allsopp noted of "the grafting part of the business" or of "blue-sky" editions.[362] The work of such firms was not limited to newspapers, and the so-called Goodspeed histories of the regions of Arkansas were cut from the same cloth.

The task of being a circus critic was one country editors took seriously. "There is a fascination about a circus that appears to be irresistible to many persons, and they will go if takes their last dollar," editorialized the *Southern Standard*.[363] Especially around harvest season, no topic occupied rural editors more than circus criticism.

The Orton Circus probably was the "miserable, drunken, quarrelsome set of bruisers" that the *Southern Standard* said it was.[364] But a number of factors could go into the press's equation. Did the circus advertise? "The coming of a circus to town was always a source of both profit and pleasure to the office," Fred Allsopp recalled.[365] The full-page advertisement for Cooper, Bailey & Co. in the *Southern Standard* on November 13, 1875, was doubtless paid for in cash and lots of free passes. However, once the circus departed, the newspaper told readers of burglaries that had taken place while people were at the shows.[366] One response to deceptive circuses was the passage of city ordinances requiring circuses to parade through town before setting up. This early form of consumer protection legislation was an antidote to fanciful advertisements. After one circus failed to reach Arkadelphia, the editors congratulated the town on saving $2,000.[367]

Editors promoted other aspects of community life as well. All declared their towns the best, their gin scales to be fair, and their health perfect. Neighboring towns, readers were told, did not measure up. Prescott, a visiting editor told his readers, needed to incorporate so the town could "remove all the dead swine laying around the streets."[368] Since Arkansas was hit by epidemics of yellow fever and smallpox into the 20th century, editorial reticence was often less than honest. Three of the major promotions of the late 19th century were fire protection and other municipal services, cultural development, and sports.

Getting a fire engine was the first sign of urban maturity. Massive conflagrations hit every town in Arkansas repeatedly, even with fire engines. Steeling the merchants' determination to build in brick, together with city ordinances about fire walls and abating smoking chimneys, were issues for editorials.

Nineteenth-century editors were serious about culture, and newspapers assumed the mantle of cultural guardians. For many towns, getting a town band established ranked high on the agenda. Four bands from Helena, Marianna, and Marvell were featured in the local celebration of America's Centennial in 1876.[369] The *Southern Standard* described Arkadelphia's Aeolian Brass Band as "being always ready by good practice, to discourse sweet music to the people of Arkadelphia in every style they may wish."[370] No town of its size was better served than Harrison, where *Times* editor J.R. Newman, the son of Boone County's first printer, was band director and father to a highly musical family. APA members were entertained by this family orchestra when the Association visited Harrison in 1915.

History was important, too, and many newspapers printed long essays, often the first published histories of towns, counties, and regions. A number of 19th-century newspapers are known today only because some reader saved a copy for posterity.

Community sports were a new development in Arkansas. Hunting, fishing, and horseracing dominated antebellum life. After the war came baseball. Based on town ball, which had been played before the war in several forms around the state, baseball was planted by the Union army into an already fertile ground. One team during Reconstruction that styled itself the Ku Klux Klan failed to amuse the Republican sheriff at Fort Smith who arrested the players. Baseball challenged in a more public way than hunting or fishing the sanctity of the Christian Sabbath, and that led to arrests.

Editors reported scores regularly and by the end of the 19th century were often active participants. Cicero Brown at the *Marshall Republican* even used the crowing rooster, usually reserved for election victories, to record Marshall's 38 to 8 victory over Valley Spring.[371] When the Joplin (Missouri) press explained away their team's loss to Siloam Springs as due to the long train ride, editor A.W. Perrine would have none of it. The Joplin boys did not play "real ball and were just outclassed at every turn."[372] A July 4th game in 1876 in Helena against the Mechanics and nine picked players from outside the town drew a large crowd, and "precaution had been taken to keep out the rabble which generally takes possession of the ground, by having ropes across the places of entrance and active members of the club to keep guard."[373] "Very quiet and interesting" was the assessment of J.T. Gage at Huntsville's *Democrat* of a game in which the editor had his little finger torn from the next finger, one player had a finger broken, another was left with one out of joint, and one player, struck on the cheek, had to leave when his eye swelled shut. Gage urged all his readers to come to the next game, when the Huntsville Kids took on the Alabam Nine.[374]

Probably no one refereed more games of baseball and football than Erwin Funk. Young Funk and old E.W. McCorkle of the Arkadelphia *Siftings Herald* used to slip off to games while ostensibly attending APA meetings in Little Rock.[375] Funk later recalled that seeing Presidents Cleveland and Roosevelt should have been the most memorable event while attending the APA's meeting in St. Louis for the World's Fair, instead it was watching a Pirates/ Cardinals game with Honus Wagner making a diving one-hand catch and then throwing out a runner at home.[376] One project that journalism instructor Walter J. Lemke undertook during his retirement was a history of the Fayetteville Angels minor league team.

Town editors engaged in good and bad repartee with their colleagues. The *Southern Standard* editors had once practiced their trade in Camden, Arkadelphia's rival for the cotton trade. Hence, every piece of bad news about that town made its way into their newspaper. By the summer of 1875, they reported that "numbers of substantial brick buildings are vacant." One of Camden's attractions, Burstin's Celebrated Mineral Well, they claimed had water flavored by the oozing from an old tannery.[377] Their favorite target was the local stage line. John T. Chidester was a noted antebellum stage-line owner whose Camden home is still a local landmark. Although he worked for the Confederacy, after the war he went in partnership with E.H. Searle, the Republican judge who threw *Standard* editor J.W. Gaulding in jail for criticizing his court proceedings. But even before that incident, the newspaper referred to "Old Chidester's broken down stages."[378] Afterwards, it wrote, "Among all the negligent and careless managers of stage lines, we think that 'Old Chit' leads the van."[379]

A battle of a different order took place between the Bentonville *New Bentonian*, and two Fayetteville newspapers, the *Sentinel* and the *Democrat*, over the subject of chamber pots. "Their ill feigned modesty," the neutral *Arkansas Blade* asserted, "is like the affected shyness of a courtisan [*sic*]. One would judge from the hollow mockery that is indulged in, from the high sounding phrases, the bad odor of the theme and withal, their familiarity with the subject that their respective editorial craniums consisted of the veritable article."[380]

Editorial wars, like that between Camden and Arkadelphia, were fought over economics. Equally common were political wars. The 1876 *Helena Daily World* of William R. Burke warred with what he styled the "defunct Shield."[381] Many exchanges were jocular. Wrote Bob Crockett at De Witt:

> Folsum [sic] of the Augusta Vidette thus lacerates our pericardium:
>
> According to Crockett's Gleaner, hail stones fell in De Witt last week measuring 10½ inches in circumference and weighing 4½ ounces. That's right, 'Bob,' if you 'tell one tell a whopper.'
>
> Just as we expected! We know that some damphool would accuse us of lying! But we've got you dear boy! We had that hailstone varnished to exclude air and prevent melting and have been using it as a paper-weight ever since and can show it! Lying—quotha! Come again Bro. Folsum![382]

The bane of all editors was the economy. The Panic of 1873 hit hard in Arkansas, dragging down Little Rock's new banks to ruin and bankrupting every railroad in the state. Forthwith the *De Witt Indicator* accepted coonskins, muskrat skins, bee's wax, tallow, and cord-wood for subscriptions. Apparently, these were not forthcoming and the newspaper was sold to the county Republican committee and thereafter perished.[383] "Arkansas is an unhealthy climate for newspapers," intoned the *Standard*, which not only took in wheat for subscriptions but also sold itself to the patent medicine industry.[384]

Preprinted pages were called "patent" after the medicine companies that provided the bulk of the advertising. The idea had begun in Wisconsin as an auxiliary service for distributing state official matter. Ansel Nash Kellogg took this idea further in Chicago, offering a variety of reading matter flanked largely by patent medicine advertisements. The Chicago fire of 1871, which temporarily wiped him out, created grave problems for a number of Arkansas newspapers already dependent on this material. One form, called boiler plates, came in columns that could be inserted at will on any free page. Ready-print consisted of two printed pages to which the local publisher added merely his nameplate and banner.

In the early days there was competition. The *Arkansas Gazette* created its own concern, the Arkansas Newspaper Union, which operated on the premise that Arkansas-related auxiliary sheets would be more desirable to rural editors.[385] However, A.N. Kellogg and Western Newspaper Union engaged in cost-cutting practices, leading the *Gazette* to sell out to Western. By the end of the 19th century, most Arkansas newspapers were supplied by A.N. Kellogg Newspaper Company, which merged with the Western Newspaper Union in 1908. In that year, sales to 180 newspapers justified the large building in Little Rock that bore its name. The remoteness of northwest Arkansas led newspapers in that section to rely on Kansas City.

The services filled their pages primarily with advertisements for patent medicines because this was the first industry to advertise specific name-brand products nation-wide. By agreeing to accept these pages, the publishers signed a "red-line" contract that forbade them from criticizing an industry run by "toadstool millionaires," where advertising ethics were unknown and where the consumer got at best various combinations of alcohol and opiates. Arkansas's leading prohibitionist, George Thornburgh (APA president, 1891) relied heavily on such advertisements in his *Arkansas Methodist*. Indeed, a cursory examination of the religious press reveals a much higher rate of such obnoxious advertising than the general average. Even worse, some newspapers ran the content of these advertisements as if it were news: "In Diarrhoea, Dr. M.A. Simmon's Liver Medicine is invaluable. It gives Tone to the Stomach, Aids Digestion and Assists Nature off all... [*sic*]"[386]

What flanked the advertisements was not really news. Syndicate literary material was often denounced as being almost utterly without any redeeming qualities. Much of it indeed was "evergreen," consisting of recycled homilies, jokes, and sage advice. The great principle being not to offend, the syndicates eliminated almost everything of interest. Most material was regionally selected, and the few extant issues of one black newspaper, the *Arkansas Mansion*, indicate that the black press was serviced by a black syndicate.

W.S. Torey, who defended the service at the APA's 1894 meeting, claimed that the Little Rock branch house did a fine job in providing coverage of state events. John H. Page, at the 1893 meeting, observed: "The country publisher, if he should choose to do so, can sit in his office and do absolutely nothing but get up the local page and yet publish a paper congenial to his taste in every respect."[387] Those who followed this advice were not well respected in the profession.

The patent pages generated an increasing amount of negative comment early in the 20th century when the nation discovered from scientific studies just what was in those nostrums. Even before the creation of the Food and Drug Administration, the APA's 1904 historian, T.M. Woods, reported an increase in home print. Calling ready-print "one of the greatest drawbacks the country press had to contend with," he cited both the editor's lack of control over the contents and the inferior nature of the finished product: "a six-column folio filled with local occurrences is far more satisfactory to a majority of the subscribers than a seven-column quarto with from four to seven pages printed abroad, filled with stale boiler-plate matter that has been published from time to time for the past fifty years."[388]

APA President Robert O. Schaefer in 1923 took editors to task for what he saw as the sorry state of Arkansas: "What occupies the space under your editorial 'mast head,' where the editorials used to be? Is it any wonder that our legislature is full of incompetents when our editorial column is full of Wine of Cardui and Vick's Salve? How can a national congressman get direction from your columns when in reaching out to feel the public pulse he feels only the throb of a column of press notices sent out by the Department of Agriculture?"[389]

Even selling out did not save many newspapers, and pleas for subscribers to pay rang out regularly. "We are out of meat, money, and other things, we are out at the elbow. We are out of patience, and seriously contemplate running our face for about two hundred post cards with which to remind those who owe us. Pay up," pleaded J.P. Fagan of the Jacksonport *Arkansas Statesman*. Perhaps because his motto was "Truth Before Favor," the newspaper became the *Dispatch* before suspending.[390] One wonders whether the explanation for reducing the *Tuckerman Times* to a half sheet on July 18, 1907, was really "to give us some relief from the heat caused by working the big press."[391] Permanent relief came when the newspaper suspended completely in 1909.

In order to survive against the competition, owners had to be creative and adaptive. One of the most enduring was William A. Wenrick at the *Mountain Wave* of Marshall. Founded in 1892, the *Wave* had a troubled early history until 1897, when W.A. Wenrich, "a well known printer" from Cumberland, Maryland, became first its business manager and then in 1898 the full owner, a position he maintained for the next 50 years.[392] In 1898, he added to his four pages of home print a Christmas insert, one of the earliest to appear in a rural area. Apparently, Wenrich's innovation did not take, and by March 1899 he had to reduce the newspaper's

The Arkansas Press Association *in Nashville, October 31, 1895. The woman fourth from the left in the front is Sallie Robinson-Stanfield, the first woman known to use a hyphenated surname in Arkansas. After her first husband died, she married J.C. Riley of the* Walnut Ridge Blade. *(Courtesy Marilyn Zweig)*

Republican *Office, Huntsville (Madison County). The* Republican *started out as the* Democrat, *moved to St. Paul and then back to Huntsville. In a 34-year period it had eight different owners. Pictured here about 1908 are Mr. and Mrs. E. Grant Hutchinson and their three children. In 1919 Albert Hawn (APA president, 1931) of the* Democrat *bought the* Republican *and consolidated the two papers as the* Madison County Record. *(Courtesy* Madison County Record)

The Beebe News, *circa 1940. A typical small town newspaper advertised itself for news, commercial printing, and office supplies. (APA Archives)*

The Carroll County Progress *office, c. 1900. Founded in 1879, the* Progress *had a number of different owners before being consolidated with William J. Douglass's* North Arkansas Star *in 1916. This photograph, reproduced from a broken glass negative, testifies to the increasing presence of women as compositors by 1900. (Courtesy Carroll County Heritage Center/Shiloh Museum of Ozark History)*

The Springdale News, *1903. John P. Stafford was especially proud of his skylight. Prior to the advent of electricity, skylights helped compositors immensely. (See modern version on page 328.) (Courtesy Maudine Sanders Shiloh Museum of Ozark History)*

Pulling the "Great Archimedean Lever." *This Washington hand press was still in use when Frederick Allsopp went to work at the* Nevada County Picayune *in the 1880s (see vignette on page 98). (Frederick W. Allsopp,* Little Adventures in Newspaperdom*)*

Star Herald *correspondents of 1914. Only one person was missing from this correspondents' party in 1914. Represented here were the communities of Ingram, Elevenpoint, Noland and Hoover's Landings, Alberta, Harmony, Demun, Maynard and Ravenden Springs, Reyno, and Biggers. After 1920 women began to outnumber men as correspondents. (Courtesy Pocahontas* Star Herald*)*

The Bentonville Democrat *office, 1888. Information on this photograph dated it to 1886, the year the newspaper was founded. However, the large American flag and the picture of Grover Cleveland place this picture to either 1888 or 1892. This solid and prosperous-looking building on the square at Bentonville testified both to the newspaper's success and its prominence in the town's life. (Courtesy Shiloh Museum of Ozark History)*

The Randolph Herald *office. This early newspaper at Pocahontas was located on the south side of the square in this frame building that also doubled as the town's post office. Oftentimes editors served in the patronage position of postmasters, but rarely after the Civil War was the post office located in the newspaper office. (Courtesy Pocahontas* Star Herald)

Pocahontas Star Herald *office, c. 1916. L.F. Blankenship, in the foreground on the right, had interests in a number of Randolph County newspapers before consolidating them in 1915. The newspaper stayed in the family's ownership until 1972. (Courtesy Pocahontas* Star Herald)

Black Rock Blade, *c. 1902. Owner J.C. Riley (center), who came from Kansas, moved the* Blade *to Walnut Ridge, where it continued to be published for a number of years. "Dark and gloomy" best describes this office. (Courtesy Thomas Moore)*

Stone County Democrat, *Mountain View, c. 1907. This newspaper, founded in 1907, at the same time as the* News, *had only a brief existence. The two newspapers consolidated only to be burned out in 1909. Owner Cebern Brooks may be the man in front of what appears to be a house and office combined. (Courtesy Butler Center for Arkansas Studies, Central Arkansas Library System)*

Oscar Franklin Craig, 1902. With his new neatly printed newspaper in hand, Craig launched a local dynasty. (Courtesy Robert D. Craig)

Advertisement, The Forrest City Times. *Many newspapers acquired stereotype plates of their presses and used them to promote advertising and job printing. The* Times *of Colonel Edward Landvoight and E.L. Vadakin was a strong newspaper in the region. (Courtesy Forrest City Museum)*

When the Newark Journal *moved in 1913, newspaper owner Oscar Franklin Craig not only had a photograph made of the event but turned it into a postcard as well. Craig, who is pictured third from the right, led the crew. (Courtesy Robert D. Craig)*

Roy Monroe Craig, 1913. When O.F. Craig decided to acquire a Linotype for the Newark Journal, *he sent his son, Roy Monroe Craig, to New Orleans to attend a Linotype school. Young Roy, at age 14, found himself the youngest Linotype graduate in the nation. (Courtesy Robert D. Craig)*

George Thornburgh. This 1907 caricature sketch showed Thornburgh's varied interests. At the time of his APA presidency in 1891 Thornburgh represented a fraternal newspaper, the Masonic Trowel. *However, he had founded the* Telephone *in Walnut Ridge before moving to Little Rock. His principal claim to fame was as head of the Anti-Saloon League, the men's equivalent of the Women's Christian Temperance Movement. After Arkansas went dry in 1916, Thornburgh became head of the state's school for the blind. (Courtesy Arkansas History Commission)*

J.C. Graham, compositor, Mineral Springs Vim. *On October 3, 1929, the nation's oldest member of the International Typographical Union celebrated his 87th birthday, "pounding long primer" as usual at his case at the* Mineral Springs Vim *of W.E. Brown, "one of the best men I have ever known and for the best little paper." Graham, who had worked on old Washington hand presses as well at the* Memphis Avalanche, *observed: "I will not be able to work much longer. My people are all dead and gone and I am the only one left of a large family." (*Arkansas Publisher, *October 1929)*

Adah Roussan, the wife of Osceola Times *founder Leon Roussan, became an honorary member of the APA in 1879 and remained active for more than 40 years. Her shop motto was "Good paper, good ink, good work and prompt delivery." The neatness and order of this office contrasted to the usual clutter and mess. (Courtesy Marilyn Zweig)*

The Blade
Devoted to all the boundless resources of Northern Arkansas.
Hoc Signo Vinces
Souvenir Edition. | WALNUT RIDGE, ARKANSAS. | August, 1905.

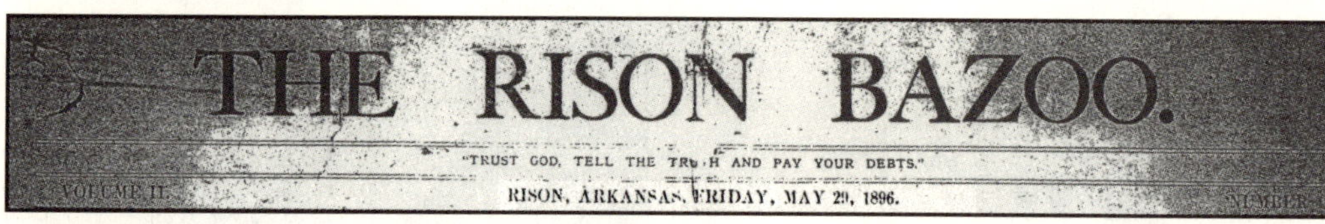
THE RISON BAZOO.
"TRUST GOD, TELL THE TRUTH AND PAY YOUR DEBTS."
VOLUME II. | RISON, ARKANSAS, FRIDAY, MAY 29, 1896. | NUMBER

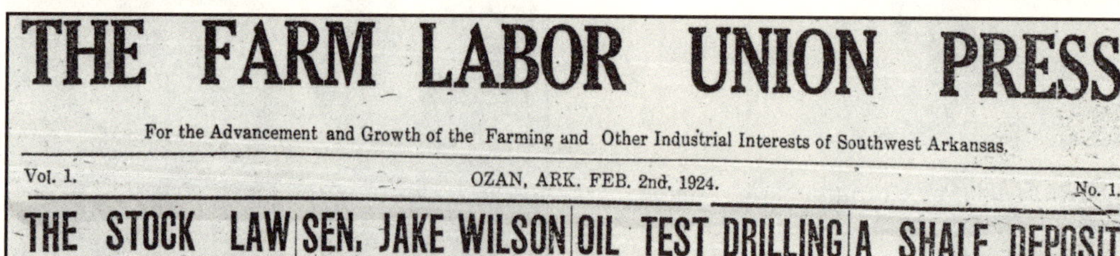
THE FARM LABOR UNION PRESS
For the Advancement and Growth of the Farming and Other Industrial Interests of Southwest Arkansas.
Vol. 1. | OZAN, ARK. FEB. 2nd, 1924. | No. 1.
THE STOCK LAW | SEN. JAKE WILSON | OIL TEST DRILLING | A SHALE DEPOSIT

BINGEN SOCIAL VISITOR.
Vol. 7. | Bingen, Hempstead County, Ark., July 10, 1891. | No. 42.

THE WASHINGTON PRESS.

VOLUME 13. WASHINGTON, HEMPSTEAD COUNTY, ARK., SATURDAY, JUNE 8, 1889. NUMBER 23.

Commercial Job Printing. **The Monitor.** Advertising Rates Reason-able.

Vol. 1. CENTRE POINT, HOWARD COUNTY, ARKANSAS, FRIDAY, SEPTEMBER 5, 1902. No. 34

THE LOCKESBURG ENTERPRISE.

O. T. GRAVES OWNER. LOCKESBURG, ARKANSAS, WEDNESDAY. OCT. 5, 1910 32nd

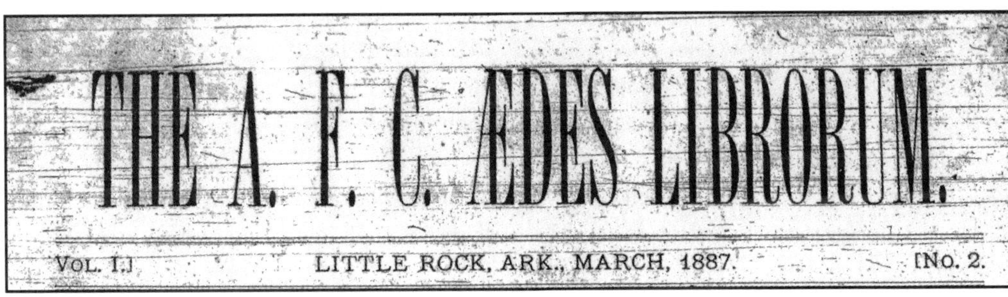

THE A. F. C. ÆDES LIBRORUM.

VOL. I.] LITTLE ROCK, ARK., MARCH, 1887. [NO. 2.

Washington Telegraph.

OL. XXVIII, Devoted to Internal Improvement, Agriculture, and the Dissemination of General Information. NO.

HN P. ETTER, WASHINGTON, ARKANSAS. WEDNESDAY. DECEMBER 16, 1868. PUBLISHER AND PROPRIET

PIKE CITY CANNON BALL.

PIKE CITY, PIKE COUNTY, ARKANSAS, AUGUST 7, 1897.

size.[393] A 1901 examination of his books showed that subscribers owed him $700, "a princely sum of money for a struggling country editor."[394] Erwin Funk recalled that early in the 20th century one Benton County publisher whose newspapers claimed a circulation of 2,000 told him he had only received $400.00 on subscriptions.

Nineteenth-century editors were among the leaders in institutionalizing the celebration of Christmas, complete with gift-giving, Santa Claus, and hymns and carols. Across Arkansas the popularity of the celebration varied greatly. Plantation areas and towns led the way, but conservative Protestants in the rural areas were not convinced. Indeed, the pioneer Christmas of the 19th century was no Christmas at all.

Even before the Civil War, the Christmas tree appeared in Fayetteville, and, increasingly, the dictum found in Louisa May Alcott's *Little Women*, that it would not be Christmas without presents, caught the attention of editors. In the rural areas, where for a half-century the standard purchased gift for a child was an orange, there was less to promote. Well into the 20th century, rural celebrations were times of community gathering. "A box supper given Saturday night at Battle Axe to raise funds for a Christmas tree brought $42.75," the *Swifton Sentinel* reported in 1910, "Quite a great deal of spirit was displayed—some boxes selling for as much as $5.00."[395]

Small-town editors tried to energize their merchants into both acquiring gift items and then advertising them in the newspaper. New York cartoonist Thomas Nast was one of the major protagonists of Santa Claus, and it was another editor, writing in the *New York Sun* in 1897, whose "Yes, Virginia, there is a Santa Claus" response to the question of Santa's existence gave the journalistic seal of approval to the custom.

By the beginning of the century, editors began running children's letters to Santa, and some unknown young child usurped Fannie Borland's place as Arkansas's youngest published author. Completing the picture was the distribution of special Christmas inserts that contained the music of Christmas hymns and carols. These were provided from the ready-print suppliers. The great turn-of-the-century popularity in sending Christmas cards prompted many newspapers to print personalized cards for the wealthier classes. Youthful printer Dee Brown got his first job because Tom Newman at Harrison needed someone to help print the cards.[396] As it turned out, Brown had to work the square getting orders from local businesses. Indeed, by the century's end, American merchants were passing out calendars and other printed items mass produced in Germany or the east but personalized at the local printer's.

Either New Year's or the newspaper's anniversary was a good time to remind readers to pay up. One way to go after delinquent subscribers was to sue, but publishers who thought they planned to stay in the community preferred gentle persuasion. "It is the home paper that keeps the people of the community in touch with others by giving them all the news of their own neighborhood and country. For that alone they are of value and worth far more than the small subscription price," the *Tuckerman Times* cut from an exchange.[397]

Occasionally, a publisher got aggressive. Harry Lee Williams, on disposing of the *Times* at Jonesboro and planning to start up the *Tribune*, placed the names of all his deadbeats in the hands of the Sprague Collection Agency of Chicago. Perhaps it was the out-of-town name or their less-than-friendly warnings, but, "By the time a subscriber received the third letter he began to entertain the fear that his favorite mule would be attached, and, grabbing his hat, hastened to the newspaper office to pay." One man from Buffalo Lick, 20 years in arrears, came in and paid it all. The editor thought that anyone doing that ought to get the newspaper free for the rest of his life, but the man shouted, "I don't want the damned thing!"[398]

Although the cash system was discussed, the prevailing practice both of the weeklies and of the *Gazette* and *Democrat* remained sending the newspaper until the subscriber ordered it stopped. In 1908, a number of newspapers adopted the policy of stopping delivery if the subscriber did not promptly renew, and, the historian reported, "nearly all have been gratified at the result."[399]

A growing sense of professionalism in the 20th century prompted Erwin Funk to take aim at confessions of editorial poverty designed to entice readers to pay up. Funk, who campaigned ceaselessly for editors to be businessmen, thought it "an insult to the newspaper fraternity" and a "decidedly poor advertisement from any viewpoint" to confess to poverty: "The public hates a loser; don't forget that, and put up a bluff that will at least make you look like a winner in your own paper."[400]

The vital statistics of Arkansas newspaper life were recorded in creation and failure. In 1870 there were 56 newspapers, almost all but a handful being weeklies; in 1885 the numbers stood at 10 dailies and 147 weeklies. The year 1909 represented the high water mark, with 315 assorted publications (early estimates included monthlies and quarterlies). Probably half of the 19th-century newspapers lasted less than two years. R.W. Leigh, who rejoiced in writing obituaries for the APA's Proceedings, noted, "The *Echoing Nemesis* of Eureka Springs has ceased to be a rebounding avenger in religion and politics and its little toes are snugly tucked beneath the daisies." In Izard County, he reported that the "rather rapid transit" of the *Franklin Tidings* which had passed through three owners in less than 40 days. Another newspaper in that county was the *Magnet*, established in Newburg, "'to fill a long felt want.'" Failing to draw subscribers, it moved to Oxford where it became the *New Magnet*: "Result—the green grass grows over its grave and there is no cash on hand to buy a tomb to mark its last resting place. I pause for tears."[401]

There were so many of these failures that one essayist took the association historian to task for recording only "his start and his finish, whether he is a member of the Association or not."[402] Left out, the essayist complained, were the yearly accomplishments of living newspapers. Nevertheless, virtually the only basis for determining what was going on in the state came from this source. Early historian J.N. Smithee could carry it all in his head; by 1904, historian T.M. Woods explained that he mailed out inquiries and got about a 50 percent return. In that year, there were seven suspended newspapers and 13 start-ups. One of the suspensions, he noted, came because "the proprietor had a horror of dying rich; hence he decided to give up the newspaper business on that account."[403]

Burton Bunch, the APA's orator in 1916, addressed his problems at Lead Hill:

> It is, really, a town. You can find it on the maps. Some maps. On Boone county maps. It is a small dot there, but to those of us who live there for years, it almost is the universe. It has done much for me. It as given me a wife who is kind enough to continue as such for six years; it has given me a father-in-law who is very accomodating; it has fed me many country cured, hickory-smoked hams and it has given me thousand of hours of good bass fishing. And best of all, it has given me a newspaper experience such as few other men in the world have had. That's why I sold out![404]

In reality, too many editors ignored the business side. Taking produce might have fed the editor's family, "but it was an awful wrestle to get the cash to redeem the ready-print from the express office, or pay printers the balance of their wages not taken out in trade at the stores."[405]

A run of hard luck, the death or illness of an editor, or a change in local politics could produce either a closing or a consolidation. In a consolidation, the competitor bought the name, good will, and subscription list, but not always the plant. When the *Searcy Times* suspended in 1905, former *Times* editor W.C. Dungan kept enough material for his job office, but the rest went to J.J. Baugh of the *Citizen*. "Short crops and hard times" was the reason why the *Times* failed.[406] By the end of the 20th century most newspapers in Arkansas presented a tangled genealogy.

Few newspapers ever foretold their planned demises, but the *Bingen Social Visitor*, founded and published by merchant J.R. Wolf in a small Hempstead County hamlet, ended its 26-year career on December 23, 1910. In between the news that Thomas Willard had dressed 663 pounds of pork and a report on a planned Confederate reunion, Wolf wrote his newspaper's obituary: "There wil be no issue of the VISITOR next week. Likely under its present management it will not resume publication. All who are behind in their subscriptions will please pay. Those who have paid in advance will have amounts due them refunded."[407] Thus ended the newspaper history of Bingen.

The newspaper business was not healthy, either financially or physically. J.W. Clyde, founder of the *Chicot Times* (1871) died of yellow fever in the fall of 1873. That feared killer mostly was limited to the outbreaks of 1873 and 1878; but tuberculosis remained the industry's greatest problem. One prominent late 19th-century victim was D.A. Brower, who edited the *Arkansas Gazette* during the late 1880s and early 1890s. After his death in Colorado on July 18, 1892, the newspaper sent a floral wreath showing a floral design of the figure "30."[408]

In 1908, APA president William E. Spencer of the *Clarendon Sun* missed being able to give the annual address in person. "I had fallen a victim to the great white plague," he explained, and after suffering a hemorrhage of the lungs, turned his newspaper over to his brother-in-law, W.T. Bonner, and, since Arkansas had no sanitariums, moved to Colorado.[409] Another victim of the plague, J.W. Adams of the *Pine Bluff Graphic*, moved to Albuquerque, New Mexico, where he recovered and later returned to Arkansas in 1906.[410] The last case known to the author was that of Edward Raymond "Marty" Stafford at the *Springdale News*, who lost one lung to the disease and spent the years from 1937 to 1945 recovering at Booneville and in Arizona.

The besetting problem, especially with printers, remained an addiction to strong drink. In Little Rock, "Paradise Alley," the narrow walkway in back of the building the *Gazette* occupied between 1887 to 1908, "was famous in song and story—between drinks—and in police annals, as well as in newsboy history," Allsopp recalled.[411] At the start of the Spanish-American War, a patriotic printer began organizing a company of volunteers. A newspaper notice mentioned that by the next Monday the company would be "full," and, recalled Fred Allsopp, "a number of the captain's volunteers were gloriously drunk before the time mentioned."[412] Among rural journalists, W.A. Wenrick lost a hand in a printing accident while under the influence of alcohol. His subsequent abstinence oath was long remembered in Marshall.[413]

"Curls, Crinoline, Chignon and Calico"

When Opie Read introduced a female typesetter into his first novel, he was merely confirming what had already happened around the state. Female typesetters, "with all the appliances of curls, crinoline, chignon and calico," appeared in Little Rock in 1871.[414] From then until Linotype machines temporarily displaced them after 1900, an increasing number of women found work in this branch of printing.

One of the first women to undertake more advanced work was Mrs. George L. Brown, whose husband founded the *Ozark Banner* in 1874. Even before his death from tuberculosis in May 1876, Mrs. Brown "conducted the editorial department of the paper with signal ability." That summer Mrs. Brown became the first woman admitted to membership of the Arkansas Press Association. She continued the *Banner*, marrying printer J.W. Cummins, but Ozark was a small town and the newspaper was "stricken with the disease on non-support, a disease that used to be epidemic amongst country newspapers" and died.[415]

Other women editors appeared as well. Sallie Robinson-Stanfield, the first hypenated woman in the state known to this author, edited the *Cleveland County Herald* at Rison during the 1890s. Her husband, W.J. Stanfield, assumed management in 1897. After his death in 1906, she sold the concern but bought it back in 1912, selling it four years later when she married J.C. Riley of the *Walnut Ridge Blade*. Erwin Funk spoke of her as one of Rison's "best loved citizens," while Allsopp observed that she "not only edited the paper and managed the business, but she educated her children in the printing and newspaper business."[416]

The first woman to edit a daily in Arkansas was Miss Louise Payne. Sam E. Marrs, who had purchased the *Democrat* at Fayetteville from the Moore brothers, started in 1893 "a delightfully bright and newsy little daily" under her direction.[417] Others active at the turn of the century included Mrs. Sue L. James and Miss Willie Hicks. Nanna Wood, another Northwest Arkansas journalist, assisted "the great luminary of Northwest Arkansas [H. L. Cross], to scatter the Italian Climate broadcast in our beautiful state."[418] Miss Wood read a paper on women in journalism at the 1897 APA convention, perhaps because the year before it had been suggested that females be excluded from membership.

After Cross gave up the *Sun* to come to Little Rock, his daughter, Mrs. Frank Peel, continued its publication until selling out to W.H. Plank at the *Democrat*. According to her,

There was a pretty editress,
Who pushed a facile pen;
In news work she achieved success
Surprising to mere men;
But as she wrote there came desire
To bake a cherry pie,—
To sit and crocket by the fire,—
Which made her heave a sigh.
The call of home became too strong
For woman to resist;
She sold her paper for a song
To her antagonist;
Then gratified her heart's desire
With matrons smart to vie
In knitting by the cheerful fire,
Or making cherry pie.

Informed sources, however, reported that Mrs. Peel "not only cannot bake a pie, but never was in a kitchen in her life."[419]

Daughters sometimes followed the trade of their fathers. The indomitable Valentine Dell ("he could never be bribed to hide or distort the truth") was assisted from 1879 to 1885 by his daughter.[420]

The Progressive impulse of the early 20th century found expression in Ada A. Hite of the Fort Smith *City Item*. Her father, R.C. Hite, formerly of the *Memphis Appeal* and after the Civil War of the *Public Ledger*, relocated to Clarksville after the yellow-fever epidemic, and then became a founder of the Fort Smith *News-Record*. At age 73 a daily became too much for him, so he established the *City Item*. Father Hite was fearless in the cause of prohibition, but his daughter, a shut-in after a crippling accident, did much of the work. Among her projects were supporting the public schools, maintaining the cemetery, and adding the Colored Annex to Sparks Memorial Hospital (named for the pioneering Fort Smith journalist).[421] She continued the newspaper for decades after her father's death.

The usual process by which women attained prominence was when a husband's death brought the widow into the office. Mrs. Adah Roussan, the relict of Leon (APA president, 1893), was not only postmistress of Osceola but also, in Funk's judgment, "one of the best known and brightest newspaper women of the southwest." When she gave the annual oration at the 1915 APA meeting in Harrison, "What is the Matter with Arkansas?" she offered a sophisticated analysis on both the economic and cultural aspects of Arkansas's failure to thrive, starting with the absence of a state pride.[422]

The state-pride theme was not new. Robert Ward Johnson called attention to it after the Civil War, and William M. Quesenbury's poem on Arkansas offered analysis and solutions. For many Americans, the joke book *On a Slow Train through Arkansas* (1903) or the story, music, and print of the Arkansas Traveler defined what was still called the Bear State even if bruins were extinct. Perhaps for that reason, many Arkansas news stories reflective of pioneer conditions were reprinted around the nation.

The Big Story

A late 19th-century editor spelled out what it took to put out a proper newspaper:

> All a fellow has to do is to be able to write poems, discuss the tariff and money questions, umpire a baseball game, report a wedding, saw wood, describe a fire so that readers will shed their wraps, make a dollar do the work of ten, shine at a dance, measure calico, abuse the whiskey habit, test whiskey, subscribe to a charity, go without meals, attack free silver, defend bi-metalism, sneer at snobbery, wear diamonds, invent advertisements, overlook scandal, appraise babies, delight pumpkin

---

The Perils of Being an Editor

John P. Stafford of the *Springdale News* was one of the most modern-looking editors in Arkansas. But he was also active in Springdale's Christian Church. This is what he heard from one reader:

> Ozark, ark, 6/29.1893
> John P. Staford
> Springdale ark. Sir.
>
> When you became partner with Mr. Renner, I told him not to send me the News any longer, not but what I did not like to aid him in any way I could, but because I did not want anything to do with you, or your newspaper and that I should advise my friends to let the News severely alone. I hope you will understand that I consider you too exceedingly filthy for me to even allow your little Campbellite* Sheet to enter my house. You can send your paper to some of your rotten egg fraternity of the Campbellite* Sect, but I warn you not to send it to me again. Remember I stand just where I told to your face.
>
> D.C. Hardin

*The term *Campbellite* referred to either to members of the conservative Church of Christ or the more liberal Disciples of Christ (Christian Church), and for over a century constituted "fighting words."

---

raiders, minister to the afflicted, heal the disgruntled, fight to the finish, set type, mold opinion, sweep the office, speak at prayer meetings and stand in with everything and everybody.[423]

Still at the heart of the editor's arsenal were his exchanges. Copies of other newspapers were obtained by sending out copies to those who would reciprocate. As a result, some stories took their time in getting around. By the early 20th century, editors came to prefer paragraphs rather than the long editorial columns of days past. The front page slowly lost its advertising, but the second page was still where state and local news was concentrated. The third page was given over to business notices and lesser local stories. Advertisements and canned material, plus any overflow, ended up on the last page. Country correspondents' columns could be found everywhere.

The weekly grind of writing and collecting locals, cutting articles from exchanges, and writing editorials could all change without warning if a big story broke. Then the coverage the newspaper gave the event became critical to its reputation. "Kidnappers Write Mr. C.C. Hachett; 'The Death Gang' Threaten to 'Blind' Walker Hatchett and to Dynamite and Burn Mr. Hachett's Property," ran a headline in the *Leslie News*.[424] White County in 1876 made national news when the Cobbites, a fanatical religious group, reacted to legal proceedings against them by cutting off a head and posting it on their property.[425]

Tornadoes, fires, and floods led to record sales, if the newspaper itself was not among the victims. The cyclone of May, 1898, that swept through Washington County warranted an entire page under the headline, "Terrible Tornado Sweeps Through the Country Near Springdale." The *News* managed to get three woodcuts illustrating damaged buildings.[426]

The late 19th century saw the rise of the penny press in the big cities. Geared to the masses and filled with stories of sordid sex and violence, the penny press influenced Arkansas editors. One Little Rock weekly of the 1890s was the *Tribune*. Editor K.O. Gould, a former *Gazette* foreman and "a fearless slinger of picturesque English," on one occasion was soundly battered by an irate woman armed with an umbrella.[427] Criminal trials in particular excited editors. O.C. Ludwig at the *Clarksville Enterprise* in 1883 printed the complete speeches of the attorneys in the celebrated case of the *State v. Jim and Coon Warren*.[428] Publishing pictures of criminals was an expense editors felt to be justified. Capital punishment was carried out by hanging, and hangings were public, attracting crowds that numbered in the thousands. While the penny press pandered to the public's prurient interests, some Arkansas editors were appalled. Opie Read told the story of a woman who spent all day in the hot sun with a babe in arms in order to see a hanging. While she was intent on the spectacle, the child died.

One of the most conspicuous aspects of late 19th-century reporting was in the treatment of racial news. Over and over, blacks were treated as subhuman. Even the Hot Springs *Citizens Bulletin*, a progressive organ, in exposing conditions at the local poor house, played the race card. "Young Girl Locked in with Lunatics, One a Naked Negro," ran the newspaper headline."[429] When, in the early 20th century, Governor Jeff Davis preached genocide, he was merely fulfilling the rhetoric too many editors had come to deploy in their everyday coverage of news events involving blacks.

The late 19th-century editor also believed in giving readers not only what they wanted but what the editor liked. Erwin Funk, who enjoyed traveling, wrote lengthy reports on his trips, as did other wandering editors. Funk had a sister who was a missionary in China. Her journal appeared in the *Rogers Democrat* as well, justified, no doubt in the editor's mind, by the knowledge that foreign missions were all the rage in churches.

Many editors of weekly newspapers doubled as "stringers" for a variety of state and regional metropolitan newspapers. Hence, earth-shaking events not only appeared in the next week's newspaper, but also caused the editor to rush to the telegraph office and file perhaps as many as three reports. The income derived from this work kept many a small-town editor afloat financially as well as connected to the larger journalistic world. To take but one example, Effie Giacomini, the wife of Thomas Paul Giacomini of the *Graphic* at Clarksville, also worked for the *Arkansas Gazette*, the *Arkansas Democrat*, the Fort Smith *Times Record* and *Southwest American* as well as the Associated Press. In addition, she wrote a column and had her own radio show.

Enter the Country Correspondent

One of the important developments of the late 19th century was the rise of regular rural correspondents. This idea spread slowly in Arkansas at first. Typical for the 1870s was having a traveler—usually a lawyer or merchant—report on the state of the crops from some remote part of the county. If something unusual happened, it might prompt a reader to write a letter, but even deaths and marriages outside the editor's purview were infrequently covered. All this changed by the 1880s and 1890s.

One probable explanation for the delayed development of an institution already common in the Midwest and North is that, in the first decade after Reconstruction, the Democrats allowed the public school system to collapse. "I know of no subject, except politics, that receives as much attention as education," one writer observed.[430] During the 1880s schools made a comeback, and the largely male teaching corps seem to have been prime candidates for writing local news. A second factor was the greatly improved postal system with new post offices appearing every few miles. While this made it easier for correspondents to get their reports in, it also meant an increased circulation for daily newspapers. "It is useless to try to compete with the metropolitan papers" for general news, Springdale's John P. Stafford concluded in 1904. Instead, he extended his local coverage to include the two adjourning counties.[431]

A case study in development could be made from the *Mountain Wave* at Marshall. By W.A. Wenrick's first full year, 1898, the *Wave* had over a dozen writers, "our assistant editors," as he called them.[432] "Will you please admit us to your happy band of correspondents?" asked a would-be correspondent from Duff:

> "We have long been a constant reader and admirer of that newsy paper, the Wave, but have never before attempted to join its circle of correspondents with our mite. So if we make mistakes, gentle reader, please consider our knowledge of newspaper writing as very limited and pass us by; and though we do not pose as a 'Bab' or 'Bill Arp' we shall try to give you a few happenings from our thriving little village. Health is generally good…"[433]

Health, the correspondent from Western Grove noted, was "very good"; at Richland the writer, tired of this standard beginning, started with, "The creek still runs down hill."[434]

The Duff correspondent who mentioned the writings of Bill Arp* showed that this first batch of correspondents had some exposure to wider themes in Southern writing. Such writers often tried their hands at humor. "Jolly" from Snow Ball described a pretty/ugly party. "Miss Maud is much the prettiest, even the old blind man could see that and he has been

* Bill Arp was a popular Southern writer who used provincial speech patterns and wrote in dialect. His stories filled Southern newspapers from the Civil War to the end of the century. *Bill Arp from the Uncivil War to Date. 1861-1903* (Atlanta, 1902) is available electronically.

blind for several years." There were several candidates for ugliest man, but none "of them being able to look half so ugly as Dr. Rumbley, even the Sheriff of Searcy county could not look ugly ... they say that the young Dr. is nearly bald headed and they fear he will finishing combing his hair out."

In contrast to either the elaborate wedding descriptions newspapers used for town society or the increasingly formal notices that correspondents sent in, "Jolly" reported, "The good people of this settlement were alarmed by the news that Mr. Henderson Syniard and Miss Tead Woods had been pronounced husband and wife. This wedding strictly shocked one young man in this community. It is now thought that he will recover. The man has our sympathies. He has sold his crop, thinking that he would need the proceeds thereof pretty soon."[435]

Newspapers did not use the correspondents' real names. Instead, there were nicknames. The *Springdale News* had Mulkeepmo, Don't Worry, and Celsus.[436] Most writers took the names of the communities that they covered. Speculation sometimes flourished, especially when two reported on the same event. Romances carried on through these columns were not unknown. Men outnumbered women into the 1920s. "Ladies do not make the best correspondents, although I have some very good ones," John P. Stafford observed in 1904. His favorite correspondent was a young mill hand who had never missed a single issue in five years and whose "items are always well written and are ready for the compositor as soon as they reach the office."[437] By contrast at one newspaper, a badly written local caused the editor to write at the bottom of the copy, "tell this man to learn how to write," which message the compositor set in print.[438]

While most editors rewrote the copy before sending it to the printer, others did not. Compositors and later Linotype writers hated setting the unedited originals. Written on cheap tablet paper supplied by

the newspaper, they were often filled with grammatical mistakes. Dee Brown wondered why the Newmans at the *Harrison Times*, who edited all their other writers, avoided the entries from the Bear Creek correspondent. Brown learned why when the correspondent came into town for a new supply of paper and envelopes: "She was wearing a man's leather jacket with cartridge loops on the sides and I could see the brass heads of cartridges sticking out of them. Her checked skirt was not quite long enough to conceal a peg leg. I learned from John that the correspondent had lost her leg in a gun battle that developed during a family feud up near Bear Creek. From that day I always set her letters with great care, letting the participles dangle and the misspelled words stand as she wrote them."[439]

Teacher-correspondents could hardly avoid discussing the state's woeful educational system. "Daisy," the Western Grove correspondent for the *Wave*, had opened her school and openly advertised: "Come all young men and young women who are longing for an education. We have kind hearted people who will help you. Surely there is not a sensible young man or woman but what had rather have an education than not to have. Listen, if you will; most every day we hear some one say, 'I wish I could call back the past; I would go to school and obtain an education.'" For good measure, she gave the names of her new scholars and their families.[440] By contrast, the 1882 correspondent from Roller's Ridge for Bentonville's *New Bentonian* (the successor to the *Bentonian* but which later reverted to the first title), had no news: "No school to report. Our school house got burned down a week or two ago, and we will have to rebuild."[441]

John P. Stafford, who advised his colleagues to use teachers as correspondents, added this caveat,"if you can get one who does not want to consume all his [*sic*] space in writing of school matters."[442] Stafford was a pioneer in organizing his correspondents, holding on August 1, 1906, the first meeting of the *Springdale News* Correspondents' Association.

The country correspondents were an important part in the rise of American democracy. Antebellum newspapers had been so concerned with politics that the day to day doings of plain people rarely made it into print. Country correspondents, however, were encouraged to report everything. Pleas Reeves at Duff got his name in the newspaper for having a new stone chimney erected: "Pleas said he was tired of holding his chimney on his shoulder."[443] Births, marriages and deaths were certain to be recorded as well as the openings and closings of schools and the results of revivals. A good country correspondent could produce an excellent obituary.

The historical value of these contributions caught the attention of Powell S. Carden in his 1898 speech at the annual meeting: "Frequently it is through the efforts of the intelligent correspondent that some idea is obtained of the beliefs and superstitions held by the rural population relative to political, ecclesiastical, or social questions."[444] The newspaper with a well-developed system of correspondents found another circulation benefit. Many who moved away kept their subscriptions to "the old home paper."[445]

There were, however, some things reserved to the editor. "No editor except those who wait for all things, need ever work with a loose waistband to his trousers," S.A. McNish, who tried his hand with newspapers at Stamps and Beebe, told APA members in 1899, "He is the recipient of the seasons first and best fruits and a three line local brings more to his table."[446] The first flowering of cotton required strong proof. Some farmers tried to pass off althea (rose of Sharon) on city-bred editors. Then came the first bale of cotton ginned. Across much of the state there was a better than even chance that a black man might win that honor; if so, it would be one of the few times outside of a lynching that a white newspaper would put his name in print.

Rural correspondents added to the South's stock of *lusus naturae* (freaks of nature): a common hen egg that came with a handle or if it displayed the letter "W" was proof of a coming war; snake stories came in abundance. The Duff correspondent reported: "The spider question has been settled, but there is another one even more serious."[447] "I can still visualize old Henry Lollar, who lived south of the S curve on the Greenland Road (South School Avenue)," recalled one-time Fayetteville newspaper boy Arthur Friedman, "on his way to the paper office with a huge turnip nestling in a homemade basket slung on his arm, determined to convince the editor that it was the largest one grown, not only in Fayetteville, but Washington County as well."[448]

There were historical mysteries as well. A long-lost Spanish mine supposedly existed on the north side of White River near Eureka Springs, according to one I.N. Yontsler, alias Ike Carson.[449] The increasingly religious hegemony found expression in the alleged discovery of the famous petrified man of Pike County, whose sin had been to go fishing on Sunday. "The story, though a little fishy, is seriously told and is believed by many," the *Standard* reported, "A number of persons were foolish enough to get on their horses and start at once to see the miracle."[450]

One drawback to the correspondents was that

the editor was responsible for their comments. The Reverend-editor J.D.C. Cobb, the "Nestor of Northeast Arkansas journalism," was visited shotgun in hand by an irate farmer from Brookland who took exception to a correspondent's joke about his daughter. Fortunately, the staff disarmed the man. Cobb refused to reveal the correspondent's name, as did Harry Lee Williams when a justifiably enraged husband from the New Haven community, pistol in hand, stormed the office after a correspondent reported the man, who had married an unwed mother, was "raising children on the halves."[451] To avoid such situations, some editors, like John P. Stafford, edited out anything likely to give offense.[452]

By 1900, the mark of a good newspaper was its size and content. The *Rogers Democrat* of Emanuel and Erwin Funk started as a seven-column folio on four pages. Then it went to eight columns on eight pages. At that point, it became desirable to acquire a Linotype machine, just like the metropolitan newspapers used. The *Democrat* also started paying its correspondents.[453] On March 9, 1916, Funk apologized to readers. Two rules at the *Democrat* had been broken: an advertisement had appeared on the first page, and a country correspondent had been carried over until the following week. "The advertisers came too strong for us" was the reason for these lapses.[454] In short, the good newspaper by 1916 looked nothing like those of two decades earlier. At the opposite extreme, there still remained the four-page, six-column, patent-insides newspaper with few correspondents and little local news that was struggling to survive.

Since Arkansas was and remained one of America's most rural states, the country press remained strong. "Here's to the country press!" proclaimed the young John P. Stafford in 1898, "May it grow apace until it becomes powerful enough to crush all foes of liberty, truth, and justice, and help to usher in the era of human brotherhood, wherein peace and love shall be the dominant elements in an enlightened, truly cultured civilization."[455] Unfortunately, despite successes, it never attained fully Stafford's vision.

Opie Read and the Arkansas Country Editor

No one knew more of the ways of journalism than writer Opie Read, and the two novels he wrote based on his Arkansas years offer illuminating insights and potent descriptions on the way things were when the lines between the country and metropolitan press were just emerging.[456]

The first of these, *Len Gansett*, was set in a fictional "village consisting of a dozen dwellings, three rude storehouses, and the office of the 'Weekly Picket,'" which consisted of "rough oak boards, set up endwise. The house had been built when the lumber was green, and the consequent shrinkage had left cracks so large that the editor was never placed under the necessity of raising a window for want of air. A placard on the door bore the following announcement: 'Having purchased a complete outfit of latest styles of types, we are prepared to do all kinds of job printing.' A strong man, at one load, could have carried away all the types owned by the Hon. Mr. Dockery, yet the editor was prepared to do all kinds of work. The hand-press was old and battered, and the 'cases,' judging from their ancient appearance, might have been used in Jacobite garets in the reign of William III."

Editor Dockery tried somewhat unsuccessfully to distinguish himself with his homespun surroundings. He "wore jean trousers and a sort of linsey waistcoat, but his coat was 'store made.'" Of his subscribers he said: "There is nothing in this world so unreasonably exacting as a man's subscribers. They expect him to be a saint, and at the same time be familiar with all phases of sin; damned if they do, damned if they don't." Advertisers gave trouble as well: "'See that man?' (pointing); 'well, he's another enemy of printers' ink. Ever since I started the "Picket" he has been an advertiser. In the last issue of my paper I thoughtlessly placed another merchant's ad. above his, and, sir, he 'kicked' like Adam's off ox. I wouldn't have minded his 'kicking,' but he ordered his advertisement out. How do people exact a man to run a paper when advertisers act that way?" The loss of revenue transcended matters of money: "'Why, sir, a paper without advertisements is a pretence! I wouldn't let such a sheet come into my house. Advertisements are the ballast, while the reading matter are the sails. Without advertisements a paper flops and flounders like a wounded fish—damned if it does, damned if it don't.'"

After Dockery engineered for himself a demand that he run for the legislature, the newspaper passed to the protagonist, Len Gansett. Dockery offered to write "leaders" but Gansett thought otherwise. Dockery exclaimed: "'My dear young man, let me warn you against making such a mistake. A newspaper without a leader is like a man without a coat. What are you going to fill it up with?'

> "'With local news, editorial paragraphs, amusing articles, and careful selections.'"
>
> "'That's very well, but you've got to have leaders. What the people want is strong political articles, mainly on legislative matters. What was it the poet said? " We must legislate, we must legislate, or we must perish."'"

In Read's novel, a local farm girl came to work in the *Picket* office. The printer, who "was known to the Guttenberg trade as 'Hungry Pete,'" undertook her instruction in sorting up her case. At first she could set type only by constant reference to the reprint copy; then she reached the point where she could correct her own galleys. The printing office, editor Gansett declared, "is a great school, as far as it goes, and that its methods are practical, although they are technical. I studied punctuation at school, but I find that the printing-office, in this branch especially, is far better than any school. A good printer, in the matter of punctuation, is better than an ordinary professor."

While many printers never rose above the mechanics of their trade, Gansett nevertheless observed: "whenever a printer attempts to enlarge his sphere he generally succeeds." Frederick Allsopp later agreed with this assessment.[457] Read's old printer took a dimmer view of editors: "A man's that a failure in everything else generally makes a good editor." The veteran tramp printer also reflected Read's own views on Victorian morality, asserting that two-thirds of the Sunday school books "are written by the rattiest old bums—I mean drunkards—who want to raise a stake. I know a fellow who writes dime novels half the week, and Sunday-school books the other half."

Read also had his characters reflect on the value of the delinquent tax list. "It keeps us moving," the printer observed, "Used up nearly all the sorts in the office." To the complaint that setting it was "dry work," the printer replied: "Dry to the reader but pretty moist to the publisher."

Later in the novel, the first editor, now out of politics, returned to town and started a second newspaper. The *Eagle of Freedom* set up shop in a weather-boarded shed with a dirt floor: "A number of people who knew the pinched condition of Dockery's finances were surprised when the prospectus of his new newspaper appeared; but they need not have been, for Dockery, when he had not money enough to do anything else, always started a paper."

The novel ends with Gansett married to his female printer, while Dockery is taken in tow by a scheming school teacher, who turned him into a grocer. When the railroad comes to town, all ends happily with a burst of prosperity.

More biographical is Read's other saga of the press, *Emmett Bonlore* (1891). The first part of this novel followed the protagonist's career as editor and proprietor of the *Arkansas Weekly Back-Log*. Based on Read's real-life experiences in Conway (and hence the title *Back-Log* being a tribute to the Conway *Log Cabin*), the novel realistically evokes the world of the country publisher.

Bonlore, a Kentuckian, came to Arkansas after repeated disasters elsewhere. Just after he had written that never before had his newspaper been in so flourishing a condition, it suspended. His second try in another town, although fortified by ready-print, "fell into that yawning gulf whose crumbling edge seems ever near the cast-iron feet of the Washington hand press." His third effort took place in a fictionalized Conway.

Both the plot of the novel and the speeches of this editor/hero reveal, with familiarity and to some extent contempt, the political and economic limitations of the small town. Said Bonlore: "It matters not how deserving of success a man may be, nor what a good influence as an educator his paper may exert, for, let the advertiser suspect that a rival sheet, inferior in everything that goes to make up a newspaper, has a larger circulation, and, immediately losing sight of the former's good qualities, he bestows his patronage upon the latter. This is right, for it is business." Another example of the state of the Fourth Estate came during a train robbery: "What have you got?" demanded one of the robbers. "You compel me to remind you of a joke that the newspapers have worn out," was Bonlore's response, "I haven't anything. I'm a newspaper man."

A second character in the novel, a tramp printer afflicted with a stammer, claimed he could "edge up as many ems as the next man." His pay, eight dollars for two weeks, was spent in buying a new shirt and for "a brief season of convivial stuttering, a deep sleep, a treacherous stomach, and a sensitive head filled with repentant thoughts." The printer's tendency to engage in drunken episodes left Bonlore with no newspaper one week.

Like Read himself, Bonlore soon left the small town for the luster of the city. "I am tired of Rigville," Bonlore exclaimed, "Even if the *Back-Log* were to be successful there, it would, after all, be but a poor achievement. There is but little difference between the failure and success of a country paper."

In Read's case, moving on meant first Little Rock and then Chicago, where he became one of America's most popular (if not very profound) novelists. However, to the end of his life he remained a part of the fraternal world of journalists. As for country editors, more than a few, both in the 19th century and later, did succumb to lure of the city. The 19th-century list is endless, for virtually everyone involved in a city press started in the country. In the 20th century, Guy Stafford became a Los Angeles city editor; Karr Shannon moved from Melbourne to Little Rock; and Tom Dearmore left Mountain Home for Washington and then San Francisco.

In both of Read's romantic novels, editors struggled to become independent of politics and local pressures. In the real world, many newspapers were adjuncts of small printing offices or the editors were local politicians, often lawyers, whose interest in journalism waned after election time.

Off on a Lark

The ceaseless monotony of the office could be broken by attending the meetings of the Arkansas Press Association. Although supported largely by state press and the larger weeklies, the Association reached out to the country editors. "We would like very much to attend and get acquainted with the boys," explained the *Russellville Siftings* in 1895, "but as the requisite $7 for membership fee is not forthcoming, we will have to decline this year with a promise to be with the boys in '96."[458] Other than a single issue, no other record exists of this newspaper.

The young people who flocked from other states to open newspapers in Arkansas readily joined the

APA in order to make or renew ties of friendship, while the old timers enjoyed celebrating their ancient rivalries. Meetings provided a place for camaraderie, and thanks to the free railroad passes, the excursions, for those who could afford the time, were nearly a free vacation. So great was the desire to attend these meetings that Thomas Newman, the founder of Boone County's press, gained the nickname "the great walking editor" for hoofing it half way across the state to attend APA conventions.

Only as the century drew to a close did these meetings become family affairs. Elbert Smithee, who accompanied his father to the 1884 Fayetteville convention, complained to his mother that things were "awfully dull." Apparently, the debate, banquet, and ball or even an excursion to Eureka Springs failed to interest him. However, "there are more dogs here than I have ever seen; on the street, in front of the hotel are about twenty dogs fighting and playing."[459]

One of the problems facing APA members on their late-19th-century excursions was having their luggage labeled "APA." Those initials also stood for the American Protective Association, an anti-immigration, anti-Catholic group. Some railroad porters of Irish extraction, believing the excursionists were part of this group, sabotaged the baggage.[460]

One of the worst experiences befell Dr. M.M. McGuire of the *Independent Arkansian* of Dardanelle. While this future APA president (1881-1882) was attending the APA convention in 1875, his partner, D.P. Cloyd, and Captain R.W. Wishard had a "personal difficulty" over a paragraph that had appeared in the newspaper. Cloyd killed Wishard but was acquitted by a jury. Then McGuire's newspaper office was destroyed by fire in 1876, and the doctor was seriously injured trying to save it.[461]

The APA increased the opportunity to attend by holding meetings in various parts of the state. Within its first 12 years, the APA had met twice in Searcy and Hot Springs, and once in Arkadelphia, Fort

Smith, and Fayetteville. Such meetings attracted regional attention, not only from the members, but also from the politicians and town leaders who went all-out to entertain and publicize their communities and regions. In subsequent years, the APA met in Helena (1885), Pine Bluff (1886), Texarkana (1888), Bentonville (1889), Batesville (1891), Camden (1892), Mammoth Spring (1895), Springdale (1896), and Paragould (1897). Perhaps the most unusual meeting was that of 1904, held in the Arkansas World Fair Building in St. Louis. "A State, a town, a city, a people can be judged by its press," J.N. Smithee intoned in 1885, and each meeting was invariably followed up by articles in the press discussing the communities the editors had seen.[462]

As part of that commitment, the APA met in joint session with other state bodies. The 1898 meeting at Eureka Springs was one of the most exciting. This was a tri-state meeting with Missouri and Texas. There had been tornadoes and heavy rains. The White River, which had to be crossed to reach Eureka Springs, was at flood stage and the railroad bridge was believed to be weakened and unsafe for the heavy Pullman cars from Texas. Although some went back, others were transferred over the bridge on flatcars pulled by handcars in an operation that took three hours. Some men walked from the bridge to the spa, as railroad flares lighted the way. Eventually, some 300 people managed to reach the Crescent Hotel. Among them was banquet speaker Walter Williams, later the founding dean of journalism at the University of Missouri and three other future presidents of the National Editorial Association.[463]

The APA's programs sought to instruct and improve as well as entertain. "Most convention programs," Erwin Funk recalled, "were heavy with long essays on the glories of the quill and pen and the insistence that the editor was the real leader of every community, even though the poorest paid."[464] Early on the redoubtable Peter Donan, whose oratory on the meaning of a newspaper soared to Olympian heights, laid down four rules that newspapers should follow. First, "we should put our business on a business footing," and not be "dead-head pack mules" for other's political or economic schemes. Second, "Stop the abuse of each other." Third, was to "abolish the system of indiscriminate puffery." And last, was to "squelch the dead-beat advertisers."[465] Particularly valuable technical advice for editors who were novices to printing came from Louis B. Audigier, who explained type and press workings and gave useful suggestions such as urging printers to buy from only one foundry as no two manufacturers ever made their type exactly the same size. Audigier brought country printers into the world of the Hoe Lightning Press and the Bulloch Web Press.[466]

The 1886 convention also offered Jacob Frolich, Jr.'s essay, "How to Run a Country Newspaper," that ran the entire gambit of blows the country editor faced. The first requirement was a well-printed newspaper. "A good roller boy is an artist," Frolich noted. The first page should contain miscellaneous reading matter with "plain but distinct head lines to all articles over a half column in length" as well as several columns of advertisements. The second page would feature editorials "long and short," in from two to four columns. Frolich favored "wholesome articles upon State policy," that were based on "good grounds, and have patriotic tendencies." Denouncing abuse, he exhorted, "The editor that deals in these unholy and heartless sayings, who craves scandal, delights in throwing mud at any one prominent, simply because it is in his power to do so, will find, when perhaps too late to amend, that 'man reaps as he sows.'" Frolich recommended copying the well-expressed thoughts of others to supplement the editor's own opinions.

The third, or local, page "should be the pride of all connected with the office—stop the press at any time to insert a local occurrence." That page should list the "movements of everybody and everything;" a country editor, Frolich insisted, "can never weary the reader or tire his eyes with local news." Endorsing country correspondents, he told editors to "dress them up," and eliminate "their effusions as we would any other matter," especially those "likely to produce unkind feelings or do harm."

Frolich advised editors that "A considerable use of adjectives" about friends and advertisers might cause a "fried partridge to light on his table." He also called for agricultural articles, Sunday readings, and funny sayings—as long as they were chaste. Since the newspaper was "teacher and preacher combined," "Let your paper be freighted with instructive, wholesome and newsy reading matter, and plenty of well-paying advertisements."

The subject of how to get advertisements was a main concern for the country editor. Frolich's advice was to go hunt them up. "People expect to be drummed these days," he noted, adding, "you must walk and talk in the interests of your business."

Unfortunately, Frolich found Arkansas to be full of barely readable sheets set by some "slouch of a printer." "Ink must have been scarce too, or perhaps its rollers were made by Faust & Guttenberg." The roller boy was "evidently a shoemaker's apprentice, and the pressman a blacksmith's help." "Dead stereotype plates" that were "ready to die of shame when an advance-paying subscriber casts a withering glance over the paper," marked a doomed offering, "no matter how high-sounding its name may be."

The heart of shop-talk invariably got around to the matter of money. "Try to collect your accounts monthly," was advice that none achieved then and few could boast of before 1950. Frolich found no problem with accepting a heifer, soap, or produce. Most of all, the editor should be prompt in all his printing, whether in getting out his newspaper or in job printing. Frolich endorsed a clean shop: "Ere you seek joyous recreation, see that all your cases are full—dead jobs distributed, and for pity's sake don't let them stand lose on the stone pieing by piece-meal. Clean the standing galley, oil the bed of the press, see that the rollers are ready for use, for a man might want a job in a hurry. Let your office be in complete order ere you hie yourself to the riverside, even though it be Saturday noon and the fish as reckless as the average Legislator, swallowing unbaited hooks."[467]

Frolich's early effort covered almost all the ground, its main tenets being a fountain of usable quotations and ideas good for at least a century. In time, each of his major topics became the subject of specialized presentations. Even the great Walter Williams, by then Dean of the University of Missouri School of Journalism, who addressed the APA in 1910, could add but little to Frolich's comprehensive treatment.[468]

Some of those present took the advice to heart. In 1905, J. Arthur Livingston (APA president, 1911) of the Russellville *Courier Democrat* implored publishers to insist on having *Inland Printer* or other trade publications in the print shop: "The first time I ever got up courage enough to submit a piece of work to a trades paper for criticism I was surprised to get a favorable comment, and from that day on I began to take a greater interest in my profession and was continually striving to outdo my former efforts."[469] Livingston's insistence of a well-printed newspaper laid the foundations for Russellville becoming an important printing center later in the 20th century.

The single most telling testimonial on the full impact of APA membership came from its 1932 president, Alfred Hawn of the *Madison County Record* at Huntsville. Hawn's career there started in 1892: "My early training was of the crudest sort, in a shop poorly equipped and with a paper variously managed by owners who cared nothing about progress and who were content with meager profits." This he endured for 20 years. "Under the head of the paper my name appeared as Alfred Hawn, publisher. No designation as to editor. Well, I was really correct in the deletion, for the paper didn't even have good publisher." After joining the APA, "I soon began to get a different understanding, different vision; consequently, I placed a very different estimate on the business of publishing a newspaper; I changed my heading to show that Alfred Hawn was also editor of the Record, and ever since I have been proud to be known as Editor Hawn." In addition to "inspiration and edification," Hawn testified to the "invaluable information as to shop work and business management I never could have received otherwise."

One of the ideas he implemented was the cash-in-advance subscription list. It took courage, for of his 1,300 subscribers, 75 percent were in from one to seven years in arrears. Fearful that he might only end up with 500, Hawn actually lost only 50.[470]

For a number of years the APA had the office of Censor. Chosen secretly by the president and secretary in order to "exalt the standard of journalism in Arkansas," the Censor's duty was to criticize the style and arrangements, not the politics, of all the state's newspapers. Later, contests would serve the same goal. The specific results were not part of the printed record, but general criticism was recorded. That one of the principal failings was trying "'to publish a ten-column paper in a six-column town,'"[471] actually speaks highly of the integrity and ambition present in this Golden Age. Indeed, one of the joys of reading the scant surviving copies from this era is that the country press had not yet fallen into a monotonous routine.

Convention attendees would hear other unpleasant truths. Josiah H. Shinn, best known as an educational leader and historian, took his 1885 audience to task for selling out high ideals: "We puff all and every kind of character at one dollar a line. We sell patent medicines that we know are worthless, at fifty dollars a square. We advise our friends in our papers to take the lotions which we would advise him privately to burn. We hesitate to speak unpalatable truths, for fear twenty subscribers will haul off their names. Great Scotland, is this the editorial goal? If so, then order out the hearse and carry me to the graveyard with solemn step and the slowest music."[472]

In the early 20th century a Committee of Awards under Earle W. Hodges was set up, making its first presentations in 1908. There were 25 awards, including one for the "most popular lady at the convention," won by Mrs. Bernie Babcock of *The Sketch Book*. Many of the awards were donated by printers or suppliers. Hence, the *Log Cabin Democrat* won $15 in ready-print sheets for its award-winning essay on "Advantages of Using Ready-Prints." Among the other winners were the *Springdale News*, the "handsomest newspaper in Arkansas," the *Rogers Democrat*, the "neatest all-home-print weekly," and

Erwin Funk, who wrote the best essay on "Why Every Publisher Should be a Member of the Arkansas Press Association."[473]

Funk later recalled that no decent essays on the topic had been written, and he was prevailed upon to produce one overnight. At five o'clock the next morning he was seated at a typewriter at the Old State House, and by nine the piece was finished. Funk appreciated the $10 gold piece, but wondered, "If mine was the best, some of the other stories must have been awful punk." But he was not ashamed of it: "That is the way most good newspaper stories are written, and I probably wouldn't have turned in a better one if they had given me a month."[474]

The goal of elevating the rural press led to the formation of the National Editorial Association (NEA) in New Orleans in 1885. Founder Benjamin Briggs Herbert foresaw that dailies were to become the "gatherers of general news, of great events, and wielders of the destinies of states and nations..." But the community press was equally important, recording "the record of home history and the storehouse from which the true history—and its underlying philosophy—the inward, everyday life of the people and its objects and motives, must be drawn."[475]

This national body, which with the APA had its free railroad excursions in the 19th century, grew in importance. R.W. "Bob" Leigh of the *Morrilton Headlight* was elected executive secretary at the NEA's first convention in Cincinnati.[476] The NEA came to Arkansas for the first time in 1902, meeting in conjunction with the APA. It was Erwin Funk's first NEA convention. Held in Hot Springs at the Eastman Hotel, the convention attracted over 750 attendees. The banquet cost the simply enormous sum of $10 a plate, and, Funk recalled, with seven different wines on the menu, "a number of editors became unduly noisy and in a fight between a colored waiter and a northern publisher, the latter was struck over the head with a wine bottle and spent several days in the hospital."[477] Thereafter Erwin Funk became a major NEA promoter in Arkansas, even venturing to Seattle (including an excursion to Alaska) for the 1909 meeting. The popularity of the group with Arkansas editors increased tremendously. In 1918, the NEA again came to Arkansas, meeting in Little Rock and Hot Springs. Visiting editors got a railroad tour of the state. Later its name was changed to the National Newspaper Association (NNA), but it remained the Washington watchdog for the country press, now defined as the community press.

Although the APA was organized primarily by the Little Rock press and both the *Gazette*'s J.N. Smithee and the *Democrat*'s James Mitchell served as presidents, 29 of the first 43 presidents (1873-1920) were drawn from small-town weeklies. Nevertheless, with each passing year a growing gap separated city and country. At the 1900 meeting, the association passed a resolution requesting the NEA to report on why the metropolitan press "kept aloof" from the NEA.[478] The concern was real. By the middle of the 20th century, many in the metropolitan press corps looked down on the APA as an association of country bumpkins. The *Arkansas Gazette* regularly declined to participate in the APA's Better Newspaper contests on the grounds that they would win all the awards. These tensions did not diminish in the new century.

Conclusion

In his 1899 presidential address, James Mitchell called his audience's attention to some startling statistics. Poor, despised, butt-of-every-cheap-joke Arkansas had a larger number of newspapers according to population and a larger circulation than any other Southern state except Florida and Texas. At least one of the state's 256 publications could be found in every county except Calhoun.[479] Arkansas was proud to be an editor's Land of Opportunity.

Geography and personality determined the fate of country editors. Some towns grew to where sufficient demand existed for a daily. Publishers who entered into that world lost interest in their weekly over time, even as the rural communities that supported weeklies were drawn into the urban vortex and lost both their character and often even their residents. Economic decline hit the Ozarks as early as the 1890s, and timber towns began thinning by the 1910s. Despite the optimistic expectations of editors, only coal and bauxite mining took firm root. Economic decline or stagnation led to newspapers dying off or consolidating.

The strong personalities who shaped the lives of many newspapers also helped give definition to their communities. The first generation often looked quickly for the main chance. Easily disillusioned if rapid success was not easily obtained, they moved on. However, by 1900 Arkansas was becoming populated by men (and some women) who were devoted to their regions and determined to persevere. Erwin Funk, Maud Duncan, John P. Stafford, W.O. Troutt, W.B. Folsom, J.A. Livingston, Frank Robins, Max Hampton, and many more had their foundations laid in the waning years of the Victorian age.

Or, as S.A. McNish phrased it, "God bless all the old pink bald-headed country editors, they are things of beauty and a joy forever. And you dear pretty things, just budding into the ranks of country journalism, may your shadows never grow less on a diet of turnip greens and cord-wood on subscription."[480]

Chapter V

The City Press: Modernization Arrives, 1875-1920

"Newspaper men, by a system of false education, are taught to believe that a scandal is a topic of legitimate discussion. The publication of any matter that tends to make an edition marketable is said to be enterprise. I was taught to believe in the ethics of that school, but I now see how shameful are its precepts."
Opie Read, *Emmett Bonlore* (1891).

"I had been cautioned by Old Dick Johnson to be more careful. He said that a newspaper caught in a lie was worse off morally than a man, in that a newspaper could not blush."
Opie Read, *I Remember* (1939).

"It is a fact that they [newspaper men] are more progressive, and entertain more liberal views, than the great majority of people. They are always found in the advance of every work which tends to promote the intellectual, moral and material interest of the State. They favor and advocate immigration, with a view to settling up our vacant lands; they unite in the advocacy of manufacturing enterprises, the building of railroads, the clearing out of our rivers, the establishment of public schools, and all other projects which will tend to make the State great and powerful."
J.N. Smithee, *Proceedings of the Arkansas Press Association...1877.*

"...a daily paper where everthing is done with a rush and a rattle."
Clio Harper Diary, December 25, 1895.

"There are only two forces that can carry light to all corners of the globe—the sun and the Associated Press."
S.L. Clements (Mark Twain), Speech, September 19, 1906.

Introduction

Revolutionary changes took place in the press between the end of Reconstruction and the beginning of the 1920s. Even as early as 1910 the metropolitan newspaper had achieved a recognizable degree of maturity. Three important aspects present in Arkansas were the rise of the reporter, the modernization of printing, and the independence of the press from politics. Prior to the appearance of radio, the printed word, the "art preservative of all arts," reigned as the *lingua franca*, the universal language, of communication, thanks in large part to a growing literacy. Specialized publications reached out to special-interest groups, ranging from the State Horticultural Society to the students of intriguing puzzles.

All these elements were reflected in the Arkansas Press Association, which retained its premier position as the state's first and most active special-interest body. In place of the few men at those early meetings who mostly were already acquainted with each other, conventions early in the new century had grown to include an ever-increasing number of the country editors, their wives, children, and staff members. The most progressive members of the Association were ready to move beyond socialization and into professionalization.

The Return of a Native

The great antebellum editor William Minor Quesenbury came to grief in Texas after the Civil War. He was out of the newspaper business in Navasota and was probably in trade when the crash hit. "Wm Quesenbury has been sold out House & Home. He is evidently wrecked," Robert Ward Johnson reported to David Walker in Fayetteville, "Neither by work nor credit has he been able to save it." Johnson went on to explain that he and law partner Albert Pike had launched a campaign to raise funds from Cush's former friends. "He is a gentleman & was one of us," he added, in one of the nicest tributes ever made about an Arkansas editor.[481]

The consortium Johnson and Pike put together raised close to $400, and on October 19, 1875, the Shreveport *Caddo Star* reported on Cush's progress: "Inexorable time had left its traces upon his brow, but the same warm impulsive heart beat within his generous bosom as of yore." The editor predicted "his numerous friends will warmly welcome his return. He is an old newspaper man, and one of the spiciest writers we have ever known. Some of his productions in verse will live as long as Arkansas has a history or a literature."[482] And the best was yet to come.

Cush first arrived in Van Buren. "We had not been married a great while when my husband's cousin, William, came one morning to take breakfast with us and stayed eight months," a relative recalled."[483] The reason for this stay was that being sold out in Texas did not end Cush's financial woes. He had signed pre-war surety bonds for and together with George W. Clarke and J.W. Washbourne. With Clarke decamped to Mexico City, where he published a bilingual newspaper, and Washbourne being dead, the federal government came after Cush. A judgment of $33,396 and costs could not be satisfied from Cush's nonexistent estate, and after 1877 he was free but poor.[484]

At least two job offers came in. J.S. Dunham wanted Cush to stay and work in Van Buren for the *Press*, and Elias C. Boudinot offered "chief control" and half the profits of his Vinita newspaper, the *Indian Progress*.[485] Instead, Cush settled in as the art instructor at Cane Hill College, probably in order that his children could attend it. His wife's family seems to have provided him with a house, and with an organ in the parlor and some chickens, hogs, and cattle on the place, Cush made do. He also undertook a number of portraits and scenic views of Arkansas during his tenure there, of which only two survive.

Cush had not been in Arkansas long when Colonel Smithee gave an address on the history of Arkansas journalism at the APA's fifth annual meeting. Cush was not altogether pleased and took out an advertisement addressed to John F. Wheeler at the *Western Independent*:

> President Smithee has acted a noble part toward our profession, that we all, saint or sinner, must acknowledge. (As to the saint qualification used in this expression, I know no typo who could as honestly as yourself strike his ribs just outside his heart and say, "I am he." Let not your face grow redder, father-friend, at this averment.) President Smithee has gathered, systematized and fixed, as if in a geological stratum, the newspaper history of Arkansas. It would be harsh, if not untrue, to say there are fossils in this stratum. Still, are there not some omissions which might or should be explained?

Cush reminded his readers that Wheeler had been associated with the *Arkansas Intelligencer* before moving on to Fort Smith, and Cush took issue with being described as "a spoiled child of genius; "he should have said, to do justice to some others, a 'despoiled child.'" Reprinted by the *Arkansas Gazette*, Cush's advertisement marked his journalistic return to the state.[486]

The result was that the APA forthwith asked Cush to "ascend Parnassus and from thence soar into the cerulian empyrean to catch for us the brightest scintillations of poesy" at the 1878 annual meeting in Hot Springs.[487] Cush spent almost a year getting ready. The meeting ran late, and Cush asked to be excused, but to no avail. Cutting as he read, he gave the delegates a truncated version of his "pome." Even heavily cut, it was, the *Gazette* reported, "filled to overflowing with a brilliant admixture of the humorous and the pathetic, and that peculiarity of sarcasm and invective characteristic of the gentleman."[488]

Delighted by the reception and in no hurry to get home, Cush gave a full reading in Little Rock on July 12. "All who love a good laugh ought to go and hear him," the *Gazette* advised. After the event, the newspaper offered a fuller assessment, noting:

> The pome, then, is a rhythmic satire on many of the follies and vices of the times peculiarly applicable to Arkansas life, together with a strange, weird medley of poetic thoughts, odd fancies and eccentric conceits. It is written in a humorous strain and pleasing style, and is brim full of good hits and happy jeux d'esprits. The Major delivers in with comical expression and grotesque intonation so peculiar to him and which alone can give the desired emphasis and impressiveness to its varied parts. But no description can convey a full idea either of the merits of the pome or the manner of its delivery. To be appreciated they must both be seen and heard together; and as the Major designs to read the pome at various parts of the State, we recommend all who want to enjoy a good thing, and appreciate one of nature's truest and most unsophisticated children.[489]

By September, Cush was in Fayetteville, and prodded by John F. Wheeler he decided to have the work printed in pamphlet form at the *Gazette* job office. The finished project ran to 39 pages, but one wishes Cush had illustrated it as well. J.N. Smithee apparently thought the same, for in 1897, long after Cush's death, he printed the poem in the *Gazette* with illustrations by staff artist Elmer Burrus. These were of the generic order; not the satirical sort Cush would have supplied.[490]

What Cush attempted in his work was a complete history of the state that aimed at resolving the perennial image problem: "What stigma rests on Arkansas?/What crime or foul disgrace upon her?" Along the way he visited the major towns and scenic sights, finding, for example, in Little Rock, the city of roses, "The red is in the ladies' cheeks,—/The men, they wear it on their noses!"

Raising up Arkansas and overcoming these problems was a task for strong editors:

> *And what your hard-earned recompense?—*
> *Much fame "gifts, gold and frankincense?"*
> *No, by the Gods! complaints, advice,*
> *Grumbling at error and "high price,"*
> *Warm censure for "mistaken views"*
> *And, most of all, outstanding dues,—*
> *Dues, paltry in the debtor's head,*
> *To you, your raiment and your bread.*
> *Strange, men of honor will forget*
> *Existence of an honor-debt,*
> *Evade with promises, deny,*
> *And last, when closely cornered, lie!*
> *Delinquent! the disgraceful name*

Of him who only moves by shame
Of strong, nay hot words well burnt in
Like live coals on a terrapin.

Doubtless these were not some of the lines cut at the initial reading. Moving rather like the coda of the last movement of a majestic symphony, Cush arrived at his great apotheosis:

The song is sung—if such it may be called—
As unmethodical, rude, backwoods song
Discordantly discoursed or rather bawled:—
But be it what it may, it will not long
Remain in memories amid the throng
Of busy life pursuits,—a passing flaw
Upon the stream of time,—and, right or wrong,
From it one truth, a rock-truth, we may draw,—
'Tis this: GOD LOVES NOT HIM THAT LOVES NOT ARKANSAS!

Although Arkansas would continue to produce poets of local, regional and even international renown, not one ever stormed these Arkansas Olympian heights. Its closing line took on a new life in the 20th century, appearing in books and on the floor of the Arkansas Senate.

As for Cush, in 1881 he left Cane Hill and settled in Neosho, Missouri. He came back to Arkansas for Albert Pike's last visit in 1884. Pike had avoided Little Rock, his former home, since "the place and people are so changed that I do not like to see it," going to Van Buren instead. Cush came down, and later called it "a time when all were kind."[491]

When Cush died in 1888, there were many outpourings of grief. The neighbor of his last years, M.E. Benton, a noted Democratic politician and the father of painter Thomas Hart Benton, spoke of Cush as "a connecting link between yesterday and today of western and southern history. Well informed, genial, honest, truthful, he was a valued man to use in his age of insincerity. He was typical of a class of good, true men who lived in the '40s and '50s in Tennessee, Kentucky, Arkansas, and Missouri. With no care for the morrow, no desire for acquired wealth, bubbling up with great good humor, faithful to friends."[492] James H. Van Hoose, who had known Cush from the Fayetteville days, cited his love for his native state.[493] The most extensive treatment came from Albert Pike:

> As a writer he was strikingly original, expressing his opinions and fancies in clear, strong, pure, epigrammatic English. He thought well and wrote well when some grotesque conception did not become his master and lead him into extravagancies. I do not know where he got his command of language. No man ever wrote me such letters, so quaint and forcible, so full of acute remarks and bold expressions of opinion, of exuberant mirthfulness and queer fancies and grave reflections and sagacious axioms, expressed in incomparable language.[494]

In retrospect, if the full measure of Cush's output were known, he would rank as one of America's leading newspapermen of the mid-19th century.

The Press and Politics

The "Thou Shall Not" Constitution of 1874 set the course of Arkansas for years to come. Its negativism, most often directed at taxes, effectively terminated public education and state support for economic development. The office of governor, reduced to a term of two years, was rendered largely honorific. Yet for many, Reconstruction had been worse. At the APA's third meeting, President Smithee observed, "We want to forget the past and build up Arkansas. We want to keep pace with the progress of the age, and the press is the great lever after all which must determine whether we will or not."[495]

Although the Democrats came back into power, the election of Augustus H. Garland as governor marked the triumph of a special kind of Democrat. The "New Departure" movement that Garland embodied wished to give a business orientation to the party. Since racist rhetoric cost the South Northern investment and now served no political purpose, New Departure Democrats were willing to preserve African-American constitutional rights, provide them with some public services, and even to welcome them into the party. Most importantly, the New Departure leaders did not support repudiation of the state debt.

The first divisive issue came in 1878, when Robert Ward Johnson attempted to regain his old Senate seat. Johnson had worked hard to thwart Radical Reconstruction and then moved to Washington to practice law and attempt to recoup his lost fortune. He came back to Arkansas after Reconstruction's end only to clash head on with J.D. Walker, the nephew of David Walker and a leading figure from the much-neglected northwest.

The Johnson faction consisted, in the language of the times, of Bourbons, a reference to the last of the French kings, who never learned and never forgot. This representative of the old antebellum planter order enlisted the support of the *Arkansas Gazette*, whose ownership in the late 19th century became a merry-go-round.

William E. Woodruff, Jr., who embraced this group, owned the *Gazette* from 1873 to 1876, when he sold it to W.D. Blocher and John D. Adams. Since neither was a practical newspaper man, they hired James Mitchell to edit the newspaper. Mitchell's father had accompanied Cush to California in 1850, and this son had been one of Cush's students. After serving as a captain in the Confederate army, James Mitchell taught literature at Arkansas Industrial University in Fayetteville. Apparently, 19th-century Arkansas ranked professors above captains, for he remained until death "Prof. Mitchell." He was a chip off the old block. His father, a Cane Hill farmer, had become involved in a long and devastatingly expensive lawsuit simply because he believed it to be right. The son lasted at the "old harlot" 18 months before he and Blocher purchased the upstart competitor, the *Arkansas Democrat*.

That newspaper had started out as the *Evening Star*, with Dan O'Sullivan, the first of crew of colorful Irishmen in Arkansas, at the helm. O'Sullivan earlier had failed with a weekly called the *Chronicle* and had worked for the *Liberal*. Then he had founded the *Evening Star*, which claimed the largest circulation in Little Rock. One of its accomplishments was publishing W.D. Blocker's history of Arkansas's finances, a weighty tome that later appeared as a separate publication. In early 1877 the newspaper passed on to the "quaint and forcible" John McClure, the former chief justice formerly of the *Republican*.[496]

During a time of uncertain editorship, a not uncommon feature of those days, the *Hot Springs Telegraph* had charged the editor, presumably McClure, with being a "sore-head, dyspeptic, erratic radical," and the *Gazette* chimed in, claiming that the *Star* "has nothing to do but snap and snarl at the Democratic party." The *Star* replied: "Slander the Democratic party! That is impossible. We haven't command of language sufficient to do that. This truth is enough. It makes a record of brutality that excites the envy of the Turks, who have for years plundered and murdered the Jews of Romania."[497]

J.N. Smithee, who had left the *Gazette*, acquired the *Star* on April 12, 1878, and renamed it the *Daily Arkansas Democrat*. Smithee then kicked over the traces and called for debt repudiation and endorsed Greenbackism (inflating the money supply through printing paper money)—all suspect positions for the Bourbons. "Take an old man's advise," said John F. Wheeler from Fort Smith, "keep in the broad road of democracy and don't get close to the edge as you have done once or twice."[498] It was advice Smithee failed to heed.

Johnson had the support of the *Gazette*, and he made the rounds in the state, speaking in favor of farmers' issues and running on his long experience and connections. Dispassionate observer Opie Read considered him a man of honor. Walker, who had no record, ran a youth campaign but was known as the nephew of the state's leading Whig. Mitchell at the *Democrat* was one of his strongest supporters.

The election of senators still rested with the legislature, and at first it appeared to be a close race. However, Johnson found himself deserted by many former friends and lost. Then came the scandal. It had been believed that a few black Republicans would hold the balance of power. Banker Logan Roots, a former Republican congressman and federal marshal, was accused of trying to bribe some of the these men to vote for Johnson. The story left Johnson broken-hearted, and the great man died shortly thereafter. As for Roots, who "never failed to liberally reward the newspaper for any services rendered him," he went on to become probably the richest man in Arkansas and was spoken of as a possible vice presidential nominee.[499]

After Garland headed off to Washington as a senator in 1877, William R. Miller, the first native Arkansan elected governor, continued in the New Departure vein. However, large segments of the party felt increasingly restive over the debt problem. William M. Fishback, a major stockholder in the Little Rock and Fort Smith Railroad, argued vigorously that the railroad bonds, although authorized by the voters, were a fraud on the state. The state supreme court accepted this contention, thus removing Fishback's company from one of its major liabilities. Then the state land commissioner, the APA's founding father, J.N. Smithee, refused to accept state levee bonds for payment and was sustained by the high court. Emboldened by these victories, repudiationists pushed to get rid of the old Holford bonds left over from the antebellum bank failure.

Supporters of repayment were tainted because the main owners of the Holford bonds had distributed shares for years in an effort to get legislative action. Fishback, "The Great Repudiator," proposed a constitutional amendment to forbid the state ever from paying either principal or interest on the Holford bonds.

Fishback's principal opponents were Senator Garland, John D. Adams, and Uriah M. Rose (founder of the Rose law firm). The first round, in 1880, went against the repudiators as voters narrowly rejected the proposal. A much-discussed compromise put forth by John D. Adams, the sometime *Gazette* owner, and Jared E. Redfield called for Arkansas to be bound only for the amount the bank had actually received. The Adams-Redfield plan, as it was styled, never passed the legislature, but it did contribute to a street confrontation some have called the last duel in Arkansas. In May 1878, Smithee triggered the encounter when in the *Democrat* he called Adams at the *Gazette* "a corrupter of men and a debaucher of women.[500]"

As observer Opie Read recalled the events a half-century later, a crowd anticipating trouble had gathered that Sunday morning along Main and Markham Streets. Mayor John G. Fletcher ordered the people to disperse, and Methodist minister the Rev. A.R. Winfield, a future (1885-1887) editor of the *Arkansas Methodist*, tried to steer the loungers to church. Instead, Ferd Hamilton, a steamboat pilot, wondered who was making book and wanted to put his money on Adams. In addition to Read, newspapermen Charles Blackburn and Harry C. Warner were there.

Suddenly the shout went up, "Here comes Smithee! Yonder's Adams!" Approaching each other from opposite directions, they opened fire at 30 feet. Smithee was hit and fell into the street, while Adams rushed forward, pistol in hand: "If it weren't for your wife and children I'd finish you, you damned slanderer!" To which the fallen Smithee replied: "Finish me, damn you!"

Adams turned away, and Smithee was taken home where the physicians pronounced him "painfully but not dangerously wounded." It was Read who wrote up the story for the *Democrat*, and it was Smithee, not pleased by the suggestion that he had tried to take cover behind a sign, who subsequently fired his reporter.[501]

Smithee was a candidate for governor in 1880, running on a "Young Arkansas" platform and promising economy and reform. Others in the race at the Democratic convention (primaries being a thing of the future) were William Fishback and Thomas J. Churchill, as well as incumbent governor Miller, who wanted a third term. Fishback was pushing his amendment, but Smithee did a hatchet job by calling up Fishback's flip-flop on secession at the 1861 convention. Both men and Miller lost out to Thomas J. Churchill, the son-in-law of Robert Ward Johnson and Arkansas's best-known living Civil War general.

Temperance was becoming an issue for the first time. When the *Gazette* admitted Churchill did not support that cause, *Arkansas Methodist* editor Rev. A.R. Winfield denounced whiskey as the cause of all the world's evils. After the *Gazette* admitted that the general was "a man fond of his drink," Winfield claimed D.A. Brower at the *Gazette* was really a Republican who was trying to deliver Arkansas over to the whiskey-drinkers, gamblers, and Sabbath-breakers. Brower's response, "Is This Man Without Shame, Drunk or Crazy?" denounced all the charges as "Winfieldian hogwash, of an unsavory brand."[502]

Governor Churchill was an antique character who named his estate "Blenheim" in honor of the great battle won in 1704 by John Churchill, the first Duke of Marlborough. Once, during the Civil War, after he had a horse shot out from under him by a Union battery even though he had not ordered an attack on it, he complained that the war had "degenerated into positive impoliteness."[503] All but one of the slate of state officers opposed repudiation, and William E. Woodruff, Jr. was the party's nominee for state treasurer. "He will make, as his father many years ago made, a faithful and efficient officer," the *Gazette* predicted.[504]

In addition to opposing repudiation, Churchill and the New Departure Democrats courted the black voters, urging them to become Democrats. Their organ, the *Gazette*, apologized for the Confederate flags flown at the Democratic convention, and reported favorably on the first commencement at Union Public High School, held at the opera house, where whites sat in the galleries and blacks had the floor.[505] The Redeemers had created a black college at Pine Bluff (known successively as Branch Normal, AM&N, and UAPB), and "nothing could be more encouraging for the future."[506] "It is very much regretted," the newspaper noted, when M.E. Childress, a Negro census taker, was unable to perform his job in Faulkner County due to white opposition.[507]

In the 1880 election, the Democrats won easily. Churchill continued to support black civil rights and maintain law and order. In contentious Perry County the killing got so far out of hand that Churchill called out the militia and sent General Robert Newton (son of the only Whig congressman) to occupy the county seat. Opie Read went along as a war correspondent. Newton appointed Read a militia major, and then as Read's superior demanded to see the dispatches Read had written. "What do I get for this?" Read inquired. After learning that his pay was the same as in the regular army, he handed over the manuscript: "Read the stuff and let the war go on."[508] The press was so well represented in the militia that while in Perryville there appeared the *Quapaw Times*, "Devoted to the Suppression of Disturbances," and which was "published to-day and maybe to-morrow."[509]

Churchill was limited to one term when his enemies found shortages in his accounts as state treasurer. Churchill blamed accounting errors, and with the state's record keeping being mired in medieval procedures, he may have been correct. Even more embarrassing for the Redeemers was the charge that William E. Woodruff, Jr., had embezzled some $2,000,000 from the state. The evidence was greatly controverted, and Woodruff was acquitted in the first three of his four trials. His conviction at the fourth was then overturned by the state supreme court. Leading the attack on Woodruff was James Mitchell at the *Arkansas Democrat*, who called the acquittals "an outrage upon justice and common honesty."

In 1882, the repudiationist wing elected as governor J.H. Berry, a one-legged Confederate veteran, and two years later Arkansas voters adopted the Fishback Amendment wiping out the Holford debt. Garland called repudiation "the memorial blunder, if not the crowning crime, of the age."[510] The net affect of these repudiations was to make the state unable to borrow money until well into the 20th century. Indeed, even the state's uncontested indebtedness to the federal government remained unpaid until the 1890s.

One feature of the 1874 constitution had been to deny towns and cities adequate taxing power. Little Rock lived off the proceeds from taxing illegal gambling, but paving streets or establishing drainage, sewers, or municipal lighting were beyond help. The first telephone arrived in 1879, but visitors were appalled by the lack of municipal services. Editors complained to no avail.

Meanwhile, despite being out of power within the state, Republicans staged a comeback. Their leading editor at the capital was that ancient antebellum figure, W. Jasper Blackburn of the *Blackburn's Free South* and the *Little Rock Republican*, "a powerful writer, when you get him started."[511] One of Blackburn's causes was opposition to capital punishment, a view shared by Opie Read and Colonel A. Curl of the *Malvern News*.[512] Blackburn's fearless reporting of Democratic abuses and his pointed repartee kept Democratic editors on their toes. When the editor of the *Rogers New Era* tried to dredge up the sins of Reconstruction, Blackburn replied: "We have had nothing to do with it. Were not in the State in those days. But it could not have been worse or more imbecile than some more recent Democratic rule of which we know something."[513]

Despite adverse conditions overall, the early 1880s witnessed tremendous growth as railroad construction led to new towns popping up everywhere. The upland areas filled up rapidly in this decade, causing in the hills many who had been squatting for decades finally to get titles to their farms. Exploration for minerals was all the rage, with silver, manganese, zinc, and lead figuring prominently.

Yet a combination of continued abuse of power, especially on the county level, and farm prices that fell steadily until the end of the century led to yet another farmer revolt. The Agricultural Wheel, which banned from membership "senile editors" but established newspapers all over the state, supported cooperative stores and self-help. The Brothers of Freedom, who feared the marketplace, called for direct political action. After the two groups merged, they plunged into state politics, notably in the election of 1888.

Since most blacks in Arkansas were farmers and still had the right to vote, and since the moribund Republican party had little to offer them, both Democrats and Wheelers reached out for this crucial minority. When the Democrats saw that it was more likely blacks would vote for a Wheel candidate for governor, they ceased to encourage racial moderation. The gubernatorial election of 1888 was fought not over farm issues but over race. Wheel gubernatorial candidate C.M. Norwood, a one-legged Confederate veteran, became the supreme race traitor. "The mask has been torn off and the authors of the crimes of the Reconstruction era stand forth in bold relief," cried the *Arkansas Gazette*.

Election day was marked by probably the worst fraud and certainly the most violence in Arkansas history. In Crittenden County, black county officials fled for their lives across the Mississippi River to Memphis, and a white mob armed with Winchester rifles supervised the election. Murdering blacks was the order of the day, and to keep Pulaski County safe, 6,000 bogus ballots were counted and then tossed into the Arkansas River to prevent an investigation. The jubilant Democrats declared James P. Eagle the new governor and forthwith began to eliminate blacks politically and otherwise from Arkansas life. Conway County's black legislator was taken off a train and fed to the catfish of the Arkansas River.

One counted-out congressional candidate was John Clayton, the popular brother of Powell Clayton. After learning how the election had been stolen at Plumerville, Clayton went to investigate and was murdered by an assassin who later became a famous local hero.[514] The subsequent giving of the state printing to APA historian Robert Leigh's *Morrilton Headlight* may have been the party's reward for good hard work.

Eagle did not enjoy good relations with the *Arkansas Democrat*, and when he was succeeded in 1897 by Daniel Webster Jones, Clio Harper, then serving as city editor of the *Democrat*, confided to his diary: "Now I can with impunity pay my respects to his excellency, the Governor, for the first time in two years, without fear of being cursed or kicked out of the office …"[515]

Soon thereafter came three devices to get rid of black voters: the Australian or written ballot, which effectively disfranchised those who could not read; the poll tax, which required each voter to prove he had paid the $1 a year tax before he could vote; and the white primary, which made the Democratic party from 1906 to 1944 a private club open to whites only. In 1917, Earle W. Hodges, the Secretary of State, and a former publisher at Mammoth Spring, Imboden, and Pocahontas and APA secretary for 12 years, ran for governor on a platform that promised whites they could determine where blacks might live. Hodges had missed his opportunity on this issue, for white mobs had already decided that issue in hundreds of towns that posted signs reading, "Nigger, Don't Let the Sun Set on You in ________."

The racial as well as the political climate reached a white heat with the appearance of Jeff Davis at the end of the century.[516] Although no kin to the Confederate president, Davis always wore Confederate gray. One simple confused voter called him "the greatest and longest-lived man that ever was." A college graduate and lawyer, Davis claimed to speak for the common white man. He made class war on the "high-collared crowd" and gloried in trampling on all the decencies of life.

Davis became state attorney general in 1897 and made a name for himself by taking on the trusts, especially the insurance companies, whom he literally drove out of Arkansas. Then he attacked the building of the new state capitol Arkansas desperately needed. Borrowing Populist rhetorical style, but without much of its substance, Davis never failed to quote the *Helena World*, which had called him a "Carrot-headed, red-faced, loud-mouthed, strong-limbed, ox-driving mountaineer lawyer and a friend to the fellow who brews 40-rod bug-juice back in the mountains."

More than any other politician, he played the race card. Early in his career "I told the boys around Morrilton, Russellville and Plumerville, that if they elected me, I would fill the penitentiary so full of niggers their feet would be sticking out of the windows." A firm opponent of black education—"Every time you educate a 'nigger' you spoil a good field hand"—he vetoed funding for AM&N. Then in 1905, on the occasion of President Theodore Roosevelt's visit to Little Rock, Davis defended lynching as sound public policy. Roosevelt was incensed, and lectured the governor in front of the crowd of 40,000 persons. Davis boycotted the lunch. For even though no blacks had been invited (unlike Grant's 1880 appearance), Davis would not sit down with Republican Powell Clayton.

Davis became the first governor to win more than two terms, and then in "the vilest and meanest state campaign ever witnessed in Arkansas," according to the *Democrat*, unseated incumbent United States Senator James H. Berry.

What was remarkable about Davis's career is that so few newspapers supported him. Both the *Arkansas Gazette* and the *Arkansas Democrat* vied with each other in denouncing his antics. They gave full play to all his scandals—selling pardons, being expelled from Little Rock's Second Baptist Church, and accepting bribes—but to no avail. Davis turned their opposition into a positive.

Early on, one editor had warned, "if the *Arkansas Democrat* and several other papers don't let up abusing Jeff Davis, they will elect him governor." During the three terms he was governor, neither side let up. "Squirrel-headed editors" were the enemy of his common people, while the *Gazette* was "that old red harlot. I had rather be caught with a dead buzzard under my arm or a dead polecat." As for the other Little Rock newspaper, "I have a little boy, God bless him, a little pale-faced, white-haired fellow… If I find that boy is a smart boy, I am going to make a lawyer out of him, and if I find that he has not a bit of sense on earth I am going to make an editor out of him and send him to Little Rock to edit the *Arkansas Democrat*."

Davis delighted in telling audiences about his dogs, and how an old, blue, speckled dog called Old Lead would bark and all the others would then follow

Old Lead's bark. "This is the way with these newspapers in Arkansas. The *Gazette* and *Democrat* emulate Old Lead in this campaign; they open up, and the little country papers all over the state break out, 'yow, yow, yow;' they do not smell a thing on earth, but they hear Old Lead bark." And Davis did another daring thing. Breaking a 30-year sacred tradition, he refused to use the columns of the *Gazette* to announce his candidacies.[517]

One of Davis's ploys was to write libelous material, submit it to a newspaper that correctly refused to print it, and then attack the newspaper as unfair to him.[518] Arkansas had liberal libel laws, but most editors had been sued, and Erwin Funk called libel suits "an ever present threat in the newspaper game."[519]

America was well into the Progressive Era when Arkansas finally got a progressive governor in 1909 in the person of George Washington Donaghey. Arkansas then passed initiative and referendum amendments in 1910, finished the state capitol, and caught up with public health measures. Donaghey was defeated in his bid for a third term in 1912 by Joseph T. Robinson. Meanwhile, Senator Jeff Davis died in Washington, and in poetic justice John N. Heiskell, the editor of the *Arkansas Gazette*, served until the legislature elected Robinson. George W. Hays, the eventual new governor, won by virtue of delayed (and doubtless fraudulent) returns from Phillips County. In 1916, university professor Charles H. Brough defeated three other candidates, among them Earle W.

Hodges, and restored progressivism. Brough supported both prohibition and women's suffrage, both of which were enacted.

The press had its own progressive issue. Despite or perhaps because of the involvement of members of the profession in the legislature, that body seemed to find great pleasure in being hostile to the profession. One legislator said that informing a blacksmith was a better way to advertise than a public notice in a newspaper, and both the state and the counties regularly threw obstacles in the way of publishers collecting their just debts.[520] Hence, in 1915, a select committee of APA members wrote the Publicity Act and then oversaw its passage using the initiative process. Besides serving the financial interests of newspapers, it also served to inform the public on just how their tax moneys were being spent. Interestingly, a small but significant number of editors who were associated with courthouse gangs opposed the measure.

World War I ushered in a sharp break with the Victorian age. The certainties of the old science were undermined by Albert Einstein's relativity theory; almost overnight all the once-dominant rules of literature, art, and music were overthrown. By 1919, even baseball had been tarnished by the "Black" Sox scandal; national prohibition was proving unenforceable; and America now lived in fear of communism. Even if a journalist, in the person of Warren G. Harding, was in the White House, the heroic age of journalism was virtually over.

Giants of the Press

In the years between the end of Reconstruction and the 1920s, three men stood out, dominating the state scene.

James Newton Smithee, the first of these, was the founding president of the Arkansas Press Association. Born in 1842 on a farm in what is now Sharp County, he had less than three months of schooling before being apprenticed to John C. Morrill at the *Des Arc Citizen* where he stayed for four years. After working in Pine Bluff, he had a half interest in the *Prairie County Democrat* at the now-defunct town of Brownsville. At the start of the Civil War he enlisted in William E. Woodruff, Jr.'s battery and ended the war as first lieutenant in W.D. Blocher's artillery battalion. Some sort of labor dispute occurred when Smithee, who allegedly was a charter member of Local 92 of the typographers' union, joined the *Gazette*'s management. But Smithee remained faithful to the union and ended up holding "every office within its bestowal."[521]

Smithee become the office foreman at the *Gazette* and served on Elisha Baxter's staff during the Brooks-Baxter War. From 1874 to 1878, he was commissioner of state lands, founding the *Arkansas Democrat* upon his retirement. After his failed gubernatorial bid, he bought the *Gazette* in 1882 but did not long remain in charge. A government job took him to Denver and briefly out of Arkansas politics.

Smithee's radicalism proved to be a striking contrast to conservatism that had marked the newspaper under a succession of subsequent owners. When Fred Allsopp started with the *Gazette*, D.A. Brower was president of the Gazette Printing Company, with George R. Brown as vice president. Brower was another victim of tuberculosis, dying in 1893; Brown was a printer who had worked at the *New York Daily Tribune* under Horace Greeley before coming west ("young man") and had arrived in Little Rock as a true carpetbagger, with all his possessions in that flimsy piece of luggage. Brown had many interests, including his own company that regularly bid on the state printing contract. In 1888, H.G. Allis, a banker, assumed the role of a largely absentee owner for a corporation that included the most prominent Democrats in Arkansas.

Although not involved in the day-to-day

operations of the newspaper, Allis was the author of an editorial famous in the infamous annals of Arkansas prison lore, when he castigated the three prison commissioners, one of whom was Governor Simon Hughes, as the "Three Blind Mice."[522] Allis and all his investments went to ruin in the Panic of 1893, and he ended up in prison. Among those who managed the newspaper were Jacob Frolich, Jr., E.L. Givens, and W.M. Kavanaugh. It was during the Frolich years that labor troubles erupted and the printers walked out, almost causing the newspaper to miss an issue. The *Gazette* hired strikebreakers from a group known as the Printers' Protective Fraternity and remained union-free for some years.

Then, in 1896, Smithee returned to Arkansas and reacquired the *Gazette*, editing it until the end of 1899. Smithee made the newspaper again a union shop, supported free silver, and attacked railroad abuses with so much intensity that R.D. McMullen, state senator from Yell County, charged into Smithee's office where his assassination attempt failed after Fred Allsopp hit the senator's hand and caused the bullet to miss.[523] Smithee not only endorsed the union movement but also championed a host of Populist reforms.

To those with long memories, Smithee's radicalism led to the charge that the *Gazette* had become "hypercritical." Smithee replied that "the 'Old Lady's' age and experience should be a sufficient rejoinder to any notion of the sort," adding that "for all her age and experience, the 'Old Lady' may be more of an herb and ointment doctor than diagnostician." Doctoring to the needs of the age required telling the truth, "though it tears the hide off our backs." The *Gazette*, he asserted, "assumes the part of one who addresses himself to friends whom he loves and who have known him for many years."[524]

However, the state's political powers did not share his vision, and the election of banker W.B. Worthen in 1900 as head of the Gazette Publishing Company reversed the course again. Among the oldest employees were Fred Allsopp, who rose to become business manager in 1896, and Dickison Brugman, who had been around for almost ever. "Some of these days I will be too old to work and I want little 'Dick' Brugman to succeed me as editor of the *Gazette*," C.C. Danley had told the child who started setting type during Reconstruction and was still working in 1936 when he put together the historical material in the *Gazette*'s Centennial edition.[525]

Dick Brugman deserves further mention for his part in one of the pre-Smithee disasters that befell the *Gazette*. Sam Jones, a Southern evangelist, came to Little Rock to preach. Jones, as was his style, lashed Little Rock as "the wickedest city in the United States." Allsopp wrote an editorial taking exception to the attack and encouraging people to save the Sabbath from desecration by boycotting Jones. Brugman was then assigned to cover the revival, and wrote of Jones's "acrobatic movements about the stage, necessary to illustrate his minstrel jokes. The infants seemed to enjoy the fun as much as the grown folks." Incensed, Jones and his supporters launched a boycott against the newspaper, causing it a temporary loss of subscribers. Jones continued to return yearly to Little Rock until his death in 1906.[526] The *Gazette* was not the only newspaper to get burned on matters religious.

As for Smithee, in his later years he worked on what he believed (quite incorrectly) to be a great novel, "Aaron Lewis: A Story of the Southwest."[527] Obviously mentally deranged and in "sore financial straits," he had fallen on the ice in New York during the winter of 1901-02. His wife and family lived separately from him in Denver. After returning to Little Rock, he stayed at the Merchants Hotel. Claiming he was being bothered by stray cats, he borrowed a pistol from a friend and on the evening of the 4th of July during a fireworks display fired a 32-

calibre bullet through his right temple. The body was not found until the next day. "For cripples, paupers and mendicants I have no use," he wrote, and recalling that the Confederacy had gone down to defeat at Helena and Gettysburg on the 4th of July, added, "it is befitting that my taking-off should end today." He wanted to be cremated, as "all dead bodies should be thus disposed of." Neither his wife nor any of his six children came to his funeral. There was, the *Democrat* intoned, "a warmth and congeniality about his nature which readily attracted friendship from all classes with whom he came in contact."[528] He was at his genial best in siring and nurturing the infant Arkansas Press Association.

James Mitchell at the *Arkansas Democrat* was a tower of consistency when compared to the changing policies at the *Gazette*. Unwilling to serve as the pliant tool for special interests, Mitchell soon acquired a great reputation for integrity. He opposed the Fishback Amendment as a fraud and found fault with the free silver movement and its 1896 Democratic presidential nominee, William Jennings Bryan. This economic conservatism contrasted with his very advanced stand in favor of women's rights that led him to declare for "the absolute equality of man and woman under law." "Some glorious day in the near future the world will demand a larger share of justice and rights for women and greater equality of rights and privileges as to persons and property now denied her," he declared.[529]

Mitchell not only editorialized on the subject, but on Thanksgiving Day, 1895, turned the entire newspaper over to women. Led by Mrs. Ex-Governor Eagle, "the women took possession, absolute with the exception of the composing and press rooms," Clio Haper recorded in his diary. "The fair creatures actually swarmed through the sanctum sanctorum, and the way financial editorials, poems of home, dissertations on morality, and any thing but news flowed from their facile pens was a caution to

Bohemians." Harper noted that the project's planning had taken two weeks, "and had we died at the time, and an autopsy been held, 'Woman's Edition,' would have been graven on our hearts." Harper managed to skip out to the theater on the pretense of visiting police headquarters but lamented that "a world of matter of all kinds of uninteresting subjects was left over" that would have to be inserted later under the stereotyped heading, "The foregoing article was unavoidably crowded out etc."[530] By contrast, the *Gazette* called women's suffrage a "dangerous innovation" with "destructive tendencies."[531]

Mitchell served the APA as president in 1899, and in his presidential address he denounced the use of patent insides both for reasons of business and journalistic integrity. Calling on newspaper owners to become better businessmen, he observed, "When a newspaper man suffers a scurvy politician to 'work' him out of twenty five dollars for a straw hat and a dollar subscription the sense of humiliation that must come over him when he counts up the transaction must be appalling."

One of the worst failings was to succumb to the lure of office-seeking: "For if in a moment of weakness you should yield to the first temptation and should seek and gain even a small office, the virus will possess you and permeate your entire system and then though you had the strength of ten Ulysseses—you are undone, and unless God helps you, Calypso shall bind you fast and hold you in her island. The history of our profession is laden with the wrecks of men who in an evil hour exchanged the certainty of a competence and the sure prospect of building up a business for the almost certain disaster of a public career." However, Mitchell was among the hundreds of editors who served as postmasters, holding that position during the Cleveland years.

Mitchell called for editors to be in touch with the people, but not to be "a Polly Parrot" or one who "floats along like a dead log in the current of the river." Early in his career, he confessed, he had worked hard to put out an interesting newspaper. "After I had several experiences in libel suits and damage suits, several challenges to fight duels, hundreds of complaints, threats and accusations, and scores of letters thundering 'stop my paper,"—I concluded that there was something of more importance that what to put in the paper. That something is what to keep out of the paper." Mitchell called for giving the benefit of the doubt and giving "the justice that gives everyone his due, freely and without constraint."[532] While the modern reader may find that this latter point sounds platitudinous, much news at the time was reported in inflammatory and judgmental terms, especially where crimes or blacks were concerned.

Finally, Mitchell stood four-square for progress:

> I proclaim to you as a necessary element in your faith the gospel of optimism. Beware of the pessimist—the man who is always wailing of the calamities that are upon us and the dire disasters that are coming. There will always be evil in this world so long as the human race exists—always wrongs and abuses, tyranny, injustice and oppression. But this old world is better today, in the closing of the 19th century than it ever was since the beginning of time. It is getting better as it grows older; Because
>
> *Through the ages one increasing purpose runs*
> *And the thoughts of men are widened with the*
> *process of the suns.*
>
> Hold fast to this doctrine, proclaim it at all times, and you will help yourself, your country and humanity. Stand up for your state and for every movement and for every cause that will add to it greatness and renown.[533]

Arkansas Secretary of State O.C. Ludwig, who did not follow Mitchell's strictures on politics, pronounced Mitchell "scholarly, forcible and chaste in all his editorial utterances. A man of convictions he maintained his views with courage and honesty, and was one of the few city editors ready to welcome to his own private editorial rooms the boys of the country press as if he had a personal interest in them. He was in many respects a great man, aside from his newspaper ability."[534] Clio Harper took Christmas dinner with the family in 1894. His own family was highly dysfunctional, and Harper was awed by people with "happy, sunny dispostions" and financial security. "Such a family is my ideal," he pronounced.[535] Mitchell's second partner, James R. Bettis, shared his interests and served as APA president in 1887.

Edgar L. Givens, a sometime rival *Gazette* editor, shared Ludwig's views. Mitchell's editorials "were clothed in that perfect English, of which he was an acknowledged master," and made effective use of sarcasm and ridicule. "It was always easy to foretell where the *Democrat* would stand on any issue turning upon a question of good morals, honest government or public enterprise."

One good example was Mitchell's support for constitutional reform. The Constitution of 1874 was full of "harsh and restrictive provisions which stand as a lion in the pathway of progress."[536] Another losing cause was gun control. The pistol toter, as those who carried weapons were called, was "a heathen and a barbarian."[537] There were limits to enlightened attitudes. After the bloody and fraudulent election of 1888, in which so many blacks were victimized, Mitchell explained that it was their fault because they had not listened to their "true friends."[538]

Givens predicted that "the future historian of Arkansas will accord him a deservedly prominent place among the able, useful and distinguished men of the state, and the press of Arkansas will cherish and perpetuate his memory as one its strongest and brightest ornaments," but it was not to be.[539] In the absence of a scholarly biographical study, Mitchell's place in history rests mostly on hearsay.

The *Democrat* was owned by Mitchell and W.D. Blocher and, after the latter's death in 1879, by Mitchell and James R. Bettis until 1890. The business prospered, becoming in Edgar Givens's judgment "one of the best newspaper properties in the South."[540]

The early years were hard. "While I am not rich," he wrote his wife, "I have plenty and am making more," estimating his income for 1883 at between $4,000 to $5,000.[Readers should multiply probably by at least 15 to get an idea of his wealth. Reporters generally made between $9 and $25 a week, or at the most $1,300 per annum.] In addition, Mitchell in 1883 held over $2,000 in state warrants whose redemption was delayed because there was no money in the treasury.

A series of disasters hit the newspaper early in the 20th century. Mitchell died in 1902. Clio Harper, then the newspaper's city editor, ascribed the death in his diary to Governor Jeff Davis's successful reelection: "To the arch demagogue, and political buffoon whose jest is venom and whose laugh a plague, I charge the death of one of the noblest, strongest, most loyal, and best men that ever lived."[541] Three years later, the entire plant burned. The newspaper had labor troubles as well over the eight-hour day. The ITU had gone on record in favor of this reform as early as 1865 at a time when even a 12-hour day was rarely practiced. The union had succeeded in getting the hours down to 10 by the 1890s.

The 1905 campaign for the eight-hour day had ramifications in Arkansas. The *Democrat*, which was unionized on its commercial side, tried to put out the newspaper with non-union men, thus gaining the nickname of "Democ-Rat." The Central Trades and Labor Council began a secondary boycott of firms that advertised in the newspaper. Harper, still serving as city editor, grew increasingly at odds with W.S. Mitchell, who was "trying to get out the sheet with 'scab' labor, and a pretty poor try it was, too. It was almost impossible to secure competent men and the linotypes were down half the time. Sometimes the afternoon paper, due at 3 o'clock, would not get out until 7."

In 1906, the Mitchell heirs sold it to the Little Rock Publishing Company of which Clio Harper was secretary and George C. Naylor a vice president and general manager. The Panic of 1907 hit the newspaper a hard blow. By the summer of 1910, "things got pretty gloomy," Harper confessed. Then George Naylor and his brother sold their controlling interest to Frederick Allsopp, business manager of the *Gazette*. Shortly therafter, George Naylor was stricken with paralysis and died. Allsopp imported H.D. Bord from the Scripps-McRae chain, who brought in, as Harper put it, "a lot of big unassimilated ideas" but found "that he had no money to work with." Taking the hint, Harper sold his stock.[542] In his later years, J.N. Heiskell denied that the *Gazette* had purchased the *Democrat* but did not rule out that those associated with the *Gazette* may have made the purchase.[543] In 1911, John M. Branham and Elmer E. Clarke purchased the newspaper, with K.A. Engel as

their business manager.[544]

Although the Mitchell family sold off the newspaper, they maintained their ownership of the Democrat Printing and Lithographing Company. DP&L remained one of the prominent printing firms in state. As for the *Arkansas Democrat*, it never regained its late-19th-century leadership. First under Clarke, and later under Engel, it settled for being a pale shadow of the *Gazette* around the state and as Little Rock's evening newspaper.

John Netherland Heiskell completed the triumvirate. The grandson of Frederick S. Heiskell, who founded the *Knoxville Register* in 1816, Ned, as close family members called him, was born in 1872 and grew up in Memphis where at age 10 he published a family newspaper. At age 17, he enrolled at the University of Tennessee, where by skipping his sophomore year he graduated in three years. His senior thesis was entitled "The Use of the Subjective in English." Then he joined the *Knoxville Tribune* as a reporter at a salary of nine dollars a week, payable only after he "qualified" by working two weeks with no pay. While still a student, Heiskell had begun his career in a most uncharacteristic way for a man who had no interest in sports when he covered a football contest between the University of the South and the University of Tennessee, receiving two dollars in compensation.[545]

The *Tribune* gave Heiskell good experience even if it was a poor newspaper that relied heavily on syndicate "stuff," as he called boiler-plate. A three-dollar-a-week raise caused him to move over to the *Knoxville Sentinel*, where, despite his youth, he carried the title city editor. Then he moved to Memphis when the *Commercial Appeal* raised the ante by another three dollars. In June 1899, he took a job with the Associated Press's division headquarters in Chicago. A year later he was sent to Louisville, where he held a position comparable later to that of bureau chief.[546]

At some point, the story got started that Heiskell had been forced to resign from the AP after he killed the news that the *U.S.S. Maine* had gone down in Havana harbor. After columnist Bill Ladd of the Louisville *Courier-Journal* printed the story in 1949, Heiskell replied: "My long career has not been without errors of judgment or without failures, but it remains for you to traduce my journalistic reputation. This gauzy invention published in your column will never be forgotten. Now that you and the *Courier-Journal* have given it currency, it will be retold and republished even after I have passed away. Such is the work of your hands." The *Maine* went down on February 15, 1898, at which time Heiskell was still in Memphis at the *Commercial Appeal*![547]

In 1902, a Little Rock relation, Maxwell Coffin, was visiting in Memphis with Ned's mother. She and her husband had just received $15,000 from the sale of utility stock, and he told her the *Arkansas Gazette* was for sale. "Ned had told me that his ambition was to own a newspaper," his mother recalled, "so I wrote to him that night." The total purchase price was probably about $100,000, and in addition to the $15,000, Ned contributed $2,000 he had saved, his mother mortgaged a house she owned, and his parents assumed a debt of $80,000. The principal minority stockholder was business manager Fred W.

Allsopp. On June 17, 1902, the sale was consummated, and the new regime took over on July 1, with Ned as editor-in-chief and his younger brother Fred as managing editor.[548]

"Mr. J.N.," as the older Heiskell brother was called, was a model of decorum, dignity, and discretion. He presided over the editorial page, making it reflect "his humane, progressive views and of the cosmopolitan interests of a widely-traveled man."[549] No one in the *Gazette*'s long history took greater pride in having the newspaper fulfill its longtime role as the recorder of the state's history. At the time Arkansas had no university archives and only an impoverished Arkansas History Commission, so Heiskell began collecting Arkansiana, acquiring a large and varied library, later the basis for the Chronicles of Arkansas series. Perhaps because of his college background in English, Heiskell insisted on good and correct writing. Generations of reporters lived in fear of making an error, for even as he approached his hundredth year he read each day's newspaper, even (sometimes) the sports, with a critical eye.

With wide experience in what went into making a good newspaper as well as youth and energy, "Mr. J.N." studied to improve his newspaper. His arrival in Little Rock coincided with the death of James Mitchell, and over the next decades the *Gazette* pulled ahead of the *Democrat*. In his first editorial, he told readers that "the *Gazette* will strive to be a newspaper. News is the mental food of the human race." Developing this metaphor and paraphrasing Shakespeare he added, "When the humblest and poorest man unfolds a real newspaper he opens a window through which he may look out upon the universe." Heiskell promised to provide a Democratic newspaper, but not one that would consist of "parrot-like recitation of the various resolutions of the party platform." He concluded by stating: "This newspaper has outlived many lives. It has begun a new one this morning."[550]

Certainly there was much to do. The front page was covered with advertisements, which all the best city newspapers and many Arkansas weeklies had banished from the place that now had become the home only to news. Even worse, a casual reader on June 22 would have seen a large bold headline first running above all the news stories stating that Albert Pfeifer had Sterling thimbles on sale. Equally antiquated were its building and its equipment.

A case of sorts could be made that another antiquated part of the purchase was Frederick W. Allsopp. It was Allsopp as both a minority stockholder and business manager who kept those advertisements on the front page and dragged his feet on every proposed improvement.

While Ned went upstairs to the editorial sanctorum, Fred managed the city room. In his memoir, novelist James Street, at first a reporter there, witnessed "a Southern lady from any angle, her Confederate limbs hidden under a Victorian petticoat and seen only in stormy weather when she kicks up her heels in an eye-catching crusade for her principles."[551]

The Heiskell brothers poured every cent back into the newspaper immediately. First came a new press. Then on the *Gazette*'s 87th birthday, November 20, 1906, the newspaper went to a full seven-day schedule. Allsopp was not in favor of the move, "but the times and outside competition demanded it."[552] As long as there was no Monday *Gazette*, the company had responded to important stories by issuing extras put out at no cost to subscribers in order to meet the competition. The Sunday newspaper, which by 1920 was twice the size of a weekday issue, also had four times the advertising. It slowly displaced the old weekly (and later bi-weekly) version that eventually expired on December 30, 1952. In 1908, the *Gazette* introduced colored comics to Sunday readers, and the next year gave aficionados the popular comic strip, *Mutt and Jeff*. The new regime reorganized the sports and society sections, giving them independent status.

The best sign of the new prosperity was the erection of a fine new three-story Beaux Arts building at 3rd and Louisiana streets designed by Mrs. J.N. Heiskell's father, George Mann.

Long forgotten is that both the *Gazette* and the *Democrat* had competition from 1917 to 1927 from the *Little Rock Daily News* of Robert Presly Robbins. Robbins had extensive experience in Jonesboro and Batesville before trying his hand at a daily.

In the early years of the Heiskell family ownership, Fred was the most visible. In contrast to his taciturn older brother, Fred was a lively fellow whom Allsopp called "a number-one news man, a brilliant, whole-souled fellow, who wins the hearts of all with whom he comes in contract."[553] Fred undertook editing the All Over Arkansas column and was one of the contributors to a collectively written mystery story, *Rival Stars, or, The Mystery of the Missing Million* (1914). His early death in 1931 was a major loss to the profession.

The most important aspect of J.N. Heiskell's early years was his political stance. Since he was not a native, never even having been to Little Rock prior to the purchase, he inherited no political agenda. He opposed Jeff Davis and received a satisfying reward for his efforts by filling the last days of the dead senator's term of office. Thereafter, Heiskell took the *Gazette* away from political endorsements. Issues were important; individual politicians were not. The day of personal journalism had at last ended.

A Nose for News

One of the key elements in the rise of the daily was the reporter. In Opie Read's days in the late 1870s, a reporter's routine consisted of getting the names of arriving businessmen and politicians from the steamboats and hotels. Read had submitted short paragraphs of fiction disguised as news when times were dull, and Charlie George followed suit.[554] Dickison Brugman, "the dean of Little Rock journalists" in Allsopp's estimation, "could come as near extracting the meat out of a good story, or making for the reader an entertaining story out of nothing, as any man on earth."[555]

By the 1880s, newspapers fed the public's fascination with crime, violence, and sex by covering the doings of the local police court. By the century's end, the daring reporter was coming into his own. Robert J. Brown, who during his *Gazette* days covered 11 official hangings in less than two years, followed in underwater detail the construction of a bridge across the Arkansas River by going down personally in a caisson. On one day this intrepid (and overworked) reporter supplied 12 columns of news![556] Staff shortages were endemic, and in the pre-Heiskell days at the *Gazette*, reporter Guy Bilheimer found himself alone in the editorial room except for the telegraph operator. "He wrote," Allsopp recalled, "heads for Associated Press dispatches with one hand, local items with the other, and talked over the 'phone to correspondents all at the same time."[557] Over at the *Arkansas Democrat*, Clio Harper began to feel overworked from "my manifold duties of city editor, sporting editor, reporter, exchange editor, society editor, theatrical critic, and producer in general of 'stuff' to fill in the chinks between the news."[558] Little Rock's newspapers aspired to metropolitan status but were perilously understaffed throughout the 19th century.

The job Harper most enjoyed and that contributed most to his education was that of dramatic critic. In early 1895, when the Capitol Theater cut out its advertising with the *Democrat*, the newspaper responded by dropping both advance notices and criticism. Fortunately for Harper, the theater manager still honored his newspaper pass. Reporters even in smaller towns shared in the largess.

Newport and Jonesboro, for example, were disproportionately blessed with theatrical events, mainly because the towns were convenient stopping points on the railroad for one-night stands. Harry Lee Williams of Jonesboro was, like Harper, well educated in matters theatrical.

Another of Allsopp's reporter stories concerned the 1921 escape from prison of condemned bank robber and murderer Tom Slaughter just prior to his electrocution. The news arrived late at night, and only night editor Clyde L. Dew was on the premises. Dew stopped the press run, jumped in a taxi and raced to the prison to get the facts, then returned to write a two-column story, which the printers set as fast as he wrote it in order to get the newspaper out nearly on schedule.[559]

"The Associated Press cuts a small figure with us for far as Arkansas news is concerned," the young Frederick Allsopp had been informed, and for many years this remained true.[560] Indeed, the Associated Press drew its stories from the metropolitan press. As both the *Democrat* and the *Gazette* established their own sources of information, the country weeklies remained valuable more for their opinions and less and less for their news stories.

One of the popular novels of the early 20th century was Evelyn Waugh's *Scoop* (1938). In journalistic slang the title meant beating the competition to print with a hot story. Clio Harper, writing in 1895, explained it this way: "All the time on qui vive for something sensational, the sweet morsel which the modern reading public covet, all the time the newsgather's ear, eye, and instinct strained to utmost tension to secure some startling item which the other fellows may miss, technically called a *scoop*—these things give the business an enchanting interest."[561] In the Slaughter case, it seems that the escapee had left behind in his cell a long letter addressed to the *Arkansas Democrat*. It was a real scoop when the *Gazette* got a copy of the letter and published it ahead of the newspaper to which it had been addressed.[562]

Newspapers embraced the typewriter, and by the late 19th century reporters typed their stories. The image from motion pictures and plays of "ancient typewriters and battered desks surrounded by a sea of strewn paper and topped by a pall of tobacco smoke spiced by the scent of corn whiskey" were words actually used to describe the *Gazette*'s newsroom in the early 20th century under Fred Heiskell's direction.[563]

In addition to the reporters working for individual newspapers, correspondents remained important. William Ami Webber, a Union army lieutenant who in Arkansas naturally rose to rank of colonel as well as being the APA's president in 1885, arrived as a special correspondent for the once-famous *Chicago Inter-Ocean*. Webber tried all parts of Arkansas for the big chance, and among his ventures at different times were the *Saline County Digest* at Benton; the *Malvern Meteor*; a Republican organ, the Little Rock *Daily Progress*; and at a now forgotten zinc-mining town, the *Maryhattianna Herald*. Webber's membership in the APA dated from 1876 to 1922, and in addition to serving as president, he was secretary from 1878 to 1883 and historian from 1919 to 1921.[564]

Many reporters led double lives. Z.T. Hedges, a reporter for the *Democrat*, also worked as a correspondent for out-of-town newspapers and sold stories to national periodicals including *Saturday Night* and the *Waverly*. Despite the rise of the Associated Press and other news services, correspondents continued to flourish. John T. Ginocchio ranked first, serving in 1889 as the first head of the Little Rock bureau of the Memphis *Commercial-Appeal*. He also kept posted the *St. Louis Globe-Democrat*, the *Kansas City Star*, as well as New York and Chicago newspapers. Allsopp noted, "He is the authority on political news, and no Arkansas

newspaperman is better posted on general affairs than this alert writer."[565]

There were special correspondents for country newspapers as well. In 1892 Alex C. Hull at the *Boone Banner* worked up a consortium of 25 newspapers to send Clio Harper to cover the world's fair, the Columbian Exposition at Chicago. Harper, who was only 20 years old, had never ridden on a railroad train and had never been to Chicago or any other city when he bravely set forth to cover one of the most exciting and culturally influencial events in 19th-century America. Most of the newspapers failed to pay him on time, but Harper found a variety of work to keep himself fed and clothed. Arriving before the fair opened, he remained six months until it ended, having churned out 163 letters by July 31, for which he received only $9. However, the *Arkansas Democrat* picked up his work. Harper met virtually every Arkansan who came to the fair, including the APA delegates, whom he found to be "a nice set of fellows." *Democrat* owners George Naylor and James Mitchell were so impressed that shortly after Harper turned 21 he was offered and took the post of city editor at the *Arkansas Democrat*.[566] One of Harper's most important journalistic pieces was his biography of Arkansan Caroline Shaw Brooks, whose butter sculpture was one of the highlights of the Exposition.[567]

In addition to a paid staff, the city press picked up stories from around the state by using stringers. Allsopp, who began as a stringer in 1883, received a job offer from George Russ Brown written in all capital letters on a Remington No. 1 typewriter. Important news was to be sent by telegraph and needed to arrive by six o'clock in the evening to make the first edition at midnight. The train would do for lesser stories. The instructions called for him to "send all the news and take no sides in politics."[568]

When high school and college sporting events attained near religious status in the 20th century, the need to get the scores in print gave many youngsters their start. But if a lad proved able at that, he might get a chance to cover some other local event. Such was the experience of printer Dee Brown, who learned on arriving in Harrison that at the Newman-owned *Times*, "Tom hires and John fires, they say." Brought in to help with the Christmas rush, he stayed to do some reporting. Brown picked up from a local correspondent a story (incorrect, as it turned out) that a geologist had become lost in an Ozark cave. Convinced that he had a national event on his hands along the order of Floyd Collins in Tennessee, Brown wrote exaggerated feature stories until it turned out the geologist was back in Kansas City.[569]

All reporters constantly faced moral dilemmas. "The conscientious journalist will not accept courtesies for which he cannot return a *quid pro quo*," Allsopp observed.[570] But where and how to draw the line was gray area. In 1895, George Tilles, the state agent for the Mutual Life Insurance Company, gave a banquet for the local press that Clio Harper described as "one of the swellest affairs ever given in the city." The "feast of reason and flow of soul—also champagne—was kept up until 2 o'clock Sunday morning."[571] This "Talk with Tilles" was not without political significance, for within two years Jeff Davis would base his political career in part on bashing insurance companies.

The adoption of a Code of Ethics at the APA's 1923 convention contained a section entitled "Respecting Confidences," but its vague language offered no meaningful guidelines. Members found it much easier to denounce the "mushroom papers and disreputable sheets" that came out prior to elections.[572]

While editors and the business manager dealt with the more powerful forces, temptation existed as well for the lowly reporter. The more involved the reporter became with the individuals making news, the more likely impartiality would be lost. Ginocchio, Allsopp observed, was "on easy terms with all the Bryans, Roosevelts, Wilsons, Lloyd Georges, and Clemenceaus of Arkansas politics."[573] By the 1920s the words reporter and cynic, if not married, were at least in common-law habitation. Clio Harper, who understood he would have a clerkship when Alex C. Hull became Secretary of State, followed William E. Woodruff down the primrose path of journalists who believed politicians and paid for it: "I shall never again dabble in the rottenness and corruption of politics, which is but another name for an undignified, soul-destroying scramble for office, and not a man can participate in it that he is not more or less brought under the sway of its vitiating influence."[574]

In the coverage of news events, especially of crimes involving minorities of any stripe, reporters acted often as judge, jury, and sometimes even executioner. The age of personal journalism consisted not only of inflammatory editorials but also of prejudicial and biased reporting.

If the early 20th century dawned as "the day of Unions," reporters remained outside the pale.[575] In the mid 1890s, W.M. Kavanaugh and Frederick Allsopp organized a press club to provide a gathering place for the Fourth Estate. It sported a billiard table and a reading room, but many of the members played cards—for money—to the utter scandal of members representing the religious press. This first club did not long endure.[576]

Prior to the arrival of radio and television, metropolitan newspapers sometimes provided free news by means of photographic slides. News on such events as presidential elections, the World Series, or boxing matches would be transcribed from Morse code to slides and then projected onto outdoor screens. Crowds of people would gather in the street to read the headlines and then hopefully buy the next newspaper for the full story.

The late 19th century saw a dramatic increase in the use of cartoons. The works of nationally famous Thomas Nast appeared in both the *Gazette* and the *Democrat*.[577] P.H. Bernays crafted two cartoons locally in 1880, but the real start of local cartooning came at the Smithee-run *Gazette* when from December 27, 1896, until May 1897 Elmer Burrus served as the first staff cartoonist in Arkansas.[578]

Little is known about Burrus, but his work appeared on the front page and from the start reflected Smithee's vigorous campaign against how the railroads, and Jay Gould of the St. Louis and Iron Mountain in particular, were corrupting and exploiting Arkansas.

Burrus also carried the title "Gazette Artist," and his drawing of Governor Dan W. Jones reading his inaugural address served as a practical demonstration on how pictures could be used to cover events. In contrast to the cumbersome way William Quesenbury made woodcuts, Burrus was able to take chalk and draw directly on plates.[579]

Cartoons also appeared outside Little Rock. One of the earliest was by James Shaver at the *Nashville News* on September 8, 1888, drawn to support the gubernatorial bid of Democrat James Eagle. The

Arkansas Gazette, *sometime between 1876 and 1878. A number of important individuals are in this photograph. Major W. D. Blocker and Major John D. Adams flank editor James Mitchell in the front. The four women worked in the bindery. On row one, the second from the left is George Woodruff, a grandson of founder William E. Woodruff; next to him is reporter George B. Rose, later a noted lawyer and writer. Scattered elsewhere in the photograph are a number of persons prominent in the ITU. (Courtesy Butler Center for Arkansas Studies, Central Arkansas Library System)*

Arkansas Gazette *business office, 1906. By 1900 the business office had become separate from the editorial, reporting, and printing sides. At the Gazette, Frederick Allsopp presided for more than 40 years. (Courtesy J.N. Heiskell Collection, UALR Archives and Special Collections)*

"REGISTER FOR 'HOBO' PRINTERS.

" 'NOTICE: It is requested that none but tourists register in this chart.

Name, Where From	*What Conveyance*	*Condition of Chewing*	*How Finances*	*Where Bound*	*Remarks for Enlightenment of the Craft*
Sam Cribbs, Kansas (laugh, damn you).	Blind Baggage.	Route overworked.	Too heavy to carry (I will have my joke).	Heaven is my destination.	Let bleeding Kansas bleed; I'll not try to stanch its wounds.
Tom Harper, Hades (called also Memphis).	The cinder path.	Good.	Money! Money! I've heard that before.	To some haven of rest where they toil not, but have plenty.	Memphis is a good town to be from.
Ernest Newell, Louisiana.	Side door Pullman.	Fit for the best.	Not burdened with the fithy stuff.	This will do; I'm not particular.	This printing business is no job for a clergyman's son.
Ed Douglass, Bosting.	The trucks (I blush to say it).	Good, if one is fond of beans.	Light—exceeding light.	Any place will suit me; I've lived in Bosting.	Experience comes with travel. If I wasn't a tourist, I'd turn out tomorrow.
Albert Duncan, Texas.	Lightly (I tripped along the ties).	Nothing to brag on.	Bad.	Where work is lightest.	Have no advice to give nor excuses to offer.
Walter McNeil, Missouri.	In a stock car with some other hogs.	Awful.	Awful.	Any place but Missouri.	Keep away from Joplin, Mo.
Will Elkins, St. Louis.	In the varnished cars.	The service in the dining car was rather good.	If I was any more prosperous I couldn't stand it.	Monte Carlo, maybe.	When the bang tails run your way, money certainly comes easy.

" 'NOTICE SOME MORE.—Tourists without bullion will please mention the name of "Peso" Jones; it rolls well under the tongue and breathes of money. Also a slight reference to "Shorty" Thomas would come in handy if you desire to perish in the sight of plenty. Shorty is sure a tight-wad.' "

Doubtless Frederick W. Allsopp cleaned up the language before publishing this register. (Frederick W. Allsopp, Little Adventures in Newspaperdom*)*

Display advertising, 1880s. This advertisement was for a hatter. (Frederick W. Allsopp, Little Adventures in Newspaperdom*)*

Arkansas Gazette Building, 1908. Little Rock. architect George R. Mann, who also designed the State Capitol, incorporated floral and fruit designs typical of Louis Henry Sullivan. Recognized at the time as one of the finest newspaper buildings in the South, it was owned by Peter Hotze and family until 1936. In 2002 the building was renamed the Textron Building. (Courtesy J.N. Heiskell Papers, University of Arkansas at Little Rock Archives and Special Collections)

J.N. Heiskell, c. 1904. The prim young man who bought the battered Gazette *set the newspaper's course for most of the 20th century. His objective became to make it into an Arkansas version of* The New York Times. *(Courtesy J.N. Heiskell Papers, University of Arkansas at Little Rock Archives and Special Collections)*

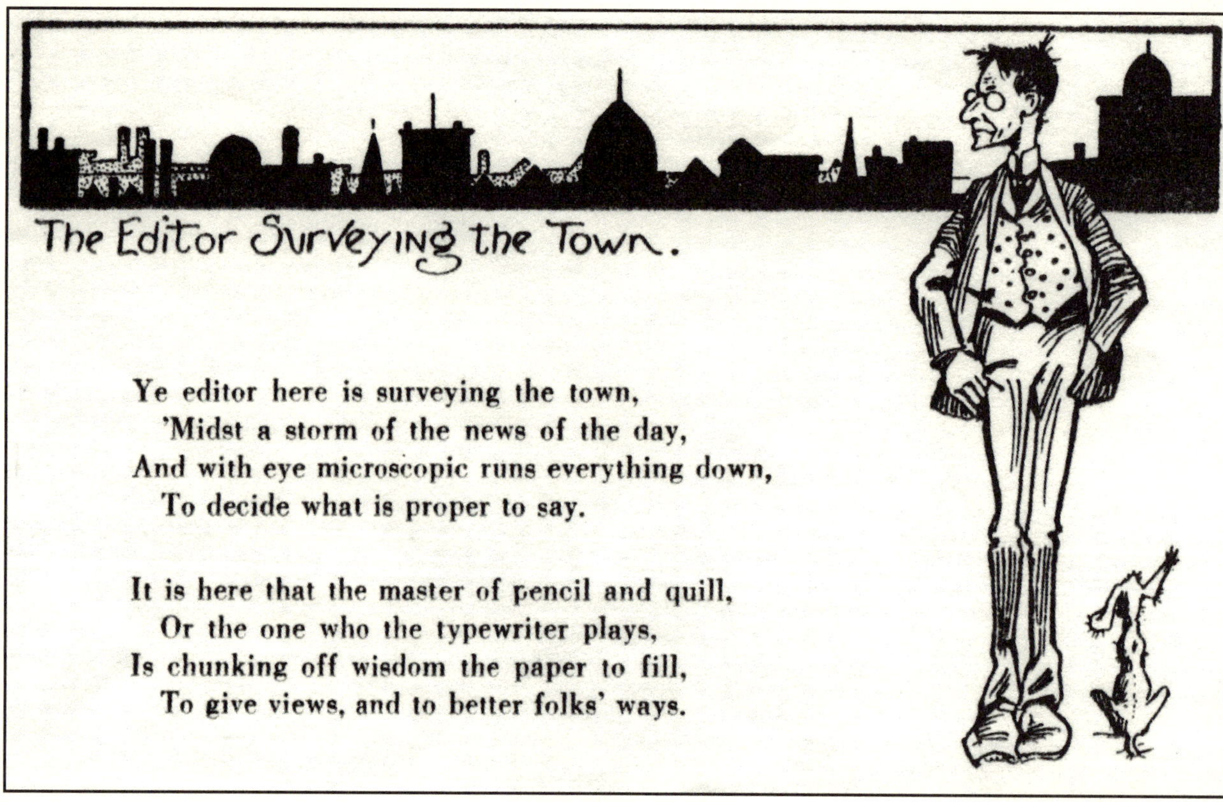

J.N. Heiskell, c. 1907. This caricature and the accompanying poem by Frederick W. Allsopp show Heiskell in a less formal pose. (Frederick W. Allsopp, Little Adventures in Newspaperdom*)*

MPANY. Leute 320 Mainstr.

M. M. Cohn & Co.,

Ankunft dernenen Waaren.

Herr M. M. Cohn, der augenblicklich in New York, schickte uns eine schöne elegante Auswahl von seinen modernen Frühjahrs Waaren.

Auch empfingen wir eine gute Auswahl von fertigen Herren und Damenkleidern, wie modernen Hüte. Wir laden das verehrte deutsche Publikum höflichst ein, uns zu besuchen.

M. M. Cohn & Co.,

308 u. 310 Main Straße : Little Rock, Ark

Jedersoll sich ansSpaaren gewöhnen

Numerous firms advertised in the German-language Arkansas Echo, *March 22, 1901. The advertisement for M.M. Cohn & Co. translates as "Arrival of New Goods. Mr. M.M. Cohn, who is at the moment in New York, sent us a beautiful and elegant selection of fine modern spring goods. Also we possess a good selection of ready-to-wear men's and women's clothes as well as stylish hats. We most humbly invite our most honored German patrons to visit it."*

A nose for news: Frederick W. Allsopp not only wrote a sketch of the proboscisatorily challenged Harry Watkins but also identified him by name in one copy of his book (see text on page 150). (Frederick W. Allsopp, Little Adventures in Newspaperdom, *1922)*

John D. Adams. This sometime owner of the Arkansas Gazette *and Little Rock businessman had many friends and admirers as well as bitter enemies. A famous street fight between J.N. Smithee and Adams has sometimes been called the last duel in Arkansas.*

Major Charles Gordon Newman, 1907. Pine Bluff editor Newman cuts out more copy to fill out his newspaper. (Courtesy Arkansas History Commission)

Pine Bluff Commercial, *c. 1900. The elegantly attired Major Newman (with top hat third from the right) stands with presumably a group of his staff and carrier boys outside the office. (Courtesy* Pine Bluff Commercial)

Commercial Printing Co., Pine Bluff, c. 1920. In the days before central heat, the potbellied stove located in the middle room served as the heat source. (Courtesy Pine Bluff Commercial)

Horace. G. Allis, c. 1890. In 1874 Allis was the business manager for the Little Rock Evening Star, *the newspaper that eventually became the* Arkansas Democrat. *Then in 1882 he became the secretary of the Gazette Printing Company, the corporate owners of the* Arkansas Gazette. *Allis had many other endeavors, including the Capital Theatre, Little Rock's streetcar line, and railroad investments, all of which he lost in the Panic of 1893. He did write editorials at times, and his attacks on the convict-lease system helped turn public opinion against that inhumane practice. (Courtesy J.N. Heiskell Collection, UALR Archives and Special Collections)*

W.S. Mitchell, 1907. Mitchell in this caricature is seen popping through the window of the Democrat Printing and Lithographing Co. The still-standing building adorns downtown Little Rock. William was one of James Mitchell's sons and directed the Arkansas Democrat's *printing side prior to the divorce of the newspaper from the printing firm. (Courtesy Arkansas History Commission)*

George R. Brown, 1907. Brown, the author of the line, "Once a printer, always a printer," came from New York. Starting as a sub-compositor at the Gazette, *he rose to become company president. In Little Rock he was remembered as the town's chief booster, serving as Secretary of the Board of Trade. Brown had his own printing company as well as interests in several different newspapers. (Courtesy Arkansas History Commission)*

Two veteran newspapermen, Dickison Brugman and Opie Read, c. 1920. Read, after finding success in writing novels, moved out of day-to-day journalism; Brugman, who started his career before the Civil War, worked mostly at the Arkansas Gazette. *(Courtesy Arkansas History Commission)*

L.S. "Sharpe" Dunaway. The best known newspaperman in Arkansas at the turn of the century, he worked at different times for the Arkansas Democrat *and the* Arkansas Gazette. *He authored two books, one a biography of Jeff Davis, the other a collection of stories notable for his treatment of the Elaine Race Riot. (Courtesy Arkansas History Commission)*

*Editors and printers in the 19th century knew when to use the apostrophe, hence its correct use in Col. Ed. Landvoight's news' stand. Landvoight, a Confederate veteran and head of the local United Confederate Veterans' camp, opposed the Ku Klux Klan at Forrest City during the 1920s. His news' stand business was probably profitable, for the Memphis & Little Rock Railroad (Rock Island) crossed the St. Louis & Iron Mountain (Missouri Pacific) at Forrest City, resulting in layovers for travelers. (*Arkansas Publisher, *May 1928)*

Clio Harper, c. 1890. The founder of the Arkansas Publisher *started his writing career in Kansas as a country correspondent. After working on the* Boone Banner *and covering the Columbian Exposition for a group of Arkansas newspapers he went to work at the* Arkansas Democrat. *In addition to founding a publishing company, he served as a Little Rock alderman. (Courtesy Lawrence Harper)*

Karl Joseph Meurer. *The longtime editor of the German-language newspaper used a Linotype machine with German gothic characters to print his newspaper. It survived both internal controversy within the German community and the repressive effects of World War I, but it could not survive the gradual acculturation of Arkansas's German population or Meurer's death in 1930. (Courtesy family of Karl Meurer)*

Paradise Alley. Located behind the pre-1908 Arkansas Gazette *building, the site was a legendary location for the vices sometimes associated with the printing trades. (Courtesy UALR Archives and Special Collections)*

The Arkansas Optic.

Edited and Published by the Deaf Mute Institute, a Free School for the Deaf Children of Arkansas.

VOL. XLII. LITTLE ROCK, ARK., OCTOBER 10, 1922. NO. 1

THE GLOBE.

SILOAM SPRINGS, BENTON COUNTY, ARKANSAS, JULY 8, 1882. VOL. I.

The Pike County Courier.

DEVOTED TO THE INTERESTS OF PIKE COUNTY. $1.00 p

Murfreesboro Arkansas Friday, January 23, 1909 No

THE NASHVILLE NEWS.
SEMI-WEEKLY.

Vol. XX. NASHVILLE, HOWARD COUNTY, ARKANSAS, SATURDAY, MAY 7, 1898. No. 31.

The Evening Reporter.

Vol. 1 Hope, Ark., Wednesday Evening November 7, 1894 No. 183.

Ward & Key, Family Medicines. The Star of Hope. Ward & Key. Leading Druggists.

VOLUME IV. HOPE, ARK., AUIST 29, 1903. NUMBER 46.

BY STAR PRINTING CO. *FOR HOPE AND F ARKANSAS.* Subscription Price, $1.50 per Year.

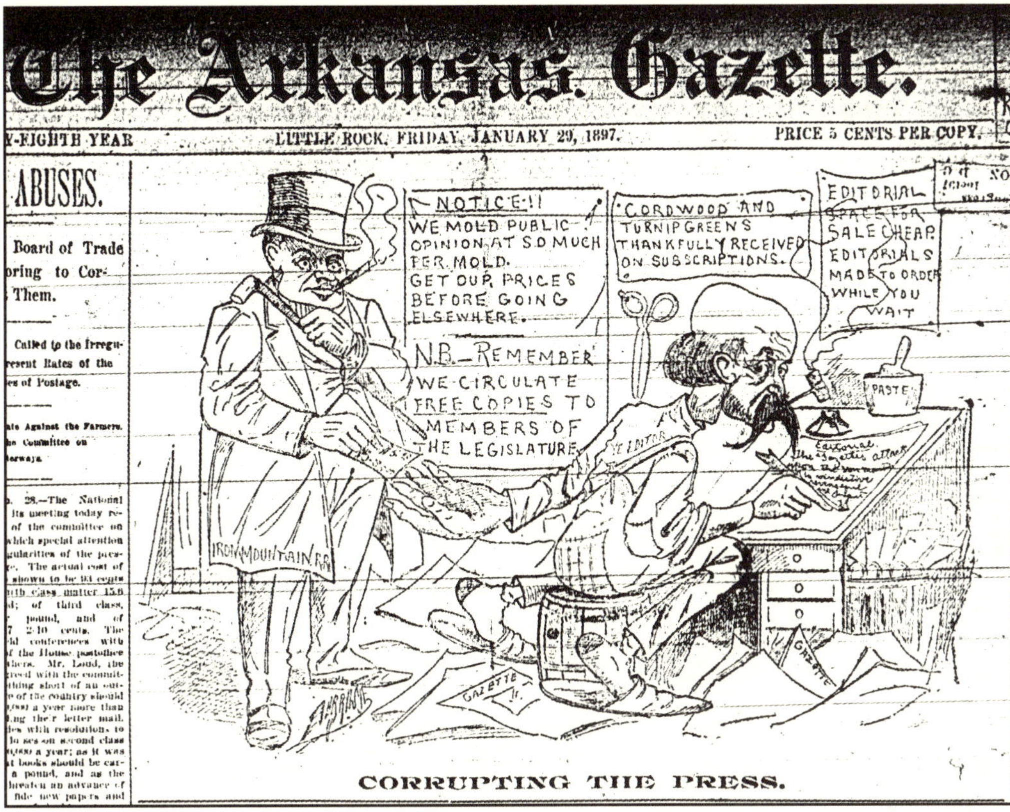
The Arkansas Gazette.

-EIGHTH YEAR LITTLE ROCK, FRIDAY, JANUARY 29, 1897. PRICE 5 CENTS PER COPY.

ABUSES.

Board of Trade
ring to Cor-
Them.

Called to the Irregu-
resent Rates of the
es of Postage.

CORRUPTING THE PRESS.

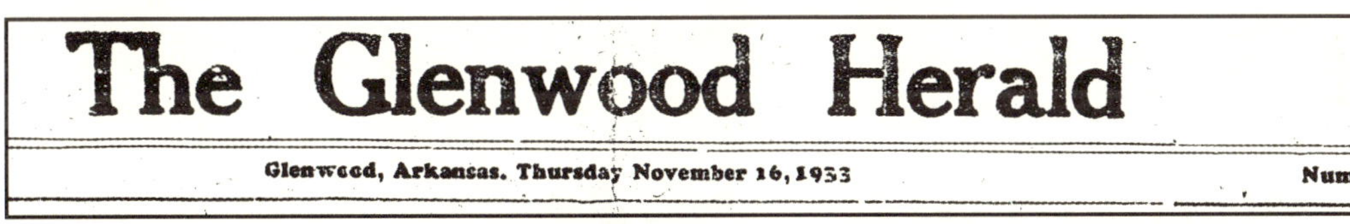
The Glenwood Herald

Glenwood, Arkansas. Thursday November 16, 1933

The Hardy Herald

HARDY, SHARP COUNTY, ARKANSAS, OCTOBER 14, 1927 WEEKLY—

Pike County---"The Garden Spot of Southwest Arkansas"

Pike County Courier

COUNTY SEAT WEEKLY NEWSPAPER

VOLUME 44 MURFREESBORO, ARK., DECEMBER 1, 1933 NUMBER 48

THE BAPTIST VANGUARD

A Religious and Educational Journal

THE OFFICIAL ORGAN OF THE MISSIONARY BAPTIST CONVENTION, CONSOLIDATED, (THE VOICE OF 100,000 BAPTIST IN ARKANSAS)

VOLUME 60 LITTLE ROCK, ARKANSAS OCTOBER 10, 1944 NUMBER

Telephone 102

Please bring or call all local, personal or social items to The Journal Office.

Located at 207 South Louisiana Street (Across from Frisco Depot)

SOUTHWEST JOURNAL

Volume 1 Hope, Arkansas, Wednesday, May 15, 1940 Number 1

25c Per Month

Delivered in Hope each Tuesday afternoon and Friday morning. By mail in Hempstead, Nevada, Lafayette and Howard counties, $1.50 a year. Elsewhere, $2.00 per year.

THE NEVADA NEWS

FOR DEFENSE BUY UNITED STATES SAVINGS BONDS

The Prescott Daily News Established 1907 The Nevada News Established 1905 Both Papers Consolidated January 8, 1942

VOLUME XXXVIII—No. 6 Thursday, June 11, 1942 Prescott, Nevada County, Arkansas

PRESCOTT DAILY MAIL

An independent, Democrat newspaper dedicated to the interests of Prescott and Nevada County.

VOLUME I PRESCOTT ARKANSAS, MONDAY AFTERNOON, NOVEMBER 3, 1047. NUMBER 68

THE BLEVINS NEWS

IN THE HEART OF THE CANTALOUPE BELT

VOLUME VIII.—NO. 7. BLEVINS, HEMPSTEAD, COUNTY, ARKANSAS, FRIDAY, APRIL 4, 1930. $1.50 PER YEAR

ARKANSAS EVENING HERALD

OLUME II. HOPE, ARKANSAS, MONDAY, JANUARY 28, 1918 NO. 301

The Daily Picayune

OL. 1—NO. 91 PRESCOTT, ARKANSAS, MONDAY, APRIL 18, 1921 PRICE FIVE CENTS

Classified advertising, in getting results, is just as effective as the Allied Armies in making a charge.

FOUR STATES PRESS

AND TEXARKANA COURIER

THE WEATHER.

Arkansas and East Texas—Saturday, rain, moderate temperature; Sunday probably fair, cooler.

ASSOCIATED PRESS FULL LEASED WIRE SERVICE TEXARKANA, U. S. A., SATURDAY, NOV. 16, 1918. ESTABLISHED IN 1875

Arkansas Developer

DEVOTED TO THE COMMERCIAL, MANUFACTURING, AGRICULTURAL, HORTICULTURAL, MINERAL AND TIMBER INTERESTS OF ARKANSAS AND THE INDIAN TERRITORY.

VOL. 1.--NO. 13. FORT SMITH, ARKANSAS, SATUR— SEP—MBER 29, 1894. SUBSCRIPTION PER YEAR ONLY 75 CENTS.

Arkansas Echo.

Allgemeine Zeitung für Wahrheit und Klarheit auf politischem und socialem Gebiete.

rgang 1. Little Rock, Donnerstag, den 21. Januar 1892. Nummer 4

The big picture in PARAGOULD

Picturing the People and Progress of Northeast Arkansas & Southeast Missouri

Spanish-American War prompted the *Pine Bluff Graphic* to issue a cartoon as well.[580] Doubtless others could be found were it not for the many lost issues.

When Frederick Allsopp listed the reporters of his acquaintance, he ended with a tribute to Harry Watkins, who both literally and figuratively had "a nose for news":

True poets of majestic rhyme
Must be descended from the muse,
But journalistic heights you climb
With simply this: A Nose for News;
So he who pines to join the press,
A news proboscis must possess.[581]

Opie Read and Ottmar Mergenthaler

Opie Read, Arkansas's premier 19th-century reporter-novelist, had a wild Arkansas ride. After his Carlisle and Conway experiences, Read accepted J.N. Smithee's offer of the city editorship at the *Democrat*, that is, he became the newspaper's sole reporter of local news. Read's genius was in creative writing, but Smithee said, "And what I want is news. Whenever a man comes to town, especially a man who has any political influence in his neighborhood, print his name. Yes, news, and no sketches, you understand."[582] While supposedly engaged in hard-nosed reporting, Read sat at the feet of such old giants as Richard H. Johnson, Thomas C. Peek, and others of antebellum ink. His greatest piece of straight writing, was, in his opinion, giving the story of the Smithee-Adams fight, which proved to be not at all to Smithee's liking. When Smithee finally hobbled back to the office, one of his first acts was to fire his city editor, allegedly for reporting incorrectly on another story.

The unemployed reporter then received an offer to go to Memphis and report on the yellow fever epidemic. Read went into the jaws of the most feared epidemic the 19th century experienced. His dispatches made him famous and resulted in another Little Rock job. The *Gazette* had been purchased by A.H. Sevier, who brought in Richard H. Johnson and the ubiquitous Thomas C. Peek as editors. Read worked at the *Gazette* probably until 1882, when he was replaced by Dan O'Sullivan.

In one of Read's recollections, he described how the state auditor and the governor came to blows in a barbershop and had to be separated by a policeman. Both men threatened Read with horrible consequences if the story was printed, but print it he did, and both apologized for their behavior.

Read became even more famous for another story. Short of news one evening, he invented, whole cloth, a story in which the old cannon on the statehouse grounds turned out to have been loaded and when struck by lightning sent forth its ancient ball that killed a man riding on horseback some two miles away. Read then made the mistake of identifying the dead man as Bradly Bunch. There was, in fact, such a man, a longtime legislator, and the next day Read was besieged by no less than ex-governor Henry M. Rector who wanted the full particulars of the death of "Poor old Bradly, tenderest man that ever lived!" Forced to confess that the story was a fabrication, Read was instructed to come to Rector's home where he met the living Bradly Bunch: "I read about being killed by that old cannon, but as I was about thirty miles down the river at the time the thing went off I was pretty well satisfied that I wasn't the man." The three then celebrated the event with some "old stuff," "log-distilled away back in 1812, sworn statement."[583]

Read's creative writings dealt with people and problems of the times and while humorous often carried a moral. Out-of-state newspapers began to pick these pieces up for filler, and although Read got no additional money, he thought they reflected well on the *Gazette*. Having married and needing more money, Read approached Johnson for a raise. Read argued his stories made the *Gazette* more valuable as an advertising medium, but Johnson replied, "if we had any more advertisements than we have now we'd have to enlarge the paper and that would be an expense."[584] Another of Johnson's views was: "Now mirth is one of the best features of life: it is the stimulating spice of the hearth-stone, but it's tragedy that makes the newspaper."[585] Read did not accept this view and on June 4, 1882 he and his brother-in-law started their own newspaper entitled the *Arkansas Traveler*, where Read's humorous sketches reigned supreme. Then, in the novel *Emmett Bonlore*, Read drew on all his experiences in creating a fictional hero who sought and succeeded in producing a quality newspaper free from personalities and cliques. Read became one of America's most popular novelists, making the Chicago Press Club, an exclusive group limited to 250 members, his headquarters. In 1893, Clio Harper reported Read's income at about $350 a month, or more then 10 times what a reporter would make.[586]

Read represented a type of reporter in Arkansas who had greater aspirations than merely listing the arrivals and departures and reporting as news what was really glorified advertising. Dan O'Sullivan, "best remembered by his tendency to quote Latin on every occasion when he could possibly inject a phrase from the dead language," finally left Little Rock to become the drama editor for the *Chicago Tribune*.[587] Novelists James Street, Charles Portis, and Dee Brown followed Read away from journalism and into literature, and all drew on their newspaper experiences.

Specialization grew apace in the late 19th century. By the early 20th century, the city press

---

A Week in the Life of a City Editor

After Clio Harper came to Little Rock and became city editor of the *Arkansas Democrat* at age 21, he wrote of his routine in his diary on May 27, 1894:

> My life is uneventful and devoted to living out a daily, well defined, and rather prosaic routine of existence. Up at 6 o'clock every morning, at work by 6:45, 8 to 9 around the hotels and police court, 10 to 12 state house and circuit and federal courts, write from 12 to 1, possibly eat dinner, probably go without, tell 3 o'clock odds and ends, after 3 till 6 or later, get copy for the next day, 8 to 11, or midnight attend some kind of entertainment, reception, meeting, or what not. Sunday morning. I sleep till 8 o'clock, eat breakfast, go to Sunday school and church, dinner at 1, afternoon at office reading, writing letters, and getting copy for Monday, church at night, preceded by Christian Endeavor, and there I am.

Other entries in the diary show that this routine indeed could vary. On October 2, 1894, after Little Rock was struck by the tornado, Harper hired a horse and followed the storm's track across town, writing up a page and a half of that evening's *Democrat*. And there was the occasion when Governor-elect James P. Clarke, whom the *Democrat* opposed politically, ordered Harper to leave the governor's office, explaining, "I want nothing to do with his g—d—slanderous sheet or anything connected with it. The d—rag will publish any lie without compunction, especially against me. We don't want you here." Harper took his revenge by reporting Clarke's exact words in the evening newspaper. The war between editor and governor continued for the next four years and perhaps beyond.

---

sported a business editor, religious editor, sports editor, society editor, agricultural editor, and political editor who worked under a city editor, a managing editor, an associate editor, and an editor-in-chief.

Read went on to become a prolific if not profound novelist, but writing sketches and human interest stories did not disappear. The *Gazette* from about 1882 to 1895 had Colonel M.L. De Mahler, who covered the state, largely on foot, writing under the name Potomac. Of mysterious origins, though probably from Virginia, he was "a linguist, a traveler, an artist, a geologist, as well as a graceful writer," but "peculiar in appearance and manners." His coming into a community always created a certain amount of excitement, for De Mahler styled himself "a development promoter," and that meant that some local story would soon appear in the far-away but ubiquitous *Arkansas Gazette*.[588] "His style of composition was original, but not popular," Allsopp recalled, "His sentences were complex, long-drawn-out and burdened with foreign words and idioms."[589] Compositors despised setting his copy, but saved their worst curses for Sam W. Williams, whose recollections of antebellum days graced an earlier chapter. Williams's "most miserable scrawl" resulted in them getting double compensation.[590]

Meanwhile, the mechanical world was undergoing revolutionary changes. On July 3, 1886, German inventor Ottmar Mergenthaler demonstrated his typesetting machine to Whitelaw Reid, the publisher of the *New York Tribune*. Sitting down at a keyboard, an idea copied from typewriters, an invention itself only about 10 years old, Mergenthaler tapped at the keys, thus setting into operation levers, tubes, gears, and molds that then spit out a thin metal slug, the face of which presented eight words of type.

"Ottmar, you have done it," Reid is alleged to exclaimed, "a line o' type." The greatest machine ever invented, William Jennings Bryan said, except for the Philadelphia Republican Machine.[591] Thus was born the Rube Goldberg-like Linotype machine that reigned for the next 90 years. There were many competitors, and Mark Twain, for one, lost a fortune on a failed model.

Clio Harper saw his first machine at the Columbian Expostion: "Today I saw a linotype in operation. It is truly a most wonderful machine. All the operator has to do is to manipulate the keyboard, and the machine sets, spaces, and distributes the type automatically, stereotyping each line separately. It is capable of doing the work of four hand compositors."[592] Other members of the Arkansas press doubtless witnessed this wonder during the APA's stay in Chicago in June.

However, when Harper went to work at the *Democrat* later in 1893, hand composition still prevailed. The panic of that year hurt the industry by reducing advertising and circulation. W.S. Mitchell, the *Democrat*'s business manager, told Harper that when conditions improved in perhaps two years, he hoped to get several typesetting machines and change over to a morning newspaper.

One cause for the *Democrat*'s delay was that from 1893 to 1896 it had to contend with the *Daily Press*. That too much competition resulted in too many weak newspapers was as true in town as it was it was in the country. Shortly after the *Press* succumbed, two Linotype machines arrived. Harper reported they could set 80,000 ems at less cost than 45,000 ems under the old system. The drawback was "that necessarily means more work for me to provide copy for the hungry maws, about twice as much as formerly being required." Meanwhile, W.S. Mitchell told Harper he was pushing ahead with the view of making the newpaper one of the leading organs in the South. As for Harper, he expressed to his diary the hope that the management would recognize that the two "rapacious Mergenthalers" could not be fed by "one lone Pooh-bah reporter."

Hot metal revolutionized the daily press

immediately by speeding up the setting of type. One old printer, offered a job learning the new machine, declined: "I'm a printer; I'm no piano-player."[593] At first, the Linotype displaced women, who had become increasingly common as typesetters, for running one of these machines was considered man's work. Having a blacksmith handy helped.

As Linotypes became common with dailies, the advantages of having a job-printing establishment connected to the newspaper diminished, for no longer were the newspaper and the job printing likely to be done by the same printers. The *Gazette* and the *Democrat* were both shed of job printing in less than a decade.

By 1890, the Mergenthaler Linotype Company turned out the Standard model that dailies purchased, although none in Arkansas had yet taken that step. The first machine installed in Little Rock was a Simplex at the commercial firm of H.G. Pugh Company. The Simplex and the Thorne had reputations for breaking type. In 1895, L.D. Freeman, who had worked for the *Memphis Avalanche* and the *Wynne Ripsaw*, before moving to Harrisburg and establishing the *Modern News*, bought one of these early machines, possibly the first such purchase for a weekly newspaper. It took weeks to get the monster from Memphis to Harrisburg, but it performed so badly Freeman reluctantly abandoned it.

The first typesetting machine in Benton County was installed by *The Bentonville Sun* around 1900. It was, Erwin Funk believed, a Simplex. The machine's cylinder had "real metal type, each letter in a groove" and had to revolve for each letter. It had other problems as well, notably with keeping the type clean. "A dustpan to gather the type on the floor was requisite equipment."[594]

Early in the 20th century came the Junior Mergenthaler. The first Junior in Arkansas was installed by John P. Stafford at the *Springdale News* in 1909. He had seen one displayed at the APA's Fort Smith meeting and wrote to users in Oklahoma and Texas for their opinions. Their favorable reports convinced him to go ahead.

After the Junior arrived, a machinist arrived from New Orleans and spent two days teaching Stafford's son how to operate and service it. Although the Junior came with a book of instructions, Stafford advised APA members to spend the extra amount to get the expert.[595] Another option the company offered was to train an employee in their school at New Orleans. At Newark, O.F. Craig, who bought a Junior in 1915, sent his son, Roy M. Craig, age 13, to New Orleans for instruction, where he became the youngest person in the country to complete the course. "Don't Knock Our Operator," the senior Craig later told readers, "remember that every line of type in this issue of the paper except about two columns was set on the Linotype by the editor's 13-year-old son, Roy, who never operated a Linotype in his life until last Monday."[596]

Like every innovation, cost-cutting helped sell machines. Stafford was able to discharge two young female compositors, but he hired another female who soon could set five galleys a day. Stafford put the costs for the gasoline engine that also powered the presses and folder at $15.00 per month, with an additional $4.00 needed for fuel to melt the recycled lead.

Stafford noted that he was able to run more matter, probably at less cost. Merganthaler estimated that the average cost of composition was less than 12 cents per thousand ems, compared to the 35 cents per thousand standard for compositors. Another advantage was in job work. Formerly time-consuming tabular work—in Stafford's illustration preparing the results of the county's primary election—was done in one evening. There was no fear of running out of figures or of a worker dropping any of the characters. (One issue of the *Jonesboro Sun* had an entire page blank when a devil slipped and fell.)

Another great benefit was the improvement the

machine made in scheduling. Prior to 1909, Stafford, whose newspaper went to press at noon on Thursday, printed four of his eight pages on Monday. Late news and country correspondents filled in the last four pages. The result was that sometimes he had to carry over some of this matter: "Those of you who make a feature of country correspondents know what it is to carry items over." With the Junior, these problems diminished: "A big bunch of copy on Thursday morning has no more terrors for us, and the Junior grows fat on it."

In his 1910 article, Stafford surveyed the state and found that there were nine machines in use in Arkansas. Among the enterprising publishers who had bought the first Juniors were L.B. White of the *Times-Courier* at Benton, Ed McCorkle of the *Star of Hope*, and W.W. Turner of the *Nashville News*. "We couldn't think of going back to hand composition," testified Adah Roussan of the *Osceola Times*.[597] At Harrisburg, L.D. Freeman had a crew excavate a hole under his non-working monster, dropped the machine into the hole, covered it with concrete, and set his new Linotype in its place.[598]

Erwin Funk at the *Rogers Democrat* followed Stafford's lead in 1910 but was far less enthusiastic about the results. "It was a rather erie [*sic*] looking contraption with each matrix having its own wire channel instead of a magazine. Each matrix had a different length, and as they swung around the wires it looked like a crowded merry-go-round on a busy day." Funk found that while it worked satisfactorily, it could cast only a 13-em slug, with the result that "the longer lines had to be butted." In 1919 he replaced it with the then-industry-standard model No. 8. The company's salesman had the Junior thrown out and demolished with a sledgehammer in order to keep the parts out of the market.[599]

James Holt, the Memphis representative of the American Type Foundry Co., counterattacked in 1917. The cost of these machines, which ran from $2,600 to $3,300, was roughly equal to the entire cost of a proper hand composition office. He concluded that "in a vast majority of instances they are an expensive luxury."[600] Nevertheless, a 1920 survey by W.A. Webber concluded that approximately 185 line casting or typesetting machines were in use.[601]

The Linotype, the Eighth Wonder of the World, as it was sometimes called, brought new interest to newspaper offices. At Newark, a meeting of Confederate veterans "by special invitation marched in a body to the Journal office where they inspected and witnessed the operation of the new Linotype machine recently installed and had some of the mysteries of the wonderful machine explained to them."[602]

Improvements in presses continued apace. "A printer of fifty years ago would be a novice in many a printing establishment today," Louis B. Audigier told the APA members in 1886, pointing to the Hoe Lightning Press, that gave 20,000 copies an hour or the Bulloch Web Press that printed on both sides.[603]

In 1889, the *Arkansas Gazette* replaced its two-revolution flat bed press with a second-hand Web Perfecting Press at a cost of some $10,000. Of the first Hoe four-and eight-plate pattern, it was 30 feet long and "looked more like a threshing machine than the present type of press," Allsopp recalled. Nevertheless, it was "a source of wonder to the people, and thousands visited the place at night to see it in operation and to watch the process of making into metal curved plates the matrix impressions formed from the type."[604] It was not replaced until 1903, at which point it was so obsolete that it had to be broken up and sold for junk, bringing $135.15. Allsopp took to poetry to commemorate its passing, for "I was attached to the machine, and disliked to see it go in this way, as it was like parting with an old friend."[605]

However, across rural Arkansas, the Washington press, the Vaughn Ideal, a Prouty, or a Country Campbell prevailed. Indeed, Arkansas was "a dumping ground for any old press or machine that they could not sell elsewhere," Hillory Jennings of the Keystone Typefoundry Co. told APA members.[606] By the 20th century the drum cylinder press was common, with 1903 being a banner year. J.W. Underwood believed that when the circulation of a weekly reached 1,000 or more, the hand press became too slow.[607] However, James Holt told the APA members in 1917 that the two-revolution machine was a better investment, primarily because of its greater speed. Increasingly, the Washington hand press could be found only in small and poor rural offices. Jennings told of selling a new press to Charles Gordon Newman at the *Pine Bluff Commercial* that replaced his old Campbell: "Jennings, please wait until I get out of the office before you smash that press again. It was the foundation of my business and I tell you it is dear to me."[608]

A few years later, Alex H. Washburn of the *Hope Star* proclaimed: "Watching a modern press perform, tugging at its roll of blank paper, and writing, writing, until it tosses the finished paper into the hands of the waiting newsboy—is a lesson in magic."[609]

The waiting newsboy was another important

aspect of the 19th century. In the major cities, many poor children lived entirely from their newspaper earnings; in Arkansas, although urban slums were not unknown, newspaper boys were drawn from all classes. As the century drew to a close and town photographers became ubiquitous, it became common to assemble the carriers and staff for a group photograph.

The carrier's world was revolutionized as well by an important invention, the bicycle. At first a play toy for the rich, it became after 1880 a popular transportation medium, with over a million machines being produced a year by the century's end. Instead of walking door-to-door, the carrier learned—or tried to learn—how to throw a newspaper from his machine on to a customer's porch or sidewalk without the newspaper breaking a window, or landing in the fish pond or in a puddle, and all without breaking stride in his peddling. Those delivering morning newspapers had to arise early, for, in increasing defiance of proper etiquette, many patrons expected to read the newspaper over breakfast. Boys working for evening newspapers went right from school to the office to pick up their bundles.

Often it became the custom for an older boy to supervise the carriers. The newspaper assigned routes, but delegated to the carriers the keeping of books and the collecting of subscriptions. While often touted as providing lessons in business education, this system also insulated newspapers from financial loss.

In addition to the carrier's income from sales, it remained customary for subscribers to give Christmas or New Year's presents. Newspapers themselves gave fancy dinners. The ancient custom of printing for the carriers a New Year's greeting or carriers' address survived into the early 20th century, and Major John D. Adams, for one, gave a five dollar gold piece to his carrier.[610] Frederick Allsopp took to poetry to describe the process:

The carrier, up with the lark,
With paper bundle, and light heart,
Goes out to meeting the smiling morn',
And to perform his useful part.
'Tis he who brings the news to you.
Oftimes your paper strikes the lawn,
Or finds a mud-hole, wet and torn,
Instead of landing at your door,
But all the news would die still-born,
Except for this same car-ri-er!

The Rise of the Unions

The invention of the Linotype and the new presses changed the world of printers. The man who refused to learn to play a piano could still find work for half a century in the smaller country offices. The tramp printer, a familiar feature of the 19th century, endured until after World War II. In the offices at Little Rock, Hot Springs, and even small towns, union rules required that anyone showing up and holding a valid card could be given work if a regular employee had worked his allotted time. Tourist-printers, to use their preferred term, ranked their places of employment, and some of their comments were posted on the walls of a closet in the composing room at the *Gazette*. It was, Fred Heiskell observed, "a huge autograph album, where names of tourists who travelled years ago, are inscribed, and where there are many evidences of the wit and the happy-go-lucky disposition of the old-time journeyman printer."[611] Because it was the morning newspaper, the *Gazette* attracted the most "tourists." Mixed in with "Weary Willie" Waterhouse, "Bughouse" Smith, and "Gadget" Reves were a few women, notably Miss Martha Throop.[612]

One long-remembered story was of a tramp printer at the *Arkansas Methodist*, who started work one morning but, on looking out the window, saw in the freight yards of a local railroad an empty boxcar. Putting his stick and rule in his pocket he "announced he was going to New Orleans and made a bee line for the open boxcar door."[613] Because tramps were union members and represented no threat, locals enjoyed their visits. In 1905 Little Rock members passed the hat, raising $5.50, "to be used in getting a brother out of Argenta [the future North Little Rock]."[614]

Union affairs for each newspaper were decided in that "ancient and honorable institution" called "chapel," supposedly named in honor of William Caxton having set up the first English press in Westminster. A "daddy" presided over these meetings. In 1887 the union sustained the *Gazette*'s "daddy" for fining a member who had insulted him.[615]

In the late 19th century the standard rate for hand-composition was 35 cents per thousand ems of 8-point straight matter. Those who set "head"(lines) and "ad"(vertisements) were paid more but were required to turn part of that over to the chapel. Printers commonly arrived an hour early to measure their "strings," in order to calculate their earnings, and to distribute back into the cases the type or "takes" from the previous day. Welfare in the 19th century was of the self-help variety, and printers looked after their own.[616] The ITU bought lots at Little Rock's Oakland cemetery and supported a retirement home in Colorado. One interment at the cemetery was Dan Taylor, the stereotyper who lived in the third-floor room at the *Democrat*'s printing office and was burned to death in the 1905 fire.[617] Another was of tramp printer Ed. C. Devine, who had deposited his card in January and hopped a freight on April 2, only to fall off and be killed at Judsonia.[618]

Health problems abounded, and the average life expectancy of a printer was 38 years. "It was necessary at least once a month," an old-timer recalled, "to use a pick and shovel to remove from the floor of some of the composing rooms the accumulation of tobacco juice."[619] Master printers belonged to Typothetae, which its members shortened to "Teapot."[620]

Since union identification ran high, no day was more important than Labor Day. All members were expected to parade, and at the 1891 parade a special marshal made sure no "rats" were in the procession. There was no national law fixing this date (or that of Thanksgiving), and in 1895 the ITU tried to get a state law passed.[621] The best remembered of these parades was that of 1930 when the city's fire department, in the lead, apparently thought they had been called to a fire and headed off full speed down Main Street with the floats following as fast as they could. The march was supposed to have ended at Fair Park, but some never reached it at all, and the city's streets were littered with pieces of floats from lost paraders. The ITU's float ended up behind that of the hod carriers.[622]

From the start the ITU supported other union activities, including the Knights of Labor in the 1880s and the American Federation of Labor in the early 1900s. By 1901 a fine of $1 was leveled against those found drinking non-union beer or patronizing non-union barber shops.[623] That same year W.L. Oury started the *Union Labor Bulletin*, which he edited until 1922 and which under other owners endured for most of the century. Oury "was never too busy to engage in a 'talk fest,'" and always had a place for a tourist to flop.[624] Another of the union's concerns, and one shared by the major printing firms, was that the legislature in the late 19th century continually let out-of-state bidders carry off the state's printing. Only in 1905 did the printers win a victory on this issue. Another victory for the union came in 1907 when the national body decided to meet in Hot Springs. By that time the Little Rock union boasted a woman's auxilary.

The next change in labor conditions came in 1919 when the national proposed a 44-hour workweek. This was to have been implemented in 1920, the same year that saw the rise of the Open Shop movement and initiated a decade not very favorable for unions. In Arkansas, both the Western Newspaper Union and the *Arkansas Democrat* refused to sign contracts, and protracted strikes followed.[625] The union survived these difficulties, and under its longtime secretary-treasurer, Elmer "Ma" Grant, was in prosperous condition when it celebrated its 75th anniversary in 1940. At that time, there were affiliated locals in El Dorado, Fort Smith, Pine Bluff, Hot Springs, and Texarkana.

Although it is customary to think in terms of management and labor, the distinction in the printing trade at least up to the 1950s was not firmly drawn. W.M. Shelby, president of the Little Rock local in 1892, started as a devil on the first newspaper in Texarkana. After getting a union card in 1880, he tramped for a few years before settling in, first at the *Arkansas Gazette* and then as the proofreader and telegraph editor for Kellogg's ready-print plant. In 1906 he moved to Batesville and acquired the *Record*, which he owned for the next two decades.[626]

J.H. Beerstecher, president of the local in 1913, had earlier served the union as recording secretary for several years. After working in Searcy, he moved to Little Rock, where he joined the *Gazette*. In 1916 he established the *Malvern Daily Record* and in subsequent years added other newspapers. He was the only union president also to serve as president of the APA (1948).

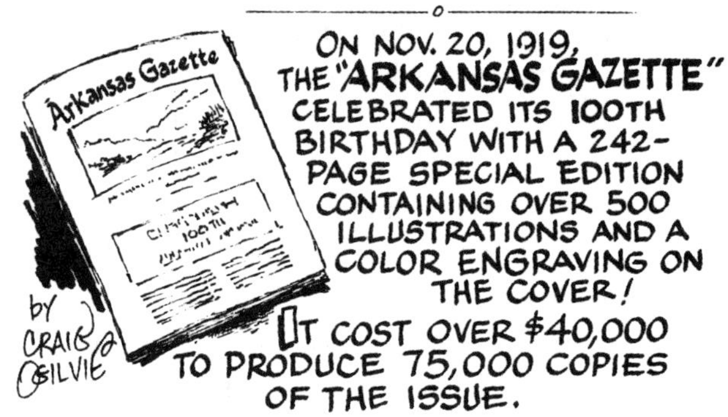

Other union members included John H. Page of the *Dardanelle Post-Dispatch*, state judge Frank H. Dodge, Labor Commissioner E.I. McKinley, Little Rock mayor H.A. Knowlton, and New Deal administrator Floyd Sharp. More typical was J.E. Purkins, whose nicknames were "Purk," "Colonel," and "Pocahontas." Purkins probably started a newspaper in the latter town in 1877 called the *Scalpel*. In the 1910s, he was at Hope, where he published the *Arkansas Evening Herald* and the *Hope Gazette*. However, most of his life was spent working at the *Arkansas Democrat*.[627]

The Growth of Dailies

In 1883, the Association's historian calculated that not one newspaper in five lived even two years. Of the 70 newspapers published in 1877 when Smithee gave his historical address, only 29 were still alive in 1883. Several dailies had already come and gone in Little Rock.

Although a few daily newspapers had appeared before the Civil War, not until the war's end did the daily form take permanent root. In 1886 the count stood at 10 dailies, 147 weeklies and two semi-weeklies.[628] By 1898 there were 26 dailies, 219 weeklies and three semi-weeklies. In that year, Arkansas had a larger number of newspapers and a larger circulation than any of the Southern states except Florida and Texas.[629] In 1909 the numbers stood at 27 dailies, 264 weeklies and 10 semi-weeklies.[630]

Circulation figures, of a sort, could be found in the *American Newspaper Directory* (subsequently known as *Ayer's* in the trade) beginning in 1869. It was the age of the circulation liar, however. In 1870, the *Republican*, which suspended at the end of Reconstruction, claimed 2,000 subscribers for its daily and 6,000 for its weekly, while the rival *Gazette* put its numbers at 1,000 and 2,500, respectively. The short-lived *Arkansas Herald* of 1874, one of those newspapers serviced by the ubiquitous Thomas C. Peek, claimed to be "the largest and widest circulated paper published in the State."[631] Reflective of the century's values, Fred Allsopp recalled, "I do not wish to give away any state secrets relative to circulations, because it is an ethic of our profession to respect such things, but I will say that it is a fact that I often carried an entire mail edition of the paper to the post-office in a sack on my back,—and I am no Sandow in strength."[632] (Sandow was known as the strongest man in the world.) Across the country, the weekly editions had much the larger circulation, and in the case of the *Arkansas Gazette*, penetrated everywhere in the state.

As dailies grew in size, a number of changes took place. At the late-19th-century *Gazette*, the pressroom was in the basement, while the editorial offices were on the second floor, which also contained the composing room. In addition, the job printing office and bindery were in the rear. Early on, the conflict between the business and editorial sides took the form of conflict over job printing. Businessmen placing job orders expected editorial favors as a reward.[633]

Even after the separation of job printing from newspaper publishing, conflicts continued. "The difference between Up-Stairs and Down is a subject which has caused many internal and uncivil wars in the print shops of the country, and it is with temerity that I approach it," Allsopp wrote. Indeed, the *Gazette* business manager once read a paper on the subject at an APA meeting, "but nearly all the audience left while I was reading it."[634] Allsopp's research convinced him that prevailing opinion considered the editor more pure and the business office a source of corruption. "I have heard of the editor editing the business manager, and also of the business department managing the editor," he observed. The two principal issues, both then, and at the time of this writing, concerned where and how to locate advertisements and what "free" news coverage to give to advertisers.

Over at the *Democrat*, where W.S. Mithchell "is visionary, but a close calculator," Clio Harper found the financial constaints to be a real strain when the legislature was in session. Too much of the newspaper was taken up "with 'slush' which nobody reads, and crowding out live news matter which would tend to make a respectable sheet." Mitchell was unwilling "to put on an extra case even if a dozen important items should come up which the regular force could not handle."[635]

It was rare that these issues reached the reader, but it did happen. On one occasion, the *Gazette*'s state editor picked up from the *Conway Times* the observation that, if a man found "a loose nut in his business, he should tighten it up." This prompted editor Fred Heiskell to add, "There are several loose nuts in this business, all of whom are in our business office." The office took offense and Allsopp replied that since the editorial side usually called them tightwads, not loose nuts, it was "another evidence of the general inconsistency of the sap-headed crowd up there. We dare the man who edits the column in the northeast corner of the 6th page to print this—*Business Office*."[636] Forthwith the exchange appeared in the newspaper. Some of the late-20th-century exchanges have not been so humorous.

Over the state, dailies arose and endured in many unlikely places. The three key elements were an adequate population, a strong trade area, and good management.

Nothing in the industry in Arkansas was ever typical, but one good example, as Dee Brown discovered, was the *Harrison Times*. In normal times, brothers Tom and John, one printer, one Linotype operator, and a girl who wrote local news constituted the staff. Tom's main role was clipping from other newspapers. The *Times* was an AP member, which meant that John would call the Little Rock office and get a five-minute report for stories to put on the front page. A number of impoverished editors who could get an early-morning metropolitan edition simply cribbed from it, but AP did provide extensive feature coverage editors could use if other news fell short.[637] Only as printing demands increased around Christmas did the brothers need more help in the printing plant.

In Harrison, the competition was with the weekly *Headlight*, not another daily. Hence, the struggle in the smaller communities was waged with indifferent advertisers and an apathetic public, not rival dailies. By contrast, an entirely different battlefield existed in the larger places.

Fort Smith

Fort Smith was a slaughterhouse of 19th-century Arkansas journalism.[638] After the Civil War the federal district court moved there from Van Buren as the Fort's former rival faded into a mere Fort Smith suburb. Afro-American, Republican, German, labor, and religious newspapers tried western Arkansas waters. Home first to the most corrupt federal court in American history and then to Isaac Parker, the hanging judge, Fort Smith moved from being one of Arkansas's most wide open communities to one of its most conservative.

John F. Wheeler, the founder of Fort Smith journalism, lived until 1880, active almost to the end. Wheeler and James H. Sparks were partners before and after the Civil War in the *Herald*. Sparks served as the second president of the APA from 1876 to

1877. In 1877 Sparks, who had acquired full ownership, leased the newspaper to J. Frank Gallagher and James E. Breitz who failed to make a go of a daily. James Saunders and Lawrence Lamb revived the *Herald* as a daily in 1880 but it suspended in 1883. The *Western Independent*, the *Daily Tribune*, and the *Elevator* were among the best known of probably two dozen casualties.

John and J. Henry Carnall were the proprietors of the *Fort Smith Elevator*. Its complex banner carried the curious motto, "Yes, while I live, no rich or noble Knave Shall walk the world, in credit to his grave."

George Rainey Williams, who started with the *Dardanelle Post*, was brought to Fort Smith by William M. Fishback, who became Arkansas's governor in 1893. Williams, who eventually lost his *Fort Smith Daily Times*, was APA president in 1890. A brilliant chess player and "pungent writer," his nickname was "Geranium."[639] W.O. Troutt of the *Jonesboro Sun*, who started his career at Spiro, Oklahoma, recalled that the *Times* "changed hands about every other first of the month when its bills became payable."[640]

All the issues of the day were fought out in these newspapers. On January 12, 1891, the *Evening Call*, the town's official newspaper at the time, reported the arrest of barber Albert Numrich, who had shaved a customer at the Hotel Main on Sunday morning, in patent violation of Arkansas law.[641] There was much editorial support for blue laws, even from newspapers whose Sunday edition (printed on Saturday) was nevertheless sold, distributed, and read on Sunday.

One success in the late 19th century was the *News Record*, begun in 1893 as a daily by a group of practical printers led (in age) by R.C. Hite. "The members of this firm threw all of their energies into their business," Allsopp recalled, "and by way supplementing their industry kept their heads clear from booze, a feat which some of their predecessors had been unable to accomplish."[642] The newspaper started with $10 in cash and the use of a press belonging to a weekly newspaper, the *Republican*. Of its four pages, two were ready-print. In 1894, A.J. Kendrick from Chicago purchased the good will. He bought first a Linotype machine, then a fast press, added another Linotype, and finally installed a folding machine. All this required a new building on Rogers Avenue costing $15,000. Instead of four pages, it became a six-column, eight-page affair.[643]

The *News Record* covered the great cyclone that hit the town on the evening of January 11, 1898. A headline was made with a black box and four different sizes of type were employed to summarize the disaster. The only picture was a sketch of "Working in the Debris" drawn by Ida Boles.[644] The *News Record* consolidated with the *Times* in 1909 to make the *Times Record*. The *Southwest American* was the work of Colonel W.E. Decker, who came from Ohio by way of Oklahoma. Allsopp called it "a modern journal with Associated Press leased wire, other news services and special correspondents at important points."[645]

When Decker decided to sell out in the early 1920s, he did not want control to go his arch-rival, J.S. Parks of *Times Record*, so the sale was made to a Tulsa firm. However, it turned out that firm was just a front for Parks, and Fort Smith thereafter became the largest monopoly market in Arkansas. As for Decker, he headed off to California in a caravan of open touring cars. He lost one fortune during the Depression in California real estate but reportedly made another in raising turkeys.[646]

Pine Bluff

Pine Bluff pictured herself as the queen city of the Delta. Its postwar record was also cluttered with failures. One was the *Pine Bluff Press* of Wyatt C. Thomas and Major Charles Gordon Newman. Before the *Press* died, Newman started the *Pine Bluff Commercial* after first having gone to Cincinnati and acquiring a new outfit. Active in APA from the start, he served as president in 1878 while still with the

Press. In 1887, he started an evening daily. At first Newman got wire service second hand from the Western Newspaper Union in Little Rock. Then, in 1907, he signed up with the Associated Press under what was called the pony system, each item having, he said, as much information as Mabel's postcard: "Having a good time, wish you were with us." Then he went to telephone wire service and finally in 1917 to full AP service. The newspaper was a success, and Newman remained in complete control until 1902 when his son-in-law, E.W. Freeman, joined him.[647] Newman was a colorful character, and at the Fourth of July celebrations in Little Rock in 1899, that also included the groudbreaking for the new state capitol, Newman, a capitol commission member, read the Declaration of Independence "in a manner so convincing," Clio Harper confided to his diary, "that had he been prosecuting King George before an Arkansas jury, they must have returned a verdict from the box sentencing the royal malefactor to be drawn and quartered or boiled to death in alcohol."[648]

Newman apparently believed the statement which he placed at the head of the editorial column—"Founded by Charles Gordon Newman, in 1868"—which was only partly true for the *Press* and not at all for the *Commercial*. Arkansas journalism history had several unfortunate parallels. The *Arkansas Gazette* miscalculated its age and volume numbers, but the worst offense was committed by the *Arkansas Democrat* in 1921, when it published a 50th anniversary issue in complete defiance of history by claiming both to date uninterruptedly from 1871 and to being the lineal descendant of William E. Woodruff's 1846 newspaper of the same name![649]

The second enduring newspaper of Pine Bluff started as the *Weekly Graphic* of 1886. Read Fletcher, a notable character with a long history of involvement in the town's newspapers as well as a local correspondent for the *Gazette* and *St. Louis Globe-Democrat*, was the first editor. Before the Civil War, Fletcher was traveling down the Mississippi River with Congressman Thomas C. Hindman who gave Fletcher a message about needing a fighting editor at Napoleon. "Nowadays," Fletcher wrote very much prematurely in 1876, "brains, tact, talent, good morals, cultivation, mental process and the observance of the 'small, sweet courtesies of life' so eloquently hailed by Sterne, are the powerful weapons which win applause."[650]

If not unique, it was certainly distinctive of Fletcher that he put his editorials on the front page. One of his causes was gun control: "There is too much indiscriminate 'pistol toting,' and the revolver is too conspicuous in this community," he proclaimed in 1887.[651] Two years later J.W. Adams acquired the *Graphic*, converting it to a daily. His brother, George H. Adams, continued this morning newspaper that also had Associated Press service. Neither of the Adamses nor E.W. Freeman were Pine Bluff natives, and both George and E.W. had arrived from Kentucky together. Adams was the first head of the state organization of Associated Press newspapers. In its declining years, the *Graphic* switched to United Press. "Serve It with Every Breakfast" was the newspaper's motto, and it expired on March 11, 1942, as Allied planes where hitting Japanese bases and Pine Bluff was just about to experience an enormous wartime growth that would have prolonged its life.[652]

Helena

Helena was one of Pine Bluff's rivals for the trade and industry of the Delta. Its complex newspaper history grew even more complicated after the Civil War. W.S. Burnett, a Mississippi native and former apprentice at the *Democratic Star* and *Southern Shield*, started up the *Western Clarion* on April 1, 1865. There may have been a daily version as well. Although he began his career as a Republican, by 1871 he had switched sides. One of the founders of the *Helena Weekly World*, he took that newspaper into daily status. After selling out to William R. Burke, he tried a rival organ, the *Helena Daily Mail*. After it suspended he stayed away from the business until 1885, when he repurchased the *World*.[653] The *World* later passed into and out of the hands of a corporation before Pine Bluff's George H. Adams bought it in 1906. The next year the newspaper's city editor, J.M. Scott, was assassinated. In 1910, Adams sold the *World* to Charles M. Young (APA president, 1933), whose family owned it for most of the rest of the century. The *World* long claimed to have purchased the first Linotype machine outside of Little Rock in Arkansas. In addition to many weeklies, other dailies in Helena included the *Daily Independent* (1874), *Daily Tribune* (1877), and some the names of which even Allsopp had forgotten.[654]

Hot Springs

Another of the regional centers was Hot Springs. The special clientele of spa customers produced a superheated newspaper environment. Gambling, prostitution, and quackery took root there, nourished by some in the press and condemned by others. Dailies started there as early as 1873. The *Daily and Weekly Telegraph*, of which W.A. Webber (APA president, 1885) was a sometime publisher, once ran a Confederate flag as a heading for a story on Union veterans. The war had not yet become a time of fraternal reunion, and most the issues were suppressed. Those that survived sold as souvenirs.[655]

The *Weekly Horse Shoe* turned into a daily in 1882, but its editor, Charles Matthews, was shot to death in a street duel on September 22, 1882. A subsequent editor, Major Mose C. Harris, was jailed in 1883 for criticizing the circuit judge in the case and was run out of town when he wrote of the Flynn-Doran War rival gambling interests fought. Although expelled from the APA, he reportedly later collected $2,500 in damages against Hot Springs in federal court.[656] A merger with the *Hornet* resulted in the

People's Hornet-Horse Shoe. Editor J.L. Wadley (APA president, 1902) renamed the newspaper the *News* and converted it from being "the only Republican daily in the South" into a Democratic organ. Like his predecessors, he was on the side of clean government in a dirty town.[657]

Another early daily was the *Sentinel*. Its owners on February 25, 1878, were William R. Burke of Helena and George Russ Brown, the longtime *Arkansas Gazette* employee. Ten days later, one of Hot Springs's great fires ended their career. A subsequent owner was John G. Higgins, who in 1899 founded the *Record* and later merged the two into a morning newspaper with Associated Press service. The 1922 fire of May 10 caused the newspaper to miss an issue.

The third important newspaper started as the *Semi-Weekly Bulletin* in 1906. Its founder was Robert O. Schaefer (APA president, 1922), a 20-year-old reporter who left the *News* to found the *Citizens Bulletin*. "We Stand for Honest Elections and a Square Court," it announced in dedicating itself to political reform and progressive causes. The established *Sentinel Record* called it a "fly-by-night publication [that] will take the same course of many of its forerunners."[658] Nevertheless, it grew from its narrow campaign origins to become the *Daily Bulletin*.

Honest elections were not popular with Garland County officials, so under "The Infant Editor" the editorial office stocked a small arsenal of weapons.

Schaefer took on the political establishment over election fraud when excelsior instead of ballots was found in supposedly already counted ballot boxes. Jailed on contempt-of-court charges, Schaefer had his story picked up by the *St. Louis Post-Dispatch*, which pictured the prisoner-editor working away from behind bars.

Another notable event in the *Bulletin*'s history concerned woman reporter Alta Smith. She was returning from the court house on a snowy day when the street-car conductor slipped and fell out of the moving vehicle, leaving three women aboard. Miss Smith tried to stop the car but her actions only made it go faster, so she contented herself with ringing the gong fiercely as the runaway car careened on. She continued to experiment with the controls and eventually found one that stopped it. The Hot Springs Street Railway System presented her with a gold badge and lifetime free rides. The story of Arkansas's Nelly Bly received considerable attention in the state's press.[659]

As the *Bulletin* matured, it slowly changed. Humor appeared. "Brutal Fight Occurred Last Night" was about a fight between a dog and a badger at a livery stable down from the Arlington. The newspaper acquired the Hearst Service for national news; had a Christmas issue by 1908; and undertook to promote a town Chautauqua. By the time it became the *New Era* in 1911, the bold motto had long been gone.[660]After acquiring the *Daily News* it became the town's established afternoon newspaper. Clyde Palmer acquired both the *Sentinel Record* and the *New Era* in 1929, and Hot Springs, like Fort Smith, became a monopoly town.

The dependence of Hot Springs on tourism resulted in newspapers rather different from those elsewhere. Arkansas affairs were not as important as Illinois news for many readers. During much of the 20th century, Mayor Leo P. McLaughlin ruled Hot Springs and Garland County. Gambling ranked second only to the baths in the town's life, and corruption spread from the county machine to infect the entire state.

As the statistics indicate, there were other dailies in 19th-century Arkansas. As some towns added dailies, others lost them. Redistribution of population after 1900 was the prime factor, but community support and the quality of the newspaper itself helped determine survival. In short, Arkansas possessed a metropolitan and state press in Little Rock, larger dailies in Fort Smith, Pine Bluff, Helena, and Hot Springs, and smaller dailies in towns ranging from Arkadelphia to Texarkana.

There are Many Mansions

In 1881, there appeared in Little Rock a newspaper entitled the *Arkansas Weekly Mansion* with C.O. Jacko as "editor-in-chief." "A white lady, by the name of Mrs. E.J. Chapman, who often passes by our office," Jacko wrote, "seeing that we were unable to afford the luxury of painted sign, had one painted, and sent to us by her little boy and girl." Thus did the second most prominent black newspaper in Arkansas get launched.[661]

Jacko went on to the short-lived *Independent* but the *Mansion* was revived with Henry Simkins as editor. Simkins announced his intention to expand his four-page, seven-column newspaper to eight columns, and he had a regular correspondent at Lonoke. The *Mansion* had patent insides that apparently came from a source that regularly supplied black newspapers with reading material that proved to be far more valuable than the common run. But Henry Simkins is important for other reasons. Not only did he join the APA, but he took part in the group's 1883 excursion to Texas and wrote a multi-sectioned report on the trip. The tantalizingly incomplete report found Simkins to be the expected victim of discrimination in notoriously bigoted Texas, but a number of the press gang, including Mrs. Mary

W. Loughborough of the *Arkansas Ladies Journal*, "never forgot to ask Simkins, how are you getting along [and] upon the whole we had a nice set of gentlemen and ladies, there was no disposition on the part of our gang to make it unpleasant for us."[662]

Long forgotten was that during the 1880s American life was still integrated. Public-accommodation laws existed and were enforced. Major league baseball was integrated well over a half-century before Jackie Robinson supposedly broke the color barrier. And at the *Mansion*, Simkins defended using the lower case for negro "as the word was born in derision. For our part we prefer choosing the least of the evils and be called colored people. Nationally we are all Afro-Americans."[663]

One of the leading issues of the day was debating the meaning of the United States Supreme Court's ruling in the Civil Rights Cases. What the court effectively said was that while states were barred from discriminating, private parties were free to do as they pleased. Simkins declared his support for the decision and castigated other black editors for wanting, to use a modern term, affirmative action.[664] Unfortunately, the court's decision proved to be the first step in undoing all civil rights for the black people of the South.

Simkins, who could hold his own editorially with any writer in the state, may have come to grief when he advised black men in Howard County to "stand firm and if our women are beaten and outraged riddle the perpetrator of it with bullets, let the consequences be as it may." Unfortunately, for the next half-century the consequences led to whites lynching blacks in ever-increasing numbers.[665]

At the APA's Fayetteville meeting in 1884, Henry Simkins and Mose C. Harris of Hot Springs were expelled without explanation. The *Mansion* merged with the *Herald* and soon disappeared. Simkins's policy of not collecting the subscription price of $1.50 in advance doubtless did not help.[666]

Perhaps two dozen or more black newspapers appeared around the turn of the century in Helena, Fort Smith, Pine Bluff, and in small Delta towns. In 1893, as separate and unequal triumphed, a Negro Press Association was formed, largely to protest the emerging new order. William Buford of the *Arkansas Dispatch* was president and F.W. White from Searcy's *Arkansas Mule* was secretary. At the 1894 meeting, there were speeches by Judge M.W. Gibbs and other notables in opposition to segregation legislation. The white press gave the Association scant coverage.[667] The full content of these meetings and of the newspapers represented is unknown, but in the repressive atmosphere of the times both the black press and its association soon perished. In 1976, archivist Amanda Saar combed through a variety of sources in identifying 183 black publications up to that time. All the usual forms—school, religious, special interest groups, and general newspapers were represented—but copies exist for only a handful.[668]

Women founded newspapers directed at their sex. Mary W. Loughborough's *Arkansas Ladies Journal* of 1884 was followed by Clara A. McDiarmid's *Woman's Chronicle* that championed bestowing the right to vote and also served as the official organ of the state's Women's Christian Temperance Union (WCTU). Catherine Cunningham, a sometime *Chronicle* editor, was instructed by legislators to "go home and attend to house and babies," but the APA was more solicitous. Both regular and honorary memberships were extended to women in the press, and to Miss Georgine Woodruff, a daughter of the *Gazette*'s founder.

German-language newspapers were also represented within the APA. The name *Arkansas Staats-Zeitung* (City News) was used for three newspapers, the first dating to 1866, the second in 1869 and 1870, and the last from 1877 until World War I. Phil Dietzgen had charge of it from 1877 until around 1900. He was followed by George Doerner,

who stood over six feet in height, weighed more than 250 pounds, and had five fingers and a thumb on each hand and reportedly six toes on each foot.[669] One rural newspaper of the late 19th century was the *Logan County Anzeiger* (Advertiser).

Dietzgen, the *Arkansas Staats Zeitung* editor in 1891, apparently offended the state's German Catholics, who then created the *Arkansas Echo*. The *Echo*'s first issue was delayed when someone broke into the office, pied all the forms and scattered the type. When the belated first issue of the *Echo* appeared, it insinuated that Dietzgen was responsible. He sued for libel, but the jury found for the *Echo*.[670] Dietzgen found a good opportunity to counterattack when on April 21, 1892 the *Echo*, in publishing a report of an upcoming marriage, made a blunder in its use of the past tense, thereby suggesting that the couple had been sexually intimate before the marriage. Dietzgen called attention to this in postcards sent to Father Bonaventura, one of the newspaper's founders. The *Echo* turned the postcards over to the federal prosecutor and the grand jury indicted Dietzgen for obscenity. Although acquitted, Dietzgen suffered another indignity when *Echo* editor Karl Meurer assaulted him on the streets. After knocking Dietzgen to the ground, Meurer promptly turned himself in to the authorities and pled guilty to assault.[671] That did not end the war, however, for Dietzgen next attacked the *Echo*'s treasurer, Adolph Arnold. Arnold, who ran a second-hand store, charged Dietzgen with criminal libel over a poem that had appeared in the newspaper. The case turned over whether the term *staufp-schule* meant a "darning school" or a whorehouse. Two days of testimony found the German community divided on this fine point, and Dietzen was again acquitted.[672]

The *Echo* was printed on a Linotype with German Gothic characters. Its motto, "Allgemeine Zeitung fur Wahrheit und Klarheit auf dem Politichen und Socialen Gebiete," (A Popular Newspaper for Truth and Clarity in the Political and Social Spheres) aptly defined its mission. Editor Karl Meurer was born in Wipperfürth in 1849 and came to Arkansas in 1881, the "emigration year" for Germans in Arkansas. Meurer had a thorough education and a command of seven languages. Although a staunch Catholic, he gave some space to Lutherans and to all German club activities. In the early years, he encouraged and mobilized Germans to become active in politics. Perhaps his greatest achievement was in surviving the vicious anti-German prejudices during World War I. "He held the *Echo* upright through all the difficult years," his son recalled.[673]

There were many similarities between the *Echo* and the better country newspapers. Peter Wilhelm Schmitz, its correspondent from Brown, wrote "folksy items."[674] Greatly concerned with what the editor saw as an already vanishing history, it published a series of pioneer stories and tales. One extended series came from the pen of missionary Father Eugene Weibel. Collected and published separately, it was translated into English in 1967.[675]

Some of the principal themes of the early years centered on problems of acculturation. Many of the Germans were Catholic, and anti-Catholic prejudice remained active. Although Germans could be found in the mines of western Arkansas, most were farmers.

One article discussed how a man was cheated out of his land; another explained the problem of retaining land secured from the railroad companies.[676] The church was often the center of German culture in Arkansas, and parish events were regularly reported. The first golden wedding anniversary of a German couple, Gerhart and Elizabeth Kordsmeir, was a highlight event.[677] The newspaper defended Catholic schools, encouraged first-generation families to learn English and second-generation families to retain German, and offered readers a joint subscription plan with the *Arkansas Democrat*.[678]

At its peak just before World War I it claimed a circulation of 1,300. Besides providing national and international news, it offered "a useful background for a person seeking naturalization in the United States."[679]

Another category was labor newspapers. The Agricultural Wheel and the Populist party produced dozens of short-lived organs around election times. The *Southern Economist* of Searcy, which was six years old in 1893, had as the slogan of its publisher and editor Homer Prince, "Free Silver or Bust." Bust it did, and both the newspaper and its editor were unknown to Allsopp.[680] More enduring and more narrowly focused was the *Union Labor Bulletin*, founded in 1898 by W.L. Oury. His father, of the same name, had the *Forrest City Times* from 1871 to 1885. After they moved to West Plains to publish the *Gazette*, the son moved to Little Rock where he was foreman of the job printing plant of the *Arkansas Gazette* and secretary of the typographers' union. As Allsopp was forced to testify, "Deeply rooted in 'Bill' Oury's system were the principles of union labor."[681] Labor's organ survived well into the last quarter of the 20th century.

In the old APA all were deemed welcome. The newspaper became the universal medium for every cause or special interest, and counted among the state's press were the publishers of virtually any sort of respectable journal, including those published monthly.

One type of publication that appeared in the late 19th century was the predecessor of the shopper. A number of stores bought from the patents a small ready-print paper, added their own advertisements and pretended this constituted a newspaper. The postal authorities, who held control over second-class mailing permits, took a dim view of such "newspapers," but how to resolve the conflict between legitimacy and government control worried some editors. Apparently the first in Little Rock was the *Daily Advertiser* that started in 1904 and endured for three or four years.[682]

The religious press was another important component. The state's leading ministers played roles of importance in the state's political affairs. The most conspicuous religiously affiliated figure in the APA was Methodist layman George Thornburgh, who settled in Lawrence County after the Civil War. Thornburgh's first newspaper was the *Walnut Ridge Telephone*. A lawyer, legislator, and colonel in the Brooks-Baxter War, he moved to Little Rock, bringing along with him the *Masonic Trowel*, a fraternal newspaper, of which he was the longtime editor. Thornburgh was one of the organizers of the state's Anti-Saloon League and the acknowledged leader of the prohibitionist movement. In addition, he was a part-owner and manager of the *Arkansas Methodist*. His election as APA president in 1891 reflected the broad nature of the old APA as well as a growing anti-alcohol sentiment within the formal body. In 1918, Thornburgh was elected superintendent of the Arkansas School for the Blind, which also published a newspaper. Thornburgh's grandson was John Workman, the religious editor and columnist of the *Arkansas Gazette* prior to its demise in 1991.

Although the state had a number of Baptist editors and newspapers, none played a role in the

THE "ARKANSAS BAPTIST," FOUNDED IN 1859 IN LITTLE ROCK BY REV. P.S.G. WATSON, WAS THE STATE'S FIRST RELIGIOUS NEWSPAPER.

APA comparable with that of Thornburgh in the 19th century or A.C. Millar in the 20th. In the late 19th century, the leading publication was the *Arkansas Baptist*. However, a split within the ranks of state Baptists led to the permanent secession of the more conservative Missionary Baptists. They had control of the *Arkansas Baptist* and merged it with another organ to form the *Baptist and Commoner*. It came under the control of Brother Ben Bogard, a powerful preacher and determined opponent of anything liberal. Baptists adhering to the Southern Baptist Convention then founded a new organ, the *Baptist Advance*, with J.S. Compere from a famous Baptist family as editor.

Virtually every denomination, white or black, represented in Arkansas sported an organ, and most used newspaper format into the 1950s. Although none of their editors played important roles in the APA, the religious press in the 19th century was actively against the publication and even the reading of newspapers on Sunday. In the 1920s, the still-powerful religious press undertook crusades on behalf of banning the teaching of evolution, stopping the sale of gasoline on Sundays, forbidding mixed bathing, the sale of one-piece bathing suits, and cigarettes. In some denominations, the religious press supported the Ku Klux Klan.

Ironically, church newspapers, and the *Arkansas Methodist* was the leader in this cause, might have been hostile to saloons, but their advertising revenue was largely derived from patent medicines that were heavily laced with both alcohol and opiates.

Another type of publication with APA affiliation was of the literary sort. Robert J. "Bert" Brown, a younger brother of George Russ Brown, one was of the first who tried to fill this long-felt need. *The Grand Opera House Program* of 1882 was his first effort in this direction, and others included *The Life*, a Sunday literary newspaper, *Arkansas Life*, and a humorous journal appropriately entitled *Arkansas Toothpick*. Brown, whose other ventures included the weekly *Star* at Stuttgart and the *Daily Globe* at Hot Springs, ended his creative efforts with *Revolution*, a philosophical journal, in 1900.[683] The *Saturday Bee*, which started in 1895, enlisted at times Fred Allsopp and O.C. Ludwig. It "stung everybody who had been connected with [it]," Allsopp lamented.[684]

By far the best known of perhaps some two dozen literary organs was the *Sketch Book*, a high-class pictorial and literary magazine of the early 20th century edited by Mrs. Bernie Babcock. Mrs. Babcock, the author of *The Soul of Ann Rutledge*, a once-famous novel about Abraham Lincoln's alleged childhood sweetheart, had a long career as a writer, including a stint as editor of a newspaper in Pulaski Heights, the state's first suburb. The *Sketch Book* got nice reviews if few readers. An APA member, she spoke at the 1907 meeting.

The most enduring literary newspapers were of the humorous order. After Opie Read had the distinction of being fired, first by Colonel Smithee from the *Arkansas Democrat*, and then by Dick Johnson from the *Arkansas Gazette*, he responded by starting his own newspaper, the *Arkansas Traveler*. Doubtless the most-used name for journals in the state's history, the Arkansas Traveler of story, song, and painting formed a triptych of cultural humor of the sort Victorian Arkansas was anxious to suppress. Read rummaged though the rural press for good material, and then mined it for a national audience. There was so much animosity to his exploitation of Arkansas's rusticity that Read moved the newspaper to Chicago. His own interests soon turned to writing novels, and the newspaper eventually expired. Read, however, retained his interest in the state that gave him his start. He contributed a humorous piece to the *Arkansas Gazette*'s centennial edition in 1919 and wrote J.N. Heiskell a complimentary letter after the publication of the Arkansas Centennial edition in 1936. Heiskell replied that he was looking forward to starting a regular series on the state to be entitled "The Chronicles of Arkansas." Although Read was long dead in the 1950s when Margaret Ross was assigned to write the series, it carried the kind of historical material in which he delighted.

Another humorous publication that long delighted those with a taste for the arcane and macabre was the weekly *Arkansaw Thomas Cat* of Jefferson Davis Orear of Hot Springs. Styled as a "Journalistic Highball for people now on earth," the *Thomas Cat*, its editor confessed, was "not built for babies or convention club women. Every issue is Necromantic Narrator of the Nigesceant, Noxious, Nozzling Nuisance of a Nation swollen with ignorance and pride."

Orear, in addition to being something of a village atheist, also tackled controversial topics. In 1917, an exposé on a Hot Springs man led to a $40,000 damage suit being filed against the newspaper. Although the plaintiff won, the jury awarded him but one dollar.[685] Orear was an active member of the APA, and for the 1921 meeting devised an imaginary menu. Among the entrées was Compote of Cigar Snipe, Tobacco Flavor; the vegetables included Stewed Bunions; and one of the dining room rules was, "Biscuits riveted together can be opened with a chisel supplied by a waiter. The use of dynamite is strictly forbidden."[686] Most humor publications were of short duration, but this one began publication in 1890 and survived for more than 40 years.

Other cultural publications appeared outside the APA's wide umbrella. *Musical Topics*, "Devoted to the Advancement of Music, Art and Literature," began publication as a monthly in Little Rock in July 1901. Its subscription rate was 50 cents for 16 pages. In addition to musical criticism (including a review of Ignace Jan Paderewski's new and now forgotten opera *Manru*), it included the "V.M.I. [Virginia Military Institute] March" for piano by Charles J. MacHenry. While not considered newspapers today, such publications graced the various historians' reports in the APA's published proceedings. Frederick W. Allsopp listed dozens of such publications that invariably failed to find their niche in filling a long-felt need.

Educational journals were among the first specialized publications. Started in October 1871 and enduring for a few years was the *Belle Grove School Journal* from Fort Smith, apparently the first publication from a public school. J.M. Lucey, its founder and high school principal, later became the state's best known Catholic priest and an early historian of the church in Arkansas. Miss Nannie Haglin was one of the editors, reflecting the growing importance of women in education.[687] Numerous other professional journals came and went. The *Arkansas School Journal* started in 1880 with J.L. Denton, the state superintendent of public instruction, as editor. Denton grew so depressed over the cause of education in Arkansas that he committed suicide in 1882.[688]

Some colleges issued their own publications in hopes of recruiting students and attracting financial support. *The Endeavor*, a three-column tabloid, was published monthly by the faculty of Arkansas Cumberland College at 50 cents a year. The state's first college newspaper was from the Masonic school Albert Pike had sponsored before the Civil War. St. John's failed to thrive, but the *College Record*, founded in 1872 by its students, pointed the way for other college publications.[689]

One common 19th-century arrangement could be

found at Hendrix College in Conway where the *Hendrix College Mirror*, founded in 1890, was the work of the Franklin and Harlan Literary Society, and the *Bulldog*, founded in 1912, was the school newspaper. By far the best-titled student newspaper was the *Petriculanian* from Little Rock College, the predecessor institution to the University of Arkansas at Little Rock (UALR).[690]

College newspapers pre-dated sometimes by a quarter of a century the creation of journalism departments. Usually under the sponsorship of a faculty member, students elected the editor who then chose the staff. Such journals reflected institutional values and had little editorial freedom. The University of Arkansas had ongoing problems over content and personalities, reflective of its divergent constituencies. On the other hand, Jonesboro's little state agricultural high school of 1910 boasted the *Aggie Herald* in 1921 that became the *State College Herald* in 1932 and *The Herald* once the institution became Arkansas State University in 1967. The institution's journalism department was contemporaneous with its Fayetteville counterpart. Northeastern Arkansas's answer to Walter J. Lemke was for 38 years Leland W. "Tex" Plunkett, whose English professor-father had taught the college's first journalism classes. Tex's role as newspaper sponsor led one president to attempt his firing, but the president departed instead. Among the best known of Plunkett's students were Gene Foreman, editor of the *Philadelphia Inquirer*, and Roy Ockert, who edited the *Batesville Guard*, the *Russellville Courier* and the *Jonesboro Sun*, as well as teaching journalism at Arkansas College in Batesville and Arkansas State University.

Printing was invariably done off campus. When Jonesboro's Arkansas State College in 1933 acquired two printing presses and two second-hand Linotype machines, it had a complete setup some 15 years ahead of Fayetteville.[691] Having the equipment led to the creation of a printing department that strengthened Jonesboro's already strong printing community, and it prepared the way for Jonesboro to become a national printing center in the late 20th century.

Other institutions had publications as well. The Deaf Mute Institute in Little Rock published the *Arkansas Optic* for at least 40 years. The mutes performed all the mechanical work, and editor F.B. Yates was a paid-up APA member.[692]

Agriculture journals were a venerable part of American journalism, and several were attempted in Arkansas. Among W.A. Webber's long list of newspapers was the *Rural and Workman*, a small, three-column journal "for farmers, mechanics and workmen." The newspaper's vice president was Dr. M.M. McGuire, the APA's president in 1881-82. Webber and McGuire attempted to use their extensive connections to promote the newspaper. The subscription rate was $1.50, but a prospective subscriber could take it and the *Russellville Democrat* for only $2.00. Such piggyback arrangements were common in the 19th century.[693]

"Some of our readers are disposed to criticise the make-up of the Rural and Workman, by insisting that we give no news," Webber noted. And it was valid: "We confess that we are in no sense a newspaper." News belonged to weekly and daily newspapers; *Rural and Workman*'s mission was "to aid the farmer and the workmen in their respective callings" and to "share with their better to do neighbors, more of the pleasures and comforts of home, the family altar and fireside." Webber printed Tennyson's new poem, "Freedom" and reported that the apples Red June, Astrachan, Early Harvest, and Ben Davis did well at Judsonia.[694] *Arkansas Developer* from Fort Smith became the official organ of the State Horticultural Society during the 1890s, but that organization was badly divided when prohibitionists sought to eradicate Arkansas's growing wine industry.[695]

As American life became more specialized, each

interest or occupation organized. The newspaper format soon gave way to that of the magazine or journal. The bankers sported the *Arkansas Banker*; the doctors dug into the *Journal of the Arkansas Medical Society*. There was even a publication on construction news of which R.O. Schaefer was editor. On the eve of the Great Depression, Parke-Harper Publications specialized in this field. Among their titles were *The Arkansas Sheriff*, *The Southern Peace Officer*, *The Homemaker*, *The Southern Musical Journal*, the *A.O.U.W. Guide*, *The Arkansas Realtor*, *The Arkansas Christian*, *Sanatorium Outlook*, the *Arkansas Churchman*, *Arkansas Farm and Marketing*; and even the *Commonwealth College Fortnightly* and *The Quapaw Scout*. At least two of the editors from that collection were active in the APA: H.L. Cross (APA president, 1903), who after his retirement from the *Bentonville Sun* edited the *A.O.U.W. Guide* for the Ancient Order of United Workmen, and Mrs. Florence B. Cotnam of *The Homemaker*.

This section winds down with the *American Puzzler* of 1886. Started at London, in Pope County, it included among its editors R.L. Blakely, O.C. Ludwig (APA president, 1894) and E.E. Smithee (son of J.N. Smithee). Measuring only six by nine inches, Allsopp heard that "its contents were said to be a high order and instructive to devotees of mystic lore."[696]

Conclusion

In 1931 W.O. Troutt, who had made the *Jonesboro Evening Sun* a successful small-town daily, recalled his first newspaper of 30 years earlier outside of Fort Smith at Spiro, Oklahoma. Troutt had paid $150.00 for a Washington hand press on which he had published a five column quarto with ready print insides. His idea of a headline read: IMPORTANT NOTICE, and the story explained that he would accept wood, potatoes, onions, pumpkins, or corn for subscriptions. He persevered, and after selling out for $600.00 went to Jonesboro where he bought the *Sun* and converted it into a daily.[697] Troutt's story was typical. Hardly a single 19th-century publisher had had any experience with a daily press before deciding to start one. Opie Read, who fictionalized the process in *Emmett Bonlore*, had his hero start by getting Associated Press service. That was too expensive for almost all the small-town dailies. They continued to rely on ready print sources or crib from other newspapers.

The rise of the daily gradually resulted in a new kind of editor. What was commonly known as "The old-time master" by the 1930s, he of "fancy scrolls of his pen and flowery manner in which he could connect up words in reporting marriages, births, death or social items of the community or the pleasing manner in which he could tell of the good qualities and boost to the skies the politician or county orator," could not thrive under the constant pressure of a daily deadline. "Personal journalism," as J.H. Sparks defined it in 1878, was gradually replaced by the demand that Smithee had made to Read, for news, strictly factual news.

With the passing of Colonel Donan and others of this ilk, the APA changed. Erwin Funk recalled that in the days of his APA youth, convention programs "were heavy with long essays on the glories of the quill and pen and insistence that the editor was the real leader of every community, even though the poorest paid."[698] But the increasing expense of Linotypes and other equipment needed for establishing a newspaper office drove the profession into the business world. In those great group pictures taken in the early years of the 20th century, one can see in the faces and clothes of the people all the newspaper types assembled together, some looking back to their glorious past struggles, and others pointing ahead to brave new worlds.

Chapter VI

Publishing for Profit: The Press in the 1920s

"Reporters, not editors, make a newspaper."
J.N. Heiskell, quoted in Ray Reid, "Romances of American Journalism," *Editors & Publisher and the Fourth Estate*, December 1, 1928.

"At the present time we have but few editorial writers whose opinions sway a State or Nation, not from lack of ability but because today the average reader thinks for himself, or doesn't think at all."
J.B. Parker, *Conway News*, 1929.

"We are confident that [the Ku Klux Klan] will find few adherents here, for it is one organization the residents of Marked Tree can do without."
Marked Tree Tribune, September 10, 1926.

"If you think it is any fun to print a newspaper on a job press, standing in water knee deep, try it once."
A.B. Avery, Lake Village *Chicot Spectator*, 1927.

The APA: "from a club of enjoyment, [it] has blossomed out as a school of instruction and business."
Colonel Ed Landvoight, Forrest City *Times-Herald*, 1928.

Introduction

As America settled into William G. Harding's "Normalcy" after World War I, a different Arkansas began to emerge. Except in those parts of eastern Arkansas still experiencing agricultural growth due to the expansion of drainage projects, a sluggish rigidity and "stand-pat" attitude emerged. No longer was it possible to "grow up with the country," for agricultural maturity had been reached, and in reality a state of decline was already well underway. Soil exhaustion caused by poor farming practices, blights, diseases, poor marketing by the state's orchards, and a failure to industrialize characterized the early 1920s.

Across America, the 1920s saw a continuation of the "joiner" attitude. Older organizations were transformed in hopes of making them more useful, and new bodies emerged to fill new needs. The progressive impulse, although moribund in the Washington of Warren G. Harding and Calvin Coolidge, thrived at the state and local levels. "Better roads to better schools," the slogan for gubernatorial winner John E. Martineau in 1926, identified two issues many local editors strongly promoted. In addition, many small towns tried to encourage industrialization, for, as President Calvin Coolidge proclaimed, "The business of America is business." As usual, editors were in the forefront of the age.

The Ku Klux Klan and the Press

The "War to End All Wars" coincided with what was viewed at the time as one of the greatest Progressive victories imaginable—Prohibition. Arkansas was already a nominally dry state, which in reality meant that local bootleggers now had a monopoly on production and sales. Across much of rural Arkansas, the blandishments of preachers made little dent against strongly held cultural values fortified by the need to survive economically, while townspeople knew or learned quickly where to drive to pick up glass canning jars and leave their money in its place. Local law enforcement officials often were elected not to enforce the law, and if they were not pliable, the profits were so great that juries could be corrupted. Over-diligent officers—like the deputy sheriff for the eastern district of Craighead County—would be gunned down. National prohibition simply expanded the market as hearse after hearse carried something other than the dead from Arkansas to St. Louis and Chicago.

The massive anything-but-passive resistance that greeted Prohibition was a fertile seedbed for one of the most colorful and misunderstood activities of the age, the reappearance of an organized Ku Klux Klan in Arkansas.

The origins of the early 20th-century Klan lay in history and fiction. For Southern whites, the early years of the century were spent in blotting out every recollection of Reconstruction while cementing blacks into the neo-slavery world of "Jim Crow." It was in this atmosphere that a popular novel, *The Clansman* (1905) by Thomas Dixon, stirred the imaginations of filmmaker D.W. Griffith, who used it in *The Birth of a Nation* (1915). Then, an impressionable former Methodist circuit rider, William Joseph Simmons, recreated the Klan as a fraternal body—at first public—that fit right in with the Masons, the Elks, and the American Legion. Only after he hired two former war bond salespeople did this group begin to find its niche in American life, for they instinctively divined the fears of middle-class Americans and capitalized on it to the maximum.

Nationally, Arkansas ranked near the bottom in Klan activity, largely because this Klan was made up of small-town and urban businessmen rather than farmers. Similar to another new club, Rotary, except that it met at night, it was a club that businessmen joined with every sincere intention of doing good. It is important to note that in contrast to Reconstruction, when blacks and Republicans were the main enemies, Republicans were well-represented in leadership, very few racially motivated actions were undertaken in Arkansas, and the Klan was often weakest in the plantation counties.

The first recorded appearance of the Klan came in Prescott in mid-December 1921; in the weeks before Christmas, Klansmen in their white robes visited churches in half-a-dozen towns to leave donations, fooling almost no one, for everybody knew everybody else's shoes and pants. Since this Klan was nominally secret, most newspapers kept a discreet distance even if, as was often the case, the editor or publisher was a member.

One might deduce that in Conway a strong case could be made that J.B. Parker of the *Conway News* was a Klansman. Parker had dedicated his newspaper to "stand for RIGHT against wrong": taking on Sabbath desecration, the Missouri Pacific's "menacing freight yard," kissing ("an unclean and dangerous habit"), the teaching of evolution, and other evils of the day.[699] Compulsory Bible reading (adopted in Arkansas during the 1930s) and flag saluting were two of his favored causes.[700] He noted the first official appearance of the Klan in Conway in January 1922, when they endorsed a local judge in his war against crime. The crimes in this case consisted of unspecified Sabbath violations (one in Jonesboro was cutting grass) but possibly selling cigarettes to minors, and either the possession or sale of whiskey. Parker struck an ecumenical note, for alongside the Klan's statement were other similarly worded endorsements from the men's Bible classes of the Baptist and Methodist churches.[701]

After a rally of some 4000 Klans members in Little Rock in April 1922, Parker quoted approvingly the Rev. H.G. Knowles of the capital's First Christian Church: "Surely we cannot object to several thousand of our leading citizens resorting to secret, yet withal lawful measures, to uphold law and enforce it throughout the land."[702] And under the headline "Mysterious Visitors in Mayflower Vicinity," Parker told of a Klan group from Conway who traveled by automobile to that notorious community where they issued warnings against "bootleggers and distillers and other law breakers."[703] Forthwith, a Klan appeared at Hendrix College; not surprisingly, since Dr. Alexander Copeland Millar, a former college president and longtime APA member, was an early supporter.[704] Yet Parker avoided direct endorsement and even printed an advertisement during the summer of 1922 from a group opposing the Klan. In short, Parker kept his secret thoughts to himself and his newspaper open.

During the organization's early months, agendas were strictly local. Hence, in the oil boom counties of south Arkansas, labor unions, the businessmen's favorite enemy, were the Klan's targets. At El Dorado they drove out a lawyer representing the International Workers of the World. Klans in Ouachita and Union counties, where oil riches had broken down the social order, made war on prostitution and the open sale of liquor.[705] In Little Rock and Fort Smith, Catholicism was the main issues. Klansmen in Fort Smith forced the recall of Mayor Fagan Bourland, and all Klans united in calling for the expulsion of Catholic teachers from the public schools.[706] In Benton County the impetus came from opposition to the creation of local road districts.[707] Elsewhere, Klans went after wife beaters, adulterers, and gamblers.

The acceptance that greeted the early Klan was reflected in a report in the *Batesville Record* in the fall of 1923. Apparently the Klan did not arrive until the fall of 1922, but the next year it gave Independence County a big bang, or perhaps more correctly, a big cross. In mid-September the Batesville and Newark Klans held a public initiation at the fair grounds with over 6000 persons in attendance. "Many well known citizens were recognized as they drove their cars through the entrance and gave the password to the sentinels," the newspaper's reporter noted. At eight o'clock a mammoth cross lighted by electricity glowed forth as the Klan members marched in, the crowd having been augmented by the arrival of a large contingent from a Methodist protracted meeting. The lead speaker was the Rev. J.O. Johnson of Peoples Baptist Church at Little Rock, who explained the objects and principles of the organization. He repudiated any acts of violence, and while claiming that the organization was not against Jews and Catholics but only for Americans, declared it the group's goal to see "that the Protestant religion and protestantism rules, in this, a Protestant country." "The scene from a distance was beautiful," the enthusiastic reporter noted, "and at the same time imparting to the uninitiated a feeling of awe and mystery."[708]

A little is known about the Newark Klan, which seems to have been merely the operating arm of the local Masons. Their lodge was used for a meeting hall, and white Klan uniforms were discovered there in the 1950s when the building was torn down. With no Catholics and only one well-liked Jew in town, this Klan focused on local gambling and petty thievery. The Big Bottom Klan was especially active in charitable work. In a show of strength, they visited each of Newark's major churches, marching silently up the aisle during services, sporting an American flag and leaving a donation with the minister. Throughout the state, the KKK song entered the repertory of singing schools.[709] The *Newark Journal* recorded these activities without comment.

One newspaper that did comment early on was the *Forrest City Times and Herald*. Part of the trouble started over an election to the Chamber of Commerce. On August 9, 1922, a front-page headline read KLAN PLACES BOYCOTT ON TIMES-HERALD. Seven men, whom the newspaper listed, came in and cancelled their subscriptions after a local Klan meeting decided to "stop the *Times-Herald*." "We have no apology to offer, no retraction to make," editor John T. Durst noted, "We have no desire to retain on our list those who believe in a 'muzzled' press, or in the un-American practice of 'boycotting.'"[710] In contrast to the mountain counties, the Delta contained more Catholics and especially a large Jewish merchant class.

Perhaps the most notable struggle took place in Searcy County, where social divisions exacerbated by the Civil War still flourished. At first, things went peacefully. On July 8, 1923, at the end of a revival at the Christian Church, 20 robed Klansmen marched down the aisle and presented a check for $20. On their way out, the obviously well-rehearsed choir sang "Onward Christian Soldiers".[711] But on October 27, a Searcy County farmer died of gunshot wounds after a riot at a Klan meeting in St. Joe. Minister J.H. Tudor, who later purchased the *Marshall Republican*, had introduced Dr. L.M. Copeland, a national lecturer from the Klan, at the town's opera house. Copeland was unable to speak as the room was packed with Klan opponents, and the shooting occurred outside after the meeting had broken up. "The county has been considerably excited as a result of the series of Klan meetings, which have drawn large crowds," the *Mountain Wave* noted. Opponents created The Order of Anti-Poke Noses to fight the "Hoods."[712] A third county newspaper, the anti-Klan *Eagle*, appeared and soon claimed a circulation of over 1,000.

What was at stake in Searcy County economically was the survival of hill farmers who made wildcat liquor. "Are not most all of the men who are operating stills and selling and drinking liquor members of the anti-Klan?" a Klan manifesto asked.[713] In addition to causing a death, Klan members were alleged to have ordered the beating of Frederick Houghton, a former Democratic candidate for assessor. Sheriff "Big Dan" Patterson, also a Democrat, arrested four men for this action. When Patterson announced his decision to run for reelection, a hailstorm of protest from Klan supporters appeared. Patterson campaigned on an anti-Klan platform, closing it with a poem that a Klan supporter said "would make Shakespeare get out of his grave and climb a telephone pole."[714] Three months later, on the eve of the delinquent tax sale, Patterson committed suicide in his office in the courthouse.[715]

The historian of the Klan in Arkansas observed, "no town was too small, no election too minor, for the Klan to become the preeminent issue."[716] Obviously, a survey of 75 counties is beyond the scope of this work, but one important point needs to be noted: while the Klan excluded blacks (as well as Chinese, Jews, Catholics, and immigrants in general) from membership, it was not a major factor in the state's race-relations records. The Elaine Race Riot, the Nodena and Jonesboro lynchings, and other racially charged events in the Delta came earlier; indeed, planters were now worried about black flight diminishing their labor supply. The Klan's Arkansas historian noted that the first violent episode consisted of the Texarakana Klan whipping a black man for "fooling about a white woman," but the Klan in that border town early fell afoul of the law and must have lacked much social prestige.[717]

The collapse of the Klan came once it entered state politics. Its state Wizard, James A. Comer, a former Bull Moose Republican, had visions of becoming a kingmaker. By holding a Klan primary prior to the Democratic primary (which in the mostly one-party state decided office holders), Comer gained great initial power. In Little Rock the entire Klan slate, headed by Sheriff Homer Adkins, a future governor, was elected. Defeated Klan candidates rebelled, however, and one gubernatorial candidate, Tom Terral, unable to get any Arkansas Klan to admit him to membership, found a compliant group in his native Louisiana. The "Klansman without a home" was elected governor in 1924.

The idea, as William M. Shelby at the *Batesville Record* phrased it, "for a very small minority to rule the democratic party and dictate party nominees" was "the rock upon which we fear the political ship may be wrecked."[718] O.F. Craig at Newark, who seldom agreed with his county editorial compatriots, wrote: "The Journal has no fight to make upon the Ku Klux Klan so long as it confines itself to fields of morality, charity and fraternalism, but when it enters politics, attempts to run the government, as it did in Oklahoma, and attempts to dictate to free-born American citizens as how they shall vote, as has been done in Arkansas, it is high time for somebody to speak out in protest."[719] Even more devastating was the attack made by the Forrest City newspaper. Under the headline "A SAMPLE OF KU KLUX PROPAGANDA," Durst found a Northern Klan newspaper that claimed both Robert E. Lee and Jefferson Davis were agents of the Pope and that took exception to Lee's face being carved on Stone Mountain. As the Forrest City editor noted, "Klan organs publish many columns of misstatements, as groundless as the article referred to. We are sure our readers realize the utter futility of attempting to deny all, or any of them."[720] After losing a local election, the Klan in St. Francis County filed suit. A recount showed they had lost by an even greater margin.[721] Meanwhile, emboldened by Terral's victory, other politicians and newspapers took up the challenge. A splinter group called the Mystic Knights appeared, but it was a power struggle in the women's division that finally precipitated the group's collapse in Arkansas.

Although brief in duration, the Klan episode engendered longstanding hard feelings in many communities. It reinforced for many the image of closed-minded small-town Arkansas.

Taking Stock, 1920–1930

There had been a recognition even before World War I that the age of great heroes was passing. Perhaps this sense prompted Fred Allsopp to capture from his own knowledge and from that of the older veterans he knew the materials that went into writing the *History of the Arkansas Press for a Hundred Years and More* (1922).

Frederick William Allsopp (1867–1946), a native of Wolverhampton, Staffordshire, England, was 12 when his family arrived in Prescott, the county seat of Nevada County. After first selling newspapers from a newsstand, he went to work setting type in the office of the *Prescott Picayune* before moving in 1886 to Little Rock, where he eventually rose to become business manager and in 1902 a major stockholder in the *Arkansas Gazette*. He had other interests as well, for Allsopp and Chapple was Little Rock's leading bookstore. Allsopp, who never held the office of editor, turned his attention to writing books in his later years. In addition to two volumes of press history, he authored a biography of Albert Pike and collected and published much poetry and folklore. In trying his own hand at poetry, he produced a nine-stanza tribute entitled "Lines to the 'Old Lady.'" The *Arkansas Gazette*'s annual birthday was long a celebrated event in Little Rock and in newspaper circles generally. "If I have done anything good in this world, it is through my connection with the *Gazette*," he said shortly before his death. His personal recollections were recorded in *Little Adventures in*

Newspaperdom (1922).

Allsopp's press history sought both to characterize the era of personal and political newspapers in Arkansas and to be encyclopedic at the same time. Personality, not technology, interested him most, but by 1920 the industry's emphasis had turned to publishing for profit.[722]

Makers and Shakers

The principal architect of profitable publishing was the redoubtable Erwin Funk (1877–1960) of Rogers. Born in Iowa, young Erwin started work as a carrier in Manning, Iowa, when about 13 years old. In the absence of a folding machine, the boys first had to assemble their newspapers before making deliveries. While in high school he contributed school items under an assumed name for the local newspaper. Gradually, he began writing regular articles and then worked for three months in a book bindery. Erwin was 17 when his father, Emanuel M., a lawyer, traded some land for a newspaper and put his son in charge as editor. There Erwin learned the skills of printing from the bottom (inker) up (pressman). In 1896, during the height of the free silver campaign, his father sold the newspaper and moved the family to Springdale, where he had bought the *Democrat*. The competition with the veteran editor John Stafford of the *Springdale News* proved too much, and after a few unsuccessful months, his father then traded some land in Arkansas County for the plant of the *Rogers Democrat*, which Erwin took over in early 1897. For the next 20 years, the father remained the nominal publisher while the son served as editor.

World War I took Erwin to Little Rock and France, but on his return to Rogers he bought out his father's interest, modernized the plant, and adopted the advertising pricing system known as the Franklin List or Little Black Book sold by R.T. Porte. At the APA's 1921 convention, the *Rogers Democrat* won awards for the best front-page make-up and best

newspaper from a mechanical standpoint.[723] Two years later, in an unprecedented event, the weekly repeated the wins.[724] National awards came his way as well. In 1923 the *Democrat* won a contest (sponsored by the National Editorial Association) for the best want advertisement of 15 lines, as well as coming in second in a circulation contest and fourth in a membership drive.[725]

Dr. A.C. Millar of the *Arkansas Methodist*, and for half a century the APA's official chaplain, summarized Funk's achievements:

> The Rogers Democrat, edited by Mr. Erwin Funk, is one of the best county newspapers published in Arkansas, or anywhere else, for that matter. The editorials are always timely and strong, and the news of the town and country around is given in fine form.[726]

After Funk's newspaper won the APA's award for the third time, the contest ended and in 1925 Funk was elected APA president.[727] One newspaper surmised that Funk's election was intended to bar him from contests: "You know it will not look well for an officer to gobble up the prizes."[728]

As president-elect, Funk repeated his call for "editors to do away with the poverty jokes concerning newspapers and to place the business on the same high plane as many other businesses. He told his fellow members to sell job printing and advertising on a service basis of their true value, and not on any begging plea."[729] Funk was a crusader against unpaid subscriptions and undercharged advertising. During the 1920s, he became a nationally known apostle for these causes. A man of enlarged vision who liked to travel, he served the Arkansas Press Association for five years as secretary and then in 1925–26 as president. In 1928 he was chosen as head of the National Editorial Association, where he campaigned across the country for "Better Citizens Through Better Newspapers." By his count, 1929 was a banner year, for he attended 25 banquets and 50 luncheons, giving 23 addresses and 43 short talks while covering some 28 states and managing his newspaper from long distance. When the first issue of *Arkansas Publisher* came out in September 1927, the cleverly constructed cover showed a picture of Erwin Funk's face bursting through the front page of his newspaper.

Funk's commitment to the business world of the 1920s found expression in his organizational work for the Rotary Clubs. He was the first secretary at Rogers, at that time the smallest town in America with a club. "Rotary day is always one of the outstanding events of the week for me," he confided to his diary in 1934.[730]

Funk also took good citizenship seriously. His reputation was as a liberal, and in 1926, after an editorial about a scandalous local election, four election officials filed suit against him for $40,000.[731] The suit was eventually dropped. Funk was also an advocate for women in journalism, telling the Ozark Press Association meeting in Springfield that "the successful woman publisher can hold her own with men any time, both in editorial and business management."[732]

Little wonder his doctor told him to retire, and in 1929, just before the Depression, he sold the *Democrat* to Everett W. Pate and James P. Shofner.

Funk's career was by no means over. During the New Deal he attempted to implement the Blue Eagle's newspaper code, and in 1959, the year before his death, he was in attendance at the APA's mid-winter meeting at Hot Springs diligently writing journal entries every day.

The election of Funk as president in 1925 and the publication of the *Arkansas Publisher* two years later were not fortuitous coincidences. If Funk was the apostle of modernization, Clio Harper (1872–1932) of Parke-Harper publications and Association secretary during the 1920s, recorded with an eye to detail the results of Funk's crusade. A transitional figure in Arkansas journalism, Harper encouraged modernization even as he celebrated the glories of the past.

Harper's father, a Union veteran, settled in Boone County. Young Harper attended high school in Harrison while working in the office of Alex C. Hull's *Boone Banner*. His newspaper reports on the Columbian Exposition in Chicago caught the attention of James Mitchell at the *Arkansas Democrat*, and in 1893 Harper moved to Little Rock, where he eventually became city editor, editor-in-chief, and finally a part-owner. In 1911, he left to found with A.W. Parke a news service and publishing company. He remained active in the APA, and served as its secretary from 1916 until his death. A joiner and organization man, Harper also edited a newsletter called the *Arkansas Traveler* in the interests of one of the new groups active in Arkansas in the early 1920s, the Ku Klux Klan. Harper held the title of Grand Kligrapp, the secretaryship, throughout that group's existence.[733] Harper served as a Little Rock alderman from 1912 to 1920 and was an elder in Little Rock's First Christian Church. He was, Fred W. Allsopp recalled, "a talented and industrious, God-fearing, self-made man," and while an "active and accommodating newspaper writer," he had "an idealistic side to his nature known only to his intimates" that was reflected in his poetry.

In 1920, Harper took over the publication of a four-page bulletin entitled *Arkansas Press Gossip*. Out of this grew a more formal publication that he started in 1927, entitled *Arkansas Publisher*. Like Allsopp, whom he resembled in many ways, Harper was enamored of the press and its history. Both his publications began as labors of love with very little institutional backing, principally because there was no institutional structure to back sustained activities.

Since the time of its founding, the Arkansas Press Association had assembled annually, meeting in the late spring or early summer. In addition to this meeting, it was customary to hold a press day at the state fair in the fall. Then in 1906 the first mid-winter meeting was called. But it was only after 1915 that these became annual events. In the early 1920s, some members pushed for the purchase of a club house at Glenwood-on-the-Caddo, but sufficient financial support never materialized.[734]

In the 1910s and '20s, the Association began holding its first contests, but these, too, were of short duration. The essential problem was the absence of a paid secretary to give the organization continuity. It was in that regard that Harper again reflected the transitional nature of the age. In 1927, when he started the *Arkansas Publisher*, it was at the cost of a quarter. In response to many complaints, he agreed to charge a dollar a year for 12 issues, each of which was some 15 pages long and printed on quality paper.[735] Advertisements, notably from railroads, paid most of the bills, but despite being labeled the official organ of the APA, Harper assumed the expenses personally.[736]

During his editorship, he devoured every newspaper he could get his hands on, summarizing their contents and quoting their best work. His lovingly crafted obituaries celebrated the glories of the passing leaders of the press, but he also took notice as well of up-and-coming men like Hugh Park at Van Buren or O. Klute Braswell at Berryville. Colonel Ed Landvoight at Forrest City predicted that the *Arkansas Publisher* would act as "'mother hen over a brood of chickens,' giving advice, correcting errors and protecting country papers."[737]

Women, still not organized in the state, received their due, too. *Fayetteville Democrat* editor Lessie Stringfellow Read made the December 1928 cover, as did Miss Luna Kelley of the *Lonoke Democrat* in May 1929. No less than nine prominent females graced the August 1931 cover. Leading off was Mrs. Florence B. Cotnam, of the *Homemaker*, and a political and moral force in Little Rock for many years. Lessie Stringfellow Read reappeared, as did the former Luna Kelley, now Mrs. Owen K. Davis. One of the most enduring so pictured was Mrs. Nellie Trevathan of the *Batesville Guard*. The problem of how to identify married women was evident in this issue as Harper added a "Mrs." in front of each married woman's name.[738]

Typical of the nostalgia for the past was an unsigned obituary of Charles B. Blackburn (1850–1929), written by Frederick W. Allsopp. The son of W. Jasper Blackburn, Charles Blackburn started the *Flower of Magnolia* at age 19, founded the *Hope City Times* in 1874, and then moved to Little Rock, where he and his father issued *Blackburn's Free South* from 1882 to 1895. Thereafter he worked as a proofreader for the *Arkansas Democrat*.[739]

Blackburn wrote stories and poems, was an intimate friend of Opie Read, and exemplified, Allsopp noted, "the old school." Blackburn's political writings were "marked by an incisive invective more strong than polished logic," but it was his poetry that most attracted Allsopp, and it was typical of the "old school" that Blackburn's religion tended toward "adventitious pessimism," an unorthodoxy greatly out of the style in the conformist 1920s.[740]

Across the State with the Secretary

From its earliest, the *Arkansas Publisher* had a knack of producing stories about prominent people just before they died. Indeed, some in the state in time probably came to fear being a lead story, for the next step was likely to be a "30," journalism's code for an obituary. That Harper's range was not limited to editors and writers was evident in his October 1929 cover story on J.C. Graham, reported by the International Typographical Union as the oldest active compositor in the United States. Graham, at age 87, spent his birthday "pounding long primer" for the *Mineral Springs Vim*, having started as a printer at age eight in Tennessee. Graham had joined the ITU in Memphis, where he worked for the *Avalanche* before coming to Arkansas. "I have never wanted work and have never tramped 25 miles to find it," he added.[741] Interestingly, one of his visitors was "Brooklyn Joe" Roddy, a tramp printer who claimed to have worked in more establishments than any other printer in America and who boasted that the longest he ever held a job was two weeks in Conway. "Joe," Harper noted, "wears a Stetson jauntily and is pretty much of an independent character."[742] Harper even used the good offices of the Association to inform readers that Joe needed a job.

Harper saw that tramp printers were becoming a vanishing breed, and used this story as a tribute. For Harper, it was a noteworthy news item when "Uncle Frank" Bickman, another widely known tramp printer, visited the state. Born in 1845, he had spent his life tramping and recalled being in Magnolia in 1877 to help with the first issue of the *Columbia Banner*.[743]

Harper's active involvement in the health of the industry included three tours of the state's newspapers. The first of these, in summer of 1928, took him to 145 newspapers. Since in 1929 there were 184 weeklies, 32 dailies, and "about" 20 periodicals devoted to special interests, Harper's trip was nearly encyclopedic. Unfortunately, only a small portion appeared in print. The second tour, a year later, reinforced his first impressions but consisted only in visiting offices between Little Rock and Fayetteville. Finally, in 1931 Harper, in company with APA president Alfred Hawn of the *Madison County Record* and Vice-President Tom M. Newman from the *Harrison Times*, visited six northwest Arkansas counties.

Harper began his first report by noting that mergers and consolidations were reducing the number of newspapers. In 1929 he reported that 16 counties had newspaper monopolies. Under the slogan "Fewer and Better Newspapers," he averred that the result would be more profitable newspapers that would provide better coverage.[744] Chains had begun to emerge in Arkansas, and he cited J.H. Beerstecher of Malvern with four newspapers; J.A. Thomas of Stamps who had seven, and Clyde E. Palmer with interests in El Dorado and Jonesboro. Linotype or Intertype machines were all the rage, and hand presses were on their way out. More newspapers were requiring cash-in-advance for subscriptions, but advertising rates were often too low. More pages, especially of advertising, were being printed, and special editions for various civic events were common.

For some time, Harper had engaged in a campaign to get publishers to clean up their offices: "No man can do his best work in a filthy office, cluttered up from front door to back with old exchanges, broken down machinery, discarded electros and miscellaneous debris." He also urged that more attention be given to "the long-neglected editorial column."[745] In fact, this last topic was of increasing concern to those interested in the press's higher calling. In an early *Publisher*, Harper had lauded as a "representative of the old school" Colonel J.B. Parker of the *Conway News*. Colonel Parker, he noted, "is a vigorous editorial writer and takes pride in the fact that he publishes 'a newspaper that does things.'"[746]

Harper's 3,196-mile tour in 1928 started off in south Arkansas. At first he apparently planned to write the accounts in order of his visit, but then he switched to an alphabetical listing before the series's premature end. In Grant County, Harper induced Dalton Walker of the *Sheridan Headlight* to become an APA member. In Cleveland County the *Rison Herald* was the only surviving newspaper out of four the county once boasted. Guy M. Sadler of Rison was then treasurer of the APA.

In oil-rich Ouachita County, Curtis B. Hurley, then the Association's president, published the *Camden Evening News*, a six-day daily and one of the most profitable newspapers in the state. Hurley had recently discontinued his weekly, the *Beacon-Herald*, seeing "no special advantage in having a weekly edition." This theme was to become increasingly common in Arkansas and accounted in part for the decrease in the number of newspapers. In Paragould, for example, the *Soliphone* had started as a weekly in 1893 and had been a daily early in the century, but later was issued as the weekly adjunct of the *Paragould Daily Press*. Typically, where dailies continued to publish a weekly, they assembled the

---

The Newsstand

One mark of town life for more than a century was the newsstand. Typically occupying a hole-in-the-wall structure on the square or near the leading hotel, the newsstand offered residents a chance to buy individual issues of both local and metropolitan newspapers as well as magazines, cigars and cigarettes, and, for children and many adults, comic books. Jack's Newsstand in Hope even sold beer. Often the store boasted a shoeshine parlor as well. Domino players sometimes frequented tables in the back, and baseball and other scores came in by ticker tapes. As prejudices against Sabbath desecration lessened, newsstands became a gathering place for middle-class town fathers on Sunday morning who purchased their Sunday newspapers, bought tobacco, and got their shoes shined before church.

For half a century newspapers arrived by train. At Hope, the Missouri Pacific's Sunshine Special tossed off the bundles, which sometimes fell back onto the tracks and were run over. "Why, those newspapers would be stacked three feet high in front of the counter," Bill Holt of Hope recalled. "They came by train and you had a choice: *The New York Times, Dallas Morning News, Dallas Sun Times, Shreveport Times, Texarkana Gazette, Arkansas Gazette*, or *Arkansas Democrat*."*

Often the newsstand owner was responsible for home delivery. Jack Harp, the founder of Jack's Newsstand in Hope, delivered the *Arkansas Gazette*, at first by horse and buggy. His brother Bill manned the stand while the deliveries were made. A different arrangement existed at Forrest City, where Colonel Ed Landvoight, a part owner of the *Forrest City Times* and later *Times-Herald*, also kept a newsstand.

Independent newsstands vanished from the scene after 1980. Buses replaced trains, and their schedules often did not accommodate carrying newspapers. When Jack's closed in 1982, journalist Mary Nell Turner called it "the passing of an era--a way of life already foreign to the young generation of Hope."

**Hope Star*, May 7, 1982.

---

country correspondents, culled the week's obituaries, and added a few lead stories. In areas where country correspondents were few in number, the weekly was likely to be discontinued.

Elsewhere in Ouachita County, Harper noted the *Stephens News* of Charles J. Parker, a 27-year-old establishment. The *Bearden Banner*, a Beerstecher newspaper, was put out on a Washington hand press by Myrtle Smith and another young lady.

Union County, "revolutionized by the discovery of oil," was home to one publisher but two editions, the *El Dorado Daily News* in the morning and the *Evening Times* in the afternoon. Clyde E. Palmer was the publisher, and one of his editors was the young Alex Washburn, a colorful figure in Arkansas journalism for the next 50 years. Huttig, Norphlet, Smackover, and Junction City all had newspapers. In Ashley County, Judge G.P. George owned the *Ashley County Leader*, which had "a strong position in the county." Wilmot and Crossett also had newspapers.

Arkansas County had a "successful small daily" in the Stuttgart *Arkansawyer* and a prominent weekly in the *Grand Prairie Leader*. De Witt had two newspapers, J.M. Henderson's *Enterprise* and the *New Era*. Henderson, then the county school superintendent and also the publisher of the *Journal of Rural Education*, endured to become a venerable and much-loved figure in Arkansas County. Two stories illustrated the life of this beloved figure. Henderson apparently could not distinguish red from green, and at the town's only traffic light, he invariably stopped on the green and went on the red. Townspeople could set their clocks by his routine, and on one occasion when he drove his car around a corner and hit another man, the victim apologized for being in the wrong place because he knew that Mr. Henderson always came around that corner at that time.

In Bradley County, Harper noted that the *Eagle-Democrat* at Warren had ancestors that included *The Sunbeam*, *The Eagle*, *The Whetstone*, *Free Thought*, *Flying Needle*, *The Sentinel*, *The Leader*, *The Watchman*, and the *Democrat*. A former owner was Captain J. Crawford Jolly, who had attended Columbia University and had been the 1921 president of the APA. State senator DuVal L. Purkins, the current owner, boasted "one of the largest mechanical and business staffs of any country weekly in the state."[747]

"There are six newspapers in Clark County, most of them well along in years," Harper observed in a comment that may have carried a double meaning. Philip McCorkle published the *Daily Siftings-Herald* in Arkadelphia, while Charles M. Clark carried on his father's once famous weekly, the *Southern Standard*. Gurdon had the *Times*; Okolona had the *Messenger*; and Amity, *The Owl*.

Clay County had Charles L. Payne's "live paper," the *Piggott Banner*; Corning, which Harper was unable to reach, had *The Courier*, and Ben Daulton, another redoubtable county editor, had the *Clay County Independent* at Rector.

Chicot County had *The News* at Dermott and the *Chicot Spectator* at Lake Village. The latter newspaper had not missed an issue during the 1927 flood despite water six feet high in the office.

In Craighead County, where a major newspaper war was then under way, Harper took no position. The *Jonesboro Evening Sun*, put out by the Troutts, and the rival *Daily Tribune*, owned by Clyde E. Palmer "and associates," were both "splendid publications." Elsewhere, there was the *Monette News* and the *Lake City Sun-Times*. Crawford County was represented by the Park brothers, Hugh and J.C., who had recently acquired *The Press-Argus*, another of the venerable weeklies of Arkansas, dating back to 1859.

Notice should be taken of Harper's visit to Crittenden County. In 1928 H.M. and W.H. Phelps had a monopoly in the county, publishing from their plant in Earle the *Earle Enterprise* and the *Marion-West Memphis Accelerator*. The latter newspaper's

The Fayetteville Daily Leader *office, 1928. The most modern plant in Arkansas boasted electric lighting, telephones, and typewriters. Zillah Cross Peel, the daughter of APA president H.L. Cross (1903), is at the right, as someone indicated on the print. (Courtesy Special Collections, University of Arkansas Libraries)*

Rev. A.C. Millar. Besides being president of Hendrix College and an editor of various Methodist periodicals, Millar was an active politician. At the APA conventions he held the office of chaplain. (Courtesy Arkansas History Commission)

Country correspondents at the Log Cabin Democrat, *Conway, 1926. Of the 54 correspondents pictured here next to owner Frank E. Robins, his wife and mother, 42 percent were men and 58 percent were women. Only four of the women were not wearing hats. By 1950 probably 85 percent of the correspondents were women. (Courtesy Frank Robins)*

Walter J. Lemke, c. 1935. Lemke came to the University of Arkansas to write publicity and stayed to organize the journalism department. Despite President Futrall's strict ban on smoking, Lemke is pictured here with a pipe. Students remembered him only smoking cigarettes. (Courtesy Special Collections, University of Arkansas Libraries)

Cartoon in support of Amendment 13. J.P Alley, the Arkansas-born cartoonist for the Commercial Appeal *of Memphis, contributed this cartoon, which many state newspapers used in support of an amendment to allow a school district to tax up to 18 mills. It passed in 1926 by a two-to-one margin and was added to the state constitution as Amendment 11.*

Walter J. Lemke became "Uncle Walt" to Fayetteville readers when the Leader *induced him to start a column. When it resumed at the* Democrat, *Roberta Fulbright, a prohibitionist, disapproved of the original graphic. Others then took its place. (Courtesy Special Collections, University of Arkansas Libraries)*

Officers of the APA at Fayetteville, 1929. A curious mix of old and new were caught in this photograph. Front left to right, Clio Harper, the APA's secretary; Curtis Hurley of the Camden News, *the outgoing president; Erwin Funk, NEA president; Guy M. Sadler,* Cleveland County Herald, *treasurer (who carried the treasury in his hip pocket); and Alfred Hawn,* Madison County Record, *APA president in 1931; back row, Rev. A.G. Millar, chaplain; John P. Stafford,* Springdale News, *APA president in 1929; and W.J. Lemke, University of Arkansas. (APA Archives)*

Roberta Fulbright, c. 1950. She inherited the Fayetteville Democrat *from her husband, turning it into the* Northwest Arkansas Times *in 1937.An active and progressive politician, she saw her son become president of the University of Arkansas and a United States senator. She also oversaw the creation of the Arkansas Press Women. (Courtesy UALR Archives and Special Collections)*

name was due to the fact that at the time of its founding "there was nothing in the town but filling stations."[748] In the years that followed Harper's visit, much would change, and at times some of the most interesting stories in the state would come out of this county.

The last of Harper's counties was Dallas, where Fordyce had the *Tri-County Advocate*. The *Dallas County News* was published by Roy Elliot, a future APA president (1942). The *Sparkman Times* was part of the Beerstecher chain and was printed in Malvern. Then, after promising to continue the series in the next issue, it ended.

Harper returned to the road the next year when he, APA president Curtis B. Hurley and treasurer Guy Sadler [father of future APA president William G.] journeyed from Little Rock to Fayetteville for the Association's annual meeting "via Hurley's and Sadler's faithful flivvers," and visited all the shops along the route.[749]

The first stop was Conway. The *Conway News* was one of the cleanest shops in the state, and as for Frank E. Robins's *Log Cabin-Democrat*, it cost 50 cents a month for the daily and was "strong on county correspondents." By 1941, this newspaper would lead the state with over 110 active correspondents.[750]

Next came Morrilton. President Hurley, who had lost his Camden newspaper but acquired the *Democrat*, was busy reorganizing the newspaper. The 13-year-old *Arkansas Unit* of J.F.T. Mostert was the other newspaper, "and," Harper noted, "it was gratifying to observe the spirit of co-operation between the two."

Plummerville and Pottsville, which once boasted newspapers, were now without, but Harper spoke highly of Ardis Tyson's *Atkins Chronicle*, an eight-page newspaper "well patronized by local merchants" and with a "splendid line of rural correspondents." "Splendid" seemed to be Harper's favorite word, for he applied it to both the Russellville newspapers, J.A. Livingston's *Courier-Democrat*, and Charles W. and George Dodd's *Weekly Tribune*. Dardanelle boasted "a veteran newspaper man" in George Upton, whose *Post-Dispatch* dated back to 1867. At Dover, Carl Parker put out the *Times*, "a good neighborhood paper." Lamar was home to G.E. Bennett of the *Leader*, another old-timer "and a hard worker" who "deserves a better support than he is receiving."

At Clarksville, the Johnson County seat, Mrs. J.W. Sallis was publishing the *Herald-Democrat*, of which the *Herald* part dated back to 1876. Her husband, a long-time educator, had recently died and although she was suffering from the tuberculosis that took her life later that year, the newspaper had issued a special 12-page edition during the week of the party's visit. Franklin County had the *Spectator* at Ozark. Six members of the Burrow family, descendants of the Rev. Isham L. Burrow, founder of Hendrix College, still ran that newspaper. Competition consisted of the *Democrat-Enterprise*, which was still a hand-set newspaper, but "filled with well-edited news and a fair amount of local advertising." Nearby in Crawford County, J.W. Wagner, "an incurable optimist," "appears prosperous" at the *Mulberry Times*, while the Park brothers at Van Buren had "one of the oldest and best weekly papers in Arkansas" in the *Press-Argus*.

Natives of Scott County, the Parks received their newspaper training under J.B. Cox at the *Advance-Reporter* in Waldron. J.C. had worked in Paragould; McAlester, Oklahoma; and Fort Smith, while Hugh had gone first to Magnolia and then to the *Prairie Grove Herald* where he had been editor, copy reader, printer, and assistant publisher. He, too, had spent time in Fort Smith before the family acquired the Van Buren weekly.

Fort Smith, the scene of the birth and death of more newspapers than any other place except Hot Springs or Little Rock, remained a monopoly town. The *Southwest American*, owned by J.S. Parks, George

V. Carney, and associates, came out in the morning and the *Times Record* in the afternoon, making it "one of the really big newspapers of the state."

Then the trio climbed the mountains. The highest newspaper in Arkansas was that of Maud Duncan at Winslow, whose *American* at the time of their visit was a hand-printed, four-page neighborhood newspaper.[751]

Maud Duncan was one of the most endearing people in the press "fraternity." Her second husband, G.N. Duncan, purchased the *Winslow Mirror* in 1908, changing its name to the *Winslow American*. After he died on Armistice Day, she continued publishing the newspaper until shortly before her death in 1958. Labor shortages during World War I caused her to begin setting the newspaper by hand, although she had employed an editor early in the 1920s.

One of Mrs. Duncan's claims to fame was as mayor of Winslow. In 1925 the town elected not only her as mayor but also an entire slate of women council "men" in a move that received nation-wide attention. Alleged to be the first all-woman government in America, the slate was successfully re-elected. In her later years, Duncan explained how she put out her newspaper:

> When the item is important, or has names that are hard to spell, I usually write it out before and then set up the type from the copy. But when it's just a routine story, I'll figure out the way I want it to read while I'm cleaning up the place or splitting kindling, then just sit down and "write" it as I set it up in type.[752]

Called "The Little Printer of the Ozarks," "Miss Maud" weighed less than 80 pounds in her later years. At the time of Harper's visit she housed her establishment in the Duncan Drug Store, for she was a registered pharmacist in her early years. After that building burned down in 1935, a small, unheated wooden shack served as her office and pressroom up to the time of her death in 1958. In her late years, Fayetteville journalism students, who lacked a press of their own, came down to help her put out the newspaper.[753]

The last stop on Harper's trip was at Fayetteville. Here the daily, the *Fayetteville Daily Democrat*, had been purchased by Jay Fulbright in 1913. After his death, his wife, Roberta, took the title of publisher. The managing editor was another prominent female of the age, Lessie Stringfellow Read. A Texas native and prominent club woman (she served as national press chairman for the General Federation of Women's Clubs), Lessie was invariably photographed in a typical 1920s seen-from-over-shoulder view. Like many prominent Arkansas journalists, she sold articles to national publications on the side and authored some respectable poetry.[754] At that time of Harper's first visit, the only competition consisted of two weeklies, the *Arkansas Countryman* and *The Fayetteville Republic*.

Harper's last trip in 1931 found things in Fayetteville significantly changed. One of Arkansas's great newspaper wars, between the *Democrat* and *Daily Leader*, had come and gone. Two weeklies, *The Fayetteville Republic* and the *Arkansas Countryman* (successor to the *Arkansas Sentinel*) persisted, as did Maud Duncan at Winslow. Other northwest Arkansas women editors were Mrs. J.W. Webb at the

Prairie Grove Herald (who boasted a Model Z Linotype and a pony Prunty), and Mrs. C.H. Smith with *The Sun* at Lincoln. At Springdale, John P. Stafford, a former APA president, put out the "first-class twice-a-week" *News*.

Boone County was virtually synonymous with the Newmans, Captain John R. having founded the county's first newspaper in 1869. His grandsons, Tom, John R., and Fred, published the daily *Harrison Times*. Literally next door was the *Boone County Headlight*, formerly the *Harrison Republican*, published by George L. Wright. Gone were newspapers from Alpena Pass, Everton, Elixir Springs, Lead Hill, Bellefonte, and Zinc, along with their dreams of becoming great mining centers.

In Newton County, the only county in the state never served by a railroad, the newspaper history had been "meager." Only eight newspapers had ever been published at the county seat, Jasper, and no newspapers were extant in 1931 at Deer and Mt. Judea. The *Newton County Times*, a four-page, six-column newspaper 23 years old, was owned by George L. Wright. Competition came from John "J." Milam, whose *The Informer* was recently established. Milam might best be defined as a tramp publisher. His first newspaper was apparently the *Womble Review* in 1913, but after the town was renamed Norman the newspaper became the *Montgomery County Review*. Then he latched onto the title *Informer* and had newspapers of that name at Mammoth Spring (1926), Salem (1926–30), Ash Flat (1931), Magazine (1929), and Mena (1929). Unbeknownst to Harper, Milam would find success in Jasper, where his hand-set operation prospered. He bought out the rival *Times* in 1948 and continued editing until his death in 1963.

Carroll County had four newspapers left in operation from over 40 that had once operated. The 43-year-old *Green Forest Tribune*, edited by Ertie O. Allred, was a seven-column, four-page newspaper, "all home print." At Eureka Springs, Colonel S.A. Diehl, "one of the veterans in the business," had his son Webster associated in the business. The newspaper had lost its plant to fire in 1929, and the replacement Harper rated as "one of the neatest and cleanest of all we visited." In addition to the *Daily Times-Echo*, they printed a weekly, *The Eureka Springs Flashlight*.

State senator F.O. Butt was in the newspaper business, having founded a weekly, the *Carroll Courier*, in 1929. Butt told Harper that the newspaper had been started largely as a hobby but had turned out to be financially successful. Unlike many politicians whose newspaper careers were of short duration, Butt continued his newspaper until 1942. For some odd reason, Harper made no reference to Berryville, where the young O. Klute Braswell had acquired the *Star Progress*.

Benton County had had over 55 newspapers, of which 21 were once being published simultaneously. Even in 1931, 11 newspapers fought for the market.

Bentonville, the county seat, claimed in *The Record and Democrat*, the oldest newspaper in the county. W.H. Plank issued this six-page, six-column newspaper, all home print, of neighborhood news. The *Benton County Herald*, also a weekly, had a "splendid patronage." At Rogers, Everett W. Pate owned both the *Weekly Rogers Democrat* and the *Rogers Daily News*. Pate, a future APA president (1939), was "one of the State's most progressive publishers." His plant contained a new Goss Comet press. The county's other daily was at Siloam Springs. A.W Perrine and his son, H.B., published the weekly *Herald and Democrat*, but H.B. Perrine alone owned the *Daily Register*. "The two are kept absolutely distinct in every respect," Harper noted. John E. Brown Schools (subsequently John Brown University) printed the *Interstate American* at a plant boasting four Mergenthalers and a staff of 20. They also issued a religious monthly, *The Wayshower*.

Gravette had the *News-Herald*; Decatur had the *Herald*. Harper considered old-fashioned John C.

Buckner's Decatur newspaper, two pages of ready print and the other two hand set. At Gentry, Mr. and Mrs. C.H. Reagan had the *Journal Advance*. It was four pages, seven columns, well-edited and well-patronized. In addition at the time of the visit, the Reagans were printing a four-page, three-column daily, *The Revivalist*, for a local religious meeting, "demonstrating," Harper noted, "what can be done in a country shop by a little extra effort." Again, Harper's list was not complete, for he failed to visit the *Gravette News Herald*.

Modernizing the APA

Harper's first trip to the "Great Northwest" had been occasioned by the Association's 57th annual meeting held at Mount Sequoyah in Fayetteville. Highlights of this meeting included an "inspirational address" by that familiar visitor, Dean Walter Williams, from the University of Missouri's School of Journalism, and the Association's first Past Presidents' Breakfast. Of the 10 men present, W.B. Folsom (1901) from the *Brinkley Argus* was the oldest in point of service. This would prove to be the only such breakfast for Harvey Lamar Cross (1903), who died later that year. Cross had come to Arkansas in 1890, establishing the *Benton County Sun*, which he ran until 1921. His granddaughter, Zillah Cross Peel, continued in the family calling.[755]

One interesting feature of this 1929 meeting was a woman's luncheon. Mrs. Kay Tallqvist-Root, a feature writer at the *Arkansas Democrat*, presided, and at the meeting's conclusion Mrs. Vaughn W. Root, the longtime society editor at the *Arkansas Democrat*, was elected president of the Woman's Association and Miss Zela Tucker the secretary. Clio Harper, who greeted the ladies in behalf of the Association, noted, "the past few years have seen woman take her proper place in the newspaper world." That place included not only social and club reporting, but also in advertising, news reporting, feature writing, and working in the business office and in printing. To celebrate the creation of the Woman's Association, the "feminine all-star staff" at the *Arkansas Democrat* produced an official tabloid. Plans were announced and members selected to report on the mid-winter meeting. Some of the women active in this abortive organizational effort included Lessie Stringfellow Read, Zillah Cross Peel, Peggy Leighton, Mrs. Harriette M. Folsom, and Mrs. Nellie H. Trevathan.[756] The coming Depression doomed this effort.

Results from Harper's recruiting activities were seen at this meeting in several ways. Fifteen new members were added, two of whom had been visited by the secretary on his way to Fayetteville. In addition, Harper noted that the second issue of his advertising blue book had a circulation of 3,000 copies. Only so much could be done without a full-time secretary, and by 1928, as APA President Charles Goslee observed, "this question has agitated every mid-winter meeting and general convention of the association." Goslee hoped to get the matter settled, but a select committee concluded the APA lacked adequate finances.[757] Discussed and rejected the year before had been a plan to share a field secretary with Mississippi.[758]

Secretary Harper not only held district meetings but also appears to have been the first in the APA to call for the erection of a building for the Association. Harper wanted it built on the State Fair grounds, and at the 1927 Hot Springs meeting President V.W. St.John endorsed the proposal as "a credit to us, to the fair association and our state, and that it will be more than a monument in that it will be much used for worthy purposes."[759]

Both these visionary plans came to partial fulfillment, but only after much passage of time. In his 1928 report, Harper observed that because at least half the state's newspapers were not interested in having to pay for a field secretary, only $2,000 of the

$3,600 needed to finance starting the program could be raised. Harper, who observed that much of his work during the previous year had been of the sort a secretary would undertake, called it "arduous and exacting" but of "inestimable value." One idea he put forth was to locate the secretary on a college campus in order to share expenses. Tired of the controversy, he concluded: "The question has been recurring annually for a long time, and we believe the time has come when we should decide definitely whether to proceed with the employment of a full-time field service man, or whether we shall continue to pass resolutions and talk about it indefinitely."[760]

The members preferred the second of Harper's options, and the next year Secretary Harper concluded that the hiring of a full-time field secretary "must come eventually," but that financing still was the main obstacle. After Wall Street laid a rotten egg in October 1929, Harper's assessment was something of an understatement, and the Association's slogan of "Let's Make 1930 a Banner Year" in retrospect was highly ironic.[761]

In addition to Harper's work, other modernizing elements came into play in the 1920s. One of these was in academics. In 1928, the University of Arkansas belatedly began its journalism program by hiring Walter J. Lemke. A native of Wisconsin who held a master's in journalism from Northwestern University, Lemke used the moniker "Uncle Walt" for a column he wrote, and the nickname stuck, at least off campus. Lemke was brought in to head up the university's news service and teach journalism classes. Not until 1930 was a formal journalism department established.

Lemke plunged into Arkansas with a flourish. In April 1929, he and Helen Presson of Fort Smith organized the first meeting of the Arkansas High School Press Association, for high school journalism had become increasing important. One of the first high school journalists to fall under Lemke's tutelage was Ernie Deane, the son of a South Arkansas railroad man. Others came to journalism as the children of editors and publishers. Eventually, a long list of Fayetteville graduates made their marks on Arkansas and American journalism.

Joining Lemke in 1930 was Joseph A. Thalheimer, known as "Smokey Joe" on account of his ubiquitous pipe. A graduate of Stanford and Columbia Universities, he had worked both for magazines and newspapers prior to coming to Arkansas. Indeed, such was the pay scale at Fayetteville, that during the summer months he went north to find temporary work as a feature writer for newspapers. Thalheimer became known as the "Mr. Chips of Journalism" because under the pseudonym of J.A. Lath he wrote children's books on the side. Less visible in APA affairs than Lemke, Thalheimer emphasized good writing. Over the next quarter-century, students gravitated to either Lemke or Thalheimer, depending on their interests and personalities.[762]

Modernizing the Industry

One of the best examples of 1920s trends in Arkansas could be found in the formation of newspaper chains. Consolidation had long been a feature in Arkansas, but the creation of a chain based on economics of scale began effectively with the career of Clyde Eber Palmer (1876-1957).

Like many other prominent figures in Arkansas journalism, Palmer was from out of state. Born in 1876 at Spirit Lake, Iowa, he received an eighth-grade education before working briefly as a stenographer. After serving in the Spanish-American War, he worked for the Cotton Belt Railroad and then as a credit manager in a Fort Worth men's furnishing store before becoming manager of the *Texarkana Courier* in 1919. The day after Palmer arrived in town, editor-manager John B. King left on vacation, leaving Palmer in charge. By 1925, Palmer had acquired the newspaper, which he renamed the *Four States Press* and which was published from the Texas side. In 1926 Palmer sold this newspaper to D.W. Stevick but used the profits to buy first the *El Dorado Daily News*, then the *Camden News*, and finally, in partnership with Alex H. Washburn, the *Hope Star*. From there, Palmer acquired both Hot Springs newspapers, the *Sentinel-Record* and the *New Era*. In 1933 he reacquired the Texarkana newspapers. Palmer left a complicated paper trail, for he still used the increasingly antiquated method of putting together partnerships in order to finance his purchases.

At various times he had interests in Stuttgart's *Daily Leader and Arkansawyer* (1946–51), the *Rogers Daily Post* (1923–1927), Magnolia's *Banner-News* (1939–), the *Stephens Star* (1949–), Russellville's *Courier Democrat* (1951–55), the *Fort Smith Journal* (1926–28), El Dorado's *South Arkansas Progress* (1927–63), and the *Smackover Journal* (1935–). Palmer made several miscalculations in his long career, but doubtless his biggest was the purchase of Harry Lee Williams's *Jonesboro Tribune* in 1928.[763]

By 1930 Palmer's success reached the attention of *Editor and Publisher* magazine. Palmer explained his philosophy in language common to the 1920s by praising community service and promoting general betterment. Actually, he sought to find and control markets free from competition. Defeated in Fort Smith, Rogers, and Jonesboro, he thrived in Camden, El Dorado, Hot Springs and Texarkana. At El Dorado his modern and efficient plant allowed him to print several weekly newspapers which remained profitable as long as oil fueled the prosperity of that region. In Hot Springs, where Palmer installed a 24-page Hoe Rotary Press with a capacity of 18,000 newspapers per hour, both the morning and evening newspapers were printed from one plant.[764]

In the early stages of his career, Palmer played a variety of roles in state politics and served on various boards, including, in the late 1930s, the controversial farm tenancy commission. However, his principal significance even as early as 1930 was as the man who maximized profits by promoting efficiency. During the 1920s the best example of his work was the forming of an organization called Arkansas Dailies. Starting with five members, this advertising sales agency soon grew to 16 and came to include most of the dailies in the state.

Editor and Publisher during this period paid tribute to another kind of journalism in the brothers Heiskell of the *Arkansas Gazette*. Because John (born in 1872) outlived Fred (born in 1875) by almost half a century, the younger brother's contribution to Arkansas journalism has been somewhat forgotten.

Both the Heiskells, by 1930 experienced newspapermen, continued to set forth major goals for the improvement of their newspaper. J.N. ran the editorial page, and his brother supervised the newsroom. Fred W. Allsopp, the business manager, completed the management triumvirate. In the estimation of C.P.J. Mooney, a famous editor of the Memphis *Commercial Appeal* who began his career with the *Pine Bluff Commercial*, the *Gazette* ranked as one of the three best newspapers in the United States.[765] Fred's untimely death in 1931 created a vacuum that was not easily filled.[766]

At Home on the Tripod

Across the state at large, the 1920s remained a mix of the old and new. In towns across the state, personal journalism reminiscent of the 19th century continued to thrive, primarily because each newspaper reflected the personality, or lack of such, of its editor/publisher. A few of these people had some significance either to the state as a whole or as representatives of the age.

A curious combination of these forces existed at McCrory in the person of local town native Walter W. Raney. His first newspaper, *The Home News*, was started in 1915, and at one time Raney also published the *McCrory Enterprise*. Then, in 1923 he founded the *Arkansas Central Leader*, which he ran for the next 30 years. Indefatigably industrious, Raney, a three-term mayor, at one time ran a picture show and owned McCrory's only undertaker's establishment; indeed, he was also active in the state's burial insurance association. The *Arkansas Central Leader* boasted that it was "the only newspaper published anywhere that devotes a large part of its space every week to the Confederate veterans, their widows, the Sons of the Confederate Veterans and Daughters of the Confederacy organization."[767]

Although Confederates were rapidly dying off, political capital could still to be gained from "The Lost Cause." Raney served his first term in the state senate in 1923, his last in 1947, and was largely responsible for crafting the legislation in 1927 that provided Confederate veterans and their wives with generous pensions. So well associated was he in the public mind with this cause that on one occasion he spoke to the Mississippi legislature on the subject. Arkansas had seen and would see newspapermen whose newspapers were only a publicity adjunct, but Raney was an active participant in APA meetings and had the first modern press in Woodruff County. The two Mrs. Raneys worked as well.

Politics and newspapers still mixed. Each session of the state legislature normally included from three to six active newspapermen. Interesting in this way was the 1928 election when two-term state representative William H.V. Wahlquist of the *Mammoth Spring Democrat* won a state senate seat over opponent Republican Tom Shiras, the editor of the Mountain Home *Baxter Bulletin*.[768]

Perhaps the most typical editor of the age was Max Hampton of the *Booneville Democrat*. Like so many other editors, his experiences began at childhood:

> My father practiced law for a living, ran a newspaper for amusement and dabbled in politics for sport and excitement, until I showed up. My first job was playing the devil in Dad's printing show in Booneville—both figuratively and literally. Afterwards, I served three years at hard labor as messenger boy, operator and lineman for the local telephone company, taking each job in turn as advancing age made me too big for the previous one, until I arrived at the age of seventeen.

Hampton accumulated more experience, including stints as a printer in Little Rock, running the *Midland Messenger* in Sebastian County,[769] and holding a variety of jobs in advertising. Back with the *Booneville Democrat* after 1911, Max took a different view of politics: "I allowed my name to go on the ticket for representative two years ago. Made no campaign whatever, and came out third in a field of five, with two elected!"

Like most country editors, Hampton had his own personal cause, the 4-H clubs, printing for them their own newspaper. "They repaid me by winning the National Four-H championship the next year and have been winning prizes ever since." His goal for the newspaper was "to build up the country, and the town will take care of itself."[770]

The 1920s was dominated in many ways by sports. Sports metaphors entered into political and even religious rhetoric. The new road construction and the rise of public high schools in the towns combined to raise to a new level a competitiveness that often had little to do with academics. In these developments, editors played major roles.

Erwin Funk spent 20 years as a football referee. "I started as a lineman and timekeeper. Then I secured a rule book and began studying it. I talked with officials at the University of Arkansas, interviewed coaches and players, etc. It gave me contacts with many young men I might otherwise never have known and was a welcome if strenuous break in my newspaper routine," he recalled.[771] Funk's interest in sports led to him becoming the publicity director for the state YMCA in 1919 and editor of the Camp Pike newspaper which in turn resulted in Funk spending three months in France at the end of World War I. Funk's expertise in baseball was legendary, and after Earle W. Hodges in *Public Utility News* made some mistake in print, Funk fired off a corrective letter. "After this," Hodges apologized, "we intend to stick to utility matters closely and leave baseball decisions for Funk, Judge Landis and the umpires."[772]

Most editors were not as enthusiastic and relegated sports coverage to willing high school students. Ernie Deane began his paid writing in this way, and in Jonesboro Bill Penix, who wrote sports and supervised the carriers for the *Tribune*, went on to become the editor of the *Arkansas Traveler* at Fayetteville before turning to law.

The Mechanics

The 1920s in Arkansas saw an acceleration of technology. Doubtless the best remembered case in point was the Mergenthaler Linotype machine, which was universally used by dailies and which got more adoptions by weeklies. Model 14 was probably the most popular model. Tramp printer Dee Brown found that the *Harrison Times* had two machines, one "in fairly good condition," but the other was "must have been the first off Mergenthaler's production line." Brown recalled "almost every type matrix was bent or worn, the spacebands frequently stuck in the molding box, and hot metal would squirt out on my left leg."[773] Nearby there should have been a Trim-o-saw, "an indispensable article in all well regulated shops."[774] For some odd reason, the Newmans had even purchased a National Cash Register that cost an astounding $500 and was specifically designed for recording print shop transactions.[775]

Paper was in the process of change, too. The price had climbed from two cents a pound to six, and increased attention was being given to the possibility of using Southern forests for newsprint. In early 1929 Curtis B. Hurley printed a 48-page special edition of the *Camden News* on Kraft paper manufactured locally.[776] Then in October 1934 the *Arkansas Publisher* appeared on Southern pine paper courtesy of the Southern Central Company of Memphis. The *Publisher* reported that plans were underway to make this paper available and at a cheaper price, but "when that will be, we can't say."[777] In reality, it would be nearly 10 years.

The sources for news were undergoing changes as well. With the rise of towns and the growing popularity of dailies, many weeklies concentrated on local or neighborhood news. Dailies relied heavily on the news services, the Associated Press and the United Press. There were two important developments in the way reports were delivered. First, automatic telegraph printers replaced Morse operators so that by the end of 1927 only two Morse men were left in the state.[778] The new machines sent stories at the rate of 60 words a minute, compared to 35 for the Morse system, and, since the machines received the news automatically, it was not necessary to pay an operator to stay on duty.[779]

Second, Arkansas had grown to such a level of importance that it now had its own Associated Press bureau. J.C. Stark was placed in charge of the Little Rock office with the title of "correspondent," the same term used when the AP first came to Arkansas after the Civil War. Member newspapers then formed a state association, of which George H. Adams of the *Pine Bluff Graphic* was the first president.[780] Under this system each newspaper had its territory and reported important stories to Little Rock for redistribution. The results were favorable, and almost immediately AP enlarged its bureau to four newsmen. The *Democrat* and *Gazette*, both AP newspapers, added more through lines from Arkansas to the east coast, thus increasing the volume of their reports. United Press was active in Arkansas, too, and the *Fayetteville Democrat*, "one of the best dailies in the State outside the larger cities," in Harper's estimation, subscribed to both services.[781]

Most dailies opted to use the services to provide many short stories; local events were granted more attention, especially if they were crime stories. Yellow journalism had remained to some extent in Arkansas, and while criticized in some circles, it did sell newspapers. Thus it was a matter of interest to the *Arkansas Publisher* when the *El Dorado Daily News* decided to take murders off the front page and list them under a small heading on an inside page. The *News* claimed that, nationally, crime stories amounted to between three and seven percent of coverage, and that this new policy "will be an interesting experiment for the newspaper men who are watching it over the state."[782]

A final example of 1920s modernization was the arrival of the Audit Bureau of Circulation (ABC). Historically, a newspaper's circulation ranked as an editorial opinion. Now, as national advertisers were growing in importance, they demanded audited figures before committing their money. "The day of the circulation liar is rapidly passing," editorialized the *Publisher*,[783] and at the APA's 1929 meeting Erwin Funk made a spirited appeal for an official endorsement from the Association. Following a motion from venerable ex-president W.B. Folsom, the membership endorsed APA participation. Under the system, auditors made regular inspections.

Two years later, O.E. Jones of the *Batesville Record* shared his preliminary experiences. He had expected more from the outside advertising agencies, but they turned out to be only "mildly appreciative." In the process of reviewing the *Record*'s books, Jones found he had "an unhealthy number of 'will-pay-next-fall' subscribers" whom he cut. "Great hunks were removed," he reported, but despite gloomy predictions, circulation held steady. Many paid up and only a few were permanently dropped. What did develop was a growth in non-agency advertisements.[784]

The struggle for audits reflected growing commercialism. The principal reasons for carrying nonpaying subscribers had been politics, and with each passing year the number of political newspapers declined. The *Arkansas Gazette*, which had so vigorously opposed Jeff Davis, led the way into political neutrality, but there were still many rural counties where the local newspaper was closely tied to the courthouse gang. William M. Greenwood (1864–1929), for example, had begun his career in 1883 with the *Chismville Star*. Two years later, he acquired the *Paris Express* of which he was both publisher and editor until his death. In addition, he served as chairman and secretary of the Logan County Democratic Central Committee and for three terms as mayor of Paris. Although inactive in the APA, he was a member from 1884 until his death.[785]

As audits became more common, so did promotions. Numerous awards, prizes, gifts, scholarships, and the like encouraged people to subscribe. Editors often found local causes that were calculated to increase sales. Special issues were another feature, and events like town or county centennials, county fairs, and especially Christmas issues all inspired publishers to reach out to larger audiences. "There was scarcely a paper that did not publish an issue of an increased size, all the way from 12 to 48 pages," Harper noted early in 1929.[786] The Western Newspaper Union, which provided the ready-print for many weeklies, also offered colored covers. The Waldron *Advance Reporter* expressed fully the dominant rhetoric of the 1920s in celebrating its issue: "To the wide-awake business interests of the town must be given credit for the financing of this extra large issue. Almost every business interest is represented by an advertisement. This shows a splendid spirit of progress, and the kind of spirit that makes a town grow and prosper."

The variety of ideas used to boost readership was enormous. For example, in just one issue of the *Publisher* Harper reported that the *De Queen Bee* ran a column on couples married 40 or more years; the *Hope Star* started a cooking school and held a contest for naming the office cat, giving Miss Madelyn Miller $2.50 for the name "Multiplying Maria"; the *Norman Visitor* published "by request" several chapters from Acts of the Apostles; the *Morrilton Democrat* held a contest to find the oldest mother in Conway County; the *Perryville News* awarded the Dixie School, which had only 32 pupils enrolled, a $10 prize for securing new subscriptions; the *Pine Bluff Commercial* began a column entitled "The Trouble Shooter," that promised to aid people with local problems; the competing *Pine Bluff Graphic* issued a special devoted to the industrial prospects of Star City; Alfred Hawn of Huntsville's *Madison County Record* was trying to discover the names of his newspaper's first subscribers 50 years previous; and the *Rison Herald* gave scholarship medals to high school students in Kingsland and Rison.

Another source of income publishers diligently pushed was legal notices. In 1915 the APA had used the initiative process to pass the Publicity Act. However, the law lacked enforcement teeth and was openly ignored and flaunted. As the number of defaults and embezzlements increased, largely due to secretive practices of the drainage and road districts, demands for better legislation found vent in a bill that levied a $1,000 fine or removal from office for failure to publish legally required statements. Its unanimous passage in both the House and the Senate proved to be of little consequence, for on March 28, 1929, Governor Harvey Parnell, the compliant tool of the corrupt districts, vetoed the bill.[787] The full extent of Arkansas's financial predicament did not become apparent until the Great Depression, but Representative B.H. Thomas, formerly of the *Gurdon Times*, noted that some of the special improvement districts which had not published their statements were in bad financial shape and the public was unaware of the dangers threatening.

Parnell did not veto Act No. 92, which fixed new rates for advertising, revising a price scale that had remained unchanged since 1874. The new rates for legal advertising were 50 percent higher, or $1.50 per square for the first insertion and 75 cents for each subsequent insertion. Delinquent land sales went from 25 cents to 50 cents per tract.[788] However, in the hard years ahead, publishers were to discover that the old tendency in Arkansas to ignore any inconvenient law still existed in the minds of many public officials. Indeed, not paying publishers had a long history, as numerous court cases in the 1920s attested.

Newspaper Wars

Two of the most closely watched newspaper events in Arkansas during the 1920s were the newspaper wars that erupted in Fayetteville and Jonesboro. Both attracted considerable interest not because wars themselves were unusual but because higher powers were in play.

The Fayetteville war began when former *Democrat* sports editor Homer H. "Scotty" Taylor struck it rich in Oklahoma oil and returned home in 1929 to challenge Roberta Fulbright. First he offered $25,000 for the newspaper, which by that time boasted a circulation of over 2,200. When Roberta countered with $35,000, he opted to buy his own plant. George G. Stockard, the first editor and manager of the *Fayetteville Daily Leader*, headed up a staff of six that included Mrs. Zillah Cross Peel as society editor. Walter J. Lemke undertook to write a column that defies easy description. Part of it was local gossip, both from town and the university, but considerable play was given to poets and poetry. Taylor spared no expense in outfitting the best shop to be found in Northwest Arkansas. The *Democrat* responded by beginning a Sunday edition with comics, a move that the *Daily Leader* countered.

Whether the *Democrat* was really vulnerable is unclear. Stockard, a former judge, died, and the post of editor and manager remained unfilled until January 1, 1931, when Erwin Funk was brought in. By that time, the deepening Depression doomed the experiment. Funk cut the Sunday edition, but after a few months Taylor, hard hit by falling oil prices, gave up the struggle. The competition had lasted 18 months and cost, by the *Democrat*'s estimate, some $125,000 for both newspapers.[789] The weakened *Democrat* then cut out its Sunday edition.[790]

The Age of the Circulation Liar

Nothing was more irksome to publishers than the circulation liars. Prior to the final triumph of the Audit Bureau of Circulation (ABC), outside advertisers were often at a loss to know how many persons their advertisements were reaching. One very detailed example of the practices and problems during the age of the circulation liar could be found in events unfolding at Nashville in the late 1930s.

Walter R. Haun, the advertising manager for Lion Oil Company, wrote to APA secretary Ray Kimball asking about information on the *Nashville Spotlight*. "I cannot find it in the Arkansas Blue Book," he complained, yet *Spotlight* publisher F.C. Hawkins told one source that he had a circulation of 1,500 and another that his circulation was 1,000. "I suppose since we are sustaining members of the Arkansas Press Association, we are entitled to this information," Haun noted, but added, "If it would be embarrassing to you, Ray, we will not feel hard if you are not in a position to give it to us."* In his reply, Kimball explained what he knew of the goings-on in Nashville:

> The *Spotlight* was formerly published as the *Nashville Democrat* by John Fred King. Last spring King began the publication of a daily paper by the same name and evidently discontinued its publication after a month or so because of lack of funds. Hawkins who had been publishing a weekly in Hempstead County then began publication of the *Democrat* on a weekly basis until about three weeks ago when the paper carried announcement that since the name of *Nashville Democrat* was not theirs they were changing the name to *Nashville Spotlight*. You will note that the *Democrat* was listed in the Blue Book with a circulation of 600. The *Spotlight* is not entered in the mails as second class matter so must therefore pay postage on all papers mailed. My personal opinion is that the *paid* circulation of the paper is very small. To complicate the situation further King began publication of the *Democrat* again this week. I do not know which paper is using the subscription list of the old *Democrat*. To say the least, neither paper is in a very "healthy" condition at the present time.†

Kimball underestimated Hawkins, who published the *Spotlight* until his death in 1955. His widow, Mrs. Augusta Hawkins, sold the newspaper to the *Nashville News* in 1962. At one time its circulation reached 2,000. John Fred King's *Nashville Democrat* apparently expired in 1938.

*Walter R. Haun, El Dorado, to Ray Kimball, August 29, 1938. Kimball Papers.
†Ray Kimball, n.p., to Walter Haun, September 10. 1938. Kimball Papers.

A different kind of war took place in Jonesboro. Here the market had long been divided between the morning *Tribune* of Harry Lee Williams and the *Evening Sun* of the Troutts. Williams was a political animal with an instinct for collecting local history; the Troutts were stronger on the mechanics of the profession. Then, in 1928, Clyde E. Palmer bought out Williams, who promptly headed off for Alaska. The new editor Palmer installed was Eli Whitney Collins, whom Harper lauded as an effective writer. Collins did not long remain, however, and others, including Alex H. Washburn, took his place. The *Tribune*, too, launched a Sunday newspaper in 1929, but in the vicious newspaper war that followed the Troutts came out ahead.

At stake in this struggle, if indeed not the cause of it, was Jonesboro's municipally owned utility. Another South Arkansas man, Harvey Couch, was busy putting together corporate monolith Arkansas Power and Light, largely by obtaining small town utilities for integration into his system. The *Sun* spoke for those who opposed the sale. The *Editor and Publisher* picked up the story in 1932, observing that W.O. Troutt "flatly refused a bribe offered by interests seeking to influence his editorial policy with respect to sale of the municipal power plant to privately owned power interests."[791] In early 1932, the *Tribune* filed a voluntary bankruptcy petition, but before action could be taken, Harry Lee Williams reappeared on the scene and reclaimed his newspaper. The *Tribune* would live for another decade before its final collapse.

Conclusion

The timing of historical periods and epochs is rather imprecise. So it was with the Great Depression. For Arkansans, the Flood of 1927 and the Drought of 1930 were more immediate than the slide down Wall Street's slippery slopes. But the Drought helped trigger a small-town banking collapse that rocked Arkansas badly. Often newspapers were financed or even owned by bankers, and with banks failing and notes being called in, newspapermen were at risk. In addition, many of the more successful publishers owned bank stock. Unlike limited liability common stock, bank stock made its owners responsible for bank debts.

In a publishing sense, the Great Depression for Arkansas began on December 2, 1932, when Clio Harper died. Harper had become afflicted with what his obituary described as a "type of writer's paralysis"* that eventually extended over his whole body. He had removed from Little Rock to Harrison in hopes of lessening the strain but had severely taxed himself in making his final shop tour in 1931. Doubtless the pressure of preparing a new history of the APA for the 1930 annual meeting had contributed as well, and he certainly suffered economic losses in the Depression.[792]

At any rate, for the next few years the Association had to hunker down in order to survive.

---

* There can be little doubt that Clio Harper's cause of death was an early case of Amyotrophic Lateral Sclerosis (ALS). Not until New York Yankee baseball star Lou Gehrig was afflicted later in the decade did attention begin to be focused on this ailment and it was added to the *International List of Causes of Death and Joint Causes of Death*. In order to investigate the matter further, this author petitioned and received from the Probate Court of Craighead County a court order directed to the Arkansas Department of Health, Division of Vital Records, granting him a copy of Harper's death certificate. The cause of death was described as "Progressive paralysis, Writers paralysis."

Sam Faubus: The Red Country Correspondent

One male correspondent of the 1930s and '40s was Sam Faubus, the socialist father of a future governor. Under the heading of "Greasy Creek Gleanings," he supplied the *Madison County Record* with local doings and his own poetry. In "When the World is Rid of Tyrants," he rhymed:

If the toilers of earth would get together
And dump the war-lords off their backs,
This world would be a place of pleasure
*Instead of misery, slums and shacks.**

An inveterate letter-writer to friends, politicians, newspapers, and family until his death in 1966, he tended to retain to the end the time-honored practice of country correspondents by starting off with the weather.

*Tom Wagy, "Little Sam Faubus: Hillbilly Socialist," *Arkansas Historical Quarterly*, LIII (Autumn 1994), 282.

Meeting Place, *published with permission, courtesy Charles Banks Wilson, Fayetteville. The old farmer can't wait to get home to read the community news. He visits with his neighbors at the mailboxes.*

Chapter VII

The Press Survives the Great Depression

"From the day you are born
...till you ride in a hearse
Things are never so bad
...that they couldn't be worse."
Motto of the Western Newspaper Union, 1930.

"We stand around lamenting the red ink in the business office, when it is high time
we interested ourselves in the black ink that we are serving up to our subscribers."
Alex H. Washburn, *Hope Star*, *Proceedings of the 60th Annual Meeting...1932*, 34.

"Please excuse misspelled and misused words as my typewriter is out of order,
anyway, that is your job, to spell correctly, not mine."
Anonymous correspondent to Walter W. Raney, McCrory, *Arkansas Central Leader*, January 24, 1923.

"O yes I think as years go by
That nothing could be truer
I'd vote the home town paper
My choice in literature."
Bessie Capps, Marshall *Mountain Wave*, August 10, 1956.

Introduction

The coming of the Great Depression was only gradually felt in Arkansas publishing circles. Indeed, although Wall Street laid its famous egg in October 1929, the consensus of modern Southern historians is that far more important than Wall Street's collapse was the Drought of 1930. Few Southerners, even among publishers, were heavily invested in the stock market, but the drought in wiping out gardens and crops not only hurt farm families but also the towns dependent on their trade. For newspapers, the two major sources of income first affected were advertising and job printing. The impact on subscriptions, which were commonly paid for yearly, came later, and legal advertising, so important in a time of massive foreclosures, helped sustain circulation and generated revenue.

Nevertheless, newspapers were integrated into all aspects of community life and shared the relentless deflationary downturn marked by collapse of farm commodity prices and the closing of cherished factories. As the high hopes of the 1920s turned to rubble and as each successive month brought forth official optimistic pronouncements followed by more falling prices and rising unemployment, a sense of ruin and despair generated a violent reaction against Republican president Herbert Hoover that set the stage for Franklin Delano Roosevelt's overwhelming victory in Arkansas in 1932.

After 1932, a gradual turnaround slowly began. The Arkansas Press Association survived the Depression, continuing to issue the *Arkansas Publisher*, albeit stripped of the numerous advertisements that earlier had graced its pages, and by the late 1930s the Young Turks were again agitating the Association to get moving into modernity. The hiring of the first permanent professional manager in 1938 marked their victory, and the modernizing themes of the 1920s reasserted themselves in time for the coming of World War II.

The Association Faces the Storm

In June 1932, the *Arkansas Publisher* put out an urgent request to its members to pay their Association dues. The failure of the bank in De Valls Bluff, taking with it the Association's entire treasury of $264.59, had left the Association without any operating funds.[793] But most publishers were equally short of funds. Many had lost in bank failures or faced uncertain futures as bank liquidations got under way. It was a sign of the time when the *Publisher* pleaded for members to pay the extra dollar subscription price:

> or
>
> We'd just as soon have a dollar's worth of eggs (fresh), chickens, sorghum, ham, bacon, sausage, stove wood, canned goods, fruit trees, peanuts, popcorn, tomatoes, potatoes (sweet or Irish); or anything else edible or negotiable—BUT DON'T SHIP 'EM COLLECT.

And G.S. Bennett of the *Lamar Leader* obliged:

> I have been trying for a long time to get something with which to pay my subscription to the Publisher. But it seems that all the sorghum molasses has been lapped up, the trapping season is over and I can't get hold any 'coon hides, my bootlegger is in jail, and I can't send you any bottled goods. If you do not want to accept the enclosed "George Washington" return it and I will send you a "hot" check.[794]

Meanwhile, publishers' pleas to their subscribers ranged from the desperate to the hopeful. W.B. Folsom at the *Brinkley Argus* took an entire page to tell his readers that while he would accept chickens, produce, or coon hides, those who failed to make arrangements would have to be dropped.[795] The *Beebe Sentinel* cried, "Bring us your wood on subscription if you do not have the dollar. We believe in Americanism and that the Lord helps those who help themselves and trust Him."[796] Another positive note was sounded by J.W. Wagner of the *Mulberry Times*, who printed an honor roll of those who paid their subscriptions in advance.[797]

James H. Tudor of the *Marshall Republican* made the mistake of carrying readers, feeling sure that "those behind with their dues would appreciate our effort and renew." Unfortunately, he wrote a few years later, "the majority of the delinquents are still delinquent." Tudor was willing to accept "chickens, corn, potatoes, hay, wood and cash!!" but the newspaper shrunk to four pages.[798] In order to stay in business, his son James R. left to find work in North Dakota and sent regular payments home.[799]

One of the gentlest requests to readers came from Sam Hodges, Sr., of the *Osceola Times*: "We, like every other business concern, need the money but if any of our readers are unable to pay at this time we will be glad to have you write us telling when you will be able to pay and we will try to accommodate you."[800] This was thoroughly in keeping with Sam's character. His son, Sam Hodges, Jr., later described his father as "one of the poorest businessmen I ever knew about. He was the antithesis of Scrooge. Dad had serious inhibitions about ever sending anyone a bill. He gave the paper to practically everybody unless they insisted on paying."[801] In Sam Senior's view, the newspaper was a public service. To his son he pulled out his make-up rule and explained that with that you could always make a living.

Barter arrangements did not always work out. At Atkins, Ardis Tyson's sons, Van and LeRoy, took in some moonshine in trade but unfortunately stashed it behind the stove where it overheated and exploded.[802] The *Chronicle* also had one reader who paid for his subscription for 20 years in fence posts, explaining that he planned to live that long and knew he would want to keep receiving the newspapers.[803]

As Arkansas and the nation sagged, the *Publisher* advised editors not to "'play up' stories of depression, failure and despair."[804] At the 1932 mid-winter meeting, resolutions asking editors to deliver neither "unreasoning optimism" nor "unfounded pessimism" and to "maintain an intelligent grasp upon realities" portended Franklin Delano Roosevelt's much-quoted "all we have to fear is fear itself."[805]

Nevertheless, the crisis presented opportunities. Ruby Erwin Livingston, the wife of Russellville editor J.A. Livingston, won an award of merit in the Pen Women's Contest for her poem "Drouth."[806]

That at least some of the public saw newspapers as profitable was painfully apparent in Little Rock, where, on January 5, 1932, James E. Chapple, the head bookkeeper and cashier of the *Arkansas Gazette* as well as Fred W. Allsopp's brother-in-law, was killed in a daylight robbery attempt.[807] Since time immemorial the *Gazette* had paid its workers in cash every Friday. Despite his brother-in-law's death, business manager Allsopp saw no reason to change the system, and it was not until after Allsopp's death and the arrival at the *Gazette* of Hugh Patterson in 1948 that more modern practices were begun.[808] This robbery was not the only such attempt. Jim Bland, Sr., at the Walnut Ridge *Times-Dispatch* was burglarized twice, for a total loss of $10.[809]

The local and family nature of the newspaper business formed a strong cushion for many newspapers. Hence, it was not surprising that some of the greatest difficulties were experienced by Clyde E. Palmer, who had been hailed as a progressive leader only a few years before. Palmer narrowly avoided bankruptcy proceedings in Jonesboro and Hot Springs. One early casualty was Curtis B. Hurley, who had co-signed too many notes and was forced to sell the *Camden News* to Clyde Palmer.* During the 1930s a number of weeklies in small competitive markets closed or were merged, but most of these closings seem more related to particular local circumstances rather than a general decline. Overall, the state started the Depression with about 200 newspapers and entered World War II with about 140.

One casualty was the *Arkansas Echo*. In early January 1930, Karl Meurer, its 80-year-old editor, was waiting for his son Carl to pick him up at the office. When the son was tied up in court, the editor decided to return to his office. As the elevator had closed for the night, he walked the four flights of stairs, and later was found dead of a heart attack seated at his desk.[810] After his death his son brought out a 40th-anniversary edition in 1932. Georg Koop contributed a poem, which in English read:

Forty years have you traveled
Always a trusty guide.
In every house finds your voice
A welcome "Echo."

---

* Hurley was repaid twice by a young student whom he helped attend the journalism school at the University of Missouri. Not only did Ed McLaughlin repay the loan but later he endowed the Curtis B. Hurley Chair in Public Affairs Reporting at Columbia.

Through the years have you remained
True to your motto.
Always for Truth, always for Charity,
Faith, and Justice.
In the language of your fathers
As it comes from German lips.
Honestly and forcefully
You made your message known.
To this people a true messenger
You've been these forty years.
Stay the course
Along God's blessed path![811]

As the older generation of German readers died off, the need for the newspaper ended, and shortly after the publication of the anniversary edition, it expired.[812]

Overall, newspapers suffered less than most businesses. An early optimist was E.W. Pate at the *Rogers Daily News*: "We've dried our tears because a check-up of our business for the much-lamented year just closed doesn't justify self-pity."[813] The *Jasper Informer* in remote Newton County concluded that "Arkansas newspapers are not all broke, but most of them are bent and more or less warped."[814]

Doubtless many publishers' experiences paralleled those of Ardis Tyson at Atkins. In 1929 he had traded his old Model L Mergenthaler Linotype machine in on a Model 14 with the balance of $4,832.94 being due in monthly installments of $55. During the Depression he found himself unable to continue regular payments. Apparently, a large number of the company's customers were in a similar predicament and like Tyson were able to adjust their debts and continue in operation. Finally, on February 19, 1945, the machine was paid off.[815] Ellis Reynolds, who started working for the *Chronicle* in 1934, recalled that Arkansas Gas Company and Arkansas Power and Light Company were the major advertisers. "If all delinquents had been dropped, there wouldn't have been many left," he concluded.[816]

At Marshall, James H. Tudor had two mortgages, one for his house and one on the *Republican*. With funds enough only to continue paying on one, he elected to save the newspaper and let the house go.[817] Later, Hugh Park at Van Buren was not really joking when he said that he and his brother had felt they ought to take bankruptcy but lacked the money to pay the court fees. With community support they worked their way back to prosperity. In 1933, the *Nashville News* announced, prematurely, that it would return to its regular subscription rate of $1.50 a year, "now that the depression has come to an end through the program of the President."[818]

Probably the most common early response was to reduce size. The *Trumann Democrat* of May 26, 1933, came out on green paper and as a four-column, eight-page tabloid. The Yellville *Mountain Echo* went to a six-column folio.[819] The Trumann experiment lasted only three weeks before consumer complaint forced a return to the usual eight pages.[820]

Another way to reduce costs was to revert to ready print. In early 1933 one advertiser riled some weekly publishers with an article critical of newspapers that used "boiler plates." A few months later one country editor replied in the *Publisher*, comparing the weeklies' use of "ready print," his preferred term, to the dailies' subscribing to news services.[821] Most editors who were forced to adopt this move saw it as a retrograde step and looked forward, like Sam Hodges of Osceola, to returning to home print when conditions improved.[822]

For the meantime, those editors and publishers who could afford it took the lead in trying to help raise funds locally to fight the Depression. Erwin Funk, unemployed since the collapse of the *Fayetteville Leader*, was busy at Rogers, serving first with the Emergency Relief Association, then with the distribution of clothing and other items under the Works Progress Administration (WPA), and finally for six years with the Benton County Welfare Board, during the setting up period of Social Security. Starting in 1935, he served on the Rogers Free Public Library Board, of which he became president in 1940, and during World War II he worked with the Red Cross.[823] Funk, of course, was officially retired, but other editors and publishers could be found in all these positions as well. Those who were on school boards had a particularly difficult time, for bank failures took school funds, and property-tax forgiveness laws led to closing or reduced terms for schools.

Since so many editors and publishers sat on school boards, the 1932 APA convention featured a highly articulate address on the state's problems by Marianna *Courier-Index* editor H.M. Jackson. Jackson showed that Arkansas's problems were not newly created by the Great Depression. One-third of the white pupils in the state lived in districts that failed to provide minimum standards of elementary education; and 42 percent resided in districts without high schools. In calling on other editors to get involved in the problem, Jackson declared education to be the bulwark against social and economic disintegration and "our final safeguard against the forces of unreasoned radicalism."[824]

Curiously, despite hard times, some new newspapers even appeared. The *Hot Springs Tribune* in 1933 was one, and former gubernatorial candidate W.P. "Whippoorwill Pea" Wilson started the *States Appeal* in Conway.[825]

One greatly disordered county was Crittenden, formerly an overwhelmingly rural county opposite Memphis. But the growth of highways brought many motorists to the Hanrahan Bridge, where cars shared crossing the Mississippi River with the trains. West Memphis grew into a notorious border town lined with filling stations.

Prior to 1931, H.M. "Uncle Henry" Phelps of the *Earle Enterprise* held a monopoly in the county. Phelps, who had started the *Imboden Gazette* in 1903 and later moved to Marked Tree before settling in Earle, started the *Marion-West Memphis Accelerator* where amidst nothing but gas stations it expired.

Then came the *Crittenden County Times* of C.H. Brown. Brown was one of the more interesting characters in Arkansas journalism, being an inveterate inventor. He was less successful in developing his ideas, and much of the work of putting out the newspaper fell to Margaret Woolfolk. Inspired to write by her high school journalism teacher and with family funds sufficient to send only her brother to college, she became a fulltime employee in 1936.

Two political factions soon emerged to battle for control of the county. After 1936, the *Times* had to contend with the *West Memphis News* of Fred L. Hedges. Hedges, who also owned the *Star-Herald* at Hughes, sold out in 1939 to a corporation headed by John A. Cooper, a planter and lawyer better known later for his retirement communities in Sharp and Benton counties. Things were heating up as the nation moved closer to war.

For Arkansas as a whole the Depression proved to be far worse than in many other states. Arkansas's banking collapse cast a wide net. Prior to the Bank Holiday in 1933, 204 banks had closed. The state's most spectacular crash was taken by financier and highway bond profiteer A.B. Banks, when his Little Rock flagship bank and 66 others scattered all over the state suspended on November 17, 1930. The next year the *Publisher* received its exchange copy of the *Harrison Times* wrapped in sheets of bank checks.[826]

K. August Engel at the *Arkansas Democrat* was one owner who lost heavily in the crash. At one point, he asked one of his compositors if there was a story about the banks closing. When the man reported it was true, Engel said, "Because if they are, I'm broke."[827] Broke or not, the newspaper survived. At the *Democrat* grocers paid for their advertising by providing food for workers, each worker getting generally $3 a week.

As real money disappeared, both the *Helena Daily World* and the *Hope Star* issued their own scrip, called shinplasters in the previous century, that were redeemable for advertising, job printing, or subscriptions.[828] Some previously successful publishers were bank stockholders, who, by the law of that time, were responsible personally for their bank's debts after liquidation. W.O. Troutt at the *Jonesboro Evening Sun* was not alone among those who remained financially embarrassed for many years.[829]

For most of 1930, 1931, and 1932, Arkansas was a state without any money. Cotton prices, the basis of the state's agricultural wealth, had fallen below the price of production. With one third of the state's land delinquent and motorists refusing to pay their car licenses, the funding base that guaranteed the state's $166,410,350 debt disappeared. Junius M. Futrell, elected governor in 1932 on a platform that promised cutting the state's budget by 50 percent, could not find the money to keep up the interest payments on the bonds. In the process of defaulting, the first losers were the Confederate veterans generously served by Walter W. Raney's pension plan. Under state law, paying the bondholders naturally came ahead of paying old people. In 1933 Arkansas defaulted on its state debt, making the state technically bankrupt.

As legislators looked for ways to cut expenditures, the press came in for its share of abuse. Central to the controversy was the old issue of legal advertising. The governing Arkansas law was the much-ignored Publicity Act of 1915, which, for some unexplained reason, had been left out of the state's legal digest. Then on April 28, 1931, Attorney General Hal L. Norwood ruled that the act's omission in no way affected its validity. It was the 10th section requiring the publishing of financial reports that had long stirred editors. From the publishers' point of view, the attorney general's

An Arkansas Editor in Hollywood

On October 15, 1938, *Publishers' Auxiliary*, a leading trade magazine, published a feature story on a new motion picture. Van Buren comedian Bob Burns' new picture, *Arkansas Traveler*, had its world premiere in Little Rock. Burns might have been a controversial figure for those cultural guardians fearful of exposing the primitive in Arkansas life, but his comedy routine featured a noisemaker he called a Bazooka. During World War II GIs applied this term to portable anti-tank weapons, in time giving the word dictionary status.

Burns' picture appropriated only the name of the famous triptych of song, story and painting. The plot centered on a small-town banker who took advantage of the widowed owner of a country newspaper. Burns, who claimed he had once worked as a printer, was cast as a tramp printer who came to the widow's rescue by securing a generator so she could not only put our her newspaper but also reach the public through her radio franchise. Villainy is thwarted, and all ends happily.

Appropriately, the picture was dedicated to America's most famous country editor, William Allen White of Emporia, Kansas. For Wade W. Scott at the *Publishers' Auxiliary*, the movie glorified the industry, and he urged all editors "to impress upon the citizens of his town the value of seeing it at least once. It is one picture that glorifies the country press in a subtle way that should be welcomed by all country editors who can do their own cause a great deal of good by giving it wide publicity." Scott alluded to the controversy that surrounded Burns and admitted that "there may be a few controversial angles," but overall, "it is by far the most accurate interpretation of the country paper and small town yet produced."

opinion was good for business.[830]

A different aspect of the Publicity Act surfaced a year later. In violation of the provisions of the act, the Secretary of State had sent the printing of synopses of new state laws to Union County's three weeklies, the *Smackover Journal*, the *Huttig News*, and the *Junction City News*. Left out was the *El Dorado Daily News*, which, because it was a daily with a circulation of over 5,000, had to be paid at double the amount required for the weeklies. The *News* sued, and the court in upholding the constitutionality of the law disallowed the Secretary's actions.[831]

At the same time Norwood was issuing his opinion, Judge Junius M. Futrell, the state's governor a year later, was ordering newspapers to make bids for printing the delinquent tax lists in the drainage districts under his jurisdiction. Inasmuch as these rates were fixed by law, the press considered Futrell's move an illegal and dangerous precedent.[832] At the same time, the state's county judges were eager to collect the full 50 cents per tract for advertising delinquent taxes but to pay the newspapers only 25 cents. Some publishers were afraid to fight the county establishment, but not Alex H. Washburn at Hope. He called a publisher who caved in and accepted less than the legal amount "a hired liar about the actual facts of government, and notoriously treacherous to the cause of the common people."[833]

When Futrell was sworn in as governor in 1933, the press was well represented in his administration. Duval Purkins of the Warren *Eagle-Democrat* became the governor's secretary; Griffin Smith, a former publisher of the *Paragould Press*, was state Comptroller; and Marion Wasson, former editor and publisher of the Gentry *Journal-Advance*, was state banking commissioner.[834]

During Futrell's first legislative session, four bills impacted the press. A bill defining as legal newspapers those with a 300 net paid circulation was vetoed by the governor. The governor did sign a bill that amended the Publicity Act by authorizing weeklies as well as dailies to publish legals. The higher rate for legal advertising passed in 1929 was reduced. A new law dealing with delinquent lands was allowed to become law without the governor's signature and was promptly contested in the courts.[835] Of immediate concern was the $22,989 the state owed newspapers for printing the initiated acts and constitutional amendments during the 1932 general election. Comptroller Griffin Smith believed the newspapers could collect from the General Claims fund after July 1, 1933, if and when any money materialized. No funds were available for printing the legislature's 1933 acts.[836]

Meanwhile, with the state bankrupt, the focus of recovery shifted to Washington.

A New Deal for the Press

"Coditis," proclaimed the *Arkansas Publisher*, in discussing the first New Deal program to impact the press, the National Recovery Administration's blue eagle. Was it subtle symbolism that led the magazine to print the NRA story in red?[837] The official symbol was an art deco blue eagle, and while some critics at the time claimed the program to be Communist-inspired, historians and economists have preferred overwhelmingly to find fascist characteristics in this short-lived agency.

This first New Deal recovery program set about trying to stop the disastrous deflation by stabilizing prices and wages. In general, the law required government, management, and labor to work out a fair balance of interests which would then be enshrined in a written code. Despite the fascist charge, it was in many ways only an extension of the fair trade laws many states had passed and reflected pre-capitalist ideas that there ought to be a fair price, a fair wage, and a fair profit.

In Arkansas on March 10, Erwin Funk took over as administrator of Division 82 of the Graphic Arts

Code under a committee formed of weeklies, smaller dailies, and commercial printers. Charles M. Young of Helena, then serving as the APA president, was state chairman, and other members included such fixtures of the press as Max Hampton (Booneville), J.J. Baugh (Searcy), L.B. White (Benton), Mike Gillespie (De Valls Bluff), O.E. Jones (Batesville), Charles Goslee (Hot Springs), and printers C. Armitage Harper and J.T. Royce. No tramp printers, carriers, or apparently even union typographers were represented. Sixteen districts were set up, and meetings were held to study what ought to be done. Funk labored for nine months in an effort to create a code. At the APA's Clarksville meeting in 1934, the body made changes in its constitution in order to participate, and it adopted a 12-point program that envisioned a more active association.

After nine frustrating months, Funk resigned and C. Armitage Harper took his place. Work on the code, which bogged down on such now arcane issues as adopting the Franklin Printing Catalog (or Porte Price List), creating a cost-finding system, investigating government-produced envelopes, and collecting code assessment charges, soon stopped. In addition to a shortage of money, support for the code had dwindled. Nation-wide, the blue eagle fell from its perch when the United States Supreme Court ruled against the government in the famous "sick chicken" case of *Schechter Poultry Corp. v. United States* (1935). A unanimous Supreme Court found the codes to be an unconstitutional delegation of congressional power, that entrusting code-making to private bodies was unconstitutional, and that the "sick chickens" in the case before the court were not part of interstate commerce. Thus, such questions as whether local newspapers constituted interstate commerce or whether the First Amendment freedom of the press clause exempted newspapers from labor laws were not addressed. As for Funk, he headed off to Washington, where he briefly ran the office of the National Editorial Association.

Perhaps the most important legacy of the New Deal was the increased strength newspaper unions found under the Wagner Act and other federal laws. The Wage and Hour Law that went into effect in 1940, for example, exempted only weekly or semi-weekly newspapers with a circulation of less than 3,000. All other newspapers found that their reporters, pressmen, and staff were covered, the minimum wage being at first 25 cents an hour. A 40-hour week with time and a half for overtime was to be phased in. One of the first court cases in Arkansas involved the *Jonesboro Daily Tribune*. The case was peculiar in that the plaintiff had been placed on the job as an apprentice by the National Youth Administration that advised the newspaper it need not even pay a wage. The case was settled out of court.[838] A greater portent of the future came when stereotypers and pressmen walked out on the *Texarkana Gazette and News* in the fall of 1940.

The Association Survives and Modernizes

The death of *Arkansas Publisher* editor Clio Harper led to the assumption of the position by his son, C. Armitage Harper. Harper, who attended the university before the arrival of professors Lemke and Thalheimer, had been elected the editor of the *Arkansas Traveler*, the student newspaper, in 1924-1925, and was the grandson of another journalist, R.S. Armitage of the *Boone Banner* in Harrison. "Army," who had probably been the de facto *Publisher* editor for the two years preceding Clio's death, continued the *Publisher* with fewer pages. The literary qualities that had marked the *Publisher* in its first years continued in diluted form, for he did continue the column, "On the Nail Keg," that chronicled the activities of the state's press personnel. Like his father, he included publishers, reporters, and printers in his overview, and he also reported on the activities of special-interest publications, both economic and religious, that were not APA members.

In fact, the coming of the Depression had caused a drop-off in APA membership. President Charles M. Young of the *Helena World* addressed this issue in 1933, noting that only 33 percent of the state's 200 newspapers were members. With this rate of support and with a membership costing only $5.00 a year, the Association's income was insufficient to make it effective. In 1933, the Association started a confidential bulletin to members only, and Armitage used this as a recruiting device to boost membership. He also continued the advertising Blue Book, but bereft of the audited circulation figures.[839] Apparently, for the time being, that campaign had failed. Finally the Association abandoned printing the proceedings from the annual meetings. Despite their sometimes-weighty nature, these old proceedings had spread across in print the polemics, the personal struggles, and the humorous anecdotes that chronicled the life of the Association. The short summaries of speeches or the occasional excerpt from a presidential address that appeared thereafter in the *Publisher* were a poor substitute, but they did record much of the history of the Association.

By 1934, evidence of recovery within the organization was visible. At the Clarksville meeting, O.E. Jones of the *Batesville Guard* and *Record* was made president. The aggressive 12-point "New Deal" for the Association sought to attain a 100 percent membership, and the APA hoped to raise enough money from associate memberships to finance an advertising service, publish a weekly bulletin in addition to the monthly magazine, and issue the advertising blue book annually.

As conditions stabilized across the state, Young Turks within the Association began to campaign again for a permanent staff. Except for the leadership offered indirectly by *Arkansas Publisher*, the APA remained only a social organization, attended at its annual meetings by a small percentage of the possible members. In 1938, the Arkansas Better Newspapers Contest was cancelled due to a lack of interest, and with an annual turnover of the presidency, ambitious programs, like the 12-point plan, ended up only as faded memories.

One of the most energetic Young Turks was Donald Murray of Jonesboro. The Murrays, a large Catholic family, gave three sons and two daughters to the industry in Arkansas. Three brothers became APA presidents: Donald in 1937, A.P. (Andy) in 1952, and Francis ("Shrimp") in 1970. The smartest of the lot was one of their sisters, Martha Aline, who studied law privately and became a licensed attorney in 1929. After years of helping her brothers and then looking after her mother, she became a nun, ending her life at Holy Angels Convent in Jonesboro.

Donald, the first Murray on the scene, hit Arkansas like a comet in the waning years of the Depression. Dropping out of college in his junior year, Murray bought his first newspaper, the *Jonesboro Daily Tribune* that Clyde Palmer had abandoned. Harry Lee Williams, perhaps the quintessence of a newspaper politician, had resumed ownership briefly before disposing of it to Murray. Murray branched out in all directions almost at once. In addition to the Blue Top Engraving Company at Jonesboro, where he made single column halftones for one dollar, Murray acquired the *Lake City Sun-Times*, the *Wynne Daily Star* and the weekly *Wynne Progress*, and finally the *Pine Bluff Daily Graphic*. In 1937 he became president of the Association.

One of the earliest demands for change came from Professor Walter Lemke, whose perspective was somewhat different from that of a majority of the members. "I have never been satisfied with *The Arkansas Publisher*," he wrote Ray Kimball in 1937, "It could be made a powerful influence in holding the state press together, but since the death of Clio Harper it has seldom been worth reading. No pep."[840] Lemke had been approached by Todd Ellis at the

Russellville Printing Co. who wanted to start a new publication to be entitled "The Arkansas Press" and produced by Arkansas Tech's journalism department. Lemke did not rule out the idea, but wanted to see first what might happen to the field manager plan. Lemke was still kicking around the idea of a university-produced journal a year later and toyed with the idea again in the 1940s.[841]

In Lemke's view, Ray Kimball was the man of the hour. "I was glad to get acquainted with you here Saturday," Lemke wrote Kimball early in 1937, "The Arkansas Press has long needed new blood and new ideas. You've got modern ideas, can stand up and talk, and should be able to put the things over. If I can be of any service at any time, let me know."[842]

The unsuspecting members of the Association learned what was in store for them when the 23-year-old Donald Murray, in his 1937 presidential address, spelled out what even he considered to be an "extremely ambitious program." While "sensible of the fine old traditions that have come down to us," he declared war on the status quo, claiming, "the extent of the composite victory of the press of Arkansas in the daily battle against stagnation—against getting into a rut and staying there—will measure almost exactly the progress of the press of the state and the future development of marvelous Arkansas."[843]

The principal components were the return of the contests, an increasing number of member services, and the hiring of a salaried manager. Success in those other fields had to start with getting a manager. The brunt of the work on that job was borne by Association secretary Ray Kimball. First he attended the NEA convention in Detroit before meeting with a group of state field managers in Chicago. The "contacts made there and things learned will be worth a great deal," he reported to Murray.[844] Kimball reported that many of the tasks a field manager would undertake were actually profitable so that little financial burden would fall on the members. In addition, he suggested going ahead with contacting the university for support.[845]

It took Murray a month to reply, but the president instructed Kimball to move ahead with the manager plan through a series of district meetings, to issue the *Publisher*, and to try to meet with the university.[846] In addition, the secretary was largely responsible for securing the hotel reservations for the conventions as well as lining up the program and speakers. Judging from the correspondence, most of the work was done a few weeks in advance of the meetings.

One important element was the control of the *Arkansas Publisher*. Started, it will be recalled, as a proprietary journal, it had become the property of the Association. Whether the board fired C. Armitage Harper by promoting him to third vice president or he resigned as secretary is not clear, but on July 6, 1937, as Ray Kimball was heading off to research the manager system, he mailed materials to Armitage for insertion in the *Publisher*. Apparently miffed, Armitage dumped the journal on Ray.[847] The transition from Harper to Kimball meant that Kimball not only had to edit the publication but print it as well. That fall, Kimball seems to have been trying to put out the *Arkansas Publisher* without having the cuts, mailing lists, or advertising contracts. "Please get our minutes reduced to a record, duly signed, in order that we may have tangible evidence of the executive's [*sic*] committee action regarding transfer of activities from his [Harper's] office," Murray instructed Kimball. If Harper did not respond promptly, President Murray promised to "write him a rather stiff letter."[848]

Kimball bore up under the strain of getting out his own newspaper and virtually reinventing the Association. And his enthusiasm was catching. President Murray wrote him, "What you had to say Saturday has really steamed me up on this association business and you can count on me for 1,000 percent cooperation in putting the thing over."[849] By mid-October a series of regional meetings had been scheduled and Kimball planned to get out a *Publisher* even though insertion orders and advertising contracts were still missing.[850] Harper did provide personal material that went in the Nail Keg column.[851]

One of the most encouraging pieces of news came from Hot Springs where Murray had been told by former APA president Charles Goslee that the Palmer newspapers "would go down the line with us and would help us underwrite our budget for the first six months."[852] Apparently the regional meetings went off without a hitch. "All enthusiastic," was Murray's report after the Batesville gathering.[853] Since 23 states already used managers, the principal problem was overcoming inherited inertia.

One monkey wrench to pull out of the machinery came from the Russellville meeting when Frank Robins broached the idea of a "journalism teacher-association secretary combination" with the State Teachers' College at Conway. Kimball asked Murray about it, and Murray replied he had never heard of the matter until Kimball mentioned it. "I wonder if our friend Armitage is doing any maneuvering along that line," the president asked.[854]

For Murray and Kimball, the mid-winter meeting was critical. "We must work these things out carefully so there will be no slips," the president observed.[855] Murray had said that with the Christmas season at hand, he was "busy as hell," and Kimball in turn replied that that was "a mild phrase to describe my condition." Nevertheless, the secretary promised to "meet with you anytime and anywhere you say—the quicker the better—to thrash these matters out."[856] Replying two days later, Murray wanted the new constitution ready and distributed before holding the mid-winter meeting in Little Rock. Kimball agreed, and planned to get out another issue of the *Publisher* in preparation for the event.[857] The executive committee met on December 28 at the Marion Hotel, and in January the constitutional rewriting committee was appointed. Its members, in addition to Kimball and Murray, included Charles Goslee as chair, J.L. Bland (Walnut Ridge), R.C. Wann (Batesville), J.A. Livingston (Russellville), and Everett Pate (Rogers), all strong supporters of the idea.[858]

In order to increase attendance at the mid-winter meeting, the leaders threw in another piece of bait. At one point or another, every newspaper had had legal troubles. Hence, the Association prepared a digest of state laws affecting newspapers to be distributed to those attending.

The meeting took place on January 14-15. Bruce McCoy, the field manager for the Louisiana Press Association and president of the Newspaper Association Managers, spoke Saturday morning on "What the Field Manager Plan Is and How It Operates in Other States." This was followed by a roundtable discussion lasting almost two hours.

Armed with pledges of support for creating a manager position, the leaders then tried to consummate a relationship with the university, no easy task given the politics of the state. There existed two models, one, in which the manager had university affiliation, and the other, where the office was entirely separate.

Dr. A.M. Harding, a powerful figure statewide who carried the title Director of Extension Services and who later served as the university's president, was the principal player, but the APA made sure important board members and President Futrall were involved as well. Harding was not encouraging. In early correspondence with Kimball, Harding observed that there were dozens of projects people wanted from the university but that its budget was smaller than before the Depression. Perhaps, he thought, federal money could be obtained from W.J. Breit, the State Supervisor of Trade and Industrial Education.[859]

Harding's attempt to unload the program on a

shaky and potentially controversial federal base might have posed major problems at other times, but it remained a possibility under discussion for four months.[860] Initially, the Association wanted the university to provide $3,000 in support with the Association kicking in $2,500.[861] With the university still dragging its feet, the Hot Springs meeting in June voted to approve the plan, and another Young Turk, James Bland of the Walnut Ridge *Times-Dispatch* and the secretary to Governor Carl Bailey, became the first president under a new order the nature of which still remained obscure.

Apparently, the first proposal called for the APA to find three candidates for the office and give the university the final choice. When the university agreed only to provide office space and assistance worth $1,000 a year, leaving the Association to pay the salary of $1,400, the APA decided to take full control of the appointment.[862] Given the lack of interest from the university it is not surprising that Harding was given no role in the selection process. After the new manager was chosen, Kimball as an afterthought offered to furnish the man's references, should Harding want them.[863]

Selecting the right manager was critical. Donald Murray wrote Kimball that Everett Pate had suggested Ray for the job, and Murray thought "it would be a swell break for the association if you

---

The Manager's Nightmare, or The Eternal Pain

On November 15, 1937, C. Armitage Harper wrote APA secretary Ray Kimball concerning what he saw as a major problem. A district group meeting had been scheduled for Pine Bluff on the very same day that George Washington University was to play a football game against the University of Arkansas in Little Rock. "Army" explained that he was on the local committee for the game and had a party to attend afterward so that it would be impossible for him to come to Pine Bluff. "I am reasonably sure also that nearly all of the publishers in this territory will be interested in attending this game," he added in urging the meeting's postponement. "Football first?" was Ray Kimball's response.*

The publishers apparently went ahead with the meeting, but in time the "Hogaholics" triumphed. Across the state life in the fall revolved around the Razorbacks' schedule.

That November 21, 1937, became infamous in football legend. The Hogs' opponents were the Colonials of George Washington University, an elite academic institution that was a powerhouse in the 1930s before discontinuing football. The Hogs had visited Washington in 1936 and lost; the second confrontation found Arkansas a 19-point favorite. This game, which ended in a score of zero to zero, was fought, *Gazette* sportswriter and recent Fayetteville graduate Ben Epstein wrote, in "Arctic conditions." (Epstein moonlighted as Pat Rollo, "the undefeated middle-weight wrestling champion of Bulgaria.") All-American end Jim Benton from Fordyce, who later played for the Los Angeles Rams, was watched "closer than a Chink on the Japanese frontier," Epstein noted, in what a half century later would became politically incorrect language. As a result of the weather, Arkansas could not pass and George Washington could not run. Reflective, however, of the importance sports already had obtained, this was a front-page story.†

*C. Armitage Harper, Little Rock, to Ray Kimball, November 15, 1937, Kimball Papers.
†*Arkansas Gazette*, November 21, 1937; Orville Henry and Jim Bailey, *The Razorbacks: A Story of Arkansas Football* (Fayetteville, 1996).

---

would take the place." Murray had told Pate that "you had too good a set-up at De Queen to leave it," and Kimball seems not to have considered the idea.[864] Little is known about the final three applicants. David P. Johnson of Stillwater, Oklahoma, was not one of the finalists, being rejected "principally because of your youth."[865]

Kimball played a major role in recruiting Sam Schwieger, a former college roommate. A graduate of the University of Oklahoma, Schwieger had served for six years as the editor of a daily in Perry, Oklahoma, before coming to Arkansas. Under the manager system, Sam Schwieger set up an office on the campus at Fayetteville in the fall of 1938. By the time he left the job in 1943, the APA's membership had grown from less than half the state's newspapers to all but 12.[866]

It is evident from the interruption of the *Publisher* and the surviving correspondence that there were those who opposed the plan. Doubtless political and personal issues were involved that time has erased. In 1938, Harper was listed as the APA's third vice-president, which would have made him president in three years according to the rules of the "term," but his subsequent involvement with the Association his father had so long served was minimal. Although he found work with the *Farm Bureau Press*, he dropped out of the Association and never served as president. His family's printing firm had survived the Depression, and he remained active in printing with the Democrat Printing and Lithographing Company. In 1939, he and L.A. Henry co-authored *Conservation in Arkansas*, a pioneering conservation textbook.

Since one of Schwieger's duties was editing the *Publisher*, it is worthy of notice that during his early years the history of that publication became even more convoluted than previously. Volume Nine ended presumably with its seventh number in June 1938. Volume 10 was still being printed as late as December 1940, by which time it had swollen to 30 issues. Schwieger continued to present information about newspapers, editors, and publishers, but the extensive, graceful stories were a thing of the past. Probably because the Association's office was so far removed from the capital, both page size and content shrank and advertisements were far fewer than before 1929. The comprehensive analyses of newspapers that would have made the *Publisher* what Lemke wanted, a school of instruction, failed to materialize. Funded with less than half the projected amount, the field-manager system triumphed in the face of continued university disengagement. As for the university, by providing only office space, it lost a major chance to strengthen its journalism department.

It was during Schweiger's tenure that two of its most important services were established. In 1939, Schweiger created a clipping bureau, which read and clipped articles out of newspapers for clients for a fee. It was a profitable service for most of its existence and kept newspapers in front of hundreds of businesses, advertising agencies, government offices and others. But it became increasingly labor intensive and took up valuable office and parking space, so it was sold to GeoTel in Columbia, Missouri in 1995. Interestingly, the clipping service returned to APA as a tenant when the Association moved into its new building in 2000.

The other vital service, begun by Schweiger in 1940, was an advertising placement service. The APA became an extension of the advertising sales staffs of member newspapers, representing them to advertisers and advertising agencies. Member newspapers allowed the Association to hold back 25 percent of the revenue from the advertising it sold, 15 percent of which went to advertising agencies for their commission. While some newspapers raised their rates to APA to allow for those commissions, most newspapers adopted a "one-rate system," charging the same to everyone who bought space.

One early benefit from the connection with the

university came when law professor Robert Leflar wrote the first of a series of informational columns explaining the 12 constitutional amendments on the 1940 ballot. The columns were made available to the state's newspapers, and many picked them up.[867] Leflar continued this service for decades.

The APA's new deal for newspapers in the late 1930s mirrored national developments. Newspapers found themselves out of the age of laissez faire and into the world of government regulations. No longer could a publisher operate out of a daybook and his billfold or keep his circulation figures secret. Labor relations were changing as the federal government's encouragement of labor unions meant a return to the labor/management controversies of the previous century. The day of the tramp printer was ending as well.

Despite the rise of radio and highway advertising, so ubiquitous was the press in America that one New Deal agency well represented in Arkansas, the Civilian Conservation Corps, began creating camp newspapers. The *Flat Woods Rumble* from Jasper, the *Dirt Dauber* from Harrison, the *Camp Chatter* at Ashdown, and the *Camp Rosston News* were among the new, albeit temporary, journals that appeared during the Depression.[868]

The Golden Age of Country Correspondents

The Great Depression of the 1930s can be seen as a golden age only perhaps in retrospect. For those who lost their homes, farms, jobs, and livelihoods, the suffering, both physical and emotional, was intense. "There were a lot of lean bellies," veteran newspaperman Leland Duvall later observed. Across much of the state communities were held together by their newspapers. And rural areas depended on the mostly unpaid country correspondent to report on local affairs. Charlotte Tillar (later Schexnayder) subsequently observed, "Local citizens regard the correspondent as one having great prestige, ranking along with that of the preacher and professor. Consequently, the power of the press extends into the remotest rural areas where the correspondents likely reside."[869]

Although almost every newspaper utilized correspondents, that extent varied according to the geography of the state. In the plantation areas of the Delta, fewer correspondents could be found. Sharecroppers exhibited considerable illiteracy, moved on the average every two years, and were divided against each other by race. However, in those pockets where family ownership prevailed, correspondents, both white and black, could be found. "Among Our Colored Neighbors" was the heading used at the *Atkins Chronicle*.

From the meager evidence of the few surviving issues of mountainous Newton County's newspapers, correspondents had made few inroads there, either. It was in between these two extremes, especially in over half the state where the economy was based on small and medium-sized farms, that a vigorous culture of community existed.

The 1920s and 1930s witnessed for the first time the impact of public education into rural society. Increasing education resulted especially in more homebound literate females. If as late as 1920 the typical correspondent was a young male, by 1940 probably three-quarters were females. It was still the custom for these contributions to be anonymously presented until after World War II, but everyone knew who did the local news. Unique in Arkansas and probably in the nation was the *Clarksville Herald-Democrat*, which gave each correspondent a ten-point heading in capitals and a six-point description of the area together with the correspondent's name.[870] For this work, newspapers supplied paper, pencils, and stamps. Often the role became institutionalized, to be passed on from mother to daughter.

By the late 1920s, it became customary to hold a party for the correspondents, but attendance was rarely complete since so many lacked cars.

Altogether, much of what was reported presented a mirror of rural society. Invariably the principal items were who was sick and with what; how many were at church and Sunday school; the successes or failures of revivals (or protracted meetings); the state of the weather, especially as it pertained to crops; who had visitors or had been visiting; and the activities of the schools. Early correspondents were moral censors for their communities, opinionated on politics (as well as on religion and the weather), and sometimes, consciously or unconsciously, stylists of distinction.

Unless greatly distracted, they started with the health. "Health good—no one dead, newly married or told anything," was the news from Maddoxville.[871] That writer had a taste for catchy openings. Another read: "George Maddox butchered a hog last week and his family are all well."[872] The Brannon correspondent presented the weather with a flourish but was not well served by the printer: "The wild geese are going south and the cold weather north winds have been blowing which remind us that old winter is night [*sic*]—even at the door."[873] A white Christmas in 1926 prompted the Sunny Gap correspondent to note: "A white-mantled earth, trees with their crystal jewels; snow-covered, fairy-like houses dotting the countryside, remind one of the pictures on holiday greeting cards, only no artist's brush can paint it quite as lovely and picturesque."[874]

Although lacking formal training, many correspondents had an eye for hard news. Gus M. Oehm, the extension editor at the University's Department of Agriculture, had told the APA in 1926 that country correspondents should content themselves with nothing but neighborhood news, and that their "beat" should include the preacher, doctor, and police. Personal items alone, he explained, "do not cover all the news."[875] One Dumas writer, who had no telephone and no car, walked miles to the nearest house in order to contact the newspaper about an important story.[876] Few professional reporters would have done half as well as the *Log Cabin Democrat*'s Greasy Valley correspondent:

> The sheriff of this county, J.W. Hatchett, came over one day last week with his deputies to arrest Woodrow Elder, wanted in Alabama and no telling how many other states for car theft. Woodrow never was as good a man as his dad ought to be. Ever since he was knee high to a duck he has had the reputation of violating every criminal law he could and he has led the officers many a merry chase. The sheriff and his deputies had him surrounded in his father's home and for once Mr. Hatchett had him almost within his grasp. But our sheriff has one weakness, if it could be called a weakness. He likes women and he wouldn't harm one for his right hand. So he called to the women in the house to come out and march down the road to safety, as he expected a little shooting would take place before Woodrow would surrender. Three women marched out all with sun bonnets on and walked slowly down the road and when they were a safe distance one of them pulled up her dress and showed our sheriff her pants. Now, Mr. Hatchett knows that real women don't do that way. He had let Woodrow walk off right before his eyes. Woodrow pulled off his dress and split for the brush and when he gets into a little start, a pack of hounds couldn't catch him. We who have always known Woodrow, wouldn't doubt if he isn't now in Florida, Minnesota, California or Maine and driving a good car.[877]

The veteran male correspondent from Martinville (Faulkner County), E.H. ("Uncle Eddie") Miller, showed the ability to combine the 1926 August heat (108 in the shade) with visiting:

> It is too hot for us to start on our visit to our "wife's

kinfolks." We are planning to make this contemplative visit in the near future. We intend to visit Mt. Vernon if we can induct our good wife to remain at home and take care of our white chickens while we run over to Mt. Vernon. We will be 77 years young on August 15 and believe we can take care of ourself even among "pretty girls" and the soothing sound of "music."[878]

Miller went on to suggest that it would be useful to know the number of jars or cans of fruits and vegetables that were being put up and suggested other correspondents join him in this endeavor. He then went to work himself, walking ("hoofed it") to all 77 homes in his district and collecting information from 74 (three were away). His total count was 10,537 cans or jars, and reflected well the values Arkansans saw in their rural lives.[879] Later, the Stringtown-Macedonia correspondent, after noting that at the Rose Hill fruit farm they were still canning, observed: "What we do not need for home use, we will sell next spring. Everybody in our community have enough fruit and vegetables put up for home use, and that is the important thing."[880]

The writings of Mrs. Stevens, the correspondent quoted above, attracted the attention of Fletcher Chenault, the veteran *Gazette* feature writer, who discussed how the former Charlotte Shillcutt of Little Rock ended up at the Rose Hill fruit farm. Mrs. Stevens, one of the few who typed her submissions, was remarkable in another way, too.[881] On July 28, 1938, she confided to her readers that she had been forced to place her oldest daughter, Josephine, in the state hospital: "Her malady, as far as I can tell just from observations, is mental delusion, hallucinations and optical illusions. She sees strange sights with her eyes and goes frantic and raving crazy."[882] Later, Mrs. Stevens told of her visit to the hospital and the water therapy they were using.[883] Since mental illness was commonly treated as a disgrace that a family sought to suppress, the candor of this writer stands unique for this or indeed just about any other time.

Correspondents reflected the changing times of rural Arkansas. Across much of the state, the land available for agriculture had already been taken by 1920, and in many counties decline had been in evidence for decades. Many poor farmers abandoned the hills to take up land in the Delta, where drainage ditches accelerated land-clearing. Others began to leave for Northern factory jobs or California. County correspondents noted these developments, both directly by their reports on family visiting, and by promoting their own communities. Such correspondents played an important role in prolonging for decades a sense of community awareness in the face of one disaster after another.

Perhaps because they were not paid, correspondents displayed considerable independence. Uncle Eddie Miller, for instance, took a shot at his newspaper: "Last week the printer made us say, 'We acknowledge the weight of a copy of the 'Country Correspondent' by Mr. Oehm.' Really, we did not weigh the copy we received, but we are very thankful for it. It is light by the standpoint of avoirdupois, but from an intellectual point of view it is full of weighty matter."[884] Uncle Eddie also expressed his doubts on that old controversy, the proper method of baptism. In commenting on a service at Bogolosia on Cadron Creek, he reported a total was 66, "if," he added sarcastically, "sprinkling may be called baptism."[885]

By the 1920s, the Protestant ascendancy was in full sway. As all the women and most of the men correspondents were church members; scriptural issues frequently arose, if an editor permitted it. "Business usually begins to pick up when two men start a dispute over the Bible," the Greasy Valley correspondent noted, "but let two women lock horns over their church differences and watch the fur fly." Professing a latitudinarian point of view, Greasy Valley claimed that if he ever got narrow-minded, he wanted a Hardshell preacher friend of his "to take him gimlet and bore me for the simples and see if I have any brains." Perhaps feeling he had gone too far, he added, "I wrote the above partly in fun."[886]

From time to time controversies that erupted within the nation or the country spread into these columns. In 1925, bathing suits seem to have been a hot issue, as the exposure of female flesh and "mixed" bathing did not set well in the conservative South. Sunday baseball stirred much comment. Then in 1926 it was the bobbing of girls' hair (readers interested in this topic should consult the F. Scott Fitzgerald story, "Bernice Bobs Her Hair"). Editorially, J.B. Parker at the *Conway News* led the attack on loose women, but many female correspondents stood up for their sex. Mrs. Stevens thought it practical for women "who are helping to make both ends meet in the business and workaday world of today."[887] The Alder Branch-Quitman correspondent, after noting that her neighbors were "industrious, honest and attend to their own affairs," added, "I had forgotten—we may be very sinful, if bobbed hair is one."[888] Uncle Eddie finally got disgusted with the whole process, observing, it was time "to quit all this talk about bobbed hair. They are 'bobbing it off' regardless of what we may think or say about it."[889]

Another theme of the age was the acquisition of automobiles. Uncle Eddie took some sardonic delight in noting: "All that started to Mallettown last Sunday afternoon on Robert Martin's truck reached there safely, except Miss Nora Hendrickson, Miss Maud McKinsee and Buster Brinkley, all three of whom fell off in a mudhole near Cadron Creek Bridge."[890] And the Brannon writer observed that Professor Jacob Sandage had purchased a "tin Lizzie:" "As Jacob is a real good fellow he has our sympathy." "'He that owneth and runneth a Ford car,'" the correspondent had been informed, "'and saith that he hath no troubles is a liar and the truth is not in him.' Brother Sandage's trouble have only begun."[891]

Correspondents took on deeper issues as well. The failure of the Republicans to pass a farm bill in the late 1920s attracted comment and showed that some writers read the Memphis *Commercial Appeal* as well as the Little Rock newspapers.[892] Having suffered though the Drought and the beginning stages of the Depression under Hoover, many correspondents used their columns to support Franklin Delano Roosevelt.[893] In 1936 the Rocky Point writer, after learning that Republican nominee Alf Landon had gotten one vote, hoped that "they catch the fellow that voted for Landon. And if he is from Conway (which I can't bring myself to believe) place him in one of the show windows on Front street, so we can see what he looks like. We are sorry to know there is such an animal at large."[894] According to another correspondent, the Landon voter was a Mr. Hopkins. His fate is not known.[895] The Woodrow correspondent suggested firing the editor of the *Literary Digest*, whose famous poll had foretold the Kansas Republican governor's victory.

Female correspondents were strong supporters of Senator Hattie Caraway's re-election bid in 1938. Her Democratic primary opponent, John McClellan, offended many of them with his claim that "Arkansas needs another man in the Senate" and other "cry-baby stuff."[896]

Local politics figured in the columns as well. The Walnut Valley writer for the Dover newspaper in 1926 attacked the longstanding practice of buying votes with liquor: "...this thing of men getting booze when they go to give in their taxes, I'll say some one has a bottle to pass and if you are running for office, run away back and sit down—we don't have any such officer. We have men in the race that are clean, sober, honest men and we all know them. Put'em in and some of the whiskey men out. We don't need whiskey in office or out."[897]

Across the more remote parts of the state,

Sarah Bell "Granny" Cannon, Beaver Springs correspondent of the Siloam Springs Herald Democrat, *epitomized the country correspondent of the early 20th century. Here she sits with her husband. (Courtesy Shelly Moran)*

Free ads: a contradiction in terms

Advertising, by definition, is a paid form of mass communication by an identified sponsor. There are a few exceptions, such as public service ads. But for the most part, ads are paid for, and advertising is the primary source of revenue for newspapers.

Attempts by advertisers to gain free space in newspapers are as old as newspapers themselves. The example at left is about as blatant as ever was sent to newspapers. When Roland Hughes, publisher of *The Star-Progress* in Wynne, received the ad on May 24, 1938, he wrote to then-APA president Donald Murray of the *Jonesboro Tribune*: "In my opinion, the enclosed proof is an insult to the intelligence of editors and publishers of small newspapers. Proctor & Gamble has a radio program, giving away refrigerators, and has the gall to ask the newspapers to run free publicity for it."

President Murray, in turn, wrote to APA secretary Ray Kimball of De Queen: "The matter discussed by Roland Hughes in the letter enclosed strikes me as being one of the most vital facing the publishing industry at the moment." Subsequently Kimball appointed Hughes to lead a discussion at the summer convention.

Even today, similar attempts are made, especially by politicians. At a national convention of political consultants, one session was devoted to "The Free Medium," referring to newspapers. "Just take your candidate into town, go to the newspaper office, and they'll take your picture and run it on page one" was one of the tips offered. In response, one publisher quoted comic strip character Pogo: "We have met the enemy and he is us."

Visiting the Cleveland County Herald, *c. 1965. An oil can is prominently displayed on the left as Bill Sadler (APA president, 1972) demonstrates an old sheet-fed folder to schoolchildren. (Courtesy* Cleveland County Herald*)*

Guy M. Sadler, *sometime APA treasurer and board member, demonstrates, cigar in mouth, the Linotype he acquired in 1927 to a group of schoolchildren. (Courtesy* Cleveland County Herald*)*

Scene from the motion picture "Arkansas Traveler." Bob Burns from Van Buren starred in this popular film where a printer rescues a widowed editoress in distress. See related vignette on page 220. (Courtesy Bob Burns Museum, Van Buren)

APA convention, 1948. Kate Gillespie, the sister of Mike Gillespie (APA President 1948); Roberta Fulbright; C.G. Hall, Secretary of State; Sam Gearhart (standing); Mike Gillespie (hand in pocket). Kate, who worked closely with her brother, was famous for her hats. (Courtesy Arkansas History Commission)

Many newspapers after the Civil War used prizes and promotions. The Jackson County Democrat, *under Roy R. Craig, offered a new 1960 Chevrolet Biscayne sedan. The contest featured a $25 award for those who brought in $125 in subscriptions. Nora Lee Wilson won first place and the car. Three years later, Craig sold the weekly to the* Newport Independent. *(Photo by Ed Nave, 1960; courtesy Robert D. Craig)*

Ludlow typesetting machine at the Hope Star, *c. 1950. Ludlows were used for setting headlines. (Courtesy* Hope Star*)*

Coping with the Depression. The 1934 APA convention in Clarksville was devoted to wrestling—unnecessarily as it turned out—with the New Deal's Blue Eagle regulatory plan. Charles M.Young, Helena World, *was president; C. Armitage Harper, secretary; Erwin Funk, NRA Code administrator; K.A. Baldridge, NEA president; and O.E.* Jones, Batesville Guard and Record, *APA treasurer. (APA Archives)*

"One of our first female carriers," at De Queen, c. 1948. Females began working as carriers after World War II. (Photo by Ralph B. Kite, courtesy Anita Floyd Marshall)

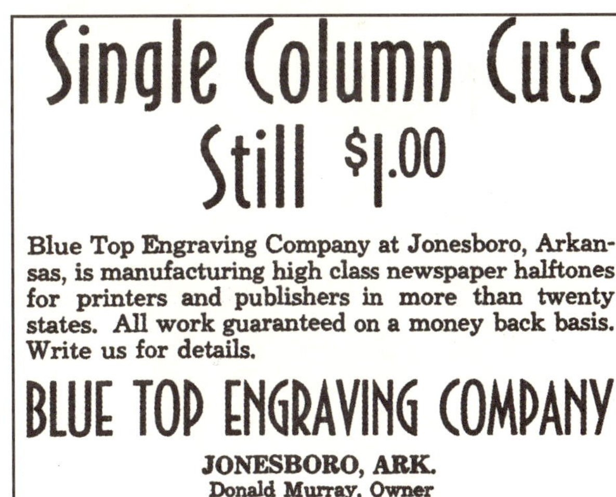

Blue Top Engraving advertisement. Donald Murray at Jonesboro ran this service before World War II. (Arkansas Publisher, *1938)*

In this cartoon from The Newark Journal's *August 13, 1934 issue, Oscar F. Craig took aim at rival editors Austin Wilkerson of the* Newport Daily Independent *and O.E. Jones of the* Batesville Guard and Record *over the dispersing of post office positions. Courtesy Robert D. Craig)*

Christmas card from APA manager Bill Miner, 1947. Miner managed to include the names of every editor/ publisher in Arkansas as well as others connected to the industry. The only known copy was saved by Roy Craig, who circled his name. (Courtesy Robert D. Craig)

Most convention events centered around meals, and delegates for half a century sported fancy membership badges. Ralph Kite, pictured here, was a pioneer in newspaper photography in Arkansas. (APA Archives)

The U.S. Postal Service commissioned a stamp from artist Charlene Blackburn to honor Baxter Bulletin *editor Tom Shiras for his work in promoting the damming of the White River. His heirs declined the honor, and the stamp was never issued. (Courtesy Judi Sharp)*

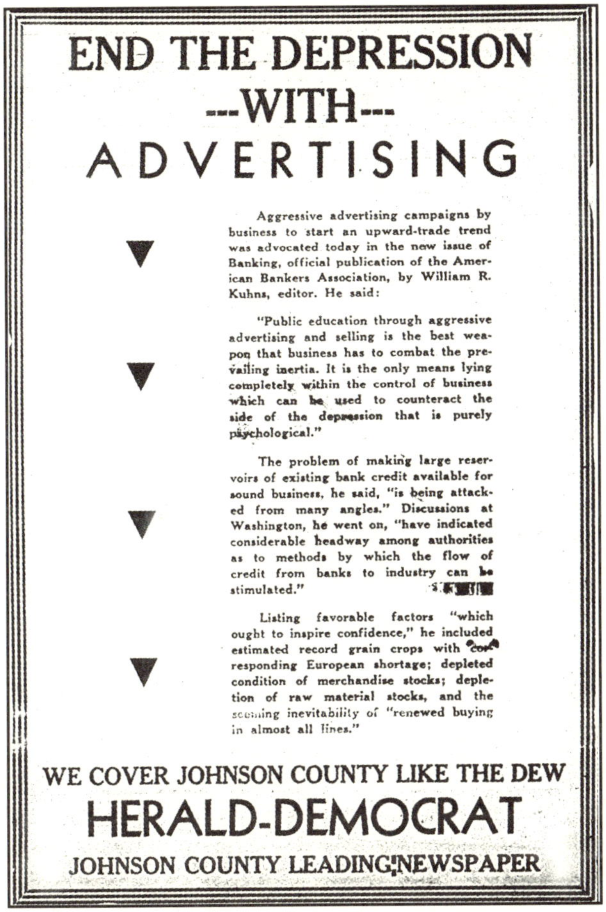

END THE DEPRESSION
---WITH---
ADVERTISING

Aggressive advertising campaigns by business to start an upward-trade trend was advocated today in the new issue of Banking, official publication of the American Bankers Association, by William R. Kuhns, editor. He said:

"Public education through aggressive advertising and selling is the best weapon that business has to combat the prevailing inertia. It is the only means lying completely within the control of business which can be used to counteract the side of the depression that is purely psychological."

The problem of making large reservoirs of existing bank credit available for sound business, he said, "is being attacked from many angles." Discussions at Washington, he went on, "have indicated considerable headway among authorities as to methods by which the flow of credit from banks to industry can be stimulated."

Listing favorable factors "which ought to inspire confidence," he included estimated record grain crops with corresponding European shortage; depleted condition of merchandise stocks; depletion of raw material stocks, and the seeming inevitability of "renewed buying in almost all lines."

WE COVER JOHNSON COUNTY LIKE THE DEW
HERALD-DEMOCRAT
JOHNSON COUNTY LEADING NEWSPAPER

Encouraging more advertising made sense as well as profit to publishers and was in line with President Roosevelt's much-quoted assurance that "the only thing we have to fear is fear itself." (Courtesy APA Archives)

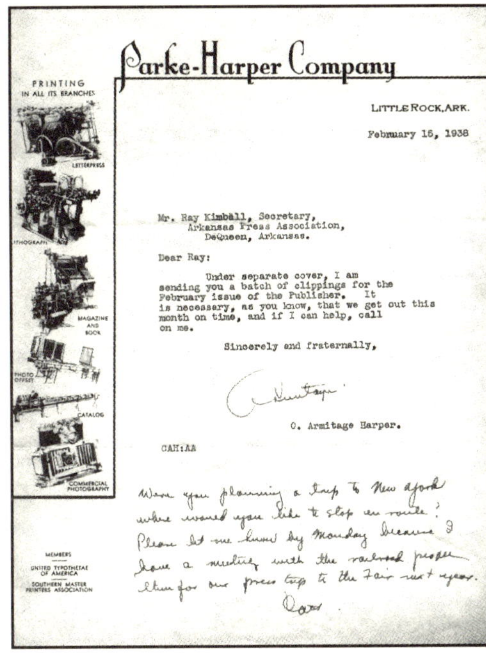

Parke-Harper Company

PRINTING IN ALL ITS BRANCHES

LETTERPRESS

MAGAZINE AND BOOK

CATALOG

COMMERCIAL PHOTOGRAPHY

MEMBERS
UNITED TYPOTHETAE OF AMERICA
SOUTHERN MASTER PRINTERS ASSOCIATION

LITTLE ROCK, ARK.

February 15, 1938

Mr. Ray Kimball, Secretary,
Arkansas Press Association,
DeQueen, Arkansas.

Dear Ray:

Under separate cover, I am sending you a batch of clippings for the February issue of the Publisher. It is necessary, as you know, that we get out this month on time, and if I can help, call on me.

Sincerely and fraternally,

C. Armitage Harper.

CAH:AA

Stationery, Parke–Harper Company, 1938, showing printing equipment. (Courtesy Anita Kimball Marshall)

Letterhead, West Memphis News, *1937, showing city's skyline. (Courtesy Anita Kimball Marshall)*

August K. Engel, longtime owner of the Arkansas Democrat; *Donald W. Reynolds, owner of the Fort Smith newspapers (subsequently Donrey Media); an unidentified man; and Walter E. Hussman, Sr. at the Southern Newspaper Publishers Association in 1940. Reynolds and Hussman had been college roommates and fraternity brothers at the University of Missouri; during World War II they were co-publishers of* Yank Magazine *for the U.S. Army in Paris, France. (Courtesy Walter E. Hussman, Jr.)*

moonshiners, who made good money during Prohibition, fought churches. The Witt Springs correspondent to the *Marshall Republican* complained, "We can't have much church or Sunday school on account of so much whiskey and disturbance."[898] When a visiting evangelist took up the issue at length, moonshiners shot up the meeting twice, killing an elderly woman the second time.[899]

There was also humor to be found in county elections, as the Walnut Valley writer noted:

> This has been a very busy and exciting week in our valley. There are so many candidates, especially for tax assessor, that even the children will ask, "was that a tax assessor," and I told them yes. So Thursday night when the two Turner boys come out to Powers' mill after dark for a load of lumber, the children saw the lights coming and their horns honking and they began to run and cry, hide mama, hide, I bet it's the tax assessors coming up here, but it was only the Turner brothers after lumber.[900]

While perhaps no cause was dearer to many correspondents than campaigning for a full attendance at Sunday School and church, some noticed other problems as well. By the 1920s, America's industrial society was impinging on the countryside. Mrs. Stevens trumpeted the concerns of residents of the Holland road and at Pickles Gap who reported filling stations were dumping oilcans and other debris along the roads, "thus putting an ugly blotch upon which was before this desecration a quiet and beautifully clean countryside."[901] She recommended boycotting the stations, but stopping the trashing of Arkansas was to become another battle lost.

Tragedies and crises found correspondents at their best. Many readers relied on the newspaper for ordinary reports on sickness and death, but events such as the great tornado of 1927 or the big flood that summer found correspondents recording the human side of these events. "We were so sorry to hear about the terrible misfortune which happened to the Jones family Tuesday evening," a Desha County correspondent wrote, "The whole community sympathizes with them in their awful loss. We join them in the general sorrow. Three shoats belonging to the Jones ate cockleburrs and passed away."[902]

Perhaps one of the most surprising comments to appear was a book review. The Woodrow writer had just received a book from her children, "written by a southern woman of Atlanta, Ga. The story, we are told, hinges on the civil war. The price is $3, and it contains 1,000 pages, but it is well worth one's money and time."[903] Unidentified was the author, Margaret Mitchell, or the title, *Gone with the Wind.*

Probably no newspaper made more use of correspondents or gave them more freedom than the *Log Cabin Democrat* at Conway. Owner Frank E. Robins' mother had been the widowed owner of the *Log Cabin* and then became the wife of J.W. Underhill of the *Conway Democrat*, resulting in the merger of the two newspapers. Her son initiated a daily in 1908, and by the 1930s the *Log Cabin Democrat* was a respectable Associated Press-subscribing small-town daily. However, it was the weekly that long overshadowed the daily. In 1926, the newspaper boasted that its 85 correspondents representing 65 communities were among the nation's leaders in this department. This translated into 17 columns of type, filling five of the newspaper's ten pages.

By 1938, the number of correspondents had grown to 114, allegedly the most of any newspaper in America. According to Robins's count, Faulkner County contained about 150 different communities, defined as churches and/or schools, each consisting of about four square miles. "Everyone of them desire to be represented in our rural news columns," he noted, and the problem was "endeavoring to prevent it from completely overwhelming us."[904] The office kept a card index on each correspondent with blanks for each week. After receiving four letters, the newspaper sent out four stamped and addressed envelopes, together with some 16 sheets of ruled paper. Finding correspondents was not the problem; rather, the reverse. In communities with more than one church, two correspondents necessarily were employed.

While the *Log Cabin* held an annual meeting for correspondents, Magnolia's *Banner-News* used quarterly gatherings. At Conway, the first gathering was held in the spring of 1926, and by the following year Uncle Eddie was pushing for another meeting and the formation of a permanent organization. "We are sure," for Uncle Eddie loved to intone in the editorial "we," that "the convention of correspondents of rural writers for the 'Cabin' was not only enjoyed and appreciated by those in attendance, but has been helpful to all of us since."[905] Another correspondent, who approved the idea, nevertheless objected to the idea of "sitting around a table discussing things and letting Mr. Robins tell us what is what and who is who. I don't know much, but what I do know, I know as good as Mr. Anybody."[906] In time the newspaper provided ice cream and cold drinks, the rest of food coming in the form of covered dishes. "I might talk at length of how the quality and tastefulness of this country food has improved during the past two decades as a result of home economics instruction and home demonstration work," Robins later observed, "but that would be another story."

Typical was the *Log Cabin*'s 13th annual meeting held in Quitman, a town in Cleburne County, that attracted 36 of the 118 correspondents for a total of some 250 guests. Following the luncheon, attendees got a history lesson on the town and some singing from the Quitman quartet. Then Frank E. Robins called the roll. Twenty-seven of the writers had not missed an issue, and 13 had missed only once. Miss Emma Duncan of Republican was cited as the "star correspondent." Not only did she have 12 consecutive years of perfect reporting, but she also displayed "perfection of manuscript and general excellence of her items."[907] After more singing, including "My Own Loved Arkansas"; some humorous readings; and a poem by Will A. Berry, the newspaper's resident poet; many went over to Buffalo Hump to see the new fire tower.

Most newspapers had far fewer correspondents than the *Log Cabin Democrat* and made somewhat less of a to-do. Nevertheless, the same year Roy Elliot at the *Fordyce Weekly News* held an open house in conjunction with the harvest festival and stock show, and gave correspondents passes to the midway shows.[908] In 1930, W.B. Folsom at the *Brinkley Argus* rented a motor coach and took 32 correspondents on a tour, stopping at the newspaper offices in De Valls Bluff, Hazen, Carlisle, and Lonoke before being welcomed in Little Rock by Governor Harvey Parnell and the city's mayor. After a visit to the state capitol and lunch at the Albert Pike Hotel came a party at the Capitol Theatre. Folsom pronounced it one of the most satisfying days in his long career.[909]

During the 1930s, the *Log Cabin Democrat* employed "Dean" W.W. Wood, who presided rather like an elder over the correspondents. Robins called him "an elderly man who is good at wisecracks and presides at the annual meeting," but in fact Wood, whose family had settled the area in 1877-78, had a good grasp of local history.

The death of a veteran correspondent elicited extensive coverage. In 1939 A.W. Perrine of the Siloam Springs *Herald and Democrat* observed:

> Soon after we came to Siloam Springs about 40 years ago and began building a foundation for the old Herald to stand on, and let it be known we wanted some reliable country correspondents, one day when Aunt Mary Bradley was telling us a thing or two about making friends in the country, Mrs.

W.L. Cannon came in and said she would look after interests over the line in the Indian Territory, and then and there started a friendship that lasted until last Sunday when this good old soul breathed her last.[910]

Five years later death claimed "Grandma" Palmer:

Forty-five years ago she came in and notified us that she was the official correspondent from the Beaver Springs, Indian Territory, neighborhood, and was more interested in the old reliable paper than we were. She joined old Aunt Mary Bradley, our correspondent in the Folker community, and organized an association of our correspondents. From that day to time of her death, she was a faithful worker for the paper, and never missed an issue. How she will be missed in her home neighborhood was elegantly told in the correspondence from that community in last week's items.[911]

All editors confronted the problem of assembling this material. At the *Log Cabin Democrat*, correspondents generated 30 galleys a week, which Robins edited himself. The task, he said, was "onerous," but it gave him, he believed, "a true picture of human nature and an accurate cross-section of the sentiments of my county. I also get many laughs, more from flashes of genuine wit than from ludicrous blunders in writing." Indeed, as noted earlier, many of his correspondents were swift to pick up any editing or printing blunders in their published copy.

Editors of country newspapers then faced the vexing question of whether and how to edit. Charlotte Tillar, who described herself as a "middle-of-road editor," explained that she left standing colloquial expressions but checked closely the names and straightened out the spelling and grammar.[912] On the other hand, many editors simply gave the handwritten copy to the Linotype operators who set it as best they could.

The question of whether the work was worthwhile vexed publishers then and now. One sturdy defender of the country correspondents was Hugh Park at Van Buren's *Press-Argus*. In a 1940 speech, Park detailed how he surveyed his readers about what they liked best. Prior to the survey Park had been running nationally syndicated columnists, but what the readers looked for was local news. The second most preferred feature was a long weekly column written by the local head of the Farm Bureau. Third place was divided among Park's own editorials, a column of social chitchat, a Sunday School lesson, and a weekly report on how to grow flowers. No one selected any of the half-dozen syndicated columnists.

Park used his survey to advance the idea that weeklies could not copy dailies. In his case, with Van Buren a virtual suburb of Fort Smith, to make the newspaper thrive it had to be distinctive. Park advised leaving European affairs to the dailies and radio and making the weekly "The Home Newspaper."[913] Robins at the *Log Cabin Democrat* had access to Associated Press stories and occasionally ran important news on the weekly's front page. However, the day of cutting and pasting from other newspapers was in sharp decline. Readers of country weeklies could learn local election results, and many newspapers ran one of the various columns of state news, but national news had disappeared. Even the Japanese bombing of Pearl Harbor failed to make its way into many country newspapers.

Another proponent of correspondents was Professor Walter J. Lemke at the University. Lemke supervised a survey conducted by one of his students, Eugene Herrington, which revealed that approximately 23 percent of the average weekly's news space went to correspondents, with a variation of between six and 40 percent. Overall, newspapers averaged one correspondent for every 47 readers, but extreme variations again existed. The *Tuckerman Record*, with 66 correspondents, had only 675 readers; the *Crittenden County Times* had only five correspondents but 1,320 subscribers.

As to who made the best correspondents, women were now overwhelmingly preferred. Three newspapers paid their writers, among them the *Crittenden County Times*.[914] All provided supplies and free subscriptions, while the Dardanelle *Post-Dispatch* offered free classified advertisements. Only about a third used yearly gatherings or meetings as a reward. The author concluded that more correspondents ought to be recruited, better editing was needed, style books would be useful, reward systems worked, and visits by the writers to offices would be of assistance.

Lemke's interest led to his creating a newsletter, *The Arkansas Community Newspaper*, to promote the improvement of weeklies. In June 1944, he produced his own study based on 60 weeklies (but not including the *Log Cabin Democrat* or the *Mena Weekly Star*). In his list, he found the *De Queen Bee* ranked first with 43 correspondents, but their words represented only 14 percent of the newspaper's makeup. The *Montgomery County Herald* with 23 correspondents gave them 25 percent of its space. In column inches, the weekly edition of Russellville's *Courier-Democrat* led with 213.

As an advocate of home news (and home print), Lemke combined the percentages contributed by country correspondents with those reporting local news. In his opinion, a country newspaper ought to devote one third of its total space to local news. Using ready print generally cut by four pages what an eight-page newspaper could have available for itself. The leader in combined county and local news was the *Montgomery County Herald* at 50 percent. Closely following were the *Van Buren County Democrat* at Clinton and the *Paris Express*.

"We were poor but we didn't know it," recalled Mary Etta (Grady) Madden, a Depression-era child from Beedeville.[915] Nowhere was this truism more in evidence than in the writings of the country correspondents during the Great Depression. Despite hard times, foreclosures, droughts, floods, bank failures, and labor unrest, they went about their duties, unconsciously ministering to the people of their communities.

Metropolitan newspapers had their correspondents as well. In imitation of the English and New York newspapers, the *Arkansas Gazette* in 1933 had a weekly nature column, entitled "Country Diarist," written by Ruth Thomas of Morrilton. Her initially unsigned reflections were greatly loved and continued until the time of her death in 1973. Roy Evans filled a different role. This Evening Shade native was another graduate from Owen C. Shaver's *Sharp County Record*, where he started work in 1920. After completing his training, he moved to the *Hardy Herald* and then to the *Batesville Record* before going to work at the *Newport Daily Independent* in 1926. Evans, who wrote a local column for nearly 60 years and even had one ready to publish after his death, also doubled as the *Arkansas Democrat*'s correspondent for the area.

The Golden Age of the Feature Writer

During the middle years of the 20th century, the metropolitan newspapers attained ever-higher standards of excellence. At the heart of this transformation was the emergence of the Sunday edition. Building on the older weekly editions, the *Arkansas Gazette* and *Arkansas Democrat* added magazine sections that solicited stories from some of the state's best writers. Modeled on *The New York Times* magazine, these Arkansas supplements almost always contained stories of state interest. Both competed with the Memphis *Commercial Appeal*, the *Kansas City Star*, as well as the St.Louis and Tulsa newspapers, which attracted readers in Arkansas. A number of country editors and writers supplemented their meager incomes through this work.

Tom Shiras of the *Baxter Bulletin* in Mountain Home was one of the most prolific writers, and one of the few whose stories have been partially republished. Known as the "walking editor," a title he inherited from Tom Newman at Harrison, Shiras contributed mostly stories about pioneer life in the Ozarks. A tireless promoter of damming the White River when not detailing primitive ways, Shiras used plain speech and often let his subjects speak for themselves. Other family members—Frances, Ginger, and Peter—were able writers as well.

Ozarks themes also appeared from Karr Shannon, who bought the *Melbourne Times* in 1932. During the 1930s he attained a statewide reputation as a cracker-barrel philosopher; after World War II, Shannon joined the *Arkansas Democrat* as a columnist. Fletcher Chenault, who worked for the *Gazette* on personal-interest stories, was another active contributor. Diana Sherwood frequently wrote articles on Arkansas history, and Otto Ernest Rayburn, the Ozarks promoter and folklore authority, wrote prolifically. Edgar B. Chesnutt, Johnny Erp, Bernie Babcock, Zillah Cross Peel, and Walter J. Lemke contributed feature stories as well.

The work of some Arkansas writers appeared in newspapers outside the state. Tom Shiras's work went to Kansas City and St. Louis; Margaret Woolfolk from Crittenden County and Esther Bindursky of Lepanto regularly supplied stories to the Memphis press. Bindursky broke into national publications, including the *National Geographic* and *Saturday Evening Post*.

From a feature-writing standpoint, the most important event of the period was the Arkansas Centennial Celebration in 1936. Despite the Depression, Arkansas made a brave showing, with the newspapers leading the way. It was the press that agitated the public well in advance of the event, and many of the state's newspapers celebrated by issuing special editions. The one put out by the *Arkansas Gazette* included original art by Howard Simon and poetry by John Gould Fletcher. Dickison Brugman drew on his immense memory and his reading of back issues in order to generate a chronological account of the state's history. Copies became treasured keepsakes, often ending up in the possession of the libraries that the New Deal helped spur. In keeping with its role of playing a seemingly perpetual second fiddle, the *Arkansas Democrat* produced its edition as well. Clyde Palmer offered $100 for a centennial song.

Most weeklies could not compete at this level, but Earl Dodd, editor of the *Greenwood Democrat*, traveled to Hot Springs over Governor Conway's "good dirt roads" in order to cover President Roosevelt's visit. Dodd had his camera with him: "I hollered at him, 'Hey, Mr. President' and took his picture."[916] At Benton, L.B. White managed on March 25, 1937 to issue a 128-page "centennial number" of the *Benton Courier* commemorating the 100th anniversary of the founding of Saline County—which had been created in 1835.

Interesting writing could be found as well in the columns generated locally. Some of the notable individuals from this period included Alex Washburn of the *Hope Star*; O. Klute Braswell of the Berryville *Star-Progress*; Ben Daulton of the *Sharp County Independent*, Curtis Hurley of the *Morrilton Democrat*; Isham L. Burrow of the Ozark *Spectator*; Eunice O'Baugh of the Pocahontas *Star Herald*; Guy Sadler of the *Cleveland County Herald*; J.E. Parrott of the *Tuckerman Record*; and James L. Bland of the Walnut Ridge *Times-Dispatch*.

Several editors wrote local histories. W.E. Orr (*White County Record*) chronicled Judsonia; Laud Payne (*Piggott Banner*) pioneered Clay County history; Karr Shannon recounted Izard County; and Klute Braswell wrote extensively on Carroll County. Later, Margaret Woolfolk undertook Crittenden County, and Robert Chowning managed both St.

Francis and Columbia Counties. Harry Lee Williams, who wrote a history of Craighead County, also authored two different versions of how the game of politics had been played. Hugh Park republished some Arkansas history classics and was the longtime printer for the Arkansas Historical Association's *Quarterly*.

Two proponents of local writing who wrote about their craft were Karr Shannon of the *Melbourne Times* and Hugh Park of Van Buren's *Press-Argus*. Shannon described how at first he had written editorials on "dignified and technical subjects. I balanced all sentences, and consulted a Webster for big words to add dignity. For nearly a year I did this. Nothing came of it other than the fact that occasionally some reader would ask me the meaning of some words I had used. I had always forgotten the meaning by the time the paper came off the press, and therefore made a sorry plight of things." Then he hit upon the formula of using plain Ozark speech, and he got rid of the editorial "we"—"highly superfluous when you are everything in the shop from janitor to ad-writer—and all the readers know it."

Shannon abhorred canned editorials, and urged writers to "let yourself loose. Don't bother too much about grammar. School teachers made grammar. Be natural about it. Shun all imitations. You may not be able to move mountains, but you can move some unsightly building from your town."[917] Hugh Park kept the "we," but shared the philosophy, entitling a collection of his writings, *The Country Editor*. Park was a close friend of actor and comedian Bob Burns and flirted with a career in radio. Although in professional meetings publishers complained about radio's competition, Park was not the only enterprising editor to find that the new medium could give wider currency to his newspaper. Ardis Tyson's "Down on the Farm" column from the *Atkins Chronicle* attained considerable circulation by being read over KARK by Bob Buice.[918] A half-century later, David Cox of the *Village Journal* of Cherokee Village regularly reported on Sharp County news for public radio station KASU.

The Rise of Journalism Education

The first student newspaper in Arkansas was the *Youth's Banner* of 1852 from Little Rock. The small three-column issue of July 5, 1852, carried to motto, "In Union there is Strength," and expressed devotion to "the advancement of Youth, Literature, and Morality." Both the newspaper and its editor and publisher, J.C. Mitchell, soon vanished without a trace. It seems not to have been affiliated with any school.[919] The contents consisted of overheated poetry and homilies.

Apparently the first college newspaper was published from St. John's College, the antebellum Masonic institution in Little Rock that failed after the Civil War. Across the Boston Mountains the transmontane state university at Fayetteville managed to get along for over a quarter-century before its first newspaper, the *University Weekly*, was started in 1906. After the football Cardinals became the Razorbacks in 1916, the *University Weekly* was transmogrified into *Arkansas Traveler* in 1920. At first, the students elected the editor, and since it was an "authorized" publication, students found it difficult to vent serious criticism. In 1912, a group of prominent students took their complaints to Fort Smith where they had printed the *X-Ray*. In retaliation for criticizing the president and faculty, 36 students were expelled. A massive boycott followed, attended by statewide publicity and ending in the students' victory.

Another protest episode in 1919 involved Brooks Hays, later a prominent Arkansas congressman, and in 1927 *Traveler* editor Theo. L. Edmiston created a stir by suggesting that illegal drinking took place on campus.[920] Even though by that time many high schools around the state had student newspapers and journalism instructors to give guidance and inspiration, the university did not respond until 1928 when it hired Walter J. Lemke. Even then, it took two more years to separate journalism from public relations and more still for the department to become independent of writing news releases. By contrast, the University of Missouri under Dean Walter Williams had created one of the leading schools in the country back in 1909.

Writing publicity releases did not entirely satisfy the young Lemke, and on July 13, 1930, he emerged as a columnist for the *Fayetteville Leader* under the heading "Ozark Moon." The first accompanying graphic showed a mountaineer drinking moonshine while propped up under a tree. A few years after the *Leader* failed, the column was revived at the *Fayetteville Democrat*, but with graphics altered to suit owner Roberta Fulbright's abstemious views. In one version the bottle was now under a tree, and readers were assured it contained only cider. Another graphic featured a hunter, dog, and log cabin.[921]

Despite the title, little of the content was Ozarkian. Some of the material alluded to university and town life; more of it featured the work of local poets, notably Rosa Zagnoni Marinoni. When the column was only a few months old, Lemke was already being referred to as "Uncle Walt," and after that name appeared on the column's title it became his off-campus nickname.[922] Early on, Lemke took up the study of local history, and William M. Quesenbury was one of his particular interests.[923] The column became unique in the annals of Arkansas journalism when it inspired its own song, "Ozark Moon," by Betty Rose. For a number of years, Lemke put together the *Moon Book*, a yearly anthology of the best poetry from the column.

Another of his activities was editing the Arkansas High School Press Association's monthly bulletin. Each month Lemke gave some 12 awards for topics ranging from best news coverage to best makeup. The first annual meeting of the Arkansas High School Press Association came in May 1929.[924] Every April the AHSPA held an annual meeting, and even during the Depression attendance averaged 300 students.[925] By 1941, over 100 high schools had newspapers. Thirty-six were printed; 54 were mimeographed, and 16 appeared as special sections of the local newspaper. Seven high schools even had their own print shops.[926] The Arkansas College Press Association followed in 1930.[927]

For all practical purposes, the journalism program at the University of Arkansas consisted of Lemke and Joseph A. Thalheimer. Despite the presence of these two revered stalwarts, the university operated the department on the starvation plan even after the Depression. The department had no money for newspaper subscriptions, so Lemke had to beg publishers to send him copies. In 1944, the university gave the department a total of $450 to cover all office expenses. One "wonders what the Missouri School of Journalism would think of that sum," Lemke once observed, adding, "nothing would give me greater pleasure than to pay for Arkansas newspaper subscriptions."[928]

One reason for the lack of money may have been Lemke himself. Robert Leflar later recalled that Lemke was "able to see through sham and to belittle hypocrisy."[929] Hence, it is not surprising that one of his favorite photographs showed him, pipe in mouth (although students later recalled him only smoking cigarettes), working at his desk, despite President John C. Futrall's ban on the use of tobacco on campus.

By 1938, the journalism program had turned out 63 majors. In that year, those working in the state included Jack Young at the *Helena Daily World*; Horace Cate at the *Jonesboro Tribune*; Johnny Erp at the *Batesville Guard*; Van Tyson at the *Atkins Chronicle*; Bill McClain at the *Pine Bluff Commercial*; W.K. Rose and Oren Stephens at the *Arkansas Democrat*; Frank Newell at the *Arkansas Gazette*; Tom Lincoln at the Clarksville *Herald-Democrat*; Herman

Teeter at the *Russellville Tribune*; and Martha Mayer and Johnnie Porter at the Fort Smith *Southwest American*.[930] Lemke kept in touch with the graduates through regular newsletters.

One 1934 graduate was Ernest C. Deane of Lewisville. Because his father was employed by the Cotton Belt railroad and had a job during the Depression, young Ernie, who had started his career in high school journalism and then as a stringer covering sporting events, was able to attend the university during the heart of the Depression. After graduation, Lemke got Deane into the Northwestern University program, where he become the first Arkansan known to take a master's degree in journalism.

One of the biggest problems Lemke and Thalheimer faced was that the school had no printing plant until 1949. In 1932, the two took 15 students, one being Ernie Deane, on a "clinic" assisting eight different dailies in the production of their newspapers. On many occasions, they sent students down to Winslow to help Maud Duncan put out the *American*. They also provided a loan service for publishers in a pinch. When J.A. Livingston at Russellville needed extended medical attention, future *Traveler* editor Bill Penix took over, scandalizing older employees by using large old block letters to headline the Japanese capture of Bataan.[931]

Lemke was apparently not satisfied with the services provided by the *Arkansas Publisher*, and for several years published the *Arkansas Community Newspaper*. One story, "There's Romance in the Names of Rural Communities," attained front-page status in the May 27, 1944 issue of NNA's *Publishers' Auxiliary*. Lemke used his forum to urge improvements in weekly newspapers, notably in promoting the use of correspondents and praising (or damning) local news coverage. The *Sharp County Independent* got taken to task for putting Crip Hall's "Capitol News" and Garrett Whiteside's

RICHARD L. SPAIN WROTE AND ILLUSTRATED A GARDENING COLUMN FOR THE ARKANSAS GAZETTE FROM 1940 UNTIL 1991, WHEN THE NEWSPAPER CLOSED.

"Washington" columns on the front page instead of inside. Lauded was the *Marked Tree Tribune* whose entire first page was made up of local news and the *Melbourne Times* for a story about the high school basketball team (coached by Elwin "Preacher" Roe) who won nine of their 19 games without having a gym, an outdoor court, practice goals, or even their own ball![932]

By 1940, college graduates were emerging as a force in state journalism. Although Charlotte Tillar attended Louisiana State University, Tom Dearmore went to Drury College in Springfield, Missouri, and Ray Kimball graduated from the University of Oklahoma, most second- or third-generation press children headed off across the mountains to Fayetteville's Old Main and later Hill Hall. Nevertheless, there were still many like Wilson Powell, who began his career cleaning out the office of Owen C. Shaver's *Sharp County Record* at age eight, or Margaret Woolfolk, who finally got to go to college—50 years after she started to work with the *Crittenden County Times*.

The Waning of the Depression

Probably only West Virginia made less of an effort to fight the Depression than Arkansas. Bankrupted by the road bonds of the previous decade, and unwilling and unable to tax, the state abdicated fighting the Depression to the federal government. All across Arkansas, federal alphabet-agencies sprang into action. The Works Progress Administration (WPA) funded new schools and civic improvements, the Civilian Conservation Corps (CCC) camps planted trees and fought erosion, the Agricultural Adjustment Act's (AAA) cotton programs paid farmers not to plant, Social Security (SSA) undertook to look after the elderly, while other programs encouraged cooperative rural canning, created agricultural resettlement communities, paid for artists to create murals in post offices, and invariably touched every person in Arkansas. A host of new rules and regulations affected businesses, including newspapers.

The receptions these varied programs got from the press varied. Few editors probably criticized the Homeowners Loan Corporation (HLC) that helped families stave off foreclosure. Harry Lee Williams was the state head, and Jim Bland (Walnut Ridge), C.B. Oldham (Clinton), and George Upton (Dardanelle) were some of the publishers who found work as county appraisers.[933]

The *Marshall Republican* used the headline "Isolated Country Made Accessible by CWA Funds" to discuss the positive impact a new road had in opening up a long-inaccessible area near St. Joe.[934] A more negative view came from Karr Shannon, who took up the case of a jack brought into Izard County in order to propagate better work animals. As Shannon recalled it, "I gave the authorities such a run of kidding about their mule that after two issues of the paper he was silently moved across the White river into Stone county in the dead hours of the night and hasn't been heard of since. The county judge was defeated on his second term the following summer on the non-braying-jack-ass platform."[935]

On the state level, machine politics resulted in elections marked by one scandal after another. In 1933, reformer Brooks Hays was denied a congressional seat in one of the most blatantly dishonest elections of the century. However, Attorney General Carl Bailey achieved nationwide fame when he turned down a $50,000 bribe to frustrate the extradition of gangster Lucky Luciano from Hot Springs. In 1936 Bailey defeated the Futrell-backed gubernatorial candidate. Because he was willing to talk to the nation's press about something small town newspapers suppressed, the sharecropper revolt being organized by the Southern Tenant Farmers' Union (STFU), Bailey gained national recognition as a reforming liberal. Not surprisingly, Young Turks like James Bland of Walnut Ridge, who served for a time as Bailey's secretary and on a variety of state boards, were big supporters.

One of the main props of the STFU was Commonwealth College outside Mena. A farm-labor school geared more to teaching agitators than tractor-drivers, Commonwealth inspired many enemies. Locals objected to the presence of mixed swimming and the wearing of shorts, while E.W. St. John of the *Mena Star* found the school full of communists. One future member of the APA who attended classes was Orval Faubus. St. John's persistent agitation eventually resulted in the state closing the institution.

All the new programs created new federal jobs, and many editors hastened to get right with Washington, or at least with Senator Joe T. Robinson, who controlled federal patronage. Those holding appointments included O.E. Jones of the *Batesville Guard* and *Record* and Paul Van Dalsem of the *Perry County News*. Van Dalsem, long a state legislator and famous (or infamous) for his 1963 remarks about the liberated woman and how she was treated in Perry County ("get her pregnant and keep her barefoot"), acquired his newspaper in 1933 but edited it only during the rare times when he was out of office.

Jones, by contrast, had several interests. Oscar F.

Craig at the *Newark Journal* sniped at the "Post Office Twins," O.E. Jones for wanting to be postmaster in Batesville and A.C. Wilkerson at the *Newport Daily Independent*, whose wife held that office at the Jackson County seat. Craig held state printing contracts eight times between 1917 and 1939, but that was state rather than federal patronage. His son, Roy Monroe Craig, worked in the campaigns of Hattie Caraway, Joe T. Robinson, Carl Bailey, and Wilbur Mills.[936] Jackson County's other editor, Ells L. Huff, loved to write long editorials and jockeyed constantly for political position. That Wilson Powell ended up at the *Batesville Guard* was largely due to Jackson County politics. Fred Hedges of Crittenden County and that then rare Republican, young James Tudor of Marshall, were among the press-politicians in the 1941 legislature.

Perhaps the most influential press-connected legislator in the late 1930s was Leo E. Nyberg. This Mississippi-born journalist went to work at the *Helena Daily World* in 1929 and married publisher Charles M. Young's daughter. Nyberg, considered one of the Delta's rare liberals, served four terms in the state House of Representatives starting in 1932. He led the successful fight to repeal state prohibition in 1933 but was best known for getting funding for a new 500-room tuberculosis sanatorium at Booneville. He was only 34 when he died of that disease in 1940.[937]

By and large, it was not an age for great editorial writing. Some of the problems stemmed from the way newspapers were put out. The state's small dailies consisted of miniscule staffs, often having only the editor/publisher gathering the news, his wife doing society, the country correspondents, and coaches or high school students providing the sports coverage. Frank Robins at Conway confessed that his goal of writing strong editorials had collapsed under the weight of editing all those correspondents. Thus, the space that once contained editorials disappeared or was replaced by syndicated material. Too typical of the age was an editorial in the Clarksville *Herald-Democrat*: "National Tire Safety Week Deserves Consideration."[938]

Garrett Whiteside's Washington column was popular, and, from Little Rock, Earl Page offered a farm letter. Some Arkansas newspapers that carried Drew Pearson's column found themselves named in a libel suit. The *Marshall Republican* went beyond the usual Sunday School lesson by offering a weekly column by Bob Jones, a Southern fundamentalist who took a very hard line on sin and race-mixing and who founded a South Carolina college later to be attended by a number of prominent Republican politicians such as Tim and Asa Hutchinson. Many newspapers, unwilling to abandon the traditional editorial space, relied on canned editorials extolling Armistice Day, motherhood, and apple pie.

Other editors or publishers were just not excited. K.A. Engel at the *Arkansas Democrat* made parking meters his primary crusade. At Jonesboro, violent church wars among the Baptists in 1931 and 1934 led to such hard feelings locally that Methodist W.O. Troutt concluded that editorials were not good for business. In Hot Springs, where the Palmer newspapers flourished along side the McLaughlin machine, gangsters gathered, prostitution and gambling disported their tawdry wares, and the county's gubernatorial vote was for sale to the highest bidder. At Camden, another Palmer town, Al Rose had been the first editor of the high school newspaper. He started writing sports for the *News* while in high school and continued that work after becoming a schoolteacher. In 1931, he became the editor and wrote for over 50 years a column entitled "Al's Alfalfa," wherein he dispensed folksy good humor. Of Jewish ancestry, he married outside the faith and became a Methodist.[939] His leading cause was the Arkansas Lions clubs, in which he held a 40-year perfect attendance record.

There were holdouts. In southwest Arkansas,

Alex H. Washburn of the *Hope Star* intoned: "A militant country newspaper stands out like the sunlight slanting against God's chosen hills." And Tom Newman at Harrison believed that "a free and militant press" could clean up Arkansas in one election. Old J.B. Parker was less sanguine. Too many newspapers "subserviently obeyed 'the machine' in return for delinquent tax lists and other political patronage," leaving voters powerless and government inefficient or corrupt.[940]

Editorial writing was responsible, however, for one the state's major political crises. Roberta Fulbright, owner of the *Fayetteville Daily Democrat* (the *Northwest Arkansas Times* after August 1937) and herself a former country correspondent, was a strong Carl Bailey supporter. After the death of university President Futrall in 1939, her son, J. William Fulbright, was appointed president. Although young, at age 34, Fulbright was a former Fayetteville star athlete, student body president, and Rhodes Scholar, then serving as a respected member of the law faculty.

After Homer Adkins, using "Take the University out of Politics" as a slogan, defeated Governor Carl Bailey in 1940, his reconstituted university's board fired Fulbright. *Traveler* editor Ellis Stafford, a son of *Springdale News* founder John P. Stafford, denounced the firing as did some newspapers around the state. Roberta Fulbright, who wrote an occasional column for her newspaper, then started a long war against Adkins, finding him a shade worse than Huey Long or Adolph Hitler. J. William Fulbright won a congressional seat in 1942 and two years later defeated Adkins in a runoff to become a United States senator.

However, the declining role the press was playing in politics was reflected by a 1940 study in the *Arkansas Publisher*. It showed that in the controversial gubernatorial election of that year, of the 35 dailies, nine supported Bailey, six were for Adkins, and 20 were neutral. Of the 164 weeklies, 12 were for Bailey, 16 were for Adkins, and 138 were neutral.[941] All of this came at a time when newspapers were again beginning to pay attention to foreign affairs and discuss the meaning of American values. "Our part is to awaken the consciousness of the people to the blessings of self-government as compared to life under totalitarian rule," Everett W. Pate of the *Rogers Daily News* told APA members in 1940. How this was to be done "without specifically calling names or attaching blame" Pate did not make clear.[942]

At the *Arkansas Gazette*, editor J.N. Heiskell still supported the poll tax, and in elections popular participation—except for the mules that religiously paid their poll taxes and always voted in Poinsett County—was ridiculously low even by current standards. One of the last newspapers with a strong editorial position was the *Conway News*; indeed, Jacob B. Parker put his views in every story he wrote as well as in editorials and his column. Parker died in 1939, and the newspaper, a relic of times past, did not long survive him.

Technically, newspapers were getting better. At Searcy, James J. Baugh, the "Dean of Editors," steadily improved the *Citizen* during the 1930s. Baugh editorialized, at least on liquor, and had office windows broken as a result. Although the newspaper had been daily since 1890, it was not until the 1930s that it subscribed to a wire service. Baugh continued to be active until stricken at an APA convention a few months prior to his death in 1940 at age 83.[943]

Two different innovations were underway in one of most unlikely places in Arkansas, the Sevier County seat of De Queen. The *Bee*, long owned by L.A. Pearre, was purchased by A.L. Kimball and his son, Ray, in 1933 and combined with the *De Queen Daily Citizen*. The elder Kimball was primarily a printer, but Ray had interests in several newspapers and after 1939 briefly lived at Magnolia, editing the *Banner-News*. Convinced that small dailies needed a way of pooling the stories received from the wire services, Kimball took time off to research the potentials of a new technology. The result was a transmitting system that linked five daily newspapers in southwest Arkansas (Hot Springs' *New Era* and *Sentinel-Record*, the *Camden Evening News*, the Magnolia *Banner-News*, the *El Dorado Evening Times*, and the *Hope Daily Star*).

Under the system, which began operations on June 19, 1942, wire news was converted by a teletypesetter into perforated tape that could be run directly into a Linotype machine and set into type. Clyde Palmer's Hot Springs operations were the point of original reception, and then a filing editor cut down the stories and forwarded them via telegraph to a re-perforator that reproduced the tape for feeding into the Linotype machines at each daily.[944] Kimball's system (with help from Palmer and Alex H. Washburn) was the first in the nation and marked an important development in the increasing technological complexity of the press.

The second story, which also had a De Queen connection, was equally portentous. Ralph Kite, who had charge of the De Queen newspapers while young Kimball was in Magnolia, had a strong interest in photography. Although the taking of pictures was nothing new, the problem for newspapers was that photographs could be used only after they had been engraved. At a time when many weekly newspapers still charged two dollars a year or less for a subscription, and each engraving cost at a minimum of around a dollar, the cost made extensive use of photographs prohibitive.

In addition to the problem of cost, newspapers had to consider the timeliness factor. In order for Kite to get his De Queen photographs engraved, he had to send them to Lee's Summit near Kansas City, using the Kansas City Southern Railroad for a direct connection. Since at least 24 hours would elapse before the picture could be printed, many good photographic opportunities were lost. Hence, it was in those progress or county-fair editions that photographs were most likely to appear, and static scenes of businesses, individuals and scenery dominated.

Twentieth-century readers were being exposed to more photographs. In addition to picture postcards, magazines ranging from *National Geographic* to Henry Luce's *Life*, reached out to readers with pictures. Newspapers followed perforce. By the 1930s politicians supplied newspapers with their pictures, and both the news services and special-interest groups provided newspapers with ready-to-use cuts. Agricultural agencies in particular had stacks of generic pictures if editors were desperate to fill up space.

The occasional political cartoons continued to circulate. In 1926, J.P. Alley, who grew up at Benton and became famous for his "Hambone" cartoons for the *Commercial Appeal*, did a cartoon in support of the pro-education Amendment 13 that many newspapers ran.[945] But newspaper photography was still in its infancy when the Southwest News Photographers formed in the late 1930s. Ralph Kite was the editor of their publication, the *Southwest News Photographer*, and it was printed at De Queen.

One early photographic center was Jonesboro, where Donald Murray owned the Blue Top Engraving Company. And it was near Jonesboro that there occurred one of the first examples outside the metropolitan centers that proclaimed the power of photography.

Mrs. Leslie "Mutt" Alexander, née Grace Higginbotham, was a minister's daughter and valedictorian at Nettleton High School in a small and now-extinct town near Jonesboro.[946] She had married a former Jonesboro football star, and in the capacity of the good wife had left her home on the morning of July 24, 1939, to walk two doors down from her house to get water from a neighbor. Shortly thereafter, the town constable arrested her for violating the municipality's ban on public nudity. On her fateful 100-yard walk she had been wearing a pair of shorts. This case was not about bare flesh, per se, for only a few years earlier Nettleton, under the same ordinance, had fined a woman $50 for wearing slacks.

Because of the availability of local engravers, readers of the *Evening Sun* were able to see under the headline "'Shorts' Caused Her Arrest" Grace in all her allegedly indecency.[947] The *Daily Tribune* used the headline "'Shorts' Principals" in order to picture not only the "obnoxious costume," the special prosecutor who said it would "shock my morals" if Grace modeled her costume in court, and her defense attorney.[948] So great was the interest in her case that the *Memphis Press-Scimitar* sent up a reporter and "cameraman" to cover the event, and another story appeared in the *St. Louis Post-Dispatch*. Even the *Chicago Herald-Examiner* telephoned Mrs. Alexander and Nettleton's mayor for information. The Associated Press acquired the *Sun*'s negative and wired the picture around the country from Memphis, while Acme Newspictures, International Illustrated News, and Wide World News services got theirs from the *Tribune*.

In addition to the photographs, Jack Knox, the Memphis *Commercial Appeal*'s cartoonist, seized on the incident, and Mrs. Alexander became a radio celebrity, appearing on KBTM radio from Jonesboro.

The trial reflected another of those conflicts between the now-passé Jazz Age and the old morality. Squire H.F. Applegate, a former justice of the peace, and his wife were largely responsible for instigating the prosecution. Mr. Applegate wanted to begin his testimony with Adam and Eve, and did get an attack on a swimming pool "with boys and girls rolling all over each other in the sand." He ended with the argument that children would be corrupted by Mrs. Alexander's lack of clothing.

The defense wanted the court to see the costume, but initially the judge/mayor wasn't sure if "I want such indecency displayed in my court." Eventually the defense carried this point, and Grace "gracefully disrobed herself of the skirt of her three-piece play suit." In summation, the prosecutor told Grace to wear long dresses like those of Mrs. Applegate, and ended by urging that "God and our noble state be upheld." The judge/mayor pronounced her guilty.[949]

The combination of an interesting story and revealing pictures foretold the way newspapers would develop after World War II. Significantly missing was any credit given the photographers; indeed, such credits did not become common until much later in the 20th century.

Conclusion

By the late 1930s, Arkansas seemed to be back on track. One of the principal issues vexing the state was whether to consider Hollywood entertainer and Van Buren native Bob Burns an asset who popularized the state or an embarrassment who played the hillbilly image for all it was worth. Little Rock society types led the attack, and Van Buren's Hugh Park rallied to Burns's defense.

At large, the world was drifting towards war, but few cared or commented. Walnut Ridge editor James Bland reflected the popular attitudes of abhorring the fascists while believing in American neutrality. Yet, the all-seeing correspondents saw only too well the problems ahead. "Our community is almost weekly bereft of some young man entering either the army or the CCC camps," the Zack correspondent from Searcy County noted, "Newton Hancock was the last to leave, Sunday. He was a nice, quiet, industrious boy and will be missed."[950]

Chapter VIII

Wars Foreign and Domestic

"It was December 7, 1941, and I can remember it like it was yesterday. Me and my cousin were riding in the back of Uncle Neil's car when we heard it [the account of the bombing of Pearl Harbor] on the car radio. Uncle Neil turned around and said, 'Sunny, you know what that means, don't you? Daddy's going off to fight the war.' And when we saw it in the *Arkansas Gazette* we knew it was real."
Berniece (Marsh) Holder, Peach Orchard, interview with Charis R. Cook, October 6, 1999.

"Every newspaper must come to judgment and accounting for the cause that forms its image and its character. If it is to more than a mere mechanical recorder of news, if it is to be a moral force and influence and the keeper of community conscience, it must fulfill the measure of its obligation, even though in the words of St. Paul, it has to suffer affliction."
John N. Heiskell, 1964.

"I was there at the best time of the world."
Louise Bowker, October 31, 2000.

Introduction

During the late 1930s, Arkansans focused on their own difficulties—the Flood of 1937, the new regulations in agriculture, and the still-present problems of unemployment. To most Arkansans the Spanish Civil War, the Italian conquest of Ethiopia, or the *Anschluss* in Austria were far away and remote. During the 1930s, isolationism had reigned supreme in the halls of Congress. South Missouri Republican Congressman Dewey Short was one nationally famous figure in the fight, but Arkansas's delegation was inconspicuous. President Roosevelt began nudging the country into preparedness that included a peacetime draft and extensive military maneuvers in south Arkansas. Editorial reaction was muted, and even the issue of accepting an unheard-of third term for incumbent president Franklin Roosevelt did not ruffle greatly the waves. Then with the outbreak of war in September 1939, Arkansas's world began to crumble.

Detailed war news came to most Arkansans by way of the newspapers, and the evening press benefited because America's relation to Europe's time zones left morning newspapers with little but leftovers from the evening news. Radio brought the immediacy of the war into electrified urban homes; local stations had already begun to eat into newspaper advertising revenues in the late 1930s. Such competition was less a factor in the rural areas when over half the state's rural population had to rely on battery-powered instruments in the absence of rural electrification.

As America geared up for war, Arkansans

responded by leaving the state either for military service or industrial jobs in the North. During the war years, many more newspapers suspended or folded than in the 1930s, some because of communities collapsing, others because editors and printers had gone to war. One important war record consisted of the letters that former university journalism students sent to Professor W.J. Lemke. Lemke kept in touch with them through a newsletter based on the accounts he received from his former and now-scattered students.

Returning to Arkansas after the war, many young men and women still hoped to find in the state what the legislature now styled as "The Land of Opportunity." World War II proved to be a school of citizenship, and the veterans wanted politics cleaned up and economic prosperity, both in the factories and on the farms, brought about. Their struggles between 1947 and 1960 represented one of the great crusades in Arkansas history, and like the crusades in the early middle ages, there were victories and defeats. By the end of the period, technological and cultural changes both in American life and in the industry were radically altering the family newspaper system that had so long endured.

Looming over the last of these years was the Civil Rights crisis. Trouble erupted earlier in Arkansas than elsewhere in the South, resulting in a new twist on the state's reputation that long endured. White opposition to integration cemented in power publisher Orval Faubus. During the crisis and for years thereafter, many people came to believe that even their local newspaper was part of an outside conspiracy to destroy their way of life.

The Last Victorians

Three deaths on the eve of World War II marked the passing of the old order. The first to go was James J. Baugh of the *White County Citizen* in 1940. Baugh had owned the newspaper for the previous 55 years, remaining active to the end. In 1939 the *Arkansas Publisher* had hailed the 82-year-old as the "Dean of Publishers," and it was ironic that this former APA president (1904) was stricken at the 1940 annual meeting. "There is no profession in which you can see so much life, or live so close to all classes of humanity as the newspaper business," Baugh once declared.[951]

The second death was that of Dr. Alexander Copeland Millar. Like the colonels of yore, his doctorate was honorary. A longtime editor of the *Arkansas Methodist*, Millar was best remembered as the president who in his first term moved Central Collegiate Institute to Conway where it became Hendrix College. Left dispossessed was Isham Burrow, the school's founder, and his family went into journalism with the Ozark *Spectator*. Millar had long been a fixture at APA meetings, where besides serving as chaplain, he had been the APA's poet, orator, and historian. In addition, he once served as president of the Arkansas Educational Association. Politically active, he had supported temperance, education, and good roads. In 1928 he withdrew from a race for lieutenant governor, refusing to appear on the ballot with the Democratic party's presidential nominee, the New York Catholic, Al Smith.[952] Methodist minister R.E. Lee Bearden recalled: "He was, I believe, the most distinguished man I have ever seen. With his white beard and white hair, the little English tweed cap and suit, he looked for all the world like a British lord or bishop."[953]

Although the *Arkansas Publisher* would continue for some years to print Bible verses, Millar had no successor. In 1944, the state attorney general would rule that neither the *Arkansas Baptist* nor the *Arkansas Methodist* were legal newspapers, although the *Arkansas Legionnaire* was.[954] The APA made constitutional changes in the mid-1950s that confirmed what had already happened in practice: the APA was limited to secular legal newspapers.

The third critical obituary was of Harvey Couch.

For the first half of the 20th century, Couch epitomized the self-made man. Beginning as railroad clerk, young Couch saw the potential in telephones, erecting in South Arkansas a network in an area the Bell companies had not reached. After selling out, he created Arkansas Power and Light, partly through buying up small-town power plants.

Couch courted the press and was made an honorary member of the Association. The company was lavish with its advertisements, but especially during the late 1930s the unstated condition was that the newspapers back editorially private power companies against the co-ops being created by the Rural Electrification Administration (REA). Over and over, the *Publisher* used a heavy hairy hand to remind publishers that co-ops did not advertise, while Couch was "a personal friend of almost every newspaper published in Arkansas."[955] Green Forest publisher Ted Larimer estimated that without AP&L's advertisements, 30 percent of the weekly newpapers would have closed.

Couch had lost control of his company by the time of his death in 1941, but his successor, C. Hamilton "Ham" Moses, continued the same relationship with the press. Among his closest allies were Oscar F. Craig and his son Roy Monroe at Newark. As Moses wrote Roy in 1957 after a bitter fight in Jackson County, "There are few men on whose loyalty you can depend—who will stand up and be counted when the going gets tough—and I place you high on that list."[956] Subsequently, Newark became the site of a major northeast Arkansas generating plant. As an example of AP&L's influence, Jared Trevathan's *Batesville News Record* on September 23, 1948, printed what it claimed was the largest special edition ever put out by an Arkansas newspaper. Its central theme was that "Ham" was a "courageous and sincere leader." The usual local factory histories and rosy progress reports were flanked by AP&L advertisements on virtually every page.[957]

Some relics remained alive. W.B. Folsom (APA president, 1901) at Brinkley did not retire until 1948. Childless, he left his home to the city for a library. Frederick Allsopp survived War World II by only a year, but Erwin Funk continued to pop up on unexpected occasions, including later in this chapter. Among those counted as friends of the Association, none ranked higher in the immediate postwar years than Colonel T.H. Barton of Lion Oil, who plied members with strong liquid refreshment and underwrote a strong rearguard action to save the family farm through the Arkansas Livestock Show Association.

Off to War

During the fall of 1939, some called Hitler's lack of action that followed the fall of Poland "the phony war." "I well remember being awakened about 3 A.M. by the radio in my dad's bedroom the day German troops marched into Poland. Hitler was screaming a speech in his shrill voice, with a huge crowd responding every two or three minutes with 'Heil Hitler,'" Margaret Ross recalled.[958] The invasion of Norway, the fall of France, and the air battle over England that followed came while the United States remained legally at peace. Then, suddenly, the bombing of Pearl Harbor on December 7, 1941, put America at war on two fronts.

Despite the technical peace, war industries were gearing up, farm prices were rising, and newspapers made the most of their opportunities. One way was to issue special editions that featured considerable advertising. Both the *Pine Bluff Commercial* and the *Arkansas Gazette* had special sections devoted to their cities' Business and Professional Women; the *Montgomery County Herald* and nearly every other country weekly printed county-fair editions; the *Rogers Daily News* displayed fall fashions;[959] peach, watermelon, progress, and cotton editions continued apace, and newspapers inserted more and more special sections to celebrate when a new business opened. What the *Publisher* considered the largest handset edition of a newspaper came from Karr Shannon at Melbourne on June 21, 1940. The 32-page issue was occasioned by the dedication of the new courthouse and took two months to assemble.[960] At De Queen, Ray Kimball printed a two-color advertisement for one of the department stores. This required a double run on the insert page.[961]

One portent of the future was when the *Texarkana Gazette* featured an eight-page section devoted entirely to household-appliance advertising.[962] Almost all towns had fulltime electricity, and co-ops were rapidly extending their lines to serve rural customers. Another portentous special edition issued three months before Pearl Harbor consisted of a 72-page national-defense edition from the Fort Smith's *Times Record*'s new publisher, Donald Reynolds.[963] U.S. army maneuvers in south Arkansas in the summer of 1941 resulted in the military "taking" the *Nevada County Picayune* at Prescott. The 35th Division's G-2 Press Section then wheeled their equipment up to the office and put out a newspaper under simulated wartime conditions.[964] The *Southern Standard* published a bi-weekly five-column, four-page newspaper for the 130th Infantry.[965]

At the University of Arkansas, Professors Lemke and Thalheimer continued Clio Harper's war on ready-print, which in its traditional form rapidly faded away. "We will endeavor to give you one of the most newsy home printed papers in this section," editor James R. Tudor at Marshall declared as he reduced his newspaper to four pages by eliminating the four ready-print pages.[966] Actually, the market for canned material was changing more than diminishing. The Western Newspaper Union creatively marketed Christmas advertisements that could be customized for local businesses. Syndicated columnists abounded, as did comics designed in the belief that ignorant rustic readers had very primitive humor receptacles. Most dailies ran Hollywood gossip columns, for even remote rural towns like Yellville boasted a movie theater. These columns and the accompanying pictures were devoured by young females, who modeled their clothes and behavior on that of Hollywood stars.

On the eve of the war, publishers all across the state were modernizing their shops. By January 1942, the circulation of the *Pine Bluff Commercial* had passed the 10,000 mark.[967] New Linotype machines could be found in Mena, Osceola, Searcy, Newport, Stuttgart, and other towns. Mena also added a Goss Comet web press that replaced the Babcock hand-fed press used for the previous 29 years.[968] Another Goss press came to the completely modernized *Northwest Arkansas Times* plant, and the *Arkansas Gazette* celebrated its 120th birthday by installing a six-unit Goss capable of producing 37,000 48-page copies an hour. Even after the war started, new machines continued to arrive. The *Nashville News* got its third Linotype, a Model 14 Blue Streak, on its 64th birthday. Others came to the *Camden News*, the *Dermott News*, and the *Northwest Arkansas Times*.[969] The Amity *Owl* discarded its Washington Hand Press, alleged to be the last in operation in the state, and replaced it with a two-revolution Babcock in 1944.[970]

Meanwhile, the Mergenthaler Company brought out its Blue Streak Super-Display Model 35 and the Two-in-One Super Display Model 33. Publishers were doubtless awed that these new machines could be equipped with self-quaders and thermo-blo-mold coolers.[971] One of the Model 35s went to the *Arkansas Gazette* in 1942. A good example of the spirit of the age came at Rogers. After Everett W. Pate told readers he thought the daily edition could not be maintained without increasing subscription and advertising rates, readers and advertisers rallied to save the daily.

An amateur photographer, Pate was one of the leaders in the state in using pictures. After the Rogers newspaper got its own engraving plant in 1939, a total of 1,189 column inches of local photographs appeared during that first year.[972] In Little Rock, the *Gazette* installed an Associated Press Wirephoto machine, by which pictures sent by telegraph were converted by a photo-electric cell. Once received, they could be engraved and published. Photographic workshops became the rage for APA members.

A 1942 study found that the state's weekly newspapers averaged a 12.6 percent increase in circulation, while the average was 12 percent for dailies but with one having a 47 percent gain. Advertising was down for dailies by about 25 percent, but publishers were raising rates and trying to hold down costs. As of early 1942, some 22 percent of newspaper employees had been called up for service.[973]

Another sign of prosperity could be found in the Wallace Witmer lawsuit. Witmer had for 10 years been the manager of Arkansas Dailies, Inc., the collective advertising agency Clyde Palmer had created primarily to serve his own newspapers but to which most of the small dailies belonged. In October 1940, Witmer and Palmer quarreled, and Witmer left in order to create his own agency. After he immediately won contracts from the *Batesville Guard* and *Record*, the *Harrison Times*, and the Fayetteville *Northwest Arkansas Times*, Palmer got an injunction to stop the competition. On appeal, the state supreme court overturned it. Witmer had not signed a noncompetition contract, and he had not encouraged newspapers to break their contracts.[974] Apparently there was enough business independent of Palmer to justify the break.

Meanwhile, the Association's new order seemed to be working out. Membership rose to 90 percent of the state's press, and in 1941 Ray Kimball, one of the leading Young Turks, became president. Attendance records were broken with every meeting. The 1937 meeting had placed Erwin Funk in charge of a committee to revive the prize contests, and by the early 1940s participation was growing.

As the war developed, changes in personnel began to appear. Harry McDonald, a former editor of the *Lake City Sun-Times*, went to California, but did send back to his former newspaper a series of articles. Walter E. Hussman, Sr., the vice-president of Texarkana Newspapers (the morning *Texarkana Gazette* and the evening *Texarkana Daily News*), did his bit to help in the rubber shortage (caused by the Japanese capture of Malaya) by bicycling to work.[975]

Then, in short order, Arkansas journalism was decimated. President-Lieutenant Ray Kimball, who had enlisted in the Navy, was called up. The remainder of his term as president (including one board meeting) was filled by his wife, thus making Evelyn Kimball the first woman to act as president of the APA, although no official notice at the time was taken of this development.[976] The Seabees claimed another Arkansan in James R. Tudor of Marshall. He spent much of war in the Pacific, where he underwent a "catharsis" that he carried back to Arkansas.

Perhaps because of its visionary aspects, the air force attracted an unusually high percentage of Arkansas journalists. During the war, Frank Robins, Jr., the immediate past president, was joined by Sam Hodges, Jr. (Osceola), incumbent legislator Fred Hedges (Hughes), Curtis B. Hurley, Jr. (Morrilton), James L. Bland, Jr. (Walnut Ridge), J.E. Dunlap (Harrison), Robert Chowning (Wynne), Pete Shiras (Mountain Home), Carrick W. Heiskell, and many more. There were losses. Even before the war, the Livingstons at Russellville had lost their son in a plane crash. While the death of Hurley affected mostly the newspaper history of Morrilton, that of J.N. Heiskell's planned successor had important ramifications for Arkansas history.

A steady supply of labor also became a problem. "Six Brothers, all Printers, Register for Army Service Under Draft Act" ran a headline in the *Publisher*. Members of the family in question, the sons of Robert Cloyd Gray, had worked in Little Rock, Fort Smith, Russellville, and De Queen.[977]

Wartime Stresses

World War II caused all sorts of problems for the state's newspapers. First, there were local issues to consider. Labor unions scored successes in south Arkansas, both among timber workers and in factories. The new paper mill that opened in Crossett in 1937 was unionized in 1938 and shut down by a strike in 1940. The effects rippled through that company town. *Ashley County Leader* editor Macon Dunn urged arbitration: "We carry no brief for the lumber company and we are not in any way connected with the union, but our sympathy goes out to those who are in no way connected with this difference and need work to supply the absolute necessities of life for innocent women and children."[978] As local efforts to avoid trouble failed, violence—part of it racial—erupted. Among those involved was former publisher-now circuit judge Duval Purkins. The labor troubles that soon surfaced at Texarkana, Pine Bluff, and Little Rock found publishers in a less charitable mood.

The absence of editors and printers led to the closings of a number of newspapers. First affected were the small dailies. Clarksville, De Queen, Prescott, Siloam Springs, and Wynne lost their dailies. Although the term "suspension" had long been synonymous for a "30," in fact the *De Queen Daily Citizen* resumed daily publication after the war. In Pine Bluff, the venerable morning *Graphic* was taken over by Donald Murray, but he failed to reverse its decline. Murray came to grief in Jonesboro as well, and in 1943 Jonesboro became a one-newspaper town. The youngest of the Young Turks left Arkansas for good, moving to Illinois. The rest of the family settled for a time in Wynne. After the closing of the daily, they brought out two newspapers a week: the *Star* on Tuesdays, the *Progress* on Thursdays.

Weeklies suspended as well. The last Republican newspaper in Arkansas, that of James R. Tudor, suspended for the war while he was in the South Pacific. The *McGehee Times*, *Beebe Sentinel*, and *Mulberry Times* were interrupted. At Imboden, Walter C. Yeager, who had published the *Journal* since 1926, suspended the newspaper in 1944 in order to work at the Pine Bluff Arsenal. Two years later he sold it to Austin and Edith Stovall who resumed publication. One of the shortest suspensions was at the *White County Record* at Judsonia, where editor R.L. Van Meter received an early discharge and resumed publication. At Melbourne, Karr Shannon ran out of labor and first suspended and then sold the newspaper, moving to Little Rock where he remained a *Democrat* columnist for the next 20 years. Mergers resulted from the crisis as well. At Fordyce, "the exigencies of war" resulted in the *Weekly Advocate*, owned by Fred L. Snowball, being sold to C.A. VerBeck, who earlier had bought the competing *News* from Roy Elliott.[979] A story of a different sort came out of Mammoth Spring. Charley Wahlquist left for the navy in April, but the *Democrat* continued to be published, courtesy of Paul Morton at the *Salem Headlight*.

There was even talk of suspending the *Publisher*, but a new supply of paper saved the day. As for Sam Schwieger, he had married, and doubtless needing more money, moved on to work for a utility company. Apparently the university was too remote from the rest of Arkansas for maximum effectiveness, or the university was reluctant to continue granting office space; for whatever reasons, in the fall of 1943 the office was moved to Little Rock in the Boyle Building with Roy Elliott's son, Kenneth, as the editor-manager. A new treasurer, K.A. Engel, took over at the same time and remained for the next quarter-century. Elliot's service was limited, for in March 1944 he left to enter the army, and Leibert J. "Bill" Miner took his place.

Miner's first important contribution was to further confuse the chronology of the *Arkansas Publisher*, for under him every issue now stated, "Established January 1930." Some nine months later, Miner departed, and former flight instructor Albert E. "Gene" Swank from Mangum, Oklahoma, took his place.[980] Managers on musical chairs continued, however. In September 1945, Otis E. Williams took Swank's place; in January 1946, Kenneth Elliott was back at the helm only to be succeeded in September by Bill Miner, who remained in charge until his death from cancer at age 50 in 1950.

Meanwhile, the war disrupted life at home. Although Arkansas received only 1.16 percent of the federal war expenditures, what the state got was highly important. Norfork Dam, Tom Shiras's dream, was considered a wartime necessity and its construction employed over 1,200 persons. Camp Robinson (the former Camp Pike) was greatly expanded and Camp Chaffee outside Fort Smith was created. Hundreds of farmers lost their lands, disrupting rural communities but leading to surging growth in neighboring towns. The creation of the Southwestern Proving Grounds at Hope led to the doubling of the town's population almost overnight. Around the state, five air bases were established, and the camp newspaper at Walnut Ridge was printed by the *Times-Dispatch*.[981] Jacksonville, with its ordnance plant, and Pine Bluff, home to a munitions factory, were both booming.

With these defense industry plants came the Fair Employment Practices Committee (FEPC) by President Roosevelt's executive order. Although the armed services were segregated, defense industries were under mandate not to discriminate. Arkansas blacks actually got jobs at the Maumelle Ordnance Plant. According to the *Pine Bluff Commercial*, the good race relations at the Arsenal indicated that "the walls of prejudice in industry are crumbling for the simple and effective reason that the nation does not have enough manpower to do the job unless we utilize every available unit with utmost efficiency."[982]

The newspaper's implied endorsement was a minority view. The *Southern Standard* demanded the agency's abolition because segregation "makes for harmony and prevents racial friction." One letter to the *Gazette* said the agency stood for "Foul Extremists Prefer Colored," a view taken by both Senators McClellan and Fulbright. A bill to extend the FEPC after the war was fillibustered to death in the U. S. Senate.[983]

The arrival of black troops led to trouble as well. In 1941, a state highway patrolman ordered the all-black 94th Engineers Battalion marching near Gurdon to quit singing in the presence of whites. When its white officer refused, the patrolman assaulted the officer. Fearing a race riot, local whites bought up all the guns and ammunition in town and brought more from Little Rock in preparation for battle. Only the arrival of more troops and additional state police kept matters from escalating. The next year, a Little Rock policeman shot to death black Sergeant Thomas B. Foster. The Foster incident achieved international attention. City officials called it justifiable homicide, and despite vigorous black protests, a federal grand jury agreed. Both the *Gazette* and the *Democrat* supported city officials. Foster's death, the *Democrat* explained, was due to "a nationwide campaign by the black press and the National Association for the Advancement of Colored People (NAACP) to use the war to undermine white supremacy on the home front."[984]

During the war, the federal government again instituted bond drives in order to limit inflation. Yet even war-bond drives got tangled up with racism. When Roscoe Simmons, a nephew of Booker T.

Washington, was invited to Arkansas to promote better sales among area blacks, the *Marked Tree Tribune* felt compelled to allay white fears of a racial uprising by claiming that Simmons "understands southern customs and traditions."[985]

Overall, the war-bond campaigns were good to newspapers. While the exigencies of war limited the availability of consumer goods, much of the lost advertising space was taken up by the many bond drives. Each issue usually featured large advertisements that often appeared on the front page. In addition, wartime rationing required explanation. A 1944 limit of 25 pounds of sugar impacted home canning, but farmers' shoes and tires for their wagons and tractors were considered priority items. Weeklies could not hope and did not try to keep abreast of the rapidly changing war scene, but they did distill much-needed information on ever-tightening regulations to the home folks, even if vigorous black and gray markets existed in tires, gasoline, meat stamps, and other items.

Many wartime advertisements struck a patriotic theme as well. Mammoth Spring's K & K grocery store at the end of one advertisement added, "Let's Buy Mere [*sic*] War Bonds and Hang Hitler and To Jo [*sic*]." Ark-Mo Power and Light, whose hydroelectric plant was at the spring, ran "Reddy's War News," assuring readers that, "A human life depends on the smooth, even flow of electric power."[986]

Most of all, local weeklies were a major source for patriotic efforts on the home front. "Viola School Scraping Mad" was the headline the *Mammoth Spring Democrat* used to describe how 24 students "are bent on taking a Rap for the Japs, and all other enemies of our nation."[987]

Because of Arkansas's weak clout in Congress and its lack of an industrial base, much of the state was looked upon only as fertile recruiting ground for manpower. Under the heading "ATTENTION!! MEN" the state director of the United States Employment Service came to Mammoth Spring to sign up men to work in war industries.[988]

Although in time World War II would be seen as "the last good war," this attitude was not shared by all Arkansans. The *Mammoth Spring Democrat*, for example, reported that not only had Hurbie Rains not reported for duty after being drafted, but that when the first officials went out to investigate, they were attacked by the Rains family with stove wood, flatirons, pokers, and other weapons. Reinforced by FBI agents, they renewed the battle on February 12, 1942, lobbing tear gas into the farmhouse and shooting Hurbie in the leg. The entire family ended up in jail.[989]

Both during and after the war, newsprint proved to be a problem. *Arkansas Publisher* readers had been informed periodically of experiments in bringing Southern forests into production, but the Depression cut demand for paper, and Canada remained the nation's principal source. Georgian Dr. Charles H. Herty, the father of Southern paper mills, preached his gospel to Southern publishers, principally through the Southern Newspaper Publishers Association (SNPA), and on January 17, 1940, Southland Paper Mills, Inc., officially opened. Its rated capacity was 150 tons daily, or 50,000 tons per year. The first test runs of the new paper were made at newspapers in Dallas, Shreveport, and at the *Arkansas Gazette*.[990] Although the cause of Southern newsprint was of immense importance to the Arkansas press, the main impetus for getting the plant came from the SNPA, an association of the region's major dailies in which Arkansas was poorly represented. Aside from J.N. Heiskell at the *Gazette* and August Engel at the *Democrat* (a longtime director and president in 1950-51), only John S. Parks at Fort Smith (president in 1929-1930) and Clyde E. Palmer (director, 1938-1940) were involved in the organization.

The paper shortage continued after the war, and newspapers around the state traded and exchanged with one another as well as suspending new subscriptions.

Women and the War

What the war did create was an immense opportunity for women. At Malvern the publisher's daughter, Frances Beerstecher, pitched in as a Linotype operator, and girls for the first time could become newspaper "boys," as carriers frequently had been called. "There will be no future discrimination against employing girls as carriers," E.W. Pate declared.[991] Two of his Rogers carrier-girls were using their money to pay for piano lessons. An even more impressive change came when Mrs. J.H. Rinehart of Harrison took over one of the *Arkansas Gazette*'s largest motor routes with over 500 subscribers. She was required to drive 36 miles for a day that began at 2 A.M.[992] At the *Chicot Spectator*, the only man was editor D.T. Gaines; the rest of the three-person staff consisted of women.[993] During the war years, Esther Bindursky at Lepanto came into her own. Her story, "Arkansas Pine Knot," on Congressional Medal of Honor winner Sergeant Jim Hendrix, appeared in the October 20, 1945, issue of the *Saturday Evening Post*, and she won a first-place award from the National Federation of Press Women for her "Navy Edition" of the *Lepanto News-Record*.[994]

The *Publisher* took due note of these developments by initiating in January 1945 a column entitled "Skirts…In the Front Office," written by Charlotte Tillar, a Louisiana State University journalism graduate then working at McGehee. The column's title was ironic, for one of the much-debated social issues of the day was the wearing of pants by women. "Slacks are definitely not for the streets," was the ruling of the *Gazette*'s fashion editor.[995]

The *Publisher*'s first columnist, pictured in a skirt, claimed that in the popular perception women journalists were either "spineless" or "scheming." Women were believed to be incapable of covering football games or getting the facts right on accidents. Despite misconceptions, "we ladies of the press are here to stay," she proclaimed.[996] In subsequent issues she addressed issues of content, economic development, the value of exchanges, and a host of other practical concerns. In 1945 her newspaper, the *McGehee Times*, was adjudged the best weekly in the state. While the APA welcomed her work, they mistrusted the ability of single women to attend a convention in Little Rock. The APA found escorts for Charlotte and Esther Bindursky when they came to the mid-winter convention.[997]

Behind Barbed Wire

A special kind of wartime experience occurred in two Arkansas communities, Jerome and Rohwer. Acting under exclusion orders the United States Supreme Court upheld, all persons of Japanese origin were uprooted from their homes and spent much of the war behind barbed wire. All of the 10 camps had newspapers, but the one at Jerome set the highest standards. What started as a typed, mimeographed newsletter became under editor Paul Yokota a quality publication entitled the Denson (the nearest post office) *Tribune*.

Yokota, a 1941 honors journalism graduate from the University of Southern California, knew how to put out a good newspaper. In addition to reporting the details of camp life, both in English and Japanese, the editor attacked those who questioned the patriotism of the inmates, urged internees to make better use of their time, and commented extensively on camp conditions. After he left, Harry Shiramizu, a University of Hawaii political science graduate, continued the newspaper until it closed on D-Day. Overseeing the newspaper for the government was former *Gazette* reporter, Charles Lynn.[998] Neither editor applied for APA membership, but the McGehee newspaper did run a column on the camps. "We say 30," announced the newspaper in its last issue, dated June 6, 1944, D-Day.

Meanwhile the Rohwer camp sported the *Outlook*. Barry Saiki, who served the longest as editor, was a political science graduate and schoolteacher. This newspaper featured cartoonist George Akimoto, and, free from government control, Saiki provided the occasional strong editorial. A resolution adopted by the Arkansas American Legion calling on Congress to repatriate and expatriate everyone in America with Japanese ancestry produced great indignation. He also reprinted from the *McGehee Times* an editorial that criticized how some camp inmates had behaved while in that town. Saiki was gone well before the *Outpost*'s last issue of July 21, 1945.[999] Former UALR Journalism professor Edward J. Friedlander has concluded that both newspapers enjoyed remarkable freedom from censorship or outside interference. However, the presence of these detainees produced strong hatred among many plain Arkansans. By contrast, German and Italian prisoners of war, who were assigned to labor camps in eastern Arkansas, were positively welcomed as saviors for their help in harvesting the region's crops.

Carrying On

During the war, editors plunged into scrap drives in a big way, often by getting rid of ancient equipment. Food and bond drives were the order of the day in towns large and small. John Pruniski, Jr., the son of the editor of the *North Little Rock Times*, who early in the war had volunteered as an ambulance driver in North Africa and Italy, made speaking appearances in various parts of the state.[1000] And the creation of an ordnance plant in Jacksonville inspired the founding of a new newspaper, the *Jacksonville Journal*.[1001]

Some editors used their newspapers to promote American values, but just what these were could be controversial. A strong conservative social reaction was underway at home, and during the war a number of counties, mostly in the northern part of the state, went "dry." There was little loss of advertising revenue, for most newspapers were fearful of reader loss if liquor advertisements appeared in a newspaper, but the brewing industry counterattacked on the ideological front. Industry spokesman Joe Marsh, whose monthly column ran in the *Publisher*, entitled one contribution, "Many Newspapers Stress Tolerance," and concluded, "We need not fear social responsibility, for such words are the essence of democracy and enlightenment."[1002] He was talking about a "right to drink."

On the other hand, the increase in monopoly towns gave some publishers the chance they needed to avoid directly offending anyone. After the *Jonesboro Evening Sun* acquired and shut down the *Daily Tribune*, all editorials, even of the canned variety, entirely disappeared.

The *Publisher* gave space to Al Pollard, a columnist and Sunday editor of the *Democrat* before creating his own advertising firm. Pollard was president of the Benjamin Franklin, Arkansas Thrift Clubs, and used his column to promote "free enterprise," a hardly concealed attack on New Deal economics.[1003] Articles boosting free enterprise soon appeared in virtually every issue, and coincided with a considerable increase in private utility advertising. Lines were being drawn for future battles, although few readers probably noticed them.

Meanwhile, at the 1944 APA convention, De Witt's J.M. Henderson took up the mantle of the late J.B. Parker. Henderson, a longtime educator, was obsessed over the decline of morals, which he blamed on John Dewey, "an avowed communist since the Year One." Henderson denounced (with good reason) the tyranny of curve grading, before moving on to blast bad textbooks, sexology, and birth control.[1004]

By 1944, the *Publisher* celebrated the contributions of members of the profession who served in the armed forces. The *Arkansas Democrat* sported a Military-Aviation Editor, C.C. Allard. One front-page story was on a young journalism student from Lonoke who won the Congressional Medal of Honor.[1005] Maurice L. Britt, invariably called "Footsie," went on to become the state's lieutenant governor (1967-1971) but never practiced journalism. At home, editors and publishers continued to serve their communities. Lewis M. Layer of the *Dierks Banner* was not only a bank president but also served on the school board and on what became a fixture for publishers for the next 30 years, the draft board. One of the first publishers in the state to serve was Rogers's Everett W. Pate. Much publicity resulted when on April 1, 1942, he was attacked and beaten in his office by J.H. and J.M. Head after one of the brothers had been denied a deferment.[1006] Jared Trevathan was mayor of Batesville. Another mayor was Ewell H. Freeman of the *Modern News* in Harrisburg, who also could be found as secretary of the sewer commission, secretary of the school board, member of the library and welfare boards, Rotarian, Mason, and Methodist Church steward.

There was a potential conflict of interest in holding local positions. Ted Larimer of the *Green Forest Tribune*, who for some 20 years was mayor of Green Forest, once did an interview with himself. George Douthit picked up this story and gave it statewide circulation. In length of service, no one exceeded J.N. Heiskell. The owner of Little Rock Public Library card Number One, Heiskell served on the library board from 1910 to 1972.

Meanwhile, by the spring of 1944, the *Publisher* advised newspapers to begin getting ready for victory editions. Emotionally, that must have been quite a struggle for the young Charlotte Tillar, for the March 15, 1945, military edition of her *McGehee Times* listed her brother among those who would not come home.[1007]

Newspapers responded to wartime conditions. Population flight from the state led to having out-of-state correspondents, a practice still continued in some newspapers at the time of this writing. Wichita, Kansas; Flint, Michigan; Rockford, Illinois; and various towns in California lured large numbers of Arkansans. Circulation soared, with the Pocahontas *Star Herald* sending over 600 newspapers to military men and women. Officially received information on soldiers went into special columns. "Our Men in the Service" was the title used at the *Osceola Times*, even though many Arkansas women served as well.[1008]

Some soldier letters made their way into the newspapers. "This newspaper is thoroughly familiar with the roles of censorship and the reason for them," the *Marked Tree Tribune* observed. "Parents and friends may be assured that nothing will be printed which would help the enemy." Corporal Robert Smith's letter revealing details on the Guadalcanal battle was published only after "official" permission had been received. Since soldiers knew that their letters were being read by censors, a common comment was "I had better not tell you more or the censor might cut it out."[1009]

Although the weekly press did not often comment on the greater issues of the war, it did expose local mistakes. After Private Henry H. Isbell of Salem was reported to have gone Absent Without Leave (AWOL) when he was actually in the hospital with appendicitis, the *Mammoth Spring Democrat* reported the mistake and that Isbell's mother had received an official apology.[1010] The same newspaper treated D-Day by reporting how local churches would be open all day for prayer.[1011] Reports of deaths and soldiers missing in action or taken prisoners appeared regularly during the last years of the war.

The large number of former subscribers in uniform presented opportunities. The *Marked Tree Tribune* not only happily sent newspapers to military personnel but also printed the names of those whose subscriptions had expired in order to urge family members to renew for them. Instructions were printed

Max Hampton

"The Bard of Booneville" inherited the *Democrat* from his father in 1911. Under the slogan "Broad enough to have an opinion, and big enough to express it," Hampton and his wife put out a good country newspaper. In addition, he wrote short stories and poetry. Poetry was a regular feature in newspapers until the 1970s, and Hampton was probably the last poet-publisher in Arkansas.

Life's Ambition

A barefoot boy, with wistful smile, sat fishing in a stream,
And as the laddie sat and fished, perchance he dreamed a dream;
The world was wrong, he'd make it right, when he grew up some day,
He'd teach them of man's brotherhood, show them the better way.

The world was filled with greed and hate that warped the souls of men,
But he'd show them love and charity—life would be sweeter then;
So gazing there through future's haze, the boy began to plan—
'Twas the birth of life's ambition—to be a good newspaper man.

The years passed by and our wistful lad, began his work of life,
With vitriolic pen he bravely fought hate, crookedness and strife;
And as the years flew swiftly by he tried with all his skill,
To teach men of the golden rule—to respect the Master's will.

He tried to make men understand, the sweet and blessed truth,
That he had learned while fishin' on the creek as just a youth;
That life's beauty and its sweetness comes to us through God's grace
But that selfish greed and ugliness are ills of the human race.

Tonight an old man, aged and gray, looks backward through the years,
At life's trials and tribulations and its joys and hopes, its fears;
The spring of youth has left his step, his boyish face has paled,
And while he hopes the world is better, oftentimes he fears he's failed.

The passing years have numbed the brain, the crusading pen is still,
As he gazes on his office chair someone else so soon will fill;
'Tis the end of life's ambition, for our wistful little elf,
*But there's a sweetness just in knowing he's at least reformed himself.**

**Arkansas Publisher*, February 1946.

on how and what families and friends could mail to their absent loved ones. Arkansas newspapers in time could be found all over the world.[1012]

Five years after the war's end, Des Arc's *White River Journal* noted that the newspaper was sent to 22 families in California, 18 in Michigan, 17 in Indiana, 15 in Texas, 12 in Tennessee, and 11 in Illinois. "This will give you an idea of where our young boys and girls go when they finish school to make a living. Now I am wondering," editor C.J. Walls mused, "about these families. I wonder if they have done better by leaving Arkansas? I wonder how many of them would like to come back? I wonder if I would do better by joining them. I wonder if they would like to have a list of others from Des Arc who live in the same states with them? I wonder if they care whether I wonder? Do you know that Arkansas is called the WONDER STATE?"[1013] (In 1952, in order to keep people from wondering, the legislature changed the state's motto to "The Land of Opportunity.")

During the war, soldier voting was a big issue. State's rights conservative J.N. Heiskell held that a federal law to authorize soldiers to vote would violate Arkansas's poll-tax requirement. True to his convictions, Heiskell maintained that any congressional legislation to overturn state election practices was unconstitutional.[1014] During the war the divorce rate shot up, juvenile delinquency appeared as women found work in industry, and crime rose alarmingly. As usual, editors took on these targets. "Law Enforcement in White County Becomes a Joke" was the headline that won the 1944 C.E. Palmer award for the best daily for M.P. Jones of the Searcy *White County Citizen*. The contest's judge noted that "this sort of thing might not exactly be community promotion, but certainly a fearless exposé of a very nasty local situation comes under the heading of community service."[1015] The *Fordyce News* trophy for the outstanding weekly went to Guy Graves's *Marked Tree Tribune* with second place going to Graves's *Lepanto News Record*, edited by Esther Bindursky, both of which showed "plenty of evidence of hard-hitting, heads-up work." It was also a testament to the Association that the awards ceremonies, revived under the manager system, were continued uninterrupted during the war.

Overall, newspapers had survived and prospered during the great conflict, adapting to the needs of their readers. Little did the Association members know that new challenges lay ahead.

Postwar Adjustments

Following V-E and V-J Days, the trickle of returnees turned into a flood. For many it was simply a matter of getting started again. Returning veteran Ray Kimball revived the *Daily Citizen* at De Queen; J.R. Tudor, a Republican legislator in 1947, merged his suspended *Marshall Republican* with the *Mountain Wave* of the now ancient W.A. Wenrich. Jared Trevathan started the *Daily News* in Batesville; Guy Graves sold his three properties (Trumann, Marked Tree, and Lepanto) to William T. Shelton and his wife, Connie. Joining them was Connie's brother, Howard Stuck, who promptly married Marked Tree history teacher Dorothy Davis.

Another sale was made by M.J. "Mike" Gillespie, who during the late 1930s accumulated a number of local newspapers in central Arkansas. In 1946, he sold his Lonoke and Cabot newspapers to Larry Grauerholz, fresh out of the Army Air Corps. At the same time, Charles A. Price, who had taken the *Glenwood Herald* from a small, two-page newspaper into a six-column, all-home-print publication, sold out to Bill Watt, the son of Mr. And Mrs. W.O. Watt of the *Montgomery County Herald* at Mount Ida.[1016] The Layers at Dierks sold the *Banner* to Neil and June Clark—he a decorated returning veteran from Gurdon, she a journalism student from California. One of their plans was to build an apartment in the *Banner* shop. At Huttig, the *News* ran a Veterans'

Arkansas Gazette business office, 1957. Modernization of the office was the work of Hugh Patterson, for under the Allsopps, business practices were largely unchanged since the 19th century. (Courtesy J.N. Heiskell Collection, UALR Archives and Special Collections)

Horse and wagon at the Cleburne County Times, *c. 1960. Apparently, even horses had to feed the parking meter. (Courtesy* Cleburne County Times*)*

Colonel T.H. Barton, 1949. Barton, on the left, presents the Sweepstakes Trophy to Andy and Blanche Murray of the Wynne Star-Progress. *This travelling trophy was presented on Arkansas's Annual Freedoms Day, May 7, 1949, at Wynne. "Not many communities rise above the character and the abilities of their newspapers," Col. Barton said in making the award. (APA Archives)*

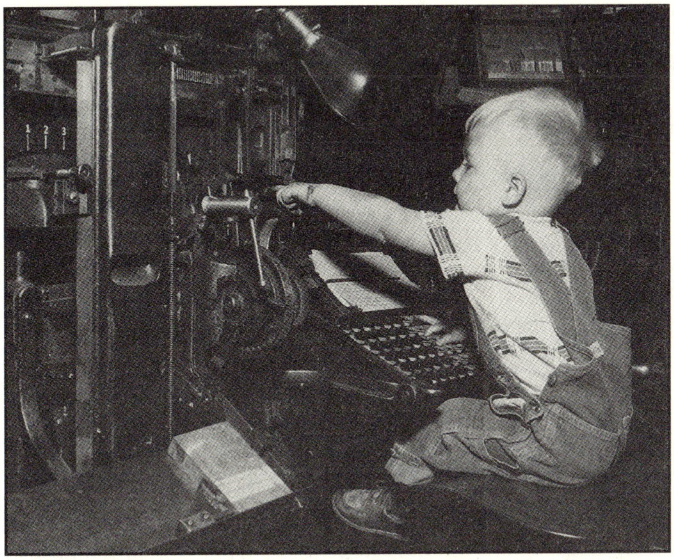

Steven Elledge, June 1953, son of Brinkley Argus *foreman Franklin H. Elledge and the grandson of* Argus *owner Mason Clifton, was two and a half when he posed for this picture at the new Linotype No. 31. (APA Archives)*

Eloise Castleberry, 1949. During Bill Miner's illness, the APA's office functioned smoothly under Elouise Castleberry, shown here holding two loving cups and a trophy. In the middle is the Sam Gearhart trophy, presented for the first time to the West Memphis News *for the best advertising; the loving cups went to the* Smackover Journal *and the* Wynne Star-Progress *for their working in promoting the Balanced Farming contest. (APA Archives)*

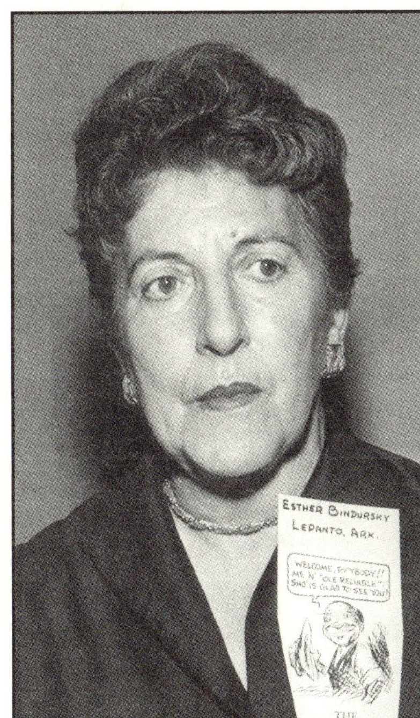

Esther Bindursky, c. 1960. This longtime Lepanto editor put out her newspaper virtually single-handedly, wrote for the Memphis Commercial Appeal, *authored articles for national journals, and became in her later years a noted photographer. (Courtesy Special Collections, University of Memphis)*

Jack (standing) and Paul Coughlin at the West Memphis News, *c. 1949. These crusading brothers received national attention for their work in promoting the GI revolt. (Courtesy Special Collections, University of Memphis)*

Howard and Dorothy Stuck (c. 1960). After Howard was stricken with polio, Dorothy assumed the reins at the Marked Tree Tribune. *Her editorial on the wrongs of segregation was a daring move in eastern Arkansas. (Courtesy Special Collections, University of Memphis)*

Margaret Woolfolk, c. 1960. The longtime editor of the Crittenden County Times *is wearing an Army Corps of Engineers hat and has the inevitable pack of cigarettes stuck in her pocket. (Courtesy Special Collections, University of Memphis)*

An APA panel at Hot Springs. Shown are: Frank Robins, Log Cabin Democrat, *Conway, moderator; Gene Foreman, Harry Haines, and Fred Wulfekuhler. Foreman, a graduate of Arkansas State College, worked at the* Pine Bluff Commercial *and* Arkansas Democrat *before moving to the* Philadelphia Inquirer; *Harry A. Haines succeeded his father, Harry W. Haines, at the* Blytheville Courier News; *and Fred Wulfekuhler owned the* Paragould Daily Press. *(Photo by Walter E. McGonagill; APA Archives)*

Four APA presidents are pictured at a convention. From left to right, Jay W. Jackson, Van Buren County Democrat, *Clinton (1968); Ted Larimer,* Green Forest Tribune *(1963); Howard Stuck,* Marked Tree Tribune, *who had to decline the presidency on account of his heath; Melvin Schexnayder,* Dumas Clarion *(1962), Val Zachariah,* Booneville Democrat; *and Porter Young,* Helena World *(1965). (APA Archives)*

Printing at Arkansas State College, c. 1950. Jonesboro led other campuses in the state in teaching printing. The development in the late 20th century of large commercial printing firms in Jonesboro was one result. Here, students view the results of installing a new Fairchild press. (Courtesy Joel Gambill)

Duplex Unitublar press at the Pine Bluff Commercial. *This tubular press could print circulars at the rate of 36,000 per hour and a standard four-page newspaper in six colors at one time. (APA Archives)*

Trophy winners, 1965. Fred Wulfekuhler, Paragould Daily Press, *garnered first place in column writing, second place in five categories, and third in three; Dorothy Stuck,* Marked Tree Tribune, *won the Press Women's Achievement Award; Cone Magie,* Cabot Star Herald, Carlisle Independent *and* Lonoke Democrat, *won the President's Award; and Roy Meyer collected three firsts, a second in one, and a third in two for Sam Hodges's* Benton Courier. *(APA Archives)*

State Senator Clyde Byrd presented the Arkansas Livestock Show's Sweepstakes Award to Senator J.W. Fulbright (right), representing the Northwest Arkansas Times. *The year's previous winner, Sam Hodges,* Osceola Times, *is in the center. (1954, Johnnie M. Gray). (APA Archives)*

The press room of the Arkansas Democrat, *c. 1950. Among those pictured are: (in the foreground) Alden Tilden, the veteran city editor; (across the table) John Scuder, Marcus George, and Roger Neunn; (standing) George Douthit, reporter; (seated front to back) Ken Francis, Bob McCord, Virginia Robinson; (seated right) Effie Laura Wooten; (standing) O.D. Gunter and Leo Martin; (standing right) Eddie Liske, the managing editor, Jon Kennedy, cartoonist, Fred Petrucelli, sports, and Matilda Touhey reporter. (Photographer unknown; courtesy Jon Kennedy)*

Paris Express *office, c. 1940. Newspaper offices typically were located downtown. By the 1960s, however, space problems led some to relocate to sites more accessible to highways or to move the printing plant to separate locations. (APA Archives)*

Cartoon by Jon Kennedy, Arkansas Democrat

Cartoon by George Fisher, Arkansas Gazette

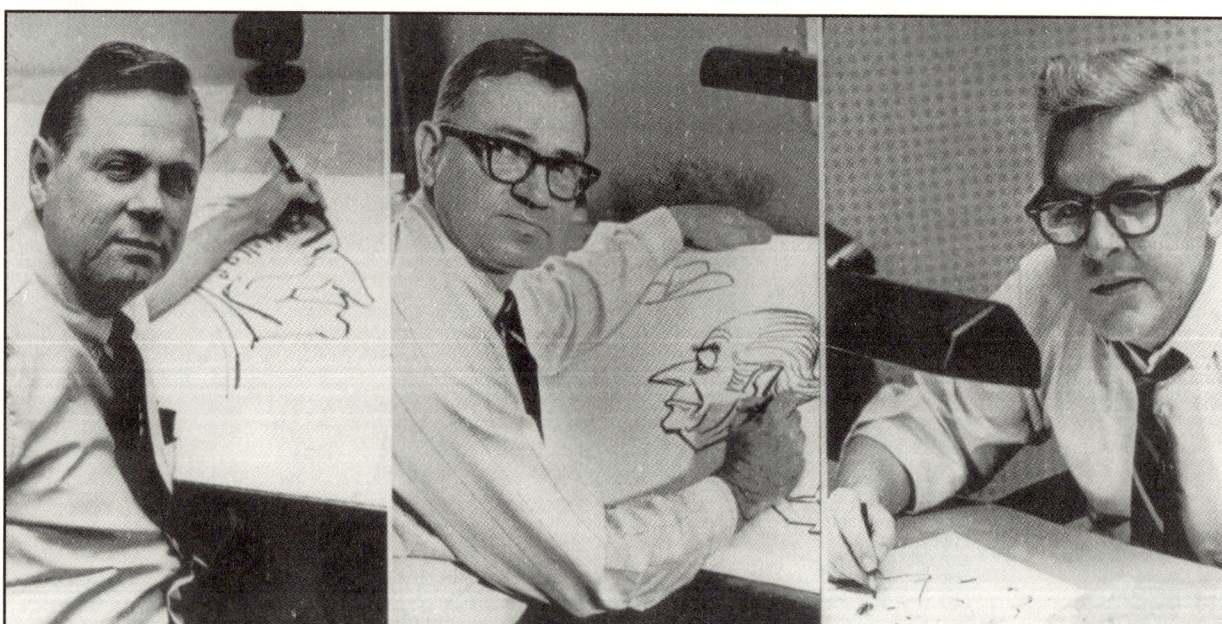

The Big Three Cartoonists: George Fisher, Jon Kennedy, and Bill Graham. (Courtesy, Jon Kennedy)

News column, while owner Fred M. Johnson continued to provide readers with his extensive hunting stories. "Big Game Hunting in Alberta, Canada" ran in five issues in 1948 and was followed by "My Thirty day Hunt in British Columbia" in 1949.

Another change came in remote Madison County. Alfred Hawn, the veteran editor of the *Record* who served as APA president in 1931, died in 1947. The new owner was a former county clerk and army major whose family had a long connection with the newspaper. Sam Faubus, a card-carrying Socialist from Greasy Creek, wrote regular letters that the newspaper published, and his son, Orval, had provided the *Record* with 29 lengthy letters during his wartime absence in Europe. After Orval Faubus bought the *Record*, he came out on September 11, 1947, with the largest edition in the newspaper's history. Faubus promised more when he could afford to replace "the antiquated machinery with which we now labor."[1017]

Changes occurred with dailies as well. Edgar Brown headed up a group that included C.E. Palmer, Ray Kimball, and W.E. Hussman that purchased the *Daily Leader* and *Arkansawyer* of Stuttgart.[1018] Forthwith, the daily installed a teletypesetter, joining the network Ray Kimball had pioneered. Featured on the cover of the March 1946 *Arkansas Publisher* was the *Jonesboro Evening Sun*'s new 16-page Goss Junior Straightline Rotary Press with a speed of 15,000 copies per hour. The *Sun*, now boasting almost 8,000 subscribers, revived its engraving plant and added Associated Press full-leased wire teletype service. Its old press headed down to Conway.[1019]

Meanwhile, the young editor of the *Charlotte* (North Carolina) *News* attracted national attention with a candid speech at the American Society of Newspaper Editors. In 1947, after turning down offers to go to Richmond and Atlanta, Harry Ashmore accepted the position as editor of the editorial page of the *Arkansas Gazette*. J.N. Heiskell, who had lost a son and heir-apparent in the war, had hired a Southern liberal who had been a Nieman Fellow at Harvard University to work for what Heiskell called "a conservative paper which sometimes disappoints conservatives."[1020] Ashmore attained national attention as the author of a well-known book, *Epitaph for Dixie* (1954), that claimed Southern distinctiveness was on the way out. His Arkansas years would challenge that assumption.

Because of all these changes, Ells L. Huff of the weekly *Jackson County Democrat*, the Association's president in 1947, concluded that newspapers were "experiencing even more difficulties now than during the war."[1021] In addition to postwar shortages of newsprint, publishers in 1947 heard about a new process called offset that did away with letter-press printing. "Everything about offset printing is about half nuts," a Texas editor reported, and "Ninety-five per cent of the operators are screwballs." But his advice was, "GET INTO OFFSET PRINTING AS SOON AS POSSIBLE."[1022]

Instead, many newspapers got into radio. Since its Arkansas inception in Pine Bluff on February 18, 1922, radio had gradually grown into a threat to newspaper advertising revenues. Because advertising ranked first in what made newspapers profitable, this loss was not taken lightly. During the 1930s, countless speakers argued various aspects of the topic at APA meetings: Should newspapers print radio schedules as a public service or only as an advertisement? How best could businesses be shown that newspaper advertising brought better returns?

Two factors came together in the late 1930s that raised the ante. First, instead of little local stations that frequently shut down in the summer and had only local talent to deploy, there were now four networks linking the country to highly publicized shows, sporting events, and news coverage. Second, thanks to rural electrification, almost all Arkansans would be able to listen at will to broadcasts, whether it be noontime blues from Helena, afternoon soap operas from the networks, or even coverage of local sporting events at night. Saturday afternoons were the province of Texaco's Metropolitan Opera broadcasts live from New York.

With the census bureau in 1946 showing radios in 90.4 percent of America's homes, newspapers decided to hop in and share the wealth. In 1944 the *Arkansas Gazette* paid $275,000 for a majority of the shares of KLRA; in 1946 Donald W. Reynolds got a permit for a new Fort Smith station, KFSA (Know Fort Smith Arkansas); and in Paragould in the early 1950s KDRS and the *Daily Press* were jointly owned. Walter E. Hussman, Sr., was president of KWFC in Hot Springs.[1023]

The Arkansas Broadcasters Association took shape after World War II, and with it, an Arkansas Associated Press Broadcasters Association. Just as with newspapers, radio stations got much of their news from AP or UP.

Television entered the picture with KFSA-TV at Fort Smith on July 19, 1953, and this new medium was only reaching early maturity when Little Rock, Arkansas, became a news focus for America in September, 1957.

"What is the public service record of your newspaper since V-J Day?"

When the September 6, 1946, Arkansas Press Association's *Confidential Bulletin* asked that question to the state's publishers, the answer already existed. The *Northwest Arkansas Times* had exposed conditions in Fayetteville's alleys and streets, promoted the county fair, worked for better housing for university students, and printed a better farms edition. At De Queen, the *Citizen* sought a modern bus depot and the installation of natural gas, published special editions on 4-H clubs and soil conservation, and started a campaign that resulted in new uniforms for the high school band. The *Arkansas Democrat* investigated irregularities in the sale of surplus war equipment, forced the State Hospital Board to open its meetings to the public, promoted a free summer camp for underprivileged girls, and pushed for free swimming lessons. In conjunction with the American Association of University Women, the *Democrat* had campaigned for election law revision that resulted in eliminating the recently adopted double primary. Similar examples of activity came from the *Star-Progress* at Wynne, the *Texarkanka Gazette* and *Daily News*, and the *Eagle Democrat* at Warren.[1024] Hugh Park's *Press-Argus* even won first prize in the National Editorial Association's 1947 Community Service contest. Park had campaigned for flood control, a playground, and other community improvements.

Reflective of these concerns, the Association greatly expanded the contests in 1945, adding seven new categories. In addition to individual advertising campaigns and presswork, awards went to agriculture and editorial excellence.[1025] Arkansas had prospered as never before during the war years, thanks to federal installations and wartime orders. Rural electrification was in full swing; colleges were crowded with returning veterans aided by the GI Bill. Evidence of a belief in impending progress appeared in every issue of the *Publisher*. "We lack a University Press in Arkansas," ran one headline, expressing a need that would remain unfilled for 40 years.[1026] "Arkansas," intoned Governor "Business Ben" Laney, "is beginning to take its rightful place as a leader among states."[1027]

Actually, Arkansas was still locked in a race with Mississippi for last in most state rankings, as many editors knew. Hence, a number of writers undertook to find other values in Arkansas life. *Arkansas Democrat* columnist Karr Shannon endeavored in his *On a Fast Train Through Arkansas* (1948) to refute every alleged slight the state had ever suffered. One of the ironies Shannon overlooked was that the closing of the legendarily slow Missouri and North Arkansas Railroad robbed large parts of the northern part of the state of all railroad service.

One fixture of Arkansas life, Colonel Thomas H. Barton, "the grand old man of oil and gas," who looked more like a Kentucky colonel than the head of Lion Oil, promoted Freedoms Day on the first of May.[1028] What had once been a day for maypole decoration (still considered satanic in some circles) had been taken over by the Communists. Freedoms Day was officially endorsed by the APA and an organization Barton carried in his back pocket, the Arkansas Livestock Show Association. For the first ceremony in 1948, Barton co-opted the APA's sweepstakes trophy, taking it up to Searcy where at Harding College he presented it to M.P. Jones of the *Citizen*. Barton got an honorary doctorate from Harding but doubtless still preferred to be called colonel.[1029] Reflective of the grim times that lay ahead, after Barton's death in 1960, Montsanto, which had acquired Lion Oil, moved its offices to St. Louis before dismantling the company.

The Bitter Battle for Better Farming

Nothing demonstrated better the idea that Arkansas's problems could be licked with proper advertising than the 1947 campaign entitled "Arkansas Balanced Farming." Launched with a flourish and sponsored by the APA, the Agricultural Extension Service, Arkansas Power and Light, and the Memphis *Commercial Appeal*, the program emphasized contour planting, and a host of other farming concerns. The winners that first year, Mr. and Mrs. Lawrence Woodard and their daughter Betty, appeared on the cover of the November issue of the *Publisher*. The immediate model was the *Commercial Appeal*'s "Plant to Prosper" program created before the war, but there were local precedents. Ralph Kite at De Queen had linked the *Bee* and *Citizen* with the Chamber of Commerce in order to have a "Farm Family of the Month."[1030]

Behind the promotion lay the idea that family farming was still economically viable. For the first 10 years or so, newspapers gladly cooperated, advertising the program on every occasion. To encourage participation the state was divided into two sections. Max Hampton (west) and M.J. "Mike" Gillespie (east), editors with long associations in promoting agriculture, coordinated the 1949 program. Those who believed in the cause suffered for the next 30 years as mechanization, changes in government agricultural policies, and increasing industrialization eroded and eventually destroyed traditional rural ways of living.

One feature of the program was its segregation. For Negro farmers, the program was called "Live-at-Home," with awards being divided between tenants and landowners. According to Gordon N. Freeman of the *Pine Bluff Commercial*, the black contest was "virtually identical" to the white. Freeman explained in a 1954 article how newspapers could support the county competitions for both whites and blacks. He urged newspapers to avoid hitting up local retail stores for prize money, but instead to go after the implement dealers, fertilizer companies, bottlers, and others who did direct business with farmers. For the black contest, he suggested getting donations from black professionals. Jefferson County was large and active enough to have prizes almost the equal of those on the state level, and it, too, had a free awards banquet.[1031] State winners were taken to Little Rock for a luncheon awards ceremony. An additional incentive was a shining trophy yearly for the newspaper that best publicized the program. One of the first white tenant winners was the Douglas Dougan family of Nevada County, and a photograph showed their smokehouse and canned goods.[1032]

"We don't need to tell you why this is important," Freeman explained to other publishers, "This and the

Home Improvement Contests will be strong factors in keeping people on the farms, in preventing Arkansas from being a state with a few big farms with a smattering of rural population."[1033] But it was not to be. In 1953 the *Osceola Times* won the APA sweepstakes award. Part of Sam Hodges's success was based on country correspondents and agricultural reporting. But Hodges soon bought the *Benton Courier* located in the midst of Arkansas's then booming bauxite belt and sold the newspaper he had inherited from his parents. "You can't sell subscriptions to machines," was his explanation.[1034]

During the mid-1950s the inroads of mechanization hit the smaller family farms. Despite the programs for balanced agriculture and industrial development, population collapse was accelerating. The Cold War played an important role, for most country boys did not go to college but headed into the military after (or before) their high school graduations; few ever came back to farm. As machines replaced day labor, the towns dependent on the rural trade suffered. Many like Osceola tried to lure Northern industry. Sam Hodges remembered one unsuccessful industrial promotion in Osceola that gloried in the town's Old South moonlight and magnolia history.

What did come were shoe factories that moved south from St. Louis after World War II. These were mostly in the northeastern and north central parts of the state. Farther south, Delta planters opposed anything that might increase pay scales, and many smaller towns were strangled by the landlords. The Rotary met for the last time in Marvell in 1973, leaving behind a half mile of empty store buildings. Gone, too, after a prolonged strangling death was the last of its several newspapers, the *Marvell Messenger*. Except in the Delta, row crops disappeared, being replaced often in the Ozarks by cattle farming, while tree farming took the place of cotton in South Arkansas. Overall, despite a birth rate higher than the national average, the state lost 40,000 persons between 1940 and 1950, and almost 250,000 between 1950 and 1960. Three congressional seats disappeared in the process.

The GI Revolt

Not all Arkansans reacted passively to the state's failure to progress. Although others participated, the GI Revolt resulted in many veterans getting into politics. The federal government had gone to some expense during the war to educate its soldiers in the principles of democracy. Yet, as Hot Springs ex-Marine Sidney McMath asked, "The returning soldier is zealous of his heritage as an American citizen, perhaps because he has so recently fought for it. When he returns to his own community from the war and finds his own people deprived of their right to vote, when he discovers that their lives and liberties are not secure, when it is threatened that if he exercises the right of citizenship and runs for public office without the consent of the political boss...What is his reaction?"[1035]

In addition, the business establishment had failed to take the necessary steps needed to move Arkansas into a new age. Governor Laney and many in the state's leadership had become more concerned about perpetuating segregation. The United States Supreme Court, in *Smith v. Allwright* (1944), had struck down the all-white primary, thus allowing blacks to be Democrats. Terrified of blacks voting, Delta politicians under Laney's leadership committed the state to paying for a double-primary system, diverting money that could have gone into state improvements.

The Battle of Hot Springs dominated the state's news from 1946 to 1948. While many other counties were machine-run, they were overwhelmingly rural and their machines generally consisted of allied families. Hot Springs, with the state's tallest skyscraper (the Medical Arts building), and the third largest city, was still ruled by Mayor Leo P. McLaughlin. Under his regime, professional gambling and prostitution flourished, as every attendee of the APA's summer meetings doubtless knew. (What APA children mostly remembered was that this was where they first experienced shrimp.) Repeatedly, aspiring state politicians railed against the town's crooked ways, but cynics (who were right) thought that to be only a ploy to blackmail McLaughlin for votes.

Styling their group the Government Improvement League but soon shorting it to GI, the veterans developed a strategy that included running for offices directly against the machine on the county level and also for the critical offices of circuit judge and prosecuting attorney that extended beyond the county. For good measure, they ran a write-in candidate for Congress in order to give them access to federal jurisdiction.

Prior to the election, the GIs proved in federal court that the machine obtained fraudulent poll-tax receipts. Nevertheless, in the tension-filled Democratic primary only McMath, whose district included Montgomery County, won. Undeterred, the veterans bolted the party and won in the general election as independents. McMath was a featured speaker at the APA's Diamond Anniversary Convention in Hot Springs's then-grand Arlington Hotel in 1947.

While Sid McMath soon became the symbol of GIs in Arkansas politics, he was not alone. Returning veteran Orval Faubus, a Madison County clerk who had been elected county judge before he left for war, expected to win the office back in 1946; instead, he was defeated by the incumbent stay-at-home Republican. Faubus landed the patronage appointment as Huntsville's postmaster and, after acquiring the *Record*, used it to spread McMath's fame.

Other revolts with less success took place in Yell, Pope, and Crittenden counties. It was in the last of these that the GIs found their editorial tribune.

John (Jack) Coughlin came to Arkansas as Guy Graves's editor at the *Trumann Democrat*. His brother Paul (Pete) followed. Both had experiences in college journalism in Missouri and in owning a weekly in LaPlata. Both served in World War II, where Pete, who took his flying lessons at Arkansas State College (Jonesboro), became nationally famous as the "Sergeant York of the Air" after capturing a large number of prisoners said to number about 150 using his ancient two-seater observation plane during the Allied landing at Scoletti in Sicily. Jack, the better writer, started as a pilot but after an injury studied at the Princeton University School of Military Government and served in Guam. Then, in early 1946 they bought the *West Memphis News* in perpetually troubled Crittenden County.

A machine ruled the county, primarily though the persons of Sheriff Cecil Goodwin and County Judge C.H. "Sly Cy" Bond; their newspaper, the *Crittenden County Times*, held the county printing. Opposing them were the "J boys," most of whom had the letter "J" in either a first or last name. The *News* got off to a strong start, going to semi-weekly status and issuing 12 pages.

At first it appeared that the GI revolt would unseat the machine. After the voting armed veterans arrived at the courthouse to watch the counting, but once the early results indicated that they were winning, they drifted away. Then, in the late night hours, the numbers were reversed, and the machine won. Charges tying the judge and sheriff to organized gambling dominated the hotly contested county election and resulted in libel suits against the brothers. Judge Bond wanted $10,000 but collected only a $500 judgment. To help pay it, the brothers' art director, George Fisher, designed satirical token dollar bills which gave the bearer 25 cents' worth of the judge's reputation. The brothers printed two thousand at first, but had to reprint three times over before saturating the market.

The sheriff's suit really proved to be a disaster for

the machine. Jailing a defense witness who testified that white men were never arrested for illegal gambling did not help the plaintiff, while the defense questioned if reporting the existence of gambling and asking the sheriff to take action could be considered malice. The jury was out for less than 30 minutes before rendering its "not guilty" verdict; one juror wanted the damages awarded to the publishers.

George Fisher, the Coughlins' artist and a native of Beebe, had attended the junior college there and at the University. Returning from the war with an English wife, Rosemary (whose nickname, Snooky, invariably appeared disguised in his cartoons), Fisher had already published cartoons in the *Army Times*, the *Arkansas Gazette*, and the *Commercial Appeal.* As head of the *News* advertising department and officially the editor of their Earle newspaper, Fisher sat in the corner "listening and smiling" as the brothers fought their war.

During the spring of 1949, a lineman came by in West Memphis to shut off the electricity at the *News*. While the brothers were "famous for not paying their bills," this was a regular practice on Thursdays in order to stop production of the newspaper. Since it took two hours to warm up the Linotype machines, such interference was a potentially deadly blow. Pete rushed out with a shotgun, said later not to be loaded, and ordered the lineman off the pole. Charged with "drawing a deadly weapon," he paid a fine but rented a generator from Memphis.[1036]

It was the Coughlin brothers who reintroduced racial issues into state politics. Under Arkansas law, while the schools were segregated by race, the tax revenues were not. In addition, the state provided each county with money designated for black and white schools. However, in the Delta, black schools not only got significantly less funding, but in 1947 $4,250,000 was diverted from black to white schools by county officials. There was never any "equal" to "separate but equal" in Arkansas.

In West Memphis, the expenditure per white student was $144.51 in 1949, and only $19.51 per black (the discrepancy was even worse out in the county). Jack wrote a story about it in the newspaper, expressing the thought that something should be done to equalize spending. Instead, when the black school burned, the district took the insurance money and used it to complete the furnishings for the brand-new white school. Enraged, Jack sold his idea for a story to *Life Magazine*. A crew of photographers captured for all America the West Memphis situation. A black student drank out of a leaking pipe that served as a water fountain; a white student (the daughter of the city manager of whom the Coughlins disapproved) was seen at the new fountain at the white school. The white school had a new gym and typing class. Some black students went to what had not burned of their old school, while others were sent to local churches. Their average was 71 to a class, and one photographed room held 370 students grouped around a potbellied stove.

The planters counterattacked with a boycott against the newspaper. Instead of being a semi-weekly, the *News* fell to four thin pages once a week. However, the planter strategy backfired for the brothers organized a counter-boycott by blacks of merchants who failed to advertise in the *News*. Jack believed he was winning and assured Little Rock's Urban League members that the board wanted to get a new school built. West Memphis voters, however, responded to the publicity about their fair city by refusing to pass a bond issue for the black school, and in the fall of 1949 it closed.[1037] Jack did receive recognition from the APA, garnering the Roy Elliott trophy in 1949.[1038]

While the brothers were churning up dangerous waters in West Memphis, Sid McMath was running for governor in 1948. One of his opponents in the race typified the power of radio. James "Uncle Mac" MacKrell was a popular radio revivalist who in 1943 started a preaching war on "the New Deal Roosevelt Socialist Party."[1039] MacKrell on occasion ran advertisements in the *Publisher* and put out publications that might have appeared to some as newspapers, a move the Association officially condemned. In the Democratic primary, McMath led the field but failed to obtain a majority. Pitted in a runoff against former attorney general Frank Holt, McMath was offered MacKrell's support for $25,000 but turned down the deal.

The runoff turned dirty as Holt launched eight racist charges against McMath. The Coughlin brothers printed much McMath material, and George Fisher contributed cartoons. However, it may have been well-placed money that insured McMath's victory by taking steps to prevent those notorious late-night, long-delayed results from altering the outcome.

At any rate, the newly elected McMath administration was committed to modernization. Initiated Act 1 of 1948 reduced the number of school districts from 1,598 to 424. Diverting funds from black schools was stopped, and funding was increased for AM&N at Pine Bluff. McMath promised some paved road for every county under a new highway program financed by bonds if voters approved. Fiscal conservative Alex Washburn at Hope, after recalling that the disastrous spending spree in the late 1920s had resulted in bonds that still were not paid off, asked, "Can Arkansas with her past record on a single bond issue feel safe in attempting to manage two issues?"[1040] Nevertheless, McMath pushed through his program and won a second term. Not surprisingly, he appeared on the cover of *Arkansas Publisher* signing a proclamation declaring "Newspaperboy Day." Despite all the earlier pronouncements, not one of the 11 carriers pictured was a girl.[1041]

McMath's rise to power coincided with the return of newspapermen to politics. Laud Payne of the *Piggott Banner*, who had left his house seat to enter the navy, returned in 1946. Others in the house included Clarence Taylor (*Phillips County Herald*), Thomas J. Allen (Brinkley *Citizen* and Clarendon *Monroe County Sun*), and Republican James R. Tudor (Marshall *Mountain Wave*). In the Senate were the venerable Walter W. Raney (*Central Arkansas Leader*) and W.M. Jackson (*McGehee Times*).

However, when McMath tried for the ill-fated third term, a variety of forces lined up against him. Most of the opposition was tied to McMath's having offended AP&L by supporting the co-ops' request for a generating plant at Ozark. His enemies created the Highway Audit Commission whose highly publicized hearing claimed fraud existed in the highway program. Political conservatism was growing, with Searcy, home to Harding College, its seedbed. There, during the 1950s and 1960s, one was greeted by highway signs reading, "Impeach Earl Warren" on one side, and "Get Us Out of the U.N." on the other. Labor unions, the income tax, and a horticultural program covertly entitled "One World of Flowers" were all regarded as part of the Communist conspiracy.

Publishers agreed, at least with the labor union part, for stereotypers had shut down Little Rock's newspapers for one day in May 1946.[1042] By far the most important strike took place at the *Gazette* starting just before Christmas 1949. The American Newspaper Guild, a member of the Congress of Industrial Organization (CIO), had been certified in September by the National Labor Relations Board. According to union accounts, the newspaper then tried to fire union members, alleging incompetence. Publisher Hugh Patterson insisted the issue was who would determine the content of the news, the *Gazette* editors or the union. One union member who refused to cross the picket lines was columnist Hardy "Spider" Rowland, and it is ironic that a man whose insider political writings made him the most read and quoted writer for the newspaper ended his career with a meek little piece on the upcoming Christmas. This, the important postwar labor dispute in Arkansas, was almost completely ignored by the *Publisher*. Three months into the strike, it noted that Robert Poteete, a former member of the editorial staff and the editor of the workers' publication, *Strike*, had taken a job with the *New York Herald-Tribune*.[1043] *Strike* initially enlisted "Spider" Rowland to continue his column, but he quit over the issue of censorship. The *Gazette*'s main union, the International Typographers Union, crossed the picket lines, and a secondary boycott failed. In time, some strikers, like Robert Douglas, were rehired and the affair largely forgotten.

The most anti-union publisher in Arkansas was Clyde E. Palmer. At Texarkana after the ITU went out on strike, the national ITU resorted to putting out its own newspaper, the *Daily News-Digest*. This strategy, which was used in a number of markets, was called the Uni-typo group. The ITU lost heavily in the venture, and on April 23, 1954, the Texarkana newspaper closed.[1044]

Arkansas publishers had in Jimmy Karam a volunteer strikebreaker. This Chicot County son of Lebanese immigrants had the reputation as a street fighter, and he hated unions. Once, during a labor dispute in Walnut Ridge, Karam showed up ready to fight. He first proclaimed himself a racial liberal and had a large black patronage at his clothing store in

A Tribute to Tom Shiras: "Arkansas' Toscanini of the Ozarks"

The death of Baxter Bulletin *editor Tom Shiras on January 17, 1947, inspired this heartfelt appreciation, signed simply "A Tribute from a Friend," which goes far in expressing the quintessence of journalism as a service profession governed by loftier standards than ordinary work and with posthumous rewards for work well done.*

"Only Heaven could possibly be a better place to live than in my beautiful Arkansas Ozarks."

Those were the words of Tom Shiras...the same Tom Shiras who came lumbering out of the hills of Kansas to become one of the great institutions of his beloved state of Arkansas.

North Arkansas is going to miss Tom Shiras. The newspaper profession for many miles around Mountain Home will miss him. For few men have climbed to such towering heights as did Tom Shiras without achieving fame and fortune in their commonest meanings.

"Unique" is the lone word that fittingly describes this great character who has just passed to the eternal editorial room above, where his typewriter will no doubt fit as harmoniously into the symphony of these heavenly hosts as any instrument ever fitted into a Toscanini orchestra.

Tom Shiras was a member of the first basketball team that Naismith had when he invented the new game. But Kansas City was too confining for his restless spirit.

Tom Shiras walked through the Ozarks calling on subscribers...picking up bits of news about them and their neighbors which he printed in his paper. He passed on advice and suggestion for better farming, and extended many helpful hints.

Soon after acquiring the *Baxter Bulletin*, Tom noticed where a prize was being offered for a name of a new safety razor, or cigarette, or some other product. He submitted a name and it won a prize—a new printing press.

All of the parts but one arrived. The local blacksmith made a substitute part that worked fine. That prized old press turned out many an issue of the Bulletin.

As Tom strode through the hill country, and later introduced the first Model T Ford, he heard all

Little Rock; after 1957, he became actively associated with Orval Faubus.

Labor unions really never had a day in the sun in Arkansas. Despite nationwide strikes by coal miners, railroad workers, telephone operators, timber workers, and just about every other union, local industries in Arkansas kept unions at bay. Part of the postwar economic strategy had been the passage of a right to work law, and nationally the Taft-Hartley Act of 1948 weakened unions, especially the ITU. Ray Kimball's labor-saving teletypesetting circle was growing into a national movement, and curiously a *Publisher* article celebrating its 10th anniversary gave all the credit to Clyde Palmer, never once mentioning Kimball.[1045]

Meanwhile, the Korean War had broken out, causing new dislocations. Louis Graves, formerly a city editor in Texarkana, had just purchased the *Nashville News* when as an ex-marine he was called back into active duty. "I guess those three things—family, friends and the News—make this the toughest war-leaving I've endured," he wrote from California.[1046]

In 1952, McMath went down to defeat, undone by Francis Cherry whose campaign gimmick was talking on the radio—for 24 hours straight on one famous occasion (July 2, 1952). By that time, the Coughlins were gone. Pete, a Reserve pilot, was back

---

kinds of stories of natural phenomena. He visited them and wrote about them for his newspaper. Other papers in other sections being asking him to report for them. The *Kansas City Star* used his items regularly, as did the *Arkansas Gazette*, the *Commercial Appeal* and others. He turned down many offers to move and work elsewhere, but to all such offers that could have brought him wealth and fame his answer was always the same—"No, I'm too satisfied here in my Ozarks."

He loved to be his own master, to work when he pleased, to rest when he pleased. He traveled a far-flung territory. No metropolitan reporter ever dug as diligently into facts and figures as Tom did when trailing a yarn.

He wrote in his own distinct style...just like he talked, in a natural, understandable and entertaining manner. As you read his copy it was almost as if you could see him standing there in front of you, telling the story in his deep bass voice. His interesting outpourings of the lives and loves of the people of the hills made you want to meet the individuals he wrote about.

He sold advertising, printing, paper stock and office supplies. But he gave away the greatest thing that a man has to give—an ever-ready smile, a hearty handshake, and sincere good wishes.

Although a giant of a man, he was blessed with a gentle nature. He was a sign and symbol of a section that appreciated his friendship. He liked people—people liked him.

It is not difficult now to imagine Tom, sitting at that venerable old Underwood, doing his greatest masterpiece. You can almost hear the words as they roll off the keys:

> "If you will walk down the golden streets to where they merge into a single golden avenue...continue down the avenue to its golden archway...there you will observe an opening in the fleecy white clouds, revealing below, in all of its glory, a sight as beautiful as all of the gold—the hills and valleys of the beautiful Ozarks of Arkansas."*

**Arkansas Publisher*, XVII (January 1947), 3.

---

in active service in Korea and Jack, the "guts of the paper," had found work selling printing presses for the American Type Foundry.[1047]

Governor Francis Cherry served only two years. The Democratic candidate who unseated him in the primary in 1954 was Orval Faubus, a former McMath highway commissioner. "One of us," proclaimed the *Publisher*, but it was less than completely true. Faubus had found owning the county weekly a useful adjunct to his political ambitions, and although he became a practical printer, his real interest was in politics.[1048] Some additional political education may have come from a printer he hired. William H.V. Wahlquist, founder of the *Mammoth Spring Democrat* (1890), the *Phillips County Herald* (1939), and father to 22 children, half of them orphans, had served for eight years in the legislature.

Politically, Orval seemed a long shot. When he first went to Little Rock intending to announce, Arkansas's kingmaker, bond profiteer Witt Stephens, told him that if he ran, his friend, Congressman Jim Trimble, would find himself in trouble. Orval left town, telling the press that he would not run "at this time." When he showed up in Little Rock again, on the last day to file, it was too late for Witt to field a candidate against Trimble. Politically, Faubus ran as a liberal, attacking, for example, the incumbent's record on welfare. Cherry had called the aged welfare recipients "deadheads" and trimmed many from the welfare roles. Faubus brought tears to eyes of his rural audiences by telling of widows who no longer had enough money to bury themselves or keep their garden and chickens. A famous photograph of the time showed the effects that followed the closing of the Confederate Home so that the land could be sold for the bauxite underlying it. The home's aged residents (all women) looked ill and out of sorts in their non-air-conditioned quonset huts at Camp Robinson where they died off rapidly during the summer, to Faubus's political advantage.

The most serious charge launched against Faubus was that he was a Communist. Former *Gazette* star reporter John F. Wells, publisher of *Arkansas Record*, was largely responsible for circulating these reports based on the Commonwealth College records that Mena editor E.W. St. John had so assiduously collected. Faubus at first tried to deny the charge. Finally, Harry Ashmore crafted a tear-jerking speech of innocent involvement Faubus read on radio. The radio time had been purchased by Edwin E. Dunaway, a prominent Urban League supporter.

Ashmore and the *Gazette* were involved in the campaign in another way. A pro-Cherry advertisement in the *Democrat* accused the *Gazette* of favoring Faubus editorially. Ashmore called the charge "a deliberate and calculated untruth" that impugned the newspaper's integrity.[1049] Faubus was doubtless helped by his GI associations, his folksy rhetorical style, and the national reaction building to the excesses of Wisconsin Senator Joseph McCarthy's anti-Communist witch hunt. Another GI, advertiser Ted Lamb, later noted for his pro-integration stance on the Little Rock school board and as a founder of the Arkansas chapter of the American Civil Liberties Union, helped Faubus win a close race. So strong was his support in Madison County that 104 percent of the registered voters turned out to cast their ballots. No one at the time had any forewarning that the Faubus the state had elected was not the Faubus it would for so long have.

Skirts in all the Offices

In 1947, the *Publisher* ran a photograph of a "scratching post" from the mid-winter meeting at the Marion Hotel. The post, which attracted much attention in the lobby, had a turnstile on top with messages about "Arkansas, the Nation's Fastest Growing State," highway safety, balanced farming, and other current topics. What was remarkable about this artifact was that it carried at the top "For

Newspaper Men & Women." Men were "back"; women were "scratching."[1050]

One of the oldest scratchers received a tribute in November 1946 when her picture appeared on the cover of the *Publisher*. Maud Duncan, Lessie Stringfellow Read proclaimed, was the "dean of women journalists."[1051] Time and the economic decline of Winslow had not treated kindly with, as Roberta Fulbright phrased it, this "tiny piece of inspired humanity who embodies the spirit of the hills, the quality of its rocks," but the newspaper still came out from time to time.[1052] At the mid-winter meeting she was given a certificate of life membership. Then the next issue had Roberta Fulbright pictured on the cover. The owner of the Fayetteville newspaper since her husband's death in 1923, she was a power in local affairs and a force to be reckoned with in state politics.[1053]

The third to be recognized was Eunice B. O'Baugh of the Pocahontas *Star Herald*. The daughter of L.F. Blankenship, she and her brother assumed management of the newspaper in 1935. Like Roberta Fulbright, she wrote a column on local affairs and other topics that interested her.[1054]

All this was prelude to the organization in 1948 of the Arkansas Newspaper Women's Association (subsequently renamed the Arkansas Press Women in 1954), an auxiliary to the APA. Roberta Fulbright, together with Walter Lemke, Bill Minor, and Eloise Castleberry, were behind a unique summer meeting in 1949 that was held on the University campus and featured seminars rather than parties. (Apparently this idea did not "take," for the Association soon reverted to its usual summertime frivolities.)

Preparatory to this meeting, Roberta issued a call to all the women to come and join. Mary Louise Wright, who had succeeded J.M. Henderson at De Witt, Esther Bindursky, Maud Duncan, and Margaret Woolfolk were among those who sent letters of support. The only opposition to the idea of a separate women's group came from Aline Murray at Wynne: "I am always opposed to segregating men and women engaged in business and professional organizations because I don't think it benefits the business or profession and works to the disadvantage of women who are trying to advance themselves and gain recognition purely on the basis of ability and qualifications." But she agreed to join.[1055]

The first meeting made Roberta Fulbright the honorary president for life, while Mrs. M.P. Jones of Searcy was the first president. Esther Bindursky (Lepanto) was first vice president; Mrs. Ray Kimball (De Queen), second vice president; Mrs. Ells L. Huff (*Jackson County Democrat*), secretary; Kate Gillespie (*De Valls Bluff Democrat*), treasurer (her brother, readers will recall, had served the APA in that capacity back in the late '20s and early '30s); and other board members were Mrs. Tom Allen (*Monroe County Citizen*) and Mrs. Walter W. Raney (McCrory). These married women did have first names, but the *Publisher* chose not to use them. Married women would have to scratch for that right, for the prevailing etiquette held that married women could use their first names only if they were divorced.

It is worthy of observation that probably two-thirds of the members were wives who had come to the profession by marriage. One of the professional single females present at the creation was Esther Bindursky, and there were some who still thought that women should concentrate on society columns. Bindursky, who both knew and sometimes deployed swear words, portended the future. As for the former Charlotte Tillar, she had married chemist Melvin Schexnayder and was out of state at the time. However, she turned her chemist-husband into a journalist, and after W.M. Jackson refused to sell them the *McGehee Times*, they bought the *Dumas Clarion*. In 1955 she was elected APW president. The APA gave the women their own page in the *Publisher*, and at the annual meeting teas and style shows predominated for many years.

While most newspaper women continued to "do" the society section and pinch hit as needed, Esther Bindursky, editor of the *Lepanto News-Record* since its founding, was honored as "Woman of the Year" in that small town in 1960. The cash award of $1575 allowed her to participate in the 1960 National Editorial Association's European Study Mission to Denmark, Sweden, Poland, Russia, and other countries.[1056]

Although the APW survived, activists of the 1970s considered it to be dominated by "do nothing old women." Affiliated with the NFPW (National Federation of Press Women), it undertook a 1978 survey of wages paid women that yielded dismal statistics. A constitutional change in 1977 opened the organization to male members. Perhaps the group's most enduring accomplishment was the publication in 1980 of *Horizons: 100 Arkansas Women of Achievement*, the sales of which supported funding an adequate scholarship.[1057]

Turmoil on the Tripod

Just as many returning GIs wanted to find fulfillment in farming or get the education they had been denied, those with a journalism background sought to own their own newspapers. Their postwar stories were often studies in frustration. William and Connie Stuck Shelton's marriage did not survive long in Marked Tree. They divorced and quietly at the beginning of 1947 she reverted to her maiden name, while he became the city editor of the *Arkansas Gazette*. Her brother Howard, who had come to assist, stayed, and after Connie headed off to a career in the diplomatic service, Howard and his wife Dorothy continued to publish the newspapers. The burden fell increasingly on the ex-history teacher, for Howard was one of those adults who fell victim to poliomyelitis during the pre-Salk epidemic years of the early 1950s. O.C. Shaver, long of the Evening Shade *Sharp County Record*, was among the older victims of this crippling disease, and in recognition of the threat polio posed, the APA created an editorial contest on the physically handicapped in 1954. At Hot Springs, the first awards were made to Gordon Freeman of the *Pine Bluff Commercial* and Bryan McGinnis of the *West Memphis News*. Noted polio victim Marjorie Lawrence, a Wagnerian soprano and resident of Hot Springs, sang at the awards ceremony.

Turmoil of a different sort came in Batesville. O.E. Jones, considered both a rising politician and good newspaperman, died unexpectedly of a heart attack in 1949. His widow, Josephine Carroll Jones, continued on, and a disabled war veteran, Paul Buchanan, took over as editor. The newspaper's business manager, Wilson Powell, did much of the local reporting and kept his hand on the pulse of the county by accompanying the county agricultural agent on his rounds. The daily *Guard* and weekly *Record* had to contend with the *News-Review*, owned after 1957 by Farrell Conner. His nine-year-old son Billy flirted with fame. A television pilot created by Harold Sherman entitled "The Amazing Adventures of My Dog Kelly" starred young Billy and featured a cameo appearance by Jimmy Driftwood. Billy's picture appeared on the cover of *Life Magazine* on August 29, 1955. Only the pilot episode was filmed, fortunately for Arkansas's bobcat population, whose unwilling participation in the pilot was achieved by trapping and killing nine of the animals. After 1958, the *Guard* and *Record* had the market to themselves.

In Russellville, the death of J.A. Livingston left a void not easily filled. His daughter, Rita Fay, had moved to New York and had no interest in returning. Leasing the newspaper, which never seems to have worked anywhere, failed, and the *Courier-Democrat* passed in 1951 to a group of partners that included both Clyde Palmer and Senator J. William Fulbright. This arrangement, too, did not work out, and in 1955 John Guion of the *Paris Express* and *Progress* acquired the daily.

In Booneville, Max Hampton resolved to retire and passed the reins to his son, Lester ("Buddy"), whose fatal heart attack in 1956 undid the arrangement. The bereaved father resumed working until his death in 1958. His wife, together with his daughter and son-in-law, Dorothy and Val S. Zachariah, assumed the reigns for the next 10 years.

Another veteran who passed from the scene disrupted the APA in the process. J.H. Beerstecher, who had constructed a mini-Palmer chain in south-central Arkansas centered on Malvern, died shortly after being made APA president in 1948. The APA could have elevated his wife, a veteran in her own right, but instead chose to select another old-timer, "Mike" Gillespie, to take over for the remainder of his term. The *Malvern Daily Record* continued under the widow and her daughters, Frances and Mrs. Alix Butler.

Disruption came to the APA in 1953 when the presidential line of succession was broken by Hugh Park, who violated APA rules by not being present at the meeting in which he was to have been elected. J.E. Dunlap of the weekly *Boone County Headlight* unexpectedly became president.

Dunlap, who had started as a high school reporter in Harrison before the war, had acquired the weekly *Headlight* from G.L. Wright. It competed with the *Harrison Daily Times* that had dropped its weekly edition in 1937. The Newman males tended to die at early ages. In 1954, Dunlap became the president and publisher of the *Times*. In time the surviving girls sold their stock to Dunlap, thus putting "30" to another dynasty.

Other changes took place at McCrory where in 1953 Walter W. Raney sold out to Harlan V. Walker. At De Witt, M.D. Braswell acquired the *Era-Enterprise* and Mary Louise Wright, a sort of female counterpart to De Witt's J.M. Henderson, became the editor. C.H. Brown sold the West Memphis *Crittenden County Times* to a group headed by Margaret Woolfolk. In 1954, the *Times* went to semi-weekly status and then became the daily *Evening Times* in 1957, ending the weekly edition in 1960. Interestingly, the state's five most prominent women editors, Mary Louise Wright(De Witt), Charlotte Schexnayder (Dumas), Esther Bindurksy (Lepanto), Dorothy Stuck (Marked Tree), and Margaret Woolfolk were all working in adjacent counties.

Two greatly contrasting events illustrated the conflicts of the age. The first came in Des Arc, where C.J. Walls, the son of *White River Journal* founder C.A. Walls, bought his first Linotype machine in 1954. Apparently, there were still two newspapers set by hand.[1058]

The other event was the appearance in the unlikely town of Paragould of a new newspaper printed entirely by offset. *The Big Picture* started as a weekly in 1948, becoming a twice-a-week and then a thrice-a-week before becoming an Associated Press daily in 1952. Iowan John J. Mueller was publisher. A 1953 plane crash cost the newspaper Stuart Mueller, the publisher's brother and the layout and makeup artist, and Steve Rizzo, the advertising manager. Although the newspaper endured for some years, Mrs. Mueller said it was "never fun again."[1059] No other newspapers followed the Muellers' early lead.

There was turmoil as well at the APA. During Bill Miner's illness, day to day continuity was provided by office manager Eloise Castleberry. Miner and Castleberry made a notable effort to revive the *Publisher*'s earlier role as chronicler of activities around the state. In addition Miner vigorously sought out an increasing amount of corporate advertising. Fortunately for the historian, he did print biographies of early presidents and material on the early history of the Association.

His successor in 1950 was William H. Parker, a University of Missouri graduate most recently of the defunct *Clarendon Herald*. Two years later William G.

On June 20, 1975, members of the Local 59 Pressmen Union went on strike in front of the Arkansas Democrat Building.

The Scratching Post, 1947. There was more than humor at this convention as APA president Ells Huff stands next to the poster proclaiming that men were back and women would now have to scratch. (APA Archives)

Revitalizing the Arkansas Democrat, *1968: president C. Stanley Berry, vice-president Marcus B. George, secretary-treasurer Ray Morrow, board member Austin McCaskiell welcome Robert McCord to the board. (APA Archives)*

APA mid-winter convention, Marion Hotel, Little Rock, 1950. Themes and banners became increasingly important in the Cold War. Notice most of the women wore hats, the fashion of the day. (APA Archives)

An original comic strip, 1956. This original comic strip panel hangs in the conference room of the APA Building. It is inscribed: "For the Little Rock Press Club, with all good wishes," and is autographed: "Milton Caniff, N.Y., Feb., 1956."

Certificates of appreciation were handed out to four veterans of the industry, c. 1950. Left to right: W.J. Lemke, J.N. Heiskell (seated), Clyde E. Palmer, and K.A. Engel. (APA Archives)

Governor Winthrop Rockefeller signs the Arkansas Freedom of Information Act, February 14, 1967. Looking on are Bob McCord, who led the effort, and co-sponsoring legislators Senator Ben Allen, Little Rock, and Rep. Leon Holsted, North Little Rock. (Courtesy APA Archives)

The APA Board of Directors, 1954. Standing left to right: Calvin Mannen, Ellis Ramsey, Andy Murray, Sam Gearhart, Bob Fisher, K.A. Engel; Seated: J.E. Dunlap and a clean-shaven Brad Govan. (Photo by Gene Prescott; APA Archives)

Jim Morriss, editor of the Springdale News, *is shown c. 1967 at his desk when the* News *was still located at 133 West Emma in downtown Springdale. He retired in 2003 after 53 years at that newspaper. (Courtesy Maudine Sanders/Shiloh Museum of Ozark History)*

Press Day at the Livestock Show and Rodeo, Marion Hotel. Editors were featured in this presentation. "A free press, the greatest builders of Democracy," Col. T.H. Barton proclaimed. (Photo by Leonard & Reynolds Studio; APA Archives)

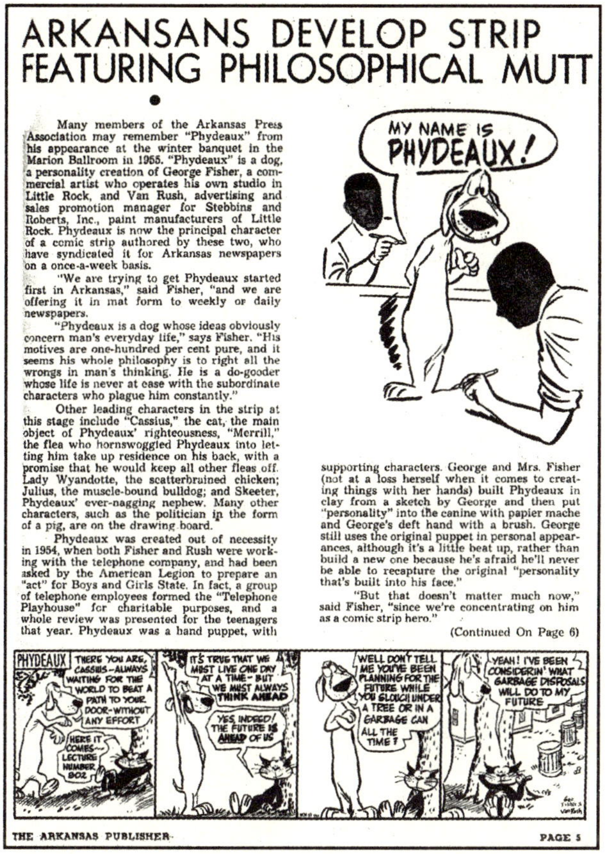

ARKANSANS DEVELOP STRIP FEATURING PHILOSOPHICAL MUTT

Many members of the Arkansas Press Association may remember "Phydeaux" from his appearance at the winter banquet in the Marion Ballroom in 1955. "Phydeaux" is a dog, a personality creation of George Fisher, a commercial artist who operates his own studio in Little Rock, and Van Rush, advertising and sales promotion manager for Stebbins and Roberts, Inc., paint manufacturers of Little Rock. Phydeaux is now the principal character of a comic strip authored by these two, who have syndicated it for Arkansas newspapers on a once-a-week basis.

"We are trying to get Phydeaux started first in Arkansas," said Fisher, "and we are offering it in mat form to weekly or daily newspapers.

"Phydeaux is a dog whose ideas obviously concern man's everyday life," says Fisher. "His motives are one-hundred per cent pure, and it seems his whole philosophy is to right all the wrongs in man's thinking. He is a do-gooder whose life is never at ease with the subordinate characters who plague him constantly."

Other leading characters in the strip at this stage include "Cassius," the cat, the main object of Phydeaux' righteousness, "Merrill," the flea who hornswoggled Phydeaux into letting him take up residence on his back, with a promise that he would keep all other fleas off. Lady Wyandotte, the scatterbrained chicken; Julius, the muscle-bound bulldog; and Skeeter, Phydeaux' ever-nagging nephew. Many other characters, such as the politician in the form of a pig, are on the drawing board.

Phydeaux was created out of necessity in 1954, when both Fisher and Rush were working with the telephone company, and had been asked by the American Legion to prepare an "act" for Boys and Girls State. In fact, a group of telephone employees formed the "Telephone Playhouse" for charitable purposes, and a whole review was presented for the teenagers that year. Phydeaux was a hand puppet, with supporting characters. George and Mrs. Fisher (not at a loss herself when it comes to creating things with her hands) built Phydeaux in clay from a sketch by George and then put "personality" into the canine with papier mache and George's deft hand with a brush. George still uses the original puppet in personal appearances, although it's a little beat up, rather than build a new one because he's afraid he'll never be able to recapture the original "personality that's built into his face."

"But that doesn't matter much now," said Fisher, "since we're concentrating on him as a comic strip hero."

(Continued On Page 6)

THE ARKANSAS PUBLISHER PAGE 5

After returning from West Memphis where he had worked for the Coughlin brothers, George Fisher eschewed journalism in order to practice commercial art. In 1955 he and Van Rush, an advertising and promotion manager for paint manufacturer Stebbins and Roberts, syndicated a new cartoon strip for Arkansas newspapers. It did not endure. (APA Archives)

Fisher cartoon, August 9, 1981. Fisher had already made the farkleberry bush the symbol of Orval Faubus. For Governor Frank White it became a banana, in reference to White's having signed the Creation Science Act. When White appointed the elderly Faubus to a state job, Fisher responded with this cartoon.

Bradley Pioneer

Serving Bradley, Walkers Creek, State Line, Canfield, N. Bossier Parish, And The Red River Valley Communities

Volume 4 — Number 12 BRADLEY, ARKANSAS, THURSDAY, AUGUST 8, 1963 PRICE FIVE CENTS

Several newspapers in Arkansas at times were owned by chambers of commerce. The Pioneer at Bradley was created by the local chamber.

Harry Ashmore strikes a pose. The editor of the editorial page of the Arkansas Gazette *became nationally famous during the Central High School crisis in 1957. (Courtesy, Special Collections, University of Arkansas Libraries)*

The famous Arkansas Gazette Library, assembled by J.N. Heiskell and presided over by Margaret Smith Ross, 1966. (Courtesy J.N. Heiskell Collection, UALR Archives & Special Collections)

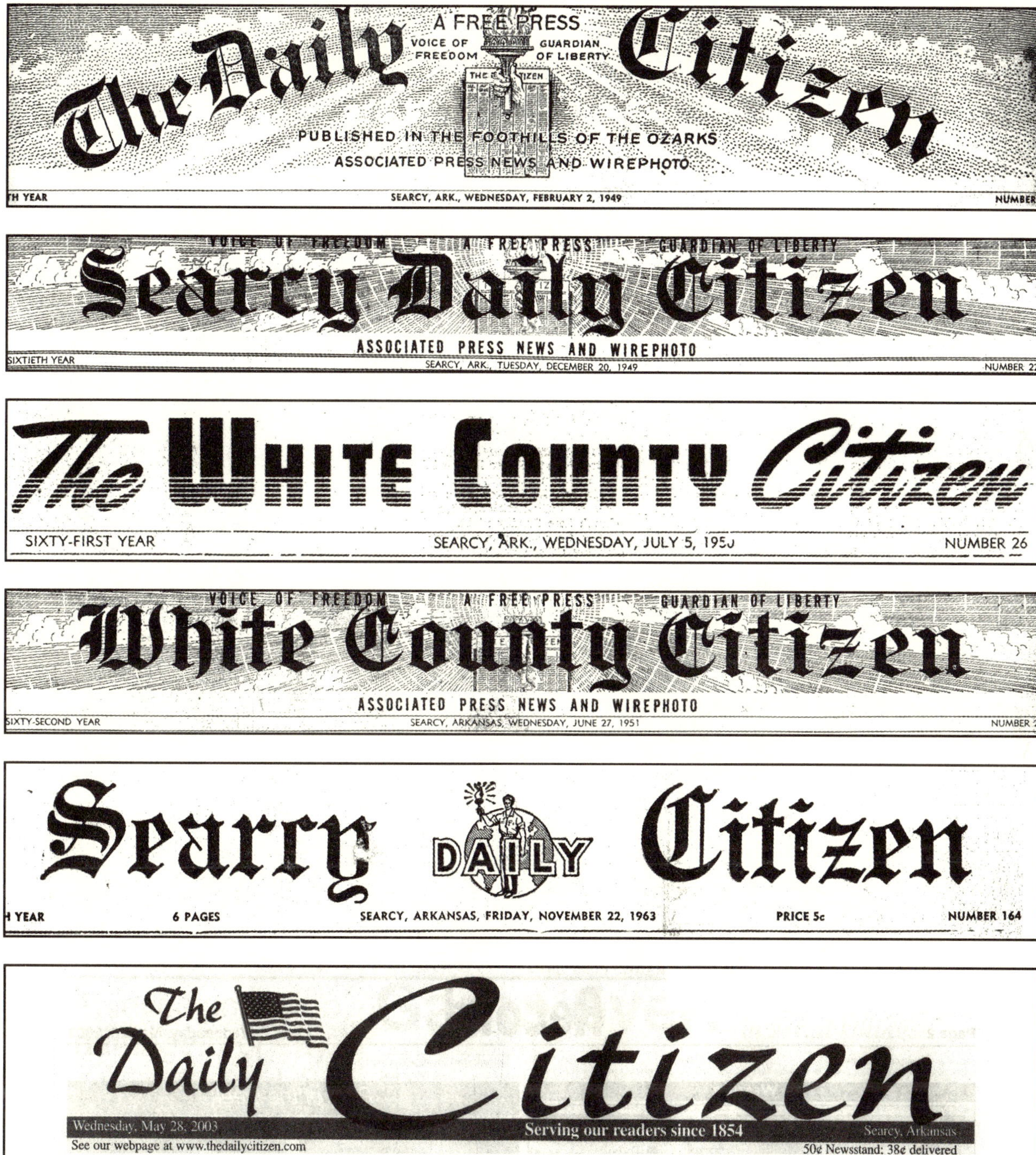

The metamorphosis of one newspaper's banners over the years.

Conley succeeded him. Conley, a former printer's devil in Booneville, had worked on newspapers at Magnolia, West Memphis, and Stuttgart and owned the *Mountain View Herald* at the time of his appointment.

Under Conley the content of the *Arkansas Publisher* shrunk even further, although nice color pictures were featured on the cover. At times the publication failed to keep a monthly schedule, and the removal of volume and issue numbers caused a loss of institutional integrity. Even the Bible quotations disappeared.

During Conley's administration, the Association found itself in an embarrassing financial predicament. One of the advantages to newspapers that the manager system offered was in the placement of advertisements. The Association dealt with advertising agencies and collected for the state's publishers, taking a small commission. In 1956, there was not enough money to pay the publishers their due; APA president Sam Hodges arranged for a loan to get the Association over the hump. After Conley left in June 1960 to work for the Brooks-Pollard Company, Ray G. Cooper, who had been at the Russellville *Courier-Democrat*, took over briefly before being followed by Jerry Russell, later well known for his use of radio jingles in political advertising, his work to preserve Civil War battlefields, and for creating the umbrella organization, the Civil War Roundtable Associates. Stability returned only in 1962 when office manager Louise Bowker, who intended to work for only one year, was promoted to manager and stayed for 20.

The Age of Orval Faubus

In 1965, when Governor Orval Eugene Faubus delivered his sixth inaugural address to the state legislature, cartoonist George Fisher drew the governor's sagging countenance on every legislator, every reporter, every portrait on the walls, and even on a baby in the audience and a mouse under the lectern. The unprecedented Faubus ascendancy was directly the result of the United States Supreme Court's unanimous decision in *Brown v. Board of Education* (1954), which overturned the segregationist ruling of *Plessy v. Ferguson* (1896). Over the next 15 years it was the Supreme Court, not the Congress, presidents, or the states, that ushered in an era of liberal social change.

In 1954, all of Arkansas's liberals on the matter of race would not have filled the Gar Hole bar at the Marion Hotel. Most were in Little Rock, like Judge Edwin E. Dunaway or advertiser Ted Lamb. Neither the *Gazette* nor the *Democrat* had anything but a generalized opposition to the civil rights movement; indeed the *Democrat* was ahead of the *Gazette* in printing black obituaries and other social news, and in hiring Ozell Sutton in 1950 as its "Negro reporter." Governor Orval Faubus, the son of a Socialist, was supposed at least to be a moderate—until political circumstances demanded otherwise.

The first reactions to the *Brown* decision varied. The *Pine Bluff Commercial*, whose influence extended all over southeast Arkansas, was, with the *Gazette*, one of the few newspapers to support the decision.[1060] Knowing that its readers would not be enthusiastic, it cautioned against violent resistance. Pine Bluff's local weekly, the *Star-Reporter*, took two different views. Editor John Robert Starr proclaimed that "non-segregation is already here," while business manager Kenneth Parsons on the same page found the decision to be an example of "the tremendous tendency toward almighty federal power."[1061] One of the strongest early attacks came from one of the state's oldest editors. Clarence Byrns of the Fort Smith *Southwest American* asserted that integration was an "unnatural association" in "direct contravention of the laws of nature," for "eagles were not meant to fly with parrots, nor the peacock with the wild geese."[1062]

Across much of Arkansas, integration was a non-issue. Fayetteville integrated to save transporting its black high school students back and forth daily to Fort Smith. The penalty it paid was being unable to play high school football in Arkansas. The University of Arkansas had already integrated its law school, sticking Silas Hunt in a little cage marked "Colored" at the back of the room and denying him access to library. Law professor Robert Leflar, who still continued preparing analyses of constitutional amendments for APA newspapers, helped engineer the collapse of this system.

What was theoretical turned practical after the Supreme Court issued *Brown* II, the enforcement decision, in which Justice Felix Frankfurter defined progress as "all deliberate speed." The *Arkansas Democrat*, which still believed that better Negro schools would solve the problem, hailed the decision, claiming that "common sense has won a victory," a "victory for orderly change paced to local conditions."[1063]

Meanwhile, segregationists in Congress adopted the Southern Manifesto declaring the *Brown* decisions unconstitutional and re-instituting the doctrine of interposition—that the states could nullify the actions of the federal government. The *Democrat* lauded the Manifesto, naively asserting that since the South (i.e, the White South) had spoken, the Supreme Court would now give up on integration. The *Gazette*, whose editorial position changed daily depending on who was doing the writing, had endorsed interposition earlier, but now called the Manifesto merely a declaration of accepted principles. Thus it was left to Bud Reid at the *Jacksonville News-Progress* to point out the Manifesto was really a declaration of war on the nation and to take the state's delegation to task for signing it: "Heaven help those within [Arkansas's] borders if the governor and other constitutional officers bend to the will of a few extremists."[1064]

The war of words took a different turn when the school board at Hoxie, a small Lawrence County town with only a smattering of blacks, decided to close its small and inadequate black school and merge the students into the white district. While the same thing was happening all across the upper South, Hoxie was less than 100 miles from the heartland of Arkansas segregation. In this unlikely little town the first major skirmish of the Age of Civil Rights struggles was played out. After local segregationists brought in James Johnson and other extremists to disrupt the process, school board attorney Bill Penix, the former journalist, got a federal injunction to stop them, thus laying the ground work for all subsequent federal court involvement in the desegregation process.

Across the Delta and South Arkansas, segregation was the Arkansas way of life, and in James Johnson of Crossett it found its Moses. Johnson was responsible for drafting a proposed constitutional amendment to nullify the Brown decision, and in 1956 he ran for governor in the Democratic primary. With polls showing 85 percent of white Arkansans opposed integration, Faubus ran to catch up with his people.

After his first strategy of trying to keep race out of the election failed, Faubus turned on Johnson and the White Citizens Councils with a vengeance. Johnson's campaign linked race with sex, added the poor Southern white male's disdain for proprieties, and delivered this message in a rhetorical style full of the fire of fundamentalism. Through television and a publication appropriately called *Arkansas Faith*, Johnson portrayed Faubus as a Communist and integrationist. Even W.L. Love (APA president, 1949) at the segregationist Warren *Eagle Democrat* found Johnson to be too extreme.[1065] Moreover, Johnson had a weakness in that his principal publicist, Curt Copeland, a sometime owner of the *Montgomery County News* and of a libelous periodical called the *Hot Springs Rubdown*, was a convicted counterfeiter with a long criminal record. While Faubus may have appeared moderate to the *Gazette*, Pete Shiras at Mountain Home's *Baxter Bulletin* found little difference between the two, damning both for their "attempt to fool the people by creating hatred and fear at a time when calm reasoning and honest self-examination are vitally important."[1066]

Meanwhile, as columnist J.R. McKinley of the *De Queen Citizen* advised his readers: "If there's a newspaper somewhere that hasn't quoted your reaction to the sgregation [*sic*] descision [*sic*], phone the editor right now and demand your rights."[1067] The APA was not kept in the dark on these matters. In 1954, at the same Hot Springs meeting where Marjorie Lawrence sang and the handicapped were recognized, Horace W. Carter, the Pulitzer Prize-winning editor of the *Tabor* (North Carolina) *Tribune*, told listeners that "segregation is economically impractical and morally wrong" and that it was their responsibility to educate the public for change.[1068]

Orval Faubus won renomination in the Democratic primary, but Johnson continued to lurk in the background, successfully promoting his nullification amendment as well as initiated acts on pupil placement and interposition. The *Southwest American* supported the two acts, but even Byrns could not stomach the amendment. Strongest in opposition was the *Baxter Bulletin*, where editor Tom Dearmore and business manager/columnist Pete Shiras predicted (correctly) that "these laws are all headed for a dead end, even if the voters of this state approve them by a tremendous majority."[1069]

A tremendous majority it was to be, and then in the new legislative session came more initiatives from segregationist East Arkansas. Worst was the Sovereignty Commission, "the most dangerous and undemocratic legislation ever introduced into the Arkansas legislature," asserted Shiras at the *Bulletin*.[1070] One future journalist, University of Arkansas student David Pryor, went to Little Rock planning to testify at a public hearing, but university officials, afraid for their budget, warned him off. Clarence Byrns, who regularly covered the solons, called the bill a menace to "everybody's rights."[1071] After the bill passed, Shiras pronounced it "a step backward" that "will cost the state dearly in future progress, in the constitutional rights of its citizens and in its reputation in the eyes of the nation."[1072] But this was heat lightning compared to what followed.

The storm hit Arkansas on September 4, 1957, when Governor Faubus called out the National Guard to defy a federal court order integrating Little Rock's Central High School. The crisis at Central High School became one of the nation's top news stories of the century, representing the first overt Southern state action in opposition to desegregation to be countered by the federal government. Media from all over the world descended on Little Rock, and the photographs of Larry Obsitnik at the *Gazette* and Will Counts at the *Democrat* became fixtures in magazines, documentaries, and textbooks. Counts won first prize in the national News Picture of the Year competition for his work.

The outside reporters in Little Rock faced culture shock, since Arkansas banned the open sale of mixed drinks. The news hounds were thirsty, and the reestablished Little Rock Press Club did quite a business. *Gazette* people were disproportionately represented, and Harry Ashmore pontificated regularly.

The segregationist mob at Central, many of whose members came from Texas, specialized in attacking newsmen. Dr. Benjamin Fine, the *New York Times* education editor, was one of those who in Faubus's words, "created some problems on the school grounds that had to be handled." After being assaulted and called a dirty New York Jew, the editor was arrested for creating a riot. An even worse fate befell black Memphis reporter Alex Wilson when he covered the withdrawal of the troops on September

23rd. After the mob yelled, "Run, nigger, run," and Wilson replied, "I fought for my country, and I'm not going to run," his severe beating was captured on film.

At the *Gazette* building, the decision about what to do rested with the man who had borne the title of editor since 1913. John N. Heiskell had lectured his Southern colleagues in 1935 on the evils of using gruesome pictures and in 1948 on not recognizing the importance of the editorial page. Now he had either to fish or cut bait. His fateful decision contributed in no small way to the demise of his beloved newspaper.

"The Crisis Mr. Faubus Made" appeared the day after the National Guard was called out and became the most famous editorial in state history. Written by Harry Ashmore and approved by Heiskell, the editorial demonstrated that the issue was not segregation or integration, it was "the supremacy of the government of the United States in all matters of law." Heiskell's personal opinion, "I won't let people like that take over my town,"[1073] reflected his elitist view of the newspaper as a public servant.

With the governor's blessing, the segregationists not only took over the town but the state as well. In December they organized a boycott against the *Gazette* and threatened businesses that continued to advertise there. The newspaper lost 18 percent of its circulation but over $1,000,000 in revenues. In parts of the state its delivery agents were terrorized.

Other newspapers that supported integration suffered as well. Victor Ray at the *Union Labor Bulletin* lost one third of his subscribers. The *Gazette* won two Pulitzer Prizes, one for the newspaper, the other for Ashmore personally, the first time that both a newspaper and a writer had been recognized at the same time. A third Pulitzer was voted to Will Counts' stirring photographs, but the selection committee's decision was overruled by the Pulitzer Board, which did not want to give three Pulitzers for the same event.

Having entered into the state politics, the *Gazette* maintained its critical stance. Not all the strong editorials were written by Ashmore, for equally active in producing the newspaper's editorials was Jerry Neill.

Many weeklies were on Faubus's side. Bill Courtney of the *Wynne Progress* gave credit to Faubus for his "political courage," noting, "I can't help liking a governor who governs."[1074] More support came from the *Helena-West Helena World*, where the aged Charles M. Young blamed the crisis on the "radical press."[1075] Clarence Byrns, curiously, supported Faubus in calling out the Guard but apparently thought their purpose was to prevent violence, not to stop integration.[1076]

There were those who shared the *Gazette*'s point of view, even in the Delta. Sam Hodges privately considered segregation a relic of medievalism, while *Pine Bluff Commercial* owner E.W. Freeman III later observed, "In Arkansas in those days, what stood between us and barbarism was the Women's Emergency Committee and the *Arkansas Gazette*."[1077] Adolphine Fletcher Terry, who had called Little Rock women together, held the meeting at her home, the former Albert Pike house. The *Pine Bluff Commercial* waged its own war, and editor Paul Greenberg won a Pulitzer Prize in 1969 for an anti-segregationist editorial. Dean Guerdon D. Nichols, who had been at the University since 1928, won the prestigious Meiklejohn Award from the American Association of University Professors for leading the opposition to Act 10 of 1958 that required all state employees to reveal the names of organizations to which they belonged. Nichols, it turned out, was a Linotypist from a printing family and had worked his way partially through the University of Wisconsin in a print shop.

Meanwhile, the *Democrat* gained readers, not because it pandered to the extremists, but merely because it did less than the *Gazette*. On the editorial page, columnist Karr Shannon wrote so much on why the Supreme Court decisions were unconstitutional that they filled an entire book. At the same time, as national advertisers decided to ignore the boycott of the *Gazette*, the *Democrat* put out a booklet contrasting five editorials from each newspaper in order to show that the *Democrat* was equally moderate. "What they neglected to mention," Margaret Ross observed, "was that those five were the only ones the *Democrat* published on the subject, while the *Gazette* hit hard every day."[1078] As for Faubus, he became not only a three-term governor—the first since Jeff Davis—but added three more terms on top of that.

The Faubus victory was so complete that every aspect of state government fell under his control, and Orval was a man who knew the names of everybody of importance as well as everyone who worked for state government. Although he continued to push for better schools, homes for retarded children, and other progressive causes, those who did not line up with him spent a lonely decade. Furthermore, he never made another serious effort to stop integration, leaving that to Johnson and the cross-burning extremists.

The press in all this mostly hunkered down and hid. Very few were as forthright as Elizabeth Burrow at the Ozark *Spectator*. She wanted to wade into the controversy but the school superintendent "had forbidden us to print anything for fear of quotes in the *Gazette* survey of state editorial opinion, but the Ministerial Alliance was afraid of violence and thought the paper's voice would reach farther than theirs. So I promised the superintendent that the column would be booby-trapped so that not one paragraph could be quoted (and two of the ministers came to help me check on it)."[1079] No one had better Arkansas credentials. Her father had been the founder of the future Hendrix College and her mother's grandfather had served in the first state legislature, but Orval "somehow makes me feel a foreigner." After this staunch Methodist discovered she was dying in 1962, she used one of her last columns to denounce the state's pervasive racism as "a malignancy worse than my cancer and I wouldn't swap with you."[1080] What would she have thought had she known her surviving brother would later sell the family newspaper to Faubus?

Critic Tom Dearmore at the *Baxter Bulletin* was something of a victim, too. Long a personal friend of Faubus's and an appointee to the publicity commission, he was told to resign after criticizing the governor. Refusing to do so, he remained, giving trouble to the end of his term. In Dearmore's case, a Nieman award, the first awarded to an Arkansan, sent him to Harvard in 1959, and except for one brief stay at the *Gazette* in 1976, he spent the rest of his career in Washington and San Francisco.[1081]

Another victim was black publisher L.C. Bates of the *Arkansas State Press*. Bates had started his newspaper before World War II, and while hardly crusading, it had denounced police brutality in Little Rock during World War II. Mostly it demanded full equality on the "separate but equal" platform. Its most daring move had been to criticize a state judge for sentences he handed down on black strikers in 1946. Bates was jailed and fined for contempt of court, but the ruling was reversed by the state supreme court.[1082] In general, the newspaper resembled most weeklies, except that its locals came from Pine Bluff, Hot Springs, North Little Rock, and other points. It carried black comics and other features, but much of its news was centered on athletics, at least until things erupted in Little Rock.

Several strong editorials appeared during the Little Rock crisis, but they were the work of S.S. Taylor or Thresa Jones. The newspaper gave coverage to the black boycott of the *Commercial-Appeal* and took Faubus to task for his television comments on threats of violence when he waved dramatically what was believed to be a copy of the *State Press*. "Where do we go from here?" the newspaper asked in disgust after the governor called out the National Guard.[1083] Its call for blacks to "Pay your poll tax, and remember that your NAACP is under attack" coincided with the legislature's finding that the NAACP was part of the Communist conspiracy.[1084] Since their newspaper depended on white advertising, the notoriety L.C.'s wife, Daisy, gained as head of the NAACP undermined its finances and forced its suspension.

Ozell Sutton, The First Black Reporter for a White-owned Daily.

The 1998 fall issue of the *Arkansas News* contained Ozell Sutton's experiences as the state's first black reporter. He was one of only 38 blacks working in the nation's newsrooms. As Sutton recalled, in 1950 the *Arkansas Democrat* wanted to hire a black reporter and contacted black lawyer Robert "Bob" Booker, who recommended Sutton, then a senior at Philander Smith College. Sutton, who worked part-time during his last semester, became a full-time employee after graduating in May. "When I reported to the *Democrat*," he recalled, "my desk was so placed as to segregate me from the rest of the staff…My desk was placed behind the city and state desks facing the wall with my back to everybody else." His job was to report the news "as it impacted the black community"; Sutton called himself "a no assignment reporter."

Six months into the job Sutton arrived at work one day to find that his desk had been moved up beside the city desk; six months after that it was moved to be in line with the desks of the other reporters. Such was the progress of integration.

Sutton soon found an issue. Neither Little Rock newspaper (nor almost any other white-owned newspaper in the South) bestowed the titles of Mrs. or Miss on African-American women. Sutton suggested to Eddie Liske, the managing editor, that a change was needed. Liske rejected the idea, and while Sutton continued to use the titles in his copy, the editors continued to strike them out. Then Sutton decided to take another tack. Instead, for example "of writing Mrs. Joanna Sutton, I reverted to using Mrs. Ozell Sutton. This way if Mrs. was deleted, the wrong person would be identified. Each day when I came to work I fully expected to be fired." Called into Liske's office one day expecting the axe, Sutton was told instead that newspaper had decided to change its policy. It was, Sutton recalled, "a small step in the eternal struggle for the dignity of African Americans."

Sutton offered this assessment of his work at the *Democrat*: "I remained a general assignment reporter with no opportunity to work in a bureau. General assignment reporters don't advance like those in charge of bureaus. I could not expect to advance to an editor or assistant editor. I did find a degree of solace in feature writing and perfected it.

"All in all mine was both a learning and a teaching experience. I learned from the white world in which I found myself and too thought a little about the world out of which I came. My presence had a profound effect on the tone and content of white reporters' stories, and on some occasions the editorials."

Although the APA had no barrier in its constitution to blacks as members, there is no evidence the Bateses ever thought of joining. Also closed was the congressional career of Southern congressional moderate Brooks Hays, defeated by a write-in segregationist, Dale Alford, in 1958.

Harry Ashmore did not long remain in Arkansas. In 1955, while he was working for Adlai Stevenson's presidential campaign, Heiskell hired Ernie Deane as a temporary replacement. After returning from managing the press corps at the Nuremburg trials, Deane had bought a newspaper in Texas before being lured back to Arkansas. Unhappy in editorial work, he soon became a columnist, and with his "Arkansas Traveler" column, covered much of the state recording local doings.[1085] James O. Powell was Ashmore's true successor, and the liberalism Ashmore had instilled remained after his departure. "The *Gazette* seldom endorses any cause or action unless it is atheistic, immoral, or pro-Communist," Governor Faubus once declared.[1086]

On the other hand, a number of editors and publishers prospered under the regime. Tom Allen became a fixture in the state senate; Paul Van Dalsem, no longer active in newspaper work, was one of the kingpins of the Old Guard; Fred McCullom (Forrest City) and J.E. Dunlap served on the important state police board, Dunlap into the Clinton years. Frances "Shrimp" Murray took over the management of Faubus's *Madison County Record* and in 1970 became APA president, the third Murray to serve. Faubus owned other newspapers, too. He acquired John F. Wells's *Arkansas Recorder* and renamed it the *Arkansas Statesman*. "This is the governor's paper, and we would like to have your ad," ran the pitch to businesses.[1087] Besides the standard racist rhetoric, the newspaper took up the cause of holocaust denial.[1088] It failed to make money, however. Faubus was a part owner of the *Piggott Banner* from 1967 to 1968 when it closed and the Waldron *Advance Reporter* from 1965 to 1968.

Despite the turmoil in the state, the APA took little official note. The first month after the crisis at Central High School, the *Publisher* carried a color cover picture of a man hunting. The next issue featured dead ducks. Only the announcement that a new newspaper, a weekly called the *Ouachita Citizen*, had been formed at Camden, with David Pryor as publisher-editor, had any relevance for the future.[1089]

At its summer meeting in 1958, APA president Calvin Mannen observed that members had "mixed emotions" on the crisis, and he declined to endorse the *Gazette*'s stance. Editorializing on the subject of higher values, Mannen thought criticizing segregation was "known to be unpopular and a sure loser at the cash register." Instead, he discussed whether newspapers should publish requests to omit flowers at funerals. The APA had Razorback coach Frank Broyles as its featured speaker.[1090]

The next year Dr. H.E. Williams, president of Southern Baptist College (currently Williams Baptist College) in Walnut Ridge, claimed America had gone down the road of socialism to the point of no return; he was followed by the former comedian of "Lum 'n Abner" fame, Chester Lauck, now an oil company spokesman, who was worried over the national debt.[1091] These causes so impressed Association members that at the suggestion of Cone Magie the APA created an "Americanism Award" for the four best editorials or columns on this theme.

One of the newspapers that ran afoul of the sensitivities of the age was the Warren *Eagle Democrat*. Local attorney Hall K. Roberts filed a $500,000 libel judgment after the newspaper reported that Roberts had been made the court-appointed attorney to defend a black rape suspect. Roberts sued because the newspaper had called him the "Negro's lawyer," and that language, he claimed, blackened his character. Chief Justice Carleton Harris wrote the majority's opinion dismissing the case with a ringing defense of a free press. Arch-segregationist "Justice Jim" Johnson predictably dissented. Former owner Duval Purkins was the newspaper's attorney.[1092]

Although Arkansas newspapers may have chosen to ignore the state's condition, life during the Faubus years was far removed from normal. The state police tapped telephones, collected rumors, and harassed supposed liberals. The witch-hunting Act 10 of 1958 required teachers and other state employees to disclose every organization to which they belonged. Although the act was challenged and overturned in court, the politically compliant administration of the University of Arkansas preferred censure by the American Association of University Professors rather than hire back professors who had been fired for not signing the disclosure forms. In an age where crewcuts ruled, Arkansas briefly sported one bearded publisher. But Marianna native Brad Govan's career was brief, both at Melbourne and (beardless) in Osceola.

The biggest problem for many editors was that the controversy shut down the state's economic development plans. Following a well-publicized divorce, Winthrop Rockefeller had moved from New York to Petit Jean Mountain, where his cattle-raising plans soon got sidetracked. Induced by Orval Faubus to become the head of the Arkansas Industrial Development Commission (AIDC), Rockefeller scored great successes before he broke with Faubus over the Central High School crisis. Rockefeller told Faubus the crisis was death to industrial promotion, and for several years thereafter new industry stayed away, especially from central Arkansas. In the post-1957 crisis years it was difficult to celebrate Arkansas; indeed, it was something many Arkansans tried to hide when going out of state. In-state, the teaching of Arkansas history began disappearing from the schools.

The Return of Mr. Funk

After a long illness Erwin Funk's wife, Mintie, died in 1953. Freed from caring for her, Erwin was again on the loose.

January 1956 found Funk in Little Rock for the APA's mid-winter meeting. His arrival even warranted his picture, "very good for a newspaper snapshot," appearing in the *Democrat*. Little did the unsuspecting APA world know that Erwin Funk kept a diary.

The featured speaker at the APA meeting was Ernie Deane, who urged the importance of editorials, and whom Funk had known since Deane's university days. Funk thought him "a good speaker and his talk was well worth while." Bob Wimberly of AP&L, longtime supporter of APA and its member newspapers, also was a featured speaker.

The next day, the Association took up an endorsement for creating a national park at the Pea Ridge (Elk Horn Tavern) Civil War battlefield site. Senator Tom Allen of the Brinkley *Citizen* "killed it. Claims he never heard of the Battle of Pea Ridge—and I expect he told the truth. Just pure ignorance or spite against Northwest Arkansas."

That May, Funk attended the Arkansas Historical Association meeting in Harrison. There he recalled a reception held at the Newman home during the APA's 1914 meeting. He and other old timers reminisced about the Newmans; "it took some time to discuss their present whereabouts—but most of them are now dead."

June found him at the APA meeting at Fayetteville, where he was now endowed with the official title of chairman of the Advisory Board of Past Presidents. Funk was not the oldest of the living presidents; that honor belonging to the long vanished R.O. Schaefer (1922). At the convention Lydel Sims, a Memphis columnist, gave, in Funk's opinion, "a clever, wise-cracking talk that went over good but was nothing out of the ordinary from my point of view."

January 1957 found him again in Little Rock, his antenna still working. Sam Gearhart, the APA president, he confided to his diary, was "a poor speaker and I thought him a very poor presiding officer." Perhaps Sam, who once sang at an APA convention, was better in that capacity. Funk met up with Earl Causey (APA president, 1964) of Star City's *Lincoln Ledger*. Funk thought the area to be "a very retired district," and asked Causey why he had been there 14 years. "He likes it," was the response. Funk did not comment on Mrs. Causey, but she was a feared feature at APA meetings, being noted especially for regularly sticking her tongue out at Louise Bowker.

Funk's last convention was in January 1958, when more than 500 publishers attended a joint meeting of the NEA and APA. Governor Faubus, Funk noted, was "not quite so egotistical as usual." After over 60 years Funk was wearing down: "why I continue to go to the conventions—not to learn how to run a newspaper but to talk about by gone days when we were all young and gay. The drawback is the number of old friends missing."[1093] It was, and is, a relevant concern. Not only were all his contemporaries gone, but so were men a few years younger like Max Hampton, Mike Gillespie, or Curtis Hurley. When Funk died on February 1, 1960, the Association's last tie to the 19th century was broken.

A Crisis for Family Newspapers

Since earliest times, newspapers too often had come to life with great hope, only to die sometimes slow but frequently rapid deaths. Long-term success invariably depended on the strength of the people who put them out. Even the first appearance of multiple ownership in the 1920s with Clyde Palmer and his imitators changed conditions little since a corresponding corporate structure remained undeveloped. However, the increases in technology, symbolized by ever more complex Linotype machines and bigger presses, represented an investment that limited startups. Furthermore, by the 1960s at an accelerating rate today's new press was tomorrow's antique. Newspapers still continued to pass down equipment, as when the *Jonesboro Sun* got a used press from the *Kansas City Star* while their old press went to Helena. But offset printing was making increased inroads, even if *The Big Picture* in Paragould gave up its daily in 1958 and its life in 1961.

That newspaper's title was also an indication of the increasing importance photographs were playing. The Scan-A-Graver of 1959 was but one of the numerous inventions that allowed for greater, quicker, and cheaper use of pictures. The multi-talented Esther Bindursky won prizes for her pictures, although she only came to photography late in her career.

As output per press grew, the need for individual small presses diminished. Guy Graves at Marked Tree had led the way before World War II in printing three newspapers (Lepanto, Trumann, and Marked Tree) from one plant. In 1946 there were 925 subscribers at Marked Tree, 750 at Trumann, and 850 at Lepanto. Two of the newspapers had to move to a Friday publication date in order to make the system work. Subsequent owner Dorothy Stuck described the equipment as a "bucket of bolts" with the result that every week the printing was occasioned by great tension. Yet by 1960, the Wynne *Star-Progress* with a re-equipped plant was printing nine weekly newspapers, six of which they owned. The days of printing at home by weeklies were drawing to an end.

Population loss led to a number of closings, and the toll included some of the most famous newspapers in Arkansas. The *Washington Telegraph* returned to the Etter family in the 1930s but suspended in 1946 and never reopened. The town, eventually a state park, had simply vanished. The death of the *Tuckerman Record* was slower. From 1924 to 1959 it was owned by John Edgar Parrott, who made it into a model country newspaper. Its circulation was never large, and Tuckerman was in an area hit hard by the end of family farming. After Parrott sold out it went through different owners before being acquired by the Richolsons of the *Newport Daily Independent*, who later closed it. Another loss was Mr. and Mrs. A.J. Hunter's *Owl* at Amity. At Huttig, home to another noted newspaper, the Johnsons suspended the *News* in 1955 and, predictably, went off hunting. Ells L. Huff, APA president in 1947, sold the *Jackson County Democrat* to the Craigs at Newark in 1959 who abandoned Newark but in turn sold the *Democrat* in 1963 to the Richolsons at the *Newport Daily Independent*. The saga of the Craig family at Newark illustrates one aspect of the changes. Printing was in the family blood, but after 1963 they were printers unable to find a community adequate to support a newspaper.

The final aspect undermining the family system was serendipitous. Just as the Newmans at Harrison died early and ran out of males interested in the newspaper, untimely deaths struck a number of other prominent families. The most dramatic case was in Conway. Frank Robins, APA president in 1924, died in 1949. His son, Frank, Jr., died a mere 10 years later. There had been a divorce, and the newspaper was thrown into receivership until the heirs reconciled and Frank Robins III became publisher. At Morrilton, Curtis B. Hurley, who lost his eldest son in the war, died in 1952. His widow and younger son Joe disposed of the newspaper to Eugene Wirges, a colorful and controversial figure in state and county politics. At Malvern, Mrs. J.H. Beerstecher and her daughters continued to operate the *Daily Record* after the death of her husband in 1948, but when she died in 1968 her daughters sold it to W.R. Whitehead and Ray Kimball.

All these trends were in their infancy. New newspapers were started up successfully. Cone Magie, who began his life in journalism with a *Gazette* delivery route, represented one in the postwar era who succeeded. Coming back to the university after the war, with bride and baby in hand, he worked several places before he and his wife founded the *Cabot Star* in 1955. The already existing newspaper, the *Herald*, maintained only an office in the town, and community leaders in the northern district of Lonoke County wanted an independent voice. The bank financed the purchase and carried the couple for many years. Fortunately, Cabot proved to be a growing area, in contrast to so much of the state, and the Magies eventually created or acquired other central Arkansan organs as well at Lonoke, Carlisle, Jacksonville, and Sherwood.

Another success story was in North Little Rock. The son of *Times* owner John Pruinski had been blighted by his wartime experiences. Robert McCord, a university graduate who as a high school student had become an accomplished photographer, was able to buy and modernize the newspaper in 1958. McCord hired George Fisher, then working as a commercial artist, to prepare weekly cartoons that were then reprinted in the *Arkansas Gazette* and even outside the state.

At Clinton, the *Van Buren County Democrat* had had absentee owners after 1934 when C.B. Oldham sold it to Curtis B. Hurley, who printed it at his Morrilton plant. The Robins family at Conway owned the *Democrat* from 1940 to 1950, at which time the newspaper was printed in Conway. In May 1951, Frank Robins, Jr., sold it to a partnership that included Jay W. Jackson and Curtis B. Hurley. After the widowed Mrs. Hurley sold her holdings, the Jacksons were able to acquire complete ownership in 1958.

Conclusion

On July 22, 1957, the APA sent a formal letter to the University of Arkansas. Disgusted over years of underfunding for the Department of Journalism, they did what rarely happened in Arkansas, going public with their complaints. Putting their money behind their words, the Association created the Walter J. Lemke Scholarship Fund. Lemke was soon to retire, whereupon he pursued his interest in history, editing the memoirs of his friend Erwin Funk, and the letters and diaries of many other Northwest Arkansans. What he thought about the *Publisher*, bereft of volume numbers and now claiming to be only a lowly trade journal, is not recorded. Like Clio Harper before him, time had left Lemke a relic of a bygone age, one who believed that makeup and advertising existed to support content.

Those valiant APA members who entered contests and attended conventions failed to see how rapidly the world was changing. With radio and television now universal, newspapers were less important as a source of news. Indeed, the censorship newspapers often imposed on their communities caused many to turn elsewhere even for local news. Often the Memphis or Little Rock newspapers printed stories about controversies that local organs deliberately chose not to cover. Ownership was still a family affair, but turnover increased rapidly, especially in declining areas. Very few of those attendees would stay in the profession or have any legacy to pass on to their children. Just ahead lay an age marked by offset printing, corporate ownership, and even publication on the World Wide Web.

L. W. "Tex" Plunkett, longtime journalsim teacher at Arkansas State College, was presented a plaque in 1968 by APA Manager Louise Bowker.

Chapter IX

O Brave New World

"These press conventions are always nice things, enabling all editors to get together for a good cry on each other's shoulders. The first fellow listens to all tales of woe without interruption, in order that he, in turn, may receive the same treatment...It is encouraging to see the methods in which many of our mutual problems have been met by certain association members."
Connie Stuck Shelton, quoted in *Arkansas Publisher*, XVII (February 1947), 10.

"What does a former newspaper woman think about when she allows her memories to surface? She thinks of Tuesdays, and the agony and the ecstacy of getting an offset weekly ready for a Wednesday morning press run. Tuesday is the Day of Days, and you can't die on Tuesdays, not if you're going to make that press run the next morning."
Ruth Rogers, Dardanelle *Post-Dispatch*, 1972.

"Arkansas' deep and abiding social problems are as they are in large measure because of superficial and unreflective journalism."
Martin Kirby, *Arkansas Advocate*, II (March-April-May 1974), 1.

"The business management is the hardest part when the chips are down."
Wilson Powell, *Batesville Daily Guard*, Interview, 1999.

"A long-standing joke was that anyone who could say Bindursky, Schexnayder and Wulfekuhler could pass any sobriety test."
Arkansas Publisher (May 1971), 10.

"If a newspaper cannot impartially report a matter of public interest such as these election contests we hardly see how it can be said that freedom of the press really exists."
Justice George Rose Smith, in *Wirges v. Brewer* (1965).

"Tom Dearmore taught me more about journalism in two years than at any other time in my life. His philosophy was: get it right, get it fast."
George Smith, e-mail, September 6, 2001.

"The real truth is that news is what I like to do."
John W. Troutt, Jr., former owner of the *Jonesboro Sun* (2000).

"You can't turn on CNN and find out what's happening in Hot Springs Village."
Delores Richardson, *Hot Springs Village Voice*, Interview, July 20, 2001.

"In any newspaper office there never comes the time when one can feel satisfied with the equipment."
Erwin Funk, 1960.

Introduction

No period in press history witnessed greater changes than the last quarter of the 20th century. The key development was the revolution in production brought about by offset printing. After computers appeared they were quickly adopted to enhance offset technology. By the century's end computers were taking over the entire operation as by successive stages newspapers began to be constructed entirely on computers before being printed. Finally, newspapers began to appear electronically over the Internet. The expenses entailed in keeping up with technology fed a drive towards corporate ownership, leading to a sharp decline in family ownership.

American society, politics, and culture underwent equally radical changes. The civil-rights cause found support in Congress in the 1960s. The collapse of the stranglehold white Southern senators had long exercised resulted in new legislation in voting rights, access to public facilities, and education. Enormous changes swept over the increasingly air-conditioned South.

Meanwhile, Americans had so thoroughly imbibed the tenets of anti-Communism that they initially endorsed America's involvement in the Vietnam War. However, support for the war waned, first in the nation's colleges, and then in the U.S. Senate in the person of Arkansas's junior senator, J. William Fulbright. Conversely, Arkansas's senior senator, John McClellan, was the sponsor of legislation to establish an official secrets act to suppress such dissent. The war's failure undermined the presidency of Lyndon B. Johnson, resulting in the election of Richard Nixon in 1968. Nixon's efforts to suppress the story of the Watergate break-in at Democratic Party headquarters, exposed by *Washington Post* reporters, resulted in his resignation before the end of his second term.

For a time in the tumultuous 1960s and 1970s, America was badly divided even over the idea of a free press. A "silent majority" blamed the messenger for the news. Conversely, on college campuses, students believed they were not really getting the news. Evidence of these trends appeared when anti-establishment newspapers appeared on college campuses and in "alternative" newspapers that surfaced in Little Rock, Fayetteville, and other towns. A reaction against social change resulted in the rise of the religious right and helped bring about the triumph of Republican Ronald Reagan in 1980.

Reagan's charm did not pass to his successor, George Bush, who was defeated in his bid for a second term in 1992 by Arkansas governor Bill Clinton. Clinton's eight presidential years were tumultuous for Arkansas. The state was overrun with reporters trying to link Clinton to anything and everything disreputable or downright criminal. Backed by rich conservatives, outside investigators tried to tie Clinton to drug-running from an obscure airport near Mena; fraud in a failing land development named Whitewater on the wrong side of the White River; and numerous murders. Clinton was accused of participating in the deaths of lawyer Vincent Foster, Jr., and even, in 2000, of Arkansas journalist Tony Moser.

Republicans impeached Clinton, not on charges related to any governmental wrongdoing, but for lying about his sex life. Although he escaped conviction, Arkansas's reputation, bad enough before 1992, remained. Attorney General Steve Clark, Secretary of State Bill McCuen, Governor Jim Guy Tucker, and longtime legislative kingpin Nick Wilson were all convicted of various crimes. In late 2000, Governor Mike Huckabee proclaimed over national television that Arkansas was a "Banana Republic," a derogatory term once used to describe small Central American countries run corruptly by outside U.S. corporations.

Arkansas's own affairs never exactly paralleled those of the nation. In 1966, Republican Winthrop Rockefeller won election as governor. A representative of the liberal wing of the party, Rockefeller championed civil rights and gave his blessing to the passage of the Arkansas Freedom of Information (FOI) Act, signing it on February 14, 1967. That law, fitting together nicely with the federal FOI act, and U.S. Supreme Court decisions on voting rights, apportionment, and libel, revolutionized the role of the press in every community in Arkansas where responsible newspapers functioned.

Rockefeller's gubernatorial successors, Dale Bumpers, former newspaper publisher David Pryor, and Bill Clinton supported moderate reform.

Only after Clinton left for Washington in 1992 did Republicans succeed in accomplishing what had already happened elsewhere in the South by capturing the governor's office as well as senate and congressional seats. The voters' adoption of term limits that same year greatly altered the legislature, but overriding all other facets of the state's political life was the greatest newspaper war in the history of the state. The victory of the *Arkansas Democrat* over the Gannett-owned *Arkansas Gazette* turned the state's metropolitan voice from moderate or liberal to conservative.

By the century's end, even the casual observer could hardly miss the evidence of the great revolutions in the press that had occurred in the previous quarter-century. Nationwide there were complaints of a sharp decline in journalistic ethics. Much of the Clinton hate literature came from reporters who failed to check their facts or evaluate their sources. Even the once highly respected *New York Times* printed sloppy and inaccurate stories.

At the local level, the triumph of a corporate mentality could result in applying cost-accounting to every aspect of newspaper production. Advertisements, banned from the front page for a century, were back, and readers could not be sure if the advertising side was not really directing news stories. In journalistic parlance, "church" (the newsroom) and "state" (the business office) were supposed to be separated by a high wall. As the new century began, a review of current literature suggested that the wall constantly was being breached.

Another challenge came from the Internet. An ever-increasing number of former or potential subscribers made a two-minute check of Web headlines the extent of their "reading." Newspapers, which had survived the much-overrated threats of radio and television, were becoming less relevant to an increasingly nonreading and busy public, especially in a time when a growing percentage of Americans had no use for politics.

Yet the century ended with many weekly newspapers stronger than ever. A determination to cover thoroughly the actions of local public decision-making bodies, to insure that the schools received proper attention, and to continue publishing the venerable country correspondents sparked many an old home newspaper. Some of the best and brightest of these remained family-owned. Every time a gap appeared, young entrepreneurs could be found to take the same risks that editors and publishers had faced in Arkansas for almost 200 years. And so the cycle continued.

Ernie Deane Makes a Convert

When Ernie Deane gave his 1956 address on the value of editorials that stirred even the venerable Erwin Funk, another affected individual in the audience was Dorothy Stuck. With her husband stricken with poliomyelitis, much of the work of putting out the *Marked Tree Tribune* had fallen on her. But she had eschewed active editorial work as something reserved for trained journalists. "Ernie convinced me so I went home and started writing," she later recalled, "I never would have started without Ernie Deane."[1094]

What she spoke to was taboo in the Delta. In

their earlier days in Marked Tree, the Stucks had pushed successfully for a black high school during the waning days of segregation. But coming out for integration required personal courage, for the following simple statement challenged the most basic beliefs of at least 80 percent of her readers:

> Truth forces us in the South to admit we live on the defensive much of the time when matters of racial equality are at issues… If we have the courage, let us face the fact that we so-called Christian people have laid the battleground for this social revolution everywhere in this nation because we have perverted the truth with rationalization, economic selfishness, social arrogance, moral cowardice and false pride.[1095]

Then Dorothy Stuck went one step further: she came out for Republican Winthrop Rockefeller, who at the time symbolized honesty in government, promoted economic development for the small towns, and became deeply committed to civil rights. "Somebody had to speak up," she thought.[1096]

In this she was not the only Arkansan to make the plunge. Rockefeller's hometown editor, Gene Wirges, stirred up a hornet's nest. The son of Joe Wirges, the longtime *Arkansas Gazette* police reporter, Gene and his wife bought the *Morrilton Democrat* in 1957 from the Hurley family. Wirges took on the Conway County machine, whose presiding leader, Sheriff Marlin Hawkins, soon became recognized statewide thanks to the cartoon work of George Fisher. Beginning in 1959 Fisher had begun drawing cartoons for the *North Little Rock Times*, and many were picked up by the *Arkansas Gazette*. Fisher created the Old Guard Rest Home, which soon housed Hawkins, Orval Faubus, Frank White, "Justice Jim" Johnson, and other worthies.

After Wirges exposed election frauds in his newspaper, country correspondents were pressured to quit, and he found himself beset by legal and financial troubles. Wirges found a champion in Roy Reed, an *Arkansas Gazette* reporter and one of Arkansas's Nieman Fellows, whose "How to Lynch a Newspaper" appeared in the *Atlantic Monthly* in 1964.[1097]

One useful weapon for Wirges's enemies was the libel suit, and since the machine effectively controlled local judges and juries, he could find protection only by making expensive appeals. *Wirges v. Brewer* reached the state supreme court in 1965 and was a ringing victory for the embattled publisher. Truth was a complete defense, Justice George Rose Smith declared, and $75,000 in damages was dismissed.[1098] Wirges later wrote a book about his experiences.[1099] In 1963, at the height of the controversy, Wirges won the prestigious Elijah Parish Lovejoy national award for courage in journalism. Hawkins turned author as well, and *How I Stole Elections: The Autobiography of Sheriff Marlin Hawkins* (1991) may be the better of the two books.[1100] The various lawsuits at one time led to a foreclosure on the newspaper, the ownership of which passed to Wirges's wife. Wirges was safe only as long as Rockefeller was paying the bills.

In contrast, there was no sympathy or kudos for Joseph H. Weston of the *Sharp Citizen* of Cave City. Weston, a rogue publisher who specialized in scandal sheets, was not a member of the APA. He had plied his trade briefly at Conway before settling outside Cave City where he injected his personality into every story he wrote. Believing that a Democratic machine ruled Arkansas and oppressed the people, Weston exposed these "crooks," "pimps," "liars," "jackasses," "killers," "drunks," and "dictators" with populist rhetoric and a complete disregard for truth.

Weston was jailed briefly for refusing to reveal his sources on one story to a Batesville grand jury, but his major accomplishment came at the end of his career, when, after accusing the Clay County sheriff of running a narcotics ring, he was prosecuted on the charge of criminal libel. In *Weston v. State* (1975), the state supreme court invoked the United States Supreme Court's rulings in *New York Times Co. v. Sullivan* (1964) and *Garrison v. Louisiana* (1968), declaring Arkansas's statute unconstitutional. Weston by that time was out of business, but to the end he remained a folk hero to the region's disgruntled.[1101]

Rewards for a more mainstream courage came after Winthrop Rockefeller revitalized the Republican Party. Although defeated in his first effort against incumbent Orval Faubus in 1964, Rockefeller was by no means discouraged. "I had a refreshing education as to just how good Arkansas newspapers really are," he told the APA mid-winter meeting after his defeat. One lesson that he had learned during the race was that weekly newspapers "are highly believable, are more thoroughly read, and have a tremendous influence on the thinking of the people in the area they serve."[1102] Rockefeller courted the press through heavy advertising, including full-page ads in every state newspaper, spending $11 million of his own money, and two years later was elected governor. Besides paying the Wirgeses' legal bills, Rockefeller saw to it that, after the Stucks sold out to Fred E. Ashcraft in 1971, Dorothy got a major federal appointment in Texas. Ernie Deane later promised never to say anything serious at an APA meeting: "I do not want to force anyone into moving to Texas."[1103]

The 1968 election saw Arkansas voters return Rockefeller to the Governor's Mansion and Vietnam critic Fulbright to the Senate, but George Wallace won Arkansas's electoral vote. In general, south Arkansas was the bastion of conservatism. From Hope, Alex H. Washburn attained a national following in 1964 for his editorial campaign against an attempt by the federal government to build his town a new post office.[1104] This former Columbia University student never regretted moving west and never gave up his "dedication to the job of making life miserable for federal politicians and bureaucrats..."[1105] His allies in the region were Louis "Swampy" Graves at Nashville and W.R. Whitehead at Magnolia.

Ironically, the same region was also home to Robert E. Fisher of the *Crossett News Observer*. "Thoughts on a Young Man's Funeral" won a national editorial writing award from Sigma Delta Chi in 1967. Prompted by the funeral of Ashley County's third Vietnam War victim, a black soldier, Fisher noted the irony of spending billions of dollars and countenancing an ever-increasing death rate to fight for freedom 10,000 miles away while denying "these very rewards for a portion of our own."[1106]

Meanwhile, a youth revolt was underway. In order to avoid controversy, University of Arkansas officials banned all outside speakers, even including state elected officials. Underground newspapers popped up there and on other campuses across the state. The sedate campus *Traveler* was stopped from going to press in the spring of 1968 when some 70 protesters blockaded the journalism building. The cause of this confrontation was the *Traveler*'s refusal to print a letter criticizing another letter that had expressed a negative view of the extensive coverage given Martin Luther King's assassination.[1107]

After a left-wing faction gained control of the campus newspaper, things changed rapidly. By 1974 the *Traveler* was, in Ernie Deane's words, "publishing obscenities so vile they must be seen to be believed."[1108] One foul word even appeared in the *Arkansas Gazette*, albeit after J.N. Heiskell's death two days after Christmas in 1972; at the *Arkansas Democrat* Jon Kennedy put a popular but obscene gesture often seen on Arkansas's highways in a cartoon depicting the Russian invasion of Afghanistan.

Obscenity was not an issue that would go away. Readers' tempers flared during the summer of 2000 when the *Arkansas Democrat-Gazette* sanctimoniously cancelled the cartoon strip "Lola" after its elderly female protagonist had problems with flatulence. Irate letters from Lola's fans condemned the move using far stronger language than had appeared in the strip.

The radical 1970s witnessed the creation of several alternative voices in Arkansas journalism. At Fayetteville, the Arkansas Student Free Press Association created *The Grapevine*. The first issue on March 18, 1970, contained only one advertisement, but this college town supplied a receptive audience, and the irreverent weekly, published for more than two decades under a variety of editors, found plenty to report and spoof. A 1980s *Grapevine* columnist, Don Eggert, noted, "These are sometimes the only places where unpopular views can be expressed, where the shennanigans of local ding-a-lings in the power structure can be exposed, and where new artists and young writers can sometimes get published."[1109]

Straight journalism best described Little Rock's *Arkansas Advocate*, founded by reporter Martin Kirby and continued by Wade Rathke, the community activist who founded Arkansas Community Organizations for Reform Now (ACORN), and Walter Nunn, later a UALR professor and book publisher. The *Advocate* enlisted a number of fine writers, including Tom Dearmore, Chris Barrier, Gene Lyons, and Robert Sarver. Advertising was minimal, and politics and culture rather than news formed its basis.

The *Advocate* also featured a number of young reporters whose in-depth work included offering horror stories on nursing homes and abuses of power. Founder Martin Kirby, who had worked for the *Democrat* and the *Philadelphia Inquirer*, broke an unspoken professional rule by dissecting the contents of a number of state newspapers. Some publishers did "not know the difference between a newspaper and an advertising throwaway," he claimed, after examining 103 issues of various newspapers for their editorial and news content. Kirby found that state news was almost totally missing, and local news was weak. Business stories, he deduced, were being inserted mostly as a favor to advertisers.

Kirby also thought that one commonly used syndicated columnist, Dr. George W. Crane, Ph.D., M.D., was an embarrassment. In one column, Crane told readers that "women seldom indulge in sex except to gain some ulterior motive" and went down the slippery slope from there. Even more distressing for Kirby was a story of some 45 column inches devoted to Professor Leland D. Callaway of Southern State College at Magnolia, who told local high school students that former President John F. Kennedy was the Anti-Christ, in part because all the Irish were really Jews; that the temple in Jerusalem was secretly being rebuilt with materials being shipped there from Sanford, Indiana; and other similar eccentric theories. What upset Kirby was that the reporter took all this (and more) down as if were true. He must, Kirby concluded, be "very young and inexperienced and very much in need of editorial guidance."

Kirby was also distressed by the coverage given the expulsion of some church members for selling liquor. The local editor declared: "We are here mainly to record the life of the community, state, nation and world, not to solve problems." Kirby could not have disagreed more: "If a journalist believes that 'recording' is somehow separate from solving, then he reduces his own role to that of a gratifier of mild curiosity... A responsible newspaper editor will demand that his staff actively seek out the community's problems and illuminate them with all the energy they can muster."

One of the best examples that fulfilled Kirby's ideals came in 1998 when the *Jonesboro Sun* was nominated for a Pulitzer Prize for its coverage of the murders of four students and a teacher at the Westside school near Jonesboro. The *Sun*'s treatment of this emotional crisis was thorough and correct, "a model of accuracy," the Freedom Forum concluded, in sharp contrast to the work of some of the reporting provided by the more than 200 members of visiting media. *The New York Times*'s national correspondent Rick Bragg, whose story appeared on page one, March 29, 1998, managed to see cows grazing from the vantage-point of the Arkansas State University administration building, a manifest impossibility unless the cows were in a parking lot or were going to or from classes. *Jonesboro: Were the Media Fair?* a publication of the Freedom Forum (the former Gannett Foundation), gave nationwide evaluation of the work of the various news organizations.[1110]

Another example of a different sort came a year earlier when on March 1, 1997, Arkadelphia was struck by a tornado that killed six people and devastated the downtown area. "We provided in-depth coverage while resolving nearly insurmountable problems," publisher Judith Collis of the *Daily Siftings Herald* recalled. Since no issue was due until Monday, she decided to print a special, and by Sunday morning, with the help of former employees and two writers from the Donrey Media Group's Little Rock bureau, a special edition hit the streets. All copies were sold immediately, and two reprintings were required to fill the need. "How do you approach reporting when the rules are changed," asked staff writer Jeff Smithpeters, who found he had to locate officials to interview while competing with television reporters from KARK, KATV, and CNN.[1111]

The other major criticism of Arkansas journalism centered on another monopoly town, Fort Smith. Rather than being buried in an obscure alternative publication, this attack in the then-prestigious *Atlantic Monthly* gave nationwide coverage to how Donrey owned the newspapers as well as radio and television stations.[1112]

One publishing venture that survived from this period was Alan Leveritt's *Union Station Times* that grew into the *Arkansas Times*. The primitive early *Times* gave way to a slick monthly magazine; then it became an alternative tabloid weekly after the demise of the *Arkansas Gazette*, where it provided a home for a number of ex-*Gazette* employees. Despite a paid circulation and a second-class mailing permit, the APA expelled the *Times* when it became free to Central Arkansas residents, leaving it with less than a 50 percent paid circulation. On the hard side, the *Times* provided a mix of investigative reporting and editorial opinion from Bob McCord, Max Brantley, Bob Lancaster, Ernie Dumas, and in 2000 John Brummett. On the soft side, the *Times* covered the state's restaurants, entertainment and tourism and was a member of the Association of Alternative Newspapers. John Robert Starr called it "a poor man's *Rolling Stone*."[1113] In 2001, the APA revised its by-laws in order to admit free newspapers if they agreed to provide audited circulation returns to prove their subscription claims, among other requirements, and the *Times* resumed APA membership.

The APA took notice of alternative journalism at its 1975 meeting when a panel consisting of Kirby, Joe Eblen, Rathke, Leveritt, and Nunn, together, rather curiously, with John Wells of the *Daily Record*, discussed this new journalism. All except Wells thought that current newspapers lacked in analysis, investigation, and creativity. Nunn defined the *Advocate*'s role as "respectable muckraking," while Leveritt claimed the *Union Station Times* was "oriented more toward people—what they may feel about their work, their loneliness, their sexuality..." Eblin complained that the old campus *Traveler* had been "a real rag" until non-journalism major Dave Baer took over. Wells, whose *Daily Record* largely recorded transactions at the state capitol, spoke up for straight reporting and attacked Wade Rathke, whose ACORN organization, he asserted, "renders a disservice by harassing government officials."[1114]

Like the populist and socialist organs of the past, the days of alternative newspapers were numbered by a growing conservatism that triumphed after 1980.

Spectrum, a Little Rock free newspaper founded by three former *Arkansas Democrat* staffers and lauded by the *Columbia Journalism Review*, covered, in addition to political issues and cultural matters, what were called alternative lifestyles. After eight years, an advertising boycott contributed to its demise in 1993. A replacement, the *Free Press*, then appeared under different ownership. It, too, has had a rocky history, even dropping from biweekly to monthly publication at one point.

Investigative reporting also appeared briefly in the public school press. One student newspaper at Conway complained about cafeteria food. However, the United States Supreme Court, in *Hazelwood School District v. Kuhlmeier* (1988), ruled that students were not real journalists and their publications need only be administrative publicity sheets.[1115] Such restraints were not needed on the University of Arkansas's Monticello campus, where the administration refused to permit even the existence of a newspaper.

More in keeping with what Arkansas was becoming was the success Alan Leveritt and his partner had with a trade publication entitled *Arkansas Business*. The last quarter of the 20th century witnessed the rise (and sometimes fall) of such firms as ALLTEL, Wal-Mart, Dillard's Department Stores, TCBY, Tyson Foods, J.B. Hunt, Systematics, and many more. *Arkansas Business*, which joined the APA in 1999, provided quality coverage of Arkansas business developments and produced in 1986 an especially effective tribute to the state's industrial growth. In 1997, it began publishing a separate northwest edition to keep up with the booming business growth in that area.

One important issue dividing the press and its readers was Watergate, the crisis that led to the resignation of President Richard M. Nixon. In late 1973, before the full evidence was in, the *Marked Tree Tribune* and *Lepanto News Record*, then owned by Fred Ashcraft, sent out survey cards to their readers. Three-quarters of those who replied supported the president, with many blaming what was now being called "the media." Readers added their own written comments, and a number took the opportunity to attack the *Tribune* and its editor.[1116]

Well into the 1970s, Arkansas possessed a number of strong-minded editors. Many of their editorials were reprinted in the *Arkansas Gazette* as a regular practice. This created a forum for opinions around the state. This useful feature did not become a part of "the best of both" at the *Arkansas Democrat-Gazette* after the *Gazette* closed in 1991.

Ideological divides between newspapers and their readers continued to occur, especially over local issues. In Delta counties the leading controversy in the waning years of the 20th century was supporting public schools. After integration finally became inevitable during the mid-1970s, segregationist academies sprang up. Denied tax-exempt status if segregated formally, they often reappeared carrying a nominal "Christian" affiliation and an almost 100 percent white enrollment. White parents then voted against the public school's millage, leaving the already troubled public school systems in worse shape than ever.

At Dumas in 1971, Melvin and Charlotte Schexnayder (APA presidents, 1962, 1981) supported the millage increase necessary to build a new high school and permit full integration of the school system. Although deeply rooted in the community, they found that their editorial position cost them lost advertising and subscriptions, and they received threats. Two decades later little had changed. In Helena, *Daily World* editor Derwood Brett (APA president, 1989) supported raising the millage rate. After receiving many threatening letters and telephone calls, he moved his family out of town until the election was over and then left himself.[1117]

It was a sign of the times when in 1999 a letter to

the *Arkansas Times* attacked columnist Bob McCord as a dangerous liberal. For the previous quarter-century McCord had been commonly perceived as a moderate conservative. Martin Kirby had so held in 1974, but the moderate conservatism of the past had become dangerous liberalism by the century's end.

Without a doubt, the most important news story of the late 20th century was the meteoric rise of Bill Clinton, who in 1993 became President William Jefferson Clinton. Although he had his enemies in Arkansas prior to his election, only a few were in the press. Articulate in speech and encyclopedic in knowledge, Clinton offended working journalists only in his propensity for arriving late for public appearances, thus throwing reporters behind in their schedules. So many journalists attended Clinton's inauguration that Dean Walls of the *White River Journal* recalled that at one reception "the room was so packed with people from Arkansas we had to remind ourselves we were not attending an Arkansas Press Association meeting or some local event back in Arkansas."[1118]

The *Arkansas Publisher* celebrated the event by including other accounts from Mary Ann Wilson at the *Osceola Times*, Ron Kemp of the Piggott, Rector, and Manila newspapers, Charlotte Schexnayder of the *Dumas Clarion*, David McCollum from the *Log Cabin Democrat*, J.E. Dunlap of the *Harrison Daily Times*, and Roy Ockert, Jr., of the *Batesville Guard*. Executive Director C. Dennis Schick added his own commentary, and Tim Schick, his son, provided photographs. Ron Kemp called it a "once-in-a-lifetime" trip, but Clinton was successfully re-elected in 1996. Daily newspapers had AP coverage, but Bill Rutherford, then working at Cabot, provided eyewitness coverage for a pool of weekly newspapers under APA sponsorship. The APA has provided such pool coverage of other state events over the years.

If by the century's end politicians were wrapping themselves in the mantle of family values, what was left of the still-independent press celebrated those editors and publishers who stood for more than the bottom line. The summer 2000 meeting of the APA featured *Freeman* (South Dakota) *Courier* editor and publisher Tim Waltner, then the president of the International Society of Weekly Newspaper Editors (ISWNE), who urged all newspapers to honor their age-old community "connectiveness," the unique feature that separated newspapers from other media.

One way to achieve connectiveness was to utilize the Internet. A nation-wide survey in 2001 undertaken by the Associated Press Managing Editors (APME) association, the Pew Center for Civic Journalism, and the National Conference of Editorial Writers revealed that 89 percent of the newspapers had been redesigned within the past five years. Some new practices included giving the reporter's e-mail address after a story. This allowed for what Dennis Schick has called "dialog journalism," for it could result in broadening a story and extending its development, perhaps into a series of stories. Another increasingly common practice was to provide website addresses, especially for government, business, and science stories. In this way, the interested reader could look up further information, while the general public's interest was served by the shorter summary.* Chris Peck, the APME president, noted that today readers "want their world and their journalism to be interactive." If history is any guide, there are lots of roads to interactive journalism.

The Freedom of Information Act

The rock upon which the century-ending press stood was the Arkansas Freedom of Information Act (FOI Act or FOIA). Signed into law on February 14, 1967, it was the great Valentine of the Rockefeller

* This author read David Ho's Associated Press story in the Cleveland *Plain Dealer*, July 27, 2001, but that newspaper neglected to provide the supportive sites. The entire report can be found in the Pew Center for Civic Journalism's website.

years. But while a signal victory, it would have been a hollow one had not courageous publishers put it to use.

In 1960, the University of Missouri established the Freedom of Information Center within the School of Journalism. Its publication, *FoI Digest*, became an insert in the March 1961 issue of *Arkansas Publisher*. However, the impetus for the legislation did not come from the APA. Perhaps because so few publishers were interested, the drive for passing an Arkansas law came from the newly activated Sigma Delta Chi, later renamed the Society of Professional Journalists (SPJ). The *Arkansas Publisher* put 11 SPJ initiates on its July 1965 cover, and the list included W.R. Whitehead, Louis Graves, Robert E. Fisher, John Robert Starr, Cone Magie, Melvin Schexnayder, and Ray Kimball; Bob McCord was the group's new president.

Forthwith, two important stories surfaced. First, the state Building Services Commission held private meetings to discuss spending $500,000 for renovating some apartments as part of a sweetheart deal. Then the University of Arkansas Board of Trustees held a secret meeting to raise salaries. Governor Rockefeller was interested in open access to records for his own reasons. Various state boards and agencies invariably deposited their state appropriations in pet banks without receiving any interest. On the other hand, some Democrats were anxious to find out how Rockefeller operated. Rockefeller's idea of subsidizing salaries of state officials out of his own pocket was considered dangerous and illegal. Additional support came indirectly from Associated Press head Al Dopking, whose reporters by following closely the law's emergence kept the issue before the public.

The proposed legislation, largely the work of McCord, Richard Allin, Bob Douglas, Ernie Valachovic, R.B. Mayfield, Sylvia Spencer, George Douthit, Cragg Hines, John Robert Starr, state senator Ben Allen, and state representatives Leon Holsted and Nathan Schoenfeld, made its way into law and immediately became a target. In April, two reporters were ejected from a city council meeting in North Little Rock Mayor Casey Laman's office when the city attorney invoked attorney-client privilege. McCord, the owner of the *North Little Rock Times*, sued, and the case, heard as *Laman v. McCord* (1968), went to the state supreme court, where the act was unanimously sustained.[1119] "To allow the (city) council to go into executive session at any time upon the pretext of consulting the city attorney about legal matters," Justice George Rose Smith wrote, "might readily open the door to repeated and undetectable evasions of the Freedom of Information Act to the public's disadvantage."

This was but the first of a wide range of cases from all parts of the state and involved everything from city councils to school boards. No publisher was more active in filing suits than John Troutt, Jr., at the *Jonesboro Sun*, who in 2001 was presented with the APA's Freedom of Information Award for three decades of litigation.

Arkansas's attorneys general played major roles in keeping the law alive through formal and informal opinions. Ray Thornton in 1971 declared that public bodies could not use secret ballots. In 1977, Attorney General Bill Clinton and SPJ president Bob Fisher joined forces to issue three FOI Act booklets directed at school boards, cities, and counties. Then, in 1981, under Attorney General Steve Clark, the separate parts were collected under the title *The Arkansas Freedom of Information Act: A Handbook*. The APA was the major force in getting the handbook in print and received major financial support from the Society of Professional Journalists, the governor's office, and the attorney general's office. Additional support came from the Arkansas Press Women, the Arkansas Scholastic Press Association, the Associated Press Managing Editors (APME), the Associated Press Broadcasters Association (APBA) and the Arkansas College Media Association. When a new edition of the handbook was needed, Attorney General

Winston Bryant appointed one of his staff members, former Searcy publisher Perrin Jones, to represent his office on the committee planning a new edition. Bryant instructed Jones that in gray areas he should err on the side of openness.[1120] Thereafter, Jones became the FOI liaison in the state attorney general's office.

By 2001, the *Handbook* had gone through 10 editions. About 25,000 copies of each edition were printed, and many were distributed statewide via the Arkansas Municipal League, the Association of Arkansas Counties, and other government agencies. Copies of the handbook were (and still are) mailed by the APA, and the governor's and attorney general's offices, to anyone who requests them. Among past recipients have been local activists, common citizens, business firms, and even prisoners. Traditionally governors send a copy to every new appointee to state boards and commissions.

By 1999, case law had grown to 28 court decisions and a much larger number of formal opinions from the attorneys general. Textual analysis could be found in University of Arkansas Law Professor John J. Watkins's book, *The Arkansas Freedom of Information Act*, whose fourth edition was scheduled to be released in 2003.[1121]

In 1994, the APA Board of Directors approved the establishment of a Libel Hotline for its members, which was expanded to include a FOI Hotline and a Legal Hotline. This hotline was manned by Williams & Anderson, the law firm of the *Arkansas Democrat-Gazette*, with John Tull and Leon Holmes as the lead attorneys. Both have spoken at APA seminars and conventions over the years, and have even testified at legislative hearings on behalf of press issues. When Tull and Holmes left Williams and Anderson in 2000 as part of a new law firm (Quattlebaum, Grooms, Tull & Burrow), the APA Hotline moved with them because they were the main contacts for the newspapers. APA pays a small monthly retainer for the service, and the Hotline is provided free to members.

The APA's Dennis Schick regularly coordinated and led FOI Act seminars around the state. Usually hosted by local newspapers, the meetings featured panel discussions by representatives from the Attorney General's Office, the Arkansas School Boards Association, the Arkansas Municipal League, and law professor John Watkins.

The cause of all these cases lay in the combination of administrative hostility to the act, the belief of public officials that it would be easier to govern in secret, and the press's vigilance. Governor David Pryor, the former newspaper publisher and legislator, called for "investigative reporting behind the scenes during the legislative session," but veteran bureaucrats were slow to change their habits.[1122]

Besides the repeated violations by the University of Arkansas board, longtime Secretary of State Kelly Bryant claimed corporate filings in his office were secret, denying access to *Gazette* reporter Tucker Steinmetz. Bryant went so far as to ignore a 1973 Pulaski Circuit Court order and accused the *Gazette*'s lawyer, Vincent Foster, Jr., of "Gestapo tactics." The state supreme court held that these records are covered under the FOI Act.

The idea of open records did not sit well in many communities. The municipal judge at Mountain Home tried to keep the *Baxter Bulletin* from publishing court convictions and fines. Indeed, the Chamber of Commerce and local realtors in 1973 even took the newspaper to task for printing news about high water on Norfork Lake and pictures of outhouses. The resultant boycott got statewide attention and prompted Batesville's irascible Paul Buchanan to wonder if losing football scores were next.

A similar crisis erupted at Hot Springs in 1976 after the now-defunct *Hot Springs News* ran a cartoon that criticized a downtown rejuvenation program.

The head of the Chamber of Commerce demanded an explanation and then organized a boycott. Banks and other businesses canceled their advertisements. Editor Barbara P. Peters wrote a spirited defense of editorial freedom, claiming that "The Chamber of Commerce most assuredly does NOT have the right to dictate editorial policy to this newspaper."[1123]

The sentiments of the Old Guard were expressed in the legislature by Representative Boyce Alford of Pine Bluff, a vigorous opponent of the law, who grumbled, "the press and the public already know too much," and by Senator Knox Nelson, who managed to get legislation passed making secret his fuel tax receipts.[1124] Journalist-legislator Charlotte Schexnayder opposed the powerful senator on this bill.

Every subsequent session of the legislature was marked by attempts to close public records and public meetings. In addition, local law enforcement officials tried to ignore it. *Gazette v. Britt* (1979) started when *Arkansas Gazette* reporter Ginger Shiras protested Hot Springs Judge Henry M. Britt's decision to hold court in secret. The *Gazette* won, and the *Publisher* ran the text of the decision in its entirety, noting editorially that by contrast in a New York case [*Gannett Co. v. DePasquale* (1979)], the United States Supreme Court had upheld closing pretrial hearings.[1125]

One way the issue was kept before the public was with cartoons, and *Gazette* cartoonist George Fisher pictured a spanked and chastened Judge Britt writing, "I will not bar the press," over and over on the blackboard.[1126] Other cartoonists, notably Jon Kennedy, Walt Skulman, Mark Davis, and Jan Gosnell, followed Fisher's lead, and probably no topic received more picturesque treatment. The 9th edition of the FOI handbook, for example, contained two cartoons by John Deering and a different one by Fisher.

During the fall of 1999, a press coalition assembled by the Donrey Media Group tested the law's practical effectiveness. Seventy-five "strangers" visited every county, asking to see jail records (specifically held to be open in *Hengel and Donrey, Inc.,d/b/a Pine Bluff Commercial v. City of Pine Bluff* [1991]); restaurant inspection reports in the county offices of the state health department; selected city revenue reports; and the contracts of selected school superintendents. The initial visits generated a 61 percent compliance rate, with cities being the most responsive (87 percent), followed by schools (72 percent), jailers (61 percent), and the county health units (51 percent).

Forthwith, stories about these "strangers" appeared in the state's press. One direct result of the project was that Dr. Fay W. Boozman, the director of the Department of Health, sent out a memorandum reminding county offices that most of their records were public and setting forth procedures to prevent future noncompliance.[1127] Another result of the coverage was that the state's teaching hospital, the University of Arkansas for Medical Sciences (UAMS), scheduled a seminar, led by the APA and attorneys from the attorney general's office, for its department heads on proper compliance. It was a testament to the act's vitality that 30 years after its enactment an anniversary luncheon at the APA's 1997 Winter Convention featured a large ice sculpture spelling out FOI, and honored Bob McCord and others responsible for the act.[1128]

Another state law attained vitality during the period. Arkansas reporters had been protected by a privilege provision (shield law) since 1935, but only in 1967 did controversy arise. After Representative Gayle Windsor said he had been offered a $1,000 bribe to vote for a casino gambling bill, a grand jury called to investigate ordered reporters Jack Baker of the *Gazette* and Michael B. Smith of the *Pine Bluff Commercial* to reveal their sources and jailed them when they refused. Released after the state supreme court agreed to hear the case, they were jailed again when the court dismissed their appeal. The case ended when the reporters' informants relieved them of their pledge of confidentiality.[1129]

Their case differed materially from that of Carol Griffee, who wrote a story about abuses at the Arkansas Soil and Water Conservation Commission that appeared in the *Arkansas Gazette*. It was a plaintiff rather than a grand jury that demanded her sources for his civil lawsuit. Circuit Judge Warren E. Wood held that the statutory protection, framed as "to any other authority," extended to civil proceedings.[1130]

In general, the rights of access for the press were strong and the protections solid. Not well understood by the public was that the FOI Act belonged to all citizens. The question for the press was whether future publishers cared enough to let reporters exercise their rights and then stand behind them.

The Last Linotype

While some Arkansas newspapers, notably Des Arc's *White River Journal*, were still setting type by hand when offset arrived in the 1950s, Linotype machines had become standard in the industry. There had been something in excess of 1,500 patents connected with Mergenthaler's invention, and the machines of the 1960s in the larger newspapers, that could hyphenate and justify automatically, were wonders compared to the Number 7 model of a half-century earlier. Nevertheless, the fundamental element, hot lead, remained.

Lithography was not new in other areas of publishing, and the technology increased greatly in the late 1940s, when the first experimental units for newspapers came into the market. The adoption of cold type was more likely to come with the founding of new firms. They had no old veterans to retrain, no capital invested in Linotype machines, and no tradition associated with putting out a newspaper. The first offset newspapers suffered by comparison with Linotype competition. Pictures printed best, hence, indeed, the banner *The Big Picture*, for Paragould's pioneering effort promised readers lots of pictures.

The hot lead and pieces of metal that constituted composition in the days of the Linotype were solid and secure compared to the scissors, razor blades, X-acto knives, and "paper dolls" of offset. It was ironic that the expression, "scissors and pot paste," long used to describe how many an antebellum editor put together his newspaper, at least required the printer to reset everything before going to press. Early offset meant trying to get the columns, advertisements, and pictures somehow straight on the page before photographing it. All too often straight lines became a thing of the past under offset. Some publishers used a bastard system. Linotypes were used to set the stories and proof the metal text. Then came pasting the proofs and photographing the finished product.

One of the principal factors influencing conversion to offset was that it facilitated the adoption of color. Fairchild Graphic Equipment's Scan-a-Color II in 1965 produced fully corrected, continuous tone prints in less than an hour. Four-color printing figured prominently in advertising inserts.[1131] Another in the long list of technological improvements was the Offsetter, which delivered justified copy from the Associated Press. In 1967, the *Rogers Daily News* became the first newspaper in Arkansas to acquire this machine.[1132]

In the office, yet another redistribution of sex roles occurred, as males tended to become cameramen or pressmen, while women moved over to typesetting and makeup. The dirt and grime that had marked the world of Linotypes gave way to cleanliness.

Also gone was the noise. Even one Linotype in operation produced a considerable roar from its hundreds of movable parts, and dailies had rooms full of these machines. It was the "clanging and carrying on that made it seem like a newspaper plant," Louise Bowker observed; "it just looks like any other business office now."[1133]

Romance was lost in the process. Don Cooper, who worked for newspapers in Batesville, Texarkana, and Hope, recalled that his powerful incentive for getting into the profession came from walking down Nashville's South Main Street and peering in the window of "Swampy" Graves's *Nashville News*, where he could "listen (and hear) the Linotypes and even feel the sidewalk shake when the press was running at top speed."[1134] Laura Shull, a longtime journalist at Russellville, lamented that the silence of offset precluded a reporter with a hot story from running into the noisy pressroom and yelling, "Stop the Presses!"[1135]

In those early days of offset, newspapers used Varitypers and Headliners before switching to the Singer Company's Justowriter. The *North Little Rock Times* was the first Arkansas newspaper to buy these glorified electric typewriters. Besides being slow, this "strike-on" method sported an inferior typeface and machines that quickly wore out. Nevertheless, many plants used them into the 1970s. An improved version came from International Business Machines (IBM). Its strike-on system used a ball, similar to that the company was putting on electric typewriters. Big Blue was so convinced this system was the wave of the future that they would only lease these machines, and few were ever found in Arkansas.

The entire technology was superseded in the late 1960s when the Compugraphic Corporation introduced photocomposition machines, the 7200 for headlines and the 2900 for text. These machines at first produced photocomposition from a tape that was fed into a machine that in turn printed the text on Ectamatic paper. Ray Kimball at De Queen was one of the first to adopt this improvement. Jay W. Jackson at Clinton recalled, "The use of full page ads by Winthrop Rockefeller in his races for governor provided some papers enough money to make down payments on Compugraphics and contributed to their early use in the state in the 1970s."[1136]

Then in 1971 came Compugraphic's Compuwriter that eliminated the tape step. Photocomposition in turn gave way to computer systems in which everything was created and seen on a video screen. Even composition became an entirely video affair. Fred Wulfekuhler's *Paragould Daily Press* went from being one of the last hot metal dailies in the state to a leader with a state-of-the-art building and the most modern equipment. The smallest daily in the world to have VDT terminals, it attracted visitors from 27 states and seven foreign countries in 1974.

By 1987, Louie Graves at Nashville had installed a "cold room" with its own air conditioning to house the computer equipment. Graves had to buy jackets for his workers, but a Compugraphic engineer told him the sealed room paid for itself several times over. Elsewhere, smoking, once omnipresent in newspaper offices, food, and aged browned coffee cups of uncertain contents were barely tolerated if not entirely banned.[1137] The sensitivity of early computers contrasted strongly with the habits of the press corps, but newspaper shops were slow in taking steps against smoking.

The Associated Press's conversion to the computer took place in 1972 when Elgin Pitts, who had sent out the first news article to originate from the Little Rock AP office in 1929 using a printer circuit, had the honor of sending the first news copy on the new facsimile machine called Datafax. Under the new system the message was sent to Dallas, where it was converted into a punched tape and then fed into a computer. Then the item was sent on to participating newspapers for reconversion into tapes.[1138] Such was the high technology of 1972.

Reflecting on these changes was Alex H. Washburn of Hope, who acquired the new-style Extel

AFR-11 Teleprinter. Washburn remembered back to 1926 when dispatches arrived via a manual Morse telegraph "ticker" amplified by an empty Prince Albert tobacco can jammed behind the instrument. That system produced some 8,000 words in eight hours but the copy had to be set again by the Linotype operator. Ray Kimball's teletypesetter circuit of 1942 had been the first step in automating the delivery of the dispatches.[1139] By 1977, AP stories arrived via Datastream at the rate of 1,200 words per minute.[1140]

Other old-time publishers shared Washburn's celebration of the new technology. C.M. Young at the *Helena Daily World*, whose career dated back to 1895, cited the convenience. Fred Troutt at the *Jonesboro Sun* called it the "greatest thing that ever happened in the newspaper industry."[1141]

From the publishing point of view, the principal advantages were supposed to be in reducing labor expenses. A compositor working with movable type could set one newspaper line a minute; using a manually-operated Linotype moved the figure to 4.9 lines a minute; a punch-paper driven Linotype increased the figure to 5.6; a computer-hyphenated and justified paper-tape-driven Linotype produced 14; a tape photocomposition system generated 80; and a photocomposition machine supposedly set 5,000. The potential from such a dramatic increase in typesetting capacity would soon be felt, but Washburn claimed that automation had resulted in better and larger newspapers. With offset he could print up to 20 pages in a single run, as opposed to the eight before. Furthermore, his staff had grown from 12 to 22.[1142]

One of the last stages of computerization came in the use of graphics. The first phase was ushered in by scanners, which translated images or text into the computer. The scanner phase, similar in many ways to bastard offset systems, endured into the 21st century, although the general direction has been toward completely digital systems. One early idea that failed was the "video-still," the selection of a specific frame recorded by a video camera. These lacked the clarity of individually shot images.

In the march to pure digitization, Arkansas was one of the leading states in the nation. In 1994, the *Jonesboro Sun* bought two Nikon-Kodak 2000 digital cameras, which cost $20,000 each. The newspaper's photography editor, Chris Ritter, was hired away by the Associated Press to become one of only two Associated Press digital camera trainers west of the Mississippi River. During the next four years he trained photographers across the western United States before joining the *Arkansas Democrat-Gazette* in 1998. That newspaper, too, had embraced the new technology under the leadership of its photography editor, Barry Arthur, and had acquired its first digital cameras in 1994.

Early digital cameras were expensive, fragile, complicated, and cumbersome, and the high-contrast, low-resolution pictures did not reproduce well. Readers during the transition days were often confronted by blurry and out-of-focus pictures. The combination of poor quality and high cost led most newspapers to continue employing the scanner technology. In 2000, Kodak introduced its D1 camera. Not only were the images better and the camera body stronger, but the price was one quarter of that of the first cameras. Although very few Arkansas newspapers were all-digital at the time of this writing, the days of the darkroom appear to be nearly over.[1143]

The prospective loss of hard-copy newspaper photography has worried historians. Several newspapers, including the *Arkansas Gazette* and the *Arkansas Democrat*, once kept important photographs, the *Gazette* having an organized library while the *Democrat*'s collection resided in dozens of filing cabinets. Few photographs predated the late 1940s, but these have long been a rich resource for researchers. Although the picture morgues of the

Memphis newspapers (which contain a number of Arkansas-related images) were given to the University of Memphis, the only Arkansas depository is the Shiloh Museum in Springdale, which houses the photographs of the *Morning News*. In the early digital age the only "print" was probably the one in the newspaper. After selecting the wanted pictures for publication, the photographer could simply erase the old images and start over. Another problem appeared when early disks failed to retain the information supposedly saved on them. But newspapers and other print media have learned to download images onto CDs and store them in archives.

The rate of introducing offset formed a bell curve, with few publisher adoptions before 1960 and with few Linotypes left by the late 1970s. Among dailies the first in the state to follow *The Big Picture* was the *Rogers Daily News*, followed by the *Springdale Daily News* and then the *El Dorado News and Times*. By 1966, five dailies and 22 weeklies had made the conversion.[1144] These changes generated controversy. "Stay with Letterpress," ran one headline in the *Arkansas Publisher*.[1145] Four years later the *Publisher* proclaimed "Offset 'Revolution' Snares Arkansas Press," as Louise Bowker reported that 20 of the 34 dailies and 74 of the 126 weeklies had gone offset, thus marking a nearly 60 percent conversion rate.[1146]

One of the early proponents of offset was Alex H. Washburn, whose *Hope Star* was the fourth daily newspaper to convert. (Fifth was the *Log Cabin Democrat*; sixth the *Searcy Daily Citizen*). Washburn emphasized he had "a fortune spent in new equipment"—and rejoiced in the improved quality of his printing.[1147] Washburn had bought a rotary offset press costing $96,000 in 1965. It replaced a Duplex 8-page flatbed press that had been new when Washburn and partner Clyde Palmer merged the *Star* and *Daily Press* in 1929. Trading in the Duplex reduced the bill by $5,000, and that press went on to a new life in Mississippi.[1148]

Weeklies were slower to change, just as they had been to adopt Linotypes in the first place. Aside from *The Big Picture*, which abandoned its daily edition to become a weekly, the earliest to convert was the *North Little Rock Times* in 1959. Second place in 1960 went to Jay W. Jackson at the *Van Buren County Democrat*. In McCord's case, he had a growing newspaper being printed in an outdated letterpress printing plant. At Clinton, the *Democrat* had been printed since 1932 mostly at Morrilton, but that arrangement had proved unworkable as Gene Wirges's problems mounted, so the Jacksons decided to adopt the new technology.

Relentlessly the march continued. "Swampy" Graves at the *Nashville News* wrote the obituary for his 69-year-old press, born shortly after 1902, and decommissioned on March 29, 1971.[1149] During the early 1970s virtually every issue of the *Publisher* noted another changeover.

Mason Clifton's story was special. Clifton had bought a half interest in the *Brinkley Argus* from W.B. Folsom in 1940, completing the purchase in 1948. The shop consisted then of one Linotype and a Babcock Standard press. Clifton added two more Linotypes and a Goss Cox-O-Type eight-page web press. Although it still took "coal chisel, handsaw, [and] hammer" to put out the weekly, Clifton thought he had a "fine plant."

Then in 1972 Wal-Mart announced plans to open a store in Brinkley, and informed Clifton that his plant was inadequate to print their advertising. Clifton promised to install an offset system in time for the store's opening. This deadline he could not meet, and he jokingly suggested to Mack Mason, his "very fine Christian pressman," that he ought to go push Wal-Mart's rising walls down. That Sunday a small windstorm did just that, giving Clifton the time he needed. After printing his last old style issue on April 18, 1974, "the pressroom where I had worked for 43 years ground to a stop—a quietness no one who hasn't gone through such a thing will ever understand."[1150]

One of the most interesting modernization stories came from Fred Causey, Jr. of the *Crowley Ridge Chronicle* and the *Hughes Star-Herald*. In 1977 Causey bought a new Harris H-125 offset press that replaced the five and one-half ton flatbed Cranston press that was at least 100 years old. "It was still in running condition the day the riggers began moving it out a few weeks ago," he observed, "And all of us felt pangs of nostalgia because it served all those years so well. It would certainly be interesting to know what the first news printed on that press was about." Although affectionately known as "Hitler" on account of its "occasional contrariness and hateful disposition," the press never once kept a newspaper from being published, and "we published the first color on it when the register gear had been off for twenty years."[1151]

The last major newspaper to capitulate to offset was Fayetteville's *Northwest Arkansas Times* in 1977.[1152] By 1986 only a few Linotypes were left in operation. "Mergenthaler's Linotype Turns 100: Goodbye Etaoin Shrdlu" was the headline C. Dennis Schick used for his obituary in the Fall 1986 issue of the *Arkansas Publisher* on that "eighth wonder of the world." "Etaoin Shrdlu" were the letters that appeared when an operator made a mistake. In order to nullify the bad line, the operator ran a finger down the first row of letters (e-t-a-o-i-n) and then the second row (s-h-r-d-l-u)]. Like the "30" for obituaries, it was part of the vocabulary of the trade. When it accidentally appeared in print, mystified readers often asked who this person was.[1153]

The prospects of uncertain change and possible layoffs did not thrill the labor force. In 1974, unionism, so thoroughly routed more than 20 years earlier, reappeared in Little Rock. Some *Gazette* staff members wanted to affiliate with the American Newspaper Guild; *Democrat* employees were being lured by the ITU, which, fearful of the loss of jobs associated with the adoption of the new technology, wanted to reach out from the shop to the office. Both moves were frustrated: new management at the *Democrat* cancelled all existing contracts, even for the union typographers, while the *Gazette* remained editorially friendly to unions and internally hostile.[1154] At the *Gazette*, Managing Editor Bob Douglas fired Dee Carithers, the head librarian, for insubordination after he learned she had acquired a union card. Douglas was justified in that Carithers was technically a member of the management, but the irony of Douglas, a prominent figure in the 1949-50 strike, fighting the union was not lost on former *Gazette* reporter Bob Stover, who covered events for the *Arkansas Times*.[1155] Like earlier efforts, this unionizing effort failed. Management in Arkansas was protected by the state's "right to work" amendment, and unions were out of favor nationally. More importantly, the move to offset eliminated the need for union printers, and after the *Arkansas Gazette* closed in 1991, Arkansas newspapers became union-free for the first time since 1865.

The end of the century saw attempts to implement a system to replace the cut-and-paste system with an electronic way called pagination in which page building would be entirely software-produced. At the same time newspapers were converting to the new narrower (50-inch web) newsprint. Even the casual reader at the dawn of the new century must have noticed the changes. The abrupt shift to the smaller size created a psychological sense of downsizing, as the late 20th century called shrinkage. Some newspapers compensated for the narrower width by adding additional pages, but others took the opportunity to reduce the amount of space devoted to news (the news hole). Early efforts at pagination resulted in mixed and mauled stories, wrong headlines, and even wrong television schedules.

Weeklies were affected as well. Jeff Dezort, the newly arrived editor of the *Newton County Times* in Jasper, discovered when he tried to introduce pagination and the new size paper simultaneously that his software would not work on the office machines. The April 5, 2001, issue of the *Times* left readers guessing. Headlines giving the names and places of the country correspondents were omitted, although the copy was there. "It will be a few weeks before the paper gets to the point where most of us are pleased," he optimistically asserted a week later.[1156]

Modern readers, confronted with newspapers whose broadsheet pages were increasingly shrinking toward tabloid size, would be advised to recall the New York *Journal of Commerce* of 1853, that placed 11 columns on an untrimmed sheet measuring about three by five feet (yes, dear readers, take out your yardsticks!).

The most recent development in the industry is CTP (computer to plate). Just as the handset typesetting and letterpress printing era ended in the early 1970s and phototypsetting was superceded by laser imagesetting around 1990, complete on-press CTPs, some theorists predict, will subsume and supplant much of the existing printing systems, making existing models as antique-like as dot matrix printers.[1157]

The Rise of Corporate Ownership

The full implications of offset were felt in two ways. First, offset generated an impetus for consolidation. During the days of the Linotype the Trumann, Marked Tree, and Lepanto newspapers were all printed at Marked Tree, but only with almost weekly difficulty. An even more daring move came in 1961 when W.M. Courtney, Harlan V. Walker (APA president, 1966), and A.P. Murray (APA president, 1952) contrived to print eight weeklies: the *Modern News* (Harrisburg), the *Cross County Times*, the *Earle Enterprise*, the *Cotton Plant Democrat*, the *McCrory Leader*, the *Marvell Messenger*, the *Augusta Advocate*, and the *Wynne Progress*.[1158] This was before offset arrived, and the project failed in two years, probably equally from the scheduling problems inherent in the system and because many of these newspapers could not survive when the towns that supported them collapsed as machines replaced people in the Delta. By 2000 only the Harrisburg, McCrory, and Wynne newspapers remained in existence.

Offset made multiple printings easy. The system was inherently more reliable and gave the first publishers who adopted it more capacity than they needed. One of the first Missouri publishers to make the change, Frank Martin of the *West Plains* (Missouri) *Daily Quill*, bought up the *Salem Headlight* and the *Mammoth Spring Democrat*, printing both in his West Plains plant. Even though Martin later disposed of these investments, the *Quill* continued in 2000 to print the *White River Current* of Calico Rock.

Improvements in printing led to changes in ownership. The Stucks at Marked Tree faced this dilemma, complicated by two other considerations. Howard had never completely recovered from his bout of polio and although in line for the APA presidency declined it on account of his health. Second, Dorothy's stands on civil rights did not exactly sell newspapers in eastern Arkansas. They decided to sell out to Fred and Hazel Ashcraft in 1971.

The costs required for the new equipment required a capitalization that favored corporate rather than family ownership. In Booneville, after the death of Max Hampton in 1958, his wife, daughter and son-in-law continued the publication. In 1960 the son-in-law, Val S. Zachariah, became editor and publisher. Although active in the APA and interested in the new technology, he decided to sell to Donrey in 1968. "The technology is going so fast that it is obsolete when it is put in the building," Perrin Jones explained in 1977 after he sold the *Searcy Daily Citizen* to

Harte-Hanks Newspapers of San Antonio, Texas.[1159]

Expenses were not as easily controlled, especially during the mid-1970s when the Hunt brothers tried to corner the silver market, driving to astronomical levels the price of a commodity essential to photography. Many printers felt that shoppers, which ran all the advertisements and carried none of the overhead of reporters or the danger of editorials, were a much safer way to make money. Indeed, the Harte-Hanks chain, which at one time acquired several newspapers in Arkansas, disposed of all their Arkansas newspapers in 1986 and the remainder of their holdings in 1996 in order to publish shoppers and produce direct mailings. The venerable *Sharp County Record*, founded in 1877 at Evening Shade and later published at Cave City, went to Ash Flat, where it degenerated into a shopper and hence no longer a legal newspaper.

Television became increasingly important for advertising, especially in politics. The first successful gubernatorial race based on television spending was that of the then unknown Dale Bumpers, who in 1970 defeated first a number of better known Democrats in the primary and then Winthrop Rockefeller in the general election. Deloss Walker, who planned Bumpers's campaign, relied on television almost exclusively.[1160] Another political strategist, former APA manager Jerry Russell, was noted for his radio jingles and carried this art form to its ultimate limits. "Pin a Rose on me, Pin a Rose me, I'm for Rosamond; Pin a Rose on me 'cause I'm proud to be from North Little Rock" helped elect a church furniture salesman over the handpicked machine candidate in a hotly contested North Little Rock mayoral election. Russell still believed in newspaper advertising and spoke to the National Newspaper Association as well as state press associations from Montana to Massachusetts on "How to Get More Political Advertising for Your Newspaper."

Publishers had come to expect every two years the ballast provided by political advertisements. Instead, revenue from this source began a steady decline. In addition, national advertisers ignored the country press. A narrowed advertising base made publishers more dependent on local sources and may have contributed to the heavy-handed attempts at censorship local advertisers sometimes tried to impose.

Underlying the changes in ownership were the demographics of Arkansas. With the agricultural revolution, the Delta was losing population rapidly. Much of this loss came from the displaced black sharecroppers and farm laborers. Many newspapers had very strong followings among blacks, "our most loyal readers," Charlotte Schexnayder recalled, and population loss meant not only a decline in subscribers but also in advertising as the towns dependent on their trade lost their retail stores. The very title in 2000 for McCrory's *Woodruff County Monitor Leader Advocate* showed the complexities of its multiple origins. Population decline also hit the southern, western, and northern counties as family farms became increasingly a rhetorical ploy of politicians rather than an actual reality. Although the state ceased losing population after 1970, in individual counties declines continued unchecked. Near the century's end, Pine Bluff managed to maintain its 50,000 population (and hence its Metropolitan Statistical Area status) only by annexing an adjoining prison.

Conversely, there were centers of growth. Northwest Arkansas grew rapidly, fueled by chicken farming, trucking, Wal-Mart, and the University of Arkansas. Central Arkansas recovered, but most of the growth came in the nearly all-white suburbs. New towns like Maumelle arose, and older farm towns like Cabot, Jacksonville, and even Conway were transformed into suburban outposts. Benton grew to such an extent that Sam Hodges converted the weekly to a daily in 1970.

Arkansas's two resort towns were a study in contrasts. Without gambling, Hot Springs struggled to find a new identity, but the retirement community of Hot Springs Village for a time boasted two newspapers, the *LaVilla News* and the *Village Voice*. In 2001 the locally owned *Voice* bought out and closed its smaller chain-owned competitor. Eureka Springs, virtually a ghost town after World War II, reinvented itself, first with the controversial Passion Play of noted anti-Semite Gerald L.K. Smith, and then with an invasion of hippies, artists, writers, and other outsiders.

The creation of Beaver, Taneycomo, Bull Shoals, Norfork, and Greers Ferry lakes spurred tourism and retirement homes for Mountain Home, Clinton, Harrison, Heber Springs, and other towns. The new retirement towns of Cherokee Village, Hot Springs Village, Bella Vista, Fairfield Bay, and Horseshoe Bend sported new weeklies.

Mountain Home's *Baxter Bulletin* remained technically a weekly even when growing population led it to come out three times a week; then it, too, went to daily status, eventually becoming a part of the Multi-Media company and then the Gannett chain. It was this combination of changing demographics and economics that underlay the structural changes of the late 20th century.

In 1972, the Donrey Media Group bought the Eureka Springs *Times-Echo* from Everett and Lucille Wheeler. The Wheelers in 1948 had purchased the former daily for $14,000 and later merged it with the weekly *Headlight*. When Donrey offered them

---

Ray Kimball

Ray Kimball, the dean of Arkansas publishers at the time of his death in 1999 at the age of 91, had a long and illustrious career in Arkansas journalism. In addition to his creating the pioneering typesetting network in 1942, Kimball at various times had interests in papers in Stuttgart, Hampton, Magnolia, and Fordyce. But it was De Queen that was closest to his heart and where he lived most of his life. With its *Daily Citizen*, De Queen reportedly was the smallest town in America with a daily paper.

When a reader of the *De Queen Bee* took Kimball to task for accepting advertising in support of a measure which the paper opposed editorially, Kimball gave the following answer of sound reasoning:

> This newspaper believes both sides in any controversy are entitled to be heard. It has never closed its columns to anyone because their views were opposed to those of the editor. It does not deny space, even to critics of its own policies, although they impugn its consistency and its sincerity. So long as an advertiser keeps within the law, avoiding personalities and offenses against the public morals and proprieties, the newspaper as a dealer (or merchant) selling a commodity or service demanded by the general public has no right to refuse to sell its space, even though it cannot endorse the use to which it is put. The secular newspaper, although privately owned, is something of a public institution. It is obligated impartially to all the people in its territory, and not simply to those who think as it thinks and see as it sees. If it has character it will take a partisan stand in its editorial column on all matters affecting the public interests, but it will keep its news columns uncolored for the presentation of facts as they are, and its advertising columns will be for sale to all without strings except that abuses already mentioned be not perpetrated. Our attitude toward advertisers or others who disagree with us, conforms to that of Voltaire when he said: "I wholly disapprove of what you say, but will defend to the death your right to say it."

$100,000 for the newspaper and later paid $35,000 for the building that had cost the Wheelers only $2500, it seemed like a good deal.[1161] Donrey was on the move, and while they would not hold on to this particular property—corporate owners often treated their acquisitions like knives at a swap meet—they would also acquire the newspapers of Arkadelphia, Booneville, Pine Bluff, Rogers and Springdale. Donrey Media Group sold most of its newspapers in 1998 but kept all of its Arkansas holdings.

Less aggressive was the older Palmer chain. After Clyde Palmer's death in 1957, his newspapers became just a division in his son-in-law Walter E. Hussman, Sr.'s WEHCO Media. With the core newspapers being located in a declining region, much of the income probably came from radio and television stations in Arkansas, Texas, and Louisiana and 12 cable television systems. WEHCO made only one Arkansas purchase, the *Arkansas Democrat*.

What is interesting about these firms is that in 1974, when the APA published Professor Robert W. Meriwether's *A Chronicle of Arkansas Newspapers Published Since 1922*, the copiously indexed book contained no entry for corporations; newspapers were assumed to be owned by individuals.

The term that described the last quarter-century was media, a plural noun that soon achieved single status and became for some a sinister monolith of misinformation that included radio, television, and newspapers. In 1969, the *Atlantic Monthly* estimated Donald W. Reynolds's (Donrey Media) worth at just under $35,000,000. Prior to his death in 1993, *Forbes* ranked him among the richest 400 persons in America with over a billion dollars of wealth. By that time, Reynolds had holdings from North Carolina to California. Reynolds was well-remembered for his invariable response to any criticism: "Well," he would say to his questioner, "how much money did you make today?"* Most of Reynolds's money went to a foundation bearing his name, and Stephens, Inc., a large Little Rock investment firm, purchased Donrey. Founder Witt Stephens had long been a major player in state Democratic politics; Jackson, his brother, embodied the state's new conservatism by turning Republican. Jackson T. "Steve" Stephens, Jr. continued in his father's conservatism. The Murphy Commission and the Arkansas Policy Center were among the forums he used to advance his pro-business and anti-tax views, and his endorsement of school vouchers. In 2001 Steve considered running against Governor Mike Huckabee, whom he felt had become too liberal. Warren Stephens, who headed Stephens, Inc., was also conservative but less in the public eye. Under Stephens, Inc.'s ownership, first the coporate headquarters of Donrey was moved from Fort Smith to Las Vegas, home of the flagship newspaper, the *Las Vegas Review-Journal*, then the name was changed to Stephens Media Group.

An indication that the Stephens family may have looked to their newspapers as more than just an investment came in 2002 when a longtime friend, ex-Fourth District Congressman Jay Dickey, who wished to unseat incumbent Mike Ross, urged Warren Stephens to have the *Pine Bluff Commercial* endorse him editorially, slant news in his favor, and refrain from printing letters critical of the ex-congressman. Stephens referred the matter to media head Sherman Frederick in Las Vegas, who ordered *Commercial* editor Tom McDonald to issue an

---

* A similar story is told of Witt Stephens, political power player and somewhat part owner of the *Arkansas Gazette*. At a lunch for local journalists Witt was reportedly interrupted by some functionary reporting on the progress of a bond sale. Witt kept relaying to the journalists how much more money he was making. After the amount got well into the millions, longtime *Arkansas Gazette* agricultural writer Leland Duvall finally commented, "Hell, Witt, that's more money than I make in a year."

immediate endorsement. Instead, McDonald chose to resign. Citing the newspaper's traditional autonomy and saying that he "felt like I was directed to participate in quiet conspiracy," he observed. "For the newspaper to be used as a political pawn didn't just smell, it reeked."[1162] Nevertheless, Dickey lost the election.

Another level of impact was felt by the state's small dailies. In 1970, almost all were family-owned; in 2000, after the sale of the *Jonesboro Sun* to the Paxton Media Group, only Batesville, De Queen, and Forrest City from among 30 dailies were left. Ended by sale to outside corporations were such dynasties as that of the Robins (*Log Cabin Democrat*), Baugh/Jones (*Searcy Daily Citizen*), Freeman (*Pine Bluff Commercial*), Wilkerson/Richolson (*Newport Daily Independent*) and Young (*Helena Daily World*). In addition, the independent dailies at Paragould, Benton, and Harrison were all sold to chains.

Weeklies felt the impact somewhat later, but relentlessly the corporate world swept into the remotest hamlets. Some firms mixed the two forms. Rust Communications of Cape Girardeau, Missouri, which bought the daily at Blytheville, acquired ten weeklies scattered over the northern part of the state; Liberty Group Publishers of Northbrook, Illinois, owned dailies at Helena, Stuttgart, and Newport (the *Independent* was reduced to semiweekly status in 2001) and the weekly at Heber Springs; American Publishing (later renamed Horizon) of Marion, Illinois, a part of Conrad Black's Hollinger group, acquired Sam Hodges's dailies at Benton and Malvern and the weekly *La Villa* at Hot Springs Village. Others were more closely focused. Westward Communications of The Woodlands, Texas, restricted its holdings to six weeklies in western Arkansas before it sold out to Donrey in 2000.

Some home-grown systems appeared as well. In many instances these multiple ownerships were rather simple. Van and Ginnie Tyson, who had succeeded Tommy Gillespie at the *Atkins Chronicle*, also published the *Dover Times*. Similarly, Bonner McCollum of Forrest City's *Times-Herald* owned the *Marianna Courier-Index*. In earlier days, before the Delta's decline, McCollum had interests in a number of Delta weeklies. One of the largest concerns was that of the Graves family. Louie Graves published the *Nashville News* twice a week as well as weeklies in Glenwood, Mount Ida, and Murfreesboro. The most aggressive example of expansion was that of the Magie family. Starting with Cone and Betty's *Cabot Star-Herald*, they added or acquired newspapers at Carlisle (*Independent*), Jacksonville (*Patriot*), Lonoke (*Democrat*), and Sherwood (*Voice*). When son Mark became president of the APA in 1999, he represented the first sibling to succeed both his parents (Cone in 1967; Betty in 1988) as president. Given the evolving nature of the industry, it is unlikely such an event will ever occur again.

By the year 2000, several newspapers changed hands because the children had no interest in carrying on the tradition. Among those selling out were E.W. Freeman III of the *Pine Bluff Commercial* (1986), Fred Wulfekuhler of the *Paragould Daily Press* (1989), Jay and Patsy Jackson of the *Van Buren County Democrat* of Clinton (1997), Melvin and Charlotte Schexnayder of the *Dumas Clarion* (1998), and John Troutt, Jr. of the *Jonesboro Sun* (2000).

Nevertheless, reinvention remained alive. At Cherokee Village, John A. Cooper's first planned retirement community, the *Cherokee Villager* began with an undated issue in the spring of 1955 intended to celebrate the opening of the community's air strip. Unfortunately, a storm kept the dignitaries from attending. Not until 1961 did this house organ begin regular monthly publication. Editor Jay Kaffka recalled ruefully that celebrating each new arrival consumed two lines of type in already crowded space. Kaffka left in 1966 to become the editor of the Game and Fish Commission's magazine. The *Villager* moved to twice-monthly publication in 1976. Bill Buckley, brought in by the company's media director, Ernie Deane, stayed only one year, but later served the company as senior editor of the company's newspapers at Bella Vista, Hot Springs, and Cherokee Village. Later he worked for the *Morning News of Northwest Arkansas* in Springdale.

In 1990, at the end of the Cooper regime, the publication became a weekly, and the next year David and Heidi Cox purchased it. Developers never permitted their house organs much freedom to report hard news. After becoming an independent newspaper, the *Cherokee Villager* soon regularly won APA contests.[1163] Cox acquired Hardy's *Community Journal* in 1997, renaming the merged newspaper the *Villager Journal*. In the absence of other county newspapers, the *Villager Journal* became a more mainstream county organ.

David Cox, who attained recognition for both his editorials and his editorial cartoons, also reported local news for KASU, the public radio station of Arkansas State University. In 2001, Cox brushed off his editorial cartooning skills and began drawing for *The Alliance* in northwest Arkansas. He also sold his newspaper to Rust Communications, who hired him to run their news operations not only for the *Villager Journal* but also for the Rust newspapers in Salem and Thayer, Missouri, just across the state line. His work also appeared in the *Arkansas Democrat-Gazette*.

Things were different at Hot Springs Village where two newspapers competed. The *La Villa News*'s predecessor was the house organ of Cooper Communities. Acquired by Sam Hodges, who took particular pride in renaming it the *La Villa News*, it passed to American Publishing Company. The competing *Village Voice* was founded by activist Mel Fluhart, who sold it to Ken and Delores Richardson. On April 1, 2001, the Richardsons bought and closed the *La Villa News*. Since Hot Springs had an existing daily newspaper, the Richardsons concentrated on local happenings and group meetings. In the virtual absence of crime, the newspaper's police columnist wrote mostly humor. All these retirement communities boasted above average income and education, and the *Voice* had some 15 local columnists.[1164]

A different sort of newspaper came out of Stamps. Dissatisfied with the local coverage provided by the *Lafayette County Democrat*, which Briner Thomas had moved from Stamps to Lewisville in 1959, Lucy and Tommy Goodwin, who met over the Internet, started the *Lafayette County Press*. They immediately focused on community news and quickly established a local loyalty.

Also reborn at the century's end were the two names from the past, the *Southern Standard* and the Amity *Owl*. Both the progenitor newspapers were long gone when Joe May resurrected both names for his Amity weekly in 1996. At Arkadelphia, the *Daily Siftings Herald* objected to his use of "Southern Standard," so May obliged by calling it merely the *Standard*, even if most readers did not. In a nod to Amity's history, A.J. Hunter's venerable "wide awake owl" hung over the banner.[1165]

Calico Rock was another community with a long if erratic newspaper history. The old *Calico Rock Progress* lost out to the new *White River Current*, founded by Barbara De Angelis in 1974. However, in 1993 a group of her employees left and got permission to revive the *Progress*. The war was brief and again Calico Rock was without a *Progress*. After De Angelis's death in 1995 she was succeeded by a daughter, Jeannie Day. The *Current*'s all-female staff of four put out a newspaper that would have met with approval from Walter J. Lemke, being strong on local news, giving space to local historian Helen Lindley, and in general serving the needs and interests of the community.

A comparison of the newspapers of 2000 with those reported in the Meriwether study of 1972

Editor/publisher Joe Weston poses with a copy of his Sharp Citizen. *Weston was not a member of the APA, but his victory in a criminal libel case benefited all newspapers. (Courtesy J.N. Heiskell Collection, UALR Archives & Special Collections)*

"The Last Hot Lead Edition," 1977. For its last hot lead edition, the Northwest Arkansas Times *in Fayetteville photographed the entire process. Here pressman J.O. Wasson is shown setting headlines at a Ludlow machine. (Courtesy Shiloh Museum of Ozark History)*

One reader's response to the death of the Arkansas Gazette: *Jill Davis, art teacher at Little Rock's Pulaski Academy, drew this illustration for her 1991 Christmas card.*

Northwest Arkansas Times *pressman Garland Speck sits with his feet on a hell-cart, where the used lead was collected prior to re-melting. (Courtesy Shiloh Museum of Ozark History)*

APA trophy winners, July 1972. A marked informality grew in Arkansas life as witnessed by the clothing of these winners. Front, left to right, Calvin Mannen, Stuttgart Daily Leader; *Margaret Woolfolk, West Memphis* Evening Times; *Ron Sloan, Monticello* Advance-Monticellonian; *Rupert Phillips,* Baxter Bulletin; *Robert Fisher,* Clarksville Graphic. *Standing:* T.C. *Sanders,* Springdale News; *Fred Wulfekuhler,* Paragould Daily Press; *Harry Wood,* Texarkana Gazette; *W.R. Whitehead, Sr.,* Fordyce News-Advocate; *Melvin Schexnayder,* Dumas Clarion. *(APA Archives)*

Dedication of the Reynolds Library, November 1982 at APA Building, 1701 Broadway. Walter Hussman, Sr., Camden; John Wells, The Daily Record, *Little Rock; Don Reynolds, Donrey Media Group, Fort Smith; and Rebecca Whitehead, Fordyce. (APA Archives)*

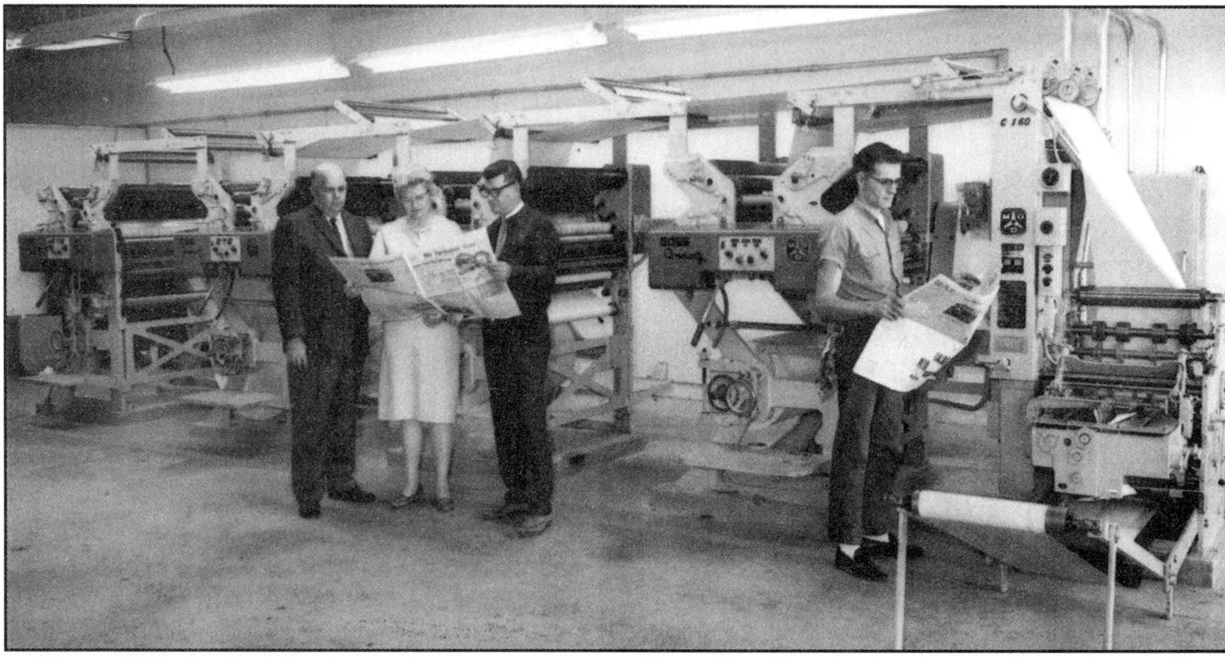

Springdale News' *new Goss press, installed in 1965. Left to right: T.C Sanders, Maudine Sanders, and Charles Sanders; Clay Bowen, pressman. (Courtesy Maudine Sanders/Shiloh Museum of Ozark History)*

A phase in the Great Newspaper War. Publisher Walter Hussman, Jr., standing beside managing editor John Robert Starr, announces that the Arkansas Democrat *will move to a morning publication schedule to compete head-on with the* Arkansas Gazette. *(Photo by Robert Ike Thomas, January 29, 1979;* Arkansas Democrat-Gazette*)*

Arkansas Gazette employees Bill Rutherford, Leroy Donald, and Bob Douglas. (Courtesy Special Collections, University of Arkansas Libraries)

The New Technology. Bill Simmons is pictured at a Hendrix computer in 1977. Note the presence of the ashtray. (Photo by George Douthit; courtesy George Douthit Papers, Special Collections, University of Arkansas Libraries)

Harry McDonald, APA president in 1969, takes a ride on an elephant at the Clyde Beatty-Cole Circus, September 24, 1969. (APA Archives)

The cover of the Arkansas Publisher *in 1970 featured this photo of Paul Buchanan,* Batesville Guard, *protecting his desk and typewriter from a leaking roof. (APA Archives)*

The 1982 flood at Clinton. Patsy Jackson points to the spot where floodwaters reached in the newspaper office. Water damaged the bound volumes of the newspaper and ruined much of the equipment. (Photo by and courtesy Jay W. Jackson)

Jay W. Jackson in his office, c. 1960. Jay and Patsy acquired complete ownership of the Van Buren County Democrat *in 1958 and installed offset printing equipment in 1960. (Courtesy Jay W. Jackson)*

APA Board members burn the mortgage of the APA Building at 1701 Broadway in the mid-1980s: (from left) Eddie Tedford, Texarkana Gazette; *John Ward,* Log Cabin Democrat, *Conway; Orville Richolson,* Newport Independent; *and Joel Irwin,* Cleburne County Times, *Heber Springs.*

Ernie Deane, 1983. Long a fixture in Arkansas life, Ernie Deane was teaching journalism at Fayetteville by 1983. Note that the elaborate name badges of the past had given way to stick-on cards. (Courtesy Fran Alexander)

revealed 21 new voices. Of these, almost half were in communities that had never sported a newspaper in the 19th century: Bella Vista, Cherokee Village, Fairfield Bay, Hot Springs Village, Maumelle, Sherwood, and White Hall were effectively new towns; West Fork (whose newspaper closed in 2002) and Junction City had newspapers only briefly in the 19th century.

Furthermore, a comparison of many individual issues in 2000 with those from three decades earlier provided strong evidence that, contrary to all the predictions about the demise of the press, there often was better news coverage, more involvement in local affairs, and more readership. One sign of the vitality of the weekly press was that at the century's end came the publication of a "magazine" insert exclusively for weeklies called *American Profile*, which over a dozen Arkansas newspapers adopted. APA Executive Director Dennis Schick was widely quoted in 1999, calling the insert "one of the most exciting ideas I have ever seen in my 40 years in the newspaper business."

In order to survive adaptation was needed. Prior to 1970, most small town newspapers also sold office supplies on the side. With the rise of Wal-Mart and large office chains, sales from this source declined. Another historic legacy was lost as publishers no longer served as the town postmasters. Austin Stovall of the *Ozark Journal* at Imboden and Bill Woods at Hazen's *Grand Prairie Herald* were among the last of the breed.

Innovation in finding new sources for profit plainly was needed. Betty Woods operated a gift store in the *Grand Prairie Herald* office; Christina Verderosa sold books at the *De Witt Era-Enterprise*; and many offices still sold wedding invitations, rubber stamps, and calling cards, and made passport photographs. Often the newspaper office was the local headquarters for an Internet provider. Several newspapers were involved in local history publications, and APA associate member D-Books Publishers of Marceline, Missouri, was one major producer of them.

In an interview with this author, former Green Forest publisher and editor Ted Larimer (APA president, 1963) observed that in today's market, only corporations could afford to buy newspapers. However, Arkansas offered many exceptions to this rule. In 1997, when C.F. Scott and Christina Verderosa purchased the *De Witt Era-Enterprise*, it was the only sale to individuals listed in NNA's *Publishers' Auxiliary*. Not all sales were nationally advertised, however, and at least a dozen recent purchases were made by individuals, including Ken Richardson in Hot Springs Village and Frank Lightfoot in White Hall.

Wars...of the Newspaper Kind

On January 8, 1968, K.A. Engel died in Little Rock. Engel had been at the *Arkansas Democrat* since 1911 and its owner since 1926. Under Engel, the *Democrat*, Little Rock's afternoon daily as well as a state presence, had stayed profitable only because he literally counted pencils. Its pay scale was much lower than that of the *Arkansas Gazette*, and it was the last major downtown employer to add air conditioning. The *Democrat* was housed in the old YMCA building, and on hot summer days the odor of aged sweat emerged. Fortunately for his financial health, Engel owned a large minority interest in KTHV-TV, Little Rock's CBS affiliate, Channel 11.

Engel devoted his entire life to the newspaper under the belief that the public wanted news and not personal opinions. The *Democrat* was not known for its editorial page. Although during the 1957 civil rights boycott the *Democrat*'s circulation briefly passed the *Gazette*'s, the *Gazette* regained the lead by 1959. The *Democrat* was considered a boring newspaper (aside from the work of the redoubtable George Douthit), whose employees were believed to crib stories from the *Gazette*. To test this thesis, an "adventurous young cub reporter fresh out of college" inserted a football result from two fictitious towns in the morning *Gazette* and watched it promptly reappear in the evening *Democrat*.[1166] After Engel's death, the newspaper passed to his nephews, C.S. Berry and Marcus B. George.

Even if the newspaper had a new Hoe Colormatic press and was to celebrate its miscalculated 100th birthday in 1971, it was in deep trouble. Throughout the 20th century, metropolitan areas had seen a drastic reduction in the number of dailies. Gone from New York were almost all the great newspaper names of history, and in cities much larger than Little Rock only single corporate ownership of both the morning and evening newspapers or joint operating agreements (JOAs: two publications, one printing plant) had become necessary. The evening newspaper in particular took broadsides from evening television newscasts and from advertisers who believed morning advertisements were more effective. Advertisers also tended to avoid Saturday publications.

Berry and George decided on a more vigorous presence, and in 1968 hired as associate editor of the editorial page Robert S. McCord, who then sold the *North Little Rock Times* to its business manager, Tom Riley. Joining Riley as editor was John Thompson from the *Pine Bluff Commercial*. In keeping with practices of the day, McCord bought five percent of the *Democrat*'s stock, becoming, for ABC purposes, a part owner. McCord's association with the *Democrat* went back to his high school days, when he started as a part-time photographer. During summers he had worked there, and after graduating from Columbia with a master's degree in 1957, Engel had hired him as a reporter and editor of the Sunday magazine. Then McCord had left to take over the *Times* in North Little Rock. A well-known conservative, McCord planned to create an intellectual and political alternate to the *Gazette*.

For news editor, Berry and George hired Gene C. Foreman away from the *Pine Bluff Commercial*. Foreman pumped much new life into the reporting side, but soon left for the *Philadelphia Inquirer*, and Jerry McConnell from the *Arkansas Gazette* took his place. The circulation, which stood at about 85,000 at the beginning of the new regime, continued to fall, reaching 60,000 in 1972 and steadily headed lower. As the bleeding continued, Berry, George, and McCord approached Hugh Patterson with a proposal for a joint operating agreement, but Patterson declined: "There was no way we could underwrite their losses."[1167] Knight Ridder and other outside investors were not interested either.

Then, in 1974, the nephews sold the *Democrat* to WEHCO Media for $3.75 million, and young Walter E. Hussman, Jr., a journalism graduate of the University of North Carolina with a master's degree in business administration from Columbia University, took charge. Berry and George promptly decamped, but McCord stayed on as executive editor. Four years later, Hussman was ready to quit and offered to sell the *Democrat* to Patterson, who refused. In 1978, McCord resigned and began producing documentaries for the Arkansas Educational Television Network (AETN).

Hussman then hired John Robert Starr as managing editor. Starr had earlier started his own weekly in Pine Bluff, worked for Orval Faubus, and then joined the Associated Press where he eventually became its Little Rock bureau chief. He had retired in order to go into journalism education when Hussman convinced him to leave unfinished his doctorate at the University of Tennessee and come back to Little Rock. Starr certainly enlivened the Little Rock scene and might be best defined as fulfilling the need for the fighting editor that Thomas C. Hindman had delivered to long-dead Napoleon. Not even during the worst of Reconstruction did any editor ever say anything approaching Starr's remark: "I'm a street fighter. Kick 'em in the nuts."

Starr expected the same aggressiveness from his staff. Foreman, he thought, might have raised the level of reporting and made the *Democrat* "the afternoon imitation of the morning mistake," but Starr wanted none of it. The *Democrat* had become too liberal in its editorials. As Starr put it, "we are no longer going to put out a newspaper to impress other newspapermen; we are not even going to put out a newspaper to impress ourselves, we are going to try to put out a newspaper to impress the people." For Starr personally, this meant an anti-establishment populism that ridiculed Hugh Patterson's son Carrick for his ability to sing and appreciate classical music; it also meant an almost pathological hatred of Arkansas's attorney general, governor, and future United States president, Bill Clinton. Starr used Hussman's money to increase the news staff from about 66 to over 100, and soon the *Democrat* was printing more local news than its rival. Starr's enthusiasm infected the staff. "We were young kids," Meredith Oakley later recalled.[1168]

On January 29, 1979, Hussman switched the newspaper from evening to morning in order to meet the *Gazette* head on and eliminate its advertising advantage. And he took a trip to Canada to study a newspaper that actually gave away free classified advertising. Returning enamored with the idea, he met with the senior staff, and although they advised against it, he went ahead and put it into operation. Sales increased, and it made the *Democrat* fatter than the *Gazette*. "A great strategy," Hussman called it in retrospect.[1169] A free Wednesday shopper, token subscription charges, and cutting the rates for major advertisers to one dollar an inch when the *Gazette* charged from $8.66 to $15.29 completed the makeover.

The war went through two phases. From 1979 to 1986 the Pattersons fought the war, mainly by ignoring Starr's daily insults. Ingrained at the *Gazette* was a belief in its innate superiority. Bob McCord, who joined the *Gazette* in 1981, was amazed to find that its editors and writers did not even clip stories from the *Democrat*, and many bragged about never reading the opposition.

In order to win, Hussman drew on the entire resources of the Palmer chain to subsidize his losses. Although much would be written about the political and philosophical differences between the two newspapers, of white backlash to civil rights legislation and of the rise of the religious right, in reality the struggle was between business offices. Given its newspaper and television holdings, the advantage from the start lay with Hussman. The *Gazette*, which did not have deep pockets, began to suffer, and in 1984 filed an anti-trust suit charging predatory practices against the *Democrat*'s free classified advertisements. Much money was spent on high-powered lawyers whom Hugh Patterson believed performed poorly, and the *Gazette* lost.[1170] Two years later, Patterson, "tired, bitter and unwilling to meet Hussman's tactics," Bob McCord recalled, sold the newspaper to the huge Gannett chain that consisted of 84 newspapers and had operating revenues of $3 billion.

The Gannett years began with the arrival of president "Big Al" Neuharth in a stretch limousine that blocked a city street. He declared that the *Gazette* now had the deeper pockets, but what followed was the rapid deterioration of the newspaper from the ideals Heiskell had held. Gannett management possessed a "cookie cutter mentality," Max Brantley recalled, and expected a 30 percent return on its investment.[1171] Editor Walker Lundy attempted to make it a sort of Arkansas *USA Today*, also a money-loser at that time. Reporter Ernie Dumas recalled that Lundy "wanted big fluffy things on the front page, light-hearted things that had nothing to do with public policy or world events, just off-beat, light stuff."[1172] The new publishers Gannett sent in also wanted more conservative editorials, but apparently Neuharth had promised Hugh Patterson to leave the editorial page alone, and the *Gazette* remained liberal to the end.

Mismanagement at all levels was rife. One Gannett import "came to work late, fiddled around, played golf, went home."[1173] One story heard in several versions dealt with the *Gazette* reporting a piece of hard news, the subject being a disappointing Dillard's department stores' earnings report. Whether from this cause or because Dillard's learned that Gannett was offering other advertisers better rates than Dillard's, that chain pulled all its advertisements and never returned.* Although the *Gazette* maintained its circulation and paid advertising leadership, Gannett had little experience in fighting wars and less patience with mounting losses, which by 1990 rose to $30,000,000. As a publicly traded company, it had to account to its stockholders.

The last publisher Gannett sent in, Maurice "Moe" Hickey, an expert in liquidation, spent 40 seconds telling employees the *Gazette* was being shut down and then left town before it happened. With no warning or farewell, the last issue—which should have been a proper obituary—rolled off the presses on October 18, 1991. The *Arkansas Gazette*, the oldest business in Arkansas as well as the oldest newspaper west of the Mississippi River, died one month and a day short of its 173rd birthday. Some 500 full-time employees and 1,700 carriers were out of work.

Gannett sold the *Gazette*'s assets to Hussman, who thereupon retooled the banner to read the *Arkansas Democrat-Gazette* with the slogan "The Best of Both." However, it was not a merger. The Old Lady, or, as in her final years, The Old Gray Lady, was dead. Initially the only two *Gazette* journalists who went to work immediately at the *Democrat-Gazette* were columnists Richard Allin and Charles Allbright, and that was because they had held their contracts with Gannett rather than with the *Gazette*. It was Starr's rule not to hire former *Gazette* employees, but Starr retired after the war's end, and Leroy Donald (business news), Irene Wassell (food editor), Karen (Knutson) Martin (features), Terry Jones (copy editor), Bill Shelton (copy editor), Steve Keesee (photographer) and others later found work at the *Democrat-Gazette*.

The meanings of the *Democrat*'s victory were many. Economically, America had become a country where only one newspaper per town could survive. As Walter E. Hussman, Jr., told the APA in 1992, the hometown newspaper had beaten the outside-owned one.[1174] Despite much criticism within the state about Gannett's mismanagement, the principal cause of Hussman's success had been his willingness to reach as deep as he needed into his pockets, his dogged determination, and his persistence.

The political implications were of statewide significance. In fairness, the *Democrat* should have been renamed the *Republican*. The indifference to personalities that had been the *Democrat*'s trademark in the days of August Engel or the lofty indifference to personalities but not issues that had marked Heiskell's *Gazette* gave way to John Robert Starr's vehemence and Paul Greenberg's reactionary retreat from his Pulitzer Prize-winning youth. Also lost was an institutional state press. The *Gazette* had circulated to every county and even under Gannett misrule still offered statewide coverage. Financially, this was a burden, and the *Democrat-Gazette* concentrated on its core market. Large parts of the state now slept very quietly as far as the *Democrat-Gazette* was concerned.

The belief that Arkansas no longer possessed a state press suggested to historians that the end of the *Arkansas Gazette* was, symbolically, the end of Arkansas history. From Fayetteville, Roy Reed turned

* Dillard's made a similar move in 2001 against television stations after stories about the practices of its security personnel appeared on national television.

his attention to chronicling the history of the *Gazette*'s final years, and the *Arkansas Publisher* did a major service to history by having former *Gazette* employees write their reminiscences while events were still fresh in their memories.

One major concern to historians was the *Gazette*'s rich photographic library, which once sported its own curator and was accessible to researchers. In Memphis, the old Memphis *Commercial Appeal* and *Press-Scimitar* photographs went to the University of Memphis, but the *Democrat-Gazette*, believing that money could be made from these pictures, did not pass their holdings over to the Arkansas History Commission or another research library. They continue to sit in the basement of the old Gazette building.

One of the major resources in Arkansas history had been the accessibility of the *Arkansas Gazette* through a thorough indexing project undertaken at Arkansas Tech University. Shannon J. Henderson, Tech's librarian, had indexed "The Chronicles of Arkansas" series as his master's thesis. Then he undertook to index the *Gazette*'s current years, starting with 1964. Finally, he went back to 1819 and carried the indexing forward into the 1890s.

After the demise of the *Gazette*, Henderson continued the project but received scant help from the *Democrat-Gazette*, which at first refused to provide him a copy of the *Gazette*'s final edition. Unwilling to index the early edition sent to Russellville, which would not be the one available on microfilm, Henderson drove to Hendrix College at Conway to get the final edition, made the entries on his computer, and returned to Russellville. Later, Hendrix librarian Delores Thompson forwarded the newspaper to him until the *Democrat-Gazette* undertook to supply copies.[1175] Henderson retired in 1993 (and died the following year) but Tech's indexing continued through 1999.

The *Democrat-Gazette* later created its own

website, with indexing being accessible through this source. The newspaper charged a fee of $1.95 per retrieved item, and access to the *Arkansas Democrat-Gazette*'s website required the researcher to have a newspaper subscription. These charges effectively ended the use of the newspaper for historical research by ordinary students or faculty.

Starr stepped down as managing editor after the 1991 victory but continued to write a column. When he died in 2000, the wounds of over two decades of caustic columns still festered. Starr was often credited with playing a major role in the *Democrat*'s victory, and people either loved or hated him. The great Latin motto, *De mortuis nil nisi bonum*, or "Do not speak ill of the dead," failed to restrain former *Gazette* feature writer and *Arkansas Times* columnist Bob Lancaster, who called Starr's columns, which he wrote up to his death, "all-too-characteristically petty, self-indulgent, inconsequential, stupid, loutish, and uncalled for."[1176]

Somewhat obscured by the demise of the *Gazette* were other wars in smaller places. One took place in Cleburne County, where the upstart *Arkansas Sun* began its career as a mimeographed sheet started by a commune at Greers Ferry on January 8, 1973, before moving eventually to Heber Springs. Known as The Group, Inc., the commune helped Heber Springs organize an Optimist Club, started a dinner theater, and supported the Chamber of Commerce. But when they registered and voted in a highly contested election, their property was burned, and a mob of leading citizens attacked their headquarters. State police had to be sent in to rescue the beleaguered members, who resettled in Little Rock. John Barnes, who bought the *Arkansas Sun* from The Group, later moved to Little Rock, where he became a stockbroker and well-known television and radio commentator. In 1980, the *Sun* was purchased by Pat and O. E. Jones of the *Batesville Guard*, who kept it until 1985. The *Sun* survived their departure, and fought the established *Cleburne County Times* edited by Joel L. Irwin (APA president, 1985). This war proved that the age of the circulation liar had not ended, and federal postal authorities twice fined the *Sun*.* It printed and paid the second class mailing on a larger number than it actually mailed, sending the rest to the city dump. The war ended in 1990 when American Publishing Company bought the two newspapers and merged them. Ownership passed in 1998 to Liberty Group Publishers after American divested itself of its smaller weeklies.

Gentry, in northwestern Arkansas, was the scene of another struggle. The *Journal-Advance* dated to the late 19th century but had led a checkered life. Marion Wasson, the one-time state banking commissioner, was briefly an owner. The *Journal-Advance* was prematurely pronounced dead in 1973 but actually survived until 1985. Then, after a short hiatus, two rivals arose to take its place. The tabloid *Gentry American* was first. Its owner, John Brimacombe, had previously published a shopper out of Fayetteville. A month later came the *Gentry Courier* of John and Martha Block. They had found a lack of support earlier for a newspaper in Farmington, but the *Courier* was full size, prompting the *American* to convert to meet the competition. Local historian Joe Carl credited the *Courier*'s victory to its having more local news.[1177]

Even more obscure was the newspaper war in Calhoun County. *The Arkansaw Plaindealer*, supposedly started in 1889 at Woodberry, had many owners along the way, including four (all absentee) APA presidents: Roy Elliott, C.A. VerBeck, William R. Whitehead, and Ray Kimball. Challenged by the rival *Hampton Herald* after 1953, it was merged in 1960 and lost its name in 1969, becoming after a bankruptcy the *South Arkansas Accent*. Alan and Jeanette Goolsby bought the newspaper out of bankruptcy and ran it until 1981, when they sold it to David Walters. In 1988, Ovid Goode purchased the *Accent* from Walters. Goode, who started his career as the first black reporter for the *Los Angeles Daily News* in 1971, just wanted to own a weekly and found this one for sale and affordable. In 1995, Goode founded the *Arkansas Tribune*, a black newspaper published from Little Rock and which he wanted to make statewide. During the mid-1990s, Hampton, which sometimes sported one working stop light, supported two weekly newspapers. Mack C. Owens Jr., the son of the *Herald*'s founder and himself the founder of the *Accent* before selling out, came back from Texas in 1993 to open the *South Arkansas Sun*. Brenda Clark, who purchased the *Sun* from Owens in March 1996, then bought the *Accent* from Goode two months later, ending a war which Goode felt had some racial overtones.

* During the *Gazette-Democrat* struggle, both newspapers' circulation figures were called into question. *Arkansas Gazette*, November 3, 11, 1989.

Another war may not even have been a war at all, for much about it remains poorly understood. This mysterious engagement, possibly fought in the smallest daily competitive newspaper market in all America, had its origins in 1970 when the Shiras heirs sold the *Baxter Bulletin* of Mountain Home to Harold E. Martin of the *Montgomery* (Alabama) *Advertiser*. George Smith, a Hope native who had been an editor at age 19, founded a weekly at 20, and went to work at the *Bulletin* under Tom Dearmore and Pete Shiras, remained editor when Martin sent up as publisher one of his bright young men, Rupert E. Phillips. Not content with his work at the *Bulletin*, Phillips in 1975 purchased Yellville's *Mountain Echo*, a newspaper that shared a market with the *Bulletin*. Martin saw this as a conflict of interest, and sent Rusty Fraser to replace Phillips. Phillips then planned a counterattack by establishing a shopper, but Fraser got his out first and Phillips moved on to greener pastures, that in Arkansas included the *Hope Star* and Arkadelphia's *Daily Siftings Herald*. Not limiting himself to Arkansas, Phillips's empire eventually stretched from his home base in Florida to the Washington, D.C. area and west to the 117-year-old *Honolulu Star-Bulletin*.

Meanwhile, the *Baxter Bulletin* flourished. From a once a week weekly, it moved by stages to twice a week and then thrice a week, becoming the largest weekly in Arkansas and the third largest in the nation before converting to a daily in 1985. Harold E. Martin had become president of Multimedia's news division, and the *Baxter Bulletin* had passed to this corporation. Multimedia's decision to convert by stages into a daily angered many readers and some advertisers. Taking advantage of the situation, Phillips in 1989 reentered Baxter County, acquiring the small *North Arkansas View*. This he converted into the *Daily News*. Phillips, who built a fine plant but spent little on the news side, kept up the war until after Multimedia was merged into Gannett in 1995. Then in 1999 the *News* shut down, its subscription list immediately passing to its competitor.

This little episode might have passed unnoticed outside the limited confines of North Arkansas had it not been that another of Phillips's maneuvers received national attention. On September 16, 1999, Gannett and Phillips announced the ending of their Joint Operating Agreement and the planned closing of the *Honolulu Star-Bulletin* under an agreement that would have netted Phillips $26.5 million. Unlike the demise of the *Arkansas Gazette*, there were other buyers, and amidst great uproar and bolstered by a strong court ruling, the *Star-Bulletin* has continued to survive. Journalist Lucinda Fleeson characterized Phillips as "Gannett's Trading Partner," and after analyzing Phillips's long and complex relations with Gannett (which, although she did not mention it, included acting as a broker during the final days of the *Arkansas Gazette*!), she implied that the Baxter County engagement may have ended up merely as a friendly tactical operation.[1178]

...And Rumors of War

At the time of this writing a second big newspaper war was being waged that lacked initially the apocalyptic qualities of that which marked the demise of the *Gazette*. In the last decades of the 20th century, northwest Arkansas was in the process of becoming one large metropolitan area of some 310,000 people bounded by Fayetteville on the south, Bentonville on the north, Springdale/Rogers on the east and with a number of other small communities east and west being swallowed up in what some called Ozarkopolis. The old rule, that a county line was "almost like a wall," was seriously weakened when thousands of newcomers poured in or people lived in one town and worked in another.[1179]

The prologue of the war began in 1937 with the *Fayetteville Democrat* being renamed the *Northwest Arkansas Times*. In 1968, the Thomson Newspapers purchased the *Times* from the Fulbrights but kept George Gearhart (APA president, 1971) in charge. The newspaper did not thrive although the region was rapidly growing.

Meanwhile, at the *Springdale News*, Edward R. Stafford, John P.'s son, went from a once a week publication to three times a week in 1948 and to a daily the next year. From 1958 to 1973, members of the Sanders family (Bob, Maudine, Charles, and T.C.) owned the newspaper. The *News* converted at first to a bastard offset, and a former vault became a darkroom. After the Sanders family sold out to the Donrey Media Group in 1973, even more changes followed.

A few miles away in Benton County, E.W. Pate of the *Rogers Daily News* and the weekly *Democrat* sold out to Charles Nutter in 1955, who in turn disposed of the newspapers to Donrey. Since Rogers and Springdale were only a few miles apart, Donrey built a new plant to print both newspapers; then it merged them in 1994, converting it to a morning schedule and opening a news bureau in Fayetteville. So armed and now styled the *Morning News of Northwest Arkansas*, this newspaper went forth to try to claim the region as its own. As early as 1990, the state press recognized that a war was underway.[1180]

The third element was at Bentonville, where the only survivor from its many newspapers was the weekly *Benton County Democrat*. In the early 1950s Wesley E. Hunnicutt was the editor/publisher. Wal-Mart acquired the newspaper in 1972, primarily in order to have its own press for printing flyers and sale advertisements. As Bentonville grew, the newspaper became a five-day daily in 1978, and added a Sunday edition in 1980. Since running a newspaper was not part of Wal-Mart's corporate strategies, in 1982 it sold the *Benton County Daily Democrat*, but not the printing plant, to James C. Walton, Sam's banker-son, and Steve Trolinger (APA president, 1994), who styled their operation Community Publishers, Incorporated (CPI). The sheet-fed and silk-screen printing operation remained with Wal-Mart under the name PMDC (Printing, Mailing & Distribution Center), but the web press later came back to CPI. Since the banner "Benton County Democrat" was a totally inappropriate name in an area now dominated by right-wing Republicans, the newspaper became the *Benton County Daily Record* in 1988. It added a Saturday issue and switched to a morning newspaper in 1993. Walton may have had little background in newspapers, but his wife, Lynne McNabb, once served as the classified advertising manager for the *Baxter Bulletin*, in Mountain Home.

There were thus three players (Fayetteville, Springdale/Rogers, and Bentonville) competing for domination in this emerging market when in 1995 Thomson Newspapers decided to sell the languishing *Northwest Arkansas Times*. Walter Hussman and James Walton offered $15 million for the property, but Thomson got $22 million from N.A.T., LC (the initials supposedly stood for *Northwest Arkansas Times*) a Stephens, Inc., entity.[1181] Had the sale stood, Stephens, which had acquired Donrey, would have controlled 85 percent of the market.

CPI cried foul, and (unlike the ill-fated *Arkansas Gazette* case) joined by the Justice Department, won its antitrust suit in federal court. On September 20, 1995, N.A.T., LC sold the *Times* back to Thomson which on the same day sold it to American Publishing Corporation, a division of Hollinger International, a Canadian firm. In 1999, American sold it to CPI, thus allowing CPI to outflank the more centrally located Donrey newspapers. Another part of CPI's strategy consisted of acquiring the weeklies of Bella Vista, Gentry, Gravette, Pea Ridge, and Siloam Springs. Attacking Donrey on its home ground, they even started the weekly *Rogers Hometown News*, appealing to those who believed Rogers's home news was being ignored.

The final element in the mix was Walter E.

Hussman, Jr. Hussman eyed the rapidly growing northwest market with envy, and drawing again on the resources of the old Palmer chain and the *Democrat-Gazette*, he moved into the market.

First, the *Arkansas Democrat-Gazette* produced its own Northwest Arkansas edition, dubbed by its enemies as the "parachute paper," although in fact it was an edition carried up to the area by truck. Since Walter Hussman now used the former *Gazette* press, he moved his old one to a new plant in Lowell and began adding successive stages of regional tailoring. Much of this tailoring was more ideological (opposition to abortion, property taxes, etc.) than in reporting school board meetings or football scores, but the edition did carry regional advertising, television schedules, and business news. Although all the players were essentially newcomers, as last to arrive Hussman generated the most hostility. "Why can't Walter be satisfied with his riches and blessings in South Arkansas instead of causing grief by coming up here?" one publisher asked.

All three newspapers were approximately the same size when in 2000 came the surprise announcement of a unique "alliance" rather improperly called at the time a joint operating agreement (JOA) between Hussman and CPI. In a normal JOA, the smaller newspaper is saved by joining its business operations with the stronger. In the CPI/*Democrat-Gazette* agreement, the *Democrat-Gazette* controlled all the business aspects (advertising, circulation, production, etc.) of the three newspapers; only those in the news departments remained CPI employees. At the time of this writing there was speculation that the Fayetteville and Bentonville newspapers might be swallowed up into one Hussman-dominated operation. Indeed, Sherman Frederick of Donrey claimed, "The Bentonville and Fayetteville papers have ceased to exist by any meaningful standard in the newspaper industry."[1182] Supporting that idea, the Audit Bureau of Circulation determined that since the two CPI newspapers were only editions of the *Democrat-Gazette* and no longer separate newspapers, it dropped them from membership.

Donrey emphasized local news, and the *Morning News* came out with zoned editions for Fayetteville, Springdale, Rogers, and Bentonville. CPI also extended its reach by acquiring the *Harrison Daily Times* and the *Newton County Times* at Jasper, and six newspapers clustered around Springfield, Mo., but these purchases two counties away reportedly were not involved in the war. Anticipating more growth, Donrey added some 28,000 square feet to its existing 33,000 square foot facility in order to house two lines of DGM 850 presses, each having 18 units and two folders, as well as reconditioned Heidelberg 1472 inserters, and more storage room for newsprint.[1183]

This war differed in many ways from that between the *Gazette* and the *Democrat*. Although some of the Donrey employees were more politically active and interested in such issues as the FOI Act, no clear ideological division existed between the two sets of foes. Nor was there a polarizing force like John Robert Starr. Instead, this was a naked struggle between two closed firms to control advertising revenues in the fastest growing region of Arkansas.

Another significant difference was the impact on the rest of the state. As Hussman shifted his emphasis to the northwest market, Little Rock readers began to complain about finding that region's news instead of local news in their morning newspaper. Thirteen column inches on the theft of the Springdale mayor's wallet or 28 inches on Bentonville's future power needs resulted in much local vocal complaint. The Little Rock-based e-newsletter *Briefing Notebook* observed that the *Democrat-Gazette* had been "in a death-swoon for the last two years," having become like the other WEHCO newspapers, "blood donors for Hussman's war elsewhere."[1184] Conversely, the Bentonville and Fayetteville newspapers now came wrapped around the *Democrat-Gazette*, which provided the state, national, and international coverage for these three newspapers. Despite both the alliance and the *Morning News* offering similar products, local loyalities continued to be important, as shown in circulation figures.

Meanwhile, as Hussman shifted personnel to the northwest, Donrey hired veteran AP reporter Dennis Byrd and established a large Little Rock bureau that began beating the *Democrat-Gazette* in key state stories. Other state newspapers, including the *Jonesboro Sun*, were "content partners," sharing in the coverage. Journalist Ernie Dumas also noted that two of Donrey's other newspapers, the flagship Fort Smith *Times Record* and the *Pine Bluff Commercial*, were being "run lean and anemic" in order to sustain the war in the northwest.

At the time of this writing, the CPI/Hussman alliance was roughly equal in circulation to the Stephens (former Donrey) newspaper. In light of the *Democrat-Gazette* war, the question might be which side could best survive sustained losses. Since both sides were closed corporations, there was no public information available, although speculations were rife. Neither side had been making money, but when a Donrey official estimated that the CPI/*Democrat-Gazette* side was losing over $10 million a year, they denied it.

¡Hola!

The first appearance of Hispanics in the Arkansas press came during the 1920s at Bauxite, a Saline County town owned by the Aluminum Company of America (Alcoa), which imported from Texas some 320 Mexicans and housed them in a section of town called, appropriately, Mexico. The house organ, the *Bauxite Bulletin*, printed news and features of the community in Spanish. This Hispanic connection ended in 1932 when the entire community was deported to Laredo, Texas, because they were the most expendable part of the town's labor force. Although migrant (bracero) labor helped pick Arkansas's cotton during the 1950s, permanent settlement did not begin until the 1980s.

The changing demographics of Arkansas reflected in the 2000 census showed that three percent of Arkansans, or 86,866 persons, claimed Hispanic ethnicity, a 337 percent increase over 1990. Just before Christmas in 2000 the first issue of *¡Hola! Arkansas* hit the streets. Offered gratis, it claimed as its motto, "The Natural State's Premiere Bi-lingual Newspaper," for it printed its stories side by side in English and Spanish. Published monthly out of North Little Rock, it had competition from a second newspaper that used only Spanish. *Arkansas Times* produced the weekly *El Latino* starting in March 2001. *El Latino* promised to serve the Hispanic community of Central Arkansas. Running on the front page was a feature entitled *Quien es quien* (Who's Who) that featured prominent local Hispanics. From Memphis, the *Commercial Appeal* put out the weekly Spanish-only *La Prensa Latina*, whose motto was "Semanario Informativo y Cultural" (weekly news and culture). While this organ had Associated Press coverage and listed Arkansas under its banner as one of the states it covered, its local news came mostly from Memphis. Other Spanish language newspapers had appeared in northwest Arkansas such as *La Prensa de Northwest Arkansas*, which was purchased by Stephens Media Group in 2003. The presence of these newspapers marked the rebirth of non-English language journals after half a century, and advertisements in Spanish could be found in many newspapers around the state.

The appearance of Hispanic newspapers coincided with a decline in the state's black press. After the demise of L.C. and Daisy Bates's *State Press* in 1959, there remained the *Southern Mediator Journal*, which first appeared in Helena in the late 1930s before moving to Little Rock where it was associated for a time with the *Twin City Press*. Then in 1973 a newspaper called the *Arkansas Tribune* appeared briefly. Perhaps the best written of the lot, it lasted only a few months before closing.

In 1984, after a 24-year gap, the *Arkansas State Press* reappeared with Daisy Bates listed as editor. Janis Kearney bought the weekly from Bates in 1988 and her sister, Janetta, succeeded her as editor in 1993, when Janis followed Bill Clinton to Washington. The *State Press* suspended in 1998. Its competition included the *Southern Mediator*, then published by Charles Dolphus and at one point briefly edited by Jess C. Henderson, a white journalist. The *Mediator* had the services for many years of J.F. Cooley, a noted civil rights activist formerly of Forrest City. Then there was the *Arkansas Tribune* (which only incidentally shared the same name as the newspaper of 1973), started in 1995 by Ovid Goode, the Hampton publisher. Another Little Rock newspaper, the tabloid *The Rock of Arkansas*, published by Patrice Cates Brown, also started in 1995 and featured primarily church and religious news. Finally, Forrest City native Curtis Varnado published *Homeland*, a weekly tabloid, which he printed in Minneapolis.

All these efforts labored under great difficulties. In 1986, the expenses associated with the *Arkansas State Press* almost cost Mrs. Bates her home, which in 2000 became a National Historic Site. *Homeland* lasted about two years. The longest-lived black newspaper, the *Southern Mediator*, closed during the 1990s but was being advertised for sale in 2001. Ovid Goode's *Arkansas Tribune* fell to monthly status. It suspended in the spring of 2001 but was revived in the fall. It was purchaed in 2002 by Stacy Williams, a Little Rock businessman, who published it on a monthly publication schedule.

The problems the black press faced were many. With the end of segregation came the closing of businesses that catered exclusively to blacks and were

often black-owned. News about blacks now regularly appeared in the state's weeklies and dailies. "We want to be mainstream," Bill Reed, the executive director of the Black Press of America division of the NNPA, explained in 1996, "even to the point of neglecting reading about events in our own communities."[1185] Obviously, the same could not be said about the Hispanic community at the time of this writing.

The APA at the Century's End

When APA manager Louise Bowker resigned in 1979 after 17 years, she had accumulated a number of awards. The Arkansas Press Women had given her their achievement award in 1961. Then she became the recipient in 1962 of the APA's Man [*sic*] of the Year Award, subsequently de-sexed to become the President's Award. She also had served in 1969 as president of the national Newspaper Association Managers (NAM). Despite never intending her APA work to be a career, she created stability during the first wave of great change brought about by offset. "It was a wonderful time to be the manager," she later recalled.[1186] Her departure was due in part to the coming of computers and her lack of interest in starting over on them. It caught the Association by surprise, and for four months, the APA office operated with no one in charge.

APA president Fred Wulfekuhler of Paragould wanted to make the APA a more active body and believed the best way to achieve that goal was to bring in an out-of-state professional. The result was the hiring of C. Dennis Schick, who had previous experience with the Oklahoma and Texas press associations but was teaching at the University of Texas in Austin at the time of his appointment.[1187] Despite having worked on newspaper staffs in Texas and Illinois, Schick held a doctorate in mass communications and thus typified the growing emphasis on academic training.

Nationwide, the trend was away from persons with only practical experience, or, as in Bowker's case, on-the-job training. Like Bowker, Schick too served as president of the national Newspaper Association Managers. He remained the APA's Executive Director at the century's end, having served over two decades, longer than any other APA manager.

Under Schick, the *Arkansas Publisher* resumed the publication of volume and issue numbers and went to a quarterly schedule. "A lasting history of the association," he called it. Timely copy would go into the weekly newsletter long called the *Confidential Bulletin* but renamed the *Member Bulletin* when associate members were added to the mailing list; photographs, general interest stories, and "the total marketing concept" would be saved for the *Arkansas Publisher*. In addition, both the *Publisher* and the bulletins would feature his own column, "Dennis Anyone?" a title he first had used for a college humor column.[1188] So important had advertising become that a second column generally appeared from the advertising manager, and in recent years a third column, on technology.

As part of the commitment to history and member service Schick in 1986 recruited retired newspaperman Gene Herrington as a field representative and sent him around the state visiting, much in the way Walter J. Lemke and Clio Harper had done before him. Herrington, a Lemke student, had worked at Marianna before joining the *Arkansas Democrat*, where he served as managing editor. Later, he worked in public relations for Arkansas Power & Light Company. Some APA presidents made the same commitment, visiting as many offices as they could during their tenure. And most presidents wrote regular columns for inclusion in the magazine.

The first major accomplishment of the Schick years was buying a building after years of renting. Schick had seen a reference in an old set of minutes to a Building Committee, and asked the APA board if they wanted to follow up on this idea. Convinced of the economy of the move, the board scrounged up the money for a down payment in 1981 and got many of its members to make five-year pledges to match their dues in order to pay off the mortgage. The Dr. Alfred Kahn house, built around 1914 and long the home of the Charles Vestal family, gave the APA a presence at 17th and Broadway, close to downtown and near the Governor's Mansion.

There were difficulties in the early years after the purchase when some members failed to honor their pledges. "There are too many slackers," Joel Irwin, APA president from Heber Springs complained in 1985, but the mortgage was paid off.[1189] Predictably, the APA outgrew the converted house even after selling the clipping service in 1995, which had swollen to eight employees, and adding more space in the back by converting the former garage into an annex.

The eve of the new century saw the sale of this building as the APA moved to within one block of the capitol, on Victory Street. The old *Arkansas Gazette* building would have been highly appropriate, but it was too expensive, too big, and had an asbestos problem. The board also wanted a permanent and well-developed museum of the newspaper industry. The *Gazette* site again would have been perfect in this regard, especially since the Arkansas Territorial Restoration, which was renamed the Historic Arkansas Museum in 2001, already had an exhibit on William E. Woodruff's early Little Rock operation only three blocks away.

The growth and development of the APA was enhanced when the new building gave the APA an entire second floor to rent. Even by 1986 dues represented only 12.5 percent of the APA's income,[1190] and like many not-for-profit bodies, entrepreneurship was necessary for survival. "Well, Dennis," a friend said in 1979, "you got the job. Now you've got to go out and raise your own salary." By 2002, the APA's budget ran to slightly over one million dollars, of which only eight percent came from dues.

Two of the most important aspects of the manager's work over the years involved legislation and advertising contracts. With the FOI Act under biennial attack and some legislators anxious to "get" the press in any way possible, the APA hired its first paid lobbyist, Herschell Parent, in 1989.[1191] The office of lobbyist then became a regular but part-time position. Starting in 1990, Milton Scott, a longtime government affairs staff member of the Arkansas Farm Bureau, became the APA's lobbyist. In addition to FOI Act concerns, other lobbying issues involved attempts to tax advertising and newspaper sales, efforts to reduce the printing of public notices or move them to the Internet, and a wide range of proposed idiosyncracisms such as product disparagement bills ("veggie libel"), mandated newsprint recycling, or a prohibition on telemarketing.

Advertising issues proved to be especially tricky. Starting in June 1982, one issue a year of the *Arkansas Publisher* for several years was devoted to this concern. The advertising world was changing greatly, in part because previous prohibitions against advertising (commercial speech) by doctors, accountants, and lawyers had been eliminated by United States Supreme Court decisions starting with *Virginia State Board of Pharmacy v. Virginia Citizens Consumer Council* (1976).[1192] Despite early fears of "hucksterism" by doctors or "ambulance-chasing" from lawyers, newspapers benefited from the growing revenue these sources generated.

Two additional advertising services were added in subsequent years, a Statewide Classified Advertising Network in 1985, and a 2x2 Network in 1998. Both have been exceptionally successful as producers of revenue, as they have for most press associations throughout the country. The Association rebates commissions to participating newspapers.

There had been talk over the years of incorporating a for-profit entity to handle the advertising and clipping services, but it had never been done before Dennis Schick became manager. Between the time he attended his first board meeting in June 1979 and heard about the situation, and the next meeting in February 1980, he filed the necessary papers and came to the meeting having established Arkansas Press Services, a for-profit entity owned by the APA.

Schick developed strategies on how to regain lost political advertisements, including creating speculative (spec) ads for statewide candidates for newspapers to sell locally. During the war between the *Arkansas Gazette* and the *Arkansas Democrat* all Central Arkansas weeklies suffered from the *Democrat*'s free service, for classifieds "represent the margin of profit" for many weeklies.[1193] While still in Texas at the university, Dr. Schick had authored a text, *How to Create Newspaper Advertising That Moves Merchandise*, and he continued occasionally to teach evening classes part-time at UALR and to conduct advertising seminars for the APA and other press associations in the United States and Canada.

Among the developments in the advertising field was the ushering in of the Standard Advertising Unit (SAU) system in 1984, which supposedly would facilitate the mass sale of advertising by standardizing column widths.[1194] Although the new system made buying advertising easier, national advertisers did not flock to the industry. Despite major and sometimes successful efforts by the National Newspaper Association (NNA), its sales branch, the American Newspaper Representatives (ANR), and the Newspaper Association of America (NAA) and its sales arm, the National Newspaper Network (NNN) to target specific product categories, newspapers remained primarily a local advertising medium. At the century's end, a trend to convert to a 50-inch web width (thus shrinking a page to 12 1/2 inches wide and a column width from 2 1/16 inches to 1 13/16) once again un-standardized column widths.

Radio and newspapers competed for local advertising dollars, and many newspapers ran effective promotions for themselves on radio stations. Television was more focused on larger businesses. Probably not unique was an expensive television advertisement heard by the author for an automobile dealership starring a small child, probably the owner's son, who told viewers to ignore all those companies with big advertisements in the newspapers and come see his father for lower prices.

Advertising had more than commercial significance. In 1986 the APA undertook a public service advertising campaign to educate voters about how the FOI Act was important to them.[1195] Another form of promoting newspapers carried the title Newspapers-in-Education (NIE), a restructuring of the earlier Newspapers in the Classroom program. Although the traditional focus had been devoted to promoting the use of dailies in the classroom, the American Newspaper Publishers Association (now the Newspaper Association of America) and the National Newspaper Association collaborated on a booklet showing how weeklies also could be teaching tools.[1196] In 1994 the APA hired Karen Brown, former teacher and wife of Bentonville publisher Mike Brown, as a part-time NIE coordinator. She worked with newspapers and teachers to develop local NIE programs. She also conducted NIE seminars, developed NIE-type programs for newspapers such as serials and coloring contests, and worked with related groups such as Arkansas literacy councils, reading organizations and Arkansas Kids Voting, for which she served as executive director.

As a third example, from 1984 to 1998 the Old State House Museum sponsored and the APA paid for the printing of *Arkansas News*, an educational newspaper. Stocked with articles on various topics about state history, it was edited by UALR history professor T. Harri Baker and Judy Dalton from the Old State House and drew on some of the best writers in the state. About 50,000 copies were printed in spring and fall editions for distribution to every fifth grader in Arkansas. Appropriately for the APA's 125th anniversary, the Fall 1998 issue was devoted to the history of newspapers and their trade association in the state. Following this issue, publication was suspended temporarily due to fire and staff changes.

Since advertising was a critical issue for the survival of all newspapers, changing patterns in the commercial world were lively topics for debate within the profession. While a perceived lack of advertising support had long been a complaint, by the 1980s some local publishers were ready to play hardball. One hard thrower—later thrown by an irate reader into his own plate glass window—was Louie Graves (APA president, 1986) of Nashville. "Are you Pogo's 'Enemy'?" he asked his fellow publishers, referring to a once-popular cartoon character that reported an astounding discovery: "We have met the enemy, and he is us." What Graves was referring to was the all-too-common practice by many newspapers of publishing almost any news release, simply to fill space cheaply. In consequence, politicians (and others) concluded that they could get their publicity for nothing. Some political consultants even referred to newspapers as "The Free Medium," and counted on getting good coverage merely by having the politician show up in town and pose for photographers.

What had President Graves particularly upset was an AIDC promotion that raised $150,000 to spend on television advertisements while newspapers were supposed to print the agency's press releases for free. Graves adopted the policy of "not running for free anything which is paid for in other media" and regularly mailed back press releases to the sender, along with a rate card. After attacking free press releases in general, Graves threw this hardball to other publishers: "Of all the things which go together to form your opinion of a candidate or a product or issue, shouldn't one of them be the treatment shown to your own newspaper?"[1197]

The next hardball was thrown out of what was presumed to be a friendly dugout and hit C. Dennis Schick, who heretofore had been deemed "great at dodging brickbats" but "more adept at catching the bouquets."[1198] In 1992, Schick took on one of the major issues troubling a number of Arkansas's newspapers, the advertising practices of the now giant Wal-Mart discount stores.

Sam Walton had based much of his early success on newspaper advertising, spending heavily (and paying publishers slowly). As the chain grew, local managers were given discretion in using their accounts, so publishers' experiences varied from town to town. It was, however, simply a question of money. In towns where the publisher and editor were integral parts of the local business community on the square or along Front Street, the rise of discount giants on the outskirts of town spelled trouble for the whole concept of community. Not for nothing were critics soon calling Wal-Mart a "Town Killer." No doubt the newspapers that got the giant chain's accounts felt better about the player than those who did not. However, in the 1980s, after acquiring its own Bentonville printing facilities, the chain had much less use for local newspapers. At the same time, in playing the role of good community citizen, Wal-Mart still expected the newspaper to cover its self-promoting civic events designed to gain free publicity. Small-town publishers were not happy.

In spite of rising negative feelings about Wal-Mart by many newspaper people, the APA named Sam Walton as its Headliner of the Year in 1985, recognizing the massive company that was soon to be the largest retailer in the world. He and Helen Walton came to the APA Winter Convention to receive the award. Following the ceremony, he had a good time talking with APA members, and commented to Dennis Schick that he would like to get together with several publishers to talk about how his people and newspaper people might work more closely together.

Schick jumped at the opportunity and readily accepted the offer. After Walton told Schick to set up a meeting, Schick alerted key publishers in Arkansas, Oklahoma, and Missouri to be on ready at any moment. However, "Mr. Sam" was always too busy opening a new store or had too full a schedule, and even though he reassured Schick personally of his desire to fulfill his promise, his health worsened and no meeting took place prior to his death in 1992.

In 1992, after renewed persistence, Schick and two other newspaper industry representatives from the Oklahoma and Alabama press associations finally were permitted to travel to Bentonville expecting to talk with Wal-Mart's advertising manager about their specific ideas for working together. But instead the visitors were ambushed. The advertising manager belittled the visitors in front of his own media buyers, criticized newspapers for making too much money, and—rejecting the delegation's attempts to explain their position and ideas—sent them on their way.

News of this meeting's failure was sent to publishers via a four-page report in the *Confidential Bulletin*. In a short addendum, Schick suggested that publishers did not need to give the company any free publicity and noted cases where local newspapers had struck back. At Berryville, the *Star-Progress*, for example, had done a price survey that showed Wal-Mart's prices were not always the lowest.

The *Arkansas Democrat-Gazette* picked up only on the addendum, presenting the story in a way highly critical of Schick. Following a hostile editorial, a columnist accused Schick of "compromising journalism ethics in the face of advertising losses," and went on to denounce the APA as "a trade organization, serving the business interests of newspapering in Arkansas, but not the people who gather and disseminate the news…"

George T. Anderson of the *Pine Bluff News*—and the APA's president—wrote an indignant reply under the head of "On uninformed bashing." Anderson first reminded the *Democrat-Gazette* that it was a major journalistic breach of ethics not to have called Schick for comments before the stories were released and at least asked for his input. Anderson then very pointedly asked how the *Democrat-Gazette* advertising and marketing directors would feel if their confidential strategies were made public.[1199]

As for the broader issue, the century ended with a surge of nationwide stories suggesting that advertising and marketing directors of major metropolitan newspapers did indeed influence news selection. In the language of the profession, there was supposed to be a high wall of separation between church (the newsroom) and state (the advertising department), but such concerns were not sacred to those afflicted with the "bottom-line" mentality, especially in newspapers where the editor was also the publisher and had direct responsibility for the bottom line.

Much of the work of the executive director centered around the two annual meetings. Press day at the Arkansas State Fair died out after World War II. As family farms declined and attendance increasingly was drawn from just eight counties in central Arkansas, the State Fair board decreased greatly its newspaper advertising. Perhaps the final indignity was when part of their small budget went to produce a mini-poster over men's urinals in Little Rock restaurants. "State fair newspaper advertising has truly gone down the toilet," one wag commented in 2000. As this book goes to press, the APA continues to attempt to regain state fair advertising for newspapers. The APA urged its members to run for free an advertisement in the form of a free admission coupon good for a family of four. Newspapers were urged to sell sponsorships or float the coupon inside sponsors' advertisements.

Arkansas newspapers and their association have been strong supporters of tourism throughout their entire existences. Newspapers with tourism facilities in their communities are especially prone to promote them whenever possible. Prior to 1989 the state had only $500,000 to promote tourism, in competition with surrounding states that had many times that amount. Subsequently, no advertising dollars were used to promote tourism within the state. Parks and Tourism staff and other supporters spent 18 months crisscrossing the state to educate people to the need for a two percent tax on tourism, which would be used to bolster the promotion budget. With the help of the Arkansas Press Association and its member newspapers, Act 38 of 1989 passed handily and put Arkansas in a much better competitive position. Further, the tax allowed tourism promotion dollars to be spent within the state for the first time, in variations of a "See Arkansas First" theme, to educate

Arkansans about tourism opportunities within their own state. Even then, newspapers helped double those dollars by agreeing to give two-for-one on paid advertising space.

In a related statewide effort, the APA and its member newspapers helped persuade Arkansans to pass a constitutional amendment in November 1996, granting a 1/8-cent sales tax dedicated to Arkansas State Parks, the Game & Fish Commision, the Arkansas Department of Heritage, and the Keep Arkansas Beautiful program.

By the century's end, the APA continued to operate on a regular schedule of two conventions. The old mid-winter meeting, now styled the Winter Convention and Trade Show, moved from January to February in order to avoid the worst winter weather; the summer convention, which before air-conditioning sometimes was held in May and more recently in June, moved to July in order to distance it more from the winter convention. The winter convention usually was held in Little Rock due to its central location and interstate accessibility, making travel more feasible in bad weather. The summer convention rotated between Hot Springs—every other year—and other vacation destinations such as Eureka Springs.

The executive director also acted as a cheerleader for newspapers. His speech, "Hats Off to Newspapers," reminded listeners of the vital roles newspapers play in people's lives. But Schick also had another rabbit up his sleeve. In "The Magic of Newspapers," he deployed his skills as a magician in order to demonstrate various points about newspapers. Schick, who also served as chairman of the Arkansas Better Business Bureau and president of the Arkansas Designated Driver Program, among other public service activities, received the Ken Graves Service Award, the highest award given by the Arkansas Society of Association Executives, in recognition of his work and his service as ASAE's president, as well as the Silver Medal Award, the highest award given by the Arkansas Advertising Federation.

Despite the rise of corporations, the family publishers remained central to the APA's success. Donrey executive Ross Pendergraft in 1980 was the first president from a big corporation. Over the next 20 years, only Eddie Telford from Palmer Newspapers in 1990, Steve Trolinger in 1994 from Community Publishers, Buddy King from Palmer Newspapers in 2000, and Charles Berry from Stephens Media Group in 2001 represented the corporate side.

One reason for corporate underrepresentation was that it took an 11-year haul, known as "The Sentence," before a person could serve as APA president. In the new age, corporate types had little ties to their communities and often worked only to win prizes that would pad their resumes, grease their way up the corporate ladder, and lead to larger bottom-line-based bonuses. At the 2003 APA Winter Convention, members approved a constitution change to allow more flexibility in serving on the Board.

In addition, there remained some degree of feudalism in the industry. On one occasion, in order better to promote an APA seminar, Schick tried contacting advertising managers directly. One irate publisher who apparently feared that employees coming to a seminar would be recruited away, or would "come back with all kinds of ideas which will cost me money," called Schick on the carpet: "Don't ever send my people any promotions directly. I'll tell them what I want them to know."

Some chains were not well represented in APA contests or conventions, provided bonuses to higher management who practiced effective cost cutting, and lived in accordance with the "bottom line" as determined at corporate headquarters. Stephens officials wanted to be thought of as a group rather than a chain, declaring that groups practiced economies of scale but left individual newspapers alone, while chains presented a canned product regardless of local needs.

On the other hand, often chain owners led in investing in improved facilities, newer equipment and staff benefits, which individual owners never could justify or never got around to adopting. "Groups are not all bad," Gene Foreman, who had worked for both groups and family-owned newspapers, concluded.[1200]

Nevertheless, in the course of interviews undertaken for this book, this author has been unable to find a single example in which a corporate takeover of a previously family-owned newspaper was greeted with anything other than gallows humor by the employees. Indeed, six months after the Paxton Media Group purchased the *Jonesboro Sun* from John Troutt, Jr., several disgruntled news employees forced a vote on whether to join the Newspaper Guild of the Communications Workers of America, a member of the AFL-CIO. By a vote of 65 to 23, employees rejected the union. Arkansas's newspapers remained union-free as the new century began.

Both professional and social qualities continued to surface at APA conventions. Award categories were expanded to reflect changing newspaper practices. Besides the grand division between dailies and weeklies, each was broken down into small, medium and large sub-contests. New awards appeared for editorial cartoons and the use of color, reflecting the increased importance of these forms. By 2003 there were 31 categories and a General Excellence; in advertising, there were 20 and a best of show.

Starting in 1980, persons who had worked for newspapers for 50 years or longer were given the Golden Fifty Award. Full-time journalists were not the only persons recognized. When Gene Herrington made his tours, he uncovered a number of country correspondents with 50 or more years of service who now are eligible for the award.

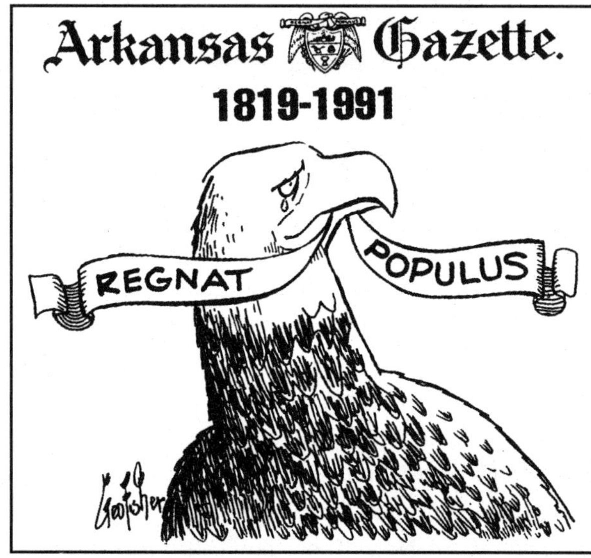

George Fisher's tribute to the Arkansas Gazette, *October 1991.*

Persons prominent in state life were designated as the Headliner of the Year, defined as "bringing good headlines to the state." The first Headliner award in 1983 went to Hillary Clinton; her husband, the governor, followed the family tradition in 1988 and in 1991, and the two of them were given the award in 1992 as President-elect and First Lady-elect. Despite their prominence, politicians were not the main recipients. Other honorees read like a who's who of Arkansas celebrities: Sam Walton (1985), William Dillard (1988), Jerry Jones (1993), Jack Stephens (1994), and Joe Ford (2001). Jennings Osborne, famous for his elaborate Christmas lighting displays first seen at his home on Little Rock's Cantrell Road and later at Disney World and Graceland, was the winner in 2000; General Wesley Clark in 2001; and University of Arkansas Athletic Director Frank Broyles in 2002. The APA also added other annual awards: the Freedom of Information Award, the Distinguished Service Award, the Journalism Educator Award and the NIE Teacher of the Year Award.

The APA also continued to be active in promoting family farming. The Arkansas Balanced Farming Contest, renamed the Arkansas Farm Family of the Year program in 1960, gave its 56th annual award in 2002. Colonel Barton was dead, Lion Oil roared no more, and Arkansas Power & Light was now swallowed up in Entergy. But the Arkansas Farm Bureau, the Cooperative Extension Service, and other agricultural agencies still promoted this activity.

The APA also provided support for the high school press. In 1996, the old Arkansas High School Press Association was renamed the Arkansas Scholastic Press Association (ASPA) in that some middle schools and junior high schools sported newspapers. After Walter J. Lemke's tenure ended, the group moved to Ouachita Baptist University in 1969, where Dr. William D. Downs, Jr., served as executive director for a quarter-century. In 1996, under Gary Lundgren the group moved back to Fayetteville. Then, in the fall of 1997, Beth Shull became the part-time executive director with an office and salary support provided by the APA in Little Rock.

In the nation at large, public school journalism was not well served by an increasingly conservative United States Supreme Court. While *Hazelwood School District v. Kuhlmeier* (1988) had upheld administrators "exercising editorial control over the style and content of student speech in school-sponsored expressive activities,"[1201] the decision had little effect in Arkansas. The Arkansas Student Publications Act of 1995 extended basic rights to students and required school boards to create policies that effectively placed the responsibility for student publications in the hands of the journalism advisor rather than leaving it at the whim of an administrator. Not all administrators were aware of the law, and a wide range of policies could be found throughout Arkansas. Another problem was that certified journalism teachers were in short supply, perhaps explaining why only 121 schools belonged to the ASPA out of some 467 programs.[1202] The Arkansas Journalism Advisors Association (AJAA), the parent body for the ASPA, tried to enhance standards through seminars and contests and an annual spring conference in Little Rock which attracted over 800 journalism students and teachers.

A name change also overtook the Arkansas College Newspaper Association, which deleted the word "newspaper" and added the word "media." Curiously, at a time when virtually every higher education institution in Arkansas proclaimed itself a university, the association kept the word "college" in its title. The Arkansas College Media Association (ACMA), whose leadership passed from campus to campus yearly, lacked the continuity seen at the public school level. Like the APA, both groups continued to hold conventions and give awards in order to promote better journalism.

During the last quarter of the 20th century, a marked decline could be found in membership, conference attendance, and participation in journalism's traditional bodies. Among those affected were the Society of Professional Journalists and the Arkansas Press Women, both of which relied on volunteer leadership. Even the Associated Press Managing Editors, which had built-in membership, had sparse attendance at its annual meetings (except for its awards banquet). Despite these general trends, the APA endured. On the other hand, new organizations sprang up. The Arkansas Press Photographers Association (APPA) was created in 1999 to serve that special interest. Like most modern organizations, the key link was its website, but the group held spring and fall meetings. The photographers submitted their clips, and the one who accumulated the most points was named Press Photogapher of the Year.

APA conventions brought news of current problems and future prospects to members. Perennial advertising promoter Charlie Mouser, a semi-regular participant for over 20 years, presented his "Mouser Rousers," telling, for example, APA sales people in 1988 that by 2000, due to the aging of the population, all newspapers would be in tabloid form; new automobiles would be sold by videotape; and so many jobs would be available that colleges would be open only in the evening or the weekends.[1203] So popular was Mouser that on two occasions the APA arranged for local newspapers to sponsor him in two-hour meetings for area retailers that started with a breakfast speech in one town and ended the same day with a dinner somewhere else and with other stops in between. One of Mouser's more memorable quotations spoke to the decline of many mom and pop stores in small communities in the wake of the Wal-Mart invasion: "The retailer who stays open only from 10 A.M. to 5 P.M. is catering to the unemployed."

Mouser was not the only on-the-road APA project. Writing coach Clarke Stallworth from Alabama held frequent seminars around the state; veteran journalist and legal expert Kathryn Shurlds from the University of Arkansas held Law for Journalists seminars in three different locations; and both advertising and FOI Act seminars were given throughout the state. The year 2002 saw the start-up of an education program of Traveling Campuses sponsored by the Southern Newspaper Publishers Association (SNPA), with APA as a co-sponsor for the Arkansas stop. Fourteen seminars were held over four days.

If newspapers, radio, and television competed for advertising revenues, they sometimes shared personnel. The most conspicuous bi-vocationalist was Steve Barnes, who started his writing career with the *North Little Rock Times* during Bob McCord's years and returned to full-time writing in 1987. Barnes, whose television career included serving as a news anchor for various Little Rock commercial stations, was well known to more enlightened television viewers because of his association with AETN, Arkansas's educational station. *Arkansas Week*, which summarized weekly developments on Friday nights, featured other state journalists as well. In AETN's early days Bob McCord did a stimulating program entitled *McCord's Arkansas* that resembled in video form the *Gazette*'s old Arkansas Traveler column.

Barnes was not the only person with statewide and even nationwide recognition. Columns by veteran Springdale reporter Brenda Blagg appeared in a number of state newspapers. Jim Davidson, a long-time professional speaker from Conway, moved from radio commentaries to popular weekly columns. He came to APA's Dennis Schick for advice and now his columns appear in some 250 newspapers in over 30 states. Davidson may be the most successful self-syndicated newspaper columnist in the country. Nationally syndicated are columnist Paul Greenberg and editorial cartoonist John Deering, both of the *Arkansas Democrat-Gazette*. All the columnists at the Arkansas News Bureau and cartoonist Vic Harville are syndicated.

In addition to syndicated columnists, many newspapers attracted local writers. Retired people, would-be commercial writers, teachers, librarians, genealogists, local historians, and humorists were all represented, albeit unevenly, around the state. The rise of this free or inexpensive writing prompted the APA in 2001 to add a new category to its Better Newspaper Contest entitled "Freelancer Recognition."

The 1990s saw the emergence of established newspapers posting an electronic version free on the Web. Some in the industry viewed these as a threat to regular readership and rejected the idea of cannibalizing their printed product by offering it free. Starting in October 2001, the *Democrat-Gazette* limited its website only to subscribers. Every newspaper struggled with the problem of how to make these editions profitable. Devices included selling advertisements on the front page and offering special inducements for Web readers to become regular subscribers. The most optimistic view was that Web editions could be great promotional devices. At Atkins, Van Tyson found he could post color pictures of school and other events that he could not afford to print in the newspaper. Some websites were locally produced; others were the work of trained specialists. In short, change was still coming rapidly. While virtually everyone in the industry agreed there was a future for this new medium, just what its relationship to print would be remained uncertain. At the beginning of the new century, the APA joined several other states in adding Web pages as a category in its news-editorial contest.

At a conference entitled "The Future of Online Journalism" held in Jonesboro on December 8, 2001, Steve Crain, a Memphis television station executive, explained that he saw WMC-TV's website as creating a place "where we can compete with newspapers on a level playing field." Lance Turner, from the niche publication *Arkansas Business*, explained that "the Web lends itself to niches." Dina Mason, formerly with newspapers in Searcy and Paragould, observed of her misnamed Web "newspaper" that "all it doesn't have is pages." Web publications already existed nationally, but the entry of television stations and in Mason's case, radio stations, into the realm of electronic imitations of regular newspapers represented a blurring of traditional distinctions. As of 2002, such entities were not granted the status of newspapers nor were they eligible for membership in the APA.

Perhaps the best proof that modernization had not completely eroded the humane qualities that had so long graced the industry came in response to a series of late-century crises. Jay W. Jackson (APA president, 1968), owner of the *Van Buren County Democrat* at Clinton, had installed his own press in 1960. He was three payments short of getting out of debt when on December 3, 1982, a monster, once-in-a-lifetime flood virtually wiped out downtown Clinton. Water came through the newspaper's walls and reached a height of over six feet in the office. Yet the newspaper kept coming out, thanks largely to the assistance that other APA members provided.[1204] Some of his major help came from Joel Irwin (APA president, 1985), Frank Robins III (APA president, 1974), and Bill Whitehead, Jr. (APA president, 1982). The APA led a campaign that raised more than $10,000 for the Jacksons.

A similar rallying around from colleagues came in 1981, when robbers broke into the *Batesville Guard* office and left a fire in their wake. New computers, still in their boxes, were lost, but the accounts receivable and circulation records, stored on a new IBM computer mounted on wheels, were rolled out by the fire chief. Almost all the historic photographs Wilson Powell had collected were charred beyond recognition.

Its press and office furniture destroyed, the *Guard* moved into temporary quarters while the rebuilding began. Nevertheless, it never missed an issue in three months. "There was a lot of character-building," general manager Pat Jones recalled. The question for the future was whether corporate owners would be as supportive as individual publishers had been.

A Century's End Assessment

In giving the keynote address on November 4, 1988, at the opening of the Walter J. Lemke Department of Journalism (funded in part by a generous donation from the Sanders family), United States Senator David Pryor lamented that changes in the high cost of campaigning had sapped politics of its soul. Pryor, for whom "the aroma of printer's ink and the thunder of an old Miehle press on Wednesday nights will always remain in my sub-conscious," did not celebrate a world where newspapers had "more glitz, more color, more advertising, fewer editorials, less local ownership, less independence," and he ended with a plea: "Please, don't let the SOUL be sapped from your profession, as is happening to mine."[1205]

By 1980, it had become commonly accepted that newspapers represented an example of a mature industry, an analogy that carried with it the implicit implication that rot was already present and that death lay somewhere in the near future. At the century's end, while the world's newspaper circulation was up by three percent, in America sales were flat. Arkansas dailies over the past 10 years had lost 72,000 subscribers, in part because after the end of the Little Rock newspaper war WEHCO recouped its losses by ending $10 subscriptions. Although after the *Gazette*'s demise, its subscribers had received the *Democrat-Gazette* for the balance of their subscriptions, many disliked the "best of both" and failed to renew their subscriptions. Even more threatening was the disconnectedness of the new Internet generation, whose idea of reading was glancing at terse headlines off a website. For a growing number of disconnected Arkansans *USA Today* sufficed. The greatest cause of alarm was that a Pew Research Center survey reported prior to September 11, 2001, that only 45 percent of Americans even wanted to know anything in the way of news from any source.

There were local exceptions. The *Arkansas Democrat-Gazette* reached 74 percent of Little Rock's homes on Sunday, the second highest penetration rate in metropolitan markets in the country. Strong weeklies continued to thrive and adapt to the new age. In the 1970s the *Sheridan Headlight* had a country correspondent who brought in her copy on her Honda motorcycle.[1206] At the century's end, the *Newton County Times* not only had correspondents for Hickory Grove, Nail, Parthenon and other county communities, but also Kansas City, Springdale, and for the entire state of California. Orpha Kilgore, who supplied the *Times* with a Former Residents column, started her career when she was 14. "I was very proud of myself. I worked very hard at it," she recalled.[1207] Yellville's *Mountain Echo* boasted a country columnist from Yakima, Washington. Danville's *Yell County Record* still continued to print Bible lessons. Minnie Claytor of Rock Creek, who might easily have stepped out from the pages of an ancient *Log Cabin Democrat*, often resorted to poetry for the *Newton County Times*. When Claytor became ill and suspended her writing, another correspondent, Ruth Norton from Piercetown, observed, "When a correspondent misses an issue, it leaves a gap in our paper. I still miss the news from Deer."[1208]

Meanwhile, only 41 single-owner newspapers out of the state's 142 newspapers remained by 2003. Robert McCord, who in his lifetime had been reporter, publisher, and editor, observed: "Publishers regard consolidation as inevitable, but the journalists who produce their newspapers will tell you that they can do a better job when the man who owns the paper sits downstairs."[1209]

There remained for reporters a sense of community through the Society of Professional Journalists (SPJ) who held their own contests. Little Rock members of the group and other media people got their biennial revenge starting in the 1960s and ending in 1999 with a roast-and-toast show called the Farkleberry Follies. Named after Orval Faubus's favorite bush, the show featured salacious scripts and cameo impersonations by society and media members. A luncheon at the 2002 APA winter convention celebrating the 40th anniversary of SPJ featured excerpts from past Follies. The nostalgia among those present gave hope that the show could somehow be revived.

Journalism continued to be a training ground for politics. Rex Nelson, Governor Mike Huckabee's press secretary, was a Ouachita Baptist University graduate who at age 23 edited Arkadelphia's *Daily*

Siftings Herald. Prior to working for the governor he had been the political editor of the *Arkansas Democrat-Gazette* and was seen frequently on AETN's *Arkansas Week* talk show. Bob Fisher (Crossett) and Perrin Jones (Searcy) both found work in the attorney general's office.

Journalists left the business for other professions, too. John Woodruff, formerly of the *Arkansas Gazette*, went to work for the Arkansas Municipal League; Derwood Brett (APA president, 1989) joined the Electric Cooperatives of Arkansas; David Russell went to GTE (CenturyTel); Ted Wagnon worked for International Paper and then Potlatch; Gene Herrington found employment with AP&L and Entergy; and George Smith, who at different times served as editor or publisher for Arkansas newspapers at Mountain Home, Hope, Paragould, Texarkana, Fayetteville, and Stuttgart, joined ALLTEL as a vice president but later returned to become the publisher at Benton when his job was eliminated. Several ex-journalists moved over to higher education: Tommy Mumert taught at Arkansas Tech, Bob Qualls at Lyon College, and Bob Douglas at the University of Arkansas; Tom Moore handled public relations at Arkansas State University. Kitty Sloan became a librarian at Paragould; Janet Nelson joined an advertising agency; and Keith Stephens became News Editor for the Arkansas Game and Fish Commission.

Any review of the concluding sections of older histories on any topic serves as a sharp reminder that the chances of anticipating history—or even of making an accurate summing up of recent events—are microscopically small. Who, for instance, could have predicted in 1980 the demise of the *Arkansas Gazette*?

Yet, the impression of this author from talking with retired veterans and visiting with currently active people is that finding and presenting the news is a compelling cause, much like preaching the gospel. Once having entered the soul, it may be discouraged but it is not defeated by obstacles that would destroy other businesses. There are the daily battles, be they fought out at the state capitol, at a school board meeting, or in an editorial board room. But a vibrant community will not let its press fail, even if it requires its reinvention. The organic metaphor of a mature industry suggests the inevitability of a dying giant oak tree, but news is by definition new, and as such a newspaper reinvents itself with every issue.

A Brave New World?

It was the intention of the author to wind down as the new century started in 2001, adding only a few key details that might clarify the history already recorded. That plan fell by the wayside the morning of Tuesday, September 11, 2001, when the worst act of terrorism in the history of the world struck New York City and Washington, D.C. This disaster changed in an hour virtually everything in American life, newspapers included. Whether indeed the new century would be a brave new world or a very bad and unpleasant world, clouded over with ancient hates but armed with modern tools of destruction, remained to be seen.

Arkansas's dozen afternoon dailies jumped at the opportunity to give same-day news coverage. Seven morning dailies (Little Rock, Conway, Fort Smith, Hot Springs, Russellville, Springdale, and Texarkana) sprang to life and produced rare "Extra" editions, on the street by mid-afternoon. The *Arkansas Democrat-Gazette*'s two afternoon extras received free distribution. More than three dozen weeklies gave rare same-day or next-day coverage of an international event.

As conditions worsened, some newspapers expanded their "news hole." In Jonesboro, publisher David Mosesso decided to increase the number of pages from 32 to 40. Half of the "A" section and all of the "B" section were given over to the attack, and four pages reached readers "wide open" (without advertisements). Reporters worked on every possible local angle. Staff writer Stephen Hankens's father, a retired Federal Aviation Administration employee, gave his insights; Stan Mitchell tracked down former ASU graduate Adam Staples, who had been attending a financial trading session before he fled down 61 flights of stairs from the World Trade Center.

The *Benton Courier* added four pages of extra news and then for 10 days ran unfolding events under the headline "Freedom Under Attack." Both the *Courier*, and its new startup, the *Bryant Banner*, organized fundraisers for the victims. One of the most direct responses came from Weiner native Rick Fahr, editor of the Russellville *Courier*, who, with the permission and support from Paxton Media Group, joined the Arkansas National Guard and went off to basic training in Oklahoma.

Those who thought print was dead must have had a rude awakening. At the *Sun*, single sales were up some 1,600 the first day and continued the strong showing. In many ways the print medium had one important role to play, for it was strong in offering detailed analyses, and newspapers were less likely to give credence to hoaxes and rumors. Local citizens seeking news dropped by the office of the weekly *White River Current* at Calico Rock. "They do look to the local paper no matter what it is or where it is," publisher Jeannie Day explained.[1210]

"It was one of those days when you would love someone to pose the question about newspapers living on borrowed time in an electronic age," managing editor Larry Fugate of the *Jonesboro Sun* observed, in noting how the *Sun* responded to the crisis. Or as associate editor Paul Holmes put it, "We doze, but we never close." For George Smith, "This was our Pearl Harbor. For the first time, our generation actually knows the feelings that our parents and grandparents had on December 7, 1941."

The problem of how to cover the event was especially complicated for weeklies, who, for over 50 years, had assumed that national affairs were no longer their concern. Some went to bed as early as Monday. While the World Trade Center towers were falling on Tuesday morning, Rusty Fraser and the staff at the *Stone County Leader* were busy attaching mailing labels.

Others had a narrow window of opportunity. "As most people did on Tuesday, September 11, 2001, I sat in front of the television mesmerized, dumbfounded, sickened, and shocked," wrote Lee McLane of the *Beebe News*. McLane, who knew little of New York, turned to the Internet for help before writing the news. "Unthinkable Terror!" was her choice for a headline, and McLane secured a photograph from Cable News Network for the September 12 issue.

The *News* was not alone in responding with same-day coverage. Many weeklies—who printed Tuesday afternoon and later—were able to generate stories, a rarity for non-daily newspapers. Editors worked feverishly, cutting planned stories, trying desperately to get a photograph of some sort to use, and often pushing their deadlines to and beyond the usual limits. The *Sheridan Headlight* was among those weekly newspapers that secured an original photograph.

New York native Christina Vederosa at the *De Witt Era-Enterprise*, who had more liberty than most because her newspaper was one of the few still home-printed, picked up on what was the most common theme: "By eight A.M. Tuesday morning, every television in De Witt was tuned in to the horrifying sights from New York City. But by one P.M. Tuesday afternoon, every car in De Witt was lined up at the gas pump." Virtually every weekly that had a chance to cover the event found their closest story to be in gasoline prices that soared on wings of rumor to Mount Everest heights. But other local themes could be found as well. Was Nuclear One at Russellville

The Arkansas Publisher

Vol. 75, No. 3 | Arkansas Press Association | Fall 2001

In Memoriam: September 11, 2001

AP Photo/Chao Soi Cheong

AP Photo/Will Nunes

AP Photo/Hasson Yim

Arkansas newspapers respond to worst terrorist attack in U.S. history...

EXTRA!
Texarkana Gazette
AMERICA UNDER SIEGE

The Beebe News
Unthinkable Terror!
Hijackers Crash Airliners into Pentagon and Twin Towers World Trade Center
Death toll could reach 10,000

Times-Herald
U.S. ATTACKED
World Trade Center twin towers collapse
Pentagon attack spreads fear in nation's capital

The Texarkana Gazette was among seven dailies that produced same-day extra editions.

The attacks occurred on a Tuesday, allowing weeklies, like *The Beebe News* to give timely coverage.

Some evening dailies, like the *Times-Herald* in Forrest City, were able to provide same-day coverage.

The Arkansas Publisher produced a rare full-color issue for its Fall number, presenting the work by newspapers of the coverage of the horrible events. Through their devotion to the news, reporters, editors, and publishers proved once again the value of newspapers in the lives of people and their communities.

safe? That facility historically had a long track record of being secretive to the newspapers nearby and downwind, and worries were well placed. Another dislocation came as the total ban on aircraft activity extended to crop-dusting, imperiling crops, especially in the Delta.

Many weeklies managed a variety of local issues. The Thursday edition of the *White River Current* contained a photograph of the gas lines, an editorial on the crisis, information on a county memorial service, and a blood drive. "Carroll County rallies for terror attack victims," the *Carroll County News* noted on the 14th; and "America is attacked—immediate effects in Pike County" the *Glenwood Herald* of September 13 told local readers.

While many weeklies managed only one story hastily assembled, others went all out. Van Tyson at the *Atkins Chronicle* summarized for his readers current national news. Randy Kemp at the Heber Springs *Sun-Times*, who had planned only one big headline, received an e-mail from former state representative Randy Thurman, then in Washington, who sent Kemp some eyewitness comments and a digital photograph of some of the damage done to the Pentagon. Following that, a local man with contacts in New York and Washington also provided original material. Kemp dropped his idea of running only one story, and all these original sources led him to fill the entire first page with immediate and valuable news. "We went past deadline but still got printed late Tuesday afternoon and our delivery was on time to all our subscribers Wednesday morning. Whew!" he recalled.[1211]

Other personal contacts surfaced as well. John Bland at the Walnut Ridge *Times-Dispatch* had a sister living in New York near the disaster, and she provided original material. The *Sheridan Headlight* ran a story from a New York resident that was passed along by her grandparents, who lived in Grant County. Weeklies often lacked the flexibility in adding pages that dailies possessed, and at Walnut Ridge a planned story on rice production got bumped a week to give more space.

Virtually every aspect of Arkansas life was touched by the events, and the press was there to catch it. A Batesville native was a flight attendant on one of the doomed flights; a Jonesboro man was among the casualties at the Pentagon. The Hector sports stringer for the *Atkins Chronicle*, Bradley Caldwell, told of the Thursday and Friday football games under the heading, "Charleston and America Win Big at Ball Games." "We as Americans took a step toward normalcy on Thursday and Friday nights as our high school and junior highs took the field," he wrote. "Suddenly the conversation changed from Osama bin Laden and a possible world war to how blind the referees are and how many yards passing John Hubbard had." Caldwell noted that the fans found their spirits lifted, and, he concluded, "just as Charleston came out victorious Thursday and Friday nights the Americans will be victorious in this war on terrorism."

Military veteran D.L. Bailey of the *Phillips County Progress* for his weekend edition of September 15 and 16 "hustled a little bit" in order to pull out all the stops. Many of his subscribers were likewise veterans, and this event particularly resonated with them. Bailey also observed that he had not heard a racial remark since the event happened. Instead, people were all pulling together.[1212] With flags flying and in short supply, the *Murfreesboro Diamond* put Old Glory on the front page together with an article on flag etiquette. The *Greenwood Democrat* reported how one woman, unable to buy a flag, had made her own.

Another response could be found in the country correspondents. Although the weather, church and company remained the major topics, Jeanne Church, the *Atkins Chronicle* correspondent at Jerusalem, caught the radically altered mood of the country: "It has only been a week since I last wrote the news.

Time hasn't passed in the normal way. So much has happened since last Tuesday. It is difficult to comprehend the suffering, sadness and horror of this terrible act. We must now depend on and hope we have leaders that are strong and will know how to handle the situation in the right way." Minnie Claytor, the Rock Creek correspondent for the *Newton County Times*, wrote: "I have never been politically minded and don't pay a lot of attention to what politicians have to say. Now they have my full attention." And Margaret Phillips, another *Times* columnist, dropped plans to write about Ozark superstitions: "It has seemed too trivial. Maybe next week."[1213]

Many readers responded to the crisis with poetry. Across the state more poetry appeared in one week than had been seen in the previous two decades. The *Eureka Springs Times-Echo* of September 18 ran a poem by seventh-grader Leah Gould on the first page. Readers supplied most of the poetry, but the *Lafayette County Press* picked up from a New York Met's baseball fan these lines: "Our hearts are broken/ But not our stride;/ Now comes the power/ Of American pride."

The first public reaction across the state was for the United States government to match or exceed the violence. "The theme on everyone's lips was 'Blow Em Up,' 'Nuke 'Em!'" Jasper United Methodist minister Robert J. Wilson recalled. But in his pastor's column in the *Newton County Times* a week after the events, Wilson urged patience and understanding, and quoted at length a former Newton County

Advertising on page one has become increasingly common as newspapers search for new sources of revenue. Shown are, from left, multiple ads on the bottom in the Lincoln Leader; *ads at top and bottom of the* Ashley News Observer, *Crossett; and a single banner at the bottom of the* Northwest Arkansas Times, *Fayetteville.*

resident, Dr. Joanie Connors, a member of the International Peace Practitioners' Network.[1214] In short, there were as many views as there were contributors to Arkansas's newspapers in the aftermath of this crisis.

In the weeks that followed, weeklies continued to feature local responses to the national threat. "Mt. Judea graduate protects president" ran a headline in the *Newton County Times*. The front page headline, "Officials reassure residents local emergency services are ready for any form of disaster," appeared in the September 26 *Sheridan Headlight*, and virtually every weekly carried a similar story.

Although it is too early to write about the longer lasting and deeper meanings of the crisis, there could be little doubt that Arkansas's newspapers had really shone. People trusted the print medium, not because

it now contained the newsbreaking stories, but because getting a story into print somehow meant that facts had been sifted to eliminate rumors and falsehoods.

There could be no doubt that a "business as usual" attitude would not soon return to America. But readers should remember that an anarchist had assassinated President William McKinley to open the 20th century, and America's involvement in World War I had ushered in "the American century," making us all citizens of the world whether we recognized it or not. As news of the disaster spread and Americans checked on their kith and kin, few families were left unaffected. It was, and is, the job of newspapers to make them connected.

The End

In 1993, George Smith, then publisher of the *Northwest Arkansas Times* in Fayetteville, came out for selling advertisements on the front page. His credo, "What the customer wants, the company will do whatever it can to see that the customer gets," reflected the marketplace mentality dominant at the end of the century.[1215] By 2000, when the Gannett chain announced that it would sell front-page space for advertisements, including its *USA Today*, Arkansas newspapers in Warren, Wynne, Paragould (*Tribune*), Prairie Grove, Lincoln, Farmington, Rison, Crossett, Prescott, West Memphis, Malvern, Fayetteville, Mountain Home, and Little Rock (*Daily Record*) had taken the plunge. Although neither the state nor the national press reported it, there was a local disturbance in Rogers: Erwin Funk, the former publisher, had turned over in his grave.

–30–

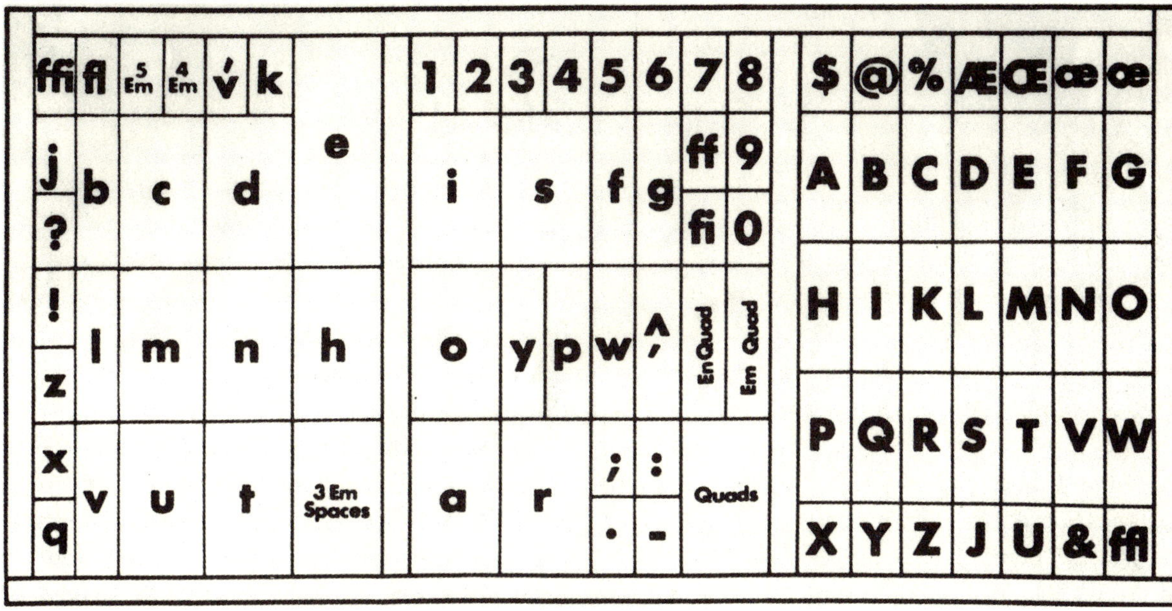

The California job case, in which hand-set type was distributed. Experienced printers could set type letter-by-letter and return it to the case with amazing speed.

The origin of the symbol -30-

It is traditional in the newspaper business to end articles submitted for publication with the symbol -30- (dash thirty dash). Attempts to find the origin of this practice have led to a dozen or more logical-sounding explanations. The following comes from the NNA publication *From Quill to Computer.*

> The origin of the symbol "30" meaning the end of a story in newspaper parlance, has never been truly established. The explanations are many and varied. One of the most plausible is that it comes from an old telegrapher's code signifying the transmission Ø- but there are other choices.
>
> Among them is an early practice of the AP to send out 30 stories each day to member newspapers. When the total had been reached, it was so indicated by the number. Another version suggests that in the days when reporters submitted their copy in longhand, X designated the end of a sentence, XX the end of a paragraph and XXX the end of a story. Similarly, early type specimen books carried an XXX logotype which compositors were supposed to use to denote the end of their "string."
>
> There are more romantic explanations, too: the code number of a telegraph operator during the Civil War who worked as a secret agent; the misprinting of the number "80" which an East Indian company supposedly used to express "farewell"; a heroic telegrapher (No. 30) who stayed at his post during a disaster for 30 hours until signing off just before his death; or even the symbol of the Spartan magistrates (the "thirty tyrants") appointed to rule Athens in ancient times.
>
> Whatever the derivation, the basic meaning has been well established.

Presidents of the APA

1873-75: J.N. Smithee, Little Rock Gazette
1876-77: J.H. Sparks, Fort Smith Herald
1878: C.G. Newman, Pine Bluff Press
1879-80: Adam Clark, Arkadelphia Standard
1881-82: M.M. McGuire, Dardanelle Arkansan
1883: E.A. Warren, Prescott Dispatch
1884: C.C. Colburn, Ozark Democrat
1885: W.A. Webber, Little Rock Workman
1886: J.S. Thomas, Des Arc Crescent
1887: James R. Bettis, Little Rock Democrat
1888: W.W. Folsom, Augusta Vidette
1889: J.R. Newman, Harrison Times
1890: G.R. Williams, Fort Smith Times
1891: George Thornburg, L.R. Masonic Trowel
1892: B.F. Jones, Russellville Democrat
1893: Leon Roussan, Osceola Times
1894: O.C. Ludwig, Little Rock Press
1895: W.M. Kavanaugh, Little Rock Gazette
1896: I.M. Patridge, Fayetteville Sentinel
1897: C.M. Kinney, Judsonia Advance
1898: James Mitchell, Little Rock Democrat
1899: W. Theo Smith, Camden Herald
1900: W.A.H. McDaniel, Wynne Democrat
1901: W.B. Folsom, Brinkley Argus
1902: J.L. Wadley, Hot Springs News
1903: H.L. Cross, Bentonville Sun
1904: J.J. Baugh, Searcy Citizen
1905: P.H. Thomas, Warren Democrat
1906: A.M. Ward, Clarksville Herald
1907: William E. Spencer, Clarendon Sun
1908: John R. Jobe, Little Rock
1909: S.B. Baird, Hamburg Eagle
1910: R.E. Bradford, Lonoke Democrat
1911: J.A. Livingston, Russellville Courier Democrat
1912: John H. Hand, Yellville Echo
1913: T.E. Wood, Marianna Courier
1914: V.A. Beeson, Morrilton Headlight
1915: Claude Mann, Malvern Times-Journal
1916: C.A. Berry, Huttig News
1917: T.L. Pound, Danville Democrat
1918: L.B. White, Benton Courier
1919: Louis Spence, Piggott Banner
1920: W.B. Williams, Brinkley Citizen
1921: J.C. Jolly, Warren Eagle Democrat
1922: R.O. Schaefer, Little Rock Southwest News
1923: Frank Robins, Conway Log Cabin Democrat
1924: H.M. Jackson, Marianna Courier Index
1925: Erwin Funk, Rogers Democrat
1926: V.W. St. John, Mena Star
1927: Charles Goslee, Hot Springs New Era
1928: Curtis Hurley, Camden News
1929: John P. Stafford, Springdale News
1930: Ed McCorkle, Hope Star
1931: Alfred Hawn, Huntsville Record
1932: Tom Newman, Harrison Times
1933: Charles M. Young, Helena World
1934: O.E. Jones, Batesville Guard-Record
1935: Max Hampton, Booneville Democrat
1936: John Sallis, Clarksville Herald Democrat
1937: Donald Murry, Jonesboro Tribune
1938: James L. Bland, Walnut Ridge Times Dispatch
1939: E.W. Pate, Rogers Daily News
1940: Frank Robins, Jr., Conway Log Cabin Democrat
1941: Ray Kimball, Magnolia Banner News
1942: Roy Elliott, Fordyce News Advocate
1943-44: E.W. St. John, Mena Star
1945: M.P. Jones, Jr., Searcy Citizen
1946: John Guion, Paris Express-Progress
1947: Ells Huff, Newport, Jackson County Democrat
1948: J.H. Beerstecher, Malvern Daily Record

1948: M.J. Gillespie, Lonoke Democrat
1949: W.L. Love, Warren Eagle Democrat
1950: Tom Allen, Brinkley Citizen
1951: C.A. VerBeck, Fordyce News Advocate
1952: A.P. Murray, Wynne Progress
1953: J.E. Dunlap, Jr., Harrison Headlight
1954: W.R. Whitehead, Magnolia Banner News
1955: R.L. Fisher, Danville Record
1956: Sam Hodges, Benton Courier
1957: Sam Gearheart, Fayetteville NW Ark. Times
1958: Calvin Mannen, The Stuttgart Daily Leader
1959: Ellis Ramsey, Beebe News
1960: Louis Graves, Nashville News
1961: Keith Tudor, Arkadelphia Southern Standard
1962: Melvin Schexnayder, Dumas Clarion
1963: Ted Larimer, Green Forest Tribune
1964: Earl Causey, Star City Ledger
1965: Porter Young, Helena World
1966: Harlan Walker, McCrory Leader
1967: Cone Magie, Cabot Star-Herald
1968: Jay Jackson, Clinton Democrat
1969: Harry McDonald, Jonesboro Sun
1970: Francis Murray, Madison Co. Record, Huntsville
1971: George Gearhart, Fayetteville NW Ark. Times
1972: Bill Sadler, Rison Herald
1973: Robert Chowning, Magnolia Banner News
1974: Frank Robins III, Conway Log Cabin Democrat
1975: Marvin Caldwell, Marianna Courier-Index
1976: Bill Woods, Hazen Grand Prairie Herald
1977: Thomas Gillespie, Atkins Chronicle
1978: Charles Sanders, Springdale News
1979: Fred Wulfekuhler, Paragould Daily Press
1980: Ross Pendergraft, Ft. Smith, Donrey Media
1981: Charlotte Schexnayder, Dumas Clarion
1982: Bill Whitehead, Jr., Fordyce News-Advocate
1983: Orville Richolson, Newport Daily Independent
1984: Tom Riley, North Little Rock, TheTimes
1985: Joel Irwin, Heber Springs, Cleburne County Times
1986: Louie Graves, Nashville News
1987: David Fisher, Danville, Yell County Record
1988: Betty Magie, Cabot Star-Herald
1989: Derwood Brett, Helena Daily World
1990: Eddie Telford, Palmer Newspapers, Texarkana
1991: Jane Christenson, Harrison Daily Times
1992: George Anderson, Pine Bluff News
1993: Ron Kemp, KMB Publishers
1994: Steve Trolinger, Community Publishers
1995: Pat Jones, Batesville Daily Guard
1996: Ron Wylie, Johnson County Graphic, Clarksville
1997: Betty Woods, Grand Prairie Herald, Hazen
1998: Bill Rutherford, Grand Prairie Herald, Hazen
1999: Mark Magie, Magie Family Newspapers, Cabot
2000: Buddy King, Palmer Newspapers, Texarkana
2001: Charles Berry, Pine Bluff Commercial
2002: Jane Graves, Nashville News
2003: Frank Lightfoot, White Hall Journal

1999
Mark Magie
Cabot Star Herald
Magie Family
Newspapers

2000
Buddy King
Texarkana Gazette

2001
Charles Berry
Pine Bluff
Commercial

2002
Jane Graves
Nashville News
Graves Publishing

2003
Frank Lightfoot
White Hall Journal

Executives of the APA

1873-1877	Jocob F. Frolich
1878-1883	W.A. Webber
1884-1885	James R. Bettis
1886-1887	R.W. Leigh
1888-1906	J.R. Jobe
1907-1916	Earle W. Hodges
1917-1918	R.O. Schaefer
May, 1919-Dec., 1932	Clio Harper
Jan., 1933-1937	C. Armitage Harper
Jun., 1937-Sep., 1938	Ray Kimball
Oct., 1938-Aug., 1943	Sam Schweiger*
Sep., 1943-Mar., 1944	Ken Elliott
Mar., 1944-Feb., 1945	L.J. Miner
Feb., 1945-Sep., 1945	Albert E. Swank
Sep., 1945-Jan., 1946	Otis E. Williams
Jan., 1946-Sep., 1946	Ken Elliott
Sep., 1947-Sep., 1950	L.J. Miner
Oct., 1950-Sep., 1952	William H. Parker
Sep., 1952-Jul., 1960	William G. Conley
Jul., 1960-Apr., 1961	Ray Cooper
Apr., 1961-Ar., 1962	Jerry Russell
Apr., 1962-Jan., 1979	Louise Bowker
May, 1979-present	C. Dennis Schick

*first full-time APA manager

Jan and Dennis Schick have been at APA since 1979, he as Executive Director and she as Administrative Assistant. They have worked as a team. Here Dennis shows Jan the first copy of newspaper columnist Jim Davidson's book, the sale of which will benefit NIE and journalism education programs around the country.

APA Headquarters

University of Arkansas, 1938-1943
(first full-time office)

Boyle Building, 1943-1955

Stephens Building, 1955-1963

Wallace Building, 1963-1978

Spring Building, 1978-1981

Broadway Headquarters, 1981-2000

Victory Headquarters (artist's rendering), 2000-present

Notes

1. Millard Grimes, *The Last Linotype; The Story of Georgia and Its Newspapers Since World War II* (Macon, 1985), 1-2.

2. Quoted in Frank Luther Mott, *American Journalism; A History: 1690–1960* (New York, 1962), 6.

3. William H. Lyon, *The Pioneer Editor in Missouri, 1808–1860* (Columbia, 1965), 7–9.

4. Morris S. Arnold, *Colonial Arkansas, 1686–1804* (Fayetteville, 1991), 79.

5. Quoted in Arnold, *Colonial Arkansas*, 79.

6. William H. Taft, *Missouri Newspapers* (Columbia, 1964), 1–11.

7. Taft, *Missouri Newspapers*, 13.

8. Jerome Loving, *Walt Whitman: The Song of Himself* (Berkeley, 1999), 36, 490.

9. Margaret Ross, *Arkansas Gazette: The Early Years, 1819–1866* (Little Rock, 1969), 3–19. Much of the rest of this chapter is derived from Ross's definitive work.

10. Even as late as the 24th president, newspapers were highly inconsistent on whether to use a "c" or an apostrophe in such names. J.B. Parker of the *Conway News* in 1924 still used the M' for Mc.

11. Ross, *Arkansas Gazette*, 12-13.

12. Judge Daniel T. Witter in 1875 remembered the place as being in the French style. See Arnold, *Colonial Arkansas*, 196. More likely Witter is right.

13. Frank Luther Mott, *American Journalism; A History: 1690-1960* (New York, 1962, 15. First in usage was the *London Gazette*, and so many American newspapers followed this example that in time the term became a generic word for newspapers.

14. Ross, *Arkansas Gazette*, 17-18.

15. Ross, *Arkansas Gazette*, 19-20.

16. Ross, *Arkansas Gazette*, 21.

17. Ross, *Arkansas Gazette*, 21.

18. Ross, *Arkansas Gazette*, 22-25.

19. *Arkansas Gazette*, July 14, 1830.

20. *Arkansas Gazette*, August 4, 1830.

21. The standard survey is Lonnie J. White, *Politics on the Southwest Frontier: Arkansas Territory, 1819-1836* (Memphis, 1964).

22. Pike, who never broke with Crittenden, knew him only in the last years of his life; Eskridge, an old settler, had arrived in 1820 and although he had been one of those Crittenden had early favored, relations rapidly soured.

23. Ross, *Arkansas Gazette*, 24-25.

24. Ross, *Arkansas Gazette*, 25-29.

25. Ross, *Arkansas Gazette*, 26-31.

26. Ross, *Arkansas Gazette*, 33.

27. Ross, *Arkansas Gazette*, 40.

28. Ross, *Arkansas Gazette*, 41-45.

29. *Arkansas Gazette*, February 4, 1823.

30. *Arkansas Gazette*, February 2, 1871.

31. Howard Cresap Key, "The Arkansas Gazette, 1819–1843: Its Literary Trends," (M.A. Thesis, University of Texas, 1935), 113–116, quoted by Ross, *Arkansas Gazette*, 47.

32. Ross, *Arkansas Gazette*, 48.

33. Ross, *Arkansas Gazette*, 54-55.

34. *Arkansas Gazette*, July 17, 1827.

35. Margaret S. Ross, ed., *Letters of Hiram Abiff Whittington: An Arkansas Pioneer from Massachusetts, 1827–1834*. (Little Rock: Pulaski County Historical Society 1956 Bulletin No. 3), 3.

36. Ross, *Arkansas Gazette*, 83.

37. Ross, *Arkansas Gazette*, 83-86.

38. Ross, *Arkansas Gazette*, 88-91.

39. Ross, *Arkansas Gazette*, 90.

40. Ross, *Arkansas Gazette*, 91-93.

41. Ted R. Worley, "An Early Arkansas Sportsman: C.F.M. Noland," *Arkansas Historical Quarterly*, XI (Spring 1952), 25-40, is a useful introduction. Leonard Williams, ed., *Cavorting on the Devil's Fork: The Pete Whetstone Letters of*

C.F.M. *Noland* (Memphis, 1979), contains the best known examples of Noland's writings.

42. Ross, *Arkansas Gazette*, 97-98.

43. Ross, *Arkansas Gazette*, 98-99.

44. Ross, *Arkansas Gazette*,100-103.

45. *Arkansas Gazette*, November 21, 1827.

46. *Arkansas Gazette*, April 7, 1835.

47. *Arkansas Gazette*, February 2, 1831.

48. *Arkansas Gazette*, May 16, 1832.

49. Ross, *Arkansas Gazette*, 99-108.

50. Walter Lee Brown, *A Life of Albert Pike* (Fayetteville, 1997), is the comprehensive modern account.

51. Brown, *Albert Pike*, 47-69.

52. Ross, *Arkansas Gazette*, 109-115.

53. Ross, *Arkansas Gazette*, 113. By 1853 the largest newspaper in America was the New York *Journal of Commerce*, measuring 3 x 5 feet! with 11 columns per page. Mott, *American Journalism*, 294-295.

54. G.W. Featherstonhaugh, *Excursion Through the Slave States* (New York, 1844), 96-97.

55. Ross, *Arkansas Gazette*, 116-117.

56. Taft, *Missouri Newspapers*, 34, has some details on our "certain John Steele."

57. Ross, *Arkansas Gazette*, 118.

58. F. Hampton Roy and Charles Witsell, *How We Lived: Little Rock as an American City* (Little Rock, 1984).

59. Ross, *Arkansas Gazette*, 122-125; Brown, *Albert Pike*, 82-83.

60. Ross, *Arkansas Gazette*, 127-129.

61. Ross, *Arkansas Gazette*, 129-134.

62. Fred W. Allsopp, *History of the Arkansas Press for a Hundred Years and More* (Little Rock, 1922), 284.

63. Taft, *Missouri Newspapers*, 50.

64. Ross, *Arkansas Gazette*, 135-156.

65. Ross, *Arkansas Gazette*, 137.

66. Brown, *Albert Pike*, 108-109.

67. A full recounting can be found in John Hallum, *Biographical and Pictorial History of Arkansas* (Albany, 1887).

68. Ross, *Arkansas Gazette*, 149-151.

69. Ross, *Arkansas Gazette*, 161-164.

70. *Arkansas Gazette*, August 21, 1839.

71. Brown, *Albert Pike*, 170.

72. Ross, *Arkansas Gazette*, 170-174.

73. Ross, *Arkansas Gazette*, 174-178.

74. Brown, *Albert Pike*, 152-153. A long account appearing in G.W. Featherstonhaugh's famous book, *Excursion Through the Slave States*... (1844), 99, had "the ruffian Wilson" then wiping the blood off his Bowie knife with his thumb and finger and resuming his seat!

75. *Arkansas Gazette*, January 10, 17, 1838.

76. Fayetteville *South-West Independent*, May 12, 1855.

77. *Arkansas Gazette*, May 17, 1843.

78. *Arkansas Gazette*, June 19, 1842.

79. Ross, *Arkansas Gazette*, 175-180.

80. *Arkansas Gazette*, July 20, 1842.

81. Ross, *Arkansas Gazette*, 181-195.

82. Ross, *Arkansas Gazette*, 195-198.

83. Ross, *Arkansas Gazette*, 198-203.

84. Ross, *Arkansas Gazette*, 198, 212-213, 217.

85. Ross, *Arkansas Gazette*, 228.

86. Ross, *Arkansas Gazette*, 226-228.

87. Brown, *Albert Pike*, 227-240.

88. Ross, *Arkansas Gazette*, 238.

89. Ross, *Arkansas Gazette*, 242-250.

90. *Arkansas Gazette*, April 3, 1844.

91. Ross, *Arkansas Gazette*, 250-261.

92. Ross, *Arkansas Gazette*, 261-265.

93. Ross, *Arkansas Gazette*, 271-276.

94. Ross, *Arkansas Gazette*, 276-286.

95. Ross, *Arkansas Gazette*, 277.

96. Ross, *Arkansas Gazette*, 281-284.

97. Ross, *Arkansas Gazette*, 284-298;

98. Ross, *Arkansas Gazette*, 288-294.

99. *Washington Telegraph*, August 15, 1855.

100. Ross, *Arkansas Gazette*, 296.

101. Allsopp, *History*, 323.

102. Ross, *Arkansas Gazette*, 305-307.

103. Dickison Brugman, "The Life Story of a Newpaper Veteran," *Arkansas Gazette*, November 7, 1931.

104. Ross, *Arkansas Gazette*, 304-309.

105. Ross, *Arkansas Gazette*, 307-323.

106. Ross, *Arkansas Gazette*, 318.

107. Ross, *Arkansas Gazette*, 322-323.

108. Ross, *Arkansas Gazette*, 318. Fannie (to use her spelling) Borland later specialized in Civil War-related poetry, with her tribute to the martyred David O. Dodd being the most remembered piece. While some of her poetry was later anthologized, all of it appeared originally in newspapers and has never been collected.

109. Ross, *Arkansas Gazette*, 337-338.

110. *Arkansas State Gazette and Democrat*, March 21, 1857.

111. Ross, *Arkansas Gazette*, 335.

112. Michael B. Dougan, *Confederate Arkansas: The*

People and Policies of a Frontier State in Wartime (University, Ala., 1976), 12-15.

113. Little Rock *Old Line Democrat*, May 24, 1860.

114. *Arkansas State Gazette*, July 28, 1860.

115. Dougan, *Confederate Arkansas*, 21.

116. Fayetteville *Arkansian*, June 8, 1860; reprinted in the *Arkansas State Gazette*, June 16, 1860.

117. Allsopp, *History*, 285.

118. My history is based on examination of extant issues. Compare with Allsopp, *History*, 284.

119. Helena *Southern Shield*, February 26,1853; September 30, 1854.

120. Allsopp, *History*, 285.

121. *Washington Telegraph*, October 24, 1855.

122. Ross, *Arkansas Gazette*, 178.

123. Allsopp, *History*, 137.

124. Read Fletcher, "Twice Told Tales; History of the Press of Pine Bluff," *Jefferson County Historical Quarterly*, VIII (No. 2, 1979), 40.

125. Batesville *North Arkansas*, August 9, November 1, 1843; January 3, February 7, 1844.

126. Batesville *Independent Balance*, April 22, 1858, July 1, 1858, May 20, 1858.

127. Batesville *Independent Balance*, August 26, 1858.

128. A.C. McGinnis, "M. Shelby Kennard and the Independent Balance, *Independence County Chronicle*, XV (January 1974), 15-33.

129. William M. Quesenbury's description, Little Rock *Daily Arkansas Gazette*, June 24, 1876.

130. Allsopp, *History*, 15, 30, 123.

131. One of the important accounts for this period is Cephas Washburn's memoir, *Reminiscences of the Indians* (Richmond, 1869).

132. Van Buren *Arkansas Intelligencer*, October 21, 1843.

133. *Arkansas Intelligencer*, October 2, 1847.

134. *Arkansas Intelligencer*, October 23, December 11, December 25, 1847.

135. Quoted in Allsopp, *History*, 410.

136. *Arkansas Intelligencer*, December 1, 1849.

137. Allsopp, *History*, 459. One copy of the *Witness* survived, none of the *Pioneer*.

138. *Arkansas Gazette*, May 3, June 21, 1836.

139. Mary Medearis, ed., *Sam Williams: Printer's Devil; Memorabilia* (Hope, Ark., 1979), 48–49.

140. *Washington Telegraph*, January 13, 1847.

141. *Washington Telegraph*, March 1, 1848.

142. *Washington Telegraph*, June 28, 1848.

143. *Washington Telegraph*, July 19, 1843.

144. *Washington Telegraph*, November 27, 1843.

145. *Washington Telegraph*, July 28, 1852.

146. *Washington Telegraph*, May 26, 1852.

147. *Washington Telegraph*, March 30, 1859.

148. Medearis, *Sam Williams*, 51–52.

149. Medearis, *Sam Williams*, 53; Allsopp, *History*, 161.

150. Fletcher, "History," 36.

151. Fletcher, "History," 37.

152. *El Dorado Union*, September 23, 1848; *The Democratic Union*, August 23, 1856.

153. *El Dorado Bulletin*, May 9, 1861.

154. *Arkansas State Gazette and Democrat*, June 6, 1857.

155. Allsopp, *History*, 96.

156. Quoted in the *South-West Independent*, January 28, 1854.

157. Quoted in *Arkansas State Gazette*, January 2, 1858.

158. Quoted in the *Arkansas Gazette and Democrat*, September 15, 1854.

159. *Arkansas Gazette and Democrat*, September 15, 1854.

160. *Washington Telegraph*, November 8, 1854.

161. *Arkansas Gazette and Democrat*, June 10, 1853.

162. Ross, *Arkansas Gazette*, 334-335.

163. *Arkansas Intelligencer*, August 18, 1849.

164. "The Carrier's Address to the Patrons of the Southwest Independent, January 1, 1854," reprinted in the *Fayetteville Daily Democrat*, January 2, 1932. Delia Wagner Price Papers, University of Arkansas.

165. *South-West Independent*, August 25, 1853. A fuller account can be found in Kim Allen Scott, "Window on the Frontier; the Early Newspapers of Washington County, Arkansas," *Flashback*, XXXIII (August 1988), 12–20.

166. *South-West Independent*, June 7, 1856.

167. Quoted in David Dary, *Red Blood & Black Ink: Journalism in the Old West* (New York, 1998), 135.

168. Quoted in the *Arkansas State Gazette and Democrat*, December 29, 1854.

169. *South-West Independent*, December 2, 1853.

170. *South-West Independent*, July 18, 1856.

171. Allsopp, *History*, 496–97.

172. *South-West Independent*, August 25, 1853.

173. *South-West Independent*, September 8, 1853.

174. *South-West Independent*, February 17, 1855.

175. *South-West Independent*, May 12, 1855.

176. *South-West Independent*, June 23, 1855.

177. *South-West Independent*, February 17, 1855.

178. Quoted in *Arkansas Gazette and Democrat*, March 9,

1855

179. *Washington Telegraph*, June 20, 1855.

180. *South-West Independent*, January 28, 1854.

181. Quoted in *Arkansas Gazette and Democrat*, March 9, 1855.

182. Richard Rudisill, *Mirror Image: The Influence of the Daguerreotype on American Society* (Albuquerque, 1971), 209–10.

183. *New York Spirit of the Times*, January 7, 1854, 555. This is another example where the original publication in Cush's newspaper has not survived. The complete story is reprinted in Swannee Bennett and William B. Worthen, *Arkansas Made: A Survey of the Decorative, Mechanical, and Fine Arts Produced in Arkansas, 1819–1870* (Fayetteville, 1991), 203–4.

184. *South-West Independent*, January 28, 1854.

185. *South-West Independent*, August 25, 1853.

186. *South-West Independent*, May 12, 1855.

187. *South-West Independent*, November 18, 1853.

188. *South-West Independent*, January 28, 1854.

189. Wm. Quesenbury to Stand Watie, January 27, 1857. Cherokee Nation Papers, University of Oklahoma.

190. Two overviews of this period are Dougan, *Confederate Arkansas* and James M. Woods, *Rebellion and Realignment: Arkansas's Road to Secession* (Fayetteville, 1987).

191. Michael B. Dougan, "The Little Rock Press Goes to War," *Arkansas Historical Quarterly*, XXVIII (Spring 1969), 14–17. *Old Line Democrat*, December 13, 1860.

192. *Arkansas State Gazette*, December 29, 1860.

193. *Arkansas State Gazette*, January 5, 1861.

194. *True Democrat*, April 13, 1861.

195. S.L. Griffith, Fort Smith, to D.C. Williams, March 30, 1861, Williams Papers, Arkansas History Commission.

196. *Arkansas State Gazette*, May 18, 1861.

197. *True Democrat*, May 9, 1861.

198. A useful summary of the Civil War can be found in Mark K. Christ, ed., *Rugged and Sublime: The Civil War in Arkansas* (Fayetteville, 1994).

199. *True Democrat*, June 12, 1862.

200. J.C. Robbins to W.E. Woodruff, November 13, 1861. William E. Woodruff Papers, Arkansas History Commission.

201. Little Rock *Daily State Journal*, January 5, 1862.

202. Address of Governor Rector to the Legislature, *True Democrat*, November 7, 1861.

203. *Arkansas State Gazette*, December 14, 1861.

204. Quoted in the *True Democrat*, December 19, 1861.

205. Brown, *Albert Pike*, 383-399.

206. William L. Shea and Earl J. Hess, *Pea Ridge: Civil War Campaign in the West* (Chapel Hill, 1992), 143-144, 274-275, 313.

207. *True Democrat*, May 22, 1862.

208. Quoted in the *Arkansas Gazette*, September 27, 1862.

209. Quoted in the *True Democrat*, September 24, 1862.

210. *True Democrat*, May 15 1862.

211. *True Democrat*, June 12, 1862.

212. *Arkansas State Gazette*, November 29, 1862; *True Democrat*, May 15, 1862.

213. *True Democrat*, April 3, 1862.

214. *True Democrat*, July 8, 1863.

215. *True Democrat*, July 4, 1861; December 31, 1862.

216. *True Democrat*, July 8, 1863.

217. *True Democrat*, October 3, 1861.

218. *True Democrat*, July 8, 1863.

219. *True Democrat*, January 30, 1862; January 7, 1863.

220. *True Democrat*, February 11, 1863.

221. Mark E. Neely, Jr, *Southern Rights: Political Prisoners and the Myth of Confederate Constitutionalism* (Charlottesville, 1999), 11–28.

222. Brown, *Albert Pike*, 401–16.

223. *Washington Telegraph*, July 2, 1862.

224. Brown, *Albert Pike*, 415-427; other jurists were Jno. (John) R. Eakin, John M'Clure (McClure), and Griffin Smith.

225. *Washington Telegraph*, January 22, 1862.

226. *Washington Telegraph*, May 7, 1862.

227. Ross, *Arkansas Gazette*, 366.

228. *Arkansas State Gazette*, February 21, 1863.

229. *True Democrat*, July 3, 1863.

230. *True Democrat*, March 13, 1862.

231. *True Democrat*, August 20, 1862.

232. *Arkansas State Gazette*, June 14, 1862

233. *Arkansas State Gazette*, October 18, 1862.

234. Quoted in Ted R. Worley, ed., *At Home in Confederate Arkansas: Letters to and from Pulaski Countians, 1861-1865* (Pulaski County Historical Society, 1955), 27.

235. Quoted in Dougan, *Confederate Arkansas*, 109.

236. Ross, Arkansas Gazette, 383.

237. Ross, *Arkansas Gazette*, 379.

238. J. Cutler Andrews, *The South Reports the Civil War* (Princeton, 1970), is the standard treatment.

239. A study of the *Washington Telegraph* can be found in Robert Freeman Smith, "John R. Eakin: Confederate Propagandist," *Arkansas Historical Quarterly*, XII (Winter

1953), 316–26.

240. *Washington Telegraph*, March 5, 1865.

241. Fort Smith *New Era*, October 8, 1863.

242. Ross, *Arkansas Gazette*, 386-389.

243. Ross, *Arkansas Gazette*, 389.

244. Leroy H. Fischer, "David O. Dodd: A Folk Hero of Confederate Arkansas," *Arkansas Historical Quarterly*, XXXVII (Summer 1978), 130-146.

245. *Arkansas State Gazette*, May 10, 1865.

246. *Arkansas State Gazette*, May 31, 1865.

247. Ross, *Arkansas Gazette*, 397-399.

248. Ross, *Arkansas Gazette*, 398–99.

249. Ross, *Arkansas Gazette*, 402. These are the lines that close the most detailed institutional history written about an Arkansas newspaper.

250. *Arkansas State Gazette*, July 4, 1866.

251. J.H. Sparks, quoted in Allsopp, *History*, 573.

252. *Arkansas State Gazette*, July 28, 1866.

253. Michael B. Dougan, "Bravo Brignoli! The First Opera Season in Arkansas," *Pulaski County Historical Review*, XXX (Winter 1982), 74-80.

254. *Arkansas Gazette*, November 20, 1870.

255. *Arkansas Gazette*, September 24, 1867.

256. *Arkansas Gazette*, March 24, 1874.

257. *Arkansas Gazette*, December 5, 1869; November 21, 1871.

258. *Arkansas Gazette*, August 25, 1874.

259. E. Merton Coulter, *The South During Reconstruction, 1865–1877* (Baton Rouge, 1947), 148.

260. Quoted in Ted R. Worley, ed. "Letters to David Walker Relating to Reconstruction in Arkansas, 1866–1874," *Arkansas Historical Quarterly*, XVI (Autumn 1957), 323.

261. The interworkings are discussed in George H. Thompson, *Arkansas and Reconstruction: The Influence of Geography, Economics, and Personality* (Port Washington, 1976).

262. Allsopp, *History*, 465.

263. Interview, Charlotte Tillar and Melvin Schexnayder, March 7, 2000. According to Allsopp, *History*, 306–306, Edward Bancroft and Theo Holt founded the first newspaper to bear this name in 1868 but did not long keep it. Bancroft then founded another newspaper in 1870 called the *Liberal*, from which Allsopp quoted Bancroft's offer to the legislature to save the state money on its printing. The offer was not accepted, and the copy Allsopp saw is not known to this author.

264. *Arkansas Gazette*, June 26, 1870. The *Fayetteville Democrat* became the *Northwest Arkansas Times* in 1937; from this list it should be noted that the *Des Arc Citizen* was moved by J.J. Baugh to Searcy where it became the *White County Citizen* and then the *Searcy Daily Citizen*; the *Van Buren Press* was merged with the *Van Buren Argus* in 1927 to become the *Van Buren Press-Argus*; the *Monticellonian*, established the year of the survey, was merged with the *Drew County Advance* in 1920; and the assets of the *Arkansas Gazette* were acquired by the *Arkansas Democrat* in 1991.

265. Margaret Ross, "Retaliation Against Arkansas Newspaper Editors During Reconstruction," *Arkansas Historical Quarterly*, XXXI (Summer 1972), 150–65.

266. Allsopp, *History*, 477.

267. Ross, "Retaliation," 150-165.

268. Harrell was apparently the man who passed on the false report that triggered the arsenal crisis. His two books were *The Brooks and Baxter War, A History of the Reconstruction Period in Arkansas* (St. Louis, 1893) and the Arkansas volume in Clement A. Evans, *Confederate Military History: A Library of Confederate States History* (Atlanta, 1899).

269. *Arkansas Gazette*, April 9, 15; October 12–15, 1871. Ross, "Retaliation," 164–65.

270. Ross, "Retaliation," 164-65. Margaret Ross says that truth cannot be found; if she could not find out, it is doubtful any future researcher will do better. Reconstruction history claims more skeletons than any other period of Arkansas history.

271. *Arkansas Gazette*, October 16, 30; November 13; December 3, 1866.

272. *Arkansas Gazette*, March 27, April 7, 1868.

273. *Arkansas Gazette*, October 17, 20, 1869. Torrans's motion had important 20th-century implications for the medical profession when the American Medical Association made it actionable for a doctor's name even to appear in a newspaper. This move was in reaction to 19th-century practices where doctors courted (and paid for) puffs from editors.

274. *Arkansas Gazette*, July 7, 1869.

275. *Arkansas Gazette*, October 14, 1873.

276. Allsopp, *History*, 506–7.

277. Allsopp, *History*, 314.

278. *Arkansas Gazette*, June 17, 1874.

279. Quoted in Allsopp, *History*, 495.

280. This author's version is based on a story in Thomas D. Clark, *The Rural Press and the New South* (Baton Rouge, 1948),1-2, and a joke told by longtime Camden editor Al

Rose.

281. Read, *I Remember*,

282. Allsopp, *History*, 141.

283. Allsopp, *History*, 140.

284. Undated clipping, Shiloh Museum.

285. Allsopp, *History*, 114, 391,

286. Lady Elizabeth Luker, "Newspapers of Jackson County," *Stream of History*, IV (January 1966), 22.

287. Erwin Funk, "Pure Baloney and No Part of my Regular Newspaper Article," Funk Papers, Special Collections, University of Arkansas.

288. *New Traditions*, October 18-24, 1981 (Clipping, Shiloh Museum).

289. Allsopp, *History*, 204.

290. Allsopp, *History*, 176.

291. *Booneville Democrat*, July 10, 1947.

292. Allsopp, *History*, 298-299.

293. *Springdale News*, April 29, 1937 [Golden Anniversary Edition], May 7, 1987 [100th Anniversary Edition], clipping, Shiloh Museum.

294. *Springdale News*, April 29, 1937.

295. *Springdale News*, April 29, 1937.

296. *Springdale News*, April 29, 1937.

297. *Springdale News*, April 29, 1937.

298. *Springdale News*, April 29, 1937.

299. *Springdale News*, April 29, 1937.

300. *Springdale News*, April 29, 1937.

301. *Springdale Morning News*, December 14, 1993.

302. Allsopp, *History*, 216-218; Robert W. Meriwether, comp., *A Chronicle of Arkansas Newspapers Published Since 1922* (N.P., 1974), 59-61.

303. *Proceedings of the Arkansas Press Association at the Fifth Annual Meeting..., 1877*, 21.

304. *Proceedings...Fifth Annual Meeting, 1877*,29-30.

305. *Proceedings...Fifth Annual Meeting, 1877*, 39-40.

306. *Proceedings...Fifth Annual Meeting, 1877*, 37.

307. *Proceedings of the Fifty-First Annual Convention...1923*, 44; Allsopp, *History*, has a picture of this press on page 72.

308. *Proceedings...Fifth Annual Meeting, 1877*, 40.

309. Kim Allen Scott, "A Printer Comes to Pettigrew," *Ozarks Watch*, VII (Summer 1993), 14-18.

310. Craig Ogilvie, "Izard County Newspapers, 1873-1971," *Izard County Historian*, II (January 1971), 16-23.

311. Ogilvie, "Izard County," 20-21.

312. *Bentonville Sun*, November 19, 1892.

313. Erwin Funk, "Final Installment of Benton County Newspaper History, *Benton County Pioneer*, IV (March 1959), 26.

314. *The Alliance Patriot*, April 23, 1891.

315. Searcy *Arkansas Banner*, August 10, 1898.

316. Searcy *Southern Economist*, August 3, 1893. Neither of these papers was known to Allsopp.

317. Conway, *The Sickle*, July 1900.

318. Pam Huett, "The Morrilton Democrat, 1896-1982," History of Journalism Paper, Arkansas Tech University. 1994.

319. *Fulton County Informer*, March 17, 1888; Allsopp, *History*, 154.

320. Jasper, *The Newton Herald*, July 7, 1898.

321. *Advance Monticellonian*, July 4, 1932.

322. *Cane Hill News*, August 6, 1903.

323. *Fort Smith New Era*, July 14, 1875.; January 21, 1880.

324. *Boone County Record*, January 12, 1872.

325. *Cleveland County Herald*, June 11, 1896.

326. *Saline County Digest*, May 24, 1877.

327. *Newton County Times*, April 2, 1927.

328. *Helena Daily World*, July 6, 1876.

329. *Dover Times*, April 22, 1926.

330. Fayetteville, *Arkansas Times*, August 31, 1882.

331. *Fayetteville Republic*, January 7, 1916.

332. Fayetteville, *The Arkansas Blade*, March 2, 1882.

333. *Osceola Times*, April 15, 1882.

334. Allsopp, *History*, 227.

335. *Crockett's Gleaner*, May 18, 1883.

336. *Mountain Wave*, May 18, 1891.

337. *Rogers Democrat*, September 14, 1916.

338. *Southern Standard*, April 17, 1875.

339. *Proceedings of the Twenty-Eighth Annual Session...1900*, 56-57.

340. Teresa Dawson, "History of the Times Dispatch of Walnut Ridge, 1910-1980," *Lawrence County Historical Quarterly*, IV (Fall 1981), 5-9.

341. Erwin Funk, "Rogers Has Seen Many Newspapers Come and Go," *Benton County Pioneer*, III (July 1958), 12.

342. *Rogers Democrat*, July 15, 1915.

343. *Proceedings of the 59th Annual Session...1927*, 20.

344. *Southern Standard*, August 18, 1877.

345. *Southern Standard*, December 15, 1877.

346. *De Witt Elector*, February 9, 1867.

347. Quoted in Allsopp, *History*, 98.

348. *Southern Standard*, May 14, 1870.

349. *Southern Standard*, September 2, 1871.

350. *Southern Standard*, July 21, 1877.

351. *Southern Standard*, March 1, 1873.

352. *Southern Standard*, April 25, 1874.

353. *Southern Standard*, June 7, 1873.

354. Quoted in *Southern Standard*, March 6, 1869.

355. *Southern Standard*, March 7, 1874.

356. *Southern Standard*, May 23, 1874; March 22, 1879.

357. Autobiography, Erwin Funk Papers, Special Collections, University of Arkansas.

358. *Leslie News*, May 9, 1919.

359. Quoted in *Southern Standard*, June 8, 1878.

360. *Crockett's Gleaner*, May 18, 1883.

361. *Rogers Democrat*, June 24, 1915.

362. Allsopp, *Little Adventures*, 120-121.

363. *Southern Standard*, November 20, 1869.

364. *Southern Standard*, March 26, 1870.

365. Allsopp, *Little Adventures*, 34.

366. *Southern Standard*, November 27, 1875.

367. *Southern Standard*, October 5, 1872.

368. *Southern Standard*, July 17, 1875.

369. *Helena World*, July 5, 1876.

370. *Southern Standard*, October 18, 1873.

371. *Marshall Republican*, June 9, 1893.

372. *Siloam Springs Herald and Democrat*, June 27, 1907.

373. *Helena Daily World*, July 5, 1876.

374. *Huntsville Democrat*, May 31, 1888.

375. *Rogers Democrat*, August 13, 1916.

376. Autobiography, Erwin Funk Papers, Special Collections, University of Arkansas.

377. *Southern Standard*, September 4, 1875.

378. *Southern Standard*, October 22, 1870.

379. *Southern Standard*, March 30, 1872.

380. Fayetteville *Arkansas Blade*, March 2, 1882.

381. *Helena Daily World*, July 6, 1876.

382. *Crockett's Gleaner*, May 18, 1883.

383. *Southern Standard*, December 18, 1875; Allsopp, *History*, 49.

384. *Southern Standard*, June 5, July 10, 1875.

385. Allsopp, *Little Adventures*, 33-35.

386. *Hot Springs Weekly News*, August 6, 1899. The news "story" stopped in mid-sentence!

387. *Proceedings of the Twenty-Second Annual Session...1894*, 50.

388. *Proceedings of the Thirty-second Annual Meeting...1904*, 27.

389. *Proceedings of the Fifty-First Annual Convention...1923*, 31.

390. "Jacksonport Newspapers," *Stream of History*, II (Spring 1964), 4-8; Allsopp, *History*, 204.

391. Jane Allen Goodwin, "The Tuckerman Times, 1907," *Stream of History*, XVI (April 1978), 27.

392. Marshall *Mountain Wave*, June 17, 1892, October 29, 1897; April 1, 1898.

393. *Mountain Wave*, March 25, 1899.

394. *Mountain Wave*, January 5, 1901.

395. *Swifton Sentinel*, December 23, 1910, in Beatrice Nicholson, "Swifton's Newspaper of 1910," *Stream of History*, XV (October 1977), 35.

396. Dee Brown, *When the Century was Young* (Little Rock, 1993), 69.

397. *Tuckerman Times*, July 18, 1907.

398. Harry Lee Williams, "Craighead County's Fourth Estate," *Craighead County Historical Quarterly* (Autumn 1964), 10-11.

399. *Proceedings of the Thirty-Seventh Annual Meeting...1909*, 24.

400. *Proceedings of the Thirty-Seventh Annual Meeting...1909*, 38-39.

401. *Proceedings of the Fourteenth Annual Meeting...* (Little Rock, 1886), 59, 63.

402. *Proceedings of the Twenty-Eighth Annual Session...* 1900, 51.

403. *Proceedings of the Thirty-second Annual Meeting...1904*, 27.

404. *Proceedings of the Forty-Fourth Annual Meeting...1916*, 26.

405. *Proceedings of the 59th Annual Session...1927*, 20.

406. *Proceedings of the Thirty-Fourth Annual Session...1906*, 21.

407. *Bingen Social Visitor*, December 23, 1910.

408. Allsopp, *Little Adventures*, 72.

409. *Minutes of the Thirty-Sixth Annual Session...1908*, 19-20.

410. *Proceedings of the Thirty-Fifth Annual Meeting...1907*, 11.

411. Allsopp, *Little Adventures*, 65.

412. Allsopp, *Little Adventures*, 52.

413. Interview with C. Edward Tudor and J. Maurice Tudor, June 3, 2000.

414. *Southern Standard*, November 25, 1871.

415. Allsopp, *History*, 149; *Southern Standard*, May 13, June 17, 1876.

416. *Cleveland County Herald*, June 11, 1896; August 26, 1897; July 10, 1902; *Rogers Democrat*, May 18, 1916; Allsopp, *History*, 107.

417. *Proceedings of the Twenty-Fifth Annual Session...* (1897), 65.

418. *Proceedings of the Twenty-Fifth Annual Session...* (1897), 65.

419. *Proceedings of the Fiftieth Annual Convention... 1922*, 50.

420. *Proceedings of the Fourteenth Annual Meeting...* (Little Rock, 1886), 26.

421. *Proceedings of the Thirty-Eighth Annual Meeting...* (1910), n.p.

422. *Rogers Democrat*, May 27, 1915.

423. Quoted in Clark, *The Rural Press*, 79-80.

424. *Leslie News*, 1912 clipping, Ozark Heritage Arts Center

425. *Southern Standard*, September 2, 1876.

426. *Springdale News*, April 29, 1937.

427. Allsopp, *History*, 383.

428. *Clarksville Enterprise*, May 25, 1883.

429. *Hot Springs Citizens Bulletin*, August 4, 1906.

430. *Southern Standard*, October 7, 1871.

431. *Proceedings of the Thirty-Second Annual Meeting...1904*, 31

432. Marshall *Mountain Wave*, September 9, 1898.

433. Marshall *Mountain Wave*, November 18, 1899.

434. Marshall *Mountain Wave*, November 18, 1899.

435. *Marshall Republican*, February 20,1891.

436. *Springdale News*, April 29, 1937.

437. *Proceedings of the Thirty-second Annual Meeting...1904*, 31.

438. Allsopp, *Little Adventures*, 179.

439. Brown, *Century*, 80.

440. Marshall *Mountain Wave*, November 18, 1891.

441. Bentonville *New Bentonian*, February 22, 1882.

442. *Proceedings of the Thirty-second Annual Meeting...1904*, 31.

443. *Mountain Wave*, November 18, 1891.

444. *Proceedings of the Twenty-sixth Annual Session...* (1898), 64.

445. *Proceedings of the Thirty-second Annual Meeting...1904*, 31.

446. *Proceedings of the 27th Annual Session...1899*, 43.

447. *Mountain Wave*, November 18, 1891.

448. *Northwest Arkansas Times*, March 6, 1982. Clipping, Shiloh Museum.

449. *Marshall Republican*, April 5, 1895.

450. *Southern Standard*, July 26, 1873.

451. Harry Lee Williams, "Craighead County's Fourth Estate," *Craighead County Historical Quarterly*, II (Autumn 1964), 6-9

452. *Springdale News*, April 29, 1937.

453. *Rogers Democrat*, September 14, 1916.

454. *Rogers Democrat*, March 9, 1916.

455. *Proceedings of the Twenty-sixth Annual Session...*(1898), 43-44.

456. Robert L. Morris, *Opie Read: American Humorist, 1852-1939* (New York), is the standard biography.

457. Allsopp, *Little Adventures*, 51.

458. *Russellville Siftings*, April 27, 1895.

459. Elbert [Smithee] to Dear Mother, May 8, 1884. Ragland Collection, University of Arkansas.

460. Erwin Funk, "APA—1896 and Now," *Arkansas Publisher*, XXIV (December 1954), 4.

461. *Proceedings...Fifth Annual Meeting...*28-29.

462. *Proceedings of the Thirteenth Annual Meeting...*, 45.

463. Erwin Funk, "An Exciting Time was 'had by all' at the 1898 Press Meet," *Arkansas Publisher*, XXV (February 1955), 4.

464. Funk, "APA," 4.

465. *Proceedings of the Thirteenth Annual Meeting...*, 48.

466. *Proceedings of the Fourteenth Annual Meeting...* 72-76.

467. *Proceedings of the Fourteenth Annual Meeting...* 87-93.

468. *Proceedings of the Thirty-Eighth Annual Meeting...* 1910, n.p.

469. *Proceedings of the Thirty-Third Annual Session...*1905.

470. *Proceedings of the 60th Annual Session...1932*, 17-18.

471. *Proceedings of the Thirteenth Annual Meeting...*, 61.

472. *Proceedings of the Thirteenth Annual Meeting ...*, 70-71.

473. *Minutes of the Arkansas Press Association Thirty-Sixth Annual Session...1908.*

474. Autobiography, Erwin Funk Papers, Special Collections, University of Arkansas.

475. Quoted in *Arkansas Publisher*, Winter 1985, 11.

476. Bob Leigh clipping file, Arkansas History Commission.

477. Autobiograpy, Erwin Funk Papers, Special Collections, University of Arkansas.

478. Clio Harper, *History of the Arkansas Press Association*, 24.

479. *Proceedings of the 17th Annual Session...(1889)*, 23.

480. *Proceedings of the 27th Annual Session...1899*, 44.

481. Robert Ward Johnson, Washington, D.C., to Hon.

David Walker, August 25, 1875. [The original of this letter was once in the J.N. Heiskell Library at the *Arkansas Gazette* but was evidently stolen. Margaret Ross transcribed it for me in 1972.]

482. *Caddo Star*, October 19, 1875, quoted in *Arkansas Gazette*, October 23, 1875.

483. Lucile Price Turner, "Bill Cush," *Arkansas Gazette* Magazine Section, November 10, 1940.

484. Criminal Case File Index Q, *United States v. William Quesenbury*, 1877. National Archives.

485. E.C. Boudinot, Washington, D.C., to Maj. William Quesenbury, January 19, 1876.

486. *Arkansas Daily Gazette*, June 24, 1876.

487. *Des Arc Citizen*, quoted in Fayetteville *Arkansas Sentinel*, June 28, 1877.

488. *Arkansas Gazette* quoted in Fayetteville *Arkansas Sentinel*, July 10, 1878.

489. Daily *Arkansas Gazette*, July 16, 1878.

490. Wm. Quesenbury (Bill Cush), *Arkansas: A Poem*. (Little Rock, 1879); *Arkansas Gazette*, February 14, 1897. The dedication was to Major John D. Adams, "a true bob-a-she-la since the days of our very innocent childhood."

491. Wm. Quesenbury, Neosho, Mo., to James S. Stuart, October 30, 1885. Historic Arkansas Museum.

492. *Daily Arkansas Gazette*, September 6, 1888.

493. Fayetteville *Arkansas Sentinel*, September 25, 1888.

494. *Fayetteville Democrat*, March 15, 1889.

495. *Proceedings of the Arkansas Press Association from its Organization in October, 1873*, (Little Rock, 1876), 21. The proceedings of the first four meetings were collected and published in 1876. Thereafter publication came annually.

496. Allsopp, *Little Adventures*, 65. Little Rock *Evening Star*, May 24, 1876; January 6, 1877. Note that M'Clure was apparently McClure's preferred spelling.

497. Quoted in Allsopp, *History*, 367.

498. *Wheeler's Independent*, September 11, 1878.

499. Allsopp, *Little Adventures*, 62.

500. Robert L. Morris, *Opie Read: American Humorist*, 64.

501. Opie Read, *I Remember*, 110-112. Fred W. Allsopp annotated one copy of his *Little Adventures in Newspaperdom*, 70, with the observation that Rev. Winfield was "a fanatic of fanatics."

502. *Arkansas Gazette*, August 21, 25, 1880; Allsopp, *Little Adventures*, 70-71.

503. Read, *I Remember*, 135.

504. *Arkansas Gazette*, June 5, 1880.

505. *Arkansas Gazette*, September 3, June 12, 1880.

506. *Arkansas Gazette*, July 21, 1880.

507. *Arkansas Gazette*, June 9, 1880.

508. Read, *I Remember*, 135-136.

509. Perryville *Quapaw Times*, August 4, 1881.

510. Quoted in Allsopp, *History* 366.

511. *Arkansas Weekly Mansion*, November 10, 1883.

512. *Little Rock Republican*, June 27, 1885.

513. *Little Rock Republican*, June 27, 1885.

514. Kenneth C. Barnes, *Who Killed John Clayton? Political Violence and the Emergence of the New South, 1861-1893* (Durham, 1998).

515. Clio Harper Diary, January 19, 1897. Private posession.

516. Raymond Arsenault, *The Wild Ass of the Ozarks: Jeff Davis and the Social Bases of Southern Politics* (Philadelphia, 1984) is the standard life. Cal Ledbetter, Jr., "Jeff Davis and the Politics of Combat," *Arkansas Historical Quarterly*, XXXIII (Spring 1974), 16-37, details the oratorical and rhetorical strategies of Davis.

517. Allsopp, *Little Adventures*, 103-105. Dating back to antebellum times, announcements were run in a separate column. The newspapers often charged for this service but generally gave the candidate a complimentary notice.

518. Allsopp, *Little Adventures*, 103.

519. *Proceedings of the Fifty-ninth Annual Meeting...1931*, 32.

520. *Proceedings of the Arkansas Press Association at the Fifth Annual Meeting...1877*, 18. Smithee said he also heard one legislator declare his opposition to public schools while another criticized immigration.

521. Unidentified clipping, Smithee file, Arkansas History Commission.

522. Allsopp, *Little Adventures*, 64-65.

523. Allsopp, *History*, 330-331.

524. *Arkansas Gazette*, December 27, 1896.

525. Dickison Brugman, "The Life Story of a Newspaper Veteran," *Arkansas Gazette*, November 7, 1931. Margaret Ross, Little Rock, to author, n.d.

526. Allsopp, *Little Adventures*, 127-132.

527. The manuscript is at the Arkansas History Commission.

528. Smithee Clippings, Special Collections, University of Arkansas.

529. Frances Mitchell Ross, "James Mitchell, Spokesman for Women's Equality in 19th Century Arkansas," *Arkansas Historical Quarterly*, XLIII (Autumn 1984), 232.

530. Clio Harper Diary, December 25, 1895.

531. *Arkansas Gazette*, May 23, 1880.

532. *Proceedings of the 27th Annual Session...1899*, 24-28.

533. *Proceedings of the 27th Annual Session...1899*, 28.

534. *Proceedings of the Thirty-seventh Meeting...(1909)*, 33.

535. Clio Harper Diary, June 29, 1912.

536. *Arkansas Democrat*, August 24, 1888.

537. *Arkansas Democrat*, August 25, 1888.

538. *Arkansas Democrat*, September 5, 1888.

539. *Proceedings of the Thirty-first Annual Session...1903*, 36.

540. *Proceedings of the Thirty-first Annual Session...1903*, 35.

541. Clio Harper Diary, August 17, 1902.

542. Clio Harper Diary, June 29, 1912.

543. Interview, Margaret Ross, October 20, 2000. After K.A. Engel's death in 1968, a *Gazette* reporter prepared a story on Engel's association with the *Democrat*, citing Allsopp's *History*, 350, who spoke of the sale being "to the owners of the *Gazette*." Margaret Ross asked Heiskell at one time if he had ever owned the *Democrat*, and he replied absolutely not. On the other hand, the anonymously authored but in-house produced *Arkansas Gazette: a history* (Little Rock, 1980), 11, states that, "Heiskell and Allsopp briefly assumed ownership, but promptly sold the publishing company as soon as a responsible buyer could be found."

544. Allsopp, *History*, 349-351.

545. John A. Thompson, "An Ambition Achieved: J.N. Heiskell Becomes Editor of the Arkansas Gazette," *Arkansas Historical Quarterly*, XLVI (Summer 1987), 156-162.

546. Thompson, "Heiskell,"162-164.

547. Thompson, "Heiskell," 164-165.

548. Thompson, "Heiskell," 165-166.

549. *Arkansas Gazette: a history*, 12.

550. *Arkansas Gazette*, July 1, 1902.

551. Quoted in *Arkansas Gazette: a history*, 10.

552. Allsopp, *Little Adventures*, 122.

553. Allsopp, *Little Adventures*, 189.

554. Allsopp, *Little Adventures*, 88.

555. Allsopp, *Little Adventures*, 88.

556. Allsopp, *Little Adventures*, 88.

557. Allsopp, *Little Adventures*, 91.

558. Clio Harper Diary, December 25, 1895.

559. Allsopp, *Little Adventures*, 206.

560. Allsopp, *Little Adventures*, 18.

561. Clio Harper, January 2, 1895.

562. Allsopp, *Little Adventures*, 206-207.

563. *Arkansas Gazette: a history*, 10.

564. *Proceedings of the Forty-Ninth Annual Convention... 1921*, 37-38. Maryhattianna combined the names of the wives of the town's three partners.

565. Allsopp, *History*, 317.

566. Clio Harper Diary, June 27, July 31, August 30, 1893.

567. Clio Harper Diary, October 29, 1893.

568. Allsopp, *Little Adventures*, 18.

569. Dee Brown, "A Tramp Printer in the Ozarks," *Arkansas Times*, X (February 1984), 62-64, 93-96, and in *When the Century Was Young* (Little Rock, 1993). The author recalls Brown delivering this as a speech to the Arkansas Historical Association.

570. Allsopp, *Little Adventures*, 35.

571. Clio Harper Diary, January 22, 1895.

572. *Proceedings of the Fifty-third Annual Meeting...1923*.

573. Allsopp, *Little Adventures*, 112.

574. Clio Harper Diary, July 18, 1896.

575. Allsopp, *Little Adventures*, 107.

576. Allsopp, *Little Adventures*, 115.

577. Greta Renee Rowbotham, "Political Cartoons in 19th-Century Arkansas Newspapers," (Master's Thesis, University of Arkansas, 1987), 22.

578. Rowbotham, "Cartoons," 60, 82.

579. Rowbotham, "Cartoons," 82; *Arkansas Gazette*, January 19, 1897.

580. Rowbotham, "Cartoons," 73-77.

581. Allsopp, *I Remember*, 89-90.

582. Read, *I Remember*, 103.

583. Read, *I Remember*, 131-133.

584. Read, *I Remember*, 173.

585. Read, *I Remember*, 179-180.

586. Clio Harper Diary, May 28, July 8, 1893.

587. Allsopp, *History*, 314.

588. *Arkansas Gazette*, February 14, 1897.

589. Allsopp, *Little Adventures*, 121-122.

590. Allsopp, *Little Adventures*, 122.

591. Allsopp, *Little Adventures*, 46.

592. Clio Harper Diary, May 19, 1893.

593. Allsopp, *Little Adventures*, 46.

594. Erwin Funk, "Pure Baloney and No Part of My Regular Newspaper Article," Erwin Funk Papers, Special Collections, University of Arkansas.

595. *Proceedings of the Thirty-eighth Annual Meeting...1910*, n.p.

596. Robert D. Craig, *A History of Newark, Arkansas: The*

Story of a Town, the Personality of a People (Newport: Craig Printing Co., 1999), 135.

597. *Proceedings of the Thirty-eighth Annual Meeting...1910*, n.p.

598. *Jonesboro Sun*, January 21, 2001.

599. Erwin Funk, "Pure Baloney and No Part of My Regular Newspaper Article," typescript, Erwin Funk Papers, Special Collections, University of Arkansas.

600. *Proceedings of the Forty-fifth Annual Meeting...1917*, 33-35.

601. *Proceedings of the Forty-eighth Annual Meeting...1920*, 13.

602. Craig, *A History of Newark*, 135.

603. *Proceedings of the Fourteenth Annual Meeting...1886*, 76.

604. Allsopp, *Little Adventures*, 56-57.

605. Allsopp, *Little Adventures*, 57-58.

606. *Proceedings of the Forty-fifth Annual Meeting...1917*, 46.

607. *Proceedings of the Thirty-first Annual Session...1903*, 37.

608. *Proceedings of the Forty-fifth Annual Meeting...1917*, 47.

609. *Proceedings of the Sixtieth Annual Meeting...1932*, 34.

610. Allsopp, *Little Adventures*, 62.

611. Allsopp, *Little Adventures*, 48-49.

612. Souvenir program, 75th Aniversary, 29. ITU Papers, UALR Archives and Special Collections.

613. Souvenir, 75th Anniversary, 27.

614. Souvenir, 75th Anniversary, 63.

615. Souvenir, 75th Anniversary, 51.

616. Allsopp, *Little Adventures*, 45-52.

617. Souvenir, 75th Anniversary, 63.

618. Souvenir, 75th Anniversary, 69.

619. Souvenir, 75th Anniversary, 28.

620. Allsopp, *Little Adventures*, 108.

621. Souvenir, 75th Anniversary, 55.

622. Souvenir, 75th Anniversary, 85.

623. Souvenir, 75th Anniversary, 59.

624. Souvenir, 75th Anniversary, 77.

625. Souvenir, 75th Anniversary, 75.

626. Allsopp, *History*, 199, 622.

627. Allsopp, *History*, 393, identifies the founder as Colonel J.H. Purkins, but in light of Purkin's nicknames, that may be a misprint.

628. *Proceedings of the Fourteenth Annual Meeting...1886*, 56.

629. *Proceedings of the 27th Annual Session...1899*, 23.

630. *Proceedings of the Thirty-seventh Annual Meeting...1909*, 24.

631. *American Newspaper Directory*, 1874, 20.

632. Allsopp, *Little Adventures*, 39.

633. Allsopp, *Little Adventures*, 33.

634. Allsopp, *Little Adventures*, 74-75.

635. Clio Harper Diary, March 10, April 6, 1895.

636. Allsopp, *Little Adventures*, 73-74.

637. Brown, *Century*, 71.

638. For a comprehensive history, see Amelia Martin, "Fort Smith Press," *Fort Smith Historical Society Journal*, XIII (September 1989), 14-25.

639. Allsopp, *History*, 643-644.

640. *Proceedings of the Fifty-ninth Annual Convention...Fort Smith, 1931*, 37.

641. Fort Smith *Evening Call*, January 22, 1891.

642. Allsopp, *History*, 428.

643. Fort Smith *Daily News Record*, May 21, 1897.

644. Fort Smith *Daily News Record*, January 12, 1898.

645. Allsopp, *History*, 430-431.

646. Jack Moseley, "Col. M.E. Decker," *Fort Smith Historical Society Journal*, XIII (September 1989), 26.

647. Allsopp, *History*, 210-213.

648. Clio Harper Diary, July 9, 1899.

649. Allsopp, *History*, 210, 346.

650. Read Fletcher, "History of the Press of Pine Bluff," *Jefferson County Historical Quarterly*, VIII (Number 2, 1979), 39-40 [from *Pine Bluff Press*, October 16, 1876].

651. *Pine Bluff Weekly Graphic*, June 25, 1887.

652. *Pine Bluff Daily Graphic*, March 11, 1942.

653. "Western Clarion, Publisher, W.S. Burnett," *Phillips County Historical Quarterly*, X (March 1972), 1-7.

654. Allsopp, *History*, 286-288.

655. Allsopp, *History*, 160-161.

656. Allsopp, *History*, 162.

657. Allsopp, *History*, 163.

658. Quoted in *Hot Springs Citizens Bulletin*, August 4, 1906.

659. Allsopp, *History*, 166.

660. *Hot Springs Citizens Daily Bulletin*, August 16, 1907; July 5, 1908; December 19, 1908; June 2, 1911.

661. *Arkansas Weekly Mansion*, March 19, 1881.

662. *Arkansas Weekly Mansion*, June 23, 1883.

663. *Arkansas Weekly Mansion*, December 15, 1883.

664. *Arkansas Weekly Mansion*, November 10, 1883.

665. Michael B. Dougan, *Arkansas Odyssey: The Saga of*

Arkansas from Prehistoric Times to Present (Little Rock, 1994), 318.

666. *Arkansas Weekly Mansion*, August 11, 1883.

667. *Arkansas Gazette*, May 12, 1893; June 15, 1894.

668. Amanda Saar, *Black Arkansas Newspaper, 1869-1975: A Checklist* (Fayetteville, 1976).

669. Allsopp, *History*, 363.

670. *Arkansas Gazette*, December 29, 1891; May 25, 26, 1892.

671. *Arkansas Gazette*, November 15, 6, 8, 1892.

672. *Arkansas Gazette*, January 19, 1894.

673. *Arkansas Echo*, January 15, 1930.

674. Sr. Herbert Huber, O.S.B., *Arkansas Echo, 1892-1906: An Arkansas German Language Newspaper* (Little Rock, 1989), 1.

675. Fr. Eugene Weibel, Sr. Agnes Voth, O.S.B., trans., *The Catholic Missions of North-east Arkansas* (State College, 1967).

676. Huber, *Arkansas Echo*, 12.

677. Huber, *Arkansas Echo*, 3.

678. Huber, *Arkansas Echo*, 4, 11, 13.

679. Huber, *Arkansas Echo*, n.p.

680. Searcy *Southern Economist*, August 3, 1893.

681. Allsopp, *History*, 614. Allsopp twice gives the date of founding as 1901, but the newspaper itself on July 12, 1935, spoke of "37 Years of Continuous Service to Arkansas."

682. Allsopp, *History*, 387.

683. Allsopp, *History*, 556-557.

684. Allsopp, *History*, 383-384.

685. Allsopp, *History*, 168-169.

686. Allsopp, *History*, 504-505.

687. *Belle Grove School Journal*, March 1872.

688. Allsopp, *History*, 374.

689. *American Newspaper Directory* (1874), 20.

690. Allsopp, *History*, 389.

691. *The Herald* [of Arkansas State University], October 19, 1996.

692. *The Arkansas Optic*, October 10, 1922, is volume XLII, No. 1; Allsopp, *History*, 374, whose book carried a May 1, 1922, dedication, pronounced erroneously that the publication had suspended. The 1922 issue was a four-column, four-page collection of stories and news. For F.B. Yates, see *Proceedings of the 22nd Annual Meeting...1894*, 22.

693. Allsopp, *History*, 639-640.

694. *Rural and Workman*, November 29, 1884.

695. Fort Smith, *Arkansas Developer*, April 13, 1895.

696. Allsopp, *History*, 301.

697. *Proceedings of the Fifty-ninth Annual Convention...1931*, 36.

698. *Arkansas Publisher*, XXIV (December 1954), 4.

699. *Conway News*, September 12, 1924; May 1, 1925.

700. *Conway News*, February 17, 1922; January 4, 1924.

701. *Conway News*, January 13, 1922.

702. *Conway News*, April 14, 1922.

703. *Conway News*, April 6, 1922.

704. Jim Lester, Jr., *Hendrix College: A Centennial History* (Conway, 1984), 112.

705. Charles C. Alexander, "White-Robed Reformers: The Ku Klux Klan Comes to Arkansas, 1921-1922," *Arkansas Historical Quarterly*, XXII (Spring 1963), 21.

706. Alexander, "White Robes in Politics: The Ku Klux Klan in Arkansas, 1922-1924, " *Arkansas Historical Quarterly*, XXII (Autumn 1963), 206.

707. Margaret Ross, "Retaliation," 150-161.

708. *Batesville Record*, September 20, 1923.

709. Craig, *A History of Newark*, 78.

710. *Forrest City Times and Herald*, August 29, 1922.

711. Marshall *Mountain Wave*, July 13, 1923. [all the following *Mountain Wave* citations courtesy of James J. Johnston].

712. *Mountain Wave*, November 2, 1923.

713. *Mountain Wave*, January 18, 1924.

714. *Mountain Wave*, March 28, 1924.

715. *Mountain Wave*, June 13, 1924.

716. Alexander, "White Robes," 207.

717. Alexander, "White-Robed Reformers," 20.

718. *Batesville Record*, July 20, 1922.

719. Craig, *A History of Newark*, 79.

720. *Forrest City Times and Herald*, September 11, 1924.

721. Alexander, "Defeat, Decline, Disintegration: The Ku Klux Klan in Arkansas, 1924 and After," A.H.Q., XXII (Winter 1963), 319. The remnants of this Klan formally disbanded in 1944.

722. Allsopp, *History*. It is essential for the careful student of journalism history not to take Allsopp's history as necessarily accurate. For instance, Jesse Lewis Russell, the sometime publisher of the *Green Forest Tribune*, found it necessary to write a corrective account of Carroll County's newspaper history. Jesse Lewis Russell, *Behind These Ozark Hills: History, Reminiscences, and Traditions Featuring the Author's Family* (New York, 1947), 157–64.

723. Clippings, June 1921, Funk Papers, Special Collections, University of Arkansas. Funk's clippings were arranged in chronological order but only occasionally

identified as to source.

724. Clippings, 1923, Funk Papers. University of Arkansas.

725. Clippings, April 1923, Funk Papers, University of Arkansas.

726. Clipping, *Arkansas Methodist*, June 14, 1923, Funk Papers, University of Arkansas.

727. Clippings, 1925, Funk Papers, University of Arkansas.

728. Clipping, 1925, Funk Papers, University of Arkansas.

729. Clipping, 1925, Funk Papers, University of Arkansas.

730. Erwin C. Funk, *64 Years of Newspapering in Arkansas* (1960), 39, 71.

731. Clippings, 1926, Funk Papers, University of Arkansas

732. Clipping, n.d. [1929?], Funk Papers, University of Arkansas.

733. *Arkansas Gazette*, December 3, 1932; Alexander, "White Robes," 200.

734. Clio Harper, *History* (Little Rock, 1930), 3.

735. *Arkansas Publisher*, I (January 1928), 2.

736. It would be hard to find, except elsewhere in newspaperdom, anything as sloppy as the institutional record keeping connected with the *Publisher*. Harper intended a volume to be 12 issues within a year's time, a goal he regularly missed. Volume I started in September 1927, but it was February 1928 before the second volume began. During the Depression, the *Publisher* was reduced to six issues a year. After Harper's death things became really deranged. What was styled as Volume 10, for the year 1940 [*sic*] contained 29 monthly issues. During the late Depression years, from 1938 to 1943, the size shrunk, only to return in 1944. That year, for some reason, the *Publisher* announced that it had been established in 1930, a statement it carried thereafter for many years. An even worse development came in 1957 when the volume and issue number were dropped entirely, thus making it impossible to be certain if all published issues were saved for binding. The *Arkansas Publisher* has to this date never been microfilmed, and missing issues abound in the early years. Some copies even bear water damage.

737. *Arkansas Publisher*, I (May 1928), n.p.

738. *Arkansas Publisher*, III (August 1931), 1.

739. The *Arkansas Union List of Newspapers* (AULN) has no entries for the *Flower*. Two issues, both for the Centennial year, exist for the *Hope City Times*, and there is one extant issue of the *Blackburn's Free South*.

740. *Arkansas Publisher*, II, (May 1929), 8–9.

741. *Arkansas Publisher*, II, (October 1929), 5.

742. *Arkansas Publisher*, II, (December 1930), 5.

743. *Arkansas Publisher*, II (May 1929), 15.

744. *Arkansas Publisher*, II (October 1929), 3

745. *Arkansas Publisher*, II (October 1929), 3.

746. *Arkansas Publisher*, II (June-July 1929), 3.

747. *Arkansas Publisher*, I (October 1928), 11.

748. *Arkansas Publisher*, I (October 1928), 11.

749. *Arkansas Publisher*, II (June-July 1929), 14.

750. *Arkansas Publisher*, XI (June 1941), 3.

751. *Arkansas Publisher*, II (June-July 1929), 14.

752. Robert G. Winn, *The Story of Winslow's Maud Duncan* (Fayetteville, 1992), 64. Carroll McGaughey interviewed Duncan for the *Arkansas Gazette*, March 3, 1952.

753. See Winn, *The Story of Winslow's Maud Duncan.* Interview with Bill Penix, June 18, 1999.

754. Dorothy D. Stuck and Nan Snow, *Roberta: A Most Remarkable Fulbright* (Fayetteville, 1997), 65–67.

755. *Arkansas Publisher*, II (December 1929), 5.

756. *Proceedings of the 57th Annual Meeting...1929*, 19-20. The author was unable to locate any copies of the tabloid.

757. *Proceedings of the Fifty-Sixth Annual Meeting...1928*, 20.

758. *Proceedings of the Fifty-Fifth Annual Meeting...1927*, 18.

759. *Proceedings of the Fifty-Fifth Annual Meeting...1927*, 19.

760. *Proceedings of the Fifty-Sixth Annual Meeting....1928*, 22.

761. *Arkansas Publisher*, II (December 1929), 2.

762. *Arkansas Publisher*, (December 1971), 5.

763. Meriwether, *Chronicle*, contains 19 references to Palmer.

764. *Arkansas Publisher*, II (February 1930), 7.

765. Ray Reid, "Romances of American Journalism," *Editor & Publisher and the Fourth Estate*, December 1, 1928, in *Arkansas Publisher*, II (February 1929), 6. Mooney was responsible for the *Commercial Appeal*'s motto, "The safety of the public lies in respect for law, an honest judiciary and an honest ballot."

766. *Arkansas Publisher*, III (April 1931), 5.

767. *Arkansas Publisher*, I (January 1928), 13.

768. *Arkansas Publisher*, I (September 1928), 13.

769. Neither Allsopp nor Meriwether report a newspaper by that name. Allsopp does mention a *Midland Post* in 1909.

Allsopp, *History*, 441.

770. *Arkansas Publisher*, I (May 1928), n.p.

771. Erwin Funk, *64 Years of Newspapering in Arkansas, 1896–1960* (Fayetteville, 1960), 38.

772. Clipping, *Public Utility News*, 1922, Funk Papers, University of Arkansas.

773. Brown, *Century*, 80.

774. *Arkansas Publisher*, I (January 1928), 6.

775. *Proceedings of the Fifty-First Annual Convention... 1923*, 43.

776. *Arkansas Publisher*, II (February 1929), 14.

777. *Arkansas Publisher*, VI (December 1934), 9.

778. *Arkansas Publisher*, I (January 1928), 4.

779. *Arkansas Publisher*, I (May 1928), n.p.

780. *Arkansas Publisher*, II (April 1929), 9

781. *Arkansas Publisher*, IV (December 1931), 5.

782. *Arkansas Publisher*, III (December 1930), 5.

783. *Arkansas Publisher*, II (December 1929), 3.

784. *Arkansas Publisher*, III (April 1931), 4.

785. *Arkansas Publisher*, I (September 1928), 15; II (April 1929), 9.

786. *Arkansas Publisher*, II (February 1929), 7.

787. *Arkansas Publisher*, II (April 1929), 5

788. *Arkansas Publisher*, II (April 1929), 4.

789. *Arkansas Publisher*, III (June 1931), 12. Funk's first editorial can be found in Funk, *64 Years*, 81–82.

790. Stuck and Snow, *Roberta*, 70.

791. *Arkansas Publisher*, IV (April 1932), 3.

792. *Arkansas Gazette*, December 3, 1932.

793. *Arkansas Publisher*, III (October-November 1930), 3; IV (June 1932), 3.

794. *Arkansas Publisher*, IV (June 1932), 3.

795. *Arkansas Publisher*, III (December 1930), 8.

796. *Arkansas Publisher*, III (December 1930), 7.

797. *Arkansas Publisher*, V (August 1933), 3.

798. *Marshall Republican*, November 8, 1935.

799. Interview, J. Maurice Tudor and C. Edward Tudor, June 3, 2000.

800. *Arkansas Publisher*, III (December 1930), 3.

801. Interview, Sam Hodges, June 23, 1999.

802. Van Tyson interview, February 15, 2000.

803. Ellis Reynolds, "Depression Hits Home," (September 29, 1999).

804. *Arkansas Publisher*, III (October-November 1930), 1.

805. *Arkansas Publisher*, IV (February 1932), 1.

806. *Arkansas Publisher*, IV (April 1932), 8.

807. *Arkansas Publisher*, IV (February 1932), 9

808. Interview, Hugh Patterson, August 15, 2000.

809. *Arkansas Publisher*, V (February 1933), 4.

810. *Arkansas Echo*, January 15, 1930.

811. *Arkansas Echo*, April 20, 1932. Translation by Dr. William Greenwald, Arkansas State University

812. *Arkansas Publisher*, IV (August 1932), 3.

813. *Arkansas Publisher*, V (February 1933), 5.

814. *Arkansas Publisher*, VI (April 1933), 5.

815. Mergenthaler Linotype Company, New York, to Messrs. Ardis Tyson and Hugh E. Matthew, November 17, 1920; Bill of Sale, February 2, 1929; Mergenthaler Linotype Company, Brooklyn, to Ardis Tyson, February 19, 1945.

816. Ellis Reynolds, "Depression Hits Home."

817. Interview J. Maurice Tudor and C. Edward Tudor, June 3, 2000.

818. *Arkansas Publisher*, V (August 1933), 4.

819. *Arkansas Publisher*, V (June 1933), 4.

820. *Arkansas Publisher*, V (August 1933), 3.

821. *Arkansas Publisher*, V (February 1933), 6; V (April 1933), 8.

822. Interview, Sam Hodges, June 23, 1999.

823. Miscellaneous clippings, 1932, Funk Papers, University of Arkansas.

824. *Proceedings of the Sixtieth Annual Meeting...1932*, 22-31.

825. *Arkansas Publisher*, V (June 1933), 4.

826. *Arkansas Publisher*, III (October 1931), 6.

827. *Arkansas Publisher*, 1975, p. 5

828. *Arkansas Publisher*, V (April 1933), 5.

829. Interview, John Troutt, May 15, 1999.

830. *Arkansas Publisher*, III (June 1931), 4-5.

831. *Arkansas Publisher*, IV (April 1932), 5.i

832. *Arkansas Publisher*, III (June 1931), 6.

833. *Proceedings of the 60th Annual Meeting...1932*, 32.

834. *Arkansas Publisher*, V (February 1933), 8.

835. *Arkansas Publisher*, V (April 1933), 6.

836. *Arkansas Publisher*, V (April 1933), 3.

837. *Arkansas Publisher*, V (June 1933), 2.

838. *Arkansas Publisher*, XI (January 1941), 6.

839. *Arkansas Publisher*, V June 1933), 1, 3.

840. W.J. Lemke, Fayetteville, to Ray Kimball, January 10, 1937. Kimball Papers.

841. W.J. Lemke, Fayetteville, to Ray Kimball, March 5, 1938. Kimball Papers.

842. W.J. Lemke, Fayetteville, to Ray Kimball, January 10, 1937. Kimball Papers.

843. *Arkansas Publisher*, IX (June-July 1937), 1-2.

844. Ray Kimball, De Queen, to Donald Murray, August 7, 1937. Kimball Papers.

845. Ray Kimball, De Queen, to Donald Murray, August 7, 1937. Kimball Papers.

846. Donald Murray, Jonesboro, to Ray Kimball, September 8. 1937. Kimball Papers.

847. Ray Kimball, De Queen, to C. Armitage Harper, July 6, 1937. Kimball Papers.

848. Donald Murray, Jonesboro, to Ray Kimball, September 28, 1937. Kimball Papers.

849. Donald Murray, Jonesboro, to Ray Kimball, September 28, 1937.

850. Ray Kimball, De Queen, to Donald Murray, October 18, 1937.

851. C. Armitage Harper, Little Rock, to Ray Kimball, February 15, 1938. Kimball Papers.

852. Donald Murray, Jonesboro, to Ray Kimball, November 9, 1937. Kimball Papers.

853. Donald Murray, Jonesboro, to Ray Kimball, December 16, 1937. Kimball Papers.

854. Ray Kimball, De Queen, to Donald Murray, December 22, 1937; Donald Murray, Jonesboro, to Ray Kimball, December 16, 1937.Kimball Papers.

855. Donald Murray, Jonesboro, to Ray Kimball, December 4, 1937. Kimball Papers.

856. Ray Kimball, De Queen, to Donald Murray, December 14, 1937. Kimball Papers.

857. Ray Kimball, De Queen, to Donald Murray, December 22, 1937. Kimball Papers.

858. Ray Kimball, De Queen, to Donald Murray, January 8, 1938. Kimball Papers

859. A.M. Harding, Fayetteville, to Ray Kimball, March 26, 1938. Kimball Papers.

860. Ray Kimball, De Queen, to Dr. A.M. Harding, August 22, 1938.

861. Donald Murray, Jonesboro, to Marion Wasson, April 23, 1938. Kimball Papers.

862. Ray Kimball, De Queen, to Dr. A.M. Harding, August 22, 1938. Kimball Papers. *Arkansas Publisher*, X (August 1938), 8.

863. Ray Kimball, De Queen, to Dr. A.M. Harding, August 22, 1938. Kimball Papers.

864. Donald Murray, Jonesboro, to Ray Kimball, March 26, 1938. Kimball Papers.

865. Ray Kimball, De Queen, to David P. Johnson, August 22, 1938. Kimball Papers.

866. *Arkansas Publisher*, XIII (September 1943), 4.

867. *Arkansas Publisher*, X (October 1938), 11.

868. W.J. Lemke, "This-'n-That," undated (1936) clipping, Lemke Papers, University of Arkansas.

869. Charlotte Tillar, "Skirts...In the Front Office," *Arkansas Publisher*, XV (August 1945), 5.

870. *Arkansas Publisher*, IV (April 1932), 3.

871. *Log Cabin Democrat*, September 16, 1926.

872. *Log Cabin Democrat*, October 28, 1926.

873. *Log Cabin Democrat*, October 28, 1926.

874. *Log Cabin Democrat*, December 30, 1926.

875. *Paragould Soliphone*, May 28, 1926.

876. Interview, Melvin and Charlotte Schnexnayder, March 7, 2000.

877. *Log Cabin Democrat*, October 7, 1937.

878. *Log Cabin Democrat*, August 12, 1926.

879. *Log Cabin Democrat*, August 12, 1926; September 30, 1926.

880. *Log Cabin Democrat*, October 28, 1926.

881. Fletcher Chenault, "Log Cabin Democrat Rural Correspondent..." reprinted in *Log Cabin Democrat*, March 17, 1926.

882. *Log Cabin Democrat*, July 28, 1938.

883. *Log Cabin Democrat*, August 18, 1938.

884. *Log Cabin Democrat*, October 28, 1926.

885. *Log Cabin Democrat*, September 16, 1926.

886. *Log Cabin Democrat*, September 30, 1937.

887. *Log Cabin Democrat*, November 4, 1926.

888. *Log Cabin Democrat*, November 4, 1926.

889. *Log Cabin Democrat*, October 28, 1926.

890. *Log Cabin Democrat*, November 4, 1926.

891. *Log Cabin Democrat*, November 4, 1926.

892. *Log Cabin Democrat*, March 24, 1927.

893. *Log Cabin Democrat*, August 25, 1938.

894. *Log Cabin Democrat*, November 12, 1936.

895. *Log Cabin Democrat*, November 19, 1936.

896. *Log Cabin Democrat*, August 25, 1938.

897. *Dover Times*, May 27, 1926.

898. *Marshall Republican*, April 5, 1935.

899. *Marshall Republican*, October 12, 1934.

900. *Dover Times*, May 27, 1926.

901. *Log Cabin Democrat*, December 3, 1936.

902. Quoted in *Arkansas Publisher*, XV (August 1945), 5.

903. *Log Cabin Democrat*, November 12, 1936.

904. Frank E. Robins, "County Correspondence Necessary for Weeklies," *Arkansas Publisher*, IX (March 1938), 4.

905. *Log Cabin Democrat*, November 25, 1926.

906. *Log Cabin Democrat*, December 2, 1926.
907. *Log Cabin Democrat*, September 1, 1938.
908. *Arkansas Publisher*, IX (November 1938), 4.
909. *Arkansas Publisher*, II (May 1930), 6.
910. Siloam Springs *Herald and Democrat*, February 16, 1939.
911. Quoted in *Arkansas Community Newspaper*, April 1944.
912. Tillar, "Skirts," *Arkansas Publisher*, XV (August 1945), 5.
913. *Arkansas Publisher*, X (July 1940), 1-3.
914. Margaret Woolfolk interview, May 2000.
915. Quoted in Dougan, *Arkansas Odyssey*, 571.
916. *Greenwood Democrat* website, http://www.greenwooddemocrat.com/history.htm.
917. *Arkansas Publisher*, IX (March 1938), 2.
918. Van Tyson, Atkins, to author, June 21, 2000 [e-mail].
919. Little Rock, *Youth's Banner*, July 5, 1852.
920. Robert A. Leflar, *The First 100 Years: Centennial History of the University of Arkansas* (Fayetteville, 1972), 349-357.
921. *Fayetteville Democrat*, January 2, 1935.
922. *Fayetteville Leader*, November 14, 1930.
923. *Fayetteville Democrat*, May 16, 1935,contains an interview with Amanda Stone, who owned her sister's diploma from the Fayetteville Female Seminary drawn by Cush.
924. *Arkansas Publisher*, II (May 1929), 7.
925. W.J. Lemke, Fayetteville, to Ray Kimball, January 10, 1937. Kimball Papers.
926. *Arkansas Publisher*, XI (January 1941), 2.
927. *Arkansas Publisher*, II (May 1930), 9.
928. *Arkansas Community News*, February 1944.
929. Leflar, *The First 100 Years*, 219-220.
930. W.J. Lemke, Fayetteville, to Ray Kimball, January 11, 1938, Kimball Papers.
931. Interview, Bill Penix, June 2000.
932. *Arkansas Community News*, February 1944.
933. *Arkansas Publisher*, V (August 1933), 5.
934. *Marshall Republican*, April 27, 1934.
935. *Arkansas Publisher*, IX (March 1938), 2.
936. Craig, *History of Newark*, 137.
937. *Arkansas Publisher*, X (April 1940), 1.
938. Clarksville *Herald-Democrat*, May 17, 1938.
939. *Arkansas Publisher*, September 1970, 7;
940. *Arkansas Publisher*, V (June 1933), 3.
941. *Arkansas Publisher*, X (October 1940), 4.
942. *Arkansas Publisher*, X (July 1940), 6.
943. *Arkansas Publisher*, X (January 1939), 1; X (September 1940), 1.
944. *Arkansas Publisher*, XII (October 1942), 3.
945. *Log Cabin Democrat*, September 30, 1926.
946. Nettleton went bankrupt and was absorbed by Jonesboro in 1958. The school district, however, is still intact.
947. *Jonesboro Evening Sun*, July 25, 1939.
948. *Jonesboro Daily Tribune*, July 27, 1939.
949. *Jonesboro Evening Sun*, July 27, 1939.
950. *Marshall Republican*, September 5, 1941.
951. *Arkansas Publisher*, X (September 1940, 1; January 1939, 1).
952. *Arkansas Publisher*, X (December 1940), 1.
953. Quoted in Thomas Rothrock, "Dr. Alexander Copeland Millar," *Arkansas Historical Quarterly*, XXII (Autumn 1963), 222.
954. *Arkansas Publisher*, XIV (May 1944), 15.
955. *Arkansas Publisher*, XI (August 1941), 1.
956. Craig, *History of Newark*, 136.
957. *Batesville News-Review*, September 23, 1948.
958. Margaret Ross, Little Rock, to author, October 15, 2000.
959. *Arkansas Publisher*, X (November 1939), 2;
960. *Arkansas Publisher*, X (July 1940), 7.
961. *Arkansas Publisher*, X (November 1938), 5.
962. *Arkansas Publisher*, X I (April 1941), 2.
963. *Arkansas Publisher*, XI (September 1941), 3.
964. *Arkansas Publisher*, XI (September 1941), 7.
965. *Arkansas Publisher*, XI (October 1941), 14.
966. *Arkansas Publisher*, X (December 1940), 7.
967. *Arkansas Publisher*, XII (February 1942), 7.
968. *Arkansas Publisher*, XI (October 1941), 15.
969. *Arkansas Publisher*, XII (September 1942), 6; XII (November 1942). 1.
970. *Arkansas Publisher*, XIII(August 1944), 4.
971. *Arkansas Publisher*, XI (June 1941), 6.
972. *Arkansas Publisher*, X (December 1940), 11.
973. *Arkansas Publisher*, XII (July 1942), 8.
974. *Arkansas Publisher*, XI (June 1941), 2.
975. *Arkansas Publisher*, XII (February 1942), 1.
976. Unfortunately, the APA board records have not survived for this or most of the other years.
977. *Arkansas Publisher*, X (December 1940), 12.
978. *Ashley County Leader*, June 27, 1940, quoted in David M. Moyers, "Trouble in a Company Town: the Crossett Strike of 1940," *Arkansas Historical Quarterly*, XLVIII (Spring

1989), 39.

979. *Arkansas Publisher*, XV (February 1945, 2.

980. *Arkansas Publisher*, XV (February 1945), 3.

981. C. Calvin Smith, *War and Wartime Changes: The Transformation of Arkansas, 1940-1945* (Fayetteville, 1986), 20-25.

982. Quoted in Smith, *War*, 128.

983. Smith, *War*, 128-129.

984. Smith, *War*, 83-84.

985. Smith, *War*, 60.

986. *Mammoth Spring Democrat*, January 15, 1943; March 26, 1943, Rhonda Simpson, "The Mammoth Spring Democrat, 1943-1945 (Unpublished paper, Arkansas State University), 10-11.

987. *Mammoth Spring Democrat*, February 12, 1943. Simpson, "The Mammoth Spring Democrat,"8-9.

988. *Mammoth Sping Democrat*, January 1, 1943, Simpson, "The Mammoth Spring Democrat," 9-10.

989. *Mammoth Spring Democrat*, April 10, 1942, Lindy Greene, "The Democrat's Coverage of World War II, 1940-1942," (Unpublished paper, Arkansas State University), 3.

990. Walter C. Johnson and Arthur T. Robb, *The South and Its Newspapers*, 1903-1953 (Westport, Conn., 1974), 208-231.

991. *Arkansas Publisher*, XII (December 1942), 1.

992. *Arkansas Publisher*, XII (September 1942), 6.

993. *Arkansas Publisher*, XIV (July 1944), 13.

994. *Arkansas Publisher*, XV (November 1945), 5.

995. Quoted in Smith, *War*, 33. Readers who remember the story of Mrs. Mutt Alexander of Nettleton who was arrested for wearing shorts should be apprised that a few years earlier a female was fined $50 for wearing slacks in town.

996. *Arkansas Publisher*, XV(January 1945), 5.

997. Interview, Melvin and Charlotte Schexnayder, March 7, 2000.

998. E.J. Friedlander, "Freedom of the Press Behind Barbed Wire: Paul Yokota and the Jerome Relocation Center Newspaper," *Arkansas Historical Quarterly*, XLIV (Winter 1985), 303-313.

999. Edward J. Friedlander, "Journalism Behind Barbed Wire: Two Arkansas Relocation Center Newspapers," (Unpublished Paper, 1999,courtesy of the author).

1000. *Arkansas Publisher*, XIV (July 1944), 15.

1001. *Arkansas Publisher*, XII (August 1942), 3.

1002. *Arkansas Publisher*, XV (March 1945), 10.

1003. *Arkansas Publisher*, XIV(March 1944), 1

1004. *Arkansas Publisher*, XIV (July 1944), 6.

1005. *Arkansas Publisher*, XIV (April 1944), 1.

1006. *Arkansas Publisher*, XII (September 1942), 1.

1007. McGehee *Times*, March 15, 1945.

1008. *Osceola Times*, May 15, 1942.

1009. *Marked Tree Tribune*, January 7, 11, 14, 1943. Tess A. Pruett, "The History, Journalistic Style and Community Service of the Tri-City Tribune During the War Years" (Unpublished paper, Arkansas State University, 1999), 2-3.

1010. *Mammoth Spring Democrat*, July 21, 1944, Simpson, "Mammoth Spring Democrat," 11-12.

1011. *Mammoth Spring Democrat*, July 21, 1944, Simpson, "Mammoth Spring Democrat, 12.

1012. Pruett, "History," 3.

1013. *Arkansas Publisher*, September 1950, 8.

1014. *Arkansas Publisher*, XIV (December 1944), 12.

1015. *Arkansas Publisher*, XIV (July 1944), 3.

1016. *Arkansas Publisher*, XVI (February 1946), 8.

1017. *Arkansas Publisher*, XVII (September 1947), 3. The standard biography is Roy Reed, *Faubus: The Life and Times of an American Prodigal* (Fayetteville, 1997). Faubus's wartime experiences are contained in *In This Faraway Land* (Conway, 1971).

1018. *Arkansas Publisher*, XVI (March 1946), 8.

1019. *Arkansas Publisher*, XVI (March 1946), 4.

1020. *Arkansas Publisher*, XVII (August 1947), 2.

1021. *Arkansas Publisher*, XVII (February 1947), 6.

1022. *Arkansas Publisher*, XVII (June 1947), 5.

1023. Ray Poindexter, *Arkansas Airwaves* (North Little Rock, 1974), 5-6, 299, 307, 318, 322, 337, 346, 349, 351.

1024. *Arkansas Publisher*, XVI(September 1946), 3, 9.

1025. *Arkansas Publisher*, XV(May 1945), 10.

1026. *Arkansas Publisher*, XVII (April 1947), 4.

1027. *Arkansas Publisher*, XVII (February 1947), 12.

1028. Barton's obituary is in the *Arkansas Gazette*, December 25, 1960. J.E. Dunlap told of Barton setting up his show outside of Harrison. Despite Boone County being legally dry, few businesses reopened that afternoon. Interview, J.E. Dunlap, June 2, 2000.

1029. *Arkansas Publisher*, XVIII (April 1948), 6-7.

1030. *Arkansas Publisher*, XIX (May 1949), 2.

1031. *Arkansas Publisher*, XXIV(January 1954), 5.

1032. *Arkansas Publisher*, XVII (November 1947), 7, 9. The author is unaware of any family connection.

1033. *Arkansas Publisher*, (January 1954), 5.

1034. *Arkansas Publisher*, October 1953, 3.

1035. Quoted in Jim Lester, *A Man for Arkansas: Sid McMath and the Southern Reform Tradition* (Little Rock, 1976),

25.

1036. *Osceola Times*, June 1, 1949. Interview, George Fisher, June 18, 2000; Interview, Paul Coughlin, July 1, 2000.

1037. *Osceola Times*, September 30, 1949.

1038. *Arkansas Publisher*, XIX(October 1949), 9.

1039. *Arkansas Publisher*, XIII (October 1943), 4.

1040. Quoted in Lester, *McMath*, 131-132.

1041. *Arkansas Publisher*, XIX (September 1949), 1.

1042. *Arkansas Publisher*, XVI (May 1946), 10.

1043. *Arkansas Publisher*, XX (April 1950), 2.

1044. Mott, *American Journalism*, 811.

1045. *Arkansas Publisher*, XXII (July 1952), 8.

1046. *Arkansas Publisher*, XX (July 1950), 2.

1047. Interview, Paul Coughlin, July 1, 2000.

1048. Interview, Tom Dearmore, September 17, 1999. Dearmore recalled helping Orval, wet with ink, get his newspaper out on one occasion.

1049. Reed, *Faubus*, 124.

1050. *Arkansas Publisher* (February 1947), 6.

1051. *Arkansas Publisher* (November 1946), 1, 3.

1052. Stuck and Snow, *Roberta*, 218.

1053. *Arkansas Publisher* (December 1946), 1, 3.

1054. *Arkansas Publisher* (March 1947), 5.

1055. Stuck and Snow, *Roberta*, 215-219.

1056. *Arkansas Publisher*, April 1960, 3.

1057. Kitty Sloan, ed., *Horizons: 100 Arkansas Women of Achievement* (Little Rock, 1980).

1058. *Arkansas Publisher*, (August 1954), 8.

1059. Interview, Kitty Sloan, July 13, 2000.

1060. Steven D. Ewart, "Arkansas Newspaper Editorial Opinion on School Integration: May 1854-October 1957," (M.A. thesis, Arkansas State University, 1971), 8.

1061. Ewart, "Editorial Opinion," 2-3.

1062. Ewart, "Editorial Opinion," 5.

1063. Ewart, "Editorial Opinion," 25.

1064. Ewart, "Editorial Opinion," 41-44.

1065. Ewart, "Editorial Opinion," 46.

1066. Ewart, "Editorial Opinion," 47.

1067. *Arkansas Publisher*, XXIV (June 1954), 3.

1068. *Arkansas Publisher*, XXIV (July 1954), 2.

1069. Ewart, "Editorial Opinion," 50-51.

1070. Ewart, "Editorial Opinion," 54-55.

1071. Ewart, "Editorial Opinion," 54.

1072. Ewart, "Editorial Opinion," 55=56.

1073. Reed, *Faubus*, 204-205.

1074. Ewart, "Editorial Opinion," 66.

1075. Ewart, "Editorial Opinion," 70.

1076. Ewart, "Editorial Opinion," 71.

1077. Jan Cottingham, "Southerner, Jew, Writer, Thinker," *Arkansas Times*, February 5, 1999, 18.

1078. Margaret Ross, Little Rock, to author, October 15, 2000.

1079. Elizabeth Burrow, Ozark, to Erwin Funk, July 25, 1958. Funk Papers, University of Arkansas

1080. Quoted in Reed, *Faubus*, 215.

1081. Interview, Tom Dearmore, September 17, 1999.

1082. *Arkansas Publisher*, (May 1946), 11.

1083. *Arkansas State Press*, September 30, 1956; September 6, 13, 1957.

1084. *Arkansas State Press*, September 20, 1957.

1085. Ernie Deane oral history tapes, Special Collections, University of Arkansas.

1086. Quoted in Reed, *Faubus*, 274.

1087. Quoted in Reed, *Faubus*, 322.

1088. Reed, *Faubus*, 268.

1089. *Arkansas Publisher*, [no volume no.]November 1957, 6.

1090. *Arkansas Publisher*, May 1958, 4.

1091. *Arkansas Publisher*, June 1959, 5.

1092. *Arkansas Publisher*, April 1960, 3; *Roberts v. Love*, 231 Ark. 886, 333 S.W.2d 897 (1960).

1093. Erwin Funk Diary, University of Arkansas.

1094. Interview, Dorothy Stuck, July 22, 2000.

1095. *Marked Tree Tribune*, April 1, 1965.

1096. Interview, Dorothy Stuck, July 22, 2000.

1097. Roy Reed, "How to Lynch a Newspaper," *Atlantic Monthly*, CCXIV (November 1964), 59-63.

1098. *Wirges v. Brewer*, 239 Ark. 317 (1965).

1099. Gene Wirges, *Conflict of Interests: The Gene Wirges Story* (North Little Rock, 1992).

1100. Marlin Hawkins, with C. Fred Williams, *How I Stole Elections: The Autobiography of Sheriff Marlin Hawkins* (N.P., 1991).

1101. Gary Delsohn, "Joseph H. Weston and His Underground Newspaper for Hillbillies," *The Quill* (January 1978), 21-23. *New York Times v. Sullivan*, 376 U.S. 254, 84 S.Ct. 710, 11 L.Ed., 2d 686 (1964) was the landmark freedom of the press case that arose from the Montgomery, Alabama, bus boycott; *Garrison v. Louisiana*, 379 U.S. 64, 85 S.Ct. 1323, 20 L.Ed., 2d 262 (1968) set a standard requiring a "high degree of awareness of probable falsity."

1102. *Arkansas Publisher* (January 1965), 8.

1103. *Arkansas Publisher* (January 1973), 10.

1104. *Arkansas Publisher* (February 1964), 11.

1105. *Arkansas Publisher* (August 1967), 3.

1106. *Arkansas Publisher* (April 1968), 4.

1107. *Arkansas Publisher* (June). 2. [Misnamed July on cover].

1108. *Arkansas Publisher*, (November 1974), 5.

1109. *Grapevine*, May 21, 1986.

1110. *Jonesboro: Were the Media Fair?* (New York, 1998).

1111. *Arkansas Publisher*, LXI (Spring 1997), 9.

1112. *Arkansas Publisher* (May 1969), 8; "The American Media Baronies, a modest Atlantic Atlas," *Atlantic Monthly*, CCXXIV (July 1969), 83-94.

1113. *Arkansas Democrat-Gazette*, May 9, 1992.

1114. *Arkansas Publisher* (January 1975), 10.

1115. *Hazelwood School District v. Kuhlmeier*, 484 U.S. 260 (1988).

1116. *Arkansas Publisher* (December 1973), 6.

1117. Interview, Derwood Brett, February 18, 2000

1118. *Arkansas Publisher*, LXVI (Winter 1992-93), 7.

1119. *Laman v.* McCord, 245 Ark.(1968).

1120. *Arkansas Publisher*, LXX (Winter 1996-97), 13.

1121. John J. Watkins, *The Arkansas Freedom of Information Act*, 3d edition (Fayetteville, 1998).

1122. *Arkansas Publisher* (May 1975), 11. *Gannett Co. v. DePasquale*, 443 U.S. 368 (1979).

1123. *Arkansas Publisher* (September 1976), 8.

1124. *Jonesboro Sun*, October 15, 1999. These are a few highlights from David Robinson's FOI Arkansas Project.

1125. *Arkansas Publisher* (December 1979), 17.

1126. *The Arkansas Freedom of Information Act: A Handbook*. July 1981, 21.

1127. *Jonesboro Sun*, October 10, 13, 15, 17, 1999.

1128. *Arkansas Publisher*, LXX (Winter 1996-97), 12.

1129. *Arkansas Publisher* (April 1967), 7

1130. *Arkansas Publisher* (July 1977), 3.

1131. *Arkansas Publisher* (September 1965), 10.

1132. *Arkansas Publisher*, (January 1968), 13.

1133. *Arkansas Publisher* (December 1977), 3.

1134. Don Cooper, Hereford, Texas, to author, September 15, 2000.

1135. Interview, Laura Shull, October 8, 1999

1136. Jay W. Jackson, Clinton, to author, November 27, 2000.

1137. *Arkansas Publisher* (Fall 1987), 18.

1138. *Arkansas Publisher*, (February 1972), 9.

1139. *Arkansas Publisher* (December 1976), 5. In yet another version of the circuit's creation, Washburn gave credit to Palmer, Kimball, and himself.

1140. *Arkansas Publisher* (December 1977), 3.

1141. *Arkansas Publisher* (December 1977), 3

1142. *Arkansas Publisher*, (December 1976), 5.

1143. Jack Zibluk, Jonesboro, to author, July 9, 2001.

1144. *Arkansas Publisher*, (March 1966), 4.

1145. *Arkansas Publisher* (July 1967), 8-9.

1146. *Arkansas Publisher* (February 1971), 10.

1147. *Arkansas Publisher* (February 1968), 5.

1148. *Arkansas Publisher* (December 1972), 5.

1149. *Arkansas Publisher*, (December 1971), 9.

1150. *Arkansas Publisher* (Summer 1987), 7.

1151. *Arkansas Publisher*, (November 1977), 9.

1152. *Arkansas Publisher* (December 1977), 3.

1153. *Arkansas Publisher* (Fall 1986), 23.

1154. *Arkansas Advocate*, II (March-April-May 1974), 1-2.

1155. Bob Stover, "*Arkansas Gazette*: Its Liberal, pro-labor editorial policy is facing a crisis of unionism," *Arkansas Times*, February 13, 1975, 16, 30.

1156. *Newton County Times*, April 7, 12, 2001.

1157. Frank Romano, "*The Era of Our Ways*," www.electronic-publishing.com (March 2002), 48.

1158. *Arkansas Publisher* (April 1961), 7.

1159. *Arkansas Publisher* (June 1977), 3-4.

1160. Interview, Dale Bumpers, August 3, 2001.

1161. William Everett Wheeler, *Backwoods Journalist: An Autobiography of a Country Journalist, 1910-2000* (Eureka Springs, 2000), 49.

1162. *Arkansas Democrat-Gazette*, June 22, 2002; Arkansas Times, July 12, 2002.

1163. *Cherokee Villager*, August 17-23, 1995. This anniversary issue contains recollections from previous editors and other historical material.

1164. Interview, Delores Richardson, July 20, 2001.

1165. Joe May to author, April 29, 2001.

1166. Margaret Ross, Little Rock, to author, November 26, 2000.

1167. Bill Terry, "The Democrat vs. The Gazette; Arkansas' Newspaper War," *Arkansas Times*, (May 1979), 30-43.

1168. Meredith Oakley, Little Rock, Butler Center, November 5, 2001.

1169. Walter Hussman, Little Rock, Butler Center, November 5, 2001.

1170. Interview, Hugh Patterson, August 15, 2000.

1171. Max Brantley, Little Rock, Butler Center, November 5, 2001.

1172. Roy Reed, "Working at the *Arkansas Gazette*: An Interview with Ernest Dumas," *Arkansas Historical Quarterly*, LX (Summer 2001), 203.

1173. Reed, "Interview," *Arkansas Historical Quarterly*, LX (Summer 2001), 203.

1174. *Arkansas Publisher*, LXV (Winter 1991-1992), 13. Hussman had moved to Little Rock at the time of the *Democrat*'s purchase.

1175. Frances Hager, Arkansas Tech University, to author, January 16, 2001. [e-mail].

1176. Bob Lancaster, "Bitch-slapping among the columnists," *Arkansas Times* (April 21, 2000), 46.

1177. Gentry *Courier-Journal*, August 1, 8, 2001; Siloam Springs *Herald and Democrat*, November 28, 1985.

1178. Lucinda Fleeson, "The Pulse of Paradise" and "Gannett's Trading Partner," *American Journalism Review*, XXIII (January/February 2001), 44-51.

1179. Interview, Jim Morriss, February 18, 2000.

1180. *Arkansas Gazette*, October 8, 1990.

1181. *Northwest Arkansas Times*, June 30, 2000.

1182. Ernest Dumas, "Newspaper War II, *Arkansas Times*, September 7, 2001.

1183. Anna America, "Northwest Arkansas: Wal-Mart boosts its home-region papers," *Presstime* (October 2001), 24-25.

1184. *Briefing Notebook*, September 10, 2001.

1185. *Arkansas Democrat-Gazette*, March 25, 1996.

1186. Interview, Louise Bowker, November 3, 2000.

1187. *Arkansas Publisher* (December 1979), 22.

1188. *Arkansas Publisher* (December 1979), 5.

1189. *Arkansas Publisher* (Winter 1985), 5.

1190. *Arkansas Publisher* (Summer 1986), 21.

1191. *Arkansas Publisher* (Winter 1988), 5.

1192. *Virginia State Board of Pharmacy v. Virginia Citizens Consumer Council*, 425 U.S. 748, 96 S.Ct. 1817, L.Ed.2d 346 (1976).

1193. *Arkansas Publisher* (Spring 1986), 21-22.

1194. *Arkansas Publisher* (June 1983), 18.

1195. *Arkansas Publisher* (Summer 1986), 19.

1196. *Arkansas Publisher* (Spring 1984), 16.

1197. *Arkansas Publisher* (Summer 1986), 5.

1198. *Arkansas Publisher* (Winter 1988), 5.

1199. *Arkansas Publisher* LXVI(Summer 1992), 5. A very critical look at Wal-Mart is by Bill Quinn, *How Wal-Mart is Destroying America and What You Can Do About It* (Berkeley: Ten Speed Press, 1998); an updated version in 2001 had a line slashed through the word "America" and "the World" written above it. A more dispassionate study is Sandra S. Vance and Ray V. Scott, "Sam Walton and Wal-Marts Stores, Inc.; A Study in Modern Southern Entrepreneurship," *Journal of Southern History*, LVIII (May 1992), 231-252. The highhanded practices of the modern Wal-Mart did not sit well with veteran publishers who remembered how in his early days Sam Walton would place lots of advertisements, but contrive to delay paying for them as long as possible. Interview, Ted Larimer, July 12, 2001.

1200. *Arkansas Gazette*, December 24, 1986.

1201. *Hazelwood School District v. Kuhlmeier*,484 U.S. 260, 108 S.Ct. 562, 98 L.Ed.2d 592 (1988).

1202. Interview, Beth Shull, April 9, 2001.

1203. *Arkansas Publisher* (Winter 1988), 7.

1204. Interview, Jay Jackson, February 17, 2000.

1205. *Arkansas Publisher* (Winter 1988), 8.

1206. *Arkansas Publisher* (August 1975), 7.

1207. Jasper, *Newton County Times*, August 9, 2001.

1208. *Newton County Times*, January 31, 2002.

1209. *Arkansas Times* (July 7, 2000), 15.

1210. Jeanie Day to author, October 10, 2001.

1211. Randy Kemp to author, September 21, 2001.

1212. Interview, D.L. Bailey, September 27, 2001.

1213. *Newton County Times*, September 20, 2001.

1214. *Newton County Times*, September 20, 2001.

1215. *Arkansas Publisher*, LXVII (Winter 1993-94), 23.

Index

Descriptive material found in parentheses after newspaper titles is an identification aid that may include date of origin, location, and/or lineage.

A

acculturation, German, 181–182
Act 10, 299
  opposition, 295
Adams, George H., 177, 178, 209
Adams, J.W., 118, 177
Adams, John D., 137–139, *154*, *157*, 172
Adkins, Homer, 191, 247
Advance (Monticello), 98
Advance-Monticellonian (Monticello), *327*
Advance-Reporter (Waldron), 202, 298
advertising, 15, 84, 93, *112*, *232*, *235*, *237*
  APA and, 227, 253
  circulation and, 210, 212, 223, 321
  color in, 315
  customized, 254
  display, *155*
  foreign language, *157*, 340
  "free," 232
  front page, *357*, 358
  issues and developments, 175, 344
  legal, 211, 220–221
  non-agency, 210
  patent medicine, 106–107
  radio, 344
  rates, 192, 211
  as revenue source, 232, 321, 339
  sales agencies, 207
  special editions as, 95
  spec(ulative), 343
  television, 321
  utilities and, 218, 253
  Wal-Mart, 318, 338, 345–346
  wartime, 258
  woodcuts in, 17, *21*, *47*
"The Age of the Circulation Liar" (vignette), 212
Agee, George O., 98
Agricultural and Mechanical Journal, 81
Agricultural Wheel, 101, 140, 182
agriculture, 58, 85, 103, 273–274, 346
Albert Pike's Letter Addressed to Major General Holmes (Pike), 70
alcoholism and addiction, 32, 52–53, 118
Alcott, Louisa May, *Little Women*, 116
Alexander, Mrs. Leslie, 249–250
Alford, Boyce, 314
Alford, Dale, 298
Allard, C.C., 261
Allard, H.C. "Cad," 86
Allbright, Charles, 334
Allen, Ben, 286
  FOI, 312
Allen, Mrs. Thomas J., 281
Allen, Thomas J., 277, 298
Alley, J.P. (cartoonist), 200, 249
Alliance, 325
Alliance Patriot (Mansfield), 98
Allin, Richard, FOI, 312, 334
Allis, Horace G., 143–144, *159*
Allred, Ertie O., 204
Allsopp, Frederick William, *110*, 143–144, 147–149, 191–192, 253
  business manager, 207
  The Editor Surveying the Town, *156*
  as historian, 94, 104, 118, 119, 151
  History of the Arkansas Press for a Hundred Years and More, 191
  Little Adventures in Newspaperdom, 191–192
  poetry and, 166, 172
"Al's Alfalfa" (Rose), 247
alternative journalism, 308–309
Aluminum Company of America (Alcoa), 340
Ambrose, D.C., 99
"Amen Corner" (Kennedy cartoon), 270
American Civil Liberties Union (Arkansas), 280
American Federation of Labor, 173
American Newspaper Directory, 174. *see also* Ayer's

American Newspaper Guild (CIO), 277, 319
American Newspaper Representatives (ANR), 344
American Profile, 331
American Publishing Company, 325, 336
  Hollinger division, 338
American Society of Newspaper Editors, 271
American Type Foundry Co., 170, 280
Anderson, George T., 346
Anti-Saloon League, 113, 182
Arkansas Advocate, 308, 309
Arkansas Advocate (1830), 24–25, 26–29
Arkansas Agricultural, Mechanical, and Normal College (AM&N), 277
Arkansas Associated Press Broadcasters Association, 272
Arkansas Banner, 35–40. *see also True Democrat*
Arkansas Banner (Searcy, continued from *Arkansas Populist*), 98
Arkansas Baptist, 78, *183*
Arkansas Blade (Fayetteville), 99, 105
Arkansas Broadcasters Association, 272
Arkansas Business, 310, 351
Arkansas Central Leader (1923), 208, 277, 283
Arkansas College Media Association (ACMA), 312, 349
Arkansas College Press Association (1930), 244
Arkansas Community Organizations for Reform Now (ACORN), 308, 309
The Arkansas Community Newspaper (newsletter), 241, 245
Arkansas Conservative, 80
Arkansas County, 197
Arkansas Dailies, 207, 255
Arkansas Democrat (1846). *see Arkansas State Democrat*
Arkansas Democrat (continued from *Evening Star, Daily Arkansas Democrat*), 15, 122, 137, 140, 177, 244
  Building, *284*
  civil rights coverage, 292–293
  James Mitchell and, 145–148
  Jeff Davis and, 142
  populist, 333
  press room, *269*
  revitalizing, 284
  sold to WEHCO Media, 322
  Supreme Court decisions, 295–296
  WEHCO Media, 323
Arkansas Democrat-Gazette, 307, 334, 352
  and CPI, 339
Arkansas Developer (Fort Smith), 185
Arkansas Dispatch, 180
Arkansas Echo (in German), 181–182, 217–218
"An Arkansas Editor in Hollywood" (vignette), 220
Arkansas Educational Association, 252
Arkansas Educational Television Network (AETN), 332, 350
Arkansas Evening Herald (Hope), 174
Arkansas Faith, 293
The Arkansas Freedom of Information Act: A Handbook, 312–313
The Arkansas Freeman, 81, 84, 85
Arkansas Gas Company, as advertiser, 218
Arkansas Gazette (1819), *20*, 20–33, 48. *see also Arkansas State Gazette*; Woodruff, William Edward
  cartoons, *75*
  move to Little Rock, 19, *20*
  in Post, 15–18, *20*
  post-war stationery, *75*
  size and format, 15, 24, 26, 28
Arkansas Gazette (1865, revived), 78–79, 81–82, 87, 101–102, 106, 118, 132, *154*, *174*, 244
  Building,1908, *155*
  business office, *154*, *264*
  civil rights coverage, 292–295
  closing of, 310, 319, 334
  correspondents, 241
  country editions, 99–100
  Harry Ashmore, 271, *290*
  J.N. Heiskell, 148–150, 295
  Jeff Davis and, 142
  modernization, 254
  political neutrality, 210
  Pulitzer Prize, 295
  Quesenbury poetry, 135–136
  radio and, 272
  Smithee and, 143–144
  sold to Gannett chain, 333
  strike, 277–279
  stringers, 122
  unions and, 319
Arkansas Gazette Library, *290*
Arkansas Herald (1819), 14
Arkansas High School Press Association (AHSPA), 206, 244
Arkansas Historical Association, *Quarterly*, 243
Arkansas history
  agrarian movement, 101
  antebellum, 42–62
  Centennial, 242
  Civil War, 63–72
  late 20th century, 304–305
  local, 42

Mexican War, 36–38
Populist movement, 101
and progress, 45
reunification, 72–76
statehood, 27, 29–30
as territory, 13–30
Arkansas Industrial Development Commission (AIDC), 299
Arkansas Intelligencer (Van Buren, 1842-59), 49, 135
Arkansas Journalism Advisors Association (AJAA), 349
Arkansas Ladies Journal (1884), 180
Arkansas Life, 183
Arkansas Livestock Show Association, 253, 273
Arkansas Locomotive (continuation of *Journal*), 91
Arkansas Magazine (1854), 55
Arkansas Mansion, 106
Arkansas Methodist, 106, 138, 139, 182, 183
Arkansas Military Land Agency, 22
Arkansas Mule (Searcy), 180
Arkansas Newspaper Women's Association, 281
Arkansas News (1984-1998), 344
Arkansas News Bureau, 350
Arkansas Newspaper Union, 106
Arkansas Optic, 185
Arkansas Patriot, 68, 70
"Arkansas Pine Knot" (Bindursky), 259
Arkansas Plaindealer (Woodberry, Hampton, 1889), 336
Arkansas Populist, 98
Arkansas Power and Light (AP&L), 213, 277
as advertiser, 218
APA supporter, 299
political influence of, 253
Arkansas Press Association, 64, 85–88, *88, 123,* 133–134, 341–351
advertising services, 227, 292, 343
alternative press panel, 309
Americanism Award, 298
annual meetings, 346, 347
The Arkansas Freedom of Information Act: A Handbook, 312
auxiliary, 281
awards and prizes, 131, 255, 263, *265, 268,* 272, 282, 348
board of directors, *287*
building, 205, 227, 342–343
censor, office of, 131
A Chronicle of Arkansas Newspapers Published Since 1922 (Meriwether), 323
clipping bureau, 227, 342 (*see also* Arkansas Press Services)
Code of Ethics, 153
constitution, 225
conventions, *234, 260, 285,* 349–350
Depression era, 222–223
editorial excursions, 86, 87, 105, *108,* 128, 152, 168
effects of war on, 255
expulsions, 178, 180
farming support, 273–274, 349
first years, 85–88
forerunners, 54–55, 83–84
high school press support, 349
history, 283
Hotlines, 313
J.N. Smithee and, 54, 143–145
lobbyists, 343
managers, 216, 223–228, 283, 292, 341–343
meetings, 104, 127–129, 135–136, 194, 225–226
membership criteria, 252, 309
membership diversity, 180–184
modernization, 205–206, 223–224, 255
mortgage burning, *330*
officers, *201*
panel, *267*
pool coverage, 311
presidents, *267,* 283
President's Award, 341
programs, 129
Publicity Act, 143, 211, 220–221
racial crisis response, 298
"scratching post," 280, *284*
segregation, 294
state law digest, 225
tourism support, 346–347
trade publications, 310
trophy winners, *327*
university and, 227–228, 301–302
Wal-Mart and, 345–346
Walter J. Lemke Scholarship Fund, 302
Arkansas Press Gossip, 194
Arkansas Press Photographers Association (APPA), 349
Arkansas Press Services (APA owned), 343
Arkansas Press Women (1954), 201, 281, 312, 341, 349
Horizons: 100 Arkansas Women of Achievement, 282
Arkansas Publisher (1927), *160,* 193–197, 222–225, *283*
advertising issues, 343
Clinton Inauguration, 311
columnists, 259, 342
cover, *329*

Fall, 2001 cover, *355*
Gazette history, 335
guest editorials, *260*
Schick and, 342
Schweiger and, 227
strike coverage, *278*
during war, *256–257*
Arkansas Record, 280, 309
Arkansas Recorder (continued as *Arkansas Statesman),* 298
Arkansas Scholastic Press Association (ASPA), 312, 349
Arkansas School Journal, 184
Arkansas Sentinel (Arkadelphia, 1850), 54
Arkansas Staats-Zeitung (City News), 180–181
Arkansas Star (Little Rock), 33–35, 46
Arkansas State College, 185
printing press, *267*
Arkansas State Democrat (1846), 36
country editions, 100
merger, 39
Arkansas State Democrat (1832-1841), 30
Arkansas State Democrat and Helena Commercial Advertiser (Helena, 1839), 44
Arkansas State Gazette (1836), 33–38, 42. *see Arkansas Gazette*
merger, 39
Whig owned, 35
Arkansas State Gazette and Democrat (1850), 39, 41–42, 46
Arkansas State Horticultural Society, 185
Arkansas State Press (1984-1998), 341
Arkansas State Press (pre-WWII–1959), 296–297, 340
Arkansas Statesman, 298
Arkansas Statesman (Jacksonport, continued as *Dispatch*), 107
Arkansas Student Free Press Association, 308
Arkansas Student Publications Act of 1995, 349
Arkansas Sun (1973), 336
Arkansas Tech University, 335
Arkansas Territorial Restoration, 22
Arkansas Times, 309
Arkansas Times (Fayetteville), 99
Arkansas Toothpick, 183
Arkansas Traveler, 120
Arkansas Traveler (1882, Opie Read), 167, 183–184
Arkansas Traveler (Arkadelphia), 54
Arkansas Traveler (college paper), 222, 243, 307
"Arkansas Traveler" (column, Deane), 298
Arkansas Traveler (Conway), 91, 96
"Arkansas Traveler" (movie), 220, *233*
"The Arkansas Traveler" (Washbourne), 41
Arkansas Tribune (1973), 341
Arkansas Tribune (1995), 336, 341
Arkansas Unit (Morrilton), 202
Arkansas Weekly Mansion (1881, Little Rock), 179–180
Arkansas Whig, 40
Arkansaw Thomas Cat (Hot Springs), *156,* 184
Arkansawyer (Stuttgart), 197, 271
Arkansian (Fayetteville), 43, 51, 78
Armitage, R.S., 222
Army Argus (Price), 71
Arnold, Adolph, 181
Arp, Bill, 122
Arthur, Barry, 317
Ashcraft, Fred and Hazel, 320
Ashley, Chester, 22, 24–25, 33, 36
senator, 37–38
Ashley County Leader, 197, 256
Ashley County Times (1866), 78
Ashley News Observer, 357
Ashmore, Harry, 271, *290,* 294, 298
Epitaph for Dixie, 271
Faubus speech, 280
Pulitzer Prize, 295
"The Crisis Mr. Faubus Made," 295
Associated Press (AP), 79, 122, 151, 177
Arkansas bureau, 209–210
computer use, 316
on FOI, 312
Associated Press Broadcasters Association, 312
Associated Press Managing Editors (APME), 311, 312, 349
Associated Press Wirephoto machine, 255
Atkins Chronicle, 202, 218, 243, 244, 324, 356
Atlantic Monthly, on Donrey Media, 309, 323
Audigier, Louis B., 129, 170
Audit Bureau of Circulation (ABC), 210, 212, 339
Augusta Advocate, 320
Australian ballot, 141
Ayer's, 97, 174

B

Babcock, Mrs. Bernie, 131, 183, 242
The Soul of Ann Rutledge, 183
Baer, Dave, 309
Bailey, Carl, 248
Bailey, D.L., 356
Baker, T. Harri, 344
Baldridge, K.A., *235*

ballot, written, 141
Bancroft, Edward, *74,* 81
banking, 41, 138
  1873 Panic and, 106
  Depression, 219–220
  Drought of 1930 and, 213
  growth, small-town, 97
  scandal, 34–36
banners, 46, 99, *114–115, 162–165, 291*
Baptist Advance, 183
Baptist and Commoner, 183
Bard, Samuel, 81
Barnes, John, 336
Barnes, Steve, 350
Barnett, A.I., 103
Barrier, Chris, 308
barter, as revenue, 217, 219–220
Barton, Thomas H., 253, 273
Bates, James Woodson, 18, 21
Bates, L.C. and Daisy, 296, 297, 340–341
Batesville, 45, 263
Batesville Eagle (Noland), 25
Batesville Guard, 98, 194, 244, 311, 329, 351
Batesville Guard and Record, 235, 282
Batesville News, 21, 45
Batesville News Record, 253
Batesville Record, 92, 173, 189, 191
Batesville Register, 100
Baugh, James J., 54, 118, 222, 248, 252
Bauxite Banner, 340
Baxter, Elisha, 76, 84–85, 86, 143
Baxter County Bulletin (Mountain Home), 152, 208, 294, 322, 327, 337
Bazzoo (Union troops, Batesville), 68
Beacon (Camden), 53
Bear Mountain News, 103
Bearden Banner, 197
The Beebe News, 109, 354
Beebe Sentinel, 216
Beerstecher, Frances, 259, 283, 301
Beerstecher, J.H., 173, 195, 197, 283
Beerstecher, Mrs. J.H., 283
Belle Grove School Journal (Fort Smith), 184
Bennett, G.E., 202, 216
Benton, M.E., 136
Benton, Thomas Hart, 136
Benton County, 204
  Welfare Board, 219
Benton County Daily Record (1988, continued from *Benton County Daily Democrat),* 338
Benton County Democrat, 338
Benton County Sun, 205
Bentonville Advance, 103
Bentonville newspaper war, 338
Bentonville Sun, 98, 119
Bernays, P.H., 153
Berry, C. Stanley, *284,* 332
Berry, Charles, 347
Berry, James Henderson, 140, 142
Berry, Will A., 239
Bertrand, Charles Pierre, 22, 24
Bettis, James R., 146, 147
Bevens, Judge W.C., 45, 49
Bickman, "Uncle Frank," 195
bicycles, 171
The Big Picture (1948, Paragould), 283, 300, 315
Bilheimer, Guy, 150
Bindursky, Esther, 242, *265,* 281, 283
  "Arkansas Pine Knot," 259
  "Navy Edition," 259
  as photographer, 300
Bingen Social Visitor, 118
The Birth of a Nation (movie), 188
Biscoe, Henry L., 30
Bishop, A.W., 85
Black, Joseph H., 53
Black Press of America (NNPA division), 341
Black Rock Blade, 111
Blackburn, Charlene, 236
Blackburn, Charles B., 138, 194–195
Blackburn, W. Jasper, 140
Blackburn's Free South, 140, 194
The Blade (Black Rock, Walnut Ridge), 99
Blagg, Brenda, 350
Blakely, R.L., 186
Bland, James L., 92, 100, 225–226, 242, 246
Bland, James L. Jr., Air Force, 255
Bland, John, 356
Blankenship, L.F., *111,* 281
Bliss, Calvin C., 76
Blocher, W.D., 83, 84, 137, 147, *154*
Block, John and Martha, 336
The Bloody Junto (Crozier), 79
Blue Book, 212, 223

Blue Top Engraving Company, 223, *235*, 249
Blytheville Courier News, 267
Bogard, Ben, 183
boiler plates, 106
Bonaventura, Father, 181
Bonner, W.T., 118
book reviews, 238
Boon(e) County Advocate (continued as *Harrison Times*), *128*
Boone Banner, 152, 160, 222
Boone County, 204
Boone County Headlight, 204, 283
Boone County Record, 99
Booneville Democrat, 94, 208, 267, 283
Boozman, Fay W., 314
Bord, H.D., 147
Borden, Benjamin J., 35, 38
Borland, Fannie, 76, 116
Borland, Fanny, 42
Borland, Solon, 35–36
  An Essay on "The Milk Sickness" of the Human Subjects, or "The Trembles" of Animals; Embracing Its History, Cause and Treatment, 36
  Know-Nothingism, 41–42
  senator, 38–39
  and violence, 40
Boudinot, Elias Cornelius, 43, 83, 134
Bourland, Fagan, 189
Bowen, Clay, *328*
Bowker, Louise, 292, *302*, 316, 341–342
Bradley County, 197
Bragg, Rick *(New York Times)*, 309
Branham, John M., 147
Branner, John L., 103
Brantley, Max, 309, 333
Braswell, M.D., 283
Braswell, O. Klute, 194, 204, 242
Breckinridge, John C., 44
Breit, W.J., 225
Breitz, James E., 176
Brett, Derwood, 310, 353
Briefing Notebook (e-newsletter), 339
Briggs, Robert, 17
Brimacombe, John, 336
Brindletails, 84
Brinkley Argus, 205, 216, 239, 318
Britt, Maurice L. "Footsie," 261
Brooks, Caroline Shaw, 152
Brooks, Cebern, *112*
Brooks, Joseph, 84
Brooks, Neill, 97
Brooks-Baxter Political War, 86, 102
Brothers of Freedom, 101, 140
Brough, Charles H., 142–143
Brower, D.A., 118, 139, 143
Brown, C.H., 219, 283
Brown, Cicero, 105
Brown, Dee, 123, 152, 209
Brown, Edgar, 271
Brown, George Russ, 143, 152, *159*, 178
Brown, Karen, 344
Brown, Mrs. George L., 119
Brown, Patrice Cates, 341
Brown, Robert J. "Bert," 150, 183
Brown, W.E., 113
Broyles, Frank, 298, 348
Brugman, Dickison "Dick," 144, 150, *159*, 242
Brummett, John, 309
Bryant, Winston, 313
Buchanan, Paul, 282, *329*
Buckley, Bill, 325
Buckner, John C., 204–205
Buerkle, Adam, *181*
Buford, William, 180
Buice, Bob (KARK), 243
Bumpers, Dale, 321
Bunch, Burton (APA orator), 117
Burgevin, Edmund, 67
Burke, William R., 85, 99, 106, 178
Burnett, George, 34
Burnett, W.S., 177–178
Burns, Bob, 220, *233*, 243
Burrow, Elizabeth, 296
Burrow, Isham L., 202, 242, 252
Burrus, Elmer, 135, 153
Burton, J.B., 53
Butler, J.E., 40
Butler, James D., 68, 79, 80
Butler, Mrs. Alix, 283
Butt, F.O., 204
Butts, William E., 44
Byrd, Clyde, *268*
Byrd, Dennis, 340
Byrns, Clarence, 292, 294, 295

C
Cabot Star (1955), 301, 324
Caddo Star (Shreveport), 134
Caldwell, Bradley, 356
Calhoun County, newspaper war, 336
Calico Rock, 325
Calico Rock Progress, 97
Calico Rocket (1903), 97
Calloway, Leland D., 308
Camden, 53, 247
Camden Beacon (1873), 96
Camden Evening News, 196, 247, 254
Camden Herald (continued as *Ouachita Herald),* 53
Cane Hill College, 134
Cane Hill News, 98
Caniff, Milton, original comic strip panel, 285
Cannon, Sarah Bell "Granny" (Beaver Springs), *232*
capital punishment, 140
Carden, Powell S., 124
Carithers, Dee (librarian), 319
Carl, Joe, 336
Carlisle, 90–91, 92
Carnall, J. Henry, 176
Carnall, John, 176
Carney, George V., 202–203
carpetbaggers, 81
carriers, news, *171,* 171–172, 277
  female, *235,* 259
Carroll County, 204, 242
Carroll County News, 356
Carroll County Progress (1879), *109*
Carter, Horace W., 284
Carthage Press (Missouri), 94
cartoonists, *270,* 314
cartoons, 153, *200*
  first in Arkansas, 45
  political, 41, 43–44
cash in advance, 34, 40, 117, 130
Casteel, John W., 98
Castleberry, Eloise, *265,* 281, *283*
Cate, Horace, 244
Causey, Fred Jr., 319
The Central Trades and Labor Council, 147
chambers of commerce, as newspaper owners, *289*
Chapple, James E., 217
Charless, Joseph, 13, 32
Chautauqua, Springdale, 95
Chenault, Fletcher, 230
  personal interest stories, 242
Cherokee Advocate, 60
Cherokee Nation, 50, 61
  alphabet (Sequoyah), 49
  move into Arkansas, 15–16, 18
  Treaty, 43
Cherokee Phoenix (Georgia), 49
Cherokee Villager (1955), 324
Cherry, Francis, 279–280
Chestnutt, Edgar B., 242
Chicago Inter-Ocean, 151
Chicot County, 197
Chicot Press, 97, *97*
Chicot Spectator, 259
Chicot Times (1871), 118
Chidester, John T., 105
Choctaw Nation, 61
Chowning, Robert, 242–243, 255
Christmas, 107, 116
"Chronicles of Arkansas," 149, 184
  indexing of, 335
Church, Jeanne, 356
Churchill, Thomas J., 139
circulation, 69, 95, 212, 255
circuses, 104, *329*
Citizen (Brinkley), 277
Citizen (Des Arc, continued in Searcy as *White County Citizen),* 54, 78, 118
Citizens Bulletin (Hot Springs, continued as *New Era*), 121, 178
City Item (Fort Smith), 119–120
civil rights, 180, 252, 306
civil rights movement, 292
Civil War, 63–76
  civil liberties *vs.* military tyranny, 69–70
  issues and themes, 64–66
  Union occupation, 72
Civilian Conservation Corps newspapers, 228
The Clansman (Dixon), 188
Clarendon Sun, 118
Clarion (in Nashville), 13
Clark, Adam, 53, *74,* 78, 82, 85, 102
Clark, Brenda, 336
Clark, Neil and June, 263
Clark, Steve, 312
Clark County, 82, 102–103, 197
Clarke, Anselm, 50

Clarke, Elmer E., 147
Clarke, George W., 49, 134
Clarksville Enterprise, 121
Clarksville newspapers, 96, 202, 256
Clay County, 197, 242
Clayton, John, 141
Clayton, Powell, 80, 84
Claytor, Minnie, 352, 357
Cleburne County, 239
  newspaper war, 336
Cleburne County Times, 264, 336
Cleveland, James M., 45
Cleveland county, 196
Cleveland County Herald (Rison), 99, 119, *233,* 242
Clifton, Mason, technology change, 318–319
Clinton, Hillary, 348
Clinton, William Jefferson, 312, 348
  Attorney General, 312
  President, 311
Cloyd, D.P., 128
Clyde, J.W., 118
Cobb, Rev. J.B., 54
Cobb, Rev. J.D.C., 125
Coger, Claude L., *131*
Colburn C.C., 94
Colby, Eli, 33, 36
Cole, Edward, 33
  suicide, 34
Collins, Eli Whitney, 213
Collis, Judith, 309
Columbia Banner (1877, Magnolia), 195
Columbia County, 243
Columbia Journalism Review, on *Spectrum,* 310
columnists, 42, 200, 241, 242, 245
  gossip, 254
  syndicated, 254, 308, 350
Comer, James A., 190–191
comics, 254
  in color, 149–150
  "Lola," cancelled, 307–308
  strip, *285*
Commercial-Appeal (Memphis), 151, 249
  black boycott, 296
Commercial Printing Company, *158*
Commercial Standard (Batesville), 45
Commonwealth College, 246
communication, written, 133
  early history, 11–12
communist conspiracy, 277
community, promotion of, 104
community press (from country press), 132
Community Publishers, Incorporated (CPI), 338, 347
  Hussman alliance, 339–340
Compere, J.S., 183
compositor. *see* newspaper production
Compugraphic Corporation, 316
computer software, for pagination, 319
computers
  in composition, 316
  for graphics, 317
confidentiality pledge, 314
Congress of Industrial Organization (CIO), 277
Conley, William G., 283, 292
Conner, Farrell, 282
Connors, Joanie, 358
Conservation in Arkansas (Harper & Henry), 227
Conservatives *vs.* Radicals, 73
consolidations, from offset use, 320
constitution, state, 30, 41, 146–147
  post-war, 73, 76, 80
  Thou Shall Not, 86
Constitutional Eagle, 81
Constitutional Journal (Helena, 1836), 44
Constitutional Union (Des Arc, 1860), 54
Constitutional Union party, 44
contributions, personal. *see also* letters to the editor
  as news, 16–17
Conway, Elias Nelson, 30, 38, 40–41, 42
Conway, Henry W., 22–23
Conway, James Sevier, 30, 33, 49
Conway News, 188, 196, 202, 248
Conway (town), 85, 92, 202
Cooley, J.F., 341
Cooper, Don, 316
Cooper, John A., 219, 324
Cooper, Ray G., 292
Copeland, Curt, 293
Copeland, L.M., 190
corporate ownership, 320–325
correspondents, 71. *see also* reporters
  country, 95, 99, 122–125, *199,* 202, 228–231, 238–241, 352
  Faubus, Sam, *214*
  female, 228, 231, 241
  Lemke survey, 240–241

metropolitan, 241
out-of-state, 261
pay, 125, 230, 241
Star Herald, 110
teachers as, 122–124
war, 139
Cotnam, Florence B., 186, 194
Cotton Plant Democrat, 320
Couch, Harvey (honorary APA), 213, 252–253
Coughlin, John "Jack," 266, 275, 280
Coughlin, Paul "Pete," 266, 275, 279–280
Coulter, E. Merton (historian), 79
"Country Diarist" (Thomas), 241
The Country Editor (Park), 243
Counts, Will (photographer), 294
Pulitzer Prize selection, 296
county fair, 103, 253
Courier-Democrat (Russellville), 130, 282
Courtney, William M. "Bill," 295, 320
Cox, David, 243
Cox, David and Heidi, 325
Cox, J.B., 202
Craig, Oscar Franklin, *112,* 169, 191, *236,* 253
Craig, Roy Monroe, 113, 169, 253
Craig, Roy R., *234*
Craighead County, 197, 243
Crain, Steve, 351
Crane, George W., 308
Crawford, Charles, 97
Crawford County, 197
"The Crisis Mr. Faubus Made" (Ashmore), 295
Crittenden, Robert, 14, 18
death, 28
political influence of, 17, 22–25
Crittenden County, 197, 202, 219, 242
Crittenden County Times, 219, 266, 275, 283
Crockett, Robert H., 62, 99, 103, 105
Cross, Harvey Lamar, 98, 119, 186, *198,* 205
Cross County Times, 320
Crowley Ridge Chronicle, 319
Crozier, R.H., *The Bloody Junto,* 79
Cruce, C.E., 98
CTP (computer to plate), 320
Cummins, J.W., 119
Cummins, William, 26, 33
Cunningham, Catherine, 180
Cunningham, J.M., 97
Cunningham, Matthew, 22, 24
Curl, A., 140
Cushman Elevator, 97
Cypert, Jesse N., 82

D

D-Books Publishers (APA associate), 331
daguerreotypes, 60
Daily Advertiser (1904), 182
Daily and Weekly Telegraph, 178
Daily Appeal (Memphis), 80
Daily Argus (1860), 50
Daily Arkansas Democrat (continued from *Evening Star; continued as Arkansas Democrat),* 137
Daily Bulletin (Hot Springs), 178
Daily Globe (Hot Springs), 183
Daily Independent (1874, Helena), 178
Daily Leader (Stuttgart), 271, 327
Daily News-Digest (ITU), 278
Daily Progress (Little Rock), 151
The Daily Record (Little Rock), 327
Daily Republican, 80–81, 82, 84, 87, 137
Daily Siftings Herald (Arkadelphia), 309, 337
Daily State Journal, 67, 71
Daily Tribune (1877, Helena), 178
Daily Tribune (Fort Smith), 176
Dallas County, 202
Dalton, Judy, 344
Danley, Benjamin Franklin, 40, 80
Danley, Christopher Columbus, 38, 40, 41–42, 76, 144
Civil War role, 64–65, 64–67
death, 79
Dardanelle Post-Dispatch (1867), 174, 176, 202
Daulton, Ben, 242
Davidson, Jim, 350
Davis, Jeff, 101, 121
race issues and, 141–142
Davis, Jill, illustration, *326*
Davis, Mark (cartoonist), 314
Davis, Mrs.Owen K. (Luna Kelley), 194
Day, Jeannie, 325, 354
De Angelis, Barbara, 325
De Mahler, M.L. "Potomac," 168
De Queen, 248, 256, 263
De Queen Citizen, 294
De Valls Bluff Democrat, 281
De Witt Elector (1866), 78, 102

De Witt Era-Enterprise, 283, 331, 354
De Witt Indicator, 106
Deane, Ernest C. "Ernie," 206, 209, 245, 298, 299, 307
  "Arkansas Traveler," 298
  in Cherokee, 324
  journalism professor, *330*
Dearmore, Tom, 127, 245, 294, 308
  Nieman Award, 296
Decatur, 204–205
Decker, W.E., 176
Deering, John (cartoonist), 314, 350
Dell, Valentine, 73, 81, 99, 119
Dembey, J.W., 73
Democrat (1890, continued from *Rogers New Era),* 93
Democrat (Bentonville, 1886), *110,* 119
Democrat (Fayetteville), 105, 119
Democrat (Huntsville), 105
Democrat (Jackson County), 234, 271, 281, 301
Democrat (Jacksonport), 93
Democrat Printing and Lithographing Company (DP&L), 148, *159,* 227
Democratic Party, 32–33
  and *Arkansas Banner,* 35–36
  New Departure, 137
Democratic Star (Helena), 45
DeMun, Auguste, 14
Denton, J.L., 184
Department of Health and FOI, 314
Depression, 213, 215–221
Dermott News, 254
Des Arc, 54
Des Arc Citizen (1854), 54, 81, 143
Des Arc Crescent (1866), 78
desegregation, 294
  federal injunction for, 293
d'Estimauville de Beau Mouchel, 36, 42
Devine, Ed. C., 173
Dew, Clyde L., 151
Dezort, Jeff, 320
Dickey, Jay, 323
Diehl, S.A., 204
Dietzgen, Phil, 180–181
Dillard, William, 348
Dillard's advertising, 334
disabilities, 42, 97
  recognition of, 282
Dixon, Thomas, *The Clansman,* 188
Dodd, David O., 76
Dodge, Frank H., 174
Doerner, George, 180–181
Dolphus, Charles, 341
Donaghey, George Washington, 142
Donald, Leroy, *329,* 334
Donan, Peter, 103
  four rules of, 129
Donrey Media Group, 237, 314, 320, 322–323, 338
  Fort Smith monopoly, 309
  and Stephens, Inc., 338
Dopking, Al (AP), 312
Douglas, Bob, 319, *329,* 353
  FOI, 312
Douglas, Stephan A., 44
Douglass, Major William F., 53–54
Douglass, William J., 109
Douthit, George, *269,* 331
  FOI, 312
Dover Times, 99, 202, 324
"Down on the Farm" (Tyson), 243
Downs, William D., Jr., 349
dresses. *see* banners
Drew, Thomas, 38–39
duels, 14, 23–24, 25, 37, 39, 67–68, 178
  Clarke-Logan, 49
  Smithee-Adams, 138–139
Dumas, Ernie, 309, 333, 340
Dumas Clarion, 267, 281, 311, 324, 327
Dunaway, Edwin E., 280, 292
Dunaway, L.S. "Sharpe," *160*
Duncan, Maud, 132, 203, 245
  Publisher cover, 281
Dungan, W.C., 118
Dunham, J.S., 50, 66, 78, 134
Dunlap, J.E., 255, 283, *287,* 298, 311
Dunn, Macon, 256
Durst, John T., 190–191
Dynasty, 38, 40

E

Eagle, James P., 141
Eagle (Batesville), 45
Eagle Democrat (Warren), 293, 298
Eagle (Searcy), 190
Eakin, John R., 48, 51, 72, 78
Earle Enterprise, 219, 320

Eblen, Joe, 309
economic development plan, 299
editions
  9-11, 353–354
  1936 Centennial, 242
  blue-sky, 104
  dailies, 32, 88, 94, 174–175, 186, 324
  extras, 18, 30, 353
  progress, 103
  special, 103, 210–211, 253–254
  Sunday, 212, 241
  twice weekly, 100
  victory, 261
  weeklies, 62, 66, 88, 196–197, 240, 241
Editor and Publisher, 207, 213
The Editor Surveying the Town (Allsopp), *156*
editorial
  philosphy, 35, 56, 186, 308
  policy, 32
  wars, 106
"Editorial Excursions" (vignette), 87
editorials, 195–196, 243, 247
  as state-wide forum, 310
editors and publishers
  black, 296–297
  country, 99, 125–127, 208, 220
  political autonomy of, 323–324
  as promoters, 104, 116
  in public service, 26, 219
  role, 16, 42, 120–121
  social issues and, 263
  sports and, 208–209
  style, 28–29, 51, 56
  women, 203–204, 283
Edmiston, Theo. L., 243
education, 219, 260
  journals, 81
  public support for, 310
  rural, 228
  segregation and, 276–277, 310
  state history, 299
Eggert, Don, 308
El Dorado, 54
El Dorado Bulletin, 53
El Dorado Daily News, 197
El Dorado Evening Times, 197
El Latino (2001), 340
elections. *see* politics
electrification, rural, 271
Elijah Parish Lovejoy Award, 306
Elledge, Steven, *265*
Elliot, Kenneth, 256–257
Elliot, Roy, 202, 239, 336
Ellis, Todd, 223
Emergency Relief Association, 218
Emmett Bonlore (Read), 126–127, 167
Engel, K. August, 147–148, 219, *237*, 247, 256, *286*, *287*
  KTHV-TV, 331
  SNPA, 258
English, Elbert H., 83
Enquirer (Borland), 42
Enterprise (De Witt), 197
  Mary Louise Wright, 281
Epitaph for Dixie (Ashmore), 271
Erp, Johnny, 242, 244
Eskridge, Judge Thomas P., 17
An Essay on "The Milk Sickness" of the Human Subjects, or "The Trembles" of Animals; Embracing Its History, Cause and Treatment (Borland), 36
Estes, R.J. "Rufe," 98
Etaoin Shrdlu, 319
ethics, newspaper, 17, 25, 37, 72, 152–153, 323
  and railroads, 103
Etter, William H., 51, 72, 300
Eureka Springs, 322
Evans, Roy, 92, 241
Evening Star (Little Rock, continued as *Daily Arkansas Democrat*), 137
Evening Times (West Memphis), 327
evolution, 183, 188
exchanges (newspapers), 16, 54, 121

F

Fagan, J.P., 107
Fahr, Rick, 354
Fair Employment Practices Committee (FEPC), 257
Fairchild Graphic Equipment, 315
The Family, 41–44, 65
  Hindman and Pike, 64
"Farkleberry Follies," 352
Farm Bureau Press, 227
Faubus, Orval Eugene, 246, 252, 271
  governor, 292–299
  liberal campaign, 280

National Guard, calling of, 294
newspaper owner, 298
Record, 275
Faubus, Sam, *214,* 271
"Sam Faubus: The Red Country Correspondent" (vignette), 214
fax machines, 316
Fayetteville, 51, 203
newspaper war, 338
Fayetteville Daily Leader, 198, 211–212, 244
Fayetteville Democrat (1860, 1869, continued as *Northwest Arkansas Times*), 51, 78, 81, 95, 194, 201, 203, 210, 244
newspaper war and, 211–212
Fayetteville Republic, 99
Fayetteville Witness (1840), 41
Featherstonhaugh, George William, 27
feature stories, 240
on mental illness, 230
feature writers, 230, 241–242
Federal Confiscation Act, 76
fiction, 52
Fin de Siecle Sickle (continued as *The Sickle),* 98
Fine, Dr. Benjamin, 294
Fishback, William F. (honorary APA), 73, 76, 138, 139, 176
Fisher, Bob, *287, 312,* 353
Fisher, George, *270,* 275–276, 301, *306,* 314
cartoon strip, *289*
untitled cartoon, *270, 289, 348*
Fisher, Robert, *327*
Fisher, Robert E.
SPJ, 312
"Thoughts on a Young Man's Funeral," 307
Fisher, Rosemary "Snooky," 276
Flanigan, Harris, 68, 72
Fletcher, John G., 138
Fletcher, John Gould, 242
Fletcher, Read, 53, 177
Flower of Magnolia (1869), 194
Fluhart, Mel, 325
Folsom, Harriette M., 205
Folsom, W.B., 132, 205, 210, 216, 239, 253
Folsom, W.W., 94
Ford, Joe, 348
Fordyce News-Advocate, 327
Fordyce Weekly News, 239
Foreman, Gene C., 185, *267,* 332, 348
The Forrest City Times, 112, 182
The Forrest City Times-Herald, 190–191, 324
Fort Smith, 49–50, 175–176, 202–203
war-time, 257
Fort Smith Daily Times, 176
Fort Smith Elevator, 176
Fort Smith Herald (1847), 50–51, 78, 176
Fort Smith New Era, 73, 81, 99, 100
Fort Smith Times (continued as *Times Record*), 50, 62, 176
Foster, Thomas B., 257
"Fourth Estate" (Macaulay), 30
Francis, Ken, *269*
Franklin List, 192
Fraser, Rusty, 337, 354
fraternal organizations, 188
Masons, 182
Rotary, 193
Frauenthal, Jo, 91
"Free ads: a contradiction in terms" (vignette), 232
free press, 27
Free Press, 310
Freedman's Bureau, 77
Freedmen, 80
Freedom Forum, *Jonesboro: Were the Media Fair?,* 309
Freedom Forum (formerly Garnett Foundationa), 308
Freedom of Information Act (FOI, Arkansas), 311–315
resistance to, 313–314
Freeman, E.W., 177
Freeman, E.W. III, 295, 324
Freeman, Gordon, 282
Freeman, L.D., 169–170
French-Spanish rule, 12
Friedlander, Edward J., 260
Friedman, Arthur, 124
Frolich, Jacob Jr., *75,* 82, 85, 86, 144
"How to Run a Country Newspaper," 129–130
Frye, William (artist), 74
Fugate, Larry, 354
Fulbright, J. William, 247, 257, *268,* 282, 307
Fulbright, Jay, 203
Fulbright, Roberta, *201,* 203, 211, *234,* 244, *248*
Publisher cover, 281
Fulton, William Savin, 24, 25, 27, 29
senator, 33, 37
Fulton County Informer, 98
Funk, Emmanuel, 125
Funk, Erwin, 132, *201*
Daily Leader and, 212
Depression era, 218–219

diary, 299–300
editor, 92
on Linotype, 170
and the NEA, 132
NRA code administrator, 221–222, *235*
observations, 93, 98, 100, 101, 103, 116, 119
on professionalism, 117
profitable publishing and, 192–193
on size and format, 89
sports referee, 105, 208–209
on traveling, 121
Futrall, John C., 215, 244, 247
Futrell, Junius M., 221, 225

G

G & D. *see Arkansas State Gazette and Democrat*
Gage, J.T., 105
Gaines, D.T., 259
Gallagher, J. Frank, 176
gambling, 29
Gannett chain, 322, 358
and Rupert E. Phillips, 337
Gantt, Edward W., 73, 82
Garland, Augustus H., 72, 83, 86, 137–138
Garland, Rufus, K., 72
Garrett, John T., 23–24
Gatewood, P.W., 97
Gaulding, Josiah W., 74, 78, 82, 102, 105
gazette, 15
Gazette. see Arkansas Gazette
The Gazette Printing Company, 143, 144, *159*
The Gazette Publishing Company, 83
Gearhart, George, 338
Gearhart, Sam, *234, 237*
Gentry, 205
newspaper war, 336
Gentry American (tabloid), 336
Gentry Courier, 336
George, Charlie, 150
George, G.P., 197
George, Marcus, 269, *284*, 332
GeoTel, 227
Giacomini, Effie, 122
Giacomini, Thomas Paul, 96, 122
Gibbs, M.W., 180
Gillespie, Katie, 234, 281
Gillespie, Mike, 222, *234*, 263, 283
Gillespie, Tommy, 324
Ginocchio, John T., 151, 153
Givens, Edgar L., 144, 146–147
Gleaner (De Witt), 103
Glenwood Herald, 263, 356
Goode, Ovid, 336, 341
Goodspeed histories, 103
Goodwin, Lucy and Tommy, 325
Goolsby, Alan and Jeanette, 336
Goslee, Charles, 205, 222, 225
Gosnell, Jan (cartoonist), 314
Gould, K.O., 121
Gould, Leah, 357
Govan, Brad, *287*, 299
Government Improvement League (GI), 275
Graham, Bill (cartoonist), *270*
Graham, J.C., *113, 195*
Graham, James, 93
The Grand Opera House Program, 183
Grand Prairie Leader, 197
Grant, Elmer "Ma," 173
The Grapevine (1970), 308
Graphic Arts Code, 221–222
Graphic (Clarksville), 122, 327
graphic materials, 17–18, *21*, 26, 37
graphics, computer, 317
Grauerholz, Larry, 263
Graves, Guy, 263
Graves, Louie, 324, 344–345
cold room, 316
Graves, Louis "Swampy," 279, 307
SPJ, 312
Gravette, 204
Greeley, Horace, 56, 88, 143
Green Forest Tribune, 267
Greenberg, Paul, 334, 350
Pulitzer Prize, 295
Greenwood, William M., 210
Greenwood Democrat, 356
Griffee, Carol, 315
Griffith, D.W., 188
Gross, Tabbs, 81, 84
The Group, Inc., 336
Guion, John, 282–283
gun control, 147, 177
Gunter, O.D., *269*

H

Hadley, Ozra, 85
Haglin, Nannie, 184
Haight, Charles, 77
Haines, Harry A., *267*
Hall, C.G., *234*
Hall, Sergeant, 13
Hallum, John, 98
"Hambone" (Alley), 249
Hamilton, Mary Ann, 27
Hampton, Harvey Theopolis, 94
Hampton, Max, 132, 222, 283, 320
 "Life's Ambition," 262
 vignette, 262
Hampton Herald, 336
Hankens, Stephen, 354
Hanly, Thomas B., 44
Harding, A.M., 225
Harding College (Searcy), 277
Harp, Jack, 196
Harper, C. Armitage "Army," 222, 224–225, 226, 227, *235*
 Conservation in Arkansas, 227
Harper, Clio, 141, 145, 147, 150, 153, *160,* 167, *201*
 Arkansas Publisher, 193–197, 202–206
 Columbian Exposition and, 152
 death, 213, 221
Harrell, John M., 83
Harris, Mose C. (APA, expelled), 178, 180
Harrison Daily Times, 311
Harrison Republican (continued as *Boone County Headlight),* 204
Harrison Times, 102, 104, 123, 128, 175, 195, 204, 283
 Linotypes, 209
Harte-Hanks Newspapers, 321
Harville, Vic (cartoonist), 350
Hawkins, F.C. and Augusta, 212
Hawkins, Marlin, 306
 How I Stole Elections: The Autobiography of Sheriff Marlin Hawkins, 306
Hawley, A.T., 52
Hawn, Alfred, 130, 195, *201,* 271
Hawthorne, Nathaniel, "The Two Widows," 45
Hayden, George B., 38, 39
Hays, Brooks, 243, 246, 298
Hays, George W., 142
Head, J.H. and J.M., 261
Headlight (Harrison), 175
Hedges, Fred L., 219, 255
Hedges, Z.T., 151–152
Heiskell, Carrick W., 255
Heiskell, Frederick S., 148, 149, 172
Heiskell, John N. "Ned," 142, 147, *148,* 148–150, *156,* 184, *286,* 298
 planned successor, 255, 271
 SNPA, 258
Helena, 44–45, 177–178
 Union troops in, 69
Helena Daily Mail, 178
Helena Daily World, 99, 106, 244, 310, 317, 324
Helena Herald (1834), 27, 30
Helena Spy, 44
Helena Weekly Clarion, 81
Helena Weekly World (1871), 85, 177–178
Helena-West Helena World, 295
Helena World, 141, 235, 267
Hempstead & Red River Inquirer prospectus, 51
Hempstead Democrat, 52–53
Henderson, J.M., 197, 260, 283
Henderson, Jess C., 341
Henderson, Shannon J. (librarian), 335
Hendrix, Jim, 259
Hendrix College, 252, 296
Henry, L.A., *Conservation in Arkansas,* 227
Herald-Democrat (Clarksville), 244
Herald Democrat (Siloam Springs), 232
 correspondents, 239–240
Herbert, Benjamin Briggs, 131
Herrington, Eugene, 240, 342, 353
Hickey, Maurice "Moe," 334
Hicks, J.C.M., 58
Hicks, Willie, 119
Higgins, John G., 178
Highway Audit Commission, 277
Hindman, Thomas Carmichael, 42, 62, 69–70
 assassination, 79
Hinds, James, 79
Hines, Craig, FOI, 312
Historic Arkansas Museum, 22
historical society, 71
History of the Arkansas Press for a Hundred Years and More (Alsopp), 191
Hite, Ada A., 119–120
Hite, R.C., 119–120, 176
Hobson, Anson W. "Legs," 53, 66, 81
Hodges, Earle W., 131, 141, 142–43

Hodges, Sam Jr., 216–217, 255, *268*, 274, 292, 295, 321, 325
Hodges, Sam Sr., 216
Hogan, "Sycamore Dan" (APA poet), 98, 101
¡Hola! (2000), 340
Hollinger Group, Conrad Black, 324
Hollinger International (Canada), 338
Holmes, Jim, 96
Holmes, Leon, 313
Holmes, Paul, 354
Holmes, Theophilus Hunter "Old Granny," 70
holocaust denial, 298
Holsted, Leon, 286
Holt, James, 170, 171
Holtzman, William F., 42, 73, 76
The Home News (McCrory), 207–208
Homeland, 341
Hope, 94, 257
Hope City Times (1874), 194
Hope Gazette, 174
Hope Star, 171, 196, *234,* 242, 337
Horizons: 100 Arkansas Women of Achievement (APW), 282
Hornet (Hot Springs), 178
Hot Springs, 97, 178–179, 322
  government move to, 68
  machine politics in, 247, 274–275
Hot Springs Rubdown, 293
Hot Springs Sentinel (1877, continued as *Sentinel Record*), 53, 178
Hot Springs Telegraph, 137
Hot SpringsTribune (1933), 219
Hotze, Peter, 155
How I Stole Elections: The Autobiography of Sheriff Marlin Hawkins, 306
How to Create Newspaper Advertising That Moves Merchandise (Schick), 343
"How to Lynch a Newspaper" (Reed, Atlantic Monthly), 306
"How to Run a Country Newspaper" (Frolich), 129–130
Hoxie (Lawrence County), 293
Huff, Ells L., 271, *284,* 301
Huff, Mrs. Ells L., 281
Huffman, John R., 97
Hughes, Roland, 232
Hughes, Simon, 144
Hughes Star-Herald, 319
Hull, Alex C., 152, 153, 193
Hunnicutt, Wesley E., 338
Hunt, Andrew Jackson, 29
Hunt brothers, 321
Hurley, Curtis B., 196, *201,* 202, 217, 242, 301
  Air Force, 255
Hussman, Walter E., Jr., 324, *328*
  Arkansas Democrat, 332
  northwest Arkansas, 338–340
Hussman, Walter E., Sr., *237,* 271, *327*
  KWFC, *272*
  WEHCO Media, *323*
Hutchinson, E. Grant and family, *108*
Hutchinson, Tim and Asa, 247

I

"I am Near Thee" (Scull), 39
illiteracy, 55, 80
The Incident (North Little Rock), 92
Independent Arkansian (Dardanelle), 128
Independent Balance (Batesville, 1856), 45
Independent (Carlisle), 342
Independent Democrat (1832), 36
Independent Southron (Helena), 45
Indexing, newspaper, 335
Indian affairs, news source, 50
Indian Progress (Vinita), 134
industrial development, 273–274
industry
  early 20th century, 100
  local and newspapers, 103
Inland Printer, 130
inserts, magazine, 331
integration, racial, 179–180, 292–293
  of Little Rock Central High School, 294–295
  press association and, 84
  during wartime, 257
  white opposition to, 252
International Society of Weekly Newspaper Editors, 311
International Typographical Union (ITU), 113, 147, *154,* 172–173, 195, 319
  strike, 278
Internet, 311
interposition, doctrine of, 293
Irwin, Joel L., *330,* 336, 342, 351
Izard, Major General George, 22
Izard County, 242

J

Jacko, C.O., 179
Jackson, H.M., 219

Jackson, Jay W. and Patsy, *267*, 316, *330*, 351
Jackson, W.M., 277
Jacksonville News-Progress, 293
James, Sue L., 119
Jefferson Enterprise (Pine Bluff), 53
Jeffersonian (Pine Bluff), 53
Jennings, Hillory, 171
Jennings, Orville, 52
John Brown University (formerly John E. Brown Schools), 204
Johnson, J.O., 189
Johnson, James "Justice Jim," 293, 299
Johnson, Judge Benjamin, 26, 38
Johnson, Richard H., 166–167
Johnson, Richard Mentor, 40, 42–44, 67
Johnson, Robert Ward, 39, 40, 42, 69, 76, 80, 137
  politics and, 137–139
  on Quesenbury, 134
  on state pride, 120
joint operating agreements (JOA), 332, 339
Jolly, J. Crawford, 197
Jones, Bob, 247
Jones, Dan W., 153
Jones, Daniel Webster, 141
Jones, Jerry, 348
Jones, Josephine Carroll, 282
Jones, Mrs. M.P., 281
Jones, Oscar E. and Pat, 92, 210, 222, 223, *235*, 246–247, 282, 351
  and *The Sun,* 336
Jones, Perrin, 313, 320, 353
Jones, Terry, 334
Jones, Thresa, 296
Jonesboro, 256
Jonesboro: Were the Media Fair? (Freedom Forum), 309
Jonesboro Register (1866), 78
Jonesboro Sun, 145, 176, *213, 271, 317, 324*
  content partner, *340*
  digital cameras, *317*
  Pulitzer Prize nomination, 308
  union vote, 348
JonesboroTribune, 116, 213, 223, 244
Journal-Advance (Gentry), 336
Journal (Imboden), 256
Journal (Napoleon, 1939), 45
Journal of Rural Education, 197
Journal (Springdale, continuation of *Springdale Yellow Jacket*), 91
journalism
  alternative, 308–309
  education, 243–245, 349
  interactive, 311
  personal, 150, 153, 207
  political training, 352–353
  training, 92, 185, 206, 227
  women in, 280–281
journals, 184–186
Judsonia, history of, 242

K

Kaffka, Jay, 324
Karam, Jimmy, 278–279
Kavanaugh, W.M., 144, 153
Kearney, B.F., 85
Kearney, Janis and Janetta, 341
Keesee, Steve, 334
Keithley, William A., 97
Kelley, Luna (Mrs. Owen K. Davis), 194
Kellogg, Ansel Nash, 106
Kemp, Randy, 356
Kemp, Ron, 311
Kendrick, A.J., 176
Kennard, M. Shelby, 45
Kennedy, Jon (cartoonist), *269, 270,* 307, 314
  "Amen Corner," *270*
Kent, Chancellor James, 28
Kilgore, James M., 52–53, 255
Kilgore, Orpha, 352
Kimball, Evelyn (Mrs. Ray), 255, 281
Kimball, Ray, 212, 223–227, 232, 245, 336
  photocomposition, 316
  SPJ, 312
  Stuttgart, 271
  war and, 255, 263
  wire service system, 248–249
"Ray Kimball" (vignette), 322
Kimbell, John D., 52–53
King, Buddy, 347
King, John Fred, 212
Kirby, Martin, 308, 309, 311
Kite, Ralph, *236, 249*
Knight, John E., 37, 39
Knights of Labor, 173
The Knights of the Pen and Scissors. *see* Arkansas Press Association
Knights of the White Camellia, 82

Know-Nothingism, 41, 50
Knowles, H.G., 189
Knowlton, H.A., 174
Knox, Jack (cartoonist), 250
Koop, George, 217–218
Ku Klux Klan, 75, 79, 82–83, 188–191, 193
  religious press and, 183

L
La Prensa de Northwest Arkansas, 340
La Prensa Latina, 340
Lafayette County Democrat, 325
Lafayette County Press (Stamps), 325, 357
Lamar Leader, 202, 216
Lamb, Lawrence, 176
Lamb, Ted, 280, 292
Lambert, David, 33–34
Lancaster, Bob, 309, 335–336
Landvoight, Edward, 112, 160, 194
  newsstand, 196
Larimer, Ted, *267,* 331
Lath, J.A. *see* Thalheimer, Joseph A.
Lauck, Chester, 298
LaVilla News (Hot Springs Village), 322
law and order, 28, 29
Lawrence, Marjorie, 282
Laws of the Territory of Arkansas comprising The Organic Laws of the Territory of Missouri and Arkansas with their Amendments and Supplements Annexed, (Woodruff), 18
Lead Hill, 117
Leflar, Robert, 228, 244, 293
legal notices, as revenue, 211, 220–221
legal printing, 13, 16, 25, 26
  federal, 18
  "Pro Bono Publico," 25
  and woodcuts, *47*
Leigh, Robert W. "Bob" (APA historian), 117, 131, 141
Leighton, Peggy, 205
Lemke, Walter J., 95, 105, *199, 201,* 301–302
  APA, 223–224, *286*
  feature stories, 242
  journalism professor, 206, 244–245, 254
  Moon Book, 244
  "There's Romance in the Names of Rural Communities," 245
  "Uncle Walt," 211, 244
  Walter J. Lemke Department of Journalism, 351
  Walter J. Lemke Scholarship Fund, 302
Len Gansett (Read), 125–126
Lepanto, 263
Lepanto News-Record, 282
Leslie News, 103
Leslie News (White County), 121
letters to the editor
  anonymous, 33
  policy, 17
Leveritt, Alan, 309, 310
Lewisburg Empire, 85
libel, 142
  Crittenden and Woodruff, 23–24
Liberal, 137
Liberty Group Publishers, 324, 336
The Life, 183
Life Magazine, 276, 282
"The Life of a Printer" (vignette), 98
Life on the Mississippi, Twain, Mark, 45
"Life's Ambition" (Hampton), 262
Lightfoot, Frank, 331
Lincoln, Tom, 244
Lincoln Leader, 357
Lindley, Helen, 325
Lion Oil, 253
  Monsanto and, 273
Liske, Eddie, *269, 297*
lithography, 315
Little Adventures in Newspaperdom (Allsopp), 191–192
Little Black Book, 192
"Little Merchants," *171*
"The Little Printer of the Ozarks," 203
Little Rock
  occupation, 72
  school board, 280
  as territorial capital, 18
Little Rock Chronicle, 85, 137
Little Rock Daily Gazette, 77
Little Rock Daily News, 150
Little Rock Press Club, 294
Little Rock Publishing Company, 147
Little Rock Republican, 140
Little Women (Alcott), 116
Livestock Show and Radio, Press Day, *288*
Livingston, J. Arthur, 130, 132, 225, 245, 255, 282
Livingston, Ruby Erwin, 217, 255
local news, 245
Log Cabin Democrat, 131, *199,* 202, 311, 324, 330

correspondents and, 238–240
Logan, John S., 49
Logan County Anzeiger (Advertiser), 181
Long-Island Star (Spooner), 13
Lonoke Democrat, 194, 324
Los Angeles Times, 96
Loughborough, Mary W., 179–180
Louisville Journal (Prentice), 32
Love, W.L., 293
Lucey, J.M., 184
Luckie, L.B., 53
Ludwig, O.C., 121, 146, 186
Lundgren, Gary, 349
Lundy, Walker, 333
lynching, 26, 102, 180, 190
as policy, 142
Lynn, Charles, 259
Lyon, William H. Jr., *The Pioneer Editor in Missouri,* 12
Lyons, Gene, 308

M

MacKrell, James "Uncle Mac," *276–277*
Madison County Record (1919 merger of *Democrat* and *Republican,* Huntsville), *108,* 130, 195, *298*
Orval Faubus, 271, 275
Magie, Cone and Betty, *268,* 298, 301, *324*
SPJ, *312*
Magie, Mark, 324
Magnolia Vindicator (1866), 78
mail system
post Reconstruction, 99
slowness of, 19, 51–52
Mallory,Samuel W., 84
Malvern Daily Record, 173, *203,* 283, 301
Malvern Meteor, 151
Malvern News, 140
Mammoth Spring Democrat (1890), 207, 280
"The Manager's Nightmare, or The Eternal Pain" (vignette), 226
Mann, George, 150, 155
Mannen, Calvin, *287,* 298, *327*
maps, 37
Marcus, E., 40
Marianna Courier-Index, 219, 324
Marinoni, Rosa Zagnoni (poet), 244
Marked Tree Tribune, 245, 258, 263, 267
on segregation, 266
Marrs, Sam E., 119
Marshall, *47*
Marshall Republican, 105, 190, 216, 218, 263
Martin, Harold E., 337
Martin, Karen Knutson, 334
Martin, Leo, *269*
Marvell Messenger, 274, 320
Maryhattianna Herald, 151
Mason, Dina, 351
Mason, Frank A., 93
Masonic Trowel, 113, 182
masthead, 46
Matthews, Charles, 178
Matthews, Jesse, 98
Matthews, W.D., 100
May, Joe, 325
Mayer, Martha, 245
Mayers, A.G., 50
Mayfield, R.B., FOI, 312
McAlmont, J.J., 78
McArthur, John (M'Arthur), 14. *see also Arkansas Herald*
McCarroll, Z.M. "Bear," 101
McCaskiell, Austin, *284*
McClain, Bill, 244
McClellan, John L., 257
McClure, John (M'Clure), *75,* 80, 81, 137
McCollum, Bonner, 324
McCollum, David, 311
McConnell, Jerry, 322
McCord, Robert "Bob," *269, 284,* 286, 301, 309, 352
AETN documentaries, 332
Arkansas Democrat, 332
political perception of, 311
SPJ, *312*
McCorkle, Ed W., 105, 170
McCoy, Bruce, 225
McCrory Leader, 320, 321
McCulloch, S.A., 97
McCullom, Fred, 298
McDiarmid, Clara A., 180
McDonald, Harry, with elephant, *329*
McDonald, Tom, 323
McGehee Times, 259, 277
McGinnis, Bryan, 282
McGuire, M.M., 128, 185
McKinley, E.I., 174
McKinley, J.R., 294
McLane, Lee, 354

McLaughlin, Leo P., 179, 247, 274–275
McMath, Sid, 275, 276–277, 279
McMullen, R.D., 144
McMurray, James, 97
McNabb, Lynne (Mrs. James Walton), 338
McNish, S.A., 124, 132
McRae, Dandridge, 82
Meador, Cincinnatus V., 73, 76
media, 323
Meiklejohn Award (AAUP), 295
Melbourne Times, 98, 242
Memphis Appeal, 72, 119
Memphis Avalanche, 113, 195
Memphis Scimitar, 50
Memphis Weekly Appeal (Pelt), 13
Mena Star (1896), 94, 98
Menefee, Nimrod, 25
Mergenthaler, Ottmar, 168
Mergenthaler Linotype, 209, 218, 254
mergers and consolidations, 195, 206–207, 219
  war-time, 256
Meriwether, Robert W., *A Chronicle of Arkansas Newspapers Published Since 1922,* 323
Merrill, A.M., 101
Messenger (Napolean, continuation of *Journal),* 35, 45
Messenger (Wittsburg), 54
Meurer, Carl, 217
Meurer, Karl Joseph, *161,* 181, 217
Meyer, Roy, *268*
Milam, John "J.," 99, 204
Millar, Alexander Copeland, 182, 189, 192, *198, 201,* 252
Miller, James, 14, 17, 22
Miller, William R., 138
Miner, Leibert J. "Bill"
  Arkansas Publisher, 257, *265,* 283
  Christmas card, *236*
Mineral Springs Vim, 113, 195
Minstrels, 84
Missouri, press history, 13, 32
Missouri Gazette and Louisiana Advertiser. see Missouri Republican
Missouri Republican (Charless), 13
Mitchell, James, 132, 145–148, 152, *154*
  politics and, 137–140
Mitchell, Stan, 354
Mitchell, W.S., 147, *159*
Modern News (Harrisburg), 169, 320
Monroe County Citizen, 281
Monroe County Sun (Clarendon), 277
Montgomery Count Herald (Mount Ida), 263
Montgomery County News, 293
Monticello (Drew County), 54
Monticello Guardian (1866), 78
Monticellonian, 81, 98
Moon Book (Lemke), 244
Mooney, C.P.J., 207
Moore, J.S., 52
Moore, N.P. Rev., 78
Moore, Tom, 353
Morals and Dogma of the Ancient and Accepted Scottish Rite of Freemasonry (Pike), 70
Morgan, Arthur F., 81
Morning News of Northwest Arkansas (Springdale), 325, 338
Morning Republican, 79
Morrill, John C., 54, 143
Morrilton Democrat (1896), 98, 202, 242, 306
Morrilton Headlight, 131, 141
Morriss, Jim, *287*
Morrow, Ray, *284*
Morse, John F., 56
Moses, C. Hamilton "Ham," 253
Mostert, J.F.T., 202
mottoes, 98–99
Mountain Echo (Fayetteville), 78, 81
Mountain Echo (Yellville), 337, 352
Mountain Wave (Marshall, 1892), 107, 122, 123, *170,* 190, 263, 277
Mountaineer (Huntsville), 53
Mouser, Charlie, 350
Mueller, John J., 283
Mueller, Stuart, 283
Mulberry Times, 202, 216
Multi-Media company, 322
  news division, 337
Mumert, Tommy, 353
Murfreesboro Diamond, 356
Murphy, Isaac, 76, 77
Murray, A.P. "Andy," 223, *287,* 320
  and Blanche, *264*
Murray, Donald, 223–226, 232, 256
  engraving company, *235*
Murray, Francis "Shrimp," 223, 298
Murray, Martha Aline, 223, 281
Musical Topics (1901), 184
Mutt and Jeff, 150

Mystic Knights, 191

N

nameplate. *see* banners
Napoleon, 45
Nashville News, 153, 170, 218, 254, 279
Nashville Spotlight, 212
Nast, Thomas, 116, 153
National Association for the Advancement of Colored People (NAACP), 257, 297
National Democrat (Douglas, 1860), 73, 76
National Editorial Association (NEA), 131–132, 192–193, 222, 272. *see also* National Newspaper Association (NNA)
  European Study Mission, 282
National Federation of Press Women (NFPW), 259, 282
National Newspaper Association (NNA), 132, 245, 321, *335,* 344
National Newspaper Network (NNN), 344
National Newspaper Publishers Association (NNPA), 341
National Union, 73
"Navy Edition" (Bindursky), 259
Naylor, George C., 147, 152
Negro Press Association, 180
Neill, Jerry, 295
Nelson, Janet, 353
Nelson, Knox, 314
Nelson, Rex, 352
Neuharth, "Big Al," 333
Neunn, Roger, *269*
Nevada County Picayune, 110
New Bentonian, 105, 124
New Era (DeWitt), 197
New Era (Hot Springs, continued from *Citizens Bulletin),* 179
New York Evening Star (Noah), 33
New York Tribune, 88, 143
Newark Journal (1902), *112*
Newell, Frank, 244
Newman, Charles Gordon, 50, 85, *157, 158,* 170, 176–177
Newman, Fred, 204
Newman, John R., 104, 128, 204
Newman, John R. (grandson), 204
Newman, Thomas R., 128, *128, 195*
Newport Daily Independent, 92, 324, 330
news, sources of, 16, 37, 50–51, 54, 59
  correspondents, 229
  news services, 209–210
  police court, 150
  radio and TV, 302
  railroads, 93
  syndicates, 106
  unions, 246
  war, 70–72, 255
News (Batesville, 1838), 45
News (Hot Springs), 178, 313
News Record (Fort Smith, continued as *Times Record*), 176
News-Record (Fort Worth), 119
News-Review (Batesville), 282
news services, 209–210, 218
news' stand, *160*
newsbooks, 12
newsboys. *see* carriers, news
newspaper association, 54–55
Newspaper Association Managers (NAM)
  C. Dennis Schick, 342
  Louise Bowker, 341
Newspaper Association of America (NAA), 344
newspaper business, 116–118, 192–194
  corporate ownership, 304, 320–325
  editorial side, 174–175
  efficiency and profit, 207
  family owned, 95–96, 300–301, 305, 320
  gender roles in, 315
  practices, 217
  revenue sources, 211, 215, 220–221, 232, 258, 321, 331
  sales promotions, 210–211, *234*
newspaper chains, 195, 206–207
Newspaper Guild of the Communications Workers of America (AFL-CIO), 348
newspaper production, 95–96, 120–121
  composition, 316
  compositors, *109, 113,* 195
  equipment for, 76, 79, 93, 94, *234,* 300
  females in, 45, 96, *109,* 118–119, *154*
  mechanical improvements in, 95, 168–169
  modernization of, 254
  noise, 315–316
  pictures, 153
  preprinted pages and, 106
  pressmen, *326, 328*
  roller boy, 98
  sheet-fed folder, *233*
  teaching, 129
  technological improvements, 209, 315–320
  teletypesetter system, 248–249

newspaper statistics, 325, 331
subscription, 29
newspaper wars, 211–213, 331–337
between business offices, 333
newspapers
agriculture and, 58
alternative, 304
armed forces, 254, 257
banking and, 34–35
bilingual, 340
black owned, 80–81, 84, 85, 179–180, 296, 336, 340–341
camp, 228
categories of, 81
consolidation of, 118
cost to readers, 100, 116–117, 130, 185
culture and, 104, 150–151, 184
developers', 324–325
educational, 344
electronic versions, 350–351
failure rate, 96, 117
fraternal, 182
free, 310
Hispanic, 340
as hobby, 54, 204
humor in, 179
labor, 182
literary, 183–184
metropolitan, 99–100
non-English, 78, *157, 161,* 180–181, 340
and post office, 25–26, 122, *236,* 331
regional, 44–62, 337–340
religion and, 24, 33, 54, 106–107, 120, 121, 144, 230–231
retirement community, 322
revenue from, 147
shoppers, 182, 321, 336, 337
specialization in, 168
sports in, 104–105
start up costs, 300
student, 184–185, 222, 243–245, 310
18th century, 12
19th century, 16–17
violence and, 34, 36, 141
white supremacy and, 102
women founded, 180
women in, 193
Newspapers-in-Education (NIE), 344
newsprint
chewing, 41
price, 209
shortage, 19, 60, 68–69, 258–259, 271
smaller, 320
sources, 68, 93
newssheets, 12
"The Newsstand" (vignette), 196
newsstands, 77
Newton, Thomas W., 36
Newton County, 204, 218, 228
Newton County Times, 99, 204, 352, 357, 358
Newton Herald (Jasper,1898), 98
Nichols, Guerdon D., 295
9-11 coverage, 353–358
Noah, Mordecai Manuel, 33
Noland, Charles Fenton Mercer "Fent," 25, 30, 42, 48
Pete Whetstone stories, 45
North Arkansas (continuation of *Batesville News*), 45
North Arkansas Star, 109
North Arkansas View (continued as *Daily News*), 337
North Little Rock Times, 332, 350
northern immigrants, 81
Northwest Arkansas Times (1937,continued from *Fayetteville Democrat*), 201, 254, 268, 337–338, *357*
"The Last Hot Lead Edition," *326*
Norton, Ruth, 352
Norwood, C.M., 141
Note-Book (Helena), 45
Novell, Joshua, 13
Nunn, Walter, 308, 309
Nutter, Charles, 338
Nyberg, Leo E., 247

O

Oakley, Meredith, 333
O'Baugh, Eunice, 242, 281
obituaries, 16, 194–195
obscenity, 307–308
Observer (Fayetteville), 78
Obsitnik, Larry (photographer), 294
Ockert, Roy Jr., 185, 311
Oden, Robert, 23
Oehm, Gus M., 229
offset technology, 304
brands, 316
color and, 315
multiple printings, 320

Offsetter, 315
Ogilvie, Craig (artist), 3, 6, 12, 19, 20, 38, 39, 49, 53, 62, 68, 74, 83, 86, 88, 91, 93, 97, 123, 128, 131, 142, 145, 148, 152, 156, 170, 171, 297, 335, 341
Old Line Democrat, 43–44, 64
  semi-weekly, 66
On a Fast Train Through Arkansas (Shannon), 272
On a Slow Train through Arkansas (1903), 120
Orear, Jefferson Davis, 156, 184
"The origin of the symbol -30-" (vignette), 359
Orr, W.E., 242
Osborne, Jennings, 348
Osceola Times, 99, *113,* 170, 216, 268, 311
O'Sullivan, Dan, 85, 86, 137, 166–167
Ouachita Baptist University, 349
Ouachita Citizen, 298
Ouachita Conference Journal, 54
Ouachita County, 196–197
Ouachita Herald (Camden), 51, 53, 68
Oury, W.L., 173, 182
Outlook (Rohwer internment camp newsletter), 260
Owens, Mark C. Jr., 336
Owl (Amity), 254, 301
Owsley (Ousley), Kit, 53
Ozark Banner (1874), 119
Ozark Democrat, 94
"Ozark Moon" (Lemke), *200,* 244
"Ozark Moon" (song), 244
Ozark Times (1932), 97

P
Page, John H., 93, 107, 174
Page Earl, 247
Palmer, Clyde Eber, 179, 195, 197, 206–207, 213, 249, 282, 286
  anti-union, 278
  in Depression, 217
  SNPA, 258
  support for APA, 225
Palmer chain, 323, 347
paper. *see* newsprint
Paradise Alley (Little Rock), 118, *161*
Paragould Daily Press, 196, 267, 324, 327
  KDRS and, 272
  technology leader, 316
Paragould Soliphone, 161, 196
Parent, Herschell, 343
Paris Express, 269, 283
Park, Hugh, 194, 202, 218, 240, 243, 283
  The Country Editor, 243
Park, J.C., 202
Parke, A.W., 193
Parke-Harper Publications, 186. *see also* Harper, Clio
  stationery, *237*
Parker, Carl, 202
Parker, Charles J., 197
Parker, Jacob B., 188–189, 196, 248
Parker, William H., 283
Parks, J.S., 202
  SNPA, 258
Parrott, John Edgar, 242, 300–301
Parsons, Kenneth, 292
Pate, Everett W., 193, 204, 225–226, 248, 254–255, 259
  draft board member, 261
  sold to Nutter, 338
patent (pre-printed), 106–107, 145
Patriot (Jacksonville), 324
patronage, 246–247
Patterson, "Big Dan," 190
Patterson, Carrick, 333
Patterson, Hugh, 217, 264, 277, 332
Paxton Media Group, 324, 348
Payne, Laud, 242, 277
Payne, Louise, 119
peace movement, 72–73
Pearl Harbor, 253
Pearson, Drew, 247
Peck, Chris (APME), 311
Peek, Thomas C., 43, 64, 67, 83, 166
Peel, Zillah Cross (Mrs. Frank), 119, *198,* 205, 211
  feature stories, 242
Pendergraft, Ross, 347
Penix, Bill, 209, 245, 293
penny press, 121
People's Friend (Rogers), 101
People's Hornet-Horse Shoe (Hot Springs, continued as the *News*), 178
"The Perils of Being an Editor" (vignette), 120
Perrine, A.W., 239–240
Perry County, 246
Peters, Barbara P., 314
Petrucelli, Fred, 269
Pettigrew Journal (1918), 97
Pew, Thomas Jefferson, 30
  alcoholism, 32

Phelps, H.M. "Uncle Henry," 197, 219
Phelps, W.H., 197
Phillips, Margaret, 357
Phillips, Rupert, *327*
Phillips, Rupert E., 337
Phillips County Democratic Committee, 85
Phillips County Herald (1939), 277, 280
Phillips County Progress, 356
photocomposition, 316
photography, newspaper, 249, 300
  archiving images, 317–318
  digitization, 317
  free slides, 153
  Gazette holdings, 335
  Kite, Ralph, *236, 249*
  power of, 249–250, 294
  silver need, 321
  workshops on, 255
Picayune (1860), 50
Pierce, H.A., 85
Piggott Banner, 277, 298
Pike, Albert, 17, 26–27, 29–30, *38,* 66–67
  Albert Pike's Letter Addressed to Major General Holmes, 70
  as "Casca," 33
  in Civil War, 70
  in Memphis, 80
  Morals and Dogma of the Ancient and Accepted Scottish Rite of Freemasonry, 70
  Prose Sketches and Poems, Written in the Western Country, 26
  and Quesenbury, 134, 135
Pine Bluff, 53, 176–177, 257
Pine Bluff American (1850), 53
Pine Bluff Commercial, 50, 85, *158,* 171, 176–177, 244, 257, 282, 292, 324, 332, 340
  anti-segregationist views, 295
  circulation, 254
  press, 268
  political endorsement, 323
Pine Bluff Democrat, 53
Pine Bluff Graphic, 118, 166, 256
Pine Bluff Independent, 53
Pine Bluff Orthopolitan (1866), 78
Pine Bluff Press, 176–177
Pine Bluff Republican, 53–54, 83, 100
Pine Bluff Vindicator, 83
Plank, W.H., 119, 204
The Plebian (Morrilton, 1878), 91
Plunkett, Leland W. "Tex," 185, *302*
PMDC (Printing, Mailing & Distribution Center), Wal-Mart, 338
poetry, in newspapers, 19, 27, 50–51, 217–218, 239
  Hampton, 262
  Marinoni, 244
polio, 282
political aphorism, 28
political cartoons, 41, 249
Political Intelligencer (1834 continued as *The Times),* 27
political strategists, 321
politics, 32
  conservative, 44
  machine, 247, 274–275, 306
  newspapermen in, 277
  and press, 17, 32, 44, 136–143, 150, 207, 247–250
  press neutrality, 210
  race and, 139–140, 275–276
  rural press and, 100–101
  state, 246–247
  television and, 321
  violence and, 23–24, 34, 141
poll tax, 141
Pomeroy's Democrat, 82
Pope, D.H., 86
Pope, John, 24, 25, 27–28
Pope, William Fontaine, 25
population, German, 78
Porte, R.T., 192
Porter, Johnnie, 245
Post-Dispatch (St. Louis), 179
Post (town), 12, 14
Poteete, Robert, 278
Powell, James O., 298
Powell, Wilson, 245, 282
Powhatan Advertiser, 54
Prairie County Democrat (Brownsville), 143
Prairie Flower (Carlisle), 91
Prairie Grove Herald, 204
Prentice, George D., 32
Prescott, 256
press
  access and protection rights, 314–315
  commercialism and, 210
  independence of, 32, 133, 136–137
  metropolitan *vs.* country, 132
  partnership model, 92

people with disabilities in, 42
state, 334–335
Press-Argus (Van Buren), 202, 240, 272
The Press Association, 84
press club, 153
press (printing), 76, 170–171, 254
army, 97
Babcock hand-fed, 254
Bulloch web, 170
Campbell, 171
Cincinnati, 24, 27, 54
Duplex Unitubular, *268*
electically powered, 95
Fairchild, *267*
gasoline powered, 95
Gos, *328*
Gos Comet, 204, 254
Gos Junior, 271
Hoe cylinder, 56
Hoe lightning, 170
Hoe rotary, 207
in-house design, 76
multiple editions, 300
Prouty, 95, 171
Ramage, 13, 14, *21*.
St. Louis, 92
steam powered, 79
Vaughn, 171
Washington hand, 95, 97, 98, *110*, *170*, 171, 197
Presson, Helen, 206
Price, Charles A., 263
Price, John G., 80, 81, 84
price reporting, current, 17
printer, tramp. *see* tramp printer
printers
master, 173
register, *155*
union, 55, 172–173
wages, 18, 172–173
printer's devil, 95
printing
modernization of, 133
offset, 271, 283, 300, 315
public, 18
standard practice, 19th century, 15
technological changes in, 320
privilege provision, shield law, 314
prohibition, 94, 106, 143, 182, 188
proofreaders, 194
Prose Sketches and Poems, Written in the Western Country., (Pike), 26
prospectus, 15, 27
Pryor, C.D., 49
Pryor, David, 294, 298, 313, 351–352
Public Ledger, 119
public service, 26, 219, 261, 272–273
Publicity Act, 143, 211, 220–221
Publishers' Association of Arkansas, 84
Publishers' Auxiliary, 220
publishing, profitable, 192–194
"puffing," 43, 104
Pulitzer Prize, 295
Purkins, Duval, 221, 299
Purkins, J.E., 74

Q
Qualls, Bob, 353
Quapaw, 14, 22
Quapaw Times, 139–140
Quarterly (Arkansas Historical Association), 243
Quesenbury, William "Cush," 11, 19, 33, 37, 42, 43–44, 55–62
artist, 41, 56
last years, 134–136
poet and essayist, 51, 56–57, 59, 61, 135–136
and proverbs, 61
on state pride, 120
in Texas, 79
war years, 66

R
race, 141
Jim Crow, 188
and politics, 139–140, 275–276
relations, 102, 121, 140–141, 179–180
riots, 190
soldiers and, 257
voting and, 141
racism, 257–258, 296
Radical Republicans, 73
Radicals *vs.* Conservatives, 73
radio
jingles, 321
KASU (public), 243
networks, 271

and newspapers, 243, 271–272, 344
politics and, 279
power of, 276–277
railroads, 44, 52, 61, 86, 99, 103
Arkadelphia and, 102–103
construction of, 140
newspaper creation and, 92–95
Rainey, James S.H., 68
Ramage, Adam, 14. *see also* press
Ramsey, Ellis, *287*
Randolph Herald (Pocahontas), *111*
Raney, Mrs. Walter W., 281
Raney, Walter W., 207–208, 283
pension plan, 220
in politics, 277
Rathke, Wade, 308, 309
Ray, Victor, 295
Rayburn, Otto Ernest, 242
Read, Lessie Stringfellow, 194, 203, 205, 281
Read, Opie, 90–92, *91,* 118, 121, 125–127, 127, *159,* 166–168, 183–184
"Editorial Excursions," 87
Emmett Bonlore, 126–127
Len Gansett, 125–126
Smithee-Adams duel, 138–139
as war correspondent, 139
ready-print, 106–107, 254
Reardon, John E., 42
Reardon, Lambert J., 37, 40
Reconstruction, 75–85, 88
and loyalty oath, 76
press and, 81–83
Unionists *vs.* ex-Confederates, 76, 78
and violence, 79–80
The Record and Democrat (Bentonville), 204
Record (1899,Hot Springs, continued as *Sentinel Record*), 178
Rector, Henry M., 43–44, 64, 67
Redfield, Jared E., 138
Reed, Bill, 341
Reed, John H., 29
Reed, Roy, 334–335
"How to Lynch a Newspaper" (*Atlantic Monthly*), 306
Nieman Fellow, 306
regulators, vigilante, 29
Reid, Bud, 293
Reid, Whitelaw, 168
religion and newspapers, 24, 33, 54, 181–183, 230–231
religious bias
anti Catholicism, 181–182, 189, 252
anti Semitism, 189, 294, 322
religious press, 182–183
reporters, 133, *341*
black, 292, 294–295, 336
and ethics, 152–153
stories about, 150–152, 166
women as, 179
Republican. see Daily Republican
Republican (Huntsville), *108*
Republican Party, 80–81
research, historical, newspapers and, 335
Revolution, 183
Reynold Library, APA Building, *327*
Reynolds, Donald W., *237, 254, 327*
Donrey Media, 323
radio station, 272
Rhea, Weston H., 54
Richardson, Ken and Delores, 325, 331
Richolson, Orville, *330*
Ridge, Major, 50
Riley, J.C., *108, 111,* 119
Riley, Tom, 332
Rinehart, Mrs. J.H., 259
Rison Herald, 196
Ritter, Chris, digital photography, 317
Rizzo, Steve, 283
Roane, John Selden, 37, 39
Roane, Samuel Calhoun, 16
Robbins, Robert Presly, 150
Roberts, Hall K., 298
Robins, Frank, 132
Robins, Frank E., *199,* 202, 225, *301*
Robins, Frank III, 351
Robins, Frank Jr., 255, *267,* 301
Robinson, Asa, 91
Robinson, Joe T., 246
Robinson, Joseph T., 142
Robinson, Virginia, *269*
Robinson-Stanfield, Sallie, *108,* 119
The Rock of Arkansas (1995), 341
Rockefeller, Winthrop, *286, 299*
governor, 307, 321
Roddy, "Brooklyn Joe," 195
Rogers, 204, 218
newspaper war, 338

Rogers Champion, 93
Rogers Daily News, 314, 338
Rogers Democrat, 100, 103, 121, 125, 192–193, 338
pictures in, 255
Rogers Hometown News, 338
Rogers New Era (1881), 93, 140
Root, Mrs. Vaughn W., 205
Roots, Logan, 85, 138
Rose, Al, 247
Rose, Betty, 244
Rose, George B., *154*
Rose, Uriah M., 71–72, 83, 138
Rose, W.K., 244
Ross, John, 43
Ross, Margaret Smith (historian), 15, 78, 184, 253, *290,* 296
Ross, Mike, 323
Roussan, Adah (honorary APA), *113,* 120, 170
Roussan, Leon, 99, 120
Rowland, Hardy "Spider," 277–278
Royce, J.T., 222
Royston, Grandison D., 72
rules and regulations, 246
Rural and Workman, 185
Rush, Van, 289
Russell, David, 353
Russell, Jerry
APA manager, 292
"How to Get More Political Advertising for Your Newspaper," 321
radio jingles use, 321
Russellville Democrat, 185
Russellville newspapers, 202
Russellville Printing Co., 224
Russellville Siftings, 127
Russellville Tribune, 245
Rust Communications, 324, 325
Rutherford, Bill, 311, *329*

S
Saar, Amanda (archivist), 180
Sadler, Guy M., 196, *201,* 202, *233,* 242
Sadler, William, 202, *233*
The Sage of Monticello, 54
Saiki, Barry, 260
Saline County, 340
Saline County Digest, 99, 151
Sallis, Mrs. J.W., 202
Sanders, 327, 328, 338, 351
Bob, Maudine, Charles, T.C.
Sarver, Robert, 308
Saturday Bee (1895), 183
Saunders, James, 176
Scalpel (Pocahontas), 174
Scan-a-Color II (Fairchild), 315
Scan-A-Graver, 300
Schaefer, Robert O., 107, *123,* 178–179, 186, 299
Schexnayder, Charlotte Tillar, 74, 81, 283
on black support, 321
inaugural coverage, 311
journalist-legislator, 314
Schexnayder, Melvin, *267*
SPJ, 312
Schexnayder, Melvin and Charlotte Tillar, 324, *335*
controversial stance, 310
Schick, C. Dennis, 311, 319, 331
APA manager, 342–347
FOI seminars, 313
How to Create Newspaper Advertising That Moves Merchandise, 343
Schick, Tom (photographer), 311
Schmitz, Peter Wilhelm, 181
Schoenfeld, Nathan, FOI, 312
Schwieger, Sam, 227–228, 256
"scissors and pot paste," 16, 71, 315
Scott, Allen M., 33
Scott, J.M., 178
Scott, Milton, 343
Scott, S.M., 54
Scott, Wade F., 220
Scripps-McRae, 147
Scuder, John, *269*
Scull, Benjamin F., 39
Seabees, 255
Searcy, 54, 190
political conservatism and, 277
Searcy Daily Citizen, 320, 324
Searcy Times, 118
Searle, Judge E.H., 82, 105
Sebastian, William King, 38
secession, 44, 64–65
segregation, 273–274, 293
in education, 273–276
Supreme Court and, 292
segregationists, 295

Semi-Weekly Bulletin (1906, Hot Springs), 178
Sentinel (Fayetteville), 105
Sentinel Record (Hot Springs), 178–179
Sevier, Ambrose Hundley, 23, 24–25, 27, 30
  Gazette owner, 166
  senator, 33, 35, 38
sex scandel, 36
Shannon, Karr, 127, 256
  On a Fast Train Through Arkansas, 272
  on Supreme Court, 295–296
  as writer, 242, 243
sharecropping system, 77–78
Sharp, Floyd, 174
Sharp Citizen (Cave City), 306, *326*
Sharp County, 243
Sharp County Independent, 242, 245
Sharp County Record, 131, 241, *282, 321*
Shaver, James, 153
Shaver, Owen C., 241, 245, 282
Shelby, William M., 173, 191
Shelton, William T. and Connie, 263, 282, 334
Sheridan Headlight, 196, 352, 354, 356, 358
Sherwood, Diana, 242
shield law (privilege provision), 314
Shinn, Josiah H., 131
shinplasters (scrip), 219
Shiramizu, Harry, 259
Shiras, Pete, 255, 294
Shiras, Tom, *152,* 208, 278–279
  feature writer, 242
  Norfolk Dam, 257
  postage stamp, 236
Shofner, James P., 193
Shull, Beth, 349
Shull, Laura, 316
Shurlds, Kathryn, 350
The Sickle (1900, continued from *Fin de Siecle Sickle*), 98
Siftings Herald (Arkadelphia), 105
Sigma Delta Chi (renamed Society of Professional Journalists), Freedom of Information Act, 312
Siloam Springs, 256
Simkins, Henry (APA, expelled), 179–180
Simmons, Bill, *329*
Simmons, Roscoe, 257–258
Simmons, William Joseph, 188
Simon, Howard, 242
size and format, 17, 89, 95, 121, 125, 149–150, 210
  Arkansas Gazette (1819), 15, 24, 26, 28
  "breaking the rule," 15, 93
  during Depression, 218
  late 20th century, 319
  war time, 69
Sketch Book, 183
"Skirts . . . In the Front Office" (1945,Tillar), 259
Skulman, Walt (cartoonist), 314
slavery, 29
Sloan, Kitty, 353
Sloan, Ron, *327*
Smith, Alta, 179
Smith, George, 337, 353, 354, 358
Smith, Gerald L.K., 322
Smith, Griffin, 221
Smith, Jefferson, 29
Smith, Mrs. C.H., 204
Smith, Myrtle, 197
Smith, William E., 51, 53, 58
Smithee, Elbert E., 128, 186
Smithee, James Newton, 54, 66, *74,* 79, 85–86, 132, 143–145
  historian, 117
  politics and, 137–139
  on the press, 128
  Quesenbury and, 134–135
Smithson, Bryan, 41
smoke signals, 11
Socialist Party, 101
Society of Professional Journalists (SPJ), 312, 349, 352
The Soul of Ann Rutledge (Babcock), 183
South Arkansas Accent, 336
South Arkansas Sun, 336
South-West Independent (Fayetteville, 1853), 34, 44, 54, 55–62
  book reviews, 62
Southern Baptist College (now Williams Baptist College), 298
Southern Economist (Searcy), 98, 182
Southern Manifesto, 293
Southern Mediator Journal, 340–341
Southern Newspaper Publishers Association (SNPA), *237, 258,* 350
Southern sectionalism, 39, 43
Southern Sentinel (continued from *Arkansas State Democrat and Helena Commercial Advertiser*), 44
Southern Sentinel (Hindman), 30
Southern Shield (Helena), 44, 78, 81
Southern Stamp (Camden), 34, 53
Southern Standard (1996, Amity), 325

Southern Standard (Arkadelphia), 53, 78, 81, 82, 85, 101–102, 103, 104, 106, 124
on segragation, 257
Southern State College at Magnolia, 308
Southern Tenant Farmers' Union, 246
Southern Worker (Huntington), 101
Southland Paper Millls, Inc., 258
Southron (1860), 50
Southwest American, 122, 176, 202–203, 294
Southwest News Photographer, 249
Southwest News Photographers, 249
Sovereignty Commission, 294
Spain, Richard L., *245*
Sparks, James H., 175–176
Speck, Garland, *326*
Spectator (Ozark), 202, 242, 296
Spectrum, 310
Spencer, Sylvia, FOI, 312
Spencer, William E., 118
Spike, S.E. "Bunk," 101
The Spirit of the Times (national), 45, 51, 60
Spooner, Alden, 13, 22
sports, 208–209
sports reporting, 104–105, 209, 226
Springdale, newspaper war, 338
Springdale Enterprise, 95
Springdale News. see Springdale Yellow Jacket
Springdale News (1887,continuation of *Locomotive*), 10, 95, 100, *109,* 120, 121, 204, *287, 327,* 328
Correspondents' Association, 124
newspaper war, 338
Springdale Yellow Jacket (1882), 91
The Spyglass (Conway), 91
St. Francis County, 242–243
St. John, A.W., 94
St. John, E.W., 246, 280
"The Life of a Printer," 98
St. John, V.W., 101, 205
St. John's College Record, 86, 243
St. Louis Republican, 99
St. Louis Type Foundry, 99
Staats Zeitung (in German), 78–79
Stafford, Edward R., 338
Stafford, Edward Raymond (Marty), 96, 118
Stafford, Ellis, 248
Stafford, Glaphyra (Bucket), 96
Stafford, Guy, 95–96, 127
Stafford, John L. (Fay), 95–96
Stafford, John P., 91, 92, 94–96, 100, 109, 120, 122, 132, *201*
on correspondents, 123, 124, 125
Linotype, 169–170
Stallworth, Clarke, 350
Standard Advertising Unit (SAU), 344
Stanfield, W.J., 119
Stanley, John Mix, 56
Staples, Adam, 354
Star Herald (Pocahontas), 110, *111,* 242, 281
The Star of Hope, 94, 170
Star-Progress (Berryville), 242
Star-Reporter (Pine Bluff), 292
Star (Stuttgart), 183
Stark, J.C., AP correspondent, 209
Starr, John Robert, 292, 309, *328*
anti-Clinton, 333
Arkansas Democrat, 332–333
columnist, 335
SPJ, 312
State Republican, 100
State Rights Democrat (Helena), 43, 45
State Rights Eagle (Camden), 42, 53
State University in Fayetteville, 85, 243
States Appeal (Conway), 219
Steele, John, 27, 28
as rogue editor, 29
Stephens, Jackson, 323, 348
Stephens, Jackson T. Jr. "Steve," 323
Stephens, Keith, 353
Stephens, Oren, 244
Stephens, Warren, 323
Stephens, Witt, 280, 323n
Stephens, Inc., 323
Stephens Media Group, 323, 347–348
and Donrey, 338
Stephens News, 197
Sterne, Laurence *(Tristram Shandy),* 56
Sterne, Thomas, 49
Stevens, Mrs. (Charlotte Shillcutt), 230
Stilwell, Arthur, 94
Stockard, George G., 211–212
Stone County Democrat (Mountain View, 1907), *112*
Stone County Leader, 354
Stovall, Austin and Edith, 256
Stover, Bob, 319
Strike (union), 278

stringers, 12, 122
Stuck, Dorothy, *268*, *282*, 283, 305, 307, 320
Stuck, Howard, 263, *267*, 282, 320
  and Dorothy, *266*
Suffolk Gazette (Spooner), 13
suffrage. *see* women
Sulphur Springs Speaker, 97
The Sun (Lincoln), 204
Sun-Times (Heber Springs), 356
supplements
  comics, 212
  magazine sections, 241
suspension, 256
Sutton, Ozell, 292, *297*
"Ozell Sutton, The First Black Reporter for a White-owned Daily" (vignette), 297
Swank, Albert E. "Gene," 257
Swifton Sentinel, 116
syndicates, 105–106

T

Tallqvist-Root, Kay, 205
Taylor, Clarence, 277
Taylor, Dan, 173
Taylor, Homer H. "Scotty," 211–212
Taylor, J.R., *161*
Taylor, S.S., 296
Tebbetts, Jonas, 58, 77
technology, *329*
  advantages, 317
  changeover rate, 318
  expense, 304, 318, 320–321
  Internet, 311
Tedford, Eddie, *330*
Teeter, Herman, 244–245
telegraph, 32, 70, 99
  automatic printers, 209
  Morse operators, 209
Telephone (Walnut Ridge), 113
teletypesetter, 248–249, 271, 279
television, 272
  advertising, 344
Telford, Eddie, 347
temperance, 35, 45, 139, 244
Tennessee State Gazette, 13
Terral, Tom, 191
Terry, Adolphine Fletcher, 295
Texarkana Courier (continued as *Four States Press*), 206–207
Texarkana Gazette, 327, 330
Textron Building, *155*
Thalheimer, Joseph A. "Smokey Joe," 206
  journalism professor, 244, 254
Thanksgiving, 57
"There's Romance in the Names of Rural Communities" (Lemke), 245
"30," 195, 359
Thirty-Fifth Parallel (Fort Smith), 50
Thomas, Briner, 325
Thomas, J.A., 195
Thomas, Ruth, 241
Thomas, Wyatt C., 176
Thompson, Delores (librarian), 335
Thompson, John, 332
Thompson Newspapers, 337–338
Thornburgh, George, 106, *113*, 182
Thornton, Ray, 312
"Thoughts on a Young Man's Funeral" (Fisher), 307
Thurman, Randy, 356
Tilden, Alden, *269*
Tillar, Charlotte, 240, 245, 261. *see also* Schexnayder
  "Skirts . . . In the Front Office," 259
Times and Advocate, 33–36
Times-Courier (Benton), 170
Times-Dispatch (Walnut Ridge), 92, 100, 242, 257, 356
Times-Echo (Eureka Springs), 322–323, 327
The Times (formerly *Political Intelligencer*), 29
Times (Jonesboro), 116
Times Record (Fort Smith), 122, 203, 254, 340
titles, use of, 58
Torey, W.S., 107
Torrans, James, 84, 85
Touhey, Matilda, *269*
tourist-printer. *see* tramp printer
trade publications, 130, 310
Trail of Tears, 53
tramp printer, 172, 195, 227
Traveling Campuses, 350
Trevathan, George, 98
Trevathan, Henry A., 98
Trevathan, Jared, 253, 263
Trevathan, Nellie H., 194, 205
Tri-Weekly Bulletin (1861), 50
Tribune (Denson, Jerome internment camp newsletter), 259
Tribune (Little Rock), 121

Tribune (Searcy), 82
"A Tribute to Tom Shiras: Toscanini of the Ozarks" (vignette), 278–279
Trim-o-saw, 209
Trimble, Jim, 280
tripod, 15
Trolinger, Sam, 338
Trolinger, Steve, 347
Trousdale, Leon, 39, 40
Troutt, Fred, 145, 213, 317
Troutt, John, 145, 213
Troutt, John Jr., 324
  Freedom of Information Award, 312
Troutt, William O., 132, *145*, 176, 186, 220, 132
Trowbridge, Samuel G., 49
True American (1855), 50
True Democrat (1852), 40–42, 53, 76, 85
  and The Family, 41
  tri-weekly, 66
True Issue (Helena), 45
Trumann, 263
Tucker, Zela, 205
Tuckerman Record, 92, 242, 300–301
Tuckerman Times, 107, 116
Tudor, James H., 190, 216, 218
Tudor, James R., 216
  in politics, 263, 277
  war and, 255–256, 263
Tull, John, 313
Turner, George P.M., 50
Turner, Lance, 351
Turner, Mary Nell, 196
Turner, W.W., 170
Twain, Mark, *Life on the Mississippi,* 45
Twin City Press, 341
"The Two Widows" (Hawthorne), 45
type
  aging of, 34–35
  American Type Founders, 170
  Binney & Ronaldson, 14
  Brevier, 98
  cases, *21, 359*
  Cherokee, 50
  diacritical, 17
  German, 161, 181
  horseshoe nails as, 91
  Oxford, 14
  shortage, 97
  St. Louis Type Foundry, 99
typesetting, 315
  capacity, 317
  intertype, 195
  Linotype, *113,* 168–170, 209, *233,* 315
  Ludlow, *234*
typewriter, 151
typo, 34–35
Typothetae, 173
Tyson, Ardis, 202, 218, 243
Tyson, Van and Ginny, 244, 324, 351

U
Unconditional Union (1864), 73, 76
Underhill, J.W., 238
Underwood, Charles, 78
Underwood, J.W., 171
Underwood, Q.K., 44, 78
Uni-typo group, 278
Union, El Dorado (continued as *Democratic Union),* 54
Union County, 197
Union Labor Bulletin (1898), 173, 182, 295
Union Station Times (continued as *Arkansas Times),* 309
Unionists, 76
unions, 147, 173, 256, 348
  in Arkansas, 279
  management and, 319
  New Deal legislation and, 222
  as news, 246
  Pressman, Local 59, *284*
  printer's, 70, 144, 172–173, 319
  stereotypers, 277
  typographer's, 55, 79, 143, 182
United Press, 177, 209–210
University of Arkansas, 225–227
  integration and, 293, 299
  student protests, 307
University Weekly (college, continued as *Arkansas Traveler*), 243
Upton, George, 202

V
Vadakin, E.L., 112
Valachovic, Ernie (FOI), 312
Van Buren, 49–50
Van Buren County Democrat, 267, 301, 324, 330, 351
Van Buren Press, 44, 50, 78, 81, 134

Van Dalsem, Paul, 246, 298
Van Hoose, James H., 136
Van Horne, Francis M., 49
Van Pelt, Henry, 13
Vance, E.H., 53
Varnado, Curtis, 341
Vederosa, Christina, 354
VerBeck, C.A., 336
Verderosa, C.F. Scott and Christina, 331
Vidette (Star City), 97
Vietnam, 307
vigilante justice, 29
Village Journal (Cherokee Village), 243
Village Voice (Hot Springs Village), 322
Villager Journal, 325
violence, 23–24, 25, 40, 50, 79–80
Voice (Sherwood), 324
voters, black, 141

W

Wadley, J.L., 103, 178
Wage and Hour Law (1940), 222
Wagner, J.W., 202, 216
Wagner Act, 222
Wagnon, Ted, 353
Wahlquist, William H.V., 208, 280
Wal-Mart, 318, 338
  and C. Dennis Schick, 345–346
Walker, Dalton, 196
Walker, David, 33, 65, 134, 138
Walker, Deloss, 321
Walker, Harlan V., 283, 320
Walker, J.D., 137
Wallace, George, 307
Walls, C.A., 283
Walls, C.J., 263, 283
Walls, Dean, 311
Walnut Ridge Blade (continued from *Black Rock Blade),* 108, 119
Walnut Ridge Telephone, 182
Walter J. Lemke Department of Journalism, 351
Walter J. Lemke Scholarship Fund, 302
Walters, David, 336
Waltner, Tim, 311
Walton, James C., 338
Walton, Sam, 345–346, 348
Wann, R.C., 225
war bonds, as revenue, 258
War Bulletin (Pine Bluff), 68
war records, Lemke, 252
Ward, John, *330*
Ward, John R., 96
Warner, Harry C., 90–92, 96, 138
Warren, E.A., *142*
Washbourne, Edward Payson
  painter, 60
  "The Arkansas Traveler," 41
Washbourne, Josiah Woodward, *48,* 49–50, 79, 134
  poet, 51
Washburn, Alex H., 171, 242, 249, 307
  on bond issues, 277
  Hope post office, 207
  in Jonesboro, 213
  on technology, 316–318
Washburn Rev. Cephas, 50
Washington, 51
  as capital, 72
Washington Post (1864), 84
Washington Telegraph (1840-1947), 51, 69, 72, 76, 78, 81, 300
Wassell, Irene, 334
Wasson, J.O., *326*
Wasson, Marion, 221, 336
Watergate, 310
Watkins, Harry, *157,* 166
Watkins, Isaac, 23
Watson, P.S.G., 183
Watt, Bill, 263
Watt, W.O., 263
Waugh, Evelyn, *Scoop,* 151
The Wayshower, 204
weather reports, 17, 59
Webb, Mrs. J.W., 203–204
Webber, William Ami, 87–88, 99, 151, 178
websites, 350–351
  Democrat-Gazette, 335
"A Week in the Life of the City Editor" (vignette), 167
Weekly Graphic (1886, Pine Bluff), 177
Weekly Horse Shoe (Hot Springs), 178
Weekly Planter (Napoleon, 1859), 45
WEHCO Media, *Arkansas Democrat,* 323, 332, 339
Weibel, Eugene, 181
Weller, Cyrus W., 35
Wells, John F., 280, 298, 309, *327*
Wenrick, William A., 107, 118, 122, *170,* 263
West Memphis News, 237, 266, *275,* 282

Western Clarion (Helena), 177
Western Frontier Whig (Van Buren, 1846), 49
Western Independent, 134, 176
Western Newspaper Union, 106, 173, 210
  customized advertising, 254
Western Pioneer (Fayetteville), 51, 53
Weston, Joseph H., 306–307, *326*
Westward Communications, 324
Wheeler, Everett and Lucille, 322
Wheeler, John F., 49, 50, *53,* 62, 65, 78, 134–135, 137, 175
Whig party, 28, 30, 32–33, 40–41
  and *Gazette,* 35
  in Van Buren, 49
White, F.W., 180
White, L.B., 170, 222
White, William Allen (Emporia, Kansas), 220
White Citizens Councils, 293
White County, 82
White County Citizen (Searcy), 54
White County Record, 82, 85, 242, 256
white primary, 141, 274
White River Arkansian (Batesville, 1858), 49
White River Current (Calico Rock), 354, 356
White River Journal (De Valls Bluff), 81, 283, 311, 315
white supremacy, 102, 257
Whitehead, Rebecca, *327*
Whitehead, W.R., Jr., 307, 336, 351
  SPJ, 312
Whitehead, W.R. Sr., *327*
Whiteley, Lambert A., 39–40
Whiteside, Garrett, 247
Whitman, Walt, 13
Whittington, Hiram Abiff, 22, 23
Whytock, Judge John, 82, 86
Wilkerson, Austin, *235*
Williams, George Rainey, 176
Williams, H.E., 298
Williams, Harry Lee, 116, 125, 213, 242
Williams, Otis E., 257
Williams, Sam W., 168
Williams, Stacy, 341
Williams, Walter (U. of Missouri), 130, 205, 244
Williams & Anderson, APA Hotline, 313
Wilson, Alex, 294–295
Wilson, Mary Ann, 311
Wilson, Nora Lee, *234*
Wilson, Robert J., 357
Wilson, W.P. "Whippoorwill Pea," 219
Wimberly, Bob, 299
Winfield, Rev. A.R., 138, 139
Winslow American (continued from *Winslow Mirror)*
wire services, 177
Wirges, Eugene "Gene," 98, 301, 306
  Elijah Parish Lovejoy Award, 306
Wishard, Captain R.W., 128
Witmer, Wallace, lawsuit, 255
Wolf, J.R., 118
Woman's Chronicle, 180
women, 231
  opportunities for, 259
  rights of, 79, 145, 180
Women's Association, 205
Women's Christian Temperance Union (WCTU), 180
Women's Emergency Committeee, 295
Wood, Harry, *327*
Wood, Nanna, 119
Wood, W.W. "Dean," 239
woodcuts, 26, 43–44, 45, *47,* 61, 121
  in advertising, 17–18
  as caricatures, 91
  original, 41
Woodruff, Alden Mills, 40
Woodruff, George, *154*
Woodruff, Georgine, 85, 180
Woodruff, John, 353
Woodruff, William Edward, 13–30, 32–33, 35, *39,* 76, 153
  assassination attempt, 24
  Gazette merger, 39
  Laws of the Territory of Arkansas comprising The Organic Laws of the Territory of Missouri and Arkansas with their Amendments and Supplements Annexed, 18
  retirement, 41
  roles, 15, 19, 25, 26
Woodruff, William Edward Jr., 66, *74,* 82–84
  Gazette owner, 78, 137
  state treasurer, 139–140
Woods, T.M. (APA historian), 107, 117
Woodward, James W., 42
Woolfolk, Margaret, 219, 245, *266,* 281, 283, *327*
  writer, 242
Wooten, Effie Laura, *269*
Workman, John, 182
Works Progress Administration (WPA), 218
World War II

conservative social reaction to, 260
defense industry, 257
Japanese internment camps, 259–260
labor shortage, 256
personnel changes, 255–254
prisoners of war, 260
women and, 259
Worthen, W.B., 144
Wright, George L., 204, 283
Wright, Mary Louise, 281, 283
writers, 241–243
Wulfekuhler, Fred, *267*, *268*, *316*, 324, 327, *342*
Wynne, 256
Wynne Progress, 295, 320
Wynne Star-Progress, *264*, *300*

X

X-Ray (student), 243

Y

Yank Magazine, *237*
Yates, F.B., 185
Yeager, Walter C., 256
Yell, Archibald, 33, 35–37
Yell, James, 53
Yell County Record, 352
Yerkes, Reuben S., 68–69, 76, 85
Yokota, Paul, 259
Yonley, T.D.W., 73
Youman, William T., 44
Young, Charles M., 178, 222, 223, *235*, 295, 317
Young, Jack, 244
Young, Porter, *267*
Youth's Banner (1852, student), 243

Z

Zachariah, Val S. and Dorothy, 267, 283, 320

ARKANSAS
WOMAN OF ACHIEVEMENT
AWARD
JANUARY 11, 1969
PRESENTED TO
DOROTHY D. STUCK
BY THE
ARKANSAS PRESS WOMEN

DE QUEEN
DAILY
CITIZEN

SERVICE AWARD
ROY EVANS
ARKANSAS
PRESS ASSOCIATION

Hope Star

THE EVENING SUN